Quantum States and Scattering in Semiconductor Nanostructures

Advanced Textbooks in Physics

ISSN: 2059-7711

Published

Trapped Charged Particles: A Graduate Textbook with Problems and Solutions
edited by Richard C Thompson, Niels Madsen & Martina Knoop

Studying Distant Galaxies: A Handbook of Methods and Analyses
by François Hammer, Mathieu Puech, Hector Flores & Myriam Rodrigues

An Introduction to Particle Dark Matter
by Stefano Profumo

Quantum States and Scattering in Semiconductor Nanostructures
by Camille Ndebeka-Bandou, Francesca Carosella & Gérald Bastard

Forthcoming

An Introduction to String Theory and D-Brane Dynamics: With Problems and Solutions (3rd Edition)
by Richard J Szabo

Advanced Textbooks in Physics

Quantum States and Scattering in Semiconductor Nanostructures

Camille Ndebeka-Bandou

Institute for Quantum Electronics, ETH Zürich, Switzerland

Francesca Carosella
Gérald Bastard

Laboratoire Pierre Aigrain, Ecole Normale Supérieure, France

World Scientific

NEW JERSEY · LONDON · SINGAPORE · BEIJING · SHANGHAI · HONG KONG · TAIPEI · CHENNAI · TOKYO

Published by

World Scientific Publishing Europe Ltd.

57 Shelton Street, Covent Garden, London WC2H 9HE

Head office: 5 Toh Tuck Link, Singapore 596224

USA office: 27 Warren Street, Suite 401-402, Hackensack, NJ 07601

Library of Congress Cataloging-in-Publication Data

Names: Ndebeka-Bandou, Camille, 1987– | Carosella, Francesca, 1976– |
 Bastard, Gérald.
Title: Quantum states and scattering in semiconductor nanostructures /
 by Camille Ndebeka-Bandou (ETH Zürich, Switzerland), Francesca Carosella
 (Ecole Normale Supérieure, France), Gérald Bastard (Ecole Normale Supérieure, France).
Description: New Jersey : World Scientific, 2017. | Series: Advanced textbooks in physics
Identifiers: LCCN 2016056720| ISBN 9781786343017 (hc : alk. paper) |
 ISBN 9781786343024 (pbk : alk. paper)
Subjects: LCSH: Nanoelectronics. | Semiconductors. | Quantum systems. | Quantum scattering.
Classification: LCC TK7874.84 .N44 2017 | DDC 537.6/226--dc23
LC record available at https://lccn.loc.gov/2016056720

British Library Cataloguing-in-Publication Data
A catalogue record for this book is available from the British Library.

Desk Editors: V. Vishnu Mohan/Mary Simpson

Typeset by Stallion Press

Email: enquiries@stallionpress.com

Foreword

The last 30 years have witnessed the prevalent use of — "quantum heterostructures" — in microelectronics (Field Effect Transistor) and optoelectronics (Quantum Well Lasers, Quantum Cascade Lasers). Advances in the area of nanostructures require a good knowledge of elementary quantum mechanics and simultaneously a feeling of how a certain electronic function is best realised (the "bandgap engineering"). Yet, the usual teaching of quantum mechanics focuses on general principles and the applications that are proposed to the students to understand this formal apparatus often fall within the field of atomic physics. The theories of quantum measurements, the decoherence, are also highlighted and for good reasons, as the measurement theory has recently been the topics of major discoveries. To be checked it requires the simpler possible quantum objects: ultra-diluted two-level systems as realised in atomic physics. However, these questions (time evolution of systems with very few degree of freedom) are irrelevant to the understanding of the electron states in semiconductor nanostructures where one deals most often with extended states perturbed by static defects or inelastic interactions with phonons.

The book is written for students and engineers who have already been exposed to elementary quantum mechanics and statistical physics. That is why our book presents an applied version of quantum mechanics that is very short on general physical questions but has the target of predicting the electron whereabouts in existing semiconductor heterostructures. To give an example, we note that many of the nanostructures display an effective cylindrical symmetry around an axis. That is why we shall devote very little space below to the spherically symmetric problems, so prevalent in atomic physics. A great deal of attention will be given to the scattering of extended states while usual courses emphasize discrete electronic states and their coupling to external fields. Our aim is to bring our readers to answer basic but relevant questions for devices; "where are the electrons in the structures, how do their energy levels vary when this or that parameter changes, what is the order of magnitude of the coupling between the electrons and the static defects or the phonons?".

While computers allow a numerical solution of a large number of problems in nanostructures, we believe it remains very important that the researchers/engineers working on these materials can analytically handle simplified cases.

To this end, we propose more than 50 exercises/problems (with solutions) where the readers will train him/herself to analytically approach actual situations. We have created most of these exercises (or we believe to have done so). Some of them have been used in different Master programmes at École Normale Supérieure (International Centre for Fundamental Physics), Pierre et Marie Curie (Sciences des Matériaux et des Nano-objets) and Paris Diderot Universities (Dispositifs Quantiques) and in different Universities abroad (TU Wien, IIS Tokyo, HKUST). We have retained a handful of classic exercises (for instance, the variational estimate of the hydrogen binding energy using a Gaussian trial function [1]) because of their pedagogical values despite the fact that some of them can be found on the Web or in specific textbooks.

The exercises/problems can be quite short with the aim of training the reader to do the calculations automatically or can be long if a certain question needs to be discussed more thoroughly. The set of exercises can be split roughly into five parts: (a) basic quantum mechanics (1)–(16); (b) energy levels in 1D structures (17)–(25); (c) (static)perturbation theory (26)–(32); (d) time-dependent problems (33)–(44); (e) scattering (45)–(54). Problems involving one-dimensional (1D) localised states are discussed more thoroughly than usually found in textbooks because a (huge) number of actual heterostructures display 1D bound states.

Throughout the years, discussions with colleagues have helped us to clarify many aspects of semiconductor heterostructures. We are much indebted to Prs K. Unterrainer, G. Strasser, J. Wang, L. Esaki, K. Hirakawa, Y. Arakawa, H. Sakaki, A. Wacker, C. Sirtori, A. Vasanelli, Y. Guldner, C. Delalande, Ph. Roussignol, J.M. Berroir, P. Voisin, M. Voos and, above all, R. Ferreira.

One of us (GB) would like to acknowledge the Technical University Vienna, the Institute of Industrial Science Tokyo and the Hong Kong University for Science and Technology for constant support all over the years. One of us (CNB) would like to acknowledge Prof. K. Hirakawa and Prof. J. Faist for their hospitality during her stay in Tokyo and Zurich.

Camille Ndebeka-Bandou[a,b], Francesca Carosella[a] and Gérald Bastard[a,c,d,e]

[a]*Laboratoire Pierre Aigrain École Normale Supérieure, France*
[b]*ETH Zürich, Switzerland*
[c]*Technical University Vienna, Austria*
[d]*Institute of Industrial Science University of Tokyo, Japan*
[e]*Hong Kong University of Science and Technology, Hong Kong*

September 2016

About the Authors

Gérald Bastard was born in 1950 near Paris. Presently he is (emeritus) Directeur de Recherche at the CNRS (French National Council for Research) and he is the head of the Theory group at the Laboratoire Pierre Aigrain (LPA-ENS). He received his PhD degree in Physics in 1979 with a study about "Magneto — optical studies of zero gap $Hg_{1-x}Mn_xTe$ alloys". In 1981–1982 he worked as a post-doc at IBM (Yorktown Heights, USA) in L. Esaki's group and since then has studied electronic states in semiconductor nanostructures. Gérald Bastard has been Visiting Professor/Scientist at IBM, MPI (Stuggart, Germany), EPFL (Lausanne, Switzerland), University of Lecce (Italy), Institute of Industrial Science (Tokyo, Japan), TU Wien (Austria), HKUST (Hong Kong, China). He has written more than 200 papers in the scientific literature, several review articles and two books: *Wave Mechanics Applied to Semiconductor Heterostructures*, published in 1988 and, together with R. Ferreira, *Capture and Relaxation in Self-Assembled Semiconductor Quantum Dots* in 2015.

Francesca Carosella is Associate Professor at Université Paris Diderot since 2008 and she performs research at the Laboratoire Pierre Aigrain (LPA, Ecole Normale Supérieure) within the Theory group. Dr. Carosella was born in 1976 in Italy. She graduated at the University of Bologna, (Italy) and obtained her PhD degree in Physics in 2005 at the University of Science and Technology of Lille (USTL) with a theoretical work about the transport properties of AlGaN/GaN heterostructure. At present her research interests are focussed on the theoretical study of the optical and electronic properties of semiconductor heterostructures; for instance, the scattering contributions to the absorption spectrum lineshape and linewidth of disordered quantum cascade structures; the electronic properties of Dirac superlattices and of heterostructures with no-common anions.

Camille Ndebeka-Bandou is a Post-doctoral Researcher and Teaching Assistant at the Institute of Quantum Electronics of the Swiss Federal Institute of Technology (ETH Zürich) and she does her research in the Quantum Optoelectronics Group of Pr. Jérôme Faist. Dr. Ndebeka-Bandou was born in 1987 in Guadeloupe. She studied Physics in Paris (France), graduated at the Université Paris Diderot in 2011 and obtained her PhD degree in 2014 with a theoretical study of the electron states in disordered semiconductor heterostructures, notably the quantum cascade structures. Since 2014, she has carried out various research projects at ETH Zürich such as the theoretical investigation of the loss mechanisms in terahertz quantum cascade lasers, the ultra-strong coupling in metamaterial cavities and the theoretical study of the bulk states in disordered two-dimensional topological insulators.

Contents

PART I
Practical Quantum Mechanics

Chapter I.1

Schrödinger Equation

Classical mechanics states that the state of a physical system is described by the knowledge of the positions and velocities at time t plus the Newton (or Lagrange or Hamilton) law for its evolution.

Quantum mechanics states the following two rules for describing a physical system.

Rule 1. The space of any physical system is described by (state) vectors conventionally noted by $|\psi\rangle$ that belong to a Hilbert space. A Hilbert space is an abstract vector space possessing the structure of an inner product: if $|\varphi_1\rangle$ and $|\varphi_2\rangle$ are two state vectors belonging to the Hilbert space, their inner product is:

$$\langle \varphi_1|\varphi_2\rangle = \iiint d^3r\, \varphi_1^*(\vec{r})\varphi_2(\vec{r}) \tag{I.1.1}$$

where $*$ denotes the complex conjugation. Hilbert spaces are complete (i.e., if every Cauchy sequence in M has a limit in M). They are indispensable tools in the theories of partial differential equations, quantum mechanics, Fourier analysis.

Rule 2. For non-relativistic particles, the time evolution of the state vectors is given by the Schrödinger equation:

$$i\hbar \frac{\partial}{\partial t}|\psi(t)\rangle = H|\psi(t)\rangle \tag{I.1.2}$$

where H is the Hamiltonian operator. For N particles, the Hamiltonian is the sum of the N kinetic energies and of the potential energies.

The latter comprise the interactions U_i between the particles and external fields plus the particle–particle interactions V_{ij}:

$$H = \sum_{i=1}^{N} \left(\frac{p_i^2}{2m_i} + U_i \right) + \frac{1}{2} \sum_{i \neq j=1}^{N} V_{ij} \qquad (I.1.3)$$

where m_i is the mass of the ith particle.

While the quantum mechanical description is seldom useful for macroscopic bodies, it proves of paramount importance for very small objects (elementary particles, atoms, nano-objects) and thus for the understanding of the behaviour of many semiconductor devices.

Most of the times in this book we shall focus on the so-called position-representation where the state vector is projected on the $\vec{r}$ basis: for N particles this defines the N particles wavefunctions $\psi(\vec{r}_1, \vec{r}_2, \ldots, \vec{r}_N, t)$.

$$\psi(\vec{r}_1, \vec{r}_2, \ldots, \vec{r}_N, t) = \langle \vec{r}_1, \vec{r}_2, \ldots, \vec{r}_N | \psi(t) \rangle \qquad (I.1.4)$$

The physical interpretation of $\psi(\vec{r}_1, \vec{r}_2, \ldots, \vec{r}_N, t)$ is

$$|\psi(\vec{r}_1, \vec{r}_2, \ldots, \vec{r}_N, t)|^2 d^3 r_1 d^3 r_2 \ldots d^3 r_N \qquad (I.1.5)$$

which represents the probability to find at time t the first particle in an infinitesimal volume $d^3 r_1$ around $\vec{r}_1$, the second particle in an infinitesimal volume $d^3 r_2$ around $\vec{r}_2$, the Nth particle in an infinitesimal volume $d^3 r_N$ around $\vec{r}_N$. It results from this definition that the wavefunctions have to be normalised:

$$\iint \ldots \int d^3 r_1 d^3 r_2 \ldots d^3 r_N |\psi(\vec{r}_1, \vec{r}_2, \ldots, \vec{r}_N, t)|^2 = 1 \qquad (I.1.6)$$

The N particles wavefunction $\psi(\vec{r}_1, \vec{r}_2, \ldots, \vec{r}_N, t)$ is the solution of the partial differential equation:

$$i\hbar \frac{\partial}{\partial t} \psi(\vec{r}_1, \vec{r}_2, \ldots, \vec{r}_N, t)$$

$$= \left[\sum_{i=1}^{N} \left(\frac{(\vec{p})^2}{2m_i} + U(\vec{r}_i, t) \right) + \frac{1}{2} \sum_{i \neq j=1}^{N} V(\vec{r}_i, \vec{r}_j) \right]$$

$$\times \psi(\vec{r}_1, \vec{r}_2, \ldots, \vec{r}_N, t) \qquad (I.1.7)$$

In the Hamiltonian function, one should replace the linear momentum $\vec{p}$ by $-i\hbar\vec{\nabla}$ where $\vec{\nabla}$ is the gradient operator:

$$\vec{\nabla} = \left(\frac{\partial}{\partial x}, \frac{\partial}{\partial y}, \frac{\partial}{\partial z}\right) \qquad (I.1.8)$$

Note that if the particles are identical, a special prescription will have to be made on the shape of $\psi(\vec{r}_1, \vec{r}_2, \ldots, \vec{r}_N, t)$. Rule of symmetrisation or antisymmetrisation of the wavefunctions depending on whether the identical particles are bosons (with integer spins) or fermions (with half integer spins) will be given:

If H is time independent, then $|\psi(t)\rangle$ can be factorised:

$$|\psi(t)\rangle = e^{-i\frac{Et}{\hbar}}|\varphi\rangle \qquad (I.1.9)$$

$$H|\varphi\rangle = E|\varphi\rangle \qquad (I.1.10)$$

In the $\vec{r}$ representation, this means that the wavefunction $\psi(\vec{r}_1, \vec{r}_2, \ldots, \vec{r}_N, t)$ can be factorised into the product of an t-dependent function by an $\vec{r}$-dependent function. Inserting this ansatz into the Schrödinger equation, one finds readily that the wavefunction should be written:

$$\psi(\vec{r}_1, \vec{r}_2, \ldots, \vec{r}_N, t) = e^{-i\frac{Et}{\hbar}}\varphi(\vec{r}_1, \vec{r}_2, \ldots, \vec{r}_N) \qquad (I.1.11)$$

In the equation $H|\varphi\rangle = E|\varphi\rangle$, the vector $|\varphi\rangle$ is such that applying H on it produces a vector that is proportional to it (in other words it is an eigenvector of H, see below).

The Schrödinger equation is linear: if $|\varphi_1\rangle$ and $|\varphi_2\rangle$ are solutions of $H|\psi\rangle = E|\psi\rangle$ then $a|\varphi_1\rangle + b|\varphi_2\rangle$, a and b being c-numbers, is also a solution corresponding to the same energy E. The linear aspect of quantum mechanics implies that particles may display wave-like behaviours, such as interference effects. The electron diffraction by a crystal of Nickel observed by Davisson and Germer in 1927 was an early spectacular confirmation of de Broglie's idea that a particle with linear momentum p is associated with a wave with wavelength $\lambda = h/p$ [2]. More recently (2002), the interference of fullerene (C_{70}) molecules passing through slits showed that more complicated objects than elementary particles can reveal wave-like behaviours [3].

A great deal of the quantum mechanical machinery rests on linear algebra in finite (or infinite) vector spaces. We summarise in the following a few linear algebra properties. Much more can be found in textbooks specifically devoted to Algebra and to Quantum Mechanics [4–11].

I.1.1.   Eigenvalues, eigenvectors of linear operators

A linear operator A is said to be diagonal in the basis $|\alpha_n\rangle$ if its matrix elements between the basis vectors are such that:

$$\langle \alpha_n | A | \alpha_m \rangle = a_n \delta_{nm} \tag{I.1.12}$$

A linear operator A is said to be diagonalisable if it is similar to a diagonal operator, i.e., if there exists an invertible matrix M such that $M^{-1} A M$ is a diagonal matrix.

The eigenvalues a_n and the eigenvectors $|\alpha_n\rangle$ of an operator A are such that:

$$A|\alpha_n\rangle = a_n |\alpha_n\rangle \tag{I.1.13}$$

If there exists a single eigenvector associated with the eigenvalue a_n, the latter is said non-degenerate. On the contrary, if several (say p) independent eigenvectors correspond to the same eigenvalue a_n, the latter is said p-fold degenerate. The eigenvalues λ of an operator A acting in an N-dimensional vector space are obtained by solving:

$$\det(A - \lambda \mathrm{Id}_N) = 0 \tag{I.1.14}$$

where $\det(A - \lambda \mathrm{Id}_N)$ is the determinant of the matrix $A - \lambda \mathrm{Id}_N$ and Id_N is the $N \times N$ identity matrix. Therefore, the eigenvalues are the zeros of the characteristic polynomial of the matrix A. For instance, the $N \times N$ identity matrix $A_{ij} = \delta_{ij}$, $i, j = 1, \ldots, N$, admits a single eigenvalue 1 that is N-fold degenerate.

The matrix A:

$$A = \begin{pmatrix} E_1 & eFd \\ eFd & E_2 \end{pmatrix} \tag{I.1.15}$$

admits two non-degenerate eigenvalues:

$$\lambda_{\pm} = \frac{E_1 + E_2}{2} \pm \sqrt{\left(\frac{E_2 - E_1}{2}\right)^2 + e^2 F^2 d^2} \tag{I.1.16}$$

The matrix B:

$$B = \begin{pmatrix} 1 & \frac{1}{2} \\ -\frac{1}{2} & 2 \end{pmatrix} \qquad \text{(I.1.17)}$$

admits a single eigenvalue $(\frac{3}{2})$ which is two-fold degenerate.

The matrix C:

$$C = \begin{pmatrix} 0 & a & a & a & a & a & a \\ a & \Delta & 0 & 0 & 0 & 0 & 0 \\ a & 0 & \Delta & 0 & 0 & 0 & 0 \\ a & 0 & 0 & \Delta & 0 & 0 & 0 \\ a & 0 & 0 & 0 & \Delta & 0 & 0 \\ a & 0 & 0 & 0 & 0 & \Delta & 0 \\ a & 0 & 0 & 0 & 0 & 0 & \Delta \end{pmatrix} \qquad \text{(I.1.18)}$$

admits the five-fold degenerate eigenvalue Δ and the two non-degenerate eigenvalues:

$$\lambda_\pm = \frac{\Delta}{2} \pm \sqrt{\left(\frac{\Delta}{2}\right)^2 + 6a^2} \qquad \text{(I.1.19)}$$

If A is a diagonalisable operator, then any power of A is diagonalisable. Let $f(x)$ be a Taylor expandable function:

$$f(x) = \sum_{n=0} a_n x^n \qquad \text{(I.1.20)}$$

Then $f(A)$ can be similarly defined and if A is diagonalisable with eigenvalues λ_i then $f(A)$ is also diagonalisable with eigenvalues $f(\lambda_i)$.

Note that not all operators can be diagonalised. For instance, the operator represented by:

$$M = \begin{pmatrix} 0 & a \\ 0 & 0 \end{pmatrix} \qquad \text{(I.1.21)}$$

is not diagonalisable.

I.1.2. Adjoint operator

The transpose A^t of the operator A is defined as

$$A^t_{ij} = A_{ji} \qquad \text{(I.1.22)}$$

The adjoint $A^\dagger$ of the operator A is defined by having its matrix element to be equal to the complex conjugates of the A^t matrix elements:

$$A^\dagger_{ij} = A^*_{ji} \qquad \text{(I.1.23)}$$

I.1.3.   Hermitian operators: observables

Rule 1. The physical observables (angular momentum, linear momentum, energy, etc.) are represented by linear operators that are hermitian (also called "self-adjoint"). A hermitian operator coincides with its adjoint: $A = A^\dagger$. In a basis $|\varphi_n\rangle$ of the Hilbert space, an observable A admits matrix elements which are such that:

$$\langle \varphi_n | A | \varphi_m \rangle = \langle \varphi_m | A | \varphi_n \rangle^* \tag{I.1.24}$$

This implies that the diagonal elements of an observable are real.

Rule 2. If an observable A is measured, the only possible outputs of these measurements are the eigenvalues of A. Immediately after a measurement the state of the system is the eigenvector associated with the eigenvalue that has resulted from the measurement. How the state of a quantum system can in effect collapse on an eigenvector of A has been the subject of intense researches and the theory of the measurement processes keeps attracting lots of attention in simple systems (say 2-level systems) [5]. In a semiconductor device, these sorts of question seldom occur because semiconductor systems are too intricate (have too many interacting variables) to allow a clear assessment of the quantum mechanical predictions one can make on simple systems.

Hermitian operators admit real eigenvalues. In finite dimensions, any hermitian matrix can be diagonalised and has as many eigenvectors as the dimension of the space can be found (spectral decomposition theorem). Moreover, the eigenvectors of a hermitian operator form an ortho-normalised basis. Several results established in finite dimensions can be extended to infinite dimensions.

I.1.4.   Unitary operators

A linear operator U whose inverse is its adjoint is called *unitary*:

$$U^{-1} = U^\dagger \tag{I.1.25}$$

The evolution operator $\exp(-\frac{iHt}{\hbar})$ where H is the Hamiltonian is unitary and of great use to study the time evolution of quantum systems. A unitary operator preserves the "lengths" and "angles" between vectors. Like hermitian operators, the eigenvectors of a unitary matrix are orthogonal. However, its eigenvalues are not necessarily real. For example, the eigenvalues of the evolution operators are $\exp(-\frac{iE_n t}{\hbar})$ where E_n are the eigenvalues of H.

I.1.5.   Projectors

A projector operator P_n on the vector $|\varphi_n\rangle$ can be written: $P_n = |\varphi_n\rangle\langle\varphi_n|$ since the only non-vanishing element of P_n is:

$$\langle\varphi_i|P_n|\varphi_j\rangle = \delta_{ni}\delta_{nj} \tag{I.1.26}$$

P_n is idempotent: $P_n^2 = P_n$. Suppose a subset B of dimension g of the set of the state vectors. Let $|b_1\rangle, |b_2\rangle, \ldots, |b_g\rangle$ be a basis of B. Then the restriction $A_{/B}$ of the operator A to the subset B is:

$$A_{/B} = P_B A P_B = \sum_{i=1}^{g}\sum_{j=1}^{g} |b_n\rangle A_{nm}\langle b_m|; \quad A_{nm} = \langle b_n|A|b_m\rangle \tag{I.1.27}$$

It follows from the spectral decomposition theorem and the definition of projector operators that if we denote by a_n and $|\alpha_n\rangle$ the eigenvalues (possibly degenerate) and associated eigenvectors of a hermitian operator A there is:

$$A = \sum_n a_n|\alpha_n\rangle\langle\alpha_n| \tag{I.1.28}$$

In other words the matrix representing A on the basis $|\alpha_n\rangle$ basis is diagonal with elements:

$$A_{nm} = \langle\alpha_n|A|\alpha_m\rangle = a_n\delta_{nm} \tag{I.1.29}$$

I.1.6.   Commuting operators

The commutator $[A, B]$ of two operators is:

$$[A, B] = AB - BA \tag{I.1.30}$$

If two hermitian operators A and B commute then there exists a basis of common eigenvectors $|\alpha_n\rangle$ where these two operators are simultaneously diagonal. Let us take an eigenvector of A associated with the eigenvalue a_n:

$$A|\alpha_n\rangle = a_n|\alpha_n\rangle \qquad (I.1.31)$$

and let us act on this vector identity with the operator B:

$$BA|\alpha_n\rangle = AB|\alpha_n\rangle = a_n B|\alpha_n\rangle \qquad (I.1.32)$$

Thus, the vector $B|\alpha_n\rangle$ is also an eigenvector of A with the same eigenvalue a_n as A. If the eigenvalue a_n is non-degenerate then $B|\alpha_n\rangle$ should be collinear to $|\alpha_n\rangle$; in other words $|\alpha_n\rangle$ is also an eigenvector of the B operator. If a_n is g-fold degenerate, let us take the g eigenvectors $|\alpha_n^i\rangle$, $i = 1, \dots, g$ corresponding to the g eigenvalues of A. In this subspace of dimension g, we write the matrix B_g whose matrix elements are $\langle \alpha_n^i|B|\alpha_n^j\rangle$. B being hermitian it can be diagonalised. Let us call $|\beta_n^i\rangle$, $i = 1, \dots, g$ the eigenvectors associated with the eigenvalues $b_i(n)$ (these eigenvalues are possibly degenerate). In the $|\beta_n^i\rangle$, $i = 1, \dots, g$ basis, B is diagonal as well as A (with the eigenvalue a_n) because $|\beta_n^i\rangle$, $i = 1, \dots, g$ are linear combinations of the $|\alpha_n^i\rangle$ vectors.

A similar result holds if B is a unitary operator. This theorem is the key ingredient to help finding the eigenvalues of H and the time evolution of the system if H does not depend explicitly on time. Suppose we know the eigenvalues and eigenvectors of a time-independent Hamiltonian

$$H|\varphi_n\rangle = E_n|\varphi_n\rangle \qquad (I.1.33)$$

And suppose we know the wavefunction at time $t = 0$: $|\psi(t = 0)\rangle$. We expand $|\psi(t = 0)\rangle$ on the $|\varphi_n\rangle$ basis:

$$|\psi(t = 0)\rangle = \left(\sum_n |\varphi_n\rangle\langle\varphi_n|\right)|\psi(t = 0)\rangle = \sum_n c_n|\varphi_n\rangle \qquad (I.1.34)$$

$$c_n = \langle\varphi_n|\psi(t = 0)\rangle \qquad (I.1.35)$$

Then the solution of the time-dependent Schrödinger equation is:

$$|\psi(t)\rangle = \sum_n c_n e^{-i\frac{E_n t}{\hbar}}|\varphi_n\rangle \qquad (I.1.36)$$

Thus, if we know how to diagonalise H, we shall be able to know exactly how the state vector evolves with time and knowing $|\psi(t)\rangle$, we shall be able to compute the time dependence of the average value of any operator B. Note that the formal solution of the time-dependent Schrödinger equation given $|\psi(t = 0)\rangle$ is:

$$|\psi(t)\rangle = \exp\left(-i\frac{Ht}{\hbar}\right)|\psi(0)\rangle \tag{I.1.37}$$

as can be directly checked if H is time independent. Then, the projection of $|\psi(t = 0)\rangle$ on the $|\varphi_n\rangle$ basis leads to the result.

Diagonalising H is usually very difficult except in a few simple cases. So, the strategy is to find simple operators B that commute with H and that are more easily diagonalisable. Let us give three examples:

Example 1. Let us consider a one-dimensional (1D) crystal. In the stationary Schrödinger equation the potential energy is periodic:

$$V(z + d) = V(z) \tag{I.1.38}$$

Consider now the translation operators

$$T_j = \exp\left(\frac{ip_z}{\hbar}jd\right) \tag{I.1.39}$$

where j is a relative integer. It is clearly a unitary operator. For any function $\psi(z)$ there is:

$$T_j\psi(z) = \psi(z + jd) \tag{I.1.40}$$

The translation operators fulfil:

$$T_jT_{j'} = T_{j'}T_j = T_{j+j'}; \quad [T_j, T_{j'}] = 0; \quad T_j^\dagger = T_{-j} = (T_j)^{-1} \tag{I.1.41}$$

Since $V(z)$ is periodic one finds readily that $[T_j, H] = 0$. Thus, there exists a common basis to H and T_j. But the eigenfunctions of T_j are easy to obtain (Floquet–Bloch theorem): since T_j is unitary its eigenvalues can always be written $\exp(ikjd)$ where k is an unknown (1D) vector. Let us denote by $\psi_k(z)$ the eigenfunction associated with the eigenvalue $\exp(ikjd)$:

$$T_j\psi_k(z) = e^{ikjd}\psi_k(z); \quad T_j\psi_k(z) = \psi_k(z + d) \tag{I.1.42}$$

These two equations show that:

$$\psi_k(z) = e^{ikz}u_k(z); \quad u_k(z + d) = u_k(z) \tag{I.1.43}$$

Hence, if $V(z)$ is periodic one can search the eigenfunctions of H in the form of the product of a plane wave and a periodic function. The Floquet–Bloch theorem thus allows to restrict to one single unit cell instead of the whole crystal, the numerical search of the solution of the Schrödinger equation.

Example 2. Consider the 1D Schrödinger equation with a potential that is an even function of z: $V(z) = V(-z)$. Consider the parity operator P such that $P\psi(z) = \psi(-z)$. The eigenfunctions of P are easy to find since $P^2 = \mathrm{Id}$. Hence, P admits two eigenvalues ± 1 and the corresponding eigenfunctions are the functions even in z (associated to $+1$) and the functions that are odd in z (associated to -1). One can readily check that $[P, H] = 0$. Hence, one can search the eigenfunctions of H in two different classes comprising respectively even and odd functions of z.

Example 3. Consider a three-dimensional (3D) problem with a potential energy that displays a cylindrical symmetry (around the z-axis). Then, it can be readily checked that the z component of the angular momentum $L_z = xp_y - yp_x$ commutes with H. The eigenfunctions of L_z are particularly easy to find. Working in polar coordinates and calling $m\hbar$ the eigenvalues (where m is *a priori* arbitrary and $\hbar$ has to show up to get the right dimension of an angular momentum) we get:

$$x = \rho\cos(\theta);\ y = \rho\sin(\theta) \Rightarrow L_z = -i\hbar\frac{\partial}{\partial\theta} \tag{I.1.44}$$

$$L_z f(\theta) = m\hbar f(\theta) \Rightarrow f(\theta) = e^{im\theta} \tag{I.1.45}$$

Now if we change θ into $\theta + 2\pi$, the wavefunction should be unchanged. Hence, the *a priori* unknown parameter m should actually be a relative integer.

To take advantage of the commutation between H and L_z, it is useful to work in cylindrical coordinates. The 3D Schrödinger equation is written:

$$-\frac{\hbar^2}{2m}\left[\frac{1}{\rho}\frac{\partial}{\partial\rho}\left(\rho\frac{\partial\psi}{\partial\rho}\right) + \frac{1}{\rho^2}\frac{\partial^2\psi}{\partial\theta^2} + \frac{\partial^2\psi}{\partial z^2}\right] + V(\rho, z)\psi = E\psi \tag{I.1.46}$$

$$\psi = \psi(\rho, \theta, z) \tag{I.1.47}$$

Since L_z commutes with H, we can immediately factorise $\psi(\rho, \theta, z)$ into $e^{im\theta} f(\rho, z)$ where f fulfils:

$$-\frac{\hbar^2}{2m} \left[\frac{1}{\rho} \frac{\partial}{\partial \rho} \left(\rho \frac{\partial f}{\partial \rho} \right) - \frac{m^2}{\rho^2} + \frac{\partial^2 f}{\partial z^2} \right] + V(\rho, z) f = E f \qquad (I.1.48)$$

Hence, instead of having to solve a partial differential equation in three variables, we have only to wonder about two independent variables.

I.1.7. Two important examples of non-commuting operators

An important case of two non-commuting operators is given by the position z and the linear momentum p_z. There is:

$$[z, p_z]\varphi(z) = \frac{\hbar}{i} \left(z \frac{d\varphi(z)}{dz} - \frac{d}{dz}[z\varphi(z)] \right) = i\hbar\varphi(z) \qquad (I.1.49)$$

This relation is valid for any function $\varphi(z)$. Hence:

$$[z, p_z] = i\hbar \qquad (I.1.50)$$

In addition, it is easily shown that

$$[z^n, p_z] = i\hbar n z^{n-1} \qquad (I.1.51)$$

Suppose there is a Taylor-expandable function $f(z)$. Then:

$$[f(z), p_z] = i\hbar f'(z) \qquad (I.1.52)$$

Another important example of non-commuting operator is given by the creation and annihilation operators of the harmonic oscillator. They are defined by:

$$a = \frac{1}{\sqrt{2}} \left(x\sqrt{\frac{m\omega}{\hbar}} + \frac{i}{\sqrt{m\omega\hbar}} p_x \right) \qquad (I.1.53)$$

$$a^\dagger = \frac{1}{\sqrt{2}} \left(x\sqrt{\frac{m\omega}{\hbar}} - \frac{i}{\sqrt{m\omega\hbar}} p_x \right) \qquad (I.1.54)$$

where ω is the angular frequency of the oscillator. If we call $|n\rangle$ the eigenstates of the harmonic oscillator associated with the eigenvalue $\left(n + \frac{1}{2}\right)\hbar\omega$, a and $a^\dagger$ are such that:

$$a|n\rangle = \sqrt{n}|n-1\rangle; \quad a^\dagger|n\rangle = \sqrt{n+1}|n+1\rangle \qquad (I.1.55)$$

Using $[x, p_x] = i\hbar$, one gets readily that:

$$[a, a^\dagger] = 1 \qquad (\text{I.1.56})$$

I.1.8. Heisenberg inequalities

Consider a hermitian operator A. We define the standard deviation σ_A by:

$$\sigma_A = \sqrt{\langle A^2 \rangle - \langle A \rangle^2} \qquad (\text{I.1.57})$$

where the average is taken on a state $|\psi\rangle$, i.e., $\langle A \rangle = \langle \psi | A | \psi \rangle$.

Consider now two operators A and B and let C be their commutator: $C = [A, B] = AB - BA$. There is an important consequence associated with the non-commutativity of operators. This is called the Heisenberg inequalities. It states that

$$\sigma_A \sigma_B \geq \frac{1}{2} |\langle [A, B] \rangle| \qquad (\text{I.1.58})$$

Thus for $A = x$ and $B = p_x$, we get:

$$\sigma_x \sigma_{p_x} \geq \frac{\hbar}{2} \qquad (\text{I.1.59})$$

There have been a number of comments about this inequality and its implications. It is a consequence of the wave-like nature of the quantum particles and inequalities similar to this one have appeared in other fields of physics (e.g., electromagnetism).

Consider the Hamiltonian of a particle of mass m^*:

$$H = \frac{p^2}{2m^*} + V(\vec{r}) \qquad (\text{I.1.60})$$

where $V(\vec{r})$ is an attractive potential (e.g., in 1D $V(x) = V_0 \left(\frac{x}{L} \right)^{2n}$ or $V(x) = -\frac{V_0}{\cosh\left(\frac{x}{L}\right)}$, etc.). The Heisenberg inequality is very helpful to explain why confining a quantum particle in a finite segment (or area or volume) necessarily implies a penalty in kinetic energy, in striking contrast with the classical analysis. The classical analysis of the previous problem tells that the lowest classical state is obtained by putting the particle at the minimum of $V(x)$ ($x = 0$ in the above examples) with a zero kinetic energy. Hence, in the two

examples given above the minimum classical energy are respectively
0 and $-V_0$. For the lowest quantum motion, we know that it will be
bound over a distance $\sigma_x \approx L$ because if we were to compute σ_x, we
would find $\langle x \rangle = 0$ and $\langle x \rangle^2 = \alpha L^2$, where the averages are over the
ground bound state of the particle implying the result $\sigma_x \approx L$. Now
Heisenberg inequality tells us that:

$$\sigma_{p_x} \geq \frac{\hbar}{2\sigma_x} \tag{I.1.61}$$

or by squaring:

$$\langle p_x^2 \rangle - \langle p_x \rangle^2 = \langle p_x^2 \rangle \geq \frac{\hbar^2}{4\sigma_x^2} = \frac{\hbar^2}{4\alpha L^2} \tag{I.1.62}$$

Thus, in the ground bound state, the average kinetic energy is non-
zero, unlike in classical physics since we find:

$$\left\langle \frac{p_x^2}{2m^*} \right\rangle \geq \frac{\hbar^2}{8\alpha m^* L^2} \tag{I.1.63}$$

We note that the more confined is the particle, the more kinetic
energy has to be paid for this confinement. As we shall see later, a
striking example of this property is the increasing ground state confinement energy of square quantum wells with decreasing thicknesses
L while, classically, irrespective of L the lowest possible energy would
have been the bottom of the well.

I.1.9.   Spin

The quantum mechanical operators associated with all the classical
observables (mechanical energy, linear momentum, orbital momentum, position, etc.) are hermitian. There are certain observables that
have no classical counterpart. The spin of a particle is one of them.
The spin of a particle is an intrinsic angular momentum that the particle displays even if it is at rest (where its classical angular momentum is zero). Fermions are characterised by spins whose projection
on a given axis is $(n + \frac{1}{2})\hbar$ where n is a relative integer. Bosons have
spin projections that are equal to a relative integer times $\hbar$. In our
case, electrons in semiconductors, we shall most often deal with spins
$\frac{1}{2}$. The Hilbert space associated with a spin $\frac{1}{2}$ has a dimension equal

to 2 (more generally, the Hilbert space associated with a spin S has a dimension of $2S + 1$). For a spin $\frac{1}{2}$, the spin eigenfunctions are labelled $| \uparrow \rangle$ and $| \downarrow \rangle$ corresponding to projection on an arbitrary axis (here called z) equal to $\frac{\hbar}{2}$ $(-\frac{\hbar}{2})$.

In the basis where the operator of the spin component along the z axis σ_z is diagonal, the matrices of σ_x, σ_y and σ_z are:

$$\sigma_x = \frac{\hbar}{2} \begin{pmatrix} 0 & 1 \\ 1 & 0 \end{pmatrix}; \quad \sigma_y = \frac{\hbar}{2} \begin{pmatrix} 0 & -i \\ i & 0 \end{pmatrix}; \quad \sigma_z = \frac{\hbar}{2} \begin{pmatrix} 1 & 0 \\ 0 & -1 \end{pmatrix} \quad \text{(I.1.64)}$$

The reader will check that these matrices do not commute. In fact:

$$[\sigma_x, \sigma_y] = i\hbar\sigma_z; \quad [\sigma_y, \sigma_z] = i\hbar\sigma_x; \quad [\sigma_z, \sigma_x] = i\hbar\sigma_y \quad \text{(I.1.65)}$$

The reader will establish that:

$$\sigma_x^2 + \sigma_y^2 + \sigma_z^2 = \frac{3}{4}\hbar^2 \mathrm{Id} \quad \text{(I.1.66)}$$

where Id is the identity matrix. More generally, for a spin S there is: $S^2 = S_x^2 + S_y^2 + S_z^2 = S(S + 1)\hbar^2\mathrm{Id}$.

The electron spin interacts with an external magnetic field leading to spin paramagnetism. Relativistic corrections to the Schrödinger equation lead to a coupling between the electron spin and the orbital degrees of freedom. This is the spin–orbit coupling that plays a detrimental role in the spintronic devices because it allows electron spin flips due to non-magnetic impurities (e.g., charged impurities).

I.1.10.   Spin–orbit coupling

A magnetic moment is associated with the electron spin:

$$\vec{\mu} = g_e \mu_B \frac{\vec{\sigma}}{\hbar} \quad \text{(I.1.67)}$$

where μ_B is the Bohr magneton ($\mu_B = \frac{e\hbar}{2m_e}$), e is the magnitude of the electron charge, m_e the electron mass and g_e the electron g factor ($g_e \approx 2$ in vacuum while in semiconductors g_e is material dependent). A magnetic moment interacts with a magnetic field $\vec{B}$. From classical physics, we know that the interaction energy is given by:

$$H = -\vec{\mu} \cdot \vec{B} \quad \text{(I.1.68)}$$

When the electron moves in an atom or in a solid, it experiences the electric field $\vec{E}$ due to the nuclei and the other electrons, but also a motional magnetic field $\vec{B}_{\text{eff}}$ where to the lowest order in $\frac{v}{c}$:

$$\vec{B}_{\text{eff}} = -\frac{\vec{v} \times \vec{E}}{c^2} \tag{I.1.69}$$

This expression, together with the interaction energy H, allows to express the spin–orbit Hamiltonian:

$$H_{\text{SO}} = -\mu_B \frac{\vec{\sigma}}{m_e e \hbar c^2} \cdot (\vec{p} \times \vec{\nabla} V) \tag{I.1.70}$$

This expression coincides with the formulation often used in atomic physics where the potential energy has a spherical symmetry:

$$H_{\text{SO}}^{\text{atoms}} = \frac{1}{2m_e^2 c^2 r} \frac{dV}{dr} \vec{\sigma} \cdot \vec{L} \tag{I.1.71}$$

Note that a factor of 2, whose origin is quite subtle (Thomas precession), has been added to the denominator; it cancels the electron g factor taken equal to 2.

The spin–orbit interaction has important consequences in atoms since it shifts levels, lifts degeneracies and therefore produces splitting of the atomic spectral lines. Since it linearly involves the potential energy, it is more important in heavy atoms where the nucleus atomic charge is the larger. In semiconductors, the spin–orbit coupling affects more the valence bands, producing shifts and splittings, than the conduction band where it contributes to a spin flip of the conduction electron (see, e.g., [55]). We shall come back to spin-flip scattering later in this book (see Section II.5.3).

I.1.11. Density of states

Suppose a Hamiltonian H and its eigenvalues E_ν where ν (discrete or continuous) is (are) the quantum number(s) that label(s) the eigenstates. The number of states $N(E)$ with energy smaller or equal to

E is:

$$N(E) = \sum_{\nu} Y(E - E_{\nu}) \qquad (\text{I.1.72})$$

where $Y(x)$ is the step function:

$$Y(x) = 1 \quad x > 0; \quad Y(x) = 0 \quad x < 0 \qquad (\text{I.1.73})$$

Let us consider the difference $N(E + dE) - N(E)$ where dE is small but larger than the energy spacing between the eigenvalues with energies around E. Then by expanding to the first order in dE, we get the density of states $\rho(E)$ such that:

$$\rho(E)dE \approx N(E + dE) - N(E) \approx dE \sum_{\nu} \delta(E - E_{\nu}) \qquad (\text{I.1.74})$$

where we have made use of the property $\delta(x) = \frac{dY(x)}{dx}$. The quantity $\rho(E)$ tells us the density of allowed quantum levels of the particular Hamiltonian H in the vicinity of the energy E.

Let us recall a very useful property of the "delta function" by considering the following integral:

$$I = \int_{-\infty}^{+\infty} dx\, a(x)\delta[\varphi(x)] \qquad (\text{I.1.75})$$

where $a(x)$ and $\varphi(x)$ are assumed to be derivable. Then it can be shown that:

$$I = \int_{-\infty}^{+\infty} dx\, a(x)\delta[\varphi(x)] = \sum_{x_n} \int_{-\infty}^{+\infty} dx\, a(x)\frac{\delta(x - x_n)}{|\varphi'(x_n)|}$$

$$= \sum_{x_n} \frac{a(x_n)}{|\varphi'(x_n)|} \qquad (\text{I.1.76})$$

where the x_n are the zeros of $\varphi(x)$ on the interval $]-\infty, +\infty[$. More generally, if the support of the integral I is the segment $[a, b]$, the sum over the x_n contains only zeros of $\varphi(x)$ that are located in $[a, b]$.

Let us give an example of calculation of a density of states: the two-dimensional (2D) free motion. We add a constant potential energy E_0 to account for the (possible) size quantisation along the third dimension:

$$H = \frac{p^2}{2m^*} + E_0 \qquad (\text{I.1.77})$$

The eigenstates are:

$$|k_x, k_y, \chi_\sigma\rangle; \quad E(k_x, k_y, \sigma) = \frac{\hbar^2}{2m^*}\left(k_x^2 + k_y^2\right) + E_0 \qquad (\text{I.1.78})$$

where χ_σ are the spin eigenfunctions ($|\uparrow\rangle$, $|\downarrow\rangle$). Each orbital state $|k_x, k_y\rangle$ can accommodate two different projections of the electron spin on a given (arbitrary) direction. Since there is no magnetic field or spin–orbit coupling, the allowed energies do not depend on the quantum number σ. Thus, we have to compute:

$$\rho(E) = \sum_{k_x, k_y, \sigma} \delta\left[E - E_0 - \frac{\hbar^2\left(k_x^2 + k_y^2\right)}{2m^*}\right]$$

$$= 2 \sum_{k_x, k_y} \delta\left[E - E_0 - \frac{\hbar^2\left(k_x^2 + k_y^2\right)}{2m^*}\right] \qquad (\text{I.1.79})$$

When the area $L_x L_y$ is very large, the summation over the allowed values k_x, k_y is converted into an integration by:

$$\sum_{k_x, k_y} \cdots \;\rightarrow\; \frac{L_x L_y}{(2\pi)^2} \iint dk_x dk_y \cdots \qquad (\text{I.1.80})$$

The rest is just a matter of easy integrals. For instance, we move to polar k coordinates:

$$dk_x dk_y = k\, dk\, d\theta; \quad 0 \le k < \infty; \quad 0 \le \theta \le 2\pi \qquad (\text{I.1.81})$$

and

$$\rho(E) = \frac{m^* L_x L_y}{\pi \hbar^2} Y(E - E_0) \qquad (\text{I.1.82})$$

The density of states is zero below E_0: obviously no states can exist that would correspond to a negative k^2. Otherwise, above E_0, the density of states is constant. We propose several exercises on the computation of the density of states in various situations (see Exercises 3 and 4).

The notion of density of states is very useful in the evaluation of statistical averages. Consider an electron gas at thermal equilibrium. The mean occupation of the state $|\nu\rangle$ with eigenvalue E_ν of H is the Fermi–Dirac function:

$$f_D(E_\nu) = \frac{1}{1 + \exp[\beta(E_\nu - \mu)]} \tag{I.1.83}$$

where $\beta = (k_B T)^{-1}$, k_B the Boltzmann constant, T the temperature, and μ the chemical potential. We want to compute the average value of a certain function of the Hamiltonian $g(H)$ taking into account the mean occupation of $|\nu\rangle$. In an eigenstate $|\nu\rangle$ of H, $g(H)$ takes the value $g(E_\nu)$. Thus:

$$\begin{aligned}
\langle g \rangle &= \sum_\nu \frac{g(E_\nu)}{1 + \exp[\beta(E_\nu - \mu)]} \\
&= \int_{-\infty}^{+\infty} d\varepsilon \frac{g(\varepsilon)}{1 + \exp[\beta(\varepsilon - \mu)]} \sum_\nu \delta(\varepsilon - E_\nu) \\
&= \int_{-\infty}^{+\infty} d\varepsilon \frac{g(\varepsilon)}{1 + \exp[\beta(\varepsilon - \mu)]} \rho(\varepsilon) \tag{I.1.84}
\end{aligned}$$

Thus, the use of the density of states allows to separate the evaluation of a certain statistical average in terms of the product of two independent quantities: the density of states which is purely quantum mechanical in nature and is independent of the carrier statistics (temperature, chemical potential, etc.) and a statistical average that depends on temperature, chemical potential, etc. but where the details of the quantum system are lumped in a single function $\rho(\varepsilon)$.

I.1.12.   Identical particles and Pauli principle

The problem of N indistinguishable particles is in classical mechanics easily solved since two particles, even identical, can always be tracked and at any time one always knows, at least formally, where is particle 1 or particle 2. In quantum mechanics instead, the impossibility of exactly following the whereabouts of the particles leads to difficulties and the part played by indistinguishability is crucial. Debates were finally closed by Pauli. The Pauli principle severely restricts the possible N electrons wavefunctions among all the possible ones. The particles fall into two categories: the fermions and the bosons. For the fermions, the N electrons wavefunctions should be antisymmetrical with respect to the interchange of two fermions. For bosons instead, the N particles wavefunctions should be symmetrical under the interchange of two particles.

Let us illustrate this feature in the case of two independent free fermions with mass m^* and spin $\frac{1}{2}$. The Hamiltonian is:

$$H = \frac{p_1^2}{2m^*} + \frac{p_2^2}{2m^*} \tag{I.1.85}$$

If there were no Pauli principle, we would write that $H = H_1 + H_2$ and the wavefunction of the two particles would factorise like:

$$\psi(\vec{r}_1, \vec{r}_2) = N \exp[i(\vec{k}_1 \cdot \vec{r}_1 + \vec{k}_2 \cdot \vec{r}_2)] \tag{I.1.86}$$

where N is the normalisation constant ($1/V^{1/2}$ for 3D motions, $1/S^{1/2}$ for 2D motions and $1/L^{1/2}$ for 1D motions). H is spin independent. Nevertheless, the quantum state is fully defined only if the spin states of the two particles are specified, like $|\sigma_1, \sigma_2\rangle$, where σ_1, σ_2 can take the values $\pm\frac{1}{2}$.

For two fermions with spin $\frac{1}{2}$, we apply the Pauli principle and antisymmetrise the wavefunction. We want to have two particles with wavevectors $\vec{k}_1$, $\vec{k}_2$ and spin projection σ_1, σ_2. The effect of interchanging the particles transforms the orbital part of the wavefunction into:

$$\tilde{\psi}(\vec{r}_1, \vec{r}_2) = N \exp[i(\vec{k}_2 \cdot \vec{r}_1 + \vec{k}_1 \cdot \vec{r}_2)] \tag{I.1.87}$$

while the spin part is now $|\sigma_2, \sigma_1\rangle$. The antisymmetrical wavefunction is therefore:

$$\psi_{AS}(\vec{r}_1, \vec{r}_2) = \frac{N}{\sqrt{2}} \{\exp[i(\vec{k}_1 \cdot \vec{r}_1 + \vec{k}_2 \cdot \vec{r}_2)]|\sigma_1, \sigma_2\rangle$$

$$- \exp[i(\vec{k}_2 \cdot \vec{r}_1 + \vec{k}_1 \cdot \vec{r}_2)]|\sigma_2, \sigma_1\rangle\} \tag{I.1.88}$$

It is interesting to remark that if we request the two particles to have identical wavevectors and identical spin projections, then there is no admissible wavefunction ($\psi_{AS} = 0$). This is another way to state the Pauli principle that two identical fermions cannot have all their quantum numbers identical.

There is a systematic way to produce antisymmetrical wavefunctions. It is to write them in the form of a (Slater) determinant, since a determinant changes sign when two columns or two lines are interchanged. Take the same problem as before. We have two particles one with wavevector $\vec{k}_1$ and spin σ_1 and the other with wavevector $\vec{k}_2$ and spin σ_2. We write the Slater determinant as:

$$\psi_{AS} = \frac{1}{\sqrt{2}} \begin{vmatrix} \text{(particle 1)} & \text{(particle 2)} \\ \varphi_{\vec{k}_1}(1)|\sigma_1(1)\rangle & \varphi_{\vec{k}_1}(2)|\sigma_1(2)\rangle \\ \varphi_{\vec{k}_2}(1)|\sigma_2(1)\rangle & \varphi_{\vec{k}_2}(2)|\sigma_2(2)\rangle \end{vmatrix} \tag{I.1.89}$$

which coincides with the previous expression. Suppose there are N fermions with spin $\frac{1}{2}$ moving in a 3D space with orbital quantum numbers $\vec{\alpha}_1, \vec{\alpha}_2, \ldots, \vec{\alpha}_N$, where $\vec{\alpha}_j$ is a short-hand notation for three quantum numbers (the three components of a wavevector for free fermions, the three integers that label the eigenstates of a 3D harmonic oscillator, a discrete quantum number for labelling the bound states of 1D heterostructure plus the two components of a 2D wavevector that labels the free particle motion in the plane perpendicular to the direction of the bound motion, and so on), and spin quantum number $\sigma_1, \sigma_2, \ldots, \sigma_N$ where $\sigma_j = \pm 1/2$: we would have written the Slater determinant as

$$\psi_{AS} = \frac{1}{\sqrt{N!}}$$

$$\times \begin{vmatrix} \varphi_{\vec{\alpha}_1}(1)|\sigma_1(1)\rangle & \varphi_{\vec{\alpha}_1}(2)|\sigma_1(2)\rangle & \cdots & \varphi_{\vec{\alpha}_1}(N)|\sigma_1(N)\rangle \\ \varphi_{\vec{\alpha}_2}(1)|\sigma_2(1)\rangle & \varphi_{\vec{\alpha}_2}(2)|\sigma_2(2)\rangle & \cdots & \varphi_{\vec{\alpha}_2}(N)|\sigma_2(N)\rangle \\ \vdots & \vdots & \vdots & \vdots \\ \varphi_{\vec{\alpha}_N}(1)|\sigma_N(1)\rangle & \varphi_{\vec{\alpha}_N}(2)|\sigma_N(2)\rangle & \cdots & \varphi_{\vec{\alpha}_N}(N)|\sigma_N(N)\rangle \end{vmatrix}$$

$$\tag{I.1.90}$$

The Pauli principle has far reaching consequences; e.g., it is at the origin of the shell structure of atoms or of the nuclei (see [6]). Here, we investigate briefly another consequence of the Pauli principle that is the spatial correlation between particles induced by the requirement of antisymmetry. Take the two independent free fermions discussed above. This time, we express the kinetic energy in terms of the centre of mass motion (mass $2m^*$) and the relative motion (mass $m^*/2$):

$$\vec{R} = \frac{\vec{r}_1 + \vec{r}_2}{2}; \quad \vec{r} = \vec{r}_1 - \vec{r}_2; \quad H = \frac{P^2}{4m^*} + \frac{p^2}{m^*} \tag{I.1.91}$$

We note that the eigenstate of H can be chosen as a product of a function of $\vec{R}$ times a function of $\vec{r}$:

$$\varphi(\vec{R}, \vec{r}) = f(\vec{R})g(\vec{r}) \tag{I.1.92}$$

In addition, $\vec{R}$ is unchanged while $\vec{r} \to -\vec{r}$ under the exchange of the two particles. Since the particles are free, both the centre of mass and reduced motions are free, characterised by plane waves with wavevector $\vec{K}$, $-\vec{K}$ and $\vec{q}$, $-\vec{q}$. The two particles Hamiltonian being explicitly spin independent, it is possible to find its eigenstates as products of space variables by spin variables:

$$\psi(\vec{R}, \vec{r}, \sigma_1, \sigma_2) = \varphi(\vec{R}, \vec{r})\xi(\sigma_1, \sigma_2) \tag{I.1.93}$$

To get an antisymmetrical wavefunction, we can choose either φ symmetrical and ξ antisymmetrical or vice versa.

If φ is symmetrical, then f being symmetrical, $g(\vec{r})$ has to be symmetrical (e.g., $\cos(\vec{q} \cdot \vec{r})$) while if φ is antisymmetrical, then f being symmetrical, $g(\vec{r})$ has to be antisymmetrical (e.g., $\sin(\vec{q} \cdot \vec{r})$). We are thus led to the remarkable conclusion that the spin state of the two particles influences directly the orbital part of the wavefunction of their relative motion despite the absence of spin-dependent term in the Hamiltonian. This consequence of the Pauli principle is at the heart of the existence of exchange interactions between electrons that are responsible for the magnetism [7] (e.g., of the transition metals like Fe, Ni).

I.1.13.   Tensorial products

Let $\mathcal{H}_1$ and $\mathcal{H}_2$ be two Hilbert spaces with dimensions N and M respectively (the dimensions are possibly infinite). $\mathcal{H}_1$ has the basis $|\chi_1\rangle, |\chi_2\rangle, \ldots, |\chi_N\rangle$ while $\mathcal{H}_2$ has the basis $|\varphi_1\rangle, |\varphi_2\rangle, \ldots, |\varphi_M\rangle$. Suppose we define the new Hilbert space $\mathcal{H}$ where $\mathcal{H} = \mathcal{H}_1 \otimes \mathcal{H}_2$ with dimension NM is called tensorial product of $\mathcal{H}_1$ and $\mathcal{H}_2$. Its basis vectors are the tensorial products $|\chi_i\rangle \otimes |\varphi_j\rangle$ since for each of the N basis functions $|\chi_i\rangle$ of $\mathcal{H}_1$, one can associate any of the M basis vectors $|\varphi_j\rangle$ of $\mathcal{H}_2$. A vector of $\mathcal{H}$ is written $|\vec{\chi}\rangle \otimes |\vec{\varphi}\rangle = \sum c_{ij} |\chi_i\rangle \otimes |\varphi_j\rangle$ with the obvious result that: $c_{ij} = \langle \chi_i | \otimes \langle \varphi_j | \vec{\chi}\rangle \otimes |\vec{\varphi}\rangle = \langle \chi_i | \vec{\chi}\rangle \langle \varphi_j | \vec{\varphi}\rangle$.

Suppose an operator A is acting in $\mathcal{H}_1$. Its action in $\mathcal{H}$ can be defined as due to the combined (generalised) operator $A \otimes \mathrm{Id}_2$ where Id_2 is the identity operator in $\mathcal{H}_2$. Similarly an operator B acting in $\mathcal{H}_2$ can be generalised as $B \otimes \mathrm{Id}_1$ to operate in $\mathcal{H}$. The identity in $\mathcal{H}$ is $\mathrm{Id}_{\mathcal{H}} = \mathrm{Id}_1 \otimes \mathrm{Id}_2$.

The physical significance is clear: in the Hilbert space, tensorial product of two Hilbert spaces, any vector has two "legs" one on $\mathcal{H}_1$ and the other on $\mathcal{H}_2$ (a vector that is entirely contained in $\mathcal{H}_1$ can be generalised as a vector of $\mathcal{H}$ provided one takes its tensorial product with $|\vec{0}\rangle_2$ the null vector of $\mathcal{H}_2$). The notation $\otimes$ is cumbersome. Very often $|\vec{\chi}\rangle \otimes |\vec{\varphi}\rangle$ is replaced by $|\chi, \varphi\rangle$.

Let us give two examples:

(1) Take a free particle. Its Hamiltonian is $H_1 = \frac{p^2}{2m^*}$. It acts in the Hilbert space $\mathcal{H}_1$ of the squared integrable functions. The second Hamiltonian H_2 will be generated by the spin degrees of freedom. It acts in the (2D) Hilbert space $\mathcal{H}_2$. But without magnetic field there is no spin-dependent term in the Hamiltonian. Nevertheless, a complete description of the electron states requires them to be labelled by the wavevector of the free particle $|\vec{k}\rangle$ if we want to consider a basis vector of H_1 and by the projection of its spin state on a prescribed axis $|\uparrow\rangle$ or $|\downarrow\rangle$. We shall write: $|\vec{k}\rangle \otimes |\uparrow\rangle, |\vec{k}\rangle \otimes |\downarrow\rangle$ or in short $|\vec{k}\uparrow\rangle, |\vec{k}\downarrow\rangle$ as the basis vectors of $\mathcal{H} = \mathcal{H}_1 \otimes \mathcal{H}_2$. Note that the spin degree of freedom while leaving unchanged the electron energy (in the absence of a magnetic field) plays however some part in all state counting procedures,

for instance in the partition function $Z = \sum_\nu \exp(-\beta \varepsilon_\nu)$ where ν labels the electron states or expressing the number of fermions solutions of a certain Hamiltonian H which admits the eigenstates ε_ν:

$$n = \sum_\nu \frac{1}{1 + \exp[\beta(\varepsilon_\nu - \mu)]} \tag{I.1.94}$$

(2) As a second example takes a 2D anisotropic oscillator:

$$H = H_1 + H_2 = \left(\frac{p_1^2}{2m^*} + \frac{1}{2}m^*\omega_1^2 x_1^2\right) + \left(\frac{p_2^2}{2m^*} + \frac{1}{2}m^*\omega_2^2 x_2^2\right) \tag{I.1.95}$$

Both H_1 and H_2 act in the Hilbert spaces $\mathcal{H}_1$ and $\mathcal{H}_2$ of the squared integrable functions. The basis functions of $H_{1,2}$ are well known (the Hermite functions $\varphi_{n_{1,2}}(x_{1,2})$) and can serve as basis functions for $\mathcal{H}$ once conveniently "tensorialised". The eigenenergies of H will be $(n_1 + \frac{1}{2})\hbar\omega_1 + (n_2 + \frac{1}{2})\hbar\omega_2$ associated with the eigenfunctions $\varphi_{n_1}(x_1)\varphi_{n_2}(x_2)$. Note that if we would have insisted in being very precise, we would have written:

$$H = H_1 \otimes \mathrm{Id}_2 + H_2 \otimes \mathrm{Id}_1 = \left(\frac{p_1^2}{2m^*} + \frac{1}{2}m^*\omega_1^2 x_1^2\right) \otimes \mathrm{Id}_2$$
$$+ \left(\frac{p_2^2}{2m^*} + \frac{1}{2}m^*\omega_2^2 x_2^2\right) \otimes \mathrm{Id}_1 \tag{I.1.96}$$

It is important to stress that some vectors of the Hilbert space $\mathcal{H}$ where H operates can be written as the tensorial product of one vector of the Hilbert space $\mathcal{H}_1$ where H_1 acts by one vector of the Hilbert space $\mathcal{H}_2$ where H_2 acts. These states are called product (or factorisable) states. But not all of the vectors of $\mathcal{H}$ where H operates are factorisable. Those that are not factorisable are called entangled states. For example, in the 2D harmonic oscillators case, the state $\frac{1}{\sqrt{2}}[\varphi_1(x_1)\varphi_3(x_2) + \varphi_3(x_1)\varphi_1(x_2)]$ is entangled. The entangled states play a great part in the modern theory of quantum cryptography [8].

Chapter I.2

Bound and Extended States

I.2.1. Propagating and evanescent states

In classical mechanics, it is relatively simple to convince oneself that a particle meets allowed and forbidden regions when time flows provided it is subjected to forces that do not depend explicitly on time. In fact, under such circumstances the potential energy is also time independent and the total mechanical energy E is conserved:

$$E = \frac{p^2}{2m^*} + V(\vec{r}) \qquad (I.2.1)$$

So, the $\vec{r}$ regions, where $E < V(\vec{r})$, cannot be visited by the particle because its kinetic energy has to be positive. The other regions such that $E \geq V(\vec{r})$ are classically allowed. In quantum description, we deal with a wave and the notion of forbidden/allowed regions becomes fuzzy. Nevertheless, the difference between what used to be (classically) allowed and forbidden regions remains for the particle wavefunction to the extent that it will be respectively propagating or evanescent depending on whether the region is classically allowed or forbidden. To make the algebra lighter we are going to study the nature of the particle wavefunction along one direction (z) and approximate the 3D potential energy by neglecting its (x, y) coordinates (in other words, we look for the behaviour along a tube in the hope that the (x, y) variations will be smooth and in first

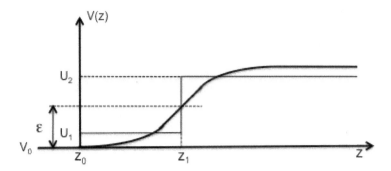

Figure I.2.1.   Potential energy profile (thick line) and step function approximating the potential profile. $V(z) = U_1$ when $z \le z_1$ (classically allowed region), $V(z) = U_2$ when $z > z_1$ (classically forbidden region). ε is the particle energy measured from V_0 and z_1 is called the classical turning point.

approximation approximated by a constant). Thus, we write:

$$V(\vec{r}) = V_0 + V(z); \quad V(z_0) = 0 \tag{I.2.2}$$

Assume $E > V_0$. Take for instance the potential $V(z)$ depicted by the blue line in Fig. I.2.1. There are two situations about $V(z)$: either $V(z) < 0$ or $V(z) > 0$. In the first case the whole z segment is classically allowed while in the second case there exists a z_1 where $E = V(z_1)$. In the second case, the region $z \le z_1$ is classically allowed and $z > z_1$ classically forbidden. z_1 is called the classical turning point since at this point the velocity of the classical particle will change sign. Let us study the simple case $V(z) = U_1$ $z \le z_1$, $V(z) = U_2$ $z > z_1$ (see Fig. I.2.1). We shall see later that one can discretise both the z-axis and the potential $V(z)$ in order to recover partially the simple results to be discussed below.

The 1D Schrödinger equation is:

$$-\frac{\hbar^2}{2m^*}\psi''(z) + [V_0 + U_1 Y(z_1 - z) + U_2 Y(z - z_1)]\,\psi(z) = E\psi(z) \tag{I.2.3}$$

Notice that to be closer from the semiconductor world the electron mass in free space is replaced by m^*, the effective mass in crystals. Equation (I.2.3) is a second-order differential equation with constant coefficients. Thus, we know its solutions exactly. We let $E = V_0 + \varepsilon$.

Let us take $\varepsilon < U_2$. For $z \le z_1$ we have the most general solution:

$$\psi(z) = A \exp\left[ik(z - z_1)\right] + B \exp\left[-ik(z - z_1)\right]; \quad k = \sqrt{\frac{2m^*}{\hbar^2}(\varepsilon - U_1)}$$

$$(\text{I.2.4})$$

while for $z \ge z_1$ there is:

$$\psi(z) = C \exp\left[-\kappa(z - z_1)\right] + D \exp\left[\kappa(z - z_1)\right]; \quad \kappa = \sqrt{\frac{2m^*}{\hbar^2}(U_2 - \varepsilon)}$$

$$(\text{I.2.5})$$

So compared to the "black" and "white" classical solution which allows motion only for $z \le z_1$ the wave-like nature transforms this into a "light grey–dark grey" kind of solution where the wave in the barrier region (classically forbidden) is damped (or magnified). Suppose now that the barrier $V(z) - V_0 = U_2$ extends to infinity. Then, the exponentially growing solution will make the normalisation of $|\psi(z)|^2$ impossible (the normalisation integral diverges). Hence, the only solution will be that $D = 0$ and for an infinitely thick barrier, the wave actually decays in the barrier. So, in the case of an infinitely thick barrier, it is true that the probability density $(|\psi(z)|^2)$ in the barrier is non-zero (in contrast to the classical result) but it decays further and further away from the classical turning point.

On the other hand, suppose that passed some z_2 the potential energy decreases again. Then $T = E - V(z)$ is less and less negative and the characteristic wavevector κ that governs the exponential decay (or increase) of the wavefunction in the barrier decreases. We have no longer any reason (the blow up of the wavefunction in the barrier) to set $D = 0$ and if it happens that there exists a z_3 where $V(z_3) = E$, then beyond that point the wave will be propagating again. So, contrarily to the classical result, the quantum wave will have finally passed through the barrier $[z_1, z_3]$ (see Fig. I.2.2). This phenomenon is called tunnelling. It is well known since a long time for the electromagnetic waves: take two dielectric dioptres separated by a thin air layer, where the first dioptre is shined by an electromagnetic wave under total reflection condition. The electromagnetic wave is damped in the air layer but if it is thin enough (say of the order of the wavelength), the wave reappears propagating in the second dioptre. This is a spectacular experiment that can be routinely made

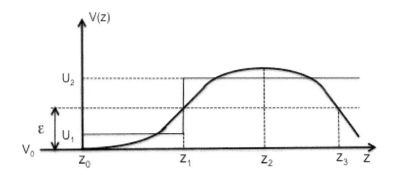

Figure I.2.2.   Profile of the potential energy $V(z)$ (thick line) and approximation of the potential profile by a piecewise constant function. The quantum wave will pass through de barrier $[z_1, z_3]$. This phenomenon is called tunnelling.

in laboratories/classes and admirably illustrates the idea that tunnel effect is nothing but the replacement of propagating by evanescent waves, irrespective of the fact they are light or matter waves.

I.2.2.   Probability current

To continue further the discussion about tunnelling, it is useful to introduce the notion of probability current. It is defined as

$$\vec{J} = \frac{\hbar}{2im^*}(\psi^*\vec{\nabla}\psi - \psi\vec{\nabla}\psi^*) = \frac{1}{m^*}\mathrm{Re}(\psi^*\vec{p}\psi) \quad \text{(3D)} \qquad \text{(I.2.6)}$$

$$J_z = \frac{\hbar}{2im^*}\left(\psi^*\frac{\partial\psi}{\partial z} - \psi\frac{\partial\psi^*}{\partial z}\right) = \frac{1}{m^*}\mathrm{Re}(\psi^*p_z\psi) \quad \text{(1D)} \qquad \text{(I.2.7)}$$

Take a plane wave $\psi(z) = Ae^{ikz}$. Then, $J_z = \frac{\hbar k_z}{m^*}|A|^2$. Instead, for a damped or exponentially growing wave $\psi(z) = Be^{\pm\kappa z}$, the probability current vanishes. It is easy to check using the Schrödinger equation that the probability current satisfies the continuity equation:

$$\frac{\partial\rho}{\partial t} + \vec{\nabla}\cdot\vec{J} = 0; \quad \rho(\vec{r}, t) = \psi^*(\vec{r}, t)\psi(\vec{r}, t) \qquad \text{(I.2.8)}$$

For a stationary state, $\rho = |\psi(\vec{r}, t)|^2$ is time independent and for 1D problem the continuity equation amounts to:

$$\frac{\partial J_z}{\partial z} = 0 \Rightarrow J_z = \text{constant} \qquad \text{(I.2.9)}$$

Let us apply these considerations to an electron propagating for $z \leq z_1$ and evanescent for $z > z_1$. We find readily:

$$J_z = \frac{\hbar k}{m^*} \left(|A|^2 - |B|^2 \right) = \frac{2\hbar \kappa}{m^*} \mathrm{Im}(DC^*) \qquad (\text{I.2.10})$$

In the case of an infinitely thick barrier we have seen that D must vanish. Hence $J_z = 0$ and $|A| = |B|$. This is the analogy for material particles of the total reflection of an electromagnetic wave by a single dioptre, the second dioptre being infinitely far away (the two situations would have been even closer if we would have taken into account the particle free motion in the (xy) plane). In the classically allowed region the probability current along z vanishes by compensation of the incident current $v_z |A^2|$ by the reflected one $-v_z |B|^2$. Hence, the reflected wave should have the same amplitude as the incident one.

As soon as the barrier has a finite thickness, D is no longer zero, the constant probability current has to reappear at z_3 to give rise to a propagating wave whose probability current will be identical to the one carried by the impinging wave.

The generalisation of the previous discussion to potentials that are not piecewise constant is relatively easy by replacing the actual z-dependent potential by a series of steps of different heights. Suppose $V(z)$ is given between z_0 and z_2, z_1 being the classical turning point (see Fig. I.2.3). We split the $[z_0, z_1]$ segment in N parts ($N = 4$ on the figure) and we replace the actual potential $V(z)$ (solid black curve) by a series of staircases of heights $[V(z_j) + V(z_{j+1})]/2$, placed at $z_j = z_0 + jd$, $j = 0, 1, \ldots, N$ where $d = (z_1 - z_0)/N$. It is clear that the solution of the Schrödinger equation in the approximate potential can be made very close from the exact solution if N is large enough. In the vicinity of the classical turning point, the approximate potential has exactly the same piecewise constant shape as discussed above. Hence, we can apply to it all the conclusions that were drawn.

I.2.3. Boundary conditions

As discussed before, the stationary solutions of the Schrödinger equation depend in a marked fashion on the boundary conditions that they should fulfil.

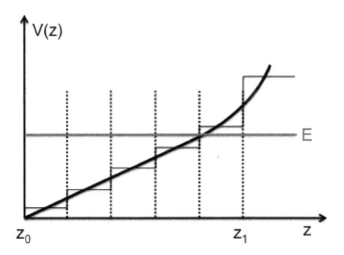

Figure I.2.3.   Potential energy profile (thick line) and its approximation by a piecewise constant potential.

- At infinity, the wavefunctions should not diverge but at worse oscillate (although this important case, since it corresponds to the free particle, is somewhat borderline).
- The wavefunction $\psi(z)$ has to be continuous since its modulus squared represents a probability density to find the particle at z. Across a finite discontinuity for the potential energy located at z_1, one can readily derive by integrating the Schrödinger equation across z_1, the following:
- The derivative of the wavefunction $\frac{d\psi(z)}{dz}$ has to be continuous in z_1.
- Later, we shall see that the usual kinetic energy term $\frac{p_z^2}{2m^*}$ is often replaced in semiconductor heterostructures by $p_z(\frac{1}{2m^*(z)})p_z$ because the effective mass is material dependent. In that case, the same integration across z_1 leads to
- the continuity of $\frac{1}{m^*(z)}\frac{d\psi}{dz}$ at z_1.

In the case of a position-dependent effective mass, one can readily show that the probability current is now:

$$\vec{J} = \frac{\hbar}{2i}\left(\psi^*\frac{1}{m^*(\vec{r})}\vec{\nabla}\psi - \psi\frac{1}{m^*(\vec{r})}\vec{\nabla}\psi^*\right)$$

$$= \frac{1}{2} \left(\psi^* \frac{1}{m^*(\vec{r})} \vec{p}\psi - \psi \frac{1}{m^*(\vec{r})} \vec{p}\psi^* \right)$$

$$= \text{Re} \left(\psi^* \frac{1}{m^*(\vec{r})} \vec{p}\psi \right) \quad \text{(3D)} \tag{I.2.11}$$

$$J_z = \frac{\hbar}{2i} \left(\psi^* \frac{1}{m^*(z)} \frac{\partial \psi}{\partial z} - \psi \frac{1}{m^*(z)} \frac{\partial \psi^*}{\partial z} \right)$$

$$= \text{Re} \left(\psi^* \frac{1}{m^*(z)} p_z \psi \right) \quad \text{(1D)} \tag{I.2.12}$$

Let us apply these boundary conditions to the potential step considered previously (see Fig. I.2.1). We shall denote by m_l (respectively, m_r) the carrier effective mass on the left-hand side (respectively, right-hand side) of the classical turning point z_1. We find, for $\varepsilon < U_2$,

$$A + B = C \tag{I.2.13}$$

$$\frac{ik}{m_l}(A - B) = -\frac{\kappa}{m_r}C \tag{I.2.14}$$

Hence the problem is underdetermined. Indeed, there is a degree of freedom associated with the intensity of the impinging probability current $\frac{\hbar k}{m_l}|A|^2$. It corresponds intuitively to the idea that if less intensity impinges on the potential step, less will be reflected. Let us factorise A in the previous expression and denote by r (t) the ratio B/A (C/A). The intensity coefficient $R = |r|^2$ will be equal to the ratio between the reflected probability flux to the impinging one (again in complete analogy with what is found in electromagnetism). We find:

$$r = \frac{1 - i\frac{\kappa m_l}{k m_r}}{1 + i\frac{\kappa m_l}{k m_r}}; \quad c = 1 + t \tag{I.2.15}$$

Hence, we get $R = 1$ and we retrieve the conservation of the probability current.

Suppose now $\varepsilon \geq U_2$. Then, the evanescent wave for $z > z_1$ should be replaced by two propagating ones. There will be now four unknown linear coefficients and still two boundary conditions at z_1. Again, we get rid of one of the unknown by setting $A = 1$, $r = B/A$. If we keep the two unknown linear coefficients there will be a current coming from $z < z_1$ as well as one coming from the right $z > z_1$. But we can as well suppress the later current if the particles are impinging from the left of the interface and we observe far on the right of that interface the transmitted current. So, we write:

$$\psi(z) = e^{ik(z-z_1)} + re^{-ik(z-z_1)} \quad z \leq z_1 \qquad (\text{I.2.16})$$

$$\psi(z) = Ce^{iq(z-z_1)} \quad z \geq z_1 \qquad (\text{I.2.17})$$

$$k = \sqrt{\frac{2m_l(\varepsilon - U_1)}{\hbar^2}}; \quad q = \sqrt{\frac{2m_r(\varepsilon - U_2)}{\hbar^2}} \qquad (\text{I.2.18})$$

and get readily:

$$r = \frac{1-\xi}{1+\xi}; \quad C = \frac{2}{1+\xi}; \quad \xi = \frac{qm_l}{km_r} \qquad (\text{I.2.19})$$

The ratio between the transmitted current to the impinging ones is

$$T = \frac{qm_l}{km_r}|C|^2 = \frac{4\xi}{(1+\xi)^2} \qquad (\text{I.2.20})$$

while $R = |r|^2$ is the ratio between the reflected current to the impinging one. Hence, we find:

$$R + T = 1 \qquad (\text{I.2.21})$$

This had to be expected since there is no loss of particle (no dissipation) in this problem. It has to be remarked that at large energies $\varepsilon \gg U_2, U_1$, R and T approach constant values that differ from the conventional results (respectively, 0 and 1) because of the effective mass mismatch. Note also the difference between the quantum result and the classical one: for $\varepsilon > U_2$, the classical particle is never reflected.

Let us turn our attention to the tunnelling through a rectangular barrier (see Fig. I.2.4). The effective masses are m_1 ($z < z_1$), m_2 ($z_1 \leq z \leq z_1 + h$) and m_3 ($z > z_1 + h$) respectively. Depending on the energy, we write the wavefunctions as linear combinations of propagating or evanescent states. For $\varepsilon < U_1$ there is no solution if the effective masses have all the same sign. For $U_1 \leq \varepsilon < U_3$, the particle is 100% reflected at the $z = z_1$ interface. For $U_3 \leq \varepsilon \leq U_2$, the wave is propagating in I and III but evanescent in II. If $\varepsilon \geq U_2$ we deal with propagating waves. When the wave propagates in I and III, we

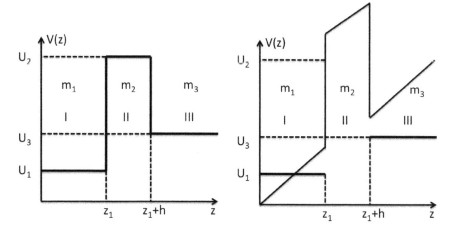

Figure I.2.4. Conduction band profile of a rectangular barrier (left panel) and a rectangular biased barrier (right panel).

choose as a boundary condition that the wave is impinging from $-\infty$ and moves to $+\infty$. One has to bear in mind the two-fold degeneracy of the motion for $\varepsilon \geq U_3$ while if $\varepsilon < U_3$ (complete reflection) there is a single quantum motion associated with the eigenvalue ε. Limiting ourselves to the cases where there exists a transmitted wave, we write:

$$U_3 \leq \varepsilon \leq U_2 \tag{I.2.22}$$

$$\psi(z) = e^{ik_1(z-z_1)} + re^{-ik_1(z-z_1)}; \quad z \leq z_1 \tag{I.2.23}$$

$$\varepsilon = \frac{\hbar^2 k_1^2}{2m_1} + U_1 \tag{I.2.24}$$

$$\psi(z) = Ae^{\kappa_2(z-z_1)} + Be^{-\kappa_2(z-z_1)}; \quad z_1 \leq z \leq z_1 + h \tag{I.2.25}$$

$$\varepsilon = -\frac{\hbar^2 \kappa_2^2}{2m_2} + U_2 \tag{I.2.26}$$

$$\psi(z) = te^{ik_3(z-z_1-h)}; \quad z_1 + h \leq z \tag{I.2.27}$$

$$\varepsilon = \frac{\hbar^2 k_3^2}{2m_3} + U_3 \tag{I.2.28}$$

$$\varepsilon \geq U_2 \tag{I.2.29}$$

$$\psi(z) = e^{ik_1(z-z_1)} + re^{-ik_1(z-z_1)}; \quad z \leq z_1 \tag{I.2.30}$$

$$\varepsilon = \frac{\hbar^2 k_1^2}{2m_1} + U_1 \tag{I.2.31}$$

$$\psi(z) = Ae^{ik_2(z-z_1)} + Be^{-ik_2(z-z_1)}; \quad z_1 \le z \le z_1 + h \tag{I.2.32}$$

$$\varepsilon = \frac{\hbar^2 k_2^2}{2m_2} + U_2 \tag{I.2.33}$$

$$\psi(z) = te^{ik_3(z-z_1-h)}; \quad z_1 + h \le z \tag{I.2.34}$$

$$\varepsilon = \frac{\hbar^2 k_3^2}{2m_3} + U_3 \tag{I.2.35}$$

Let us define:

$$\xi_1 = \frac{k_1}{m_1}\frac{m_2}{\kappa_2}; \quad \xi_3 = \frac{k_3}{m_3}\frac{m_2}{\kappa_2} \tag{I.2.36}$$

Then we get after some calculations, when $U_3 \le \varepsilon \le U_2$:

$$t = \frac{-2i\xi_1}{(1 - \xi_1\xi_3)\sinh(\kappa_2 h) - i(\xi_1 + \xi_3)\cosh(\kappa_2 h)} \tag{I.2.37}$$

$$r = \frac{-(1 + \xi_1\xi_3)\sinh(\kappa_2 h) + i(-\xi_1 + \xi_3)\cosh(\kappa_2 h)}{(1 - \xi_1\xi_3)\sinh(\kappa_2 h) - i(\xi_1 + \xi_3)\cosh(\kappa_2 h)} \tag{I.2.38}$$

$$T = \frac{\xi_3}{\xi_1}|t|^2 = \left[\frac{(\xi_1 + \xi_3)^2}{4\xi_1\xi_3} + \frac{1}{4}\left(\frac{1}{\xi_1\xi_3} + \frac{\xi_1}{\xi_3} + \frac{\xi_3}{\xi_1} + \xi_1\xi_3\right)\sinh^2(\kappa_2 h)\right]^{-1}$$

$$\tag{I.2.39}$$

$$R = 1 - T \tag{I.2.40}$$

where $\sinh(x)$ is the hyperbolic sine $(\sinh(x) = (e^x - e^{-x})/2)$.

When $\varepsilon > U_2$, κ_2 becomes imaginary and changes into ik_2. Then

$$\xi_1 \to -i\tilde{\xi}_1, \quad \xi_3 \to -i\tilde{\xi}_3, \quad \sinh(\kappa_2 h) \to i\sin(k_2 h) \tag{I.2.41}$$

$$\tilde{\xi}_1 = \frac{k_1 m_2}{k_2 m_1}, \quad \tilde{\xi}_3 = \frac{k_3 m_2}{k_2 m_3} \tag{I.2.42}$$

$$T = \frac{\tilde{\xi}_3}{\tilde{\xi}_1}|t|^2 = \left[\frac{(\tilde{\xi}_1 + \tilde{\xi}_3)^2}{4\tilde{\xi}_1\tilde{\xi}_3} + \frac{1}{4}\left(\frac{1}{\tilde{\xi}_1\tilde{\xi}_3} - \frac{\tilde{\xi}_1}{\tilde{\xi}_3} - \frac{\tilde{\xi}_3}{\tilde{\xi}_1} + \tilde{\xi}_1\tilde{\xi}_3\right)\sin^2(k_2 h)\right]^{-1}$$

$$\tag{I.2.43}$$

and $R = 1 - T$. These expressions simplify significantly when $\xi_3 = \xi_1$ since in this case we have:

$$U_3 < \varepsilon \leq U_2 \tag{I.2.44}$$

$$T(\varepsilon) = \frac{1}{1 + \frac{1}{4}(\xi_1 + \frac{1}{\xi_1})^2 \sinh^2(\kappa_2 h)} \tag{I.2.45}$$

$$\kappa_2 = \sqrt{\frac{2m_2}{\hbar^2}(U_2 - \varepsilon)}; \quad \xi_1 = \frac{k_1 m_2}{\kappa_2 m_1} \tag{I.2.46}$$

$$\varepsilon \geq U_2 \tag{I.2.47}$$

$$T(\varepsilon) = \frac{1}{1 + \frac{1}{4}\left(\xi_1 - \frac{1}{\xi_1}\right)^2 \sin^2(k_2 h)} \tag{I.2.48}$$

$$k_2 = \sqrt{\frac{2m_2}{\hbar^2}(\varepsilon - U_2)} \quad ; \quad \xi_1 = \frac{k_1 m_2}{k_2 m_1} \tag{I.2.49}$$

Several features are noticeable. The first one is tunnelling across the barrier when $\varepsilon \leq U_2$. This is a logical consequence of the wave-like nature of the electron motion. This transmission is however small. At $\varepsilon = U_2$ there is:

$$T(\varepsilon = U_2) = \left(1 + \frac{m_2^2}{4m_1^2} \frac{2m_1 U_2 h^2}{\hbar^2}\right)^{-1} \tag{I.2.50}$$

For a typical GaAs/Ga(Al)As barrier with $h = 5$ nm, $U_2 = 0.2$ eV, $m_2/m_1 = 1.1$, $m_1 = 0.07 m_0$ where m_0 is the free electron mass, there is $T(\varepsilon = U_2) = 0.26$. Very often the argument of the hyperbolic sine is $\gg 1$. This means that:

$$T(\varepsilon) \approx 16 \left(\xi_1 + \frac{1}{\xi_1}\right)^{-2} e^{-2\kappa_2 h} \tag{I.2.51}$$

This formula displays one of the main characteristic features of tunnelling which is the exponential dependence of the transmission upon the barrier thickness or evanescent wavevector in the barrier. In case of opaque barriers ($\kappa_2 h \gg 1$), it has also a technological consequence which is the sensitivity to interface defects (the departure from ideal interface) because if the barrier is locally thinner the transmission will be larger or much larger than in regions where the barrier is thicker. This creates lateral inhomogeneity in the current. Another consequence of opaque barriers is the sensitivity to defects in the barrier, which locally lowers the barrier height.

The second important feature is the existence, when $\varepsilon > U_2$ and $\xi_3 = \xi_1$, of discrete energies where the transmission reaches unity. This happens when $k_2 h = p\pi$ and is again the signature of the wave-like nature of the electronic motion. Actually, the very same phenomenon exists when one investigates the transmission of an electromagnetic wave through a dielectric slab and originates from the constructive interferences between the waves that are propagating towards $z > 0$ inside the slab with those that are reflected back into the slab at $z_1 + h$ interface. To illustrate the phenomenon of transmission through a single barrier we show in Fig. I.2.5 a plot $T(\varepsilon)$ versus ε for the parameters quoted above and we compare that transmission curve to the ones obtained when the barrier height is set to $U_3 = 0$, $U_2/4$, $U_2/2$, $3U_2/4$. Note that a non-zero U_3 mimics the application of a positive electric field to the single barrier. We

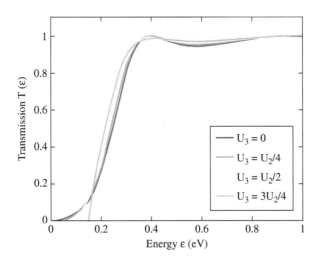

Figure I.2.5.   Energy dependence of the transmission $T(\varepsilon)$ of a quantum wave through a single barrier (red line). The transmission is compared to the ones obtained when the barrier height is set to $U_2/4$ (green line), $U_2/2$ (yellow line) and $3U_2/4$ (blue line). The material parameters are: $h = 5$ nm, $U_2 = 0.2$ eV, $m_2/m_1 = 1.1$ and $m_1 = m_3 = 0.07m_0$.

see that for a given energy the transmission decrease with increasing U_3 and that this decreases is nonlinear upon U_3.

I.2.4. Bound states

A state is bound if its wavefunction decays sufficiently rapidly at large distance in such a way that:

$$r^3|\psi(\vec{r})|^2 \to 0; \ r \to \infty \quad \text{(3D)} \tag{I.2.52}$$

$$\rho^2|\psi(\vec{\rho})|^2 \to 0; \ \rho \to \infty \quad \text{(2D)} \tag{I.2.53}$$

$$x|\psi(x)|^2 \to 0; \ |x| \to \infty \quad \text{(1D)} \tag{I.2.54}$$

In the case of an attractive potential with a strength that extrapolates to V_0 at large distance, the bound state will have an energy $E < V_0$ (see Fig. I.2.6).

The ground state of the H atom is bound: if we choose $V(\vec{r}) = -\frac{e^2}{4\pi\varepsilon_0 r}$ (i.e., $V_0 = 0$) then:

$$\psi(\vec{r}) = \frac{1}{\sqrt{\pi a_0^3}} \exp\left(-\frac{r}{a_0}\right) \tag{I.2.55}$$

where a_0 is the Bohr radius ($a_0 \approx 0.053$ nm). The corresponding energy is $E = -1R_0$ (≈ -13.6 eV).

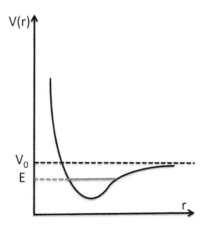

Figure I.2.6. Attractive potential energy versus r. The bound state has an energy $E < V_0$.

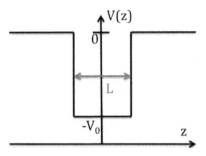

Figure I.2.7.   Scheme of a 1D square quantum well with thickness L.

Consider the 1D square quantum well (see Fig. I.2.7):

$$V(z) = -V_0; \ |z| \leq \frac{L}{2} \tag{I.2.56}$$

$$V(z) = 0; \ |z| \geq \frac{L}{2} \tag{I.2.57}$$

Then, it is readily checked that the following system of equations:

$$\chi_e(z) = A\cos(kz), \quad |z| \leq \frac{L}{2} \tag{I.2.58}$$

$$\chi_e(z) = B\exp\left[-\kappa\left(z - \frac{L}{2}\right)\right], \quad z \geq \frac{L}{2} \tag{I.2.59}$$

$$\chi_e(z) = B\exp\left[+\kappa\left(z + \frac{L}{2}\right)\right], \quad z \leq -\frac{L}{2} \tag{I.2.60}$$

$$k = \sqrt{\frac{2m^*}{\hbar^2}(E_1 + V_0)}; \quad E_1 = -\frac{\hbar^2\kappa^2}{2m^*} \tag{I.2.61}$$

is a solution of the Schrödinger equation with an energy $E_1 \leq 0$. Such a 1D square quantum well always admits one bound state irrespective of L and V_0 and may bind more than one state depending on L and V_0. Note that the very same problem in 3D leads to a qualitatively different solution. Namely, that V_0 should be large enough for the 3D well to bind one state (see Exercise 20). This is an important consideration for designing semiconductor quantum dots. Similarly, if the square quantum well is asymmetrical (say the left-hand side barrier is taller than the right-hand side one), then there might exist no bound state.

The bound states we have briefly discussed resemble much those one finds in classical mechanics. In both examples, the classical counterparts admit trajectories that are spatially bound: for the hydrogen atom, the electron trajectory is an ellipse (or a circle) while in the 1D square quantum well the particle bounces back and forth between $\pm L/2$ at a constant speed $\frac{\hbar k}{m^*}$. There is however a big difference, which is the discrete nature of the quantum motion. Bound states appear because the boundary condition at $\pm\infty$ (that the wavefunctions go to zero for the bound states) pinches the electronic wave much like a vibrating string pinched at its two ends can only admit discrete modes of vibration because the length of the string must accommodate an integer number of wavelengths. The pinched string analogy is very clear in the case of a square quantum well with infinitely tall barrier height. In that case, the boundary condition is that the wavefunction must vanish at the ends of the well, forcing the electron wavevector when the electron travels across the well to be quantised in units of π/L, where L is the well thickness. The wavevector quantisation $kL = n\pi$ leads to the energy quantisation since $E = \frac{\hbar^2 k^2}{2m^*}$.

There exists a class of bound states in classical mechanics whose quantum counterparts are not strictly bound. They are called unstable/virtual bound states or resonances. They correspond to the case where at the energy E of the bound state there exists a continuum of unbound states, spatially separated from the region where the bound particle is located (see Fig. I.2.8(a) for 1D example). As seen in Fig. I.2.8(b), the wavefunction for the stationary state at energy E is extended since at that energy the particle can be found at arbitrarily large $|r|$. In a time-dependent description, an initial bound state, looking like the bound state of a similar potential as $V(r)$ except that $V = V_0$ if $r > r_0$, would progressively diffuses towards $r > r_0$. Now, if during the time elapse (later called "tunnelling time") required for the particle to go through the potential barrier between b and c, the particle had the time to classically bounce back and forth between a and b many times, then the state is a long-lived virtual bound state/resonance. On the other hand, if the tunnelling time is comparable or shorter than the classical oscillation period, then the

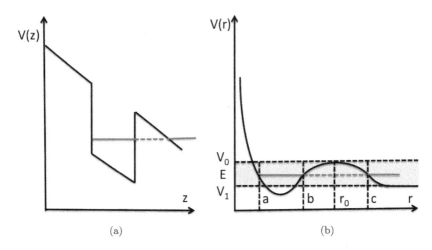

(a)   (b)

Figure I.2.8.   (a) Left panel: Conduction band profile of a biased square quantum well. The tunnelling across the triangular barrier is represented by the red dashed line. (b) Right panel: Potential energy versus r. At the energy E there is a virtual bound state. The dashed red line indicates an evanescent wave while the solid red lines indicate propagative waves.

resonance is overdamped and in practice there will be little experimental traces of it. Notice however that even long-lived resonances can be hard to detect if the detection characteristic time is too long. A good example of this is the photoluminescence of biased square quantum wells (see Fig. I.2.8(a)) where the tunnelling time across the triangular barrier can be in the 10 ps range, the classical oscillation time in the subpicosecond range, hence leading to a comfortable stability of the resonance. Yet, the photoluminescence characteristic lifetime being in the 10^2 ps range, the strong luminescence at zero electric field becomes quenched when reasonable fields are applied (say 40 kV/cm). Finally, it is worth commenting on the comparison between the classical and quantum states in the potential energy profile sketched in Fig. I.2.8(b). In the energy segment $[V_1, V_0]$ there exist two continuums of classical states in this potential profile. The first continuum comprises bound trajectories, for instance at the energy E the trajectory takes place between a and b. The second continuum corresponds to strictly unbound trajectories. For instance at the energy E the unbound trajectory occurs at $r > c$. A particle impinging from infinity with a negative velocity will go with a decreasing velocity till $r = c$ where its velocity will pass through zero to change sign and increase in magnitude corresponding to the particle returning to infinity. The two continuums of states are so to speak dissociated since the two kinds of trajectories never overlap. This is because a classical particle with energy comprised between V_1 and V_0 can never penetrate the potential barrier located between b and c. The stationary quantum states are extended and form a continuum. Among this continuum certain energies E emerge where the wavefunction while still extended shows a larger localisation in the $[a, b]$ segment. They are the quantum counterparts of the classical bound states (except for the fact that they are discrete due to the size quantisation). Their continuum aspect comes from the ability of quantum wave to exist in the barrier between a and b. Hence, by suitable linear combination of the two solutions of the Schrödinger equation one can make these states to cross the potential barrier and to become admixed with states that are essentially localised beyond c. In other words we may envision the quantum states of the potential $V(r)$ with energy E comprised between V_1 and $V_0 = 0$ (for convenience) as combinations of states that are bound and come from $V_{\text{left}}(r)$ with those that are unbound and come from $V_{\text{right}}(r)$ (see Fig. I.2.9). The states, solutions of the Schrödinger equation with V_{right}, are evanescent for $r < d$ like the discrete ones arising from V_{left} which are evanescent for $r > b$. The decay of the

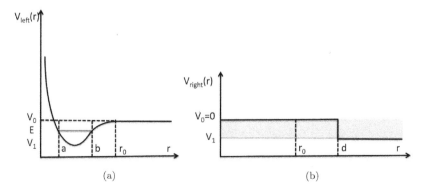

Figure I.2.9. A possible splitting of the potential that supports a virtual bound state into a part V_{left} that admits a bound state and a part V_{right} that admits a continuum of extended states. The difference $V_{\text{coupl}} = V - (V_{\text{left}} + V_{\text{right}})$ couples the discrete state to the continuum.

discrete state into the right-hand side continuum of states due to $V_{coupl} = V - (V_{left} + V_{right})$ can be analysed either semiclassically or by using the Fermi Golden rule (see Section I.3.3).

Let us study more thoroughly the 1D case because it turns out to be important for actual devices (quantum wells, lasers, detectors). Firstly, we have to determine why we chose a combination of exponentials and trigonometric functions. This is due to the structure of the stationary Schrödinger equation. In 1D it reads:

$$-\frac{\hbar^2}{2m^*}\frac{d^2\chi}{dz^2} = [E - V(z)]\chi \qquad (I.2.62)$$

Since $V(z)$ is piecewise constant, the Schrödinger equation is a second-order differential equation with constant coefficients: $\chi_e''(z) = A\chi_e(z)$. Hence, if $A > 0$, $\chi_e(z)$ is a combination of two exponentials and if $A < 0$, $\chi_e(z)$ is a combination of two exponentials with imaginary arguments or, equivalently, a combination of cosine and sine. Based on the parity property of the quantum well potential energy: $V(z) = V(-z)$, we know that the eigenfunctions can be chosen as even or odd with respect to the centre of the quantum well. For the ground state, it is sensible to assume that an even bound state χ_e (see Eqs. (I.2.58)–(I.2.61)) without zero will experience more attractive potential than any odd state χ_o that vanishes at the centre of the attractive layer. The odd wavefunction would have been chosen as:

$$\chi_o(z) = C\sin(kz), \quad |z| \leq \frac{L}{2} \qquad (I.2.63)$$

$$\chi_o(z) = D\exp\left[-\kappa\left(z - \frac{L}{2}\right)\right], \quad z \geq \frac{L}{2} \qquad (I.2.64)$$

$$\chi_o(-z) = -\chi_0(z) \qquad (I.2.65)$$

$$k = \sqrt{\frac{2m^*}{\hbar^2}(E + V_0)}; \quad E = -\frac{\hbar^2\kappa^2}{2m^*} \qquad (I.2.66)$$

To understand what will determine E, we have to remember that a second-order differential equation is not only specified by the functional relationship between χ_n'' and χ_n but also, equally, by its boundary conditions. Implicitly, we have already accounted for the non-exponential runaway of $\chi_e(z)$ at large distance from the attractive well by retaining exponentially decaying functions (their exponentially growing companions with the same energy were discarded since they would have prevented $\chi_e(z)$ to be normalisable, cf. Section I.1.1). The link between C (respectively, A) and D (respectively, B) is that χ_o (respectively, χ_c) has to be continuous everywhere, in particular at the interfaces $z = \pm L/2$. Thus, at $z - L/2$ we get:

$$A \cos\left(\frac{kL}{2}\right) = B \qquad (I.2.67)$$

Note that we gain no extra information by applying the χ_e continuity at the other interface, because we have used the parity property to build χ_e and the boundary condition at the second interface is identical to the one we got at the first interface. A second boundary condition is obtained by integrating the Schrödinger equation across the interface. One finds readily that the derivative $d\chi_e/dz$ should be continuous at $z = L/2$ resulting in:

$$A k \sin\left(\frac{kL}{2}\right) = \kappa B \qquad (I.2.68)$$

Hence, either $A = B = 0$ or

$$k \sin\left(\frac{kL}{2}\right) = \kappa \cos\left(\frac{kL}{2}\right) \qquad (I.2.69)$$

If the barrier height becomes infinite, the only possibility to fulfil Eq. (I.2.69) is that the cosine vanishes, namely

$$kL = (2j + 1)\pi, \quad j = 0, 1, 2, \ldots \qquad (I.2.70)$$

The reader will check that the states that are odd in z fulfil in the limit of an infinitely tall barrier height, the condition $kL = 2j\pi$, $j = 1, 2, \ldots$. Hence, all together we find that $kL = p\pi$, $p = 1, 2, \ldots$ corresponds to the allowed energy states of a particle that is perfectly confined in a slab of thickness L:

$$E_n = \frac{\hbar^2 n^2 \pi^2}{2m^* L^2} \qquad (I.2.71)$$

$$\chi_{e_n}(z) = \sqrt{\frac{2}{L}} \cos(2n+1)\frac{\pi z}{L}; \quad \chi_{om} = \sqrt{\frac{2}{L}} \sin\left(2m\frac{\pi z}{L}\right) \qquad (I.2.72)$$

In semiconductors, the effective masses vary from one material to the next. If we recall m_w and m_b the effective masses in the well and in

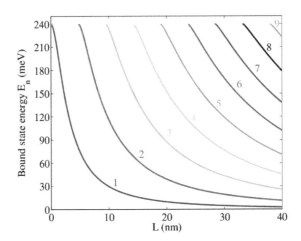

Figure I.2.10. L dependence of the bound state energies E_i, $i = 1, 2, \ldots$ of a single GaAs/Ga(Al)As quantum well where $V_b = 240$ meV, $m_w = 0.07m_0$ and $m_b = 0.09m_0$. Note that the energy origin is taken at the bottom of the well.

the barrier, it is easy to check that the conditions for bound states that are even or odd in z are respectively:

$$\cos\left(\frac{kL}{2}\right) = \frac{m_b k}{m_w \kappa} \sin\left(\frac{kL}{2}\right) \qquad (I.2.73)$$

$$\sin\left(\frac{kL}{2}\right) = -\frac{m_b k}{m_w \kappa} \cos\left(\frac{kL}{2}\right) \qquad (I.2.74)$$

$$k(E) = \sqrt{\frac{2m_w}{\hbar^2}(E + V_b)}; \qquad \kappa(E) = \sqrt{-\frac{2m_b E}{\hbar^2}} \qquad (I.2.75)$$

Figure I.2.10 shows the L dependence of the bound state if $V_b = 240$ meV, $m_w = 0.07m_0$, $m_b = 0.09m_0$.

We see that a square quantum well admits at least one bound state (even in z) since setting $L = 0$ in the previous equations is possible for the even bound states with the result that $E = 0$ is solution whereas for the odd states $L = 0$ leads to the absurd result that $k = 0$, i.e., $\chi_o(z)$ vanishes identically. We also note that the solution $E = 0$ reproduces periodically in L for both the even and odd states since there is:

$$k(E = 0)L_p = 2p\pi \qquad (\text{I.2.76})$$

$$k(E = 0)L_{p'} = (2p' + 1)\pi \qquad (\text{I.2.77})$$

Thus, when L decreases the energy of the bound levels increase till they reach the top of the well and fulfil (Eq. (I.2.77)). It is an interesting question to wonder if the continuum of unbound states $\varepsilon \geq 0$ displays specific features. To investigate this question we choose the wavefunction that corresponds to a motion from $-\infty$ to $+\infty$:

$$\chi_q(z) = e^{iq\left(z+\frac{L}{2}\right)} + re^{-iq\left(z+\frac{L}{2}\right)}; \quad z \leq -\frac{L}{2} \qquad (\text{I.2.78})$$

$$\chi_q(z) = A\cos\left[k\left(z+\frac{L}{2}\right)\right] + B\sin\left[k\left(z+\frac{L}{2}\right)\right]; \quad |z| \leq \frac{L}{2} \qquad (\text{I.2.79})$$

$$\chi_q(z) = te^{iq\left(z-\frac{L}{2}\right)}; \quad z \geq \frac{L}{2} \qquad (\text{I.2.80})$$

where $\varepsilon = \frac{\hbar^2 q^2}{2m_b}$. We get readily:

$$t(\varepsilon) = \frac{1}{C - \frac{i}{2}S\left(\xi + \frac{1}{\xi}\right)}; \quad T(\varepsilon) = |t(\varepsilon)|^2 = \frac{1}{1 + \frac{1}{4}S^2\left(\xi - \frac{1}{\xi}\right)^2} \qquad (\text{I.2.81})$$

$$C = \cos(kL); \quad S = \sin(kL); \quad \xi = \frac{km_b}{m_w q} \qquad (\text{I.2.82})$$

We see that the transmission reaches unity whenever the condition $kL = p\pi$ is fulfilled. This is the same dielectric slab effect as discussed above in the case of the single barrier. Note also that the transmission at very low energy in the continuum is vanishingly small (except if $S = 0$ at the top of the well, i.e., at the crucial L's where one state will be bound in the well by an infinitesimal increase of L). In the general case, we have this seemingly paradoxical effect that a region with attractive potential energy actually repels the electrons. This feature arises from the necessary orthogonality between the continuum states and the states bound to the well: since the well states are

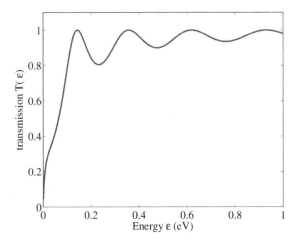

Figure I.2.11.   Energy dependence of the transmission coefficient for a 15-nm thick GaAs/Ga(Al)As quantum well. The material parameters are: $V_b = 240$ meV, $m_w = 0.07m_0$ and $m_b = 0.09m_0$. The energy origin is taken at the top of the well.

fairly localised between $\pm L/2$, the continuum states should avoid the well region to ensure orthogonality. Figure I.2.11 shows a plot of the transmission coefficient for a 15 nm thick GaAs/Ga(Al)As quantum well versus energy.

I.2.5.   The problem of plane waves

In the previous discussions, we found that propagating states, stationary solutions of:

$$\frac{(-i\hbar\vec{\nabla})^2}{2m^*}\psi(\vec{r}) = \varepsilon\psi(\vec{r}) \qquad (I.2.83)$$

are the plane waves $\psi(\vec{r}) = N\exp(i\vec{k}\cdot\vec{r})$. The trouble is that the plane waves are not normalisable in the strict sense since $\int d^3r|\psi(\vec{r})|^2$ supposed to be equal to 1 is in fact divergent. This difficulty is not new since it is routinely encountered in electromagnetism where the solutions for the fields in free space are plane waves. In both cases the difficulty is somewhat artificial since it means that the probability density is uniform in space for the quantum particle or that the electromagnetic fields are everywhere in space. To bypass this difficulty, a possible way is to enclose the particle in a finite volume Ω (a length L in 1D). This volume has to be very large compared to the relevant dimension of the physical properties we are interested in. For instance, in the case of the motion of electrons in Field Effect Transistors (FETs), Ω can be chosen as 1 μm^3 since the lengths in modern FET are largely submicronic. If we choose the solution of enclosing the free particle in a finite volume, the normalised plane waves are:

$$\psi(\vec{r}) = \frac{1}{\sqrt{\Omega}} \exp(i\vec{k} \cdot \vec{r}) \quad \text{(3D)} \tag{I.2.84}$$

$$\psi(\vec{\rho}) = \frac{1}{\sqrt{S}} \exp(i\vec{k} \cdot \vec{\rho}) \quad \text{(2D)} \tag{I.2.85}$$

$$\psi(z) = \frac{1}{\sqrt{L}} \exp(ikz) \quad \text{(1D)} \tag{I.2.86}$$

We have however to complete this definition by deciding what happens at the boundary of the domain Ω. At first sight it appears sensible to require that ψ vanishes on this boundary. Actually, a more convenient rule is to make the wave periodic (Born–von Karman):

$$\psi(x + L_x, y, z) = \psi(x, y, z) \tag{I.2.87}$$
$$\psi(x, y + L_y, z) = \psi(x, y, z) \tag{I.2.88}$$
$$\psi(x, y, z + L_z) = \psi(x, y, z) \tag{I.2.89}$$

This automatically leads to a quantisation of the possible k vectors:

$$k_x L_x = 2n\pi \tag{I.2.90}$$
$$k_y L_y = 2m\pi \tag{I.2.91}$$
$$k_z L_z = 2p\pi \tag{I.2.92}$$

with n, m, p integers. If the box is very large, then the grid of allowed $\vec{k}$ values will be very dense. With the restriction of the particle to a finite domain Ω, we have to remember that the orthogonality between different plane waves is obtained only in the limit of macroscopic L, in 1D for instance if $k \neq k'$:

$$\int_{-\frac{L}{2}}^{\frac{L}{2}} dz \psi_{k'}^*(z)\psi_k(z) = \frac{2\sin\left[(k-k')\frac{L}{2}\right]}{L(k-k')}$$

$$\Rightarrow \int_{-\frac{L}{2}}^{\frac{L}{2}} dz \psi_{k'}^*(z)\psi_k(z) \to 0 \quad \text{if } L \to \infty$$

(I.2.93)

Here $L \to \infty$ has to be understood as $(k-k')L \gg 1$, say 10^2.

Another way to handle the difficulties associated with the non-normalisable plane wave is to build wavepackets. A wavepacket is a combination of different plane waves, centred at a certain k. Since we make linear combination of the stationary eigenstates, we should explicitly account for time in the wavepacket since there will be a time evolution of the mixing between the different plane waves components. In one dimension for instance, we write:

$$\psi_k(z,t) = \frac{1}{\sqrt{2\pi}} \int dq\, g(q-k)e^{i\left(qz - \varepsilon(q)\frac{t}{\hbar}\right)}$$

(I.2.94)

where $g(x)$ is a function peaked at $x = 0$ with a certain characteristic width δ. Furthermore, $g(x)$ decays fast enough at large x. Let us study the normalisation of this wavepacket:

$$\int dz |\psi_k(z,t)|^2 = \frac{1}{2\pi} \iint dq\, dq'\, g^*(q'-k)g(q-k)e^{i\varepsilon(q')\frac{t}{\hbar}}e^{-i\varepsilon(q)\frac{t}{\hbar}}$$

$$\times \int dz\, e^{-i(q'-q)z}$$

(I.2.95)

Now we use

$$\frac{1}{2\pi} \int dz\, e^{i(q-q')z} = \delta(q-q')$$

(I.2.96)

where $\delta(x)$ is the delta distribution (such that $\int \delta(x-x_0)f(x)dx = f(x_0)$). We get:

$$\int dz |\psi_k(z,t)|^2 = \iint dq\, dq'\, g^*(q'-k)g(q-k)e^{i\varepsilon(q')\frac{t}{\hbar}}e^{-i\varepsilon(q)\frac{t}{\hbar}}\delta(q-q')$$

$$= \int dq |g(q)|^2$$

(I.2.97)

Hence, the wavepacket is properly normalised if g is normalised. But this is warranted by our demand of a sufficiently rapidly decaying g function when $z \to \pm\infty$. A convenient choice for $g(x)$ is the normalised Gaussian:

$$g(x) = \frac{1}{\sqrt{\sigma\sqrt{\pi}}} \exp\left(-\frac{x^2}{2\sigma^2}\right) \tag{I.2.98}$$

Let us now investigate the time development of the wavepacket: we make a change of variable and write $q = k + \xi$. We expand the phases of the plane waves to the first order in ξ, which is a good approximation provided $\xi \ll \delta$, the width of the g function. Under such an assumption we obtain:

$$\psi_k(z,t) = A\left(z - \frac{\partial\varepsilon(q)}{\partial q}\bigg|_{q=k} \frac{t}{\hbar}\right) e^{i\left(kz - \varepsilon(k)\frac{t}{\hbar}\right)};$$

$$A(u) = \frac{1}{\sqrt{2\pi}} \int d\xi g(\xi) e^{i\xi u} \tag{I.2.99}$$

Thus, to a good approximation, the wavepacket looks like a plane wave modulated by an envelope $A(z,t)$. This envelope moves with time like a free particle having the group velocity $\frac{1}{\hbar}\frac{\partial\varepsilon(q)}{\partial q}\big|_{q=k}$. In the specific case of a Gaussian, the amplitude can be exactly calculated:

$$A(u) = \sqrt{\frac{\sigma}{\sqrt{\pi}}} e^{-\frac{\sigma^2 u^2}{2}} \tag{I.2.100}$$

and, as expected, we find that the wavepacket of plane waves is indeed normalised. The reader will check that the average values of the particle velocity p_z/m^* and of the Hamiltonian are constant and respectively equal to:

$$\int dz \psi_k^*(z,t) \left(-\frac{i\hbar}{m^*}\frac{\partial}{\partial z}\right) \psi_k(z,t) = \frac{\hbar k}{m^*} \tag{I.2.101}$$

$$\int dz \psi_k^*(z,t) \left(-\frac{\hbar^2}{2m^*}\frac{\partial^2}{\partial z^2}\right) \psi_k(z,t) = \frac{\hbar^2}{2m^*}\left(k^2 + \frac{\sigma^2}{2}\right) \tag{I.2.102}$$

Thus, if our wavepacket is very narrow ($\sigma \ll k$), it behaves in many respects like a plane wave but can be properly normalised. In the following, we shall use plane waves enclosed in a macroscopic volume, knowing that we can recourse to the wavepacket analysis if necessary.

I.2.6. Schrödinger equation, time-dependent aspects

The time evolution of quantum states is either "trivial" if the Hamiltonian is time independent or not amenable to a simple analysis if the Hamiltonian is explicitly time dependent. In the case of time-dependent H, one has to recourse either to purely numerical computations or to approximate methods such as time-dependent perturbation theory. In the physics of simple systems (atoms) where it is possible to prepare the system in a given quantum state, there is a great deal of discussions on adiabatic theorem (slow perturbations) versus sudden perturbations. For our purposes, essentially the behaviour of charged carriers in semiconductor devices, these discussions are hardly applicable except, may be, in quantum dots. We refer the interested reader to very many excellent textbooks that discuss these aspects [1, 9, 11].

The time-dependent Schrödinger equation (TDSE) equation reads:

$$i\hbar\frac{\partial\psi(\vec{r},t)}{\partial t} = H(t)\psi(\vec{r},t) \qquad (\text{I.2.103})$$

We need a boundary condition at initial time t_0: $\psi(\vec{r}, t = t_0) = \zeta(\vec{r})$ to make the problem completely defined (the equation being first order in time derivative we need only one boundary condition on time). Suppose H does not depend explicitly on time. Then, we are allowed to look for solutions that are separable in t and $\vec{r}$. As a result, the solution of the TDSE can be written:

$$\psi(\vec{r},t) = \exp\left[-i\frac{E(t-t_0)}{\hbar}\right]\varphi(\vec{r}); \quad H\varphi(\vec{r}) = E\varphi(\vec{r}) \qquad (\text{I.2.104})$$

Since H is hermitian, it can be diagonalised and the set of its eigenfunctions χ_n used as a basis of the Hilbert space. In particular, we can project the initial state on this basis:

$$\zeta(\vec{r}) = \sum_n c_n \chi_n(\vec{r}); \quad c_n = \int d^3r \chi_n^*(\vec{r})\zeta(\vec{r}) \tag{I.2.105}$$

and get immediately the solution at any t:

$$\psi(\vec{r}, t) = \sum_n c_n \chi_n(\vec{r}) \exp\left[-i\frac{E_n(t-t_0)}{\hbar}\right] \tag{I.2.106}$$

Thus, to know the time evolution of a system subjected to a time-independent H, we need to know the stationary eigenstates of H and the initial wavefunction. That can be technically difficult but we have, at least formally, the solution.

Suppose now that H depends explicitly on time. We solve the TDSE by means of the evolution operator $U(t, t_0)$ in order to display the origin of the difficulty to find a solution:

$$\psi(\vec{r}, t) = U(t, t_0)\zeta(\vec{r}); \quad i\hbar\frac{\partial U(t, t_0)}{\partial t} = H(t)U(t, t_0); \quad U(t_0, t_0) = 1 \tag{I.2.107}$$

The formal (implicit) solution is:

$$U(t, t_0) = 1 - \frac{i}{\hbar}\int_{t_0}^t dt' H(t')U(t', t_0) \tag{I.2.108}$$

This writing allows a systematic expansion of U in power of H (Dyson series). Iterating to the second order in H gives:

$$U(t, t_0) = 1 - \frac{i}{\hbar}\int_{t_0}^t dt' H(t') - \frac{1}{\hbar^2}\int_{t_0}^t dt' H(t')\int_{t_0}^{t'} dt'' H(t'') + \cdots \tag{I.2.109}$$

These three terms are the beginning of the Dyson series expansion. If H were time independent, it could be factorised in front of all the time integrals, in whatever order we want since H will always commute with itself. As a result the $U(t, t_0)$ expansion immediately reveals the Taylor expansion of the exponential and the formal solution of the TDSE would be $\exp[-iH(t-t_0)/\hbar]$. This would allow to recover the results obtained above.

The central difficulty for a time-dependent Hamiltonian is however that we should care about the product $H(t)H(t')$ to the extent that these two operators have no reason to commute. To give an example consider an electron subjected to an electromagnetic field at the dipolar approximation:

$$H(t) = H_0 + eFx \cos(\omega t) \tag{I.2.110}$$

Then:

$$[H(t), H(t')] = eF[\cos(\omega t') - \cos(\omega t)][H_0, x] \tag{I.2.111}$$

The latter commutator is certainly non-zero since H_0 contains the kinetic energy. There exists a formal solution of the TDSE that generalises the expression for the evolution operator known for time-independent Hamiltonian. It offers however very little clue to effectively solving TDSE. The reader is referred to [10] for further details on these formal aspects. Apart from purely numerical solutions that are more and more widespread owing to the ever growing power of computers, there is a class of problems that required special attention. It is when the Hamiltonian can be split in terms of a time-independent H_0 plus a "small" time-dependent term. We shall analyse this case later by using the perturbation theory. But before, let us investigate the time evolution of the averaged quantities. Call $|\psi(t)\rangle$ the state vector at time t. The average value of an operator $A(t)$ at time t is:

$$a(t) = \langle \psi(t)|A(t)|\psi(t)\rangle$$

$$\Rightarrow i\hbar \frac{da}{dt} = \langle i\hbar \frac{\partial \psi}{\partial t}|A(t)|\psi(t)\rangle + \langle \psi(t)|A(t)|i\hbar \frac{\partial \psi}{\partial t}\rangle$$

$$+ i\hbar \langle \psi(t)|\frac{\partial A(t)}{\partial t}|\psi(t)\rangle \tag{I.2.112}$$

Manipulating the TDSE, we find easily:

$$i\hbar \frac{da}{dt} = -\langle \psi(t)|H(t)A(t)|\psi(t)\rangle + \langle \psi(t)|A(t)H(t)|\psi(t)\rangle$$

$$+ \langle \psi(t)|\frac{\partial A(t)}{\partial t}|\psi(t)\rangle$$

$$= \langle \psi(t)|[A(t), H(t)] + i\hbar \frac{\partial A(t)}{\partial t}|\psi(t)\rangle \tag{I.2.113}$$

The latter expression is known as the Ehrenfest theorem. It shows that the time evolution of an averaged observable depends markedly on whether or not this observable commutes with H. If A commutes with H (and does not depend explicitly on time) then $da/dt = 0$.

A simple application of Ehrenfest theorem is the average energy of the system. Since H commutes with itself at time t, we find that:

$$\frac{dE}{dt} = \langle \psi(t)| \frac{\partial H(t)}{\partial t} |\psi(t)\rangle \qquad \text{(I.2.114)}$$

Thus, if H is time independent we find that the averaged energy of the particle is conserved. This is the quantum counterpart of the classical result that the mechanical energy of the particle is conserved if the Hamiltonian does not depend explicitly on time. As an application of Ehrenfest theorem find (see Exercise 37) the time evolution of the operators x and p if:

$$H(t) = \frac{p^2}{2m^*} + \frac{1}{2}m^*\Omega^2 x^2 + eFx + efx\cos(\omega t) \qquad \text{(I.2.115)}$$

Chapter I.3

Approximate Methods

I.3.1. Variational method

There are very few cases where the stationary Schrödinger equation can be solved in closed forms: the free particle, the harmonic oscillator, the coulombic problem. Some problems can be solved in closed forms but are too complicated to be very useful like the motion of a charged particle in a constant electric field where one ends up with Airy functions (combinations of Bessel functions of order 1/3) or the 1D motion of a particle in a cosine-shaped potential where one faces the Mathieu functions. Thus, most often, for a given problem one should find ways to approximate the unattainable exact solution by convenient guesses called trial wavefunctions, hopefully not far from the true ground state. These guesses are much simpler for bound states than for extended states because it is easier to imagine a plausible form for a wavefunction that has to decay far from the attractive centre rather than oscillating.

Suppose a quantum mechanical system is governed by the Hamiltonian H and suppose that we have imagined a trial quantum state $|\psi_0(\lambda_1, \lambda_2, \ldots, \lambda_N)\rangle$ that depends on N parameters $\lambda_1, \lambda_2, \ldots, \lambda_N$. This trial state will have an average energy that is larger or equal to the true ground state energy E_0 of the Hamiltonian H. In fact, let us expand the (normalised) trial state on the basis of the eigenstates of H:

$$|\psi_0(\lambda_1, \lambda_2, \ldots, \lambda_N)\rangle = \sum_n c_n^0(\lambda_1, \lambda_2, \ldots, \lambda_N)|\varphi_n\rangle; \quad \sum_n |c_n^0|^2 = 1$$

$$(\text{I.3.1})$$

And let us compute the energy of our trial state:

$$\langle\psi_0(\lambda_1,\lambda_2,\ldots,\lambda_N)|H|\psi_0(\lambda_1,\lambda_2,\ldots,\lambda_N)\rangle = E_0(\lambda_1,\lambda_2,\ldots,\lambda_N)$$

$$= \sum_n E_n|c_n^0|^2 \qquad (I.3.2)$$

Thus, $E_0(\lambda_1,\lambda_2,\ldots,\lambda_N)$ is certainly larger than or equal to E_0 to the extent that $\sum_n E_n|c_n^0|^2 \geq E_0 \sum_n |c_n^0|^2 = E_0$.

The idea is to find the "best" set of parameters $(\lambda_1,\lambda_2,\ldots,\lambda_N)$ to come as close as possible from the real E_0. To do so, we need to compute effectively $E_0(\lambda_1,\lambda_2,\ldots,\lambda_N)$ and to minimise it with respect to all parameters $\lambda_1,\lambda_2,\ldots,\lambda_N$. This is achieved by writing:

$$\frac{\partial E_0(\lambda_1,\lambda_2,\ldots,\lambda_N)}{\partial\lambda_i} = 0; \quad i = 1,2,\ldots,N \qquad (I.3.3)$$

and by checking that the extremum so calculated is indeed a minimum.

Suppose now we know (exactly or approximately) the ground state of H. We want to approximate the first excited state of this Hamiltonian. If we use the previous strategy, we shall unavoidably find a state that is close from the ground state. The exact eigenstates of H are orthogonal to each other. Hence, the solution to find a plausible guess for the first excited state is to ensure the orthogonality of the trial state to the ground state. So, if we are thinking of a certain trial state $|\psi_1(\lambda_1,\lambda_2,\ldots,\lambda_N)\rangle$, we shall actually compute E_1 by using:

$$|\tilde{\psi}_1(\mu_1,\mu_2,\ldots,\mu_N)\rangle = |\psi_1(\mu_1,\mu_2,\ldots,\mu_N)\rangle$$

$$- |\psi_0(\lambda_1,\lambda_2,\ldots,\lambda_N)\rangle\langle\psi_0(\lambda_1,\lambda_2,\ldots,\lambda_N)|$$

$$\times \psi_1(\mu_1,\mu_2,\ldots,\mu_N)\rangle \qquad (I.3.4)$$

In this way we ensure that $\langle\tilde{\psi}_1|\psi_0\rangle = 0$. If our initial guess $|\psi_1\rangle$ was already orthogonal to $|\psi_0\rangle$ then $|\tilde{\psi}_1\rangle$ coincides with $|\psi_1\rangle$. Note that the required orthogonality can automatically be ensured in bi- or tridimensional problems. Take for instance a quantum dot with cylindrical symmetry. The ground state corresponds to $L_z = 0$ (S symmetry). The first excited state corresponds to $L_z = \pm1$ (P symmetry). Hence, if we take a trial wavefunction for the excited state of the form $\psi_1(\rho, z, \varphi) = f(\rho, z)e^{\pm i\varphi}$, it will automatically be orthogonal to the ground state, irrespective of our guess for the function f. In one dimension, there is in general no such symmetry that can help us except for the parity of the wavefunctions: since the ground state is even in z, the trial wavefunction for the first excited state will have to be searched among the odd functions of z.

Let us give an example and study the ground state of an electron moving in the $z \geq 0$ half space, being blocked at $z = 0$ by an infinite barrier and subjected to a constant electric field F applied along the z direction. It is a simplified version of the celebrated Fang–Howard wavefunction that describes the electron motion in the channel of a Si–SiO$_2$ transistor [12]. The simplification lays in the fact that in the actual device the electric field is affected, through Poisson equation, by the electrons themselves. Hence, the actual electric field is not homogeneous along the z direction. Our normalised trial wavefunction for the ground state is the one-parameter-dependent wavefunction:

$$\psi_b(z) = \sqrt{\frac{b^3}{2}} z \exp\left(-\frac{bz}{2}\right) \tag{I.3.5}$$

The multiplicative term z handles the boundary condition that the wavefunction should vanish at $z = 0$ since the particle cannot penetrate the barrier. Then we find:

$$E_0(b) = \frac{\hbar^2 b^2}{8m^*} + \frac{3eF}{b} \tag{I.3.6}$$

The best trial wavefunction is such that $E_0(b)$ is minimum. This happens for:

$$b_{\min} = \left(\frac{12m^* eF}{\hbar^2}\right)^{1/3} \Rightarrow E_0^{\min} = \frac{3}{2}\left(\frac{9\hbar^2 e^2 F^2}{4m^*}\right)^{1/3} \tag{I.3.7}$$

In the factor $3/2$ in front of the parenthesis of $E_0^{\min}$ (Eq. (I.3.7)), $1/2$ goes to the kinetic energy and $2/2$ to the potential energy. This complies with the virial theorem (see Exercise 10).

A characteristic feature of the energy levels is their $F^{2/3}$ variation. Actually, this can be found without much calculation by looking for a dimensionless Schrödinger equation (something we can expect since the potential energy varies like a power of the distance to the interface).

If we calculate the mean distance to the interface, we find easily:

$$\langle z \rangle_0 = \langle \psi_0 | z | \psi_0 \rangle = \frac{3}{b_{\min}} = \left(\frac{27\hbar^2}{12m^* eF} \right)^{1/3} \tag{I.3.8}$$

Hence, $\langle z \rangle_0$ decreases like $F^{-1/3}$ when F increases. For $F = 40$ kV/cm and $m^* = 0.07m_0$ we find $\langle z \rangle_0 = 8.5$ nm. Heavier effective masses (as found in Si) leads to a smaller averaged distance from the interface.

Let us now focus on the variational calculation for the excited state. Its wavefunction should also vanish at $z = 0$ and as discussed must be made orthogonal to ψ_0. A possibility is to choose:

$$\psi_1(z) = Nz(z - z_0)e^{-cz/2} \tag{I.3.9}$$

where N is a normalisation constant, z_0 an unknown constant to be determined by the orthogonality between ψ_0 and ψ_1 and c a variational parameter. The computations become tedious. At the end we get:

$$z_0 = \frac{6}{b+c}; \quad N^2 = \frac{c^5}{24 - 12cz_0 + 2c^2 z_0^2} \tag{I.3.10}$$

$$\langle T_1 \rangle = -\frac{\hbar^2}{2m^* c^3} N^2 \left(-2 + cz_0 - \frac{c^2 z_0^2}{2} \right) \tag{I.3.11}$$

$$\langle V_1 \rangle = eF \langle z \rangle_1 = \frac{6eF}{c^6} N^2 (20 - 8cz_0 + c^2 z_0^2) \tag{I.3.12}$$

Then, we express z_0 in terms of c and compute numerically the minimum of $E_1 = \langle T_1 \rangle + \langle V_1 \rangle$ versus c, the parameter b being fixed at the value $b_{\min}$. We show in Fig. I.3.1 the field dependence of E_0 and E_1 as well as $\langle z \rangle_0$ and $\langle z \rangle_1$ versus F for the material parameters given above. We note that $\langle z \rangle_1 > \langle z \rangle_0$. This implies that the electron in the excited subband would be less affected by interface defects than in the ground subband.

I.3.2.   Perturbation theory

There are few problems that are exactly (and conveniently) solvable. Hence, one should recourse to approximate treatments. We

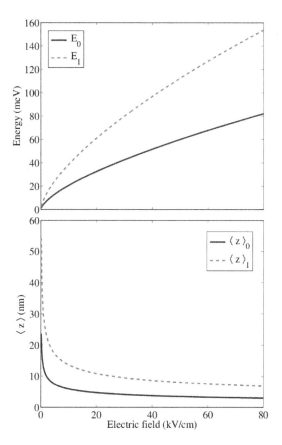

Figure I.3.1. Upper panel: Electric field dependence of the energies E_0 and E_1 of the ground and the first excited state respectively. Lower panel: Electric field dependence of mean distance to the interface $\langle z \rangle_0$ and $\langle z \rangle_1$ of the ground and the first excited state respectively. The parameter b is fixed at the value $b_{\min}$. $m^* = 0.07m_0$.

have seen that variational calculus provides relatively simple and accurate answers. But it works essentially for bound states. Here, we shall analyse another approach that is more systematic than the variational calculus but has a more restricted validity since we are going to analyse the effects of a small perturbation on the eigenstates and eigenenergies of a time-independent Hamiltonian assumed to be already diagonalised. Thus, we write:

$$H = H_0 + \lambda V; \quad 0 \leq \lambda \leq 1 \tag{I.3.13}$$

The energies and wavefunctions are expanded in ascending power of λ. The idea is to start with a small λ and at the end of the calculations to set $\lambda = 1$. There have been lots of discussions on the convergence of the series from the mathematical point of view. Since we are not going to retain more than the third order in λ in our calculations we shall not discuss the convergence problem any longer. The reader is referred to [1] for more elaborate discussions on these aspects.

We call E_n the eigenenergies and $|\varphi_n\rangle$ the eigenstates of H_0. The idea is that in the vicinity of an unperturbed energy E_n the eigenenergy of H will remain close from E_n if the perturbation is small and the eigenstates will resemble much the unperturbed $|\varphi_n\rangle$. While the first part of the statement is (approximately) true, the second part is wrong in the (many) cases of energy degeneracies, which is the rule rather than the exception. We shall see that in the case of degenerate eigenvalues the perturbed wavefunctions are to the lowest order independent of λ, showing that the action of an arbitrarily small perturbation leads to modifications of the wavefunctions that are not small. Let us first restrict our consideration to non-degenerate eigenvalues.

I.3.2.1. Non-degenerate perturbation theory

In the vicinity of $(E_n, |\varphi_n\rangle)$ we search the solution of Eq. (I.3.13) in the form:

$$E = E_n + \sum_{p=1} \lambda^p E_n^{(p)}; \quad |\varphi\rangle = |\varphi_n\rangle + \sum_{p=1} \lambda^p |\varphi_n^{(p)}\rangle \qquad (\text{I.3.14})$$

Inserting into the Schrödinger equation and equating the different terms of identical power in λ, we find, after calculations, the perturbed energies to the third order and the wavefunction up to the first in λ:

$$E = E_n + \lambda \langle \varphi_n | V | \varphi_n \rangle + \lambda^2 \sum_{m \neq n} \frac{|\langle \varphi_n | V | \varphi_m \rangle|^2}{E_n - E_m}$$

$$+ \lambda^3 \sum_{k \neq n} \sum_{m \neq n} \frac{\langle \varphi_n | V | \varphi_m \rangle \langle \varphi_m | V | \varphi_k \rangle \langle \varphi_k | V | \varphi_n \rangle}{(E_m - E_n)(E_k - E_n)}$$

$$-\lambda^3 \langle \varphi_n | V | \varphi_n \rangle \sum_{m \neq n} \frac{|\langle \varphi_n | V | \varphi_m \rangle|^2}{(E_n - E_m)^2} \tag{I.3.15}$$

$$|\psi\rangle = |\varphi_n\rangle + \lambda \sum_{m \neq n} \frac{\langle \varphi_m | V | \varphi_n \rangle}{E_n - E_m} |\varphi_m\rangle \tag{I.3.16}$$

Note that the perturbed wavefunction remains normalised up to the first order in λ included. We see on these formulae the crucial part played by the assumption of E_n being non-degenerate: if E_n were degenerate the denominators in Eq. (I.3.15) would vanish for the states having the same energies as $|\varphi_n\rangle$.

To illustrate the previous considerations, let us discuss two examples of application of non-degenerate perturbation calculus.

Example 1 (Stark effect in quantum well). Here we have:

$$H_0 = \frac{p_z^2}{2m^*} + V_{\text{conf}}(z); \quad \lambda V(z) = \lambda e F z, \; e > 0 \tag{I.3.17}$$

If $V_{\text{conf}}(z)$ is even in z (square, parabolic, $-V_0/\cosh(z/a)$, and so on, wells), the bound states have a definite parity (and the continuum states if they exist can also be made to display a given parity by combining judiciously wave coming from the left and going to the right with its opposite: a wave coming from the right and going to the left). If we insist on these parity properties this is because a number of simplifications occur in the shift of the eigenstates versus F (called Stark shift, after the discoverer of this effect in atoms). Note that the origin of the electrostatic potential has been chosen at the inversion symmetry point of the quantum well (its "centre"). We see from Fig. I.3.2 that if the unperturbed eigenstates have a definite parity, then all the odd terms in F in the Stark shift vanish identically. This is because changing F into $-F$ does not alter the physics of the problem: if we simultaneously change z into $-z$ in the Schrödinger equation, we see that $\psi(z, F)$ and $\psi(-z, -F)$ are solution of the same equation with the same energy. As we discuss below the formation of a dipole, changing F into $-F$ will change the sign of the induced dipole, but the resulting energy shift will remain the same.

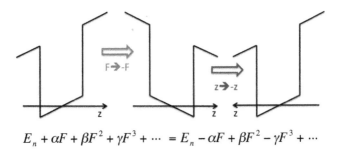

$$E_n + \alpha F + \beta F^2 + \gamma F^3 + \cdots = E_n - \alpha F + \beta F^2 - \gamma F^3 + \cdots$$

Figure I.3.2.   Parity rules of the Stark effect in a quantum well.

Let us discuss more thoroughly the weak field case. The Stark shifts are quadratic in F. The physics underlying this result is that of an induced dipole: there is no electric dipole moment before the application of the field since $\langle z \rangle$ vanishes on any unperturbed eigenstate. Applying a non-zero F polarises the wavefunctions. In fact, if we look at the perturbed wavefunction we easily deduce that there is an induced dipole. When the state is close from the nth unperturbed eigenstate, we find:

$$\langle \tilde{\psi}_n | -ez | \tilde{\psi}_n \rangle = -\langle \varphi_n | ez | \varphi_n \rangle - 2eF \sum_{m \neq n} \frac{\langle \varphi_n | z | \varphi_m \rangle \langle \varphi_m | ez | \varphi_n \rangle}{E_n - E_m}$$

$$(\text{I.3.18})$$

$$= -2eF \sum_{m \neq n} \frac{\langle \varphi_n | z | \varphi_m \rangle \langle \varphi_m | ez | \varphi_n \rangle}{E_n - E_m} \qquad (\text{I.3.19})$$

Now, if we compare this expression to the quadratic in F shift of E_n, we note that the energy shift is just $-\frac{1}{2}\vec{d} \cdot \vec{F} \equiv -\frac{1}{2}\langle \tilde{\psi}_n | -ez | \tilde{\psi}_n \rangle F$, where $\vec{d}$ is the electric dipole, as it should generate the interaction energy of an induced dipole with the field that has created it.

Note that the induced dipole $-e\langle z \rangle$ may in general have either sign depending on the signs of the energy denominators and the strength of the numerators. However, a notable exception is the quadratic shift for the ground state that is always negative (just because the energy denominators are all negative). Because any perturbation between two states leads to a repulsion between them, the ground states should experience a red shift because it is repelled by all the levels above it. This means the ground state wavefunction is polarised parallel to the field, i.e., electrons are shifted towards negative z if $F > 0$. This is a genuine quantum effect, since it is well known in the classical analysis of the electron motion in a square quantum well that the electrons accumulate near positive z (where the electrostatic potential energy is maximum and the kinetic energy minimum, hence a longer time spent by the electron on the right-hand side of the well (if $F > 0$)). The red shift of the ground state has very important practical consequences since it allows an efficient optical modulation of an electromagnetic signal. For a review of optical modulators based on Stark in quantum wells, see e.g., [13].

Example 2 ($\vec{k} \cdot \vec{p}$ approximation). As we have seen before, if the electron potential energy is spatially periodic, the eigenstates of the stationary Schrödinger equations fulfil the Bloch theorem:

$$\psi_{n\vec{k}}(\vec{r} + \vec{d}) = e^{i\vec{k}\cdot\vec{d}}\psi_{n\vec{k}}(\vec{r}); \quad \psi_{n\vec{k}}(\vec{r}) = u_{n\vec{k}}(\vec{r})\frac{e^{i\vec{k}\cdot\vec{r}}}{\sqrt{\Omega}} \qquad (I.3.20)$$

$$u_{n\vec{k}}(\vec{r} + \vec{d}) = u_{n\vec{k}}(\vec{r}) \qquad (I.3.21)$$

where n is a band index, Ω the volume of the sample and $\vec{k}$ is a wavevector that can be restricted to the first Brillouin zone. The question we address is the following. Suppose we know the eigenenergies and eigenstates at some point $\vec{k}_0$ of the Brillouin, can we know the eigenenergies and eigenstates in the vicinity of this $\vec{k}_0$? So our small parameter will be the vector $\vec{q} = \vec{k} - \vec{k}_0$. The Schrödinger equation does not help because $\vec{k}$ does not appear explicitly in this equation. However, if we write the equation fulfilled by the periodic parts $u_{n\vec{k}}$ we find:

$$\left[\frac{(\vec{p} + \hbar\vec{k})^2}{2m_0} + V(\vec{r})\right]u_{n\vec{k}}(\vec{r}) = \varepsilon u_{n\vec{k}}(\vec{r}) \qquad (I.3.22)$$

Thus, in the vicinity of $\vec{k}_0$ we can rewrite the equation for $u_{n\vec{k}}$ as:

$$[H_{\vec{k}_0} + \delta H(\vec{k}_0, \vec{q})]u_{n\vec{k}} = \varepsilon u_{n\vec{k}}; \quad H_{\vec{k}_0} = \frac{(\vec{p} + \hbar\vec{k}_0)^2}{2m_0} + V(\vec{r}) \quad (I.3.23)$$

$$\delta H(\vec{k}_0, \vec{q}) = \frac{\hbar\vec{q}}{m_0} \cdot (\vec{p} + \hbar\vec{k}_0) + \frac{\hbar^2 q^2}{2m_0} \qquad (I.3.24)$$

Now, we can use all the machinery of the perturbation expansion since the $u_{n\vec{k}_0}$'s form a basis on which we can expand the $u_{n\vec{k}}$'s. We assume the eigenvalue $E_{n\vec{k}_0}$ to be orbitally non-degenerate (the spin degeneracy is unimportant here since δH is spin independent).

The perturbation contains two terms. The scalar $\frac{\hbar^2 q^2}{2m_0}$ has only diagonal elements with respect to the band index. The term linear in $\vec{q}$ leads to both a first-order term and to a second-order term: so up to the second order in q we get the energy correction:

$$E_{n\vec{k}} = E_{n\vec{k}_0} + \langle u_{n\vec{k}_0}| \frac{\hbar\vec{q}}{m_0} \cdot (\vec{p} + \hbar\vec{k}_0)|u_{n\vec{k}_0}\rangle + \frac{\hbar^2 q^2}{2m_0}$$

$$+ \frac{\hbar^2}{m_0^2} \sum_{m \neq n} \frac{|\langle u_{n\vec{k}_0}|\vec{q}\cdot(\vec{p} + \hbar\vec{k}_0)|u_{m\vec{k}_0}\rangle|^2}{E_{n\vec{k}_0} - E_{m\vec{k}_0}} \qquad \text{(I.3.25)}$$

Now it is not difficult to see that:

$$\langle u_{n\vec{k}_0}| \frac{\hbar\vec{q}}{m_0} \cdot (\vec{p} + \hbar\vec{k}_0)|u_{n\vec{k}_0}\rangle = \frac{\hbar\vec{q}}{m_0} \cdot \langle \psi_{n\vec{k}_0}|\vec{p}|\psi_{n\vec{k}_0}\rangle \qquad \text{(I.3.26)}$$

Thus, we find that Eq. (I.3.25) can be rewritten in terms of the $\vec{p}$ matrix elements between the Bloch states:

$$E_{n\vec{k}} = E_{n\vec{k}_0} + \langle \psi_{n\vec{k}_0}| \frac{\hbar\vec{q}}{m_0} \cdot \vec{p}|\psi_{n\vec{k}_0}\rangle + \frac{\hbar^2 q^2}{2m_0} + \frac{\hbar^2}{m_0^2} \sum_{m \neq n} \frac{|\langle \psi_{n\vec{k}_0}|\vec{q}\cdot\vec{p}|\psi_{m\vec{k}_0}\rangle|^2}{E_{n\vec{k}_0} - E_{m\vec{k}_0}}$$

$$\text{(I.3.27)}$$

This expression can be compared to the Taylor expansion around $\vec{k}_0$:

$$E_{n\vec{k}} = E_{n\vec{k}_0} + \vec{q} \cdot \vec{\nabla}_{\vec{k}} E_{n\vec{k}}\Big|_{\vec{k}_0} + \frac{1}{2} \sum_{\alpha,\beta=x,y,z} q_\alpha q_\beta \frac{\partial^2 E_{n\vec{k}}}{\partial^2 k_\alpha k_\beta}\Big|_{\vec{k}_0} \qquad \text{(I.3.28)}$$

By identifying term by term, we find that:

$$\langle v_{\vec{k}_0}\rangle = \langle \psi_{n\vec{k}_0}| \frac{\vec{p}}{m_0}|\psi_{n\vec{k}_0}\rangle = \frac{1}{\hbar} \frac{\partial E_{n\vec{k}}}{\partial \vec{k}}\Big|_{\vec{k}_0} \qquad \text{(I.3.29)}$$

As expected, we find that the average velocity in a Bloch state is equal to the gradient of the dispersion relation divided by $\hbar$. Consequently, the average velocity vanishes when the dispersion relation admits an extremum.

The term quadratic in q gives us information on the effective mass of the carrier. In the Taylor expansion, the second-order term could have been rewritten $\sum_{\alpha,\beta} q_\alpha \frac{\hbar^2}{2m_{\alpha\beta}^{(n)}} q_\beta$. Then, we find:

$$\frac{m_0}{m_{\alpha\beta}^{(n)}} = \delta_{\alpha\beta} + \frac{2}{m_0} \sum_{m\neq n} \frac{\langle \psi_{n\vec{k}_0} | p_\alpha | \psi_{m\vec{k}_0} \rangle \langle \psi_{m\vec{k}_0} | p_\beta | \psi_{n\vec{k}_0} \rangle}{E_{n\vec{k}_0} - E_{m\vec{k}_0}} \qquad (I.3.30)$$

This expression shows that the effective mass always refers to a given band at a given point $\vec{k}_0$ of the Brillouin zone. Talking about the effective mass of electrons in, say, Si has little meaning unless one specifies that this mass refers for instance to the lowest lying conduction band at its minimum. We see also that the magnitude and even the sign of the effective mass is a balance between the bands that lay above the band n and those that lay below.

In this respect, one may design a toy model, the two bands semiconductor. It is characterised by a single bandgap $\varepsilon_g = E_c - E_v$ and two edges E_c and E_v. Then, as seen from (I.3.30), apart from the free electron term, the conduction and valence bands will display opposite effective mass. The seemingly oversimplified description works rather well in IV–VI material (PbTe, ...) where the band extrema occur at the L point. But it also works in the zinc blende direct gap semiconductors for the conduction and light valence band, as displayed in Fig. I.3.3 where the conduction band effective mass is plotted versus the bandgap for several semiconductors.

I.3.2.2. Degenerate perturbation theory

There are situations where the perturbation is never weak. This is when there exists degeneracy of some eigenvalue(s) of the unperturbed Hamiltonian H_0 and their corresponding eigenfunctions are coupled by the perturbation. In that case, the energy denominators in Eq. (I.3.15) will vanish for all the degenerate states. To cope with the case of an energy E_n that is g times degenerate while still being in the perturbative regime, we shall split the spectrum of H_0 into a subspace with dimension g and the rest of the spectrum. Within the subspace of the degenerate eigenvalue, we shall have to solve exactly the full Hamiltonian irrespective of the smallness of the perturbation

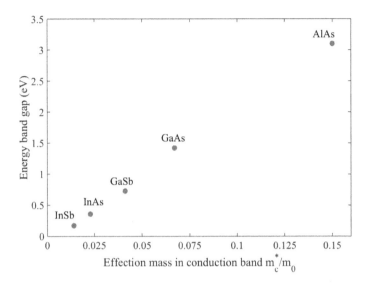

Figure I.3.3. Conduction band effective mass scaled to the free electron mass versus the energy band gap of various III–V semiconductors.

while the coupling between this subspace and the rest of the eigenstates of H_0 will be handled, if necessary, by the same technique as we used in the case of non-degenerate eigenvalues. This scheme is achieved relatively simply. We write:

$$H = H_0 + \lambda V$$

$$= H_0 + \lambda P_g V P_g + \lambda(V - P_g V P_g); \quad P_g = \sum_{\nu=1}^{g} |n\nu\rangle\langle n\nu|$$

$$(\text{I.3.31})$$

P_g is the projector on the subset of the g-fold degenerate eigenvalue E_n and $|n\nu\rangle$, $\nu = 1, 2, \ldots, g$ are the eigenvectors associated with the eigenvalue. By construction, the difference $V - P_g V P_g$ has no matrix element within the subspace of the degenerate eigenvalue. It connects the g perturbed eigenvectors that result from the diagonalisation of $H_0 + \lambda P_g V P_g$ with the rest of the unperturbed eigenvectors of H_0.

Let us then study the solution of the stationary Schrödinger equation in the $g \times g$ subspace. The matrix representing $H_0 + \lambda P_g V P_g$ has E_n on the diagonal plus the λV matrix whose matrix elements are

$\lambda \langle n\nu|V|n\mu \rangle$ $\nu, \mu = 1, \ldots, g$. The new eigenvalues and eigenvectors result from the diagonalisation of this $g \times g$ matrix. We write:

$$|n, l\rangle = \sum_\nu c^l_{n\nu}|n\nu\rangle; \quad E_{nl} = E_n + \lambda\nu_l \qquad (\text{I.3.32})$$

Depending on the physical situation, the g-fold degeneracy can be partially or completely lifted. Note that while the deviations from the unperturbed energy E_n are linear in λ, we find that the wavefunctions are independent of λ (the $c^l_{n\nu}$ are independent of λ).

In a second step, by using perturbation theory, we account for the coupling of the states of the subspace $g \times g$ to the other eigenvectors of the H_0 via the perturbation $\lambda(V - P_g V P_g)$. For instance, to the second order in λ we would get for the perturbation of E_{nl}:

$$\tilde{E}_{nl} = E_n + \lambda\nu_l + \lambda^2 \sum_{m \neq n} \frac{|\langle n, l|V|m\rangle|^2}{E_{nl} - E_m} \qquad (\text{I.3.33})$$

As a result of these virtual excursions, note that no terms linearly dependent on λ show up. Note also that a possible degeneracy of $|m\rangle$ will not affect the result since $E_m \neq E_n$.

As an example, let us consider the case of a 2D harmonic oscillator, which is a simple model for the lateral confinement in lens-shaped semiconductor quantum dots (e.g., InAs/GaAs). We have:

$$H_0 = H_{0x} + H_{0y} = \frac{p_x^2}{2m^*} + \frac{1}{2}m^*\omega^2 x^2 + \frac{p_y^2}{2m^*} + \frac{1}{2}m^*\omega^2 y^2 \quad (\text{I.3.34})$$

$$\lambda V(x, y) = \lambda A m^* \omega^2 xy \qquad (\text{I.3.35})$$

where $A > 0$ is a c-number. The eigenvalues and eigenstates of H_0 are:

$$E_{nm} = (n + m + 1)\hbar\omega; \quad \langle xy|nm\rangle = \varphi_n(x)\varphi_m(y) \qquad (\text{I.3.36})$$

where the φ_n's are the Hermite functions of order n. The degeneracy of E_{nm} is $n + m + 1$. So, the ground state is non-degenerate ($n = m = 0$), the first excited state ($n + m = 1$) is twice degenerate, the second excited is thrice degenerate, etc.

Since the 1D harmonic oscillator has a potential energy that is an even function of x or y, its eigenfunctions are even or odd in x and y. Then, we find readily that $V(x, y)$ will couple the two degenerate eigenstates corresponding to the eigenvalue $2\hbar\omega$ $(n+m=1)$. Thus, the diagonalisation of $H_0+\lambda P_g V P_g$ inside the 2×2 subspace amounts to finding the eigenvalues and eigenvectors of:

$$\begin{pmatrix} 2\hbar\omega & \lambda\alpha \\ \lambda\alpha & 2\hbar\omega \end{pmatrix}; \quad \alpha = Am^*\omega^2\langle 1,0|xy|0,1\rangle > 0 \qquad (\text{I.3.37})$$

The eigenvalues are $\varepsilon_{1\pm} = 2\hbar\omega \pm \lambda|\alpha|$. The two eigenstates are:

$$\varepsilon_+ = 2\hbar\omega + \lambda|\alpha|; \quad |\psi_+\rangle = \frac{1}{\sqrt{2}}(|1,0\rangle + |0,1\rangle) \qquad (\text{I.3.38})$$

$$\varepsilon_- = 2\hbar\omega - \lambda|\alpha|; \quad |\psi_-\rangle = \frac{1}{\sqrt{2}}(|1,0\rangle - |0,1\rangle) \qquad (\text{I.3.39})$$

If we want to study the second-order coupling with the other states, we note that the perturbation being proportional to xy can be re-expressed in terms of the creation and annihilation operators of the x and y harmonic oscillators. Since $|\psi_\pm\rangle$ contains only zero or one quantum of either oscillators, the $|\psi_\pm\rangle$ states can only be connected to states that contain at most two quanta of each oscillator. The reader will check that such states are the $|2,1\rangle$ and $|1,2\rangle$ states with an energy $4\hbar\omega$.

The states next to the $|\psi_\pm\rangle$ excited states form a triplet with an energy $3\hbar\omega$: there are $|2,0\rangle$, $|0,2\rangle$, $|1,1\rangle$. Apply the same method as above to find the new eigenstates in the degenerate set (see Exercise 27).

I.3.3.   Time-dependent perturbation theory

In semiconductor heterostructures, there exist many possible time evolutions of an initial state due to the imperfections that perturb the ideal evolutions. Note that in contrast to atomic physics, we deal with extended states in heterostructures (except for the low lying states of quantum dots) for both the initial and final states.

We want to solve:

$$i\hbar\frac{\partial}{\partial t}|\psi\rangle = [H_0 + V(t)]|\psi(t)\rangle \qquad (\text{I.3.40})$$

where H_0 is the Hamiltonian of the ideal heterostructure and $V(t)$ the perturbation that is either static or explicitly time dependent. Although qualitatively similar, the perturbative approaches of static and time-dependent potentials will be handled separately.

I.3.3.1.   Static scatterers

The potential V is actually time independent. The spectrum of $H_0 + V$ contains extended state and (sometime) a few localised states if V contains an attractive part. The eigenstates $|\psi_\nu\rangle$ of $H_0 + V$ can be written as admixtures of the eigenstates of H_0. The difficulty is to describe the effects of potential $V(r)$ on the continuum states of H_0, i.e., to find the link that exists between the projection $c^\nu_{n,\vec{k}}$ of a continuum state $|\psi_\nu\rangle$ of $H_0 + V$ on a continuum state $|n, \vec{k}\rangle$ of H_0 and the perturbing potential V. In the general case there are no answer but numerical to that question except if V is small and it is the purpose of the stationary perturbation calculus to predict the magnitude of $c^\nu_{n,\vec{k}}$.

This static description must be completed by the description of the dynamics of a given initial state under the action of $H_0 + V$. Note that in contrast with atomic physics, where good (even perfect) control of the initial states of a system is achievable, one has essentially no knowledge of the initial states in imperfect semiconductors.

Obviously, the initial state must not be an eigenstate of $H_0 + V$. Most often, one assumes that the initial state is an eigenstate of H_0. This choice is justified only if V is "weak" enough to be able to assume that a particular $|n_0, \vec{k}_0\rangle$ is plausible. Indeed, as we shall show below, as time increases the state that evolves from $|n_0, \vec{k}_0\rangle$ will admit small components on other states $|n, \vec{k}\rangle$ under the action of a small V.

Let us examine this more closely. We describe our imperfect heterostructure by a Hamiltonian $H_0 + V$. The eigenstates of the ideal heterostructure are those of H_0:

$$H_0|n\vec{k}\rangle = E_{n\vec{k}}|n\vec{k}\rangle \tag{I.3.41}$$

$$\varphi_{n\vec{k}}(\vec{r}) = \chi_n(z)\frac{1}{\sqrt{S}}e^{i\vec{k}\cdot\vec{\rho}} \tag{I.3.42}$$

n is the subband index and $k = (k_x, k_y)$ a 2D wavevector. For convenience, we shall assume that all diagonal elements of V are zero.

If this were not the case, one would define:

$$H = \tilde{H}_0 + \tilde{V} \tag{I.3.43}$$

$$\tilde{H}_0 = H_0 + \sum_{n\vec{k}} |n\vec{k}\rangle\langle n\vec{k}|V|n\vec{k}\rangle\langle n\vec{k}| \tag{I.3.44}$$

$$\tilde{V} = V - \sum_{n\vec{k}} |n\vec{k}\rangle\langle n\vec{k}|V|n\vec{k}\rangle\langle n\vec{k}| \tag{I.3.45}$$

and be in a situation where $\tilde{V}$ has no diagonal matrix elements.

At $t = 0$ $|\psi(t = 0)\rangle = |n_0\vec{k}_0\rangle$. Our task is to compute $|\psi(t)\rangle$ under the assumption that V is small. We expand $|\psi(t)\rangle$ on the basis at time t of H_0:

$$|\psi(t)\rangle = c_{n_0\vec{k}_0}(t)e^{-iE_{n_0\vec{k}_0}\frac{t}{\hbar}}|n_0\vec{k}_0\rangle + \sum_{n\vec{k}\neq n_0\vec{k}_0} c_{n\vec{k}}(t)e^{-iE_{n\vec{k}}\frac{t}{\hbar}}|n\vec{k}\rangle \tag{I.3.46}$$

The inclusion of the phases $e^{-iE_{n_0\vec{k}_0}\frac{t}{\hbar}}$, $e^{-iE_{n\vec{k}}\frac{t}{\hbar}}$ in the basis allows to eliminate H_0 from the TDSE; this is the so-called interaction representation (see Exercise 35).

$$i\hbar\dot{c}_{n_0\vec{k}_0}(t)e^{-iE_{n_0\vec{k}_0}\frac{t}{\hbar}}|n_0\vec{k}_0\rangle + i\hbar\sum_{n\vec{k}\neq n_0\vec{k}_0}\dot{c}_{n\vec{k}}(t)e^{-iE_{n\vec{k}}\frac{t}{\hbar}}|n\vec{k}\rangle$$

$$= c_{n_0\vec{k}_0}(t)e^{-iE_{n_0\vec{k}_0}\frac{t}{\hbar}}V|n_0\vec{k}_0\rangle + \sum_{n\vec{k}\neq n_0\vec{k}_0}c_{n\vec{k}}(t)e^{-iE_{n\vec{k}}\frac{t}{\hbar}}V|n\vec{k}\rangle \tag{I.3.47}$$

Projecting on $\langle n\vec{k}|$ and on $\langle n_0\vec{k}_0|$ we get:

$$i\hbar\dot{c}_{n\vec{k}}(t) = c_{n_0\vec{k}_0}(t)e^{-i\left(E_{n_0\vec{k}_0}-E_{n\vec{k}}\right)\frac{t}{\hbar}}\langle n\vec{k}|V|n_0\vec{k}_0\rangle$$

$$+ \sum_{n'\vec{k}'\neq n_0\vec{k}_0} c_{n'\vec{k}'}(t)e^{-i\left(E_{n'\vec{k}'}-E_{n\vec{k}}\right)\frac{t}{\hbar}}\langle n\vec{k}|V|n'\vec{k}'\rangle \tag{I.3.48}$$

$$i\hbar\dot{c}_{n_0\vec{k}_0}(t) = \sum_{n\vec{k}\neq n_0\vec{k}_0} c_{n\vec{k}}(t)e^{-i\left(E_{n\vec{k}}-E_{n_0\vec{k}_0}\right)\frac{t}{\hbar}}\langle n_0\vec{k}_0|V|n\vec{k}\rangle \tag{I.3.49}$$

The structure of these equations is interesting in that it reveals that if V is "small" the coefficient $c_{n_0\vec{k}_0} \propto V^0$; $c_{n\vec{k}} \propto V^1$. Thus, at this order of approximation the projection of $|\psi(t)\rangle$ on the initial state remains equal to 1 while there exist small admixtures linear in V in $|\psi(t)\rangle$:

$$c_{n_0\vec{k}_0}(t) = 1 \tag{I.3.50}$$

$$i\hbar \dot{c}_{n\vec{k}}(t) = \langle n\vec{k}|V|n_0\vec{k}_0\rangle e^{-i\frac{t}{\hbar}\left(E_{n_0\vec{k}_0} - E_{n\vec{k}}\right)} \tag{I.3.51}$$

$$\Rightarrow c_{n\vec{k}}(t) = -2i\frac{\langle n\vec{k}|V|n_0\vec{k}_0\rangle}{E_{n_0\vec{k}_0} - E_{n\vec{k}}} \sin\left[\frac{t}{2\hbar}(E_{n_0\vec{k}_0} - E_{n\vec{k}})\right] e^{-i\frac{t}{2\hbar}(E_{n_0\vec{k}_0} - E_{n\vec{k}})} \tag{I.3.52}$$

Thus, for a weak perturbation, the probability of finding the electron in the $|n\vec{k}\rangle$ state at time t if it was in the state $|n_0\vec{k}_0\rangle$ at $t = 0$ is equal to:

$$P_{n\vec{k}}^{n_0\vec{k}_0}(t) = |c_{n\vec{k}}|^2 = \frac{4|\langle n\vec{k}|V|n_0\vec{k}_0\rangle|^2}{(E_{n_0\vec{k}_0} - E_{n\vec{k}})^2} \sin^2\left[\frac{t}{2\hbar}(E_{n_0\vec{k}_0} - E_{n\vec{k}})\right] \tag{I.3.53}$$

This expression is not particularly revealing: $P_{n\vec{k}}^{n_0\vec{k}_0}(t)$ displays oscillations with time. It is proportional to V^2 and inversely proportional to the square of the energy detuning between the initial and final states.

Let us compute the survival probability in the initial state $P_{n\vec{k}_0}^{n_0\vec{k}_0}(t)$:

$$P_{n_0\vec{k}_0}^{n_0\vec{k}_0}(t) = 1 - \sum_{n\vec{k} \neq n_0\vec{k}_0} P_{n\vec{k}}^{n_0\vec{k}_0}(t) \tag{I.3.54}$$

Thus, if there exist very many states available to the particle, we may anticipate that $P_{n_0\vec{k}_0}^{n_0\vec{k}_0}(t)$ will be small at long t. In fact, in the long time limit, we shall find that the survival probability in the initial state decays exponentially:

$$P_{n_0\vec{k}_0}^{n_0\vec{k}_0} = \exp\left(-\frac{t}{\tau_{n_0\vec{k}_0}}\right) \tag{I.3.55}$$

It is interesting to note that by definition:

$$P_{n_0\vec{k}_0}^{n_0\vec{k}_0}(t + dt) = P_{n_0\vec{k}_0}^{n_0\vec{k}_0}(t)[1 - W_{n_0\vec{k}_0}(t)] \tag{I.3.56}$$

where $W_{n_0 \vec{k}_0}(t)$ is the transition rate that the system leaves the initial state between t and $t + dt$. We shall directly compute $W_{n_0 \vec{k}_0}(t)$ and find that at long time it is a constant. This will imply that the survival probability in the initial state will decay exponentially with a time constant:

$$\tau_{n_0 \vec{k}_0} = \frac{1}{W_{n_0 \vec{k}_0}(t \to \infty)} \tag{I.3.57}$$

To compute $\tau_{n_0 \vec{k}_0}$, we first evaluate the time derivative of $P^{n_0 \vec{k}_0}_{n_0 \vec{k}_0}$:

$$W^{n_0 \vec{k}_0}_{n \vec{k}}(t) = \frac{dP^{n_0 \vec{k}_0}_{n \vec{k}}}{dt} = \frac{2}{\hbar} \frac{|\langle n\vec{k}|V|n_0\vec{k}_0\rangle|^2}{(E_{n_0 \vec{k}_0} - E_{n\vec{k}})} \sin\left[\frac{t}{\hbar}(E_{n_0 \vec{k}_0} - E_{n\vec{k}})\right] \tag{I.3.58}$$

Again, nothing striking shows up. But suppose now that instead of focusing our attention on a well-defined final state we sum over all the possible final states $|n\vec{k}\rangle$:

$$W_{n_0 \vec{k}_0}(t) = \frac{2}{\hbar} \sum_{n\vec{k}} \frac{|\langle n\vec{k}|V|n_0\vec{k}_0\rangle|^2}{(E_{n_0 \vec{k}_0} - E_{n\vec{k}})} \sin\left[\frac{t}{\hbar}(E_{n_0 \vec{k}_0} - E_{n\vec{k}})\right] \tag{I.3.59}$$

To the extent that $\langle n\vec{k}|V|n_0\vec{k}_0\rangle$ is a smooth function of both the initial and final states and letting t going to infinity we find using the mathematical identity:

$$\pi\delta(x - x_0) = \lim_{L\to\infty} \frac{\sin[L(x - x_0)]}{x - x_0} \tag{I.3.60}$$

$$\frac{1}{\tau_{n_0 \vec{k}_0}} = \lim_{t\to\infty} W_{n_0 \vec{k}_0}(t) = \frac{2\pi}{\hbar} \sum_{n\vec{k}} |\langle n\vec{k}|V|n_0\vec{k}_0\rangle|^2 \delta(E_{n_0 \vec{k}_0} - E_{n\vec{k}}) \tag{I.3.61}$$

where δ is the Dirac delta function. This expression, called the Fermi golden rule, shows that at long time the system can in practice only reach the dispersion relations $E_{n\vec{k}}$ that conserve the energy (see Fig. I.3.4).

To summarise, for a weak perturbation V, we find two equivalent statements of the Fermi golden rule: either we state that the transition rate to leave the initial state is a constant or that the survival

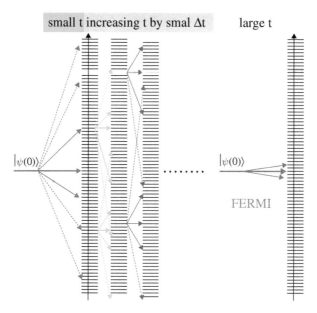

small t   increasing t by smal Δt   large t

$|\psi(0)\rangle$

$|\psi(0)\rangle$

FERMI

Figure I.3.4. Schematic representation of the Fermi golden rule: at large time t, the system can only reach the $|n\vec{k}\rangle$ states that have the same energy as the initial state.

probability in the initial state decays exponentially with time. More-over, the two time constants involved in these two statements are the same.

Let us give an example of application of the Fermi golden rule. The potential energy we consider is:

$$V(\vec{r}) = Ub\delta(z - z_0) \exp\left(-\frac{(\vec{\rho} - \vec{\rho}_0)^2}{\alpha^2}\right); \quad \rho^2 = x^2 + y^2 \quad (I.3.62)$$

b has the dimension of a length and U of an energy. Such a defect can be seen as a fairly localised perturbation along z with an effective extension $\approx \alpha$ in the layer plane around the point (x_0, y_0). The matrix element $\langle n\vec{k}|V|n_0\vec{k}_0\rangle$ is equal to:

$$\langle n\vec{k}|V|n_0\vec{k}_0\rangle = \pi\alpha^2 \frac{Ub}{S}\chi_n(z_0)\chi_{n_0}(z_0)e^{-i\vec{q}\cdot\vec{\rho}_0}e^{-\frac{q^2\alpha^2}{4}}; \quad \vec{q} = \vec{k} - \vec{k}_0 \quad (I.3.63)$$

As could have been expected from the properties of the Fourier trans-form, the matrix elements are important only if $q\alpha < 4$. We note that the in-plane translation invariance of the unperturbed Hamiltonian makes the defect position $\vec{\rho}_0$ irrelevant: when we shall apply the Fermi golden rule the phase $e^{i\vec{q}\cdot\vec{\rho}_0}$ will disappear. Such is not the case for the defect location along the growth axis. Because the heterostructure formation leads to bound states along the z-axis with eigenfunctions whose modulus display a spatial modulation, the matrix element (and its modulus squared) will be z_0 dependent. We find:

$$
\frac{\hbar}{2\pi\tau_{n_0\vec{k}_0}} = \frac{U^2 b^2 \alpha^4 m^*}{4S\hbar^2}\chi_n^2(z_0)\chi_{n_0}^2(z_0)e^{-\frac{\alpha^2(k^2+k_0^2)}{2}}\int_0^{2\pi}d\theta\, e^{\alpha^2 k k_0 \cos\theta}
$$

$$
= \frac{U^2 b^2 \alpha^4 m^* \pi}{2S\hbar^2}\chi_n^2(z_0)\chi_{n_0}^2(z_0)e^{-\alpha^2\left[k_0^2+\frac{m^*}{\hbar^2}(E_{n_0}-E_n)\right]}I_0(\alpha^2 k k_0)
$$

$$\text{(I.3.64)}$$

$$
k = \sqrt{k_0^2 + \frac{2m^*}{\hbar^2}(E_{n_0} - E_n)} \tag{I.3.65}
$$

where I_0 is the Bessel function of an imaginary argument of order 0. It admits the expansion:

$$
I_0(z) = \sum_{n=0}^{\infty}\frac{1}{(n!)^2}\left(\frac{z}{2}\right)^{2n} \tag{I.3.66}
$$

Note that if $E_n > E_{n_0}$ the initial wavevector $\vec{k}_0$ should be non-zero. If there were a single scatterer (the one located at $\vec{\rho}_0$) the level lifetime would be extremely long. But there are very many scatterers and, to the extent that one can neglect the interferences between the scattering events (this will be discussed later), we just have to multiply the previous result by N_{def}, the number of scatterers on the xy plane.

One sees that there can be inter-subband scattering ($n \neq n_0$) or intra-subband scattering ($n = n_0$). In the latter case, the elastic scattering means $k = k_0$. The magnitude of the scattering times for both processes depend firstly on whether $\chi_n^2(z_0)$ is larger or smaller than $\chi_{n_0}^2(z_0)$ and secondly on the k dependence of the scattering matrix element. Very often, it happens that the intra-subband scattering events are faster than the inter-subband scattering ones. This has significant consequences on the applicability of the Fermi golden rule as we shall discuss later in the book.

I.3.3.2. Time-dependent scattering

Very often, the time-dependent potential energy factorises as a function of time by a function that depends on $\vec{r}$:

$$V(\vec{r}, t) = V(\vec{r})f(t) \tag{I.3.67}$$

where V is hermitian and $f(t)$ a real function. A celebrated example is provided by:

$$V(\vec{r}) = eFz; \quad f(t) = \sin(\omega t) \tag{I.3.68}$$

It describes the coupling between an electron and the electric field of an electromagnetic wave at the dipolar (long wavelength) approximation.

Then under the same assumption of weak perturbation and with the same initial condition ($c_{n\vec{k}}(t = 0) = \delta_{nn_0}\delta_{\vec{k}\vec{k}_0}$) we find:

$$c_{n\vec{k}}(t) = \langle n\vec{k}|V|n_0\vec{k}_0\rangle \frac{1}{i\hbar} \int_0^t dt' f(t') e^{-i\frac{t'}{\hbar}(E_{n_0\vec{k}_0} - E_{n\vec{k}})} \tag{I.3.69}$$

Let us first consider the harmonic perturbation. We obtain:

$$c_{n\vec{k}}(t) = \langle n\vec{k}|V|n_0\vec{k}_0\rangle e^{i\frac{t}{2\hbar}(E_{n_0\vec{k}_0} - E_{n\vec{k}} + \hbar\omega)} \frac{\sin\left[\frac{t}{2\hbar}(E_{n_0\vec{k}_0} - E_{n\vec{k}} + \hbar\omega)\right]}{(E_{n_0\vec{k}_0} - E_{n\vec{k}} + \hbar\omega)}$$

$$- \langle n\vec{k}|V|n_0\vec{k}_0\rangle e^{i\frac{t}{2\hbar}(E_{n_0\vec{k}_0} - E_{n\vec{k}} - \hbar\omega)} \frac{\sin\left[\frac{t}{2\hbar}(E_{n_0\vec{k}_0} - E_{n\vec{k}} - \hbar\omega)\right]}{(E_{n_0\vec{k}_0} - E_{n\vec{k}} - \hbar\omega)} \tag{I.3.70}$$

There are two terms that evolve at very different paces. Suppose first that $E_{n_0\vec{k}_0} > E_{n\vec{k}}$. Then the first term changes with time much more rapidly than the second one, in particular when $\hbar\omega$ approaches the energy difference $E_{n_0\vec{k}_0} - E_{n\vec{k}}$. Keeping only the second term leads to a probability of finding the system in $|n\vec{k}\rangle$ if it were in $|n_0\vec{k}_0\rangle$

equal to:

$$P_{n\vec{k}}^{n_0\vec{k}_0} = |\langle n\vec{k}|V|n_0\vec{k}_0\rangle|^2 \frac{\sin^2\left[\frac{t}{2\hbar}(E_{n_0\vec{k}_0} - E_{n\vec{k}} - \hbar\omega)\right]}{(E_{n_0\vec{k}_0} - E_{n\vec{k}} - \hbar\omega)^2} \qquad \text{(I.3.71)}$$

We can now proceed exactly as before and define a survival probability in the initial state $P_{n_0\vec{k}_0}^{n_0\vec{k}_0} = 1 - \sum_{n\vec{k}} P_{n\vec{k}}^{n_0\vec{k}_0}$. In the long time limit we would find an exponential decay of the survival probability with a characteristic time $\tau_{n_0\vec{k}_0}$ equal to:

$$\frac{1}{\tau_{n_0\vec{k}_0}} = \frac{2\pi}{\hbar}\frac{1}{4}\sum_{n\vec{k}} |\langle n\vec{k}|V|n_0\vec{k}_0\rangle|^2 \delta(E_{n_0\vec{k}_0} - E_{n\vec{k}} - \hbar\omega) \qquad \text{(I.3.72)}$$

The factor $1/4$ results from the fact that the perturbation is proportional to $\sin(\omega t)$ and not to $e^{i\omega t}$. When $E_{n_0\vec{k}_0} < E_{n\vec{k}}$ it is the other component that evolves at a slower pace. Consequently, we find that the survival probability decays with a characteristic time constant equal to:

$$\frac{1}{\tau_{n_0\vec{k}_0}} = \frac{2\pi}{\hbar}\frac{1}{4}\sum_{n\vec{k}} |\langle n\vec{k}|V|n_0\vec{k}_0\rangle|^2 \delta(E_{n\vec{k}} - E_{n_0\vec{k}_0} - \hbar\omega) \qquad \text{(I.3.73)}$$

The two components of the $\sin(\omega t)$ lead either to a loss or a gain in energy for the system. In the context of light-matter interaction, the transitions corresponding to the two exponential components are associated with the absorption or stimulated emission of light. Note that the spontaneous emission is absent from our calculations since it would require to quantise the electromagnetic field.

We see that the harmonic perturbation plays a very special role since (like in classical mechanics) there can exist a resonant transfer from the exciting force to the material system (or its reverse, a loss of energy of system that is transferred to the exciting force). In the general case of a non-harmonic perturbation, it is difficult to select a particular pair of initial and final states that would "resonantly" absorb or emit energy of the perturbing potential except if it is a weakly damped sinusoid. In the latter case, the delta function in the Fermi golden rule is changed into a lorentzian function:

$$\delta(x) \rightarrow \frac{\Gamma}{\pi(x^2 + \Gamma^2)} \qquad \text{(I.3.74)}$$

For a general perturbing potential there is no other way but to find explicitly $P^{n_0 \vec{k}_0}_{n\vec{k}}(t)$ and to look at the survival probability at long time. An example of such a calculation is proposed as an exercise (see Exercise 34). Here, we handle the simple case where:

$$f(t) = e^{-\frac{t}{\tau_1}} - e^{-\frac{t}{\tau_2}} \tag{I.3.75}$$

Then, we find readily:

$$c_{n\vec{k}}(t) = \langle n\vec{k}|V|n_0\vec{k}_0\rangle \left(\frac{1 - e^{i\Omega t}e^{-t/\tau_1}}{\hbar\Omega + i\frac{\hbar}{\tau_1}} - \frac{1 - e^{i\Omega t}e^{-t/\tau_2}}{\hbar\Omega + i\frac{\hbar}{\tau_2}} \right) \tag{I.3.76}$$

$$\hbar\Omega = E_{n\vec{k}} - E_{n_0\vec{k}_0} \tag{I.3.77}$$

Since there is no resonance, we can compute $P^{n_0\vec{k}_0}_{n\vec{k}}(\infty)$ without difficulty and find:

$$P^{n_0\vec{k}_0}_{n\vec{k}}(\infty) = \frac{|\langle n\vec{k}|V|n_0\vec{k}_0\rangle|^2}{\hbar^2} \frac{(\tau_2 - \tau_1)^2}{(1 + \Omega^2\tau_1^2)(1 + \Omega^2\tau_2^2)}$$

$$= \left| \frac{\langle n\vec{k}|V|n_0\vec{k}_0\rangle\tau_1}{\hbar\sqrt{1 + \Omega^2\tau_1^2}} \right|^2 \frac{(x - 1)^2}{(1 + \Omega^2\tau_1^2 x^2)} \tag{I.3.78}$$

where $x = \tau_2/\tau_1$. We see that the probability to reach a state $|n\vec{k}\rangle$ at $t = \infty$ starting from $|n_0\vec{k}_0\rangle$ at $t = 0$ is maximum for $\Omega = 0$. It is of course zero if $x = 1$. At $x = 0$ the x-dependent factor is one while at $x = \infty$ this factor is $\Omega^{-2}\tau_1^{-2}$.

The central result of the t-dependent perturbation calculus is the irreversible departure from the initial state. One should wonder why this is so. This is because the phase space available to the system is huge. Hence, it is plausible that the probability that the system returns at time t to exactly the same quantum state as it was at $t = 0$ becomes very small at long time. This behaviour is genuine to the condensed matter where the Hilbert space of the electron (or the phonon) forms a huge continuum. For smaller systems, we shall see that in general there is no Fermi golden rule. In the last twenty years there have been tremendous efforts to grow quantum heterostructures, where by the combination of epitaxy, etching, self-organised growth, and so on, one can fabricate objects where the electronic degrees of freedom are increasingly discrete; going from the bulks to the quantum wells, then to the quantum wires to finally reach the quantum dots, where the low energy part of the electronic spectrum is discrete.

Let us see what happens to a small quantum system and to simplify the matter as much as possible let us take a 2-level system. We call $|1\rangle$ and $|2\rangle$ these two levels. We have the Hamiltonian $H = H_0 + V$ where:

$$\langle 1|V|1\rangle = \langle 2|V|2\rangle = 0, \qquad \langle 1|V|2\rangle = U \tag{I.3.79}$$

$$\langle 1|H_0|1\rangle = -\frac{\delta}{2}, \qquad \langle 2|H_0|2\rangle = \frac{\delta}{2} \tag{I.3.80}$$

Hence, δ is the energy difference between the two eigenstates of H_0 and V is the perturbation that couples them. We choose $U \geq 0$. There is no difficulty to compute the eigenstates of the complete Hamiltonian $H_0 + V$. We label them $|+\rangle$ and $|-\rangle$ and $\varepsilon_\pm$ the corresponding energies. We find:

$$\varepsilon_\pm = \pm\sqrt{U^2 + \frac{\delta^2}{4}} \tag{I.3.81}$$

If we write:

$$|\pm\rangle = c_{1\pm}|1\rangle + c_{2\pm}|2\rangle \tag{I.3.82}$$

there is:

$$c_{1\pm} = \frac{U}{\sqrt{U^2 + \left(\frac{\delta}{2} \pm \sqrt{U^2 + \frac{\delta^2}{4}}\right)^2}} \frac{\left|\frac{\delta}{2} \pm \sqrt{U^2 + \frac{\delta^2}{4}}\right|}{\frac{\delta}{2} \pm \sqrt{U^2 + \frac{\delta^2}{4}}} \tag{I.3.83}$$

$$c_{2\pm} = \frac{\left|\frac{\delta}{2} \pm \sqrt{U^2 + \frac{\delta^2}{4}}\right|}{\sqrt{U^2 + \left(\frac{\delta}{2} \pm \sqrt{U^2 + \frac{\delta^2}{4}}\right)^2}} \tag{I.3.84}$$

Since we know the stationary states of the system, there is no difficulty to compute its time evolution. We take that $|\psi(t = 0)\rangle = |1\rangle$

for simplicity and we compute the survival probability $P_1(t)$ to find the system in $|1\rangle$ at time t. If we invert Eq. (I.3.82), we get:

$$|1\rangle = d_+|+\rangle + d_-|-\rangle \qquad (I.3.85)$$

Therefore:

$$|\psi(t)\rangle = e^{-i\frac{\varepsilon_+ t}{\hbar}} d_+|+\rangle + e^{-i\frac{\varepsilon_- t}{\hbar}} d_-|-\rangle \qquad (I.3.86)$$

and finally:

$$P_1(t) = |\langle 1|\psi(t)\rangle|^2 = |e^{-i\frac{\varepsilon_+ t}{\hbar}}|d_+|^2 + e^{-i\frac{\varepsilon_- t}{\hbar}}|d_-|^2|^2$$

$$= |d_+|^4 + |d_-|^4 + 2|d_+|^2|d_-|^2 \cos\left(\frac{(\varepsilon_+ - \varepsilon_-)t}{\hbar}\right) \qquad (I.3.87)$$

So, we see that for a small system there is no irreversible departure from the initial state but instead an oscillatory behaviour. These are the famous *Rabi oscillations*. In a 2-level system, the system always comes back to its initial state periodically (except if it has been prepared in an eigenstate of H in which case it stays there for ever).

The case of zero detuning ($\delta = 0$) corresponds to $|d_\pm| = \frac{1}{\sqrt{2}}$ and to:

$$P_1^{\delta=0}(t) = \cos^2\left(\frac{Ut}{\hbar}\right) \qquad (I.3.88)$$

while at very large detuning ($\delta \to \infty$) we find a survival probability in the initial state that is close to one; the departure from one being proportional to $\frac{U^2}{\delta^2}$ and oscillating at an increasing angular frequency $\frac{\delta}{\hbar}$.

For finite systems the behaviour is intermediate between the 2-level and the macroscopic systems. For a small number of degrees of freedom, there is no irreversible departure, the system explores its phase space and can come back to the initial state but not in a periodic fashion because, in general, there are more than a single Bohr frequency in the problem and there is no reason that the different Bohr frequencies should be commensurate.

Chapter I.4

Landau Quantisation of Electron Motion in Ideal Semiconductor Bulks and Heterostructures

One of the most powerful tools of investigation of the electronic states in semiconductor heterostructures is to apply a strong magnetic field to the sample. In this chapter, we investigate the energy levels of ideal materials subjected to a static and homogeneous magnetic field B.

We adopt the simplest case of parabolic dispersion relations that lead in a bulk material to a cyclotron motion with angular frequency $\omega_c = eB/m^*$. By solving the Newton equation of motion:

$$m^* \frac{d\vec{v}}{dt} = -e\vec{v} \times \vec{B} \tag{I.4.1}$$

where $-e$ is the electron charge, we find readily, by taking the scalar product with either $\vec{v}$ or $\vec{B}$ on both sides of Eq. (I.4.1), that the projection of the electron velocity along $\vec{B}$ is constant as well as v^2. Thus, choosing $\vec{B}//\hat{z}$ we get:

$$\vec{v} = (v_0 \cos(\psi), v_0 \sin(\psi), v_z); \quad \dot{\psi} = \frac{eB}{m^*} \Rightarrow \psi(t) = \omega_c t + \psi_0 \tag{I.4.2}$$

$$x(t) = x_0 + \frac{v_0}{\omega_c} \sin(\omega_c t + \psi_0) \tag{I.4.3}$$

$$y(t) = y_0 - \frac{v_0}{\omega_c} \cos(\omega_c t + \psi_0) \tag{I.4.4}$$

$$z(t) = z_0 + v_z t \tag{I.4.5}$$

where v_0 is the modulus of the initial velocity in the (x, y) plane and ψ_0 is an initial phase. As one can see the classical solutions display a translation invariance in the plane perpendicular to the field since the centre of the in-plane oscillatory motion (x_0, y_0) is arbitrary and does not affect the particle energy. The uniform rotation around the magnetic field translates into the conservation of the z component of the angular momentum provided the origin is at the centre of the oscillation (x_0, y_0). One might think these features will be preserved in the quantum motion. However, we shall see below that it is impossible to find a gauge where the quantum motion would simultaneously display the in-plane invariance and the rotational invariance around the field. This is because the in-plane translation operators and L_z do not commute:

$$\left[xp_y - yp_x, \exp\left(-\frac{i}{\hbar}(x_0p_x + y_0p_y) \right) \right]$$

$$= (x_0p_y - y_0p_x) \exp\left(-\frac{i}{\hbar}(x_0p_x + y_0p_y) \right) \qquad \text{(I.4.6)}$$

This non-vanishing commutator will prevent to find eigenstates that are common to both the in-plane translation and L_z operators.

We want to investigate the energy levels (the Landau levels) of quasi-2D electrons (non-parabolicity effects on quantum wells Landau levels were discussed in [14]). We assume that there exists a z-dependent potential $V(z)$ that binds one or several states ($V(z)$ can be square well, a parabolic potential, a triangular potential well, and so on). It is not as easy as to build the Hamiltonian of an electron experiencing the Lorentz force as when there exists a potential energy associated with the conservative forces. Nevertheless, by comparison with the known expression of the Lorentz force, one can retrieve the correct equations of motion:

$$\frac{d\vec{r}}{dt} = \frac{\partial H}{\partial \vec{p}}; \quad \frac{d\vec{p}}{dt} = -\frac{\partial H}{\partial \vec{r}} \qquad \text{(I.4.7)}$$

if one uses for H the following expression:

$$H = \frac{1}{2m^*}(\vec{p} + e\vec{A})^2 + V(z) \qquad \text{(I.4.8)}$$

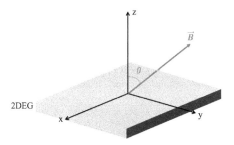

Figure I.4.1. Sketch of the orientation of the magnetic field $\vec{B}$ applied on a two-dimensional electron gas (2DEG).

where $\vec{A}$ is the vector potential associated with the magnetic field: $\vec{B} = \vec{\nabla} \times \vec{A}$. From now on we chose the magnetic field (see Fig. I.4.1):

$$\vec{B} = (0, B\sin\theta, B\cos\theta) \tag{I.4.9}$$

A possible choice for $\vec{A}$ is:

$$\vec{A} = (Bz\sin\theta, Bx\cos\theta, 0) \tag{I.4.10}$$

As we shall see below this choice privileges the in-plane translation invariance. It has to be stressed that $\vec{A}$ is an inconvenient mathematical tool because the gradient of any function can be added to it without altering the vector $\vec{B}$. Since only the field retains a physical significance, the results for physical observables should depend on $\vec{B}$ and not on $\vec{A}$, i.e., they should be gauge invariant [9, 15].

Let us define:

$$B\sin\theta = B_\perp; \quad \omega_{c\perp} = \frac{eB\sin\theta}{m^*} \tag{I.4.11}$$

$$B\cos\theta = B_\|; \quad \omega_{c\|} = \frac{eB\cos\theta}{m^*} \tag{I.4.12}$$

For completeness, we can also introduce the spin Zeeman effect $g^*\mu_B\vec{\sigma} \cdot \vec{B}$ where g^* is the effective Landé g factor of the electron ($g^* \approx -0.4$ in GaAs) and σ a dimensionless spin whose components admit the eigenvalues $\pm\frac{1}{2}$. Note that because a scalar product is rotationally invariant, we can quantise the electron spin along any direction that suits our purpose. The simplest one appears to be $\vec{B}$ (and not necessarily the growth axis). As a result, the spin variable can be entirely decoupled from the orbital variables. We know that there will exist two eigenvalues $\pm g^* \mu_B / 2$ associated with the two eigenstates $|+\rangle$ and $|-\rangle$. From now on, we leave the spin effects and concentrate on the search for the eigenstates of the orbital motion.

The Hamiltonian we have to investigate is:

$$H = \frac{1}{2m^*}(p_x + eB_\perp z)^2 + \frac{1}{2m^*}(p_y + eB_\| x)^2 + \frac{p_z^2}{2m^*} + V(z)$$

$$(\text{I.4.13})$$

Since H does not depend on y, p_y is conserved. Hence, we can search for eigenfunctions in the form:

$$\psi_{k_y,\mu}(\vec{r}) = \frac{e^{ik_y y}}{\sqrt{L_y}} \varphi_\mu(x, z) \qquad (\text{I.4.14})$$

If $\theta \neq 0$, the x and z variables do not separate in the general case ($V(z)$ arbitrary). A quadratic variation of $V(z)$ upon z (as realised in n-i-p-i structures [16]) leads to a complete solution of the problem (because the Hamiltonian becomes the sum of quadratic terms that can be suitably re-arranged). However, in the general case and if θ is not too large the system is quasi-separable. This is because for nanometric z confinement, the energy separation between the bound levels is large compared to diamagnetic Zeeman shift brought about by the magnetic field. Let us rewrite H in the form of a separable "unperturbed" Hamiltonian and a δH term that vanishes if $\theta = 0$ and contains a term that breaks the separability but is expected to be small:

$$H = H_z + H_\perp + \delta H$$

$$H_z = \frac{p_z^2}{2m^*} + V(z); \quad H_\perp = \frac{p_x^2}{2m^*} + \frac{1}{2m^*}(\hbar k_y + eB_\| x)^2 \quad (\text{I.4.15})$$

$$\delta H = \delta H_1 + \delta H_2 = \frac{e^2 B_\perp^2}{2m^*} z^2 + \frac{eB_\perp}{m^*} z p_x$$

The term in δH that breaks the separability in x and z is proportional to $\sin \theta$, is linear in B and proportional to $z p_x$. It can therefore be seen as an orbital paramagnetic Zeeman effect. The δH_2 term can also be considered as a Stark effect due to the Hall field $B_\perp p_x$. Let us remark that at the zeroth order in δH, the solutions of Eq. (I.4.15) involves only $B_\|$. This means that the energy levels will only depend on the field component parallel to the growth axis. An immediate check of this property for a given heterostructure is to rotate the sample with respect to the field and to check whether or not the physical property under consideration depends on $B \cos \theta$ or not. For a bulk material instead (and because the dispersion relations are assumed isotropic), it is easy to check that the eigenstates and eigenenergies depend only on the modulus of the field and not on its direction. Let us examine the eigenstates of $H_z + H_\perp$. Their wavefunctions factorise in x and z:

$$\varphi_\mu(x, z) = \chi_m(z)\varphi_n(x) \tag{I.4.16}$$

where:

$$H_\| \chi_m(z) = E_m \chi_m(z) \tag{I.4.17}$$

$$H_\perp \varphi_n(x) = \left[\frac{p_x^2}{2m^*} + \frac{1}{2m^*}(\hbar k_y + eB_\| x)^2\right]\varphi_n(x)$$

$$= \varepsilon_n \varphi_n(x) \tag{I.4.18}$$

$\chi_m(z)$ is the mth bound state wavefunction for the z motion associated with the energy E_m. The functions $\varphi_n(x)$ are the eigenfunctions of a harmonic oscillator problem centred at:

$$x_0 = -\frac{\lambda^2 k_y}{\cos\theta}; \quad \lambda = \sqrt{\frac{\hbar}{eB}} \tag{I.4.19}$$

λ is the magnetic length. It scales like $B^{-1/2}$ and is equal to ≈ 25.6 nm if $B = 1$ T. The eigenvalues of a harmonic oscillator do not depend on the centre of the oscillation (a classical result) but only on its angular frequency and they are equidistant [9, 15]. In our specific case of magnetic levels, we get the fundamental degeneracy of the free electron Landau levels and their even spacings:

$$\varepsilon_n(k_y) = \left(n + \frac{1}{2}\right)\hbar\omega_{c\|}; \quad n = 0, 1, 2, \dots \tag{I.4.20}$$

The eigenfunctions associated with these eigenvalues are the normalised Hermite functions:

$$\varphi_n(x) = \frac{\cos^{1/4}\theta}{\sqrt{\lambda}} \frac{1}{\sqrt{2^n n!\sqrt{\pi}}} \exp\left[-\frac{\cos\theta}{2\lambda^2}(x - x_0)^2\right] H_n$$

$$\times \left[\sqrt{\cos\theta} \left(\frac{x - x_0}{\lambda} \right) \right]$$

$$H_n(x) = (-1)^n e^{x^2} \frac{d^n}{dx^n} (e^{-x^2}) \tag{I.4.21}$$

It can be easily verified that:

$$\langle n - 1 | x | n \rangle = \int_{-\infty}^{+\infty} \varphi_{n-1}(x) x \varphi_n(x) dx = \frac{\lambda}{\sqrt{\cos\theta}} \sqrt{\frac{n}{2}} \tag{I.4.22}$$

$$\langle n | x | n \rangle = x_0 \tag{I.4.23}$$

$$\langle n - 1 | \frac{d}{dx} | n \rangle = \frac{\sqrt{\cos\theta}}{\lambda} \sqrt{\frac{n}{2}} \tag{I.4.24}$$

We have succeeded in classifying the eigenstates of $H_\parallel + H_\perp$. These eigenstates consist of Landau levels ladders that are attached to each of the zero field bound states E_n (note that the separability also applies to the unbound states for the z motion). It is remarkable that the spectrum is entirely quantised while at $B = 0$ it consists of 2D subbands of the in-plane free motion attached to each of the E_n. It is very tempting to state that the heterostructure potential quantises the z motion while the B field quantises the in-plane motion. Indeed there is no explicit dependence of the eigenenergies upon any continuous variable unlike the $B = 0$ solutions. However, we stress that the discretisation of the electron spectrum is only partly achieved because, in reality, each of the eigenvalues is "macroscopically" degenerate. In other words each eigenenergy has a degeneracy that grows proportionally to the sample area, whereas in atoms or quantum dots, some energies may be (orbitally) degenerate, but that degeneracy remains finite when the size of the system increases (in 3D radial confinement the P state are three-fold degenerate irrespective of the range of the confining potential).

I.4.1.   Landau level degeneracy

Let us compute this macroscopic degeneracy. We demand that the centre of the orbit x_0 remains in the sample, otherwise the electron energy would be much higher (since in practice it would not experience the cohesive energy felt by all the electrons that reside in this solid):

$$-\frac{L_x}{2} \leq r_0 \leq \frac{L_x}{2} \tag{I.4.25}$$

The allowed k_y values are uniformly distributed and separated by the interval $2\pi/L_y$ (periodic boundary conditions applied to the plane waves along the y axis). Thus, for a given subband index and a given Landau level, the orbital degeneracy is equal to:

$$g_{\mathrm{orb}} = \frac{L_x L_y}{2\pi\lambda^2} \cos\theta \tag{I.4.26}$$

Note that g_{orb} is exact at $\theta = 0$ ($\delta H_1 = \delta H_2 = 0$ in this case) but only approximate at $\theta \neq 0$ since the effects of δH_1 and δH_2 have not yet been evaluated.

I.4.2. Perturbative estimates of δH_1 and δH_2

We have to investigate the effects of δH on the zeroth-order eigenstates $|m, n, k_y\rangle$ of energy $\varepsilon_{m,n} = E_m + (n + \frac{1}{2})\hbar\omega_{c\parallel}$. The first term δH_1 does not affect the separability between x and z (as a matter of fact δH_1 could have been included in $H_\parallel$). The only effect is an admixture of the different z states while the in-plane motion remains unaffected and n should be conserved. For a subband that is well separated from the others, e.g., the ground subband, δH_1 can be treated by first-order perturbation theory. Thus, $\varepsilon_{m,n}$ will be shifted by Δ_m where:

$$\Delta_m = \frac{e^2}{2m^*} B_\perp^2 \langle \chi_m | z^2 | \chi_m \rangle \tag{I.4.27}$$

To make the perturbation treatment meaningful, we must have $\langle \chi_n | \delta H_1 | \chi_m \rangle \ll |E_n - E_m|$. For the states of a particle confined by a potential well of range $\approx L$, $E_n \approx \frac{\hbar^2 n^\alpha}{m^* L^2}$, where α depends on the nature of the potential energy: $\alpha = 1$ for a quadratic potential, $\alpha = 2$ for a square well with infinite barriers, etc., whereas $\langle \chi_n | z^2 | \chi_m \rangle \approx L^2$. Thus:

$$\frac{\langle \chi_1 | \delta H_1 | \chi_2 \rangle}{E_2 - E_1} \approx \frac{L^4 e^2 B^2 \sin^2\theta}{2\hbar^2 (2^\alpha - 1)} = \frac{L^4 \sin^2\theta}{2\lambda^4 (2^\alpha - 1)} \tag{I.4.28}$$

The perturbation treatment will be justified if the effective magnetic length (associated with the in-plane component of the magnetic field) remains much larger than the range of the z-dependent confining potential.

In the case of confinement by a square well with infinite barrier heights, the first-order correction to the ground state energy will be:

$$\Delta_1 = \frac{e^2 B^2 L^2}{4m^*} \left(\frac{1}{6} - \frac{1}{\pi^2} \right) \sin^2 \theta \qquad (\text{I.4.29})$$

For $B = 10$ T, $\theta = \pi/4$, $L = 10$ nm, $m^* = 0.07m_0$, we find $\Delta_1 \approx$ 0.2 meV, which is much smaller than $E_2 - E_1 \approx 168$ meV. Note however that δ_1 becomes comparable to $E_2 - E_1$ if $L \geq 50$ nm. In this case, the first-order perturbation calculus becomes insufficient. Actually the whole decoupling procedure becomes dubious because the system is too weakly bi-dimensional, either because the bound states are too dense or because the bound states supported by $V(z)$ are too close from the continuum.

The second kind of perturbing term δH_2 can be rewritten $z p_x \omega_{c\perp}$. It does not depend on y. Hence only states with the same k_y (or x_0) will be coupled by δH_2. δH_2 has vanishing diagonal element in the $|m, n, k_y\rangle$ basis since an electron placed in a bound state has no average velocity $\langle n|p_x|n\rangle = 0$. To the second order in perturbation, we get:

$$\Delta_{m,n} = \sum_{(m',n')\neq(m,n)} \frac{\omega_{c\perp}^2 |\langle \chi_m|z|\chi_{m'}\rangle|^2 |\langle n|p_x|n'\rangle|^2}{E_m - E_{m'} + (n - n')\hbar\omega_{c\|}} \qquad (\text{I.4.30})$$

Thus, δH_2 couples Landau levels of different subbands whose indexes n', n differ by one. In addition, if the confining potential along z is even in z, only subbands with opposite parities will be coupled by δH_2. Note that $\Delta_{m,n}$ becomes very large (but can no longer be described by second-order perturbation calculus) when the energy denominator in Eq. (I.4.30) vanishes. Practically, this means that two consecutive Landau levels of two consecutive subbands intersect. However, the two levels are now coupled by δH_2 and the crossing is replaced by an anticrossing. In a simple 2-level analysis, one finds the magnitude of the anticrossing A_c equal to:

$$A_c = \frac{1}{\lambda(B_c)} |\langle \chi_1 | z | \chi_2 \rangle| \frac{eB_c\sqrt{2}}{m^*} \tan\theta \qquad (I.4.31)$$

We note that A_c varies like $(B_c)^{3/2}$. The existence of anticrossing for field that is not lined up with the growth axis has led to an interesting magneto-spectroscopy of the inter-subband transitions [17]. The authors studied a 2DEG electron gas located near the GaAs/Ga(Al)As modulation-doped interface. A strong magnetic field (up to 20 T) tilted by only 4° from the growth axis of their layers was applied. By studying the cyclotron resonance absorption and its splitting into two lines when the magnetic field is such that $E_2 - E_1 = \hbar\omega_{c\parallel}$, the authors of [17] were able to observe the splitting A_c that arises because of the non-vanishing in-plane component of the magnetic field.

I.4.3.   Magnetic field-dependent density of states

We now restrict our consideration to $\theta = 0$ and take into account the spin splitting effect. The general formula for the density of states of a system with Hamiltonian H is:

$$\rho(\varepsilon) = \sum_\nu \delta(\varepsilon - \varepsilon_\nu) \qquad (I.4.32)$$

where ν labels the set of quantum numbers that specify the eigenstates of H. In our case this means the subband index $m = 1, 2, \ldots$ in E_m, the Landau-level index $n = 0, 1, 2, \ldots$, the wavevector k_y (which labels the free motion along the y axis or, equivalently, the centre of the Hermite functions) and the spin quantum number $\sigma_z = \pm 1/2$. Hence:

$$\rho(\varepsilon) = \sum_m \rho_m(\varepsilon) \qquad (I.4.33)$$

$$\rho_m(\varepsilon) = \sum_{n,k_y,\sigma_z} \delta\left(\varepsilon - E_m - \left(n + \frac{1}{2}\right)\hbar\omega_c - \sigma_z g^* \mu_B B\right) \qquad (I.4.34)$$

$$\omega_c = \frac{eB}{m^*} \qquad (I.4.35)$$

Using Born von Karman boundary conditions for the y direction, going to the macroscopic limit and accounting for the necessary location of the orbit centre in the sample (see above), we find:

$$\rho_m(\varepsilon) = \frac{S}{2\pi\lambda^2} \sum_{n,\sigma_z} \delta\left(\varepsilon - E_m - \left(n + \frac{1}{2}\right)\hbar\omega_c - \sigma_z g^* \mu_B B\right)$$

(I.4.36)

As the carrier motion is entirely quantised, the density of states is zero except at the discrete energies:

$$\varepsilon_{m,n,\sigma_z} = E_m + \left(n + \frac{1}{2}\right)\hbar\omega_c + \sigma_z g^* \mu_B B \qquad (I.4.37)$$

where it is infinite. This result is in striking contrast with the zero field situation where there is:

$$\rho(\varepsilon) = \sum_m \rho_m(\varepsilon); \quad \rho_m(\varepsilon) = \frac{m^* S}{\pi\hbar^2} Y(\varepsilon - E_m) \qquad (I.4.38)$$

where $Y(x)$ is the step function. At zero field, the quasi-bidimensional electron gas is metallic, with a gapless density of states for $\varepsilon \geq E_1$. A non-zero magnetic field dramatically alters this situation, replacing the continuous density of states ($\varepsilon \neq E_m$) by point-like singularities separated by finite gaps. Thus, depending on the respective location of the characteristic electron energy η (e.g., the Fermi energy at $T = 0$ K) and $\varepsilon_{m,n,\sigma_z}$, the electron gas will behave either like an insulator ($\eta \neq \varepsilon_{m,n,\sigma_z}$) or a metal ($\eta = \varepsilon_{m,n,\sigma_z}$). Notice that similar effects cannot be found in bulk materials because the density of states is gapless both at $B = 0$ and $B \neq 0$ (if $\varepsilon > \frac{\hbar\omega_c}{2} - \frac{1}{2}|g*|\mu_B B$).

Compared to this idealised situation, actual samples behave like a softer version of Eq. (I.4.36). It is well established that the disorder, inherent to any real sample, can be kept at bay in well-controlled 2D gases and that the broadening it produces can often be made smaller than the Landau level spacing. Qualitatively, we see easily that disorder should bluer the delta function singularities. In fact, the latter are the consequence of the independence of the Landau level energies with respect to k_y, as a result of the translation invariance in the layer plane. Disorder breaks this translation invariance and lifts the k_y degeneracy. Its effects are not easy to compute, see e.g., [12].

This is mostly due to the impossibility of using simple approximation (Born) to describe the disorder effect on Landau levels. The Landau levels broadening will be more thoroughly discussed later in the book.

I.4.4. A tractable case of lifting of the k_y degeneracy: the crossed E, B fields

We can however look at the effect of the lifting of the k_y degeneracy by investigating a much simpler problem, that of the Landau levels in the presence of crossed electric and magnetic fields. With $\vec{B} \| \hat{z}$ we can always choose $\vec{F} = F\hat{x}$ by taking the appropriate gauge. Hence, solving the Schrdinger equation, we find readily that the quantum numbers that label the eigenstates in the presence of an electric field are the same as at $F = 0$. The eigenenergies are:

$$\varepsilon_{m,n,k_y,\sigma_z} = E_m + \left(n + \frac{1}{2}\right)\hbar\omega_c - eF\lambda^2 k_y - \frac{e^2 F^2}{2m^*\omega_c^2} \qquad (I.4.39)$$

The third term is just the electrostatic potential energy of an electron at rest at the centre of the orbit and the fourth appears as a constant Stark shift. The calculation of the density of states proceeds as before and we find that the electric field-dependent density of states is constant and equal to:

$$\rho(\varepsilon) = \sum_m \rho_m(\varepsilon) \qquad (I.4.40)$$

$$\rho_m(\varepsilon) = \begin{cases} \dfrac{BL_y}{2\pi\hbar F} & \text{if } -\dfrac{eFL_x}{2} \le \varepsilon - E_m - \left(n + \dfrac{1}{2}\right)\hbar\omega_c \\[2mm] & \quad - \sigma_z g^* \mu_B B \le \dfrac{eFL_x}{2} \\[2mm] 0 & \text{elsewhere} \end{cases} \qquad (I.4.41)$$

The total number of states for fixed m, n, σ is conserved (and equal to $\frac{L_x L_y}{2\pi\lambda^2}$). Note that eFL_x is a very large number for a macroscopic sample ($L_x = 10^{-4}$ m, $F = 10^5$ V/m), much larger than the cyclotron energy ($\frac{eFL_x}{\hbar\omega_c} \approx 630$ if $B = 10$ T and $m^* = 0.07m_0$). Thus, unless F is very small, the densities of states of the consecutive Landau levels will overlap in practice. The actual density of states including all the participating Landau levels is independent of F and B and close from the zero magnetic field value. In this strong electric field case, the Landau quantisation while apparent in physical properties that probe a given Landau level becomes washed out if the experiments are insensitive to the Landau level index.

PART II

The Physics of Heterostructures

Background on Heterostructures

A semiconductor heterostructure is a stacking of two or more layers of different semiconductors. The simplest is the single heterojunction (e.g., Si/SiO_2 interface which under appropriate gating leads to a Field Effect Transistor). Nowadays that the growth techniques have much improved since the 1970s, stacks of hundreds of layers with nanometric sizes are routinely grown (e.g., GaAs/(Ga,Al)As Quantum Cascade Lasers). As mentioned, the growth techniques underwent a revolution in the mid-1960s/early 1970s when, instead of growing bulk semiconductors at thermal equilibrium out of liquid phase (Czochralski, Bridgmann methods [18]), scientists made stacks of layers by sending fluxes of elemental elements (e.g., Ga, As, Al) from heated cells on heated (580°C) substrates (e.g., GaAs). Then, as surprising as it might seem, under appropriate conditions, a bidimensional growth occurs: an As plane grows, followed by a Ga plane (GaAs monolayer) and the process is iterated. Thus, by appropriately closing and opening shutters GaAs and (Ga,Al)As layers of precise thicknesses are grown (ideally at least). We refer to [19–21] to get more information on the Molecular Beam Epitaxy, Metal Organic Chemical Vapour Deposition and Epitaxial Microstructures.

Let us briefly mention that the growth of sharp interfaces is the better realised when the two materials are lattice-matched and have compatible chemistries. As a counter-example take the Ge/GaAs interfaces. The two materials are ideally lattice-matched but, usually, the Ge/GaAs interfaces proved ill-defined because the Ge atoms diffuse through GaAs and behave like an amphoteric dopant while simultaneously Ga and As diffuse through Ge and dope it as an acceptor (Ga) or a donor (As). An almost ideal interface is found between GaAs and the (Ga,Al)As alloys: the As plane terminates say the GaAs layer and starts the (Ga,Al)As layer, thereby forming a natural boundary between the two layers. If we take InAs and GaSb instead of GaAs and (Ga,Al)As, they form interfaces that are not as sharp as GaAs and (Ga,Al)As. This is because there is necessarily the formation of an intermediate compound at the interface on account of the necessary growth stop at a plane formed by a group V element. Hence, if one grows an InAs layer, the ending plane As is followed by a Ga plane, then a Sb one etc. Thus, there is a one GaAs monolayer that exists at the InAs/GaSb interface. Symmetrically, a one InSb monolayer is formed at the GaSb/InAs interface, see Fig. II.1.1. It happens that GaAs and InSb are severely lattice-mismatched with respect to InAs and GaSb respectively. Thus, less sharp interfaces than in common anion systems can be anticipated in pairs of materials that have no common anions.

A number of heterostructures were successfully grown with lattice-matched or quasi-lattice-matched materials (lattice parameters differing by say less than 1%). Actually, growing interfaces between mismatched materials is a problem of critical thickness of the layers one wants to grow. The physics is the storage of the elastic energy and its management. Suppose one wants to grow an InAs film onto a GaAs substrate by a bi-dimensional growth. The GaAs substrate will impose its lattice parameter to the thin InAs film. Therefore, the InAs layer will accumulate a significant elastic energy

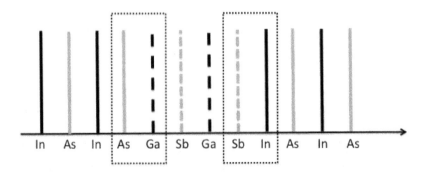

Figure II.1.1.   Ordering of the planes along the growth direction of a InAs/GaSb/InAs heterostructure. Note the monolayers GaAs and InSb at each interface.

due to the stress associated with the modification of its bond lengths (the InAs/GaAs lattice parameters differ by as much as 7%). Beyond a critical thickness L_c (≈ 1.7 monolayers in the case of InAs/GaAs), this elastic energy becomes too large and growth continues through the nucleation and coalescence of adsorbate islands (InAs quantum dots) having their own lattice parameters and floating on a very thin InAs "wetting layer" (Stranski-Krastanov growth mode [22]) containing many defects (like dislocations).

This Stranski–Krastanov (self-organised) growth of InAs quantum dots (QD's) has been an important breakthrough because it has allowed growing high quality nanometre-sized quantum dots (something impossible to achieve by etching because of traps it generates and poor surface quality, and so on), see Fig. II.1.2. It has proven possible to selectively dope the self-organised dots opening the way to a wealth of discoveries on charged electron-hole complexes in zero-dimensional structures. In addition, the discrete low energy spectra for both electrons and holes have suggested to assimilate these dots to "macro-atoms" and to try to apply to them the whole machinery of quantum optics (e.g., Purcell effect for dots in electromagnetic cavities) in the hope of realising optically controllable qubits. These attempts have been partially successful but require low temperatures

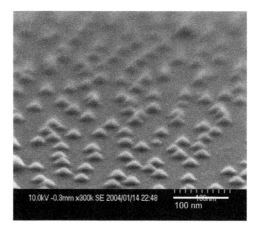

Figure II.1.2. Electron microscope image of self-organised InAs QD's grown on GaAs (courtesy K. Hirakawa).

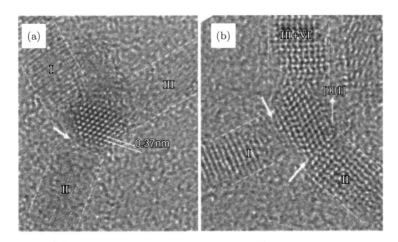

Figure II.1.3.   High Resolution Transmission Micrograph of the tetrahedral structure with one CdSe core particle and four arms: (a) viewed along the [111] direction of CdSe core; (b) viewed along the [110] direction of the CdSe core. From Qi Pang *et al.* [24].

where the phonons are frozen. Note that there exists another class of nanometre-sized QD's, grown by chemical means (i.e., out of super-saturated solution): the colloidal QD's. By this method one can grow extremely small dots (spheroids of 1–2 nm radius) or more elaborate nano-objects such as tetrapods (see Fig. II.1.3) [23].

The fact that the dots grown in supersaturated solutions are not embedded in chemically similar matrices may be a problem due to defects at their interfaces that may act as efficient non-radiative cen-tres. For reviews on quantum dots, the reader is referred to [25, 26].

MBE or MOCVD growths require expensive tools. The growth rate is a few μm/hour. One may wonder why they have proven irre-placeable in many instances. It is likely that the major advantage of the new growth methods compared to the growth at thermal equilib-rium is the capability of producing sharp interfaces, even between layers that are only several nanometres thick. Interfaces between materials grown by liquid phase epitaxy may extend over a few hun-dreds of nm. The unprecedented accuracy in interface quality has enabled to design heterostructures with specific electronic properties where quantum size effects play a prominent part. This "bandgap engineering" [27, 28] has given rise to a wealth of devices: all CD's,

DVD's are nowadays read by quantum well diode lasers that are by far the best solid state lasers in terms of current threshold and thermal stability. There is a very intense research effort to extend these successes towards ultra-violet emitting materials (e.g., based on nitride compounds) enabling larger information storage on a given CD/DVD. In effect, by playing on the layer thicknesses L (ideally controlled down to one monolayer), one plays on the confinement energies E_n of the carrier in those layers since from Heisenberg inequality one easily shows that $E_n \propto L^{-2}$. As we shall discuss below, by tailoring the widths of a double quantum well, one can induce a spatial delocalisation of the carrier over the two wells or, on the reverse, having some quantum states whose wavefunctions are very well localised in one layer in spite of tunnelling through the intermediate barrier. One can also create pseudo-parabolic wells by growing "digital alloys", where by judiciously changing the thicknesses of consecutive layers [20], one finds the effective motion of the carrier along the growth axis to be the one in a z^2 potential. As another example, let us point out the "tour de force" in growth to

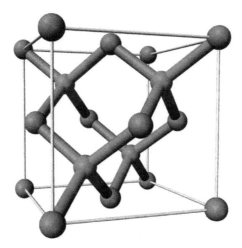

Figure II.1.4. Bulk GaAs unit cell (zinc blende lattice). The zinc blende lattice consists of two interpenetrating face centred cubic lattices shifted from one another by 1/4 of the main diagonal of the cube. In zinc blende lattice any atom (say Ga) is located at the centre of a tetrahedron whose nodes are occupied by the other kind of atom (As), https://en.wikipedia.org/wiki/Gallium_arsenide.

	InP	InAs	InSb	GaAs	GaSb
$\varepsilon_0(eV)$	1.4236	0.418	0.2352	1.5192	0.811
$\Delta(eV)$	0.108	0.38	0.81	0.341	0.752
m_{Γ_6}/m_0	0.079	0.023	0.0139	0.0665	0.0405
$E_p(eV)$	17	21.11	22.49	22.71	22.88

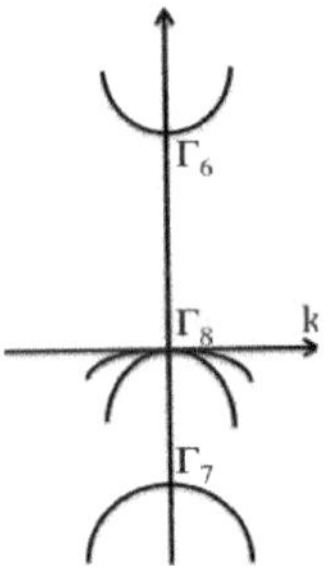

Figure II.1.5.   Table of the bandgap values ε_0, the Γ spin–orbit splitting Δ, the Γ_6 conduction band effective mass and $E_p = 2m_0 P^2$ are given for five zinc blende semiconductors with a direct bandgap where P is defined in (II.2.5).

realise a quantum cascade laser where thousands of precisely controlled layers are grown to achieve a population inversion between two subbands that belong to the conduction band [29].

The materials used for hetero-epitaxy of semiconductors are often III–V (GaAs, InP, (Ga,In)As, GaN, GaSb) or II–VI (CdS, CdSe, ZnO) materials. They can be binary (GaAs) or alloys ((Al,In)As). In the bulk form they crystallise in the zinc blende or hexagonal lattices. The primitive cell of a zinc blende lattice is shown in Fig. II.1.4. We give in the table of Fig. II.1.5 the band parameters of several binary compounds that crystallise in the zinc blende lattice. All these materials have similar band structures in the vicinity of $k = 0$ (Γ point).

Chapter II.2

Electrons States in Nanostructures

II.2.1.   The envelope function approximation

II.2.1.1.   Introduction

Take a binary heterostructure between two ideal semiconductors A and B. We assume the growth has proceeded in a bi-dimensional mode. If $A(B)$ were unlimited in the three directions of space we know that any eigenstate corresponding to the energy ε could be chosen as a Bloch state: either $|n, \vec{k}\rangle_A$ or $|m, \vec{k'}\rangle_B$. The corresponding Bloch wavefunction is of the form $\Psi^A_{n,\vec{k}}(\vec{r}) = e^{i\vec{k}\cdot\vec{r}} u_{n,\vec{k}}(\vec{r})$ where $u_{n,\vec{k}}(\vec{r})$ is a periodic function (see Section I.1.6, Example 1). n, m are bands indexes and $\vec{k}$ is a three-dimensional (3D) wavevector.

In an A/B heterostructure, because of the non-equivalence between the z and (x, y) directions, one should distinguish between k_z and (k_x, k_y). If we want to describe an extended state in an ideal heterostructure, we need to keep a single (k_x, k_y) since the heterostructure remains translation invariant in the layer plane and the Hamiltonian eigenstates can be chosen as eigenstates of the in-plane translation operators $T_{\vec{d}} = \exp(-i\frac{\vec{p}\cdot\vec{d}}{\hbar})$ where $\vec{d}$ is a two-dimensional (2D) vector corresponding to a translation in the layer plane from one unit cell to another one. In contrast, the translation invariance is broken along the z direction and we need to consider for a given energy ε both k_z and $-k_z$. Thus, for a given ε:

$$|\psi_\varepsilon\rangle = \left[\sum_n c_n |n, \vec{k}_\parallel, k_{zA}\rangle_A + d_n |n, \vec{k}_\parallel, -k_{zA}\rangle_A\right] Y(z \in A)$$

$$+ \left[\sum_m \gamma_m |m, \vec{k}_\parallel, k_{zB}\rangle_B + \delta_m |m, \vec{k}_\parallel, -k_{zB}\rangle_B \right] Y(z \in B)$$

$$(\text{II.2.1})$$

$$\vec{k}_\parallel = (k_x, k_y); \quad \varepsilon = \varepsilon_A(\vec{k}_\parallel, k_{zA}) = \varepsilon_B(\vec{k}_\parallel, k_{zB}) \tag{II.2.2}$$

Note that $\vec{k}_\parallel$ has to be real to make $|\psi_\varepsilon\rangle_{A,B}$ normalisable. Such is not the case for k_z that may be either real (propagative state) or imaginary (evanescent state). We show in Fig. II.2.1 three possible cases for k_{zA}, k_{zB}. This is the generalisation to waves in periodic potentials of what we discussed for free particles earlier. Note that in striking contrast with the free particle cases, there exists (in principle) several evanescent branches associated to different bands, i.e., different $k_{zB}(\varepsilon)$. Note also that, for a given ε, the farther away the band is, the larger the imaginary wavevector. The more remote bands contribute to evanescent states with the larger imaginary wavevectors, hence to wavefunctions that will be more and more localised near the interfaces.

There are several problems one has to handle in order to compute the electron states in semiconductor heterostructures. Firstly, one has to find out what is the role of the atomic plane at the interface and how the electrons manage to go from a material A with its band structure to a material B that is characterised by another band structure. A quantitatively important problem is how to position on the same energy scale the two band structures: this is also named the problem of the band offset.

Let us discuss heterostructures made from zinc blende (or wurtzite) materials. We know that each atom (say of the group V) is at the centre of the tetrahedron and surrounded by four atoms of the group III element (see Fig. II.1.4). This situation is possible for all the atoms in the heterostructure except those located on the interface plane (made of group V elements). For these atoms there is a new situation, which is that of having both an A and a B environment (albeit incomplete), see Fig. II.2.2. How this new feature influences the eigenstates is a matter to be investigated. Qualitatively speaking, what happens at the interfaces is unimportant for states that are

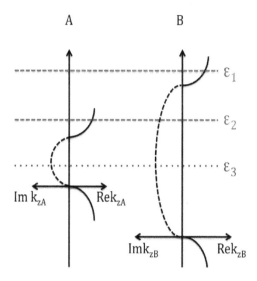

Figure II.2.1. Dispersion relations along the growth axis for both real wavevectors (propagative states, solid lines) and imaginary wavevectors (evanescent states, dotted lines). The energy ε_1 corresponds to extended states in the whole heterostructure. The energy ε_2 corresponds to a state that is extended in the A material and evanescent in the B material. The energy ε_3 would correspond to evanescent states in both kind of layers. Usually, there is no allowed state corresponding to the latter requirements.

Figure II.2.2. One-dimensional (1D) representation of A/B single heterojunction where both A and B are binary compounds. The interface is represented by the dashed vertical line. Clearly for the blue atom located at the interface, there are nearest neighbours that are neither found in A nor in B bulk materials.

tightly bound in one material. On the other hand, it can be significant if one deals with extended states over the whole structure. Thus, if one considers say a single quantum well structure, there would exist a well thickness L_0 where what happens at the interface influences the more the eigenstates (this is discussed in Exercise 21 within the envelope function approximation).

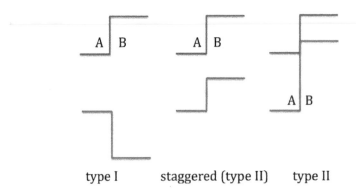

type I   staggered (type II)   type II

Figure II.2.3.   Three possible band alignments at the interface between two A and B materials. The bottom of the conduction band is represented by blue segments, the top of the valence band is in red.

The second important point is the energy difference between the top of the valence bands of the two hosts. Depending on its magnitude and on the magnitudes of the A and B bandgaps, one gets either a type I configuration where one layer (A) confines both the conduction and the valence electrons or a type II configuration where the A (respectively, B) layer confines the conduction (respectively, valence) electrons, see Fig. II.2.3. The latter situation can go to an extreme configuration (actually realised in InAs/GaSb) where the top of the valence band of one material (B) lays at higher energy than the bottom of the conduction band of the other material (A).

A complete theory of electrons states in heterostructures should be able to derive from first principles which is the band alignment between two materials and, in a given heterostructure, whether the interface atoms play (or not) a significant part. This very demanding task is seldom realised in practice, the reason being that the valence band discontinuity results both from bulk properties (how the top of the valence band of a material is placed with respect to the average electrostatic potential) and interface dipoles (the fact that there is a polarisation of the interfaces bonds compared to the bulk situation). The "all electrons" calculations performed on GaAs/AlAs short period superlattices [30] have led to a valence band discontinuity between GaAs and AlAs equal to 0.54 eV, in substantial agreement with experiments. Moreover, these calculations have shown that the thickness of an ideal interface can be as small as one monolayer (0.283 nm in GaAs): the interface dipoles are indeed localised at the interfaces and do not extend deep in each host layer. Inputting (instead of calculating) the band offset problem amounts to finding how the electron states organise in a given potential energy profile. Even that task is not trivial and there are several ways to tackle it. There are two main approaches: "the atomic descriptions" (see e.g., [31]), where the heterostructure is seen as a stack of atoms, and those that consider the heterostructure as a piecewise continuous medium, somehow "forgetting" about the atomic details (the "envelope function approximation").

Let us take as an example a quantum dot, say an InAs dot embedded into GaAs or a colloidal dot. Most of the "atomic" calculations can be termed empirical *ab initio*. Take a sp^3s^* (or sp^3s^*d) atomic parametrization of the dot atoms and the surrounding atoms, that is to say retain six orbitals per atoms (12 if the spin is included) and solve the tight binding problem assuming (or not) nearest neighbour coupling (in other words take into account that each As is surrounded by four Ga in GaAs and four In in InAs in order to comply with the tetrahedral arrangements of the bounds between atoms). The band offsets are empirically plugged in the calculation by shifting appropriately the atomic levels in Ga, As with respect to those of In, As. To determine the energy levels in the InAs dots, one takes all the atoms into account with their 12 spin-orbitals and diagonalise the Hamiltonian taking into account the shifts and the transfer integrals. Finally, one ends up with very large matrix diagonalisation. The results depend markedly on the values assigned to the unknown integrals that show up in the Hamiltonian matrix. Most of them arise from fitting the calculated band structure and optical properties of bulk materials to experiments. Not all of the parameters are known however since it was realised that certain parameters are genuine to heterostructures [32]. The "atomistic" methods are ideally suited to handle very small dots such as the tiny CdSe, CdS colloidal dots; their size is typically 1–2 nm in all directions; which means that they look like a molecule rather than a solid. The dots are dispersed in an amorphous matrix. Saturating all the dangling bonds at the surface of the dot often mimics the effect of the matrix. To do so, one imagines that there exist hydrogen atoms with a very large atomic energy that are attached to the dot [33].

A similar microscopic approach is obtained with the pseudo-potential methods [http://www.colorado.edu/zunger-materials-by-design/sites/default/files/attached-files/395.pdf] (the smoothened potentials that act on the valence electrons and result from the charged nuclei shielded by the frozen core electrons) of the different atoms (that are known from suitable adjustments from bulk semiconductors) and then solves a huge matrix that has at least the dimension of the number of atoms in the dot (plus those in the vicinity if the dot is inserted into a solid state matrix).

Obviously, "atomistic" methods face growing numerical difficulties when the dot dimensions increase. Then, in the frame of the envelope function approximation, a continuous description of the electronic states in the dot is better suited. In such a scheme, the dot eigenstates are assumed to derive from a small enough number of bands of the host materials. The relevant bands are retained and the electron state in the dot is written with a summation that runs over the retained bands. As noticed above, one should for a given energy not only consider the propagating states but also the evanescent ones if appropriate. In a quantum dot, the boundary conditions at infinity are simple since the bound states of the problem have decaying wavefunctions at large distance from the dot.

II.2.1.2. Electronic states in bulk semiconductors

Before discussing about the envelope function approximation for heterostructures it is worth recalling some general remarks about the calculations of electronic states in bulk semiconductors in the frame of the $\vec{k} \cdot \vec{p}$ method. For a more detailed analysis the reader is referred to [34].

First of all one writes the effective Hamiltonian obtained by projecting the full crystal Hamiltonian inside the basis spanned by the relevant bands

$$\{|u_{l,\vec{k}=0}\rangle, l = 1, N\} \tag{II.2.3}$$

where $u_{l,\vec{k}=0}(\vec{r})$ are the periodic parts of the Bloch function at the Γ point. The idea is to diagonalise exactly the effective Hamiltonian on a group of "close" bands and to (possibly) account for all the others up to the second order. The "close" bands are Γ_6, Γ_7, Γ_8, i.e., the topmost filled valence bands (six states spin included) at $k = 0$ and the empty Γ_6 conduction bands (two states spin included). The deeper valence band that would comply with the octet rule is rejected among the "remote" bands. The $8 = 4 \times 2$ bands under consideration are close in energy compared to the energy difference between the centre of gravity of this group at the zone centre and the other bands, see Fig. II.2.4.

Suppose that we have $2N$ "close" bands. Then, we get a Hamiltonian, including term in $\vec{k} \cdot \vec{p}$ (see Section I.3.2, Example 2), usually called the $\vec{k} \cdot \vec{p}$ Hamiltonian, which is a $2N \times 2N$ matrix. This matrix comprises constants (the energy of the N edges), terms that are linear

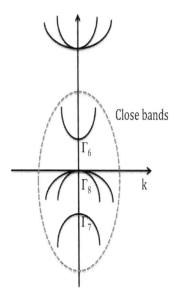

Figure II.2.4. Schematic representation of the dispersion relations of a cubic semiconductor such as GaAs. The dispersions can be accurately calculated in the vicinity of the Γ point by diagonalising the $\vec{k} \cdot \vec{p}$ Hamiltonian exactly within the close bands and by accounting for a single virtual excursion outside the set of close bands, for instance in the remote conduction band. The one band model is applicable to the (empty) conduction band Γ_6 or to the filled valence band Γ_7. The latter is of little use however.

Table II.2.1. Periodic parts of the Bloch functions at the Γ point for the eight bands retained in the Kane model.

u_i	$|J, m_j\rangle$	ψ_{J,m_j}	$\varepsilon_i(k=0)$
u_1	$\left|\frac{1}{2},\frac{1}{2}\right\rangle = |iS \uparrow\rangle$	$i|S \uparrow\rangle$	0
u_3	$\left|\frac{3}{2},\frac{1}{2}\right\rangle$	$-\sqrt{\frac{2}{3}}|Z \uparrow\rangle + \frac{1}{\sqrt{6}}|(X+iY) \downarrow\rangle$	$-\varepsilon_0$
u_5	$\left|\frac{3}{2},\frac{3}{2}\right\rangle$	$\frac{1}{\sqrt{2}}|(X+iY) \uparrow\rangle$	$-\varepsilon_0$
u_7	$\left|\frac{1}{2},\frac{1}{2}\right\rangle$	$\frac{1}{\sqrt{3}}|(X+iY) \downarrow\rangle + \frac{1}{\sqrt{3}}|Z \uparrow\rangle$	$-\varepsilon_0 - \Delta$
u_2	$\left|\frac{1}{2},-\frac{1}{2}\right\rangle = |iS \downarrow\rangle$	$i|S \downarrow\rangle$	0
u_4	$\left|\frac{3}{2},-\frac{1}{2}\right\rangle$	$-\frac{1}{\sqrt{6}}|(X-iY) \uparrow\rangle - \sqrt{\frac{2}{3}}|Z \downarrow\rangle$	$-\varepsilon_0$
u_6	$\left|\frac{3}{2},-\frac{3}{2}\right\rangle$	$\frac{1}{\sqrt{2}}|(X-iY) \downarrow\rangle$	$-\varepsilon_0$
u_8	$\left|\frac{1}{2},-\frac{1}{2}\right\rangle$	$-\frac{1}{\sqrt{3}}|(X-iY) \uparrow\rangle + \frac{1}{\sqrt{3}}|Z \downarrow\rangle$	$-\varepsilon_0 - \Delta$

in $\vec{k}$ and originate from the $\vec{k} \cdot \vec{p}$ terms inside the set of "close" bands. It may also contain terms that are quadratic in k and arise when one virtual jump from the "close" bands to the "remote" bands is taken into account.

Since the number of "close bands" is arbitrary, there are several variants of the generalised $\vec{k} \cdot \vec{p}$ Hamiltonian:

- Only the four Γ_8 edges are taken as "close" bands. All the other bands are remote and accounted for by one virtual excursion. This is called the Luttinger–Kohn Hamiltonian [35]. It is very useful to describe the hole kinematics in cubic semiconductors.
- The Γ_6, Γ_7, Γ_8 bands are taken into account but no allowance is made to virtual jumps to "remote" bands. This is the Kane Hamiltonian [36]. It is particularly useful to account for band non-parabolicity for the conduction states.
- The Pidgeon and Brown Hamiltonian combines the two preceding cases and is probably the most precise $\vec{k} \cdot \vec{p}$ Hamiltonian one can get with eight bands [14].

Of course, one can include more bands in the set of close bands. This introduces more parameters. Suppose we restrict our considerations to 8 (4×2) bands. To compute the dispersions neglecting the (small) inversion asymmetry splitting (quasi-Ge model), we need to know two gaps: the $\Gamma_6 - \Gamma_8$ and $\Gamma_8 - \Gamma_7$ gap that is actually equal to the spin–orbit splitting Δ at the zone centre. The heavier is the anion, the larger is the spin–orbit splitting. There is (by symmetry) a single $\vec{p}$ matrix element in the group of close bands:

$$\langle S|p_x|X \rangle = \langle S|p_y|Y \rangle = \langle S|p_z|Z \rangle \qquad (\text{II.2.4})$$

where S, X, Y, Z are the Bloch periodic functions at Γ point that transform under the action of local tetrahedron group as the s, x, y, z atomic functions transform under the action of the rotations group. If needed, one can introduce four remote band parameters that account for one virtual jump between the close bands and the remote bands. The $\vec{k} \cdot \vec{p}$ Hamiltonian is projected on a basis of eight states obtained as a linear combination of the eight band edge Bloch states $|S \uparrow\rangle$, $|S \downarrow\rangle$, $|X \uparrow\rangle$, $|X \downarrow\rangle$, $|Y \uparrow\rangle$, $|Y \downarrow\rangle$, $|Z \uparrow\rangle$, $|Z \downarrow\rangle$ (see Table II.2.2) [34, 36] where this basis of the $\vec{k} \cdot \vec{p}$ Hamiltonian reads as in Table II.2.1.

$k_\pm = \frac{(k_x \pm ik_y)}{\sqrt{2}}$ and P is the interband $\vec{p}$ matrix element:

$$P = -\frac{i}{m_0} \langle S|p_x|X \rangle \qquad (\text{II.2.5})$$

One can extract the dispersion relations analytically by noting that they have to be function of $k = |\vec{k}|$ only. Then, one chooses $\vec{k} \| z$ and obtains as solutions:

$$-\eta + \frac{2P^2 k_z^2}{3(\varepsilon_0 + \eta)} + \frac{P^2 k_z^2}{3(\varepsilon_0 + \Delta + \eta)} = 0 \qquad (\text{II.2.6})$$

$$\text{or} \quad \eta = -\varepsilon_0 \qquad (\text{II.2.7})$$

where

$$\eta = \varepsilon - \frac{\hbar^2 k_z^2}{2m_0} \qquad (\text{II.2.8})$$

Each of the solutions is twice degenerate (Kramers degeneracy). At $k_+ = 0$, the coupled dispersions (nonlinear in k^2) arise from states

Table II.2.2.   First order $\vec{k}\cdot\vec{p}$ matrix within the set of close bands Γ_6, Γ_7, Γ_8.

	$|iS\uparrow\rangle$	$|\frac{3}{2},\frac{1}{2}\rangle$	$|\frac{3}{2},\frac{3}{2}\rangle$	$|\frac{1}{2},\frac{1}{2}\rangle$	$|iS\downarrow\rangle$	$|\frac{3}{2},-\frac{1}{2}\rangle$	$|\frac{3}{2},-\frac{3}{2}\rangle$	$|\frac{1}{2},-\frac{1}{2}\rangle$
$\langle iS\uparrow|$	$\frac{\hbar^2 k^2}{2m_0}$	$-\sqrt{\frac{2}{3}}P\hbar k_z$	$P\hbar k_+$	$\frac{1}{\sqrt{3}}P\hbar k_z$	0	$-\frac{1}{\sqrt{3}}P\hbar k_-$	0	$-\sqrt{\frac{2}{3}}P\hbar k_-$
$\langle\frac{3}{2},\frac{1}{2}|$	$-\sqrt{\frac{2}{3}}P\hbar k_z$	$-\varepsilon_0+\frac{\hbar^2 k^2}{2m_0}$	0	0	$\frac{P}{\sqrt{3}}\hbar k_-$	0	0	0
$\langle\frac{3}{2},\frac{3}{2}|$	$P\hbar k_-$	0	$-\varepsilon_0+\frac{\hbar^2 k^2}{2m_0}$	0	0	0	0	0
$\langle\frac{1}{2},\frac{1}{2}|$	$\frac{1}{\sqrt{3}}P\hbar k_z$	0	0	$-\varepsilon_0-\Delta+\frac{\hbar^2 k^2}{2m_0}$	$\sqrt{\frac{2}{3}}P\hbar k_-$	0	0	0
$\langle iS\downarrow|$	0	$\frac{P}{\sqrt{3}}\hbar k_+$	0	$\sqrt{\frac{2}{3}}P\hbar k_+$	$\frac{\hbar^2 k^2}{2m_0}$	$-\sqrt{\frac{2}{3}}P\hbar k_z$	$P\hbar k_-$	$\frac{1}{\sqrt{3}}P\hbar k_z$
$\langle\frac{3}{2},-\frac{1}{2}|$	$-\frac{1}{\sqrt{3}}P\hbar k_+$	0	0	0	$-\sqrt{\frac{2}{3}}P\hbar k_z$	$-\varepsilon_0+\frac{\hbar^2 k^2}{2m_0}$	0	0
$\langle\frac{3}{2},-\frac{3}{2}|$	0	0	0	0	$P\hbar k_+$	0	$-\varepsilon_0+\frac{\hbar^2 k^2}{2m_0}$	0
$\langle\frac{1}{2},-\frac{1}{2}|$	$-\sqrt{\frac{2}{3}}P\hbar k_+$	0	0	0	$\frac{P}{\sqrt{3}}\hbar k_z$	0	0	$-\varepsilon_0-\Delta+\frac{\hbar^2 k^2}{2m_0}$

The energy origin is taken at the bottom of the $S(\Gamma_6)$ conduction band.

that project on the u_n's with $J_z = \pm 1/2$ but not with $J_z = \pm 3/2$ while the uncoupled solutions correspond to states that project exclusively on the $J_z = \pm 3/2$ periodic parts of the Bloch functions (Γ_8 edges). The $J_z = \pm 1/2$ states correspond to conduction electrons, light Γ_8 holes and Γ_7 holes. A typical effective mass for a light particle is $0.1m_0$. With the same approximation, the effective mass of the $\Gamma_8, \pm 3/2$ band is the bare electron mass.

This shortcoming is suppressed by allowing for one virtual excursion outside the set of close bands. As a result the $J_z = \pm 3/2$ states correspond to heavy holes (typical mass $0.5m_0$). The excursions towards remote bands are simple to handle only if $\vec{k} \| z$ since only diagonal terms are added to Table II.2.2. If $k_x, k_y \neq 0$ instead, one should introduce a whole 4×4 block. The second-order $\vec{k} \cdot \vec{p}$ matrix within the set of close bands can be found in many textbooks and review articles [34, 37, 38]. In this book, we shall be mainly dealing with conduction states in heterostructures. Thus, the Kane dispersions appear to be the optimum model to handle the conduction dispersion relations.

Restricting our analysis to small k values, one finds readily the effective masses of the various bands in the vicinity of the Γ point:

$$\frac{1}{m_{\Gamma_6}} = \frac{1}{m_0} + \frac{4P^2}{3\varepsilon_0} + \frac{2P^2}{3(\varepsilon_0 + \Delta)}$$

$$\frac{1}{m_{\Gamma_8}} = \frac{1}{m_0} - \frac{4P^2}{3\varepsilon_0}$$

$$\frac{1}{m_{\Gamma_7}} = \frac{1}{m_0} - \frac{2P^2}{3(\varepsilon_0 + \Delta)} \tag{II.2.9}$$

where no virtual jump has been taken into account. It is worth remarking the mirror effect between the conduction band and the light hole effective masses (best seen when Δ is taken to be very large in the above formulae (Eq. (II.2.9))). Note also that in a material like GaAs which is not a small band gap material ($\varepsilon_0 = 1.42$ eV at room temperature), the conduction band effective mass ($0.067m_0$) is considerably lighter than the bare electron mass. Note also that the

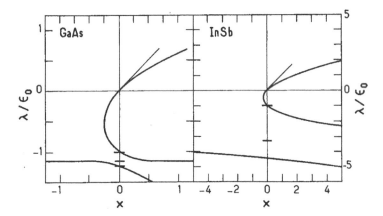

Figure II.2.5.   Energy dispersion $\lambda(k)$ scaled to the energy bandgap ϵ_0 is plotted against $x = \frac{\hbar^2 k^2}{2m_{\Gamma_6}\varepsilon_0}$ in GaAs and InSb. Notice that the negative x's correspond to the evanescent states.

Source: Bastard [34].

conduction mass vanishes if $\varepsilon_0 = 0$. Actually, the bands become linear in k in the vicinity of $k = 0$, like the photon dispersion in vacuum or graphene conduction electrons and holes dispersions. This happens in the solid solutions $Hg_{1-x}Cd_xTe$ at $x = 0.16$ and in $Hg_{1-y}Mn_yTe$ at $y = 0.07$.

The result is shown in Fig. II.2.5 for GaAs where $\Delta = 0.34$ eV, $\varepsilon_0 = 1.42$ eV and $m_c = 0.067m_0$. One sees that by decreasing the energy one first get propagating conduction electron states that become evanescent for $\lambda < 0$ and reappear for $\lambda < -\varepsilon_0$ as propagating light holes.

Besides the calculation of the dispersion relations, it is important to realise that the Bloch states in the vicinity of the Γ point display a *two scales dynamics*: the periodic parts of the Bloch functions vary with a length which is the natural crystal periodicity, while the plane wave terms vary with a wavelength $2\pi/k$, i.e., a length that is much larger than the crystal periodicity. The essence of the $\vec{k} \cdot \vec{p}$ calculation (or its associated envelope functions for heterostructures) is to study the long range dynamics while the short scale dynamics fixes the bandgaps, effective masses etc. In other words, the long range motion occurs on energy scales where it is fair to assume that the short range variables are frozen. All the $\vec{k} \cdot \vec{p}$, envelope functions, etc. are variations on that theme that has proven one of the most fruitful in semiconductor physics. To name a few examples let us mention the quantitative handling of the motion of electrons and holes in perturbed periodic fields if the perturbation is slowly varying on the scale of the natural crystal periodicity [35]. In this case, there is no interband matrix elements for the perturbing potentials. The spectra of coulombic impurities have been calculated and quantitatively agree with experiments for both donors and acceptors.

II.2.1.3. Heterostructure states

It is not so obvious that the same sort of formalism can apply to heterostructures because in ideal cases, where the interfaces are atomically sharp, the perturbations are spatially sudden and not at all slowly varying. However, for lattice-matched materials the electron states in A and B can certainly be expanded in each layer on the complete basis, e.g., spanned by all the Γ Bloch states. The restriction to a finite number of bands then follows as a reasonable approximation of the Bloch states in each layer.

The conceptual jump came from the remark that the periodic parts of the Bloch functions of the III–V materials are very similar as witnessed by the almost constant value of the P matrix element (see Figure II.1.5).

To the extent that the P matrix element is roughly the same irrespective of the material, it is *assumed* that the periodic parts of the Bloch functions are identical (improvements over that assumption were analysed by Burt and Foreman [39, 40]). So the wavefunction in the heterostructure is written:

$$\psi(\vec{r}) = \sum_n f_n^{A,B}(\vec{r}) u_{n,\vec{k}=0}(\vec{r}) \qquad (\text{II.2.10})$$

$$H|\psi\rangle = \varepsilon|\psi\rangle \qquad (\text{II.2.11})$$

$$H = \frac{p^2}{2m_0} + V_A(\vec{r})Y_A + V_B(\vec{r})Y_B \qquad (\text{II.2.12})$$

where Y_A (Y_B) are step functions that are equal to 1 if the electron is in A (B) and zero elsewhere. As a technologically very important example, let us take a 1D $B-A-B$ heterostructure and call z the growth axis. Then, expressing the wavefunction in the Kane model in both kinds of layers, we find that the envelope functions $f_n^{A,B}(\vec{r})$ are the solutions of a coupled differential system:

$$D\left(z, k_x, k_y, -i\frac{\partial}{\partial z}\right)\vec{f} = \varepsilon \vec{f} \qquad (\text{II.2.13})$$

$\vec{f}$ is a $2N$-dimensional column vector and D a $2N \times 2N$ matrix where N is the number of band edges retained in the analysis ($N = 4$ in the Kane model). We have taken advantage of the in-plane translation invariance, by writing:

$$\vec{f}(\vec{r}) = \exp(i\vec{k} \cdot \vec{\rho})\vec{\chi}(z); \quad \vec{\rho} = (x, y) \qquad (\text{II.2.14})$$

where $\vec{\chi}$ is a $2N$ column vector. The matrix D has the matrix elements:

$$D\left(z, k_x, k_y, -i\frac{\partial}{\partial dz}\right) = \left(\varepsilon_l^A Y_A + \varepsilon_l^B Y_B\right)\delta_{lm}$$

$$+ \frac{\hbar k_x}{m_0}\langle u_l | p_x | u_m \rangle + \frac{\hbar k_y}{m_0}\langle u_l | p_y | u_m \rangle$$

$$- \frac{i\hbar}{m_0}\langle u_l | p_z | u_m \rangle \frac{\partial}{\partial z} \qquad (\text{II.2.15})$$

where we have dropped diagonal terms that are proportional to $1/m_0$ because the second-order contribution absent in the Kane model are larger than these terms. Specifically, we get the first-order differential system:

$$
\begin{pmatrix}
V_s(z) & i\sqrt{\tfrac{2}{3}}P\hbar\frac{\partial}{\partial z} & P\hbar k_+ & \frac{-i}{\sqrt{3}}P\hbar\frac{\partial}{\partial z} & 0 & -\frac{1}{\sqrt{3}}P\hbar k_- & 0 & -\sqrt{\tfrac{2}{3}}P\hbar k_- \\[6pt]
i\sqrt{\tfrac{2}{3}}P\hbar\frac{\partial}{\partial z} & -\varepsilon_W + V_P(z) & 0 & 0 & \frac{1}{\sqrt{3}}P\hbar k_- & 0 & 0 & 0 \\[6pt]
P\hbar k_- & 0 & -\varepsilon_W + V_P(z) & 0 & 0 & 0 & 0 & 0 \\[6pt]
\frac{-i}{\sqrt{3}}P\hbar\frac{\partial}{\partial z} & 0 & 0 & -\varepsilon_W - \Delta_W + V_\delta(z) & \sqrt{\tfrac{2}{3}}P\hbar k_- & 0 & 0 & 0 \\[6pt]
0 & \frac{1}{\sqrt{3}}P\hbar k_+ & 0 & \sqrt{\tfrac{2}{3}}P\hbar k_+ & V_s(z) & i\sqrt{\tfrac{2}{3}}P\hbar\frac{\partial}{\partial z} & P\hbar k_- & \frac{-i}{\sqrt{3}}P\hbar\frac{\partial}{\partial z} \\[6pt]
-\frac{1}{\sqrt{3}}P\hbar k_+ & 0 & 0 & 0 & i\sqrt{\tfrac{2}{3}}P\hbar\frac{\partial}{\partial z} & -\varepsilon_W + V_P(z) & 0 & 0 \\[6pt]
0 & 0 & 0 & 0 & P\hbar k_+ & 0 & -\varepsilon_W + V_P(z) & 0 \\[6pt]
-\sqrt{\tfrac{2}{3}}P\hbar k_+ & 0 & 0 & 0 & \frac{-i}{\sqrt{3}}P\hbar\frac{\partial}{\partial z} & 0 & 0 & -\varepsilon_W - \Delta_W + V_\delta(z)
\end{pmatrix}
\tag{II.2.16}
$$

where ε_w and Δ_w are respectively equal to $\varepsilon_{\Gamma_6} - \varepsilon_{\Gamma_8}$ and $\varepsilon_{\Gamma_8} - \varepsilon_{\Gamma_7}$ in the well acting material while $V_S(z)$, $V_P(z)$ and $V_\delta(z)$ are piecewise constant functions which are equal to zero in the well material and equal to the algebraic shift of the Γ_6, Γ_8 and Γ_7 edges when going from the well to the barrier material; in other words they are the conduction, valence and spin–orbit split off offsets between the well and the barrier materials.

Note that one should replace (k_x, k_y) by $(-i\frac{\partial}{\partial x}, -i\frac{\partial}{\partial y})$ for a heterostructure involving a three-dimensional confinement.

It is illustrative to rewrite Eq. (II.2.16) in terms of an effective 2×2 Hamiltonian acting on the envelopes associated with $S \uparrow$ and $S \downarrow$ periodic parts of the Bloch functions. Expressing all the other components as functions of $f_{S\uparrow}$, $f_{S\downarrow}$, one gets:

$$
\begin{pmatrix} H_d & H_{sf} \\ H_{sf}^* & H_d \end{pmatrix} \begin{pmatrix} f_{S\uparrow} \\ f_{S\downarrow} \end{pmatrix} = \varepsilon \begin{pmatrix} f_{S\uparrow} \\ f_{S\downarrow} \end{pmatrix} \tag{II.2.17}
$$

$$
H_d = \frac{P^2}{3} \left[p_z \left(\frac{2}{\varepsilon + \varepsilon_W - V_P(z)} + \frac{1}{\varepsilon + \varepsilon_W + \Delta_W - V_\delta(z)} \right) p_z \right.
$$
$$
\left. + \hbar^2 (k_x^2 + k_y^2) \left(\frac{2}{\varepsilon + \varepsilon_W - V_P(z)} + \frac{1}{\varepsilon + \varepsilon_W + \Delta_W - V_\delta(z)} \right) \right] \tag{II.2.18}
$$

$$
H_{sf} = \frac{P^2 \sqrt{2}}{3} \hbar k_- \left\{ \left[\frac{1}{\varepsilon + \varepsilon_W - V_P(z)}, p_z \right] \right.
$$
$$
\left. - \left[\frac{1}{\varepsilon + \varepsilon_W + \Delta_W - V_\delta(z)}, p_z \right] \right\} \tag{II.2.19}
$$

where $[A, B] = AB - BA$. We see that the spin–orbit coupling leads to a mixing between the two S envelopes since the brackets in H_{sf} cancel if both Δ_A, Δ_B vanish. We also note that there is no coupling between the S envelopes if $k_x = k_y = 0$.

The boundary conditions are that $\vec{f}$ is continuous (in order to make the total wavefunction continuous as it should), in particular at the interfaces. Note that integrating the 8×8 system across one interface does not provide us with any conditions (we get once more the continuity of some of the $\vec{f}$ components). The boundary condition at infinity depends on whether we deal with bound states ($\vec{f} \to 0$ at infinity) or with extended states ($\vec{f}$ behaves like a plane wave at infinity). If we include remote bands effect the differential system becomes of the second order. In addition to the continuity of $\vec{f}$ a second set of boundary conditions are obtained by integrating D across an interface $z = z_0$.

An interesting case is obtained when the set of close bands is reduced to one. In the Kane model this amounts to assuming that $\frac{\hbar^2 k^2}{2m^* \varepsilon_w} \ll 1$ where m^* is the well effective mass and ε_w the bandgap of the well-acting material [36]. In Eq. (II.2.17)–(II.2.19), this amounts to neglecting ε in all the denominators and to discarding H_{sf}. The second-order contributions lead to a Hamiltonian acting on the two conduction envelope functions which is of the Ben Daniel–Duke type [41]. For a heterostructure with a 1D confinement this leads to:

$$\left[p_z \left(\frac{1}{2m^*(z)} \right) p_z + \frac{\hbar^2 (k_x^2 + k_y^2)}{2m^*(z)} \right] \chi(z) = \varepsilon \chi(z) \qquad \text{(II.2.20)}$$

where $m^*(z) = m_A$ if $z \in A$ material and $m^*(z) = m_B$ if $z \in B$ material, while for the 3D size quantisation one gets:

$$\left(\vec{p} \frac{1}{2m^*(\vec{r})} \vec{p} + V_b(\vec{r}) \right) \psi_c(\vec{r}) = (\varepsilon - \varepsilon_{\Gamma_6}^A) \psi_c(\vec{r}) \qquad \text{(II.2.21)}$$

$$V_b(\vec{r}) = 0 \text{ if } \vec{r} \in A; \quad V_b(\vec{r}) = V_b = (\varepsilon_{\Gamma_6}^B - \varepsilon_{\Gamma_6}^A) \text{ if } \vec{r} \in B \qquad \text{(II.2.22)}$$

For a 1D size quantisation one gets the boundary conditions:

$$\chi(z) \text{ and } \frac{1}{m^*(z)} \frac{d\chi(z)}{dz} \text{ continuous} \qquad \text{(II.2.23)}$$

while in the more general case we find that ψ_c and $\frac{1}{m^*(z)} \frac{d\psi_c}{dz}$ are continuous at any point $\vec{r}_0$ in particular at the interfaces. For quantum dots, the well/barrier interface is in general a close surface. At the point $\vec{r}_0$ this surface admits a normal $\vec{n}(\vec{r}_0)$ and a plane tangent to it. Then, integrating the effective Schrödinger equation across the normal provides the second set of boundary conditions, namely that

$\frac{1}{m^*(\vec{r})}\frac{\partial \psi_c}{\partial \vec{n}}|_{\vec{r}=\vec{r}_0}$ is continuous. This is easy to implement for simple dot geometry such as cubes, spheres, cylinders, but becomes very awkward if the dot has a complicated geometry.

II.2.2. Multiple quantum wells: transfer matrix method

II.2.2.1. Multiple quantum wells and superlattices

When there is a periodic alternation of several layers binary (AB), ternary (ABC), quaternary $(ABCD)$ superlattices, and so on, the translation invariance along the growth axis simplifies the search of the eigenstates of a stack of pN layers where p is the number of layers in a given period and N the (macroscopic) number of periods to a problem of only p layers completed by the Bloch theorem:

$$\chi(z + d) = e^{iqd}\chi(z) \tag{II.2.24}$$

where d is the superlattice period and q is the electron wavevector along the z-axis that can be restricted to the first Brillouin zone:

$$-\frac{\pi}{d} < q \le \frac{\pi}{d} \tag{II.2.25}$$

In the case of a 1D superlattice, the dispersion relations are always of the form [34, 42]:

$$\cos(qd) = f(\varepsilon) \tag{II.2.26}$$

When there is no band bending (no charges, no electric field) the function $f(\varepsilon)$ is known analytically. For a binary AB superlattice it is equal to $f_{AB}(\varepsilon)$ where:

$$f_{AB}(\varepsilon) = \cos(k_A L_A)\cos(k_B L_B) - \frac{1}{2}\left(\xi + \frac{1}{\xi}\right)\sin(k_A L_A)\sin(k_B L_B) \tag{II.2.27}$$

$$\xi = \frac{k_A}{m_A}\frac{m_B}{k_B}; \quad k_A = \left(\frac{2m_A\varepsilon}{\hbar^2}\right)^{1/2}; \quad k_B = \left(\frac{2m_B(\varepsilon - V_b)}{\hbar^2}\right)^{1/2} \tag{II.2.28}$$

In Eq. (II.2.28) the energy zero has been taken at the bottom of the A conduction band and V_b is the barrier height. As seen from

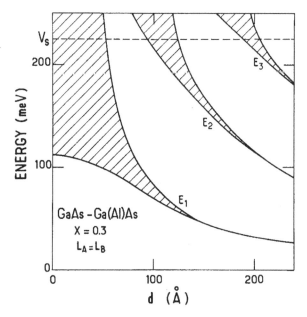

Figure II.2.6. Superlattice band structure for electrons in GaAs/Ga$_{0.7}$Al$_{0.3}$As super-lattices versus the period d of the superlattice. Equal layer thicknesses are assumed in the calculations. The allowed energy states are hatched.

Source: Bastard [34].

Eq. (II.2.28), ε must be larger than V_b for the square roots to make sense. If this is not the case ($\varepsilon \leq V_b$), one defines:

$$k_A = \left(\frac{2m_A\varepsilon}{\hbar^2}\right)^{1/2} ; \quad \kappa_B = \left(\frac{2m_B(V_b - \varepsilon)}{\hbar^2}\right)^{1/2} ; \quad \tilde{\xi} = \frac{k_B}{m_A}\frac{m_B}{\kappa_B}$$

(II.2.29)

$$f_{AB}(\varepsilon) = \cos(k_A L_A)\cosh(\kappa_B L_B) - \frac{1}{2}\left(\tilde{\xi} - \frac{1}{\tilde{\xi}}\right)\sin(k_A L_A)\sinh(\kappa_B L_B)$$

(II.2.30)

We show in Fig. II.2.6 the allowed conduction subband of GaAs/(Ga,Al)As superlattice with equal layer thickness. We see the expected trends: at large periods there is a negligible tunnelling and the bands are very narrow. By decreasing the period, the bands broaden and the gaps separating the allowed energy bands diminish.

The binary superlattice dispersion relations have two limits:

- The weakly coupled wells ($k_B L_B \gg 1$) where the bandwidths are small. Let us denote by E_n the energy of the nth bound state of an isolated well A. Expanding the solutions of Eq. (II.2.28) in the vicinity of E_n, one gets a tight binding-like dispersions relation [34]:

$$\varepsilon_n(q) = E_n + s_n + \lambda_n \cos(qd) \qquad (II.2.31)$$

$$s_n = -\frac{f_{AB}(E_n)}{f'_{AB}(E_n)}; \quad \lambda_n = \frac{1}{f'_{AB}(E_n)} \qquad (II.2.32)$$

- The strongly coupled wells: the pseudo alloy limit. We are interested in knowing how the dispersion relations evolve when L_A, L_B, d are very small while keeping the ratio $\tilde{x} = \frac{L_B}{d}$ fixed. Qualitatively we expect the subbands to become very broad and the gaps to become very small. The ground superlattice state occurs at $q = 0$ and in the limit $d \to 0$ it extrapolates to:

$$\varepsilon_1(q = 0) \to \tilde{x} V_b \qquad (II.2.33)$$

The superlattice pseudo alloys were believed to mimic true alloys without displaying the very effective alloy scattering. Unfortunately, it turned out that the requirement of very narrow layers gave rise to a detrimental interface roughness that severely limits the electron mobility.

II.2.2.2. Transfer matrix method

In general, the solutions of the Schrödinger equation in the presence of band bending in segment $[ab]$ are not known analytically. Thus, one tries to implement techniques where the band bending is approximately taken into account while simultaneously staying with piecewise constant potential. The transfer matrix method is one of such techniques (see Fig. II.2.7).

We write the 1D Schrödinger equation:

$$\left[p_z \left(\frac{1}{2m^*(z)} \right) p_z + \frac{\hbar^2 (k_x^2 + k_y^2)}{2m^*(z)} + V(z) \right] \chi(z) = \varepsilon \chi(z) \qquad (II.2.34)$$

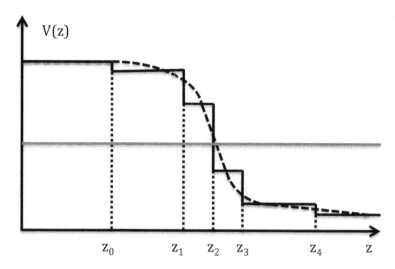

Figure II.2.7. Potential energy profile (dashed line) and its approximation by a piece-wise constant potential (solid line).

and we partition the relevant segment ($[z_0, z_4]$ in Fig. II.2.7) into $N + 1$ layers with a constant potential energy V_n and effective mass m_n. The thickness of the layers is at will, being a compromise between the accuracy (the smaller and more numerous the layers, the more accurate the description) and the computing time (less layers imply faster calculations). For simplicity, we look at the subband edges and let $k_x = k_y = 0$:

$$\chi(z) = \alpha_{n-1} e^{ik_{n-1}(z - z_{n-1})} + \beta_{n-1} e^{-ik_{n-1}(z - z_{n-1})} \qquad \text{(II.2.35)}$$

$$\text{for } z_{n-1} \leq z \leq z_n = z_{n-1} + \delta_{n-1} \qquad \text{(II.2.36)}$$

$$\chi(z) = \alpha_n e^{ik_n(z - z_n)} + \beta_n e^{-ik_n(z - z_n)} \qquad \text{(II.2.37)}$$

$$\text{for } z_n \leq z \leq z_{n+1} = z_n + \delta_n \qquad \text{(II.2.38)}$$

$$k_{n-1} = \sqrt{\frac{2m_{n-1}(\varepsilon - V_{n-1})}{\hbar^2}}; \quad k_n = \sqrt{\frac{2m_n(\varepsilon - V_n)}{\hbar^2}} \qquad \text{(II.2.39)}$$

where we have assumed that the wave is propagating both before and after z_{n-1}. In case the wave becomes evanescent either before or after z_{n-1} or both before and after z_{n-1} the relevant $k[a(\varepsilon)]$ should be replaced by $i\kappa(|a(\varepsilon)|)$. By writing the continuity of $\chi(z)$, $\frac{1}{m^*(z)}\chi'(z)$ at $z = z_n$, we get a recursion relation between (α_n, β_n) and $(\alpha_{n-1}, \beta_{n-1})$:

$$\begin{pmatrix} \alpha_n \\ \beta_n \end{pmatrix} = T_{n-1}^n \begin{pmatrix} \alpha_{n-1} \\ \beta_{n-1} \end{pmatrix} \tag{II.2.40}$$

$$T_{n-1}^n = \begin{pmatrix} \dfrac{e^{i\varphi_{n-1}}}{2}\left(1 + \dfrac{v_{n-1}}{v_n}\right) & \dfrac{e^{-i\varphi_{n-1}}}{2}\left(1 - \dfrac{v_{n-1}}{v_n}\right) \\[3mm] \dfrac{e^{i\varphi_{n-1}}}{2}\left(1 - \dfrac{v_{n-1}}{v_n}\right) & \dfrac{e^{-i\varphi_{n-1}}}{2}\left(1 + \dfrac{v_{n-1}}{v_n}\right) \end{pmatrix} \tag{II.2.41}$$

$$\varphi_{n-1} = k_{n-1}\delta_{n-1}; \quad v_{n-1} = \frac{\hbar k_{n-1}}{m_{n-1}}; \quad v_n = \frac{\hbar k_n}{m_n} \tag{II.2.42}$$

By propagating from $N_{\min}$ and $N_{\max}$, we get:

$$\begin{pmatrix} \alpha_{N_{\max}} \\ \beta_{N_{\max}} \end{pmatrix} = T_{N_{\min}}^{N_{\max}} \begin{pmatrix} \alpha_{N_{\min}} \\ \beta_{N_{\min}} \end{pmatrix} \tag{II.2.43}$$

$$T_{N_{\min}}^{N_{\max}} = T_{N_{\max}-1}^{N_{\max}} T_{N_{\max}-2}^{N_{\max}-1} \ldots T_{N_{\min}+1}^{N_{\min}+2} T_{N_{\min}}^{N_{\min}+1} \tag{II.2.44}$$

The calculations must be completed by boundary condition at infinity. In the example shown in Fig. II.2.7, we see that the actual and approximate potentials are constant for $z \leq z_0$. This means that for an energy equal to the horizontal line in Fig. II.2.7 the wave should decay exponentially in the barrier. Choosing a $z_{N_{\min}} \ll z_0$ the exponentially growing solutions must be suppressed, namely $\alpha_{N_{\min}} = 0$. At large z, for the same energy, we shall get a propagative solution. In this case we shall let:

$$\begin{pmatrix} \alpha_{N_{\max}} \\ \beta_{N_{\max}} \end{pmatrix} = \begin{pmatrix} r \\ 1 \end{pmatrix} \tag{II.2.45}$$

in order to describe a wave coming from $+\infty$ and being reflected by the potential wall $V(z)$. The numerical knowledge of the matrix $T_{N_{\min}}^{N_{\max}}$ together with the boundary conditions allow to compute $r(\varepsilon)$. In the case of a bound state as displayed in Fig. II.2.8, one should write that the wavefunction is decaying sufficiently fast for both $z \ll z_0$ and $z \gg z_7$. This means to let the coefficients of the exponentially

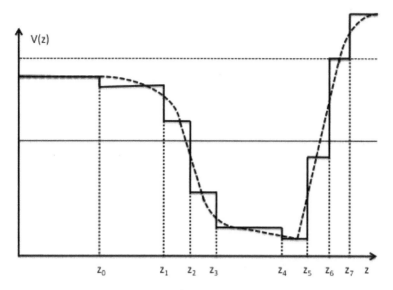

Figure II.2.8. Potential energy profile (dashed line) and its approximation by a piecewise constant potential (solid line). The solid horizontal line corresponds to a bound state while the dotted horizontal line corresponds to a reflection for a particle coming form $z = -\infty$ and returning to $z = -\infty$.

growing terms equal to zero. Thus:

$$\begin{pmatrix} \alpha_{N_{\min}} \\ \beta_{N_{\min}} \end{pmatrix} = \begin{pmatrix} 0 \\ \beta_{N_{\min}} \end{pmatrix} ; \quad \begin{pmatrix} \alpha_{N_{\max}} \\ \beta_{N_{\max}} \end{pmatrix} = \begin{pmatrix} \alpha_{N_{\max}} \\ 0 \end{pmatrix} \qquad (\text{II.2.46})$$

These two boundary conditions are compatible with the T relationships between the two external nodes only for discrete energies.

We illustrate in Fig. II.2.9 the transfer matrix technique by solving the Schrödinger equation for a biased double quantum well with $L = 7$ nm, $l = 15$ nm and intermediate barrier thickness (height) of $h = 4$ nm (224 meV). The effective masses are $0.07m_0$ and $0.08m_0$ in the well and the barrier respectively. The electric field F varies from 0 to 70 kV/cm. In the calculations we took all the δ_n equal to 1 nm. This DQW admits at $F = 0$ five bound states that are mainly localised in the narrow (E_2 and E_5) and in the wide well (E_1, E_3 and E_4). When a positive electric field is applied, the right-hand side well ($l = 15$ nm) is lifted up in energy by a quantity $\approx eF(L/2 + l/2 + h)$ compared to the left-hand side well. We indeed observe in Fig. II.2.9 that E_1, E_3 and E_4 display a quasi-linear shift with F. This shift amounts to

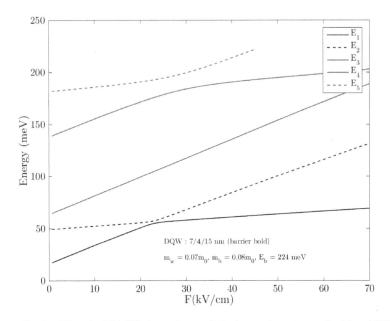

Figure II.2.9. Electric field (F) dependence of the lower eigenstates of a biased DQW. The parameters are given in the lower part of the figure.

105 meV at $F = 70$ kV/cm. However, the blue shift of the wide well levels makes them to become degenerate with the narrow well levels (at $F \approx 22$ kV/cm where $E_1 \approx E_2$ or $F \approx 25$ kV/cm where $E_4 \approx E_5$). The crossings are actually replaced by anti-crossings since we know (see Exercise 11) that in one dimension the bound state cannot be degenerate. The anti-crossings can be faint $(E_1 - E_2)$ or significant $(E_4 - E_5)$ depending on the small or pronounced delocalisations of the eigenstates (see below).

II.2.3.   Double quantum wells

The double quantum well (DQW) structure is made of two quantum wells separated by a thin intermediate barrier. A DQW is the simplest semiconductor heterostructure where the electron (or hole) tunnelling across a barrier plays a decisive part in the build-up of the electron distribution. In particular, it is possible to induce a significant spatial delocalisation of the electron distribution for certain values of the

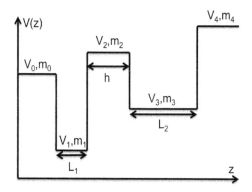

Figure II.2.10. Conduction band profile of a DQW structure.

DQW parameters. We shall first derive the equation that determines the bound states of a general DQW provided the conduction band dispersion relations are parabolic and the carrier experiences in each layer a piecewise constant potential energy (see Fig. II.2.10). Then, we shall study various limits of this general description. In particular, we shall emphasise a simplified ("tight binding") description of the eigenstates where the DQW eigenstates are built by forming linear combination of solutions of the isolated wells.

To compute the bound state of the 1D Hamiltonian

$$H = p_z \left(\frac{1}{2m^*(z)} \right) p_z + V(z) \tag{II.2.47}$$

we take the z origin at the first interface and we write:

$$\chi(z) = A e^{\kappa_0 z}, \quad z \leq 0 \tag{II.2.48}$$

$$\chi(z) = B e^{ik_1 z} + C e^{-ik_1 z}, \quad 0 \leq z \leq L_1 \tag{II.2.49}$$

$$\chi(z) = D e^{\kappa_2 (z - L_1)} + E e^{-\kappa_2 (z - L_1)}, \quad L_1 \leq z \leq L_1 + h \tag{II.2.50}$$

$$\chi(z) = F e^{ik_3 (z - L_1 - h)} + G e^{-ik_3 (z - L_1 - h)}, \quad L_1 + h \leq z \leq L_1 + L_2 + h \tag{II.2.51}$$

$$\chi(z) = H e^{-\kappa_4 (z - L_1 - L_2 - h)}, \quad z \geq L_1 + L_2 + h \tag{II.2.52}$$

$$\kappa_n = \sqrt{\frac{2m_n(V_n - \varepsilon)}{\hbar^2}}, \quad n = 0, 2, 4; \quad k_p = \sqrt{\frac{2m_p(\varepsilon - V_p)}{\hbar^2}}, \quad p = 1, 3 \tag{II.2.53}$$

By writing the continuity of $\chi(z)$ and $\frac{1}{m^*(z)} \frac{d\chi(z)}{dz}$ across the four interfaces we get after some calculations:

$$-A_1 A_2 + e^{-2\kappa_2 h} B_1 B_2 = 0 \qquad (\text{II.2.54})$$

where:

$$A_1 = \left(1 + \frac{\kappa_0 m_2}{m_0 \kappa_2}\right) \cos \varphi_1 - \left(\frac{k_1 m_2}{m_1 \kappa_2} - \frac{\kappa_0 m_1}{m_0 k_1}\right) \sin \varphi_1; \quad \varphi_1 = k_1 L_1 \qquad (\text{II.2.55})$$

$$A_2 = \left(1 + \frac{\kappa_4 m_2}{m_4 \kappa_2}\right) \cos \varphi_2 - \left(\frac{k_3 m_2}{m_3 \kappa_2} - \frac{\kappa_4 m_3}{m_4 k_3}\right) \sin \varphi_2; \quad \varphi_2 = k_3 L_2 \qquad (\text{II.2.56})$$

$$B_1 = \left(1 - \frac{\kappa_0 m_2}{m_0 \kappa_2}\right) \cos \varphi_1 + \left(\frac{k_1 m_2}{m_1 \kappa_2} + \frac{\kappa_0 m_1}{m_0 k_1}\right) \sin \varphi_1 \qquad (\text{II.2.57})$$

$$B_2 = \left(1 - \frac{\kappa_4 m_2}{m_4 \kappa_2}\right) \cos \varphi_2 + \left(\frac{k_3 m_2}{m_3 \kappa_2} + \frac{\kappa_4 m_3}{m_4 k_3}\right) \sin \varphi_2 \qquad (\text{II.2.58})$$

We show in Fig. II.2.11 the L_2 variation of the eigenenergies in the case of the structure where $L_1 = 7$ nm, $h = 5$ nm, $V_0 = V_4 = 224$ meV, $V_2 = 170$ meV, $V_1 = V_3 = 0$, $m_0 = m_4 = 0.077m$, $m_1 = m_3 = 0.067m$, $m_2 = 0.074m$ where m is the free electron mass. These parameters correspond roughly to a GaAs/Ga$_{0.7}$Al$_{0.3}$As DQW where the intermediate barrier is made of Ga$_{0.8}$Al$_{0.2}$As. One sees that anti-crossing effects occur at $L_2 = 7$ nm and $L_2 = 18$ nm. They correspond to the repulsion between levels that are mostly localised in either wells: the ground levels of each well at $L_2 = 7$ nm and the ground state of the left well with the first excited state of the right well at $L_2 = 18$ nm.

In the limit of an infinitely thick intermediate barrier ($h \to \infty$) the solution of Eq. (II.2.54) reduces to:

$$A_1 = 0 \quad \text{or} \quad A_2 = 0 \qquad (\text{II.2.59})$$

The solutions of $A_{1,2} = 0$ correspond respectively to that of the isolated single QW1 or QW2 (see Fig. II.2.12).

Let us now study the case of a thick but finite barrier. We are interested in the shift of the eigenenergy $E_n^{(1)}$ of the nth bound state

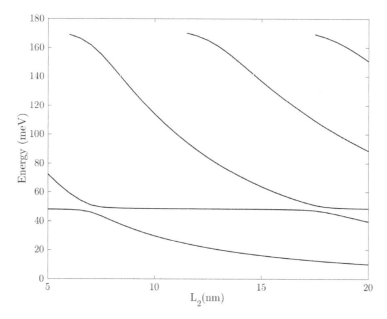

Figure II.2.11. Calculated energy levels of a DQW 7 nm/5 nm/L_2 versus L_2. The other material parameters are given in the text.

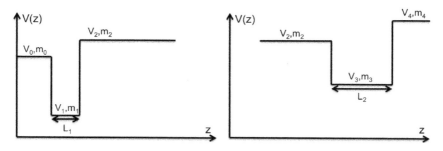

Figure II.2.12. Conduction band profiles corresponding to the $h \to \infty$ limit of a DQW: isolated QW1 and QW2 respectively.

of QW1 when isolated due to the finite tunnel coupling between the two wells. Two important cases show up depending on whether $E_n^{(1)}$ coincides in energy with $E_m^{(2)}$ (of the mth bound state of QW2 when isolated) or not.

- $E_n^{(1)}$ is not an eigenenergy of QW2. Then, we search for a solution:

$$\varepsilon = E_n^{(1)} + x; \quad |x| \ll E_n^{(1)} \qquad (\text{II.2.60})$$

and expand Eq. (II.2.54) to the lowest order in x. We find:

$$x = \frac{a_1(E_n^{(1)})B_2(E_n^{(1)})}{a_1(E_n^{(1)})A_2(E_n^{(1)})}e^{-2h\kappa_2(E_n^{(1)})}; \quad a_1(E_n^{(1)}) = \frac{dA_1}{d\varepsilon}\bigg|_{\varepsilon=E_n^{(1)}}$$

(II.2.61)

Hence, we get a shift that is exponentially small versus the barrier thickness and has a sign that depends on the particular DQW structural parameters through $B_1, B_2, \ldots$ Note that Eq. (II.2.61) is close from a first-order perturbation result. In fact as seen from QW1, the DQW situation can be written as:

$$H_{\text{DQW}} = H_{\text{QW1}} + \delta H \tag{II.2.62}$$

$$\begin{aligned}\delta H &= (V_3 - V_2)Y(z - L_1 - h)Y(L_1 + L_2 + h - z)\\ &\quad + (V_4 - V_2)Y(z - L_1 - L_2 - h)\end{aligned} \tag{II.2.63}$$

Then, to the first order in δH, $\varepsilon - E_n^{(1)}$ is equal to:

$$\varepsilon - E_n^{(1)} = \langle \chi_n^{(1)}|\delta H|\chi_n^{(1)}\rangle = \int_{-\infty}^{\infty} [\chi_n^{(1)}(z)]^2 \delta H$$

$$= C^{\text{st}} \exp[-2h\kappa_2(E_n^{(1)})] \tag{II.2.64}$$

Note that a similar dependency in $\exp[-2h\kappa_2(E_m^{(2)})]$ would occur if we would look at the shift of $E_m^{(2)}$ the eigenenergy of the mth bound state of QW2 when isolated due to the presence of QW1.

• $E_n^{(1)}$ coincides with an eigenenergy $E_m^{(2)}$ of QW2. In this case the product $A_1(E_n^{(1)} + x)A_2(E_n^{(1)} + x)$ is quadratic in x at small x. This results in a lifting of the degeneracy between $E_n^{(1)}$ and $E_m^{(2)}$ since we get two possible values x_+ and x_-:

$$x_\pm = \pm e^{-h\kappa_2(E_n^{(1)})}\sqrt{\frac{B_1(E_n^{(1)})B_2(E_n^{(1)})}{a_1(E_n^{(1)})a_2(E_n^{(1)})}}; \quad a_2(E_n^{(1)}) = \frac{dA_2}{d\varepsilon}\bigg|_{\varepsilon=E_n^{(1)}}$$

(II.2.65)

Thus, we find a lifting of degeneracy that decays with h at a much slower pace than the energy shift in the case where there is no degeneracy between the energies of the two wells. In a concomitant fashion one finds a spatial delocalisation of the eigenstates over the two wells while the localisation of the eigenstates of the coupled wells changes

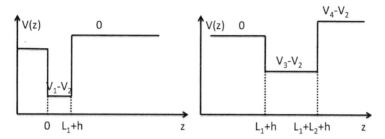

Figure II.2.13. Splitting of the DQW potential profile into the sum of the potential profiles of two single QW.

less with the tunnel coupling when there is no degeneracy. We shall return to this point below.

II.2.3.1. Tight binding analysis

The potential energy profile of the DQW can be rewritten (see Fig. II.2.13):

$$V(z) = V_1(z) + V_2(z) \qquad (\text{II.2.66})$$

$$V_1(z) = V_0 - V_2, \ z \leq 0; \quad V_1(z) = 0, \ z \geq L_1 + h$$
$$V_1(z) = V_1 - V_2, \ 0 \leq z \leq L_1 + h;$$
$$V_2(z) = V_3 - V_2, \ L_1 + h \leq z \leq L_1 + h + L_2$$
$$V_2(z) = 0, \ z \leq L_1 + h; \quad V_2(z) = V_4 - V_2, \ z \geq L_1 + h + L_2$$
$$(\text{II.2.67})$$

The stationary solutions of the Schrödinger equation are searched in the form of a linear combination of the single well problems $\chi_p^{(n)}(z)$:

$$\varphi_v(z) = \sum_{p,n=1,2} c_{p,n}^v \chi_p^{(n)}(z) \qquad (\text{II.2.68})$$

where p is the well index and n the level index. This writing introduces a first difficulty that is due to the non-orthogonality of the basis functions since the single well eigenstates centred on different well are not orthogonal:

$$\langle \chi_p^{(n)}(z) | \chi_{p'}^{(n)}(z) \rangle = \delta_{pp'}; \quad \langle \chi_p^{(1)}(z) | \chi_{p'}^{(2)}(z) \rangle \neq 0 \qquad (\text{II.2.69})$$

Secondly, the states of the continuum of the isolated wells will be counted twice for $\varepsilon \geq V_4 - V_2$.

Thus, the tight binding analysis should be restricted to the bound states of the DQW: $V_1 - V_2 \leq \varepsilon \leq V_0 - V_2$. In practice, the tight binding analysis is a variational estimate of the lowest lying bound states of the problem. By projecting in the $\chi_p^{(1)}$, $\chi_p^{(2)}$ states, we get:

$$c_{p,1}^v (E_p^{(1)} - \varepsilon_v) + \sum_{p'} c_{p',1}^v \langle \chi_p^{(1)} | V_2 | \chi_{p'}^{(1)} \rangle$$

$$+ \sum_{p'} c_{p',2}^v [\langle \chi_p^{(1)} | V_1 | \chi_{p'}^{(2)} \rangle + (E_p^{(2)} - \varepsilon_v) \langle \chi_p^{(1)} | \chi_{p'}^{(2)} \rangle] = 0$$

$$c_{p,2}^v (E_p^{(2)} - \varepsilon_v) + \sum_{p'} c_{p',2}^v \langle \chi_p^{(2)} | V_1 | \chi_{p'}^{(2)} \rangle$$

$$+ \sum_{p'} c_{p',1}^v [\langle \chi_p^{(2)} | V_2 | \chi_{p'}^{(1)} \rangle + (E_p^{(1)} - \varepsilon_v) \langle \chi_p^{(2)} | \chi_{p'}^{(1)} \rangle] = 0$$

$$\text{(II.2.70)}$$

There are three kinds of terms:

- the shifts and mixings of the eigenvalues and eigenstates in a given well due to the presence of the other well (like $\langle \chi_p^{(1)} | V_2 | \chi_{p'}^{(1)} \rangle$);
- the transfer from one well to the other (like $\langle \chi_p^{(1)} | V_1 | \chi_{p'}^{(2)} \rangle$);
- the energy-dependent corrections due to the non-orthogonality of the wavefunctions of the two wells (like $(E_p^{(2)} - \varepsilon_v) \langle \chi_p^{(1)} | \chi_{p'}^{(2)} \rangle$).

It is doable but tedious to solve the system (II.2.70) and get the eigenenergies and eigenstates of the DQW problem in the general case where there are j_1 bound levels in QW1 and j_2 bound levels in QW2.

Let us however specialise to two levels that are weakly coupled. From now on we retain one level per well say $E_p^{(1)}$ and $E_{p'}^{(2)}$ (because the system is such that these two energies are very close or even identical and as mentioned above one expects a delocalisation of the eigenstates). We find:

$$\begin{pmatrix} \tilde{E}_p^{(1)} - \varepsilon & t_{12} + s[E_{p'}^{(2)} - \varepsilon] \\ t_{21} + s[E_p^{(1)} - \varepsilon] & \tilde{E}_{p'}^{(2)} - \varepsilon \end{pmatrix} \begin{pmatrix} c_{p,1} \\ c_{p,2} \end{pmatrix} = 0 \qquad \text{(II.2.71)}$$

$$s = \langle \chi_p^{(1)} | \chi_{p'}^{(2)} \rangle \tag{II.2.72}$$

$$\tilde{E}_p^{(1)} = E_p^{(1)} + \langle \chi_p^{(1)} | V_2 | \chi_p^{(1)} \rangle = E_p^{(1)} + s_{12} \tag{II.2.73}$$

$$\tilde{E}_{p'}^{(2)} = E_{p'}^{(2)} + \langle \chi_{p'}^{(2)} | V_1 | \chi_{p'}^{(2)} \rangle = E_{p'}^{(2)} + s_{21} \tag{II.2.74}$$

$$t_{12} = \langle \chi_p^{(1)} | V_1 | \chi_{p'}^{(2)} \rangle; \quad t_{21} = \langle \chi_{p'}^{(2)} | V_2 | \chi_p^{(1)} \rangle \tag{II.2.75}$$

Hence the energies are the solutions of:

$$(\tilde{E}_p^{(1)} - \varepsilon)(\tilde{E}_{p'}^{(2)} - \varepsilon) - t_{12}t_{21} - s \left[t_{12}(E_p^{(1)} - \varepsilon) + t_{21}(E_{p'}^{(2)} - \varepsilon) \right]$$

$$-s^2(E_p^{(1)} - \varepsilon)(E_{p'}^{(2)} - \varepsilon) = 0 \tag{II.2.76}$$

We introduce x and δ such that x represents the energy measured from the centre of gravity between the two QW energies and 2δ represents their difference:

$$\varepsilon = \frac{E_p^{(1)} + E_{p'}^{(2)}}{2} + x; \quad \delta = \frac{E_p^{(1)} - E_{p'}^{(2)}}{2} \tag{II.2.77}$$

We get:

$$x_\pm = \frac{1}{2(1 - s^2)} \{ s_{12} + s_{21} - s(t_{12} + t_{21})$$

$$\pm \sqrt{[s_{12} + s_{21} - s(t_{12} + t_{21})]^2 + 4\delta^2(1 - s^2) + 4t_{12}t_{21} - 4u} \} \tag{II.2.78}$$

$$u = \delta(s_{21} - s_{12}) + s_{12}s_{21} + s\delta(t_{12} - t_{21}) \tag{II.2.79}$$

There are good reasons to neglect a number of terms in $x_\pm$. By writing down the wavefunctions of the isolated wells one can check that at large $\kappa_2 h$ there is:

$$s, t_{12}, t_{21} \approx e^{-\kappa_2 h}; \quad s_{12}, s_{21} \approx e^{-2\kappa_2 h} \tag{II.2.80}$$

Thus, if one retains the dominant terms, we find for zero detuning and thick barriers:

$$x_\pm(\delta = 0) \approx \pm\sqrt{t_{12}t_{21}} \tag{II.2.81}$$

We see that the coupling between the wells associated with the tunnelling through the intermediate barrier always increases the energy distance between the two states. We also retrieve that the splitting due to resonant tunnelling ($\delta = 0$) varies like $e^{-\kappa_2 h}$. On the other hand, like in the exact calculation, we find that at non-zero detuning, the two levels will repel each other due to the tunnelling through a quantity that varies like $e^{-2\kappa_2 h}$. The computation of the wavefunction at zero detuning shows when the tunnel coupling is taken into account that instead of remaining concentrated in one well the wavefunction delocalises over the whole structure.

II.2.3.2.   Symmetrical double quantum well

In this case, considering the tunnel coupling between the same levels in both wells, there is:

$$s_{12} = s_{21} = \sigma; \quad t_{12} = t_{21} = t \qquad \text{(II.2.82)}$$

and without any approximation we know that the $|\pm\rangle$ states of the DQW will be the symmetric and antisymmetric combinations of the two isolated QW states. This is because the Hamiltonian is now an even function of z if we chose the z origin at the centre of the DQW: the centre of the intermediate barrier. Thus, the bound states of the structures must necessarily be even or odd functions of z. We remark that the delocalisation persists irrespective of the barrier thickness h, even if the latter becomes macroscopic. This result is mathematically correct and physically absurd. The flaw lays in the assumption that two wells can physically be identical. In reality, they are not and there always exists a certain dissymmetry between the two wells; in other words in Eq. (II.2.78) δ is never zero, even if it is indeed very small. Thus, by increasing h the tunnel coupling diminishes till it becomes smaller than δ where the system enters a configuration that corresponds to the weak (perturbative) coupling between two different wells. In this situation, we know (see above) that the eigenstates are localised either in QW1 or in QW2. The criterion to decide on the localised/delocalised aspect of the eigenstates is whether the tunnelling t is large or small compared to the detuning δ. In the former case the states are delocalised over the DQW structure while in the latter case they are localised in either wells.

One can easily engineer the localisation/delocalisation of the eigenstates by biasing a symmetrical DQW. We choose the origin of the electrostatic potential at the centre of the intermediate barrier and we restrict the basis to the two bonding and antibonding combinations of E_1 states in either wells. These two states have a definite parity. Thus, the electrostatic potential has only an off diagonal contribution and the eigenstates are the solution of:

$$\begin{vmatrix} E_- - \varepsilon & eF\langle \chi_-|z|\chi_+ \rangle \\ eF\langle \chi_+|z|\chi_- \rangle & E_+ - \varepsilon \end{vmatrix} = 0 \qquad \text{(II.2.83)}$$

where $E_\pm = E_1 + \sigma \pm t$. The eigenenergies are:

$$\varepsilon_\pm = E_1 + \sigma \pm \sqrt{t^2 + e^2 F^2 \langle \chi_-|z|\chi_+ \rangle^2} \qquad \text{(II.2.84)}$$

In a first approximation the z matrix element is equal to $-(L+h)/2$, half the distance between the centre of the two wells. Thus, at large fields we find

$$\varepsilon_\pm \approx E_1 \pm eF \frac{(L+h)}{2} \qquad \text{(II.2.85)}$$

and the eigenstates are localised in either wells. In the opposite limit, we find:

$$\varepsilon_\pm \approx E_1 \pm |t| \pm \frac{e^2 F^2 \left(\frac{L+h}{2}\right)^2}{2|t|} \qquad \text{(II.2.86)}$$

where we recognise the quadratic Stark shift of the zero field eigenstates computed at the lowest order in perturbation.

We illustrate in Fig. II.2.14 the DQW problems by computing the eigenenergies of a symmetrical GaAs/GaAlAs DQW versus the intermediate barrier thickness.

II.2.4. Holes

The valence band dispersion have a negative curvature in the vicinity of the top of the band. The valence band electrons have a negative effective mass, which raises concerns regarding our capability to analyse phenomena in terms of our classical intuition. For example, take an ionised donor. It bears a positive charge and attracts conduction electrons. But the valence electrons in spite of having the same negative charge as the conduction electrons are repelled by the ionised donor because of their negative effective mass. It would be much more

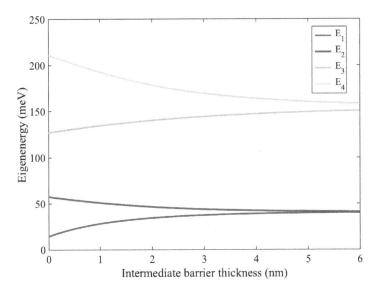

Figure II.2.14.   Eigenenergies of a symmetrical double GaAs/Al$_{0.25}$Ga$_{0.75}$As quantum well versus the intermediate barrier thickness.

convenient if we had at our disposal a formalism where the valence electrons are replaced by a quasi-particle that bears a positive mass. Although one might develop an axiomatic theory of holes, we propose here a way to create this quasi-particle using simple arguments.

Firstly, let us start by a remark: we know that at $T = 0K$ in a perfect material the valence band will be entirely filled and therefore no current will flow on account of the Pauli principle or because of symmetry (see below). At $T \neq 0$, this band will be only partially filled. Let us compute the electrical current associated with such a partially filled band:

$$\vec{j} = -e \sum_{\vec{k}} \vec{v}_{\vec{k}} f_{\vec{k}} = -e \sum_{\vec{k}} \vec{v}_{\vec{k}} \left[1 - (1 - f_{\vec{k}}) \right] = +e \sum_{\vec{k}} (1 - f_{\vec{k}}) \vec{v}_{\vec{k}}$$

$$(\text{II.2.87})$$

where $\vec{v}_{\vec{k}} = \langle \psi_{v\vec{k}} | \vec{v} | \psi_{v\vec{k}} \rangle$ is the velocity of a valence Bloch electron and $f_{\vec{k}}$ the occupation function of the state $|\psi_{v\vec{k}}\rangle$. For a filled band $\sum_{\vec{k}} \vec{v}_{\vec{k}}$ identically vanishes (because the velocity is the gradient of the dispersion and the dispersion is an even periodic function of the wavevector). Thus, for an almost filled band, we find that the electrical current can be considered as produced by positively charged carriers with an occupation statistics that is the one of the non-occupied electron states.

We are now ready to create the hole quasi-particle: we start by the definition of the current at equilibrium where $f_{\vec{k}}$ is the Fermi–Dirac function. From Eq. (II.2.87) we get

$$\vec{j}_e = +e \sum_{\vec{k}_e} \frac{\vec{v}_e(\vec{k}_e)}{1 + \exp[-\beta(\varepsilon_{v\vec{k}_e} - \mu_e)]} \qquad (\text{II.2.88})$$

where μ_e is the chemical potential of the electrons, $\beta = 1/(k_B T)$, $\varepsilon_{v,\vec{k}_e}$ is the electron energy in the valence band and we mention that we are in the electron formalism by labelling the relevant quantities by e. We now make the change:

$$\vec{k}_e \to -\vec{k}_h \Rightarrow e\vec{v}_e(\vec{k}_e) \to -e\vec{v}_e(\vec{k}_h); \quad \varepsilon_{v\vec{k}_e} \to \varepsilon_{v\vec{k}_h} \qquad (\text{II.2.89})$$

In terms of $\vec{k}_h$, the electrical current is equal to:

$$\vec{j}_e = +e \sum_{\vec{k}_h} \frac{-\vec{v}_e(\vec{k}_h)}{1 + \exp[-\beta(\varepsilon_{v\vec{k}_h} - \mu_e)]} \qquad (\text{II.2.90})$$

We now define the hole as a quasi-particle that bears a positive charge $+e$, a wavevector $\vec{k}_h$ and is a fermion characterised at equilibrium by a Fermi–Dirac function with chemical potential μ_h:

$$\vec{j}_h = +e \sum_{\vec{k}_h} \frac{\vec{v}_h(\vec{k}_h)}{1 + \exp[\beta(\varepsilon_{v,\vec{k}_h} - \mu_h)]} \qquad (\text{II.2.91})$$

We now request this definition to always coincide with Eq. (II.2.90) at any temperature and for any valence dispersion relation. For this to be true, we must have:

$$\varepsilon_{v,\vec{k}_h} - \mu_h = -[\varepsilon_{v,\vec{k}_h} - \mu_e] \qquad (\text{II.2.92})$$

$$\vec{v}_h(\vec{k}_h) = -\vec{v}_e(\vec{k}_h) \qquad (\text{II.2.93})$$

Hence, the hole energy scale is opposite to the electron energy scale and the hole velocity at a given wavevector is minus the electron velocity at the same wavevector. It has to be added that the hole spin projection on a given axis is the opposite to that of the electron (see Fig. II.2.15).

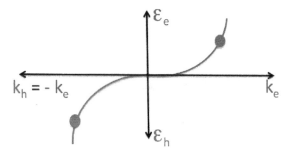

Figure II.2.15.   Electron dispersion relation versus electronic wavevector k_e (rhs panel) and hole dispersion versus hole wavevector k_h (lhs panel).

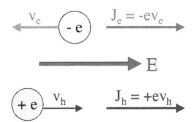

Figure II.2.16.   Summary of the effect of an electric field $\vec{E}$ on an electron and hole. The particle currents have opposite signs, but the electrical currents associated with electrons and holes add.

Of course applying the hole formalism to the conduction band (which has a positive curvature) would not make much sense because in the hole formalism a conduction electron would have a negative effective mass.

In real devices, at room temperature, there are often conduction and valence electrons. So people use a mixed description by using electrons for the conduction states and holes for the valence states. In order not to get confused, consider charged carriers in the presence of an electric field $\vec{E}$ (see Fig. II.2.16). In the presence of that field the electron and hole velocity (or the particle current) are opposite but the electrical currents add.

Chapter II.3

Beyond the Ideal World

We have so far discussed the eigenstates of ideal heterostructures: for 1D quantisation we found that the eigenstates can be written as

$$\langle \vec{r}|\Psi\rangle = \sum_n \chi_n(z) \frac{e^{i\vec{k}\cdot\vec{\rho}}}{\sqrt{S}} u_n(\vec{r}) \qquad (\text{II.3.1})$$

where the χ_n's are the solutions of a $2N \times 2N$ first- or second-order differential systems depending on whether one retains only the close bands or one accounts for one virtual excursion to the remote bands.

In the following, we shall often discuss the case where $n = 1$ (conduction electrons) and therefore have a single $\chi(z)$. The latter is the solution of:

$$\left[p_z \left(\frac{1}{2m^*(z)} \right) p_z + \frac{(p_x^2 + p_y^2)}{2m^*(z)} + V(z) \right] \chi(z) = \varepsilon \chi(z)$$

$$(\text{II.3.2})$$

where the energy zero is taken at the bottom of the conduction band of the well-acting material. With this choice $V(z)$ is zero in the well-acting material and equal to V_b in the barrier acting material, where V_b is the conduction band offset between the well and the barrier materials.

Actually, one can also add an external potential to the effective Hamiltonian, like the one produced by an electric field (biased heterostructures). We would write it:

$$V_{\text{ext}}(\vec{r}) = -e\phi(\vec{r}) \qquad (\text{II.3.3})$$

where $\phi(\vec{r})$ is the electrostatic potential in the heterostructure. It is determined by the Poisson equation and therefore linked to the fixed charges (dopants) and the mobile charges, the conduction electrons (or holes). At the simplest, one can consider that a bias is applied along the growth axis. Then, there is again a decoupling between the z and (x, y) motions in the Schrödinger equation for the envelopes χ_n. Suppose we are in such a case and that at $t = 0$, the system has been placed in an eigenstate of the effective Hamiltonian. Then, of course, the system will not evolve (apart from a pure phase: $|\psi(t)\rangle = \exp(-\frac{iE_n}{\hbar}t)|\psi(0)\rangle$) and if, in particular, there was a non-zero current associated with the initial state, this current will not degrade and will stay for ever:

$$\langle\psi(t)|j_{z,x}|\psi(t)\rangle = \langle\psi(0)|j_{z,x}|\psi(0)\rangle \qquad \text{(II.3.4)}$$

Everyone knows that this situation is not observed in semiconductors: even at very low temperatures (say 100 mK) and in the best available samples (with an electronic mobility in excess of $1000 \text{ m}^2\,\text{V}^{-1}\text{s}^{-1}$), any initial current decays. Moreover, if one could look at the electron average position $\langle\psi(t)|\vec{r}|\psi(t)\rangle$ (rather a gedanken experiment), it would randomly change with time while the electron position is supposed to change linearly with time ($\langle\vec{r}\rangle(t) = \langle\vec{r}\rangle(t = 0) + v_0 t$).

The causes of this evolution are the mechanisms that break the translation invariance in the layer plane or perturb the z-dependent potential in a random way. The random distribution of the impurities/traps in the sample or the random emission or absorption of phonons by electrons, because of their interactions with the lattice vibrations, make that the exact knowledge of the actual Hamiltonian is unreachable. Therefore, in stark contrast with simple systems like atoms, it is in general impossible to prepare an actual solid state system in a well-specified electronic state. Now, in many cases (but we shall describe counter-examples later on), the randomness is "weak", meaning that the actual eigenstates if projected on those of the ideal system have components that are significant only in a narrow energy range. This suggests that instead of attempting to define an ever-elusive initial state of the true Hamiltonian, it is much simpler to discuss the initial state of the system in terms of the known eigenstates of the ideal system. This initial state will evolve under the action of the random perturbations and we have to find ways to discuss the evolution. Note that the randomness is at the heart of the difficulties because if we were to adding a coherent/systematic term to the Hamiltonian of the ideal system, we would (hopefully) find a new set of quantum numbers and again placing the system in an eigenstate of the new Hamiltonian, there would be no evolution. The randomness can be either static (e.g., the electrostatic potential created by charged impurities that occupy random positions) or varies with time (e.g., the random time-dependent electrostatic potential created by a charged impurity that can become neutral if the static charge captures at t_0 a moving charge and becomes a dipole which, later on, ionises at t_1 to become again a single charge etc.). We shall concentrate here on the effects of the random static perturbations.

Let us then consider static scatterers (e.g., ionised impurities, interface defects). Here, the randomness lies in the positions of each scatterer:

$$V_{\text{def}}(\vec{r}) = \sum_{\vec{R}_i} v(\vec{r} - \vec{R}_i) \tag{II.3.5}$$

In effect, in a volume Ω containing N unit cells (N macroscopic), we have no way to know where the impurities/dopants are located because we have very little control on their whereabouts. Impurities diffuse, spread at a rate that is thermo-activated. Even though we placed them on a plane (delta doping) during the epitaxy, there will be some non-zero probability to find them elsewhere in the actual sample. Similarly, in the layer plane, there is no control of the impurity location. So, much like the dice thrown in the air and where despite the Newton's laws we are unable to predict the outcome of one particular facet it felt, we must consider that the probability of finding one impurity atom in a particular unit cell is evenly distributed and equal to $1/N$.

We shall always deal with diluted impurities: if there are N_{imp} impurity atoms in the volume Ω, there is $\frac{N_{\text{imp}}}{N} \ll 1$. It follows from this large dilution limit that the probability density $P(\vec{R}_1, \vec{R}_2, \ldots, \vec{R}_{N_{\text{imp}}})$ to find one impurity atom within $d\vec{R}_1$ around

$\vec{R}_1$, another within $d\vec{R}_2$ around $\vec{R}_2,\ldots$, and one within $d\vec{R}_{N_{\mathrm{imp}}}$ around $\vec{R}_{N_{\mathrm{imp}}}$ factorises (to a good approximation):

$$P(\vec{R}_1, \vec{R}_2, \ldots, \vec{R}_{N_{\mathrm{imp}}}) = \prod_{i=1}^{N_{\mathrm{imp}}} P(\vec{R}_i) = \left(\frac{1}{\Omega}\right)^{N_{\mathrm{imp}}} \tag{II.3.6}$$

Suppose now that we have to compute a certain function $f(\vec{R}_1, \vec{R}_2, \ldots, \vec{R}_{N_{\mathrm{imp}}}) = \sum_{i=1}^{N_{\mathrm{imp}}} g(\vec{R}_i)$ like the first-order energy shift of the unperturbed Hamiltonian eigenvalues due to the impurities, or an impurity-induced scattering rate between two unperturbed quantum states. In the calculations, we shall fix all the impurities sites, compute the scattering rate for a given distribution of impurities and afterwards average the result over $P(\vec{R}_1, \vec{R}_2, \ldots, \vec{R}_{N_{\mathrm{imp}}})$:

$$f(\vec{R}_1, \vec{R}_2, \ldots, \vec{R}_{N_{\mathrm{imp}}}) \rightarrow \langle f \rangle$$

$$= \int d\vec{R}_1 d\vec{R}_2 \ldots d\vec{R}_{N_{\mathrm{imp}}} f(\vec{R}_1, \vec{R}_2, \ldots, \vec{R}_{N_{\mathrm{imp}}})$$

$$\times P(\vec{R}_1, \vec{R}_2, \ldots, \vec{R}_{N_{\mathrm{imp}}}) \tag{II.3.7}$$

The statistical independence between the impurity sites simplifies the previous formula:

$$\langle f \rangle = \int d\vec{R}_1 d\vec{R}_2 \ldots d\vec{R}_{N_{\mathrm{imp}}} \sum_{i=1}^{N_{\mathrm{imp}}} g(\vec{R}_i) \left(\frac{1}{\Omega}\right)^{N_{\mathrm{imp}}}$$

$$= \frac{1}{\Omega} \sum_{i=1}^{N_{\mathrm{imp}}} \int d\vec{R}_i g(\vec{R}_i) = \frac{N_{\mathrm{imp}}}{\Omega} \int d\vec{R} g(\vec{R}) \tag{II.3.8}$$

Of course in a quasi-2D situation, care has to be exercised and the integration over the impurity location runs only over the parts where we know the impurities have been placed. A very similar reasoning holds if one considers that the dopants stay on a given plane $z = z_{\mathrm{imp}}$. The random locations are now the sites on this plane and the previous formula is replaced by:

$$\langle f \rangle_2 = \frac{N_{\mathrm{imp}}}{S} \int d\vec{\rho} g(\vec{\rho}) \tag{II.3.9}$$

where $\vec{\rho} = (x, y)$. Let us compute the shift of the eigenenergy $\varepsilon_{n\vec{k}}$ to the first order in perturbation:

$$s_{n\vec{k}} = \langle \chi_{n\vec{k}} | \sum_{\vec{R}_i} v(\vec{r} - \vec{R}_i) | \chi_{n\vec{k}} \rangle$$

$$= \frac{1}{S} \sum_{\vec{R}_i} \int dz \iint d\vec{\rho} \chi_n^2(z) v(\vec{\rho} - \vec{\rho}_i, z - z_i)$$

$$= \frac{1}{S} \sum_{\vec{R}_i} \int d\xi \iint d\vec{R} \chi_n^2(z_i + \xi) v(\vec{R}, \xi) \qquad (\text{II.3.10})$$

We note that this expression is $\vec{k}$-independent but *a priori* depends on the subband index n. Let us average $s_{n\vec{k}}$ over the random positions of the impurities:

$$\langle s_{n\vec{k}} \rangle = \int d\vec{R}_1 \ldots d\vec{R}_{N_{\text{imp}}} \left(\frac{1}{\Omega} \right)^{N_{\text{imp}}}$$

$$\times \frac{1}{S} \sum_{\vec{R}_i} \int d\xi \iint d\vec{R} \chi_n^2(z_i + \xi) v(\vec{R}, \xi)$$

$$= \frac{N_{\text{imp}}}{\Omega} \iiint v(\vec{R}, \xi) d\xi d\vec{R} \int dz_i \chi_n^2(z_i + \xi) p(z_i) \qquad (\text{II.3.11})$$

where $p(z_i) = 1$ in the regions where the dopants are placed and zero elsewhere (we have assumed a uniform doping in the layer plane). We note that the volume integral and the integral over the impurity location along the growth axis can be disentangled only if the impurities are uniformly spread along z. Under such a circumstance, the integral over z_i is equal to 1 and the shift is also n-independent:

$$\langle s_{n\vec{k}} \rangle_{\text{unif}} = \frac{N_{\text{imp}}}{\Omega} \iiint v(\vec{R}, \xi) d\xi d\vec{R} \qquad (\text{II.3.12})$$

Such a constant shift can be re-absorbed in a redefinition of the energy zero and therefore has no physical significance. In the case of selective planar doping on the plane $z_i = z_0$ with:

$$p(z_i) = Y \left(z_i - z_0 + \frac{a}{2} \right) Y \left(z_0 + \frac{a}{2} - z_i \right) \qquad (\text{II.3.13})$$

where a is of the order of one monolayer (≈ 0.3 nm in GaAs), we get:

$$\langle s_{n\vec{k}} \rangle = \frac{N_{\text{imp}}}{\Omega} \iiint v(\vec{R}, \xi) d\xi d\vec{R} \int_{z_0 - \frac{a}{2}}^{z_0 + \frac{a}{2}} dz_i \chi_n^2(z_i + \xi)$$

$$\approx \frac{N_{\text{imp}} a}{\Omega} \iiint v(\vec{R}, \xi) d\xi d\vec{R} \chi_n^2(z_0 + \xi) \qquad \text{(II.3.14)}$$

Let us now discuss the important case of the scattering rate between two extended states of a heterostructure. According to the Fermi golden rule, the function f introduced above is:

$$f = \frac{2\pi}{\hbar} \sum_{n',\vec{k}'} \left| \langle n\vec{k}| \sum_{\vec{R}_i} v(\vec{r} - \vec{R}_i)|n'\vec{k}'\rangle \right|^2 \delta(\varepsilon_{n\vec{k}} - \varepsilon_{n'\vec{k}'})$$

$$= \frac{2\pi}{\hbar} \sum_{n',\vec{k}'} \delta(\varepsilon_{n\vec{k}} - \varepsilon_{n'\vec{k}'}) \sum_{\vec{R}_i, \vec{R}_j} \langle n\vec{k}|v(\vec{r} - \vec{R}_i)|n'\vec{k}'\rangle$$

$$\times \langle n'\vec{k}'|v(\vec{r} - \vec{R}_j)|n\vec{k}\rangle \qquad \text{(II.3.15)}$$

Because we deal with quasi-2D heterostructures, it proves useful to perform a Fourier–Bessel expansion (a 2D Fourier transform) of the 3D potential $v(\vec{r} - \vec{R}_i)$

$$v(\vec{r} - \vec{R}_i) = \sum_{\vec{q}} v_{\vec{q}}(z - z_i) e^{i\vec{q} \cdot (\vec{\rho} - \vec{\rho}_i)} \qquad \text{(II.3.16)}$$

$$v_{\vec{q}}(z - z_i) = \frac{1}{S} \iint e^{-i\vec{q} \cdot \vec{\rho}} v(\vec{\rho}, z - z_i) \cdot d\vec{\rho} \qquad \text{(II.3.17)}$$

where $\vec{q} = (q_x, q_y)$. Let us give a few examples: Table II.3.1 displays $v_{\vec{q}}(z - z_i)$ for three 3D potentials where $J_1(x)$ is the Bessel function of order 1 and $Y(x)$ is the step function ($Y(x) = 1$ if $x > 0$, $Y(x) = 0$ if $x < 0$). The three 3D potentials respectively correspond to:

(1) a cylindrical attractive defect extending from $-L/2$ to $+L/2$ along the z-axis with a radius ρ_0 and a depth V_0;
(2) a Gaussian attractive defect with a depth V_0 and extension α along z and β in the layer plane;
(3) a coulombic potential created by a charge Q_i in an isotropic dielectric medium characterised by a relative dielectric constant ε_r (ε_0 is the vacuum dielectric constant).

Table II.3.1. Three different 3D potential energies and their Fourier–Bessel coefficients.

$V(\vec{r})$	(1) $-V_0 Y(\rho_0 - \rho)$	(2) $V_0 \exp\left(-\dfrac{(z-z_i)^2}{\alpha^2}\right)$	(3) $-e\dfrac{Q_i}{4\pi\varepsilon_0\varepsilon_r|\vec{r}-\vec{R}_i|}$
	$\times Y(L^2/4 - (z-z_i)^2)$	$\times \exp\left(\dfrac{(\vec{\rho}-\vec{\rho}_i)^2}{\beta^2}\right)$	
$v_{\vec{q}}$	$-\dfrac{V_0}{S} Y(L^2/4 - (z-z_i)^2)$	$-\dfrac{V_0}{2S}\exp\left(-\dfrac{(z-z_i)^2}{\alpha^2}\right)$	$-\dfrac{eQ_i}{2\varepsilon_0\varepsilon_r Sq}e^{-q|z-z_i|}$
	$\times \dfrac{2\pi\rho_0^2}{q\rho_0}J_1(q\rho_0)$	$\times \exp\left(-\dfrac{q^2\beta^2}{4}\right)$	

In the cases (1) and (2), where the potentials have finite ranges in the layer plane, we find that the relevant q ranges where the $v_{\vec{q}}$ coefficients are sizeable are roughly the inverses of the spatial ranges (in the layer plane) of the perturbing potentials. The coulombic potential is particular in that it has very long range and is singular at the origin.

Using the Fourier–Bessel expansion allows to rewrite the matrix elements in the double sum above in the form:

$$\sum_{\vec{R}_i,\vec{R}_j}\sum_{\vec{q},\vec{q}'}\langle n|v_{\vec{q}}(z-z_i)|n'\rangle\langle n'|v_{\vec{q}'}^*(z-z_j)|n\rangle e^{-i\vec{q}\cdot\vec{\rho}_i}e^{i\vec{q}'\cdot\vec{\rho}_j}\delta_{\vec{q},\vec{k}-\vec{k}'}\delta_{\vec{q}',\vec{k}-\vec{k}'}$$

$$= \sum_{\vec{R}_i,\vec{R}_j}\langle n|v_{\vec{q}}(z-z_i)|n'\rangle\langle n'|v_{\vec{q}'}^*(z-z_j)|n\rangle e^{i(\vec{k}-\vec{k}')\cdot(\vec{\rho}_i-\vec{\rho}_j)}$$

$$(\text{II.3.18})$$

where v^* stands for the complex conjugate of v. The double sum over $\vec{R}_i, \vec{R}_j$ comprises two kinds of terms: those where $i=j$ and the other $i \neq j$. The diagonal terms have no fluctuating phases. Therefore, the averaging over the impurity positions will let them unchanged. On the other hand for $i \neq j$ there exists always a non-zero phase that is random. Hence, the averaging over the impurity positions lets the vector $\vec{\rho}_i - \vec{\rho}_j$ covering the whole plane perpendicular to the growth axis resulting in a vanishing sum $\sum_{i\neq j}$ in practice. Before discussing the limits of this averaging procedure, we give the average result of the double sum:

$$\left\langle \sum_{\vec{R}_i} |\langle n|v_{\vec{q}}(z-z_i)|n'\rangle|^2 \right\rangle = \frac{N_{\text{imp}}}{\Omega} \int dz_i p(z_i) |\langle n|v_{\vec{q}}(z-z_i)|n'\rangle|^2$$

$$(\text{II.3.19})$$

where $p(z_i)$ has been defined above.

Finally, we have found that N_{imp} statistically independent and dilute impurities display a scattering efficiency equal to N_{imp} times the scattering efficiency due to a single impurity. This sounds reasonable and is very well justified for a bulk material but, as we shall see, becomes questionable in modern heterostructures (e.g., narrow (30 nm) channel Field Effect Transistor) whose main characteristics is the very small size. In fact, the quasi-vanishing of the $i \neq j$ terms is based on the fact that the phases $(\vec{k}' - \vec{k}) \cdot (\vec{\rho}_i - \vec{\rho}_j)$ were changing a lot when $\vec{\rho}_i - \vec{\rho}_j$ describes the xOy plane. If indeed the in-plane area shrinks because of the increasing smaller sizes of modern devices, the random phases may remain small and the cancellation effects found in macroscopic samples will no longer be effective. Thus, a criterion to ensure a good cancellation of the random phases is:

$$(k_x' - k_x)L_x \gg 2\pi; \quad (k_y' - k_y)L_y \gg 2\pi \qquad (\text{II.3.20})$$

Suppose $L_x, L_y = 10^{-6}$ m (a small but not ultra-small heterostructure). If the symbol "$\gg$" means 10 times, then $\Delta k_x = k_x' - k_x$ should at least be $2\pi \times 10^7$ m^{-1}; smaller momentum transfers will violate the inequality. The difficulty is that, in general (see the expression of $v_{\vec{q}}(z - z_i)$), the $v_{\vec{q}}$'s are decreasing functions of q. Hence, there is a risk that our averaging procedure fails for momentum transfers that correspond to a very effective scattering. However, it is true that a zero momentum transfer corresponds to no scattering at all if only intra-subband transitions are concerned since for inter-subband transitions Δk is necessarily non-zero while for intra-subband transitions $\Delta k = 0$ means that the initial and final states coincide.

For most of the heterolayers the assumption of random impurity locations is reasonable and, in fact, very effective. This is because in these devices there are a huge number of impurities giving credence to the averaging (in other words the device can be decomposed into N subdevices where, for each, there is still a very large number of impurities). As a matter of example for an impurity concentration of 10^{16} cm^{-3} there are still 10^4 impurities in a volume of 1 μm^3. Again, in very small structures, if the number of impurities is small enough, the very notion that they are distributed at random is meaningless: for a given device that has a very small number of impurities (say 1–10), the averaging loses any meaning. Actually, the averaging can no longer be over the impurity locations in a given sample, but over very many different samples that, each, have their own impurity signature. This kind of "mesoscopic" behaviour is the situation we have to envisage in the very small/narrow devices that are nowadays being implemented to ensure faster electronics.

II.3.1. Population, velocity, energy relaxation times through rate equations

As discussed above, we split the Hamiltonian into $H_0 + U$ where U is either the electron–defect interaction V_{def} or the electron–phonon interaction $H_{\text{e-ph}}$. At time $t = 0$ we assume the system was in an eigenstate $|n\vec{k}\rangle$ of H_0 with energy $\varepsilon_{n\vec{k}}$ and velocity $\frac{\hbar\vec{k}}{m_n}$ where m_n is the in-plane effective mass in the nth subband or more generally $\frac{1}{\hbar}\frac{\partial\varepsilon_n(\vec{k})}{\partial\vec{k}}$ if non-parabolicity is important. But no one can in practice prepare the system in such a well-defined eigenstate and some averaging will have to be performed to account for this ill-defined initial state. We look at the long time regime where the Fermi golden rule can apply. We define $W_{n\vec{k}\to n'\vec{k}'}$ the constant transition rate at long time t for the system to undergo a transition from $|n\vec{k}\rangle$ to $|n'\vec{k}'\rangle$. Thus, the survival probability $p_{n\vec{k}}$ to find the system in the quantum state $|n\vec{k}\rangle$ at time t fulfils:

$$\frac{dp_{n\vec{k}}}{dt} = -\frac{p_{n\vec{k}}}{\tau_{n\vec{k}}}; \quad \frac{1}{\tau_{n\vec{k}}} = \sum_{n',\vec{k}'} W_{n\vec{k}\to n'\vec{k}'} \qquad (\text{II.3.21})$$

where we have focussed on the quantum evolution due to U, irrespective of any initial state filling or final state availability. $\tau_{n\vec{k}}$ is the lifetime of the state $|n\vec{k}\rangle$. Suppose now that we have a partial knowledge of the initial state and that $p_{n\vec{k}}(0)$ is the probability that the initial state is $|n\vec{k}\rangle$. Then, we would define an average life frequency as

$$\left\langle \frac{1}{\tau_{n\vec{k}}} \right\rangle = \sum_{n',\vec{k'}} P_{n'\vec{k'}}(0) \frac{1}{\tau_{n'\vec{k'}}} \tag{II.3.22}$$

However, Pauli exclusion principle precludes any transition to an occupied state. Thus, the actual probability variations are given by the previous expression if $|n'\vec{k'}\rangle$ was empty or are equal to zero if $|n'\vec{k'}\rangle$ was occupied.

In general, in condensed matter because there are so many electrons, one is more interested in the time evolution of the macroscopic (measurable) quantities like the population N_n of the nth subband or the energy of the electron gas or the current carried by all the electrons instead of the current carried by one particular electron. At time t, the population $N_n(t)$ is equal to:

$$N_n(t) = 2 \sum_{\vec{k}} f_{n\vec{k}}(t) \tag{II.3.23}$$

where the factor 2 comes from the spin degeneracy and $f_{n\vec{k}}$ is the occupation factor of the orbital state $|n\vec{k}\rangle$ (with a given spin). If the system were ideal and isolated, we know that $f_{n\vec{k}}(t)$ would be either 0 or 1 because we would know that there are as many quantum states occupied (spin included) as we have particles. But the real (macroscopic) electronic systems interact with energy and (sometime) particle reservoirs and these complicated exchanges make them reaching thermal equilibrium. In doing so, a great deal of the quantum features are lost and if the system is at thermal equilibrium at time t, $f_{n\vec{k}}(t)$ is a Fermi–Dirac distribution function. We now see that the real evolution of our quasi-2D system is less and less describable in terms of pure quantum evolution (survival probability) because of these repeated interactions with thermostats/surroundings and between the electrons. It is however true that the population $n_n(t)$ will irreversibly vary because of the possibility for an electron in the nth subband to escape to other subbands. If we make provision to warrantee that the final states of the transitions are empty and if we also take into account the refilling of the nth subband arising from transitions from the n'th subband to the nth one, one ends up with a time evolution of N_n such that N_n has varied during dt by an amount dN_n where taking the spin degeneracy into account there is:

$$\frac{dN_n}{dt} - -2 \sum_{\vec{k},n',\vec{k'}} W_{n\vec{k}\to n'\vec{k'}} f_{n\vec{k}} (1 \quad f_{n'\vec{k'}}) - W_{n'\vec{k'}\to n\vec{k}} f_{n'\vec{k'}} (1 - f_{n\vec{k}})$$

(II.3.24)

It can be readily checked that the total number of electrons is conserved, i.e.,

$$\frac{d}{dt}\left(\sum_n N_n\right) = 0 \qquad (II.3.25)$$

A similar approach can be used to define the energy loss rate or velocity loss rates. During dt a given elemental evolution from $|n\vec{k}\rangle$ to $|n'\vec{k'}\rangle$ would lead to variations:

$$dt W_{n\vec{k}\to n'\vec{k'}} \left(\varepsilon_{n'\vec{k'}} - \varepsilon_{n\vec{k}}\right) \quad \text{in energy} \qquad (II.3.26)$$

$$dt W_{n\vec{k}\to n'\vec{k'}} \left(\frac{\hbar\vec{k'}}{m_{n'}} - \frac{\hbar\vec{k}}{m_n}\right) \quad \text{in velocity} \qquad (II.3.27)$$

By adding the increments associated with scattering out and scattering in the state $|n\vec{k}\rangle$, we get the net variations associated with a given pair of states $|n\vec{k}\rangle$, $|n'\vec{k'}\rangle$:

$$dt \left[W_{n\vec{k}\to n'\vec{k'}} f_{n\vec{k}}(1 - f_{n'\vec{k'}}) - W_{n'\vec{k'}\to n\vec{k}} f_{n'\vec{k'}}(1 - f_{n\vec{k}})\right]$$
$$\times \left(\varepsilon_{n'\vec{k'}} - \varepsilon_{n\vec{k}}\right) \quad \text{in energy} \qquad (II.3.28)$$

$$dt \left[W_{n\vec{k}\to n'\vec{k'}} f_{n\vec{k}}(1 - f_{n'\vec{k'}}) - W_{n'\vec{k'}\to n\vec{k}} f_{n'\vec{k'}}(1 - f_{n\vec{k}})\right]$$
$$\times \left(\frac{\hbar\vec{k'}}{m_{n'}} - \frac{\hbar\vec{k}}{m_n}\right) \quad \text{in velocity} \qquad (II.3.29)$$

Finally, by summing over all the pairs of states $|n\vec{k}\rangle$, $|n'\vec{k'}\rangle$ we get the expressions for the energy and velocity loss rates:

$$\frac{d\langle E\rangle}{dt} = -2 \sum_{n\vec{k},n'\vec{k'}} [W_{n\vec{k}\to n'\vec{k'}} f_{n\vec{k}}(1 - f_{n'\vec{k'}}) - W_{n'\vec{k'}\to n\vec{k}} f_{n'\vec{k'}}(1 - f_{n\vec{k}})]$$
$$\times (\varepsilon_{n'\vec{k'}} - \varepsilon_{n\vec{k}}) \qquad (II.3.30)$$

$$\frac{d\langle \vec{V} \rangle}{dt} = -2 \sum_{n\vec{k},n'\vec{k}'} \left[W_{n\vec{k} \to n'\vec{k}'} f_{n\vec{k}} (1 - f_{n'\vec{k}'}) - W_{n'\vec{k}' \to n\vec{k}} f_{n'\vec{k}'} (1 - f_{n\vec{k}}) \right]$$

$$\times \left(\frac{\hbar \vec{k}'}{m_{n'}} - \frac{\hbar \vec{k}}{m_n} \right) \tag{II.3.31}$$

where $\langle E \rangle$ and $\langle \vec{V} \rangle$ are the total energy and velocity of the electron gas and the factor 2 is again for the spin degeneracy (we have implicitly assumed that the elastic or inelastic scatterings are spin-conserving). Considering Eq. (II.3.24) and Eqs. (II.3.30), (II.3.31), we see immediately that the energy relaxation should *a priori* occur at a smaller or much smaller rate than the velocity or population relaxation rates since the elastic scatterers do not contribute to energy variations but do participate in the velocity and population changes (when inter-subband scatterings take place).

The rate equation approach has the advantage of its (relative) simplicity. It raises however questions like finding the meaning of $f_{n\vec{k}}$ or why should one average over the initial and final states. It should work fine when the systems we deal with are "moderately quantum", meaning that their energy spectra display clear quantum fingerprints (like discrete energy levels) but where the coupling to the surrounding/thermostats or between the particles is sufficiently efficient to wash out the quantum evolution (survival probability, etc.) and replaces it by that of distribution functions. The rate equations poorly handle early time evolutions; by early we mean the evolution that takes place over times shorter than the typical time scale of the inelastic interactions (phonons, carrier-carrier scattering). At short time, the quantum evolution prevails. At long time, the multiple interactions have washed out many quantum details and the distribution function approach becomes relevant. To give an example, a typical electron–optical phonon interaction occurs on a subpicosecond time scale. Hence, for $t < 10^{-1}$ ps, a quantum description of the evolution due to static scatterers should prevail. For t larger than few picoseconds, rate equations should well describe the system evolution including elastic and inelastic scatterers. A deeper insight in the time evolution of an open system is obtained if one uses the density matrix approach to the evolution or the Keldysh Green function formalism. In both these approaches, a complete formulation of the effect of a random potential acting on an open system is fully analysed, albeit in an extremely complicated way [43].

II.3.2. Rate equations with elastic and inelastic processes

Assuming that the coupling between electrons and impurities and phonons is weak the transition rates are given in the long time limit by the Fermi golden rule. This is called the Born approximation.

- For elastic scattering one finds:

$$W^{\text{static}}_{n\vec{k}\to n'\vec{k}'} = \frac{2\pi}{\hbar}|\langle n\vec{k}|V_{\text{def}}|n'\vec{k}'\rangle|^2\delta(\varepsilon_{n\vec{k}} - \varepsilon_{n'\vec{k}'}) \qquad (\text{II.3.32})$$

Suppose we concentrate on intra-subband scattering. Equation (II.3.24) becomes:

$$\frac{dN_n^{\text{intra}}}{dt} = -2\sum_{\vec{k},\vec{k}'} W^{\text{static}}_{n\vec{k}\to n\vec{k}'}(f_{n\vec{k}} - f_{n\vec{k}'})$$

$$= -\frac{4\pi}{\hbar}\sum_{\vec{k},\vec{k}'}|\langle n\vec{k}|V_{\text{def}}|n\vec{k}'\rangle|^2\delta(\varepsilon_{n\vec{k}} - \varepsilon_{n\vec{k}'})(f_{n\vec{k}} - f_{n\vec{k}'})$$

$$(\text{II.3.33})$$

and by exchanging $\vec{k} \leftrightarrow \vec{k}'$ we find that the intra-subband transitions do not affect the population. Thus, Eq. (II.3.24) can be rewritten

$$\frac{dN_n}{dt} = -\frac{4\pi}{\hbar}\sum_{\vec{k},\vec{k}',n'\neq n}|\langle n\vec{k}|V_{\text{def}}|n'\vec{k}'\rangle|^2\delta(\varepsilon_{n\vec{k}} - \varepsilon_{n'\vec{k}'})(f_{n\vec{k}} - f_{n'\vec{k}'})$$

$$(\text{II.3.34})$$

for elastic scattering. Moreover, if the distribution functions only depend on the energy of the carriers (like e.g., the equilibrium ones) in the same way (i.e., with the same temperature if they are Fermi–Dirac distributions) there is no change on the subband population induced by elastic scattering. Note that in an operating device, because of the bias, there is a preferred direction for the carrier

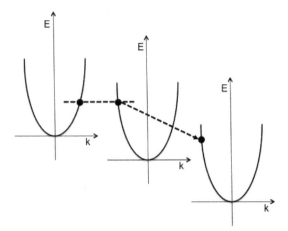

Figure II.3.1. Elastic scattering between 2 subbands in a biased heterostructure (horizontal dashed line). Before exchanges can balance the populations an inelastic scattering depletes the second subband (oblique dashed line). If definable, the temperature in the second subband is likely be smaller than in the first subband.

motion: the upper subbands lose populations to the benefit of the lower ones and even elastic scatterings contribute to the depopulation of the upper subbands: the very efficient emptying of the lower states to even lower states prevents a refilling of the initial subband (see Fig. II.3.1). This amounts to neglecting the $f_{n'\vec{k'}}$ in Eq. (II.3.34).

When we look at the expression for the total velocity of the electron gas (Eqs. (II.3.30) and (II.3.31)), we find that there is no average velocity at thermal equilibrium for elastic scatterers. It is only if one creates an anisotropy in the equilibrium distribution function that a finite velocity can show up. The same remark as done above for the population applies to the average velocity, namely that the biasing of the structure implies a different population for the various subbands and, in fine, a non-zero velocity.

- For the electron–phonon interaction we shall assume that the phonons remain at thermal equilibrium[1] described by a

---

[1] This is almost invariably true, except for the zone centre Longitudinal Optical phonons in GaAs where the phonon lifetime is very long (several picoseconds). This implies a lack of thermalisation for these phonons if they are created too fast, as happens due to the electronic relaxation. The persistence of "hot phonons" in turn impedes the electronic relaxation.

Bose–Einstein distribution function: for a phonon with wavevector $\vec{Q}$ and energy $\hbar\omega_{\vec{Q}}$ the average occupation of this phonon mode is:

$$n_{\text{BE}}(\omega_{\vec{Q}}) = \frac{1}{\exp(\beta\hbar\omega_{\vec{Q}}) - 1} \tag{II.3.35}$$

where $\beta = (k_B T)^{-1}$, k_B is the Boltzmann constant and T is the lattice temperature. The high temperature limit ($\hbar\omega_{\vec{Q}} \ll k_B T$) corresponds to a large phonon population for this mode: $n_{\vec{Q}} \approx \frac{k_B T}{\hbar\omega_{\vec{Q}}} \gg 1$. In the opposite limit, there are few phonons: $n_{\vec{Q}} \approx e^{-\beta\hbar\omega_{\vec{Q}}} \ll 1$. This low temperature limit applies in particular to Longitudinal Optical (LO) phonons in III–V compounds: even at $T = 300$ K ($k_B T \approx 25$ meV), the number of thermally activated LO phonons is smaller than 1 while there are many acoustical phonons (a typical acoustical phonon energy is 1 meV).

The electron–phonon interaction can be cast in the general form:

$$H_{\text{e–ph}} = \sum_{\vec{Q}} u_\alpha(\vec{Q})e^{-i\vec{Q}\cdot\vec{r}}a^\dagger_{\alpha\vec{Q}} + u^*_\alpha(\vec{Q})e^{i\vec{Q}\cdot\vec{r}}a_{\alpha\vec{Q}} \tag{II.3.36}$$

where a given phonon mode α (longitudinal optical, transverse acoustical, and so on) is taken into account. $u_\alpha(\vec{Q})$ is the coupling strength between the electron and the phonon modes α, $a^\dagger_{\alpha\vec{Q}}$, $a_{\alpha\vec{Q}}$ are the creation and annihilation operators of a phonon in the mode α with a wavevector $\vec{Q}$. The transition rate for emission and absorption of phonons are:

$$W^{\text{emiss}}_{n\vec{k}\to n'\vec{k'}} = \frac{2\pi}{\hbar}\sum_{\vec{Q}}\left[1 + n_{\text{BE}}(\omega_{\vec{Q}})\right]|\langle n\vec{k}|e^{-i\vec{Q}\cdot\vec{r}}|n'\vec{k'}\rangle|^2|u_\alpha(\vec{Q})|^2$$
$$\times\,\delta(\varepsilon_{n'\vec{k'}} - \varepsilon_{n\vec{k}} + \hbar\omega_{\alpha\vec{Q}}) \tag{II.3.37}$$

$$W^{\text{abs}}_{n\vec{k}\to n'\vec{k'}} = \frac{2\pi}{\hbar}\sum_{\vec{Q}} n_{\text{BE}}(\omega_{\vec{Q}})|\langle n\vec{k}|e^{i\vec{Q}\cdot\vec{r}}|n'\vec{k'}\rangle|^2|u^*_\alpha(\vec{Q})|^2$$
$$\times\,\delta(\varepsilon_{n'\vec{k'}} - \varepsilon_{n\vec{k}} - \hbar\omega_{\alpha\vec{Q}}) \tag{II.3.38}$$

Thus, if we consider a given electronic transition $n\vec{k} \to n'\vec{k'}$ and a given phonon mode α with a given wavevector $\vec{Q}$, we find:

$$\frac{W^{\text{emiss}}_{n\vec{k}\to n'\vec{k'}}(\vec{Q})}{W^{\text{abs}}_{n'\vec{k'}\to n\vec{k}}(\vec{Q})} = \frac{1 + n_{\text{BE}}(\vec{Q})}{n_{\text{BE}}(\vec{Q})} = e^{\beta\hbar\omega_{\alpha\vec{Q}}} \tag{II.3.39}$$

We showed previously that the static scatterers do not affect the energy loss rate. Also, if we look at the electron–phonon contributions to the energy loss rate, we find that the system will show no evolution ($\frac{d\langle E \rangle}{dt} = 0$) if:

$$f_{n\vec{k}} = \frac{1}{1 + e^{\beta(\varepsilon_{n\vec{k}} - \mu)}} \qquad (\text{II.3.40})$$

where μ is the electron chemical potential. The equilibrium phonons have brought the electrons to an equilibrium characterised by an electronic temperature that is the same as the lattice temperature. In actual devices, it may happen that the electron and phonon populations quickly equilibrate within themselves but with different temperatures. The system then reaches a stationary solution that is not thermal equilibrium. Most often, the electrons are warmer/hotter than the phonons, which requires that an external source supplies this extra energy. If one stops the energy supply to the electrons (e.g., by suppressing the Joule heating of the electron gas), a further evolution will ultimately bring the two systems to the same temperature. Close enough from the equilibrium, after linearising the energy loss rate equations, one finds that the electronic temperature relaxes exponentially in time to the lattice temperature (see Exercise 49).

Extensive experimental and theoretical studies of the energy loss rates of electrons and holes quasi-2D gases have been undertaken in semiconductor heterostructures. Based on the only assumption that the Fermi golden rule applies to describe the electron–phonon scattering, a quantitative agreement between modelling and experiments has been demonstrated provided that hot phonon effects are taken into account [44].

II.3.3.   Analysis of the relaxation times in rate equations

From now on, we concentrate on the level lifetime and the population relaxation time and attempts to evaluate their characteristic times. However, we shall occasionally make comparison between the population relaxation times and the velocity or energy relaxation time.

In the Fermi golden rule expression, we always need to evaluate matrix elements of the form:

$$\langle n\vec{k}|e^{i\vec{q}\cdot\vec{\rho}}g_{\vec{q}}(z-z_i)|n'\vec{k'}\rangle \quad \text{or} \quad \langle n\vec{k}|e^{i\vec{Q}\cdot\vec{\rho}}e^{iQ_z z}|n'\vec{k'}\rangle \qquad \text{(II.3.41)}$$

for impurity and phonon scattering, respectively. These two matrix elements are respectively equal to:

$$\langle n|g_{\vec{q}}(z-z_i)|n'\rangle\delta_{\vec{k},\vec{k'}+\vec{q}} \quad \text{and} \quad \langle n|e^{iQ_z z}|n'\rangle\delta_{\vec{k},\vec{k'}+\vec{Q}} \qquad \text{(II.3.42)}$$

II.3.3.1. Impurity form factor

Let us discuss the impurity form factor for ionised impurities:

$$g_{n,n'}(q,z_i) = \langle n|g_{\vec{q}}(z-z_i)|n'\rangle = \int dz \chi_n(z)\chi_{n'}(z)e^{-q|z-z_i|} \qquad (\text{II.3.43})$$

where χ_n, $\chi_{n'}$ have been chosen real.

For $n = n'$ (intra-subband scattering), $g_{nn}(q,z_i)$ is a strictly decreasing function of q. At $q = 0$, $g_{nn}(0,z_i) = 1$. On the other hand for $n \neq n'$, $g_{nn'}(0,z_i) = 0$. More precisely when $q \to 0$:

$$g_{nn'}(q\approx 0,z_i) \approx -q\int dz\chi_n(z)\chi_{n'}(z)|z-z_i| \qquad (\text{II.3.44})$$

In the large q limit there is:

$$\exp(-q|z-z_i|) \approx \frac{2}{q}\delta(z-z_i) \Rightarrow g_{nn'}(q\to\infty,z_i)$$

$$\approx \frac{2}{q}\chi_n(z_i)\chi_{n'}(z_i) \qquad (\text{II.3.45})$$

Since $g_{nn'}(q,z_i)$ will have to be latter integrated to compute the population (and other) relaxation times, it is convenient to find a smooth function of q that interpolates $g_{nn'}(q,z_i)$. In order to approximate the $g_{nn'}$'s we can attempt:

$$g_{nn}(q,z_i) = \frac{1}{1+\alpha q}; \quad \frac{1}{\alpha} = 2\chi_n^2(z_i)$$

$$g_{nn}(q,z_i) = \frac{1+bq}{1+dq+eq^2} \qquad (\text{II.3.46})$$

The second expression is more precise than the first one, in particular close to $q = 0$ which is a region that contributes mostly to the relaxation frequencies. The second form of g_{nn} requires one numerical computation for a certain q_0. Let us call $g_0 = g(q_0, z_i)$. Then the unknowns b, d and e are determined through:

$$g_0 = \frac{1 + bq_0}{1 + dq_0 + eq_0^2}; \quad b = 2e\chi_n^2(z_i); \quad d = b + \int dz |z - z_i| \chi_n^2(z)$$

$$(\text{II.3.47})$$

Along the same line one can approximate $g_{nn'}(q, z_i)$ by the rational fraction:

$$g_{nn'}(q, z_i) = \frac{aq}{1 + bq + cq^2} \qquad (\text{II.3.48})$$

$$a = -\int dz |z - z_i| \chi_n(z) \chi_{n'}(z); \quad \frac{a}{c} = 2\chi_n(z_i)\chi_{n'}(z_i) \qquad (\text{II.3.49})$$

$$g_0 = g_{nn'}(q_0, z_i) = \frac{aq_0}{1 + bq_0 + cq_0^2} \qquad (\text{II.3.50})$$

We show in Fig. II.3.2 a comparison between the numerically calculated $g_{nn}(q, z_i)$ and its approximants (first and second expression) in the case of a single GaAs/Al$_{0.25}$Ga$_{0.75}$As quantum well of thickness 15 nm. Figure II.3.3 displays a similar calculation for $g_{nn'}(q, z_i)$ in the same structure for $n = 1$ and $n' = 3$.

It is worth pointing out the important role played by the location of the doping plane. We see that the effect of the coulombic scattering can be somewhat controlled by a careful placement of the dopants. For instance, putting the dopants at a node of χ_n suppresses the $1/q$ variation of $g_{nn}(q, z_i)$ and $g_{nn'}(q, z_i)$ at large q and replaces it by a faster decay. This feature is illustrated in Fig. II.3.4 where we show $g_{11}(q, z_i)$ for the structure used in Figs. II.3.2 and II.3.3 for several value of z_i.

A spectacular realisation of this property of a strong dependence of velocity scattering rate versus the impurity location is the modulation doping [45]. For a single GaAs/(Ga,Al)As heterojunction the low temperature mobility of the 2D gas located at the interface between GaAs and (Ga,Al)As has been increased to ≈ 300 m^2 V^{-1} s^{-1} while the low temperature mobility of bulk GaAs is only few m^2 V^{-1} s^{-1}. In the case of optical properties of multi-heterojunctions (quantum wells, superlattices), we shall see that the whole absorption lineshape sensitively depends upon the location of the dopant plane.

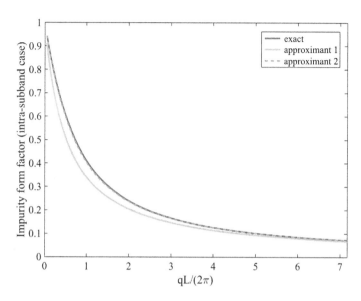

Figure II.3.2. Comparison between the numerically calculated $g_{11}(q, z_i)$ and its approximants (first and second expression) in the case of a single $GaAs/Al_{0.25}Ga_{0.75}As$ quantum well of thickness $L = 15$ nm. The impurity location is at the centre of the quantum well ($z_i = L/2$).

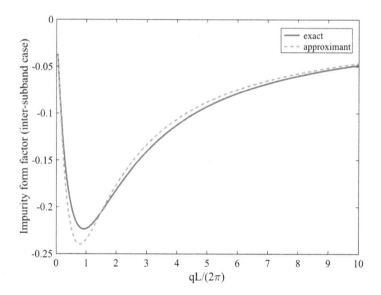

Figure II.3.3. Comparison between the numerically calculated $g_{13}(q, z_i)$ and its approximant in the case of a single $GaAs/Al_{0.25}Ga_{0.75}As$ quantum well of thickness $L = 15$ nm. The impurity location is at the centre of the quantum well ($z_i = L/2$).

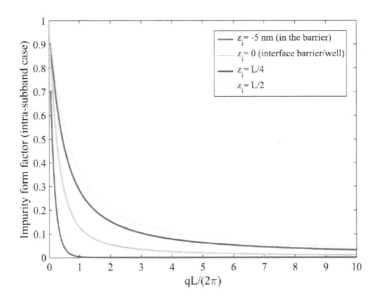

Figure II.3.4.   Impurity form factor $g_{11}(q, z_i)$ is plotted against $qL/(2\pi)$ for various locations (z_i) of impurities in a single GaAs/Al$_{0.25}$Ga$_{0.75}$As quantum well of thickness $L = 15$ nm.

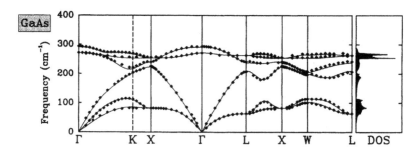

Figure II.3.5.   Calculated phonon dispersions and densities of state for GaAs by *ab initio* method. The dots denote the experimental data.

Source: Giannozzi *et al.* [46].

II.3.3.2.   Phonon form factors and transition rates

Since the unit cells of bulk III–V and II–VI materials have two atoms (e.g., Ga and As for GaAs), the phonons spectrum comprises acoustical and optical branches (see Fig. II.3.5). Acoustical branches extrapolate to zero energy when $\vec{Q}$ vanishes and display dispersion relations that are linear versus the modulus of the phonon wavevector $\vec{Q}$. The optical branches extrapolate to a finite energy at vanishing $\vec{Q}$. Acoustical phonons correspond to in-phase oscillations of the two atoms in the unit cell near $Q = 0$ while the optical phonons correspond to the two atoms of the unit cell vibrating in phase opposition. Since in III–V and II–VI materials the two atoms of the unit cell are different and the bounds between atoms are slightly polar, this means that the LO vibrations create a macroscopic electric field that couples very efficiently to the electrons.

In case of heterostructures, there are phonon modes that are "bulk-like" and others that can be termed "confined phonon modes" or "interface" modes. Since we deal with heterostructures that comprise thousands to billions of unit cells, we shall in this introductory book retain the bulk-like description for the phonons. More information on phonons in nanostructures can be found in [47]. The electron–phonon form factor depends on which particular phonon branch is considered. When energy allowed, the most effective electron–phonon scattering is the Fröhlich coupling between the electrons and the LO phonon modes in polar samples (i.e., III–V or II–VI materials). The interaction with acoustical phonons is either the deformation potential (LA modes) or the piezo-electric coupling (for details see [37,48]). For Fröhlich and deformation potential interactions, the potentials $u_\alpha(\vec{Q})$ are, respectively, equal to:

$$u_{\text{Fröhlich}}(\vec{Q}) = -i\frac{C_F}{Q}; \quad C_F = e\sqrt{\frac{\hbar\omega_{\text{LO}}}{2\Omega\varepsilon_0}\left(\frac{1}{\varepsilon_r(\infty)} - \frac{1}{\varepsilon_r(0)}\right)}$$

$$u_{\text{DP}}(\vec{Q}) = D_c\sqrt{\frac{\hbar Q}{2\Omega\rho c_s}} \tag{II.3.51}$$

where Ω is the volume of the crystal, D_c the deformation potential for the conduction band, ε_0 is the vacuum dielectric permittivity (MKS units are used), $\varepsilon_r(\infty)$ and $\varepsilon_r(0)$ are the high frequency and zero frequency relative dielectric constants respectively, ρ is the mass density and c_s the sound velocity assumed to be isotropic. The LO phonons have been assumed dispersionless. Typical figures for GaAs are: $\rho = 5320 \text{ kg m}^{-3}$, $c_s = 5000 \text{ m s}^{-1}$, $D_c = -7.23 \text{ eV}$, $\varepsilon_r(0) = 12.9$,

$\varepsilon_r(\infty) = 10.89$, $\hbar\omega_{LO} = 36$ meV. In Eq. (II.3.51), $\vec{Q}$ is a 3D vector. A property common to the Fröhlich and deformation potential interactions is the small and large Q_z dependences of the z form factor $\langle n|e^{-iQ_z z}|n'\rangle$. Namely:

$$\langle n|e^{-iQ_z z}|n'\rangle \approx \delta_{nn'} \quad \text{when } Q_z \to 0 \qquad (\text{II.3.52})$$

$$\langle n|e^{-iQ_z z}|n'\rangle \approx \frac{1}{|Q_z|} \quad \text{when } Q_z \to \infty \qquad (\text{II.3.53})$$

In addition, the particular shape of the Fröhlich interaction allows an interesting rewriting of the Fermi golden rule. Remember that the LO phonons are assumed dispersionless: $\omega_{ph}(\vec{Q}) = \omega_{LO}$. Hence, the delta function in the Fermi golden rule is Q-independent, as well as the Bose–Einstein occupation functions. Thus, for instance for the scattering rate corresponding to the emission we get:

$$W^{\text{emiss LO}}_{n\vec{k}\to n'\vec{k'}} = \frac{2\pi}{\hbar}\left[1 + n_{\text{BE}}(\omega_{LO})\right]\delta(\varepsilon_{n\vec{k}} - \varepsilon_{n'\vec{k'}} - \hbar\omega_{LO})C_F^2$$

$$\times \frac{L_z}{2\pi}\int_{-\infty}^{+\infty} dQ_z \frac{\langle n|e^{-iQ_z z}|n'\rangle\langle n'|e^{iQ_z z}|n\rangle}{Q_z^2 + (\vec{k} - \vec{k'})^2}$$

$$(\text{II.3.54})$$

where L_z is the macroscopic length along the growth direction. We can get rid of the integral over Q_z by writing explicitly the matrix element. This results in:

$$W^{\text{emiss LO}}_{n\vec{k}\to n'\vec{k'}} = \frac{\pi}{\hbar}\left[1 + n_{\text{BE}}(\omega_{LO})\right]\delta(\varepsilon_{n\vec{k}} - \varepsilon_{n'\vec{k'}} - \hbar\omega_{LO})C_F^2$$

$$\times \frac{L_z}{|\vec{k} - \vec{k'}|}I_{nn'}(|\vec{k} - \vec{k'}|) \qquad (\text{II.3.55})$$

$$I_{nn'}(|\vec{k} - \vec{k'}|) = \iint dz dz' \chi_n^*(z)\chi_{n'}(z)\chi_n(z')\chi_{n'}^*(z')e^{-|\vec{k}-\vec{k'}||z-z'|}$$

$$(\text{II.3.56})$$

Note that the length L_z actually disappears from the transition rate because C_F^2 is proportional to $1/L_z$. In a very similar way we would get:

$$W^{\text{abs LO}}_{n\vec{k}\to n'\vec{k'}} = \frac{\pi}{\hbar} n_{\text{BE}}(\omega_{\text{LO}})\delta(\varepsilon_{n\vec{k}} - \varepsilon_{n'\vec{k'}} + \hbar\omega_{\text{LO}})$$

$$\times C_{\text{F}}^2 \frac{L_z}{|\vec{k} - \vec{k'}|} I_{nn'}(|\vec{k} - \vec{k'}|) \qquad (\text{II}.3.57)$$

We can make the same remark for $I_{nn'}$ as we made for the impurity form factor regarding the asymptotic behaviours:

$$I_{nn'}(x=0) = \delta_{nn'}; \quad I_{nn'}(x\to\infty) \approx \frac{2}{|x|}\int_{-\infty}^{+\infty} dz |\chi_n(z)\chi_{n'}(z)|^2$$

$$(\text{II}.3.58)$$

and again find convenient approximations of $I_{nn'}$ (see Eqs. (II.3.46) and (II.3.47)). We pointed out in Eq. (II.3.39) that for a given initial state $|n\vec{k}\rangle$ the ratio between the transition rates for emission and absorption (disregarding any population effect for the initial and final states) is $\frac{W^{\text{emiss LO}}_{n\vec{k}\to n'\vec{k'}}}{W^{\text{abs LO}}_{n\vec{k}\to n'\vec{k'}}} = e^{\beta\hbar\omega_{\text{LO}}}$. Thus, the absorption of phonons is most of the time negligible for the level lifetime when no attention has been paid to the availability for the final state (empty) and the initial state (occupied). As we shall see, these occupation factors reduce the difference between emission and absorption (see Fig. II.3.6). As for the interaction with Longitudinal Acoustical (LA) phonons by the deformation potential, we find also an analytical expression for the transition rates if one takes isotropic acoustical phonon dispersions: $\omega_{\text{LA}}(\vec{Q}) = c_s Q$. Let us define Q_0 as the z component of the

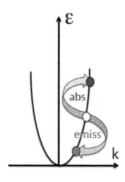

Figure II.3.6.   Absorption and emission of one LO phonon in an intraband transition.

phonon wavevector that ensures energy conservation of the total electron+phonon system, given that the in-plane components are related to the initial and final electron wavevectors:

$$Q_0 = \sqrt{\left(\frac{\varepsilon_{n\vec{k}} - \varepsilon_{n'\vec{k'}}}{\hbar c_s}\right)^2 - (\vec{k} - \vec{k'})^2} \qquad \text{(II.3.59)}$$

Then, the emission rate of LA phonons is equal to:

$$W_{n\vec{k}\to n'\vec{k'}}^{\text{acous emiss}} = \frac{D_c^2}{S\rho\hbar^3 c_s^4 Q_0}[1 + n_{\text{BE}}(c_s Q_0)](\varepsilon_{n\vec{k}} - \varepsilon_{n'\vec{k'}})^2 |\langle n|e^{iQ_0 z}|n'\rangle|^2$$

$$\text{(II.3.60)}$$

Similarly, we find the absorption rate of LA phonons equal to:

$$W_{n\vec{k}\to n'\vec{k'}}^{\text{acous abs}} = \frac{D_c^2}{S\rho\hbar^3 c_s^4 Q_0} n_{\text{BE}}(c_s Q_0)(\varepsilon_{n\vec{k}} - \varepsilon_{n'\vec{k'}})^2 |\langle n|e^{iQ_0 z}|n'\rangle|^2$$

$$\text{(II.3.61)}$$

We note that an almost equality between the absorption and emission rates shows up at relatively low temperature, say 80 K or so. This is because the number of "relevant" acoustical phonons is very quickly $\gg 1$. In this respect, there is a marked contrast between the acoustical and optical phonon scatterings.

II.3.4. Consequence of the Born approximation on the additivity of scattering frequencies

It has to be realised that using the Born approximation automatically implies that (1) the scattering frequencies due to different static scatterers add and (2) that the same is true if we consider adding the electron–phonon interaction to static scatterers.

To prove (1), let us write the defect Hamiltonian as a sum:

$$V_{\text{def}}(\vec{r}) = V_{\text{def}}^{(1)}(\vec{r}) + V_{\text{def}}^{(2)}(\vec{r})$$

$$= \sum_{\vec{\rho}_{i1}, z_{i1}} V_{\text{def}}^{(1)}(\vec{\rho} - \vec{\rho}_{i1}, z - z_{i1}) + \sum_{\vec{\rho}_{i2}, z_{i2}} V_{\text{def}}^{(2)}(\vec{\rho} - \vec{\rho}_{i2}, z - z_{i2})$$

$$\text{(II.3.62)}$$

Thus, the matrix element $\langle n\vec{k}|V_{\text{def}}(\vec{r})|n'\vec{k'}\rangle$ is equal to:

$$\langle n\vec{k}|V_{\text{def}}(\vec{r})|n'\vec{k'}\rangle$$

$$= \sum_{z_{i1}}\langle n\vec{k}|V_{\text{def}}^{(1)}(\vec{\rho}, z - z_{i1})|n'\vec{k'}\rangle \sum_{\vec{\rho}_{i1}}\exp[i(\vec{k'} - \vec{k}) \cdot \vec{\rho}_{i1}]$$

$$+ \sum_{z_{i2}}\langle n\vec{k}|V_{\text{def}}^{(2)}(\vec{\rho}, z - z_{i2})|n'\vec{k'}\rangle \sum_{\vec{\rho}_{i2}}\exp[i(\vec{k'} - \vec{k}) \cdot \vec{\rho}_{i2}]$$

$$(\text{II.3.63})$$

It is then clear that when we shall square the modulus of this matrix element and average over the defect positions, we shall get the scattering frequency due to V_{def} equal to the sum of the scattering frequencies when either the defects 1 or the defects 2 are acting only plus a crossed term. It is easy to see that this crossed term will involve the real part of

$$\left\langle \sum_{\vec{\rho}_{i1}}\exp\left[i(\vec{k'} - \vec{k}) \cdot (\vec{\rho}_{i1} - \vec{\rho}_{i2})\right]\right\rangle_{\text{aver}} \qquad (\text{II.3.64})$$

If the scatterers (1) and (2) are uncorrelated, the previous sum vanishes after averaging over the impurity/defects locations. So, the scattering by interface defects and that due to coulombic impurities will add to the extent that the interface defect positions and that of impurities are statistically uncorrelated. As a counter-example, one may imagine that the impurities segregate at the interface and stay preferentially (because of strain or whatever) near interface defects. Then, rule (1) would not apply because the vector $\vec{\rho}_{i1} - \vec{\rho}_{i2}$ would always remain close to a certain value and in no case would cover the whole plane with an equi-probability.

To show that the proposal (2) is correct, we write:

$$\langle |\langle n\vec{k}|V_{\text{def}}(\vec{r}) + H_{\text{e-ph}}|n'\vec{k'}\rangle|^2\rangle_{\text{aver}}$$

$$= \langle |\langle n\vec{k}|V_{\text{def}}(\vec{r})|n'\vec{k'}\rangle|^2\rangle_{\text{aver}}$$

$$+ \langle |\langle n\vec{k}|H_{\text{e-ph}}|n'\vec{k'}\rangle|^2\rangle_{\text{aver}} + A + A^* \qquad (\text{II.3.65})$$

$$A = \langle |\langle n\vec{k}|V_{\text{def}}(\vec{r})|n'\vec{k'}\rangle\langle n'\vec{k'}|H_{\text{e-ph}}|n\vec{k}\rangle\rangle_{\text{aver}} \qquad (\text{II.3.66})$$

Then, the crossed terms disappear for two reasons: on the one hand, the average over the random positions of the impurities leads to a cancellation of A. Simultaneously H_{e-ph} can only connect states whose phonon populations differ by one unit. However, the V_{def} matrix elements are non-zero only if the phonon populations in the initial and final states are the same. Therefore, A has to vanish and proposal (2) is established.

Chapter II.4

Screening at the Semi-classical Approximation

A gas of mobile electrons (ions) at thermal equilibrium subjected to an external potential energy $V_{\text{ext}}(\vec{r}) \equiv -e\varphi_{\text{ext}}(\vec{r})$ deforms itself in order to minimise its total energy (for ions $-e$ should be changed in e_{ion}). For instance, a ionised donor creates a positive electrostatic potential. It is plausible (and true) that the electrons will be attracted by the ionised donor, resulting into an accumulation of negative mobile charges around the impurity compared to the uniform electron density that prevails in the absence of donor. The spatial rearrangement of the mobile carriers is called screening. The deformation induces a charge density $-en_{\text{ind}}(\vec{r})$ that creates, from Poisson equation, an induced electrostatic potential energy $-e\varphi_{\text{ind}}(\vec{r})$. This adds to the external potential energy $-e\varphi_{\text{ext}}(\vec{r})$, leading in turn to another deformation of the electron density. Ultimately, there is a total potential energy $-e\varphi_{\text{tot}}(\vec{r})$ and the central question is to find the relationship between $\varphi_{\text{ext}}(\vec{r})$ and $\varphi_{\text{tot}}(\vec{r})$. Often, the induced charge density (and therefore the induced electrostatic potential) is linearised with respect to the external potential energy.

Screening effects are important because they alter the scattering efficiency of the defects: if we think about scattering of mobile electrons by defects $\sum_{\vec{\rho}_i, z_i} V_{\text{def}}(\vec{\rho} - \vec{\rho}_i, z - z_i)$ the V_{def} are the total ones, i.e., the external plus the induced electrostatic potentials. An early attempt to handle the screening effects is the Debye–Hückel model of "strong" electrolytes. It was based on classical statistical mechanics. Screening effects in metals has been handled by a variety of techniques from the Thomas–Fermi model (semi-classical approximation) to many-body formalism. There has been a large amount of work devoted to the screening effects in quasi-2D electron gases (see e.g., [12]).

In the following, we consider the semi-classical approach for the screening of an external potential by a 2D gas under the condition that all the electrostatic potentials vary very slowly with position. This procedure is the equivalent of the Debye–Hückel model of the screening in electrolytes but for a quasi-2D situation. In a Hartree-like treatment, we want to solve the effective Hamiltonian:

$$\left(-\frac{\hbar^2}{2m^*}\frac{\partial^2}{\partial z^2} - \frac{\hbar^2 \nabla_2^2}{2m^*} - e\varphi_{\mathrm{sc}}(z) - e\varphi_{\mathrm{tot}}(\vec{r}) \right) F_\nu(\vec{r}) = \varepsilon_\nu F_\nu(\vec{r})$$

(II.4.1)

where $\varphi_{\mathrm{sc}}(z)$ is the [band bending + band offset] potential of the ideal 2D gas and $\varphi_{\mathrm{tot}}(\vec{r})$ is the total electrostatic potential that includes the external part and the reaction of the 2D gas to this external part.

II.4.1.   Case of a single subband occupation

We first consider a single subband (Electric Quantum Limit) labelled E_1 and write:

$$F_\nu(\vec{r}) = \chi_1(z)g_\nu(\vec{\rho}); \quad \vec{\rho} = (x, y)$$

(II.4.2)

The g_ν fulfils the effective 2D equation:

$$\left[-\frac{\hbar^2 \nabla_2^2}{2m^*} - e\langle\varphi_{\mathrm{tot}}\rangle_{11}(\vec{\rho}) \right] g_\nu(\vec{\rho}) = (\varepsilon_\nu - E_1)g_\nu(\vec{\rho})$$

(II.4.3)

$$\langle\varphi_{\mathrm{tot}}\rangle_{11}(\vec{\rho}) = \int_{-\infty}^{+\infty} dz\chi_1^2(z)\varphi_{\mathrm{tot}}(\vec{r})$$

(II.4.4)

In the quasi-classical approximation, the potential energy is assumed to vary very slowly with position, in such a way that around each point $\vec{\rho}$ it is sensible to assume that, apart a shift in its energy zero due to the electrostatic potential energy, the particle is free to move.

Hence, the quasi-classical eigenvalues are:

$$\varepsilon_\nu = E_1 - e\langle\varphi_{\text{tot}}\rangle_{11}(\vec{\rho}) + \frac{\hbar^2 k^2}{2m^*} \tag{II.4.5}$$

Assuming thermal equilibrium at temperature T, we can immediately compute the 2D electron density at the point $\vec{\rho}$:

$$n_2(\vec{\rho}) = -\frac{2e}{S} \sum_{\vec{k}} \frac{1}{1 + \exp\left[\beta\left(E_1 - e\langle\varphi_{\text{tot}}\rangle_{11}(\vec{\rho}) + \frac{\hbar^2 k^2}{2m^*} - \mu\right)\right]}$$

$$= -e\frac{m^* k_B T}{\pi\hbar^2} \ln(1 + e^{\beta[\mu + e\langle\varphi_{\text{tot}}\rangle_{11}(\vec{\rho}) - E_1]}) \tag{II.4.6}$$

Hence, the 3D charge density at point $(\vec{\rho}, z)$ is $n_3(\vec{r}) = n_2(\vec{\rho})\chi_1^2(z)$. The 3D induced charge density δn_{ind} is just the difference of the 3D charge densities with and without $\langle\varphi_{\text{tot}}\rangle_{11}$. Hence:

$$\delta n_{\text{ind}}(\vec{r}) = -e\chi_1^2(z)\frac{m^* k_B T}{\pi\hbar^2} \ln\left(\frac{1 + e^{\beta[\mu + e\langle\varphi_{\text{tot}}\rangle_{11}(\vec{\rho}) - E_1]}}{1 + e^{\beta(\mu - E_1)}}\right)$$

$$= \chi_1^2(z)\delta n_{2,\text{ind}}(\vec{\rho}) \tag{II.4.7}$$

This induced charge density in turn creates an induced electrostatic potential:

$$\varphi_{\text{ind}}(\vec{r}) = \int d^3 r' \frac{\delta n_{\text{ind}}(\vec{r'})}{4\pi\varepsilon_0\varepsilon_r|\vec{r} - \vec{r'}|}$$

$$= \frac{1}{2\varepsilon_0\varepsilon_r S} \sum_{\vec{Q}} \frac{e^{i\vec{Q}\cdot\vec{\rho}}}{Q} \int dz' e^{-Q|z-z'|}\chi_1^2(z')$$

$$\times \int d^2\rho' e^{-i\vec{Q}\cdot\vec{\rho'}}\delta n_{2,\text{ind}}(\vec{\rho'}) \tag{II.4.8}$$

We can average the 3D induced potential over the E_1 charge distribution. We obtain:

$$\langle\varphi_{\text{ind}}\rangle_{11}(\vec{\rho}) = \int_{-\infty}^{+\infty} dz\chi_1^2(z)\varphi_{\text{ind}}(\vec{r})$$

$$= \frac{1}{2\varepsilon_0\varepsilon_r S} \sum_{\vec{Q}} \frac{e^{i\vec{Q}\cdot\vec{\rho}}}{Q} g_s^{11}(Q) \int d^2\rho' e^{-i\vec{Q}\cdot\vec{\rho'}}\delta n_{2,\text{ind}}(\vec{\rho})$$

$$\tag{II.4.9}$$

where $g_s^{11}(Q)$ is the screening form factor:

$$g_s^{11}(Q) = \iint dz dz' \chi_1^2(z) \chi_1^2(z') e^{-Q|z-z'|} \qquad \text{(II.4.10)}$$

We now linearise the induced charge density with respect to $\langle \varphi_{\text{tot}} \rangle_{11}$. We find:

$$\delta n_{2,\text{ind}}(\vec{\rho}) \approx -\frac{e^2 m^*}{\pi \hbar^2} \frac{e^{\beta(\mu-E_1)} \langle \varphi_{\text{tot}} \rangle_{11}(\vec{\rho})}{1 + e^{\beta(\mu-E_1)}} \qquad \text{(II.4.11)}$$

Let us define the 2D Fourier component of the induced and total electrostatic potentials:

$$\langle \varphi_{\text{ind}} \rangle_{11}(\vec{Q}) = \frac{1}{S} \int d^2\rho \langle \varphi_{\text{ind}} \rangle_{11}(\vec{\rho}) e^{-i\vec{Q}\cdot\vec{\rho}} \qquad \text{(II.4.12)}$$

$$\langle \varphi_{\text{tot}} \rangle_{11}(\vec{Q}) = \frac{1}{S} \int d^2\rho \langle \varphi_{\text{tot}} \rangle_{11}(\vec{\rho}) e^{-i\vec{Q}\cdot\vec{\rho}} \qquad \text{(II.4.13)}$$

We find readily:

$$\langle \varphi_{\text{ind}} \rangle_{11}(\vec{Q}) = -\frac{e^2 m^*}{2\varepsilon_0 \varepsilon_r \pi \hbar^2} \frac{g_s^{11}(Q)}{Q} \frac{e^{\beta(\mu-E_1)}}{1 + e^{\beta(\mu-E_1)}} \langle \varphi_{\text{tot}} \rangle_{11}(\vec{Q}) \qquad \text{(II.4.14)}$$

Hence, we obtain the Fourier component of the total 2D electrostatic potential as a function of those of the 2D external potential:

$$\langle \varphi_{\text{tot}} \rangle_{11}(\vec{Q}) = \frac{\langle \varphi_{\text{ext}} \rangle_{11}(\vec{Q})}{1 + \chi_{11}(Q)}; \quad \chi_{11}(Q) = 2\frac{g_s^{11}(Q)}{Q a_B^*} \frac{e^{\beta(\mu-E_1)}}{1 + e^{\beta(\mu-E_1)}} \qquad \text{(II.4.15)}$$

where a_B^* is the effective Bohr radius. For a degenerate electron gas ($\mu - E_1 > 3k_B T$), the arguments of the exponential are large and positive and we find:

$$\chi_{11}(Q) \approx 2\frac{g_s^{11}(Q)}{Q a_B^*} \qquad \text{(II.4.16)}$$

This expression, obtained in the long wavelength limit (or $Q \to 0$), coincides with the limit of the full screening expression at infinite Fermi wavevector [12, 34]. At elevated temperature instead ($\mu - E_1 \ll 0$), the exponentials are very small and we get:

$$\chi_{11}(Q) \approx g_s^{11}(Q)\frac{Q_{\text{Db}}}{Q}; \quad Q_{\text{Db}} = \frac{ne^2}{S k_B T \varepsilon_0 \varepsilon_r} \qquad \text{(II.4.17)}$$

At $T = 300$ K, with $n/S = 10^{11}$ cm^{-2} and $\varepsilon_r = 12.4$, we find a Debye screening that is quite effective since $1/Q_{\text{Db}} \approx 17.1$ nm.

The screening effects have important consequences in that they suppress the $Q \to 0$ divergence of the coulombic scattering: the Fourier–Bessel expansion of a 3D coulombic potential is

$$V_{\text{ext}}(\vec{r}) = -\frac{ee_i}{2\varepsilon_0 \varepsilon_r S} \sum_{\vec{Q}} \frac{e^{i\vec{Q}\cdot(\vec{\rho}-\vec{\rho}_i)}}{Q} e^{-Q|z-z_i|} \qquad (\text{II.4.18})$$

where we have considered a coulombic centre with charge e_i located at $(\vec{\rho}_i, z_i)$. Hence, for intra-subband scattering we shall have to average $V_{\text{ext}}(\vec{r})$ over the $\chi_1^2(z)$ charge distribution to finally get:

$$\langle V_{\text{tot}} \rangle_{11}(\vec{Q}) = -\frac{ee_i}{Q + QA_{11}(Q)} e^{-i\vec{Q}\cdot\vec{\rho}_i} g_{\text{imp}}^{11}(Q) \qquad (\text{II.4.19})$$

$$g_{\text{imp}}^{11}(Q) = \int dz \chi_1^2(z) e^{-Q|z-z_i|} \qquad (\text{II.4.20})$$

We readily see that $QA_{11}(Q) \to C \neq 0$ when $Q \to 0$. Thus the $Q = 0$ coulombic divergence is actually suppressed by the screening.

Suppose we take instead a short-range potential (for which stricto sensu the semi-classical limit is not applicable): $V_{\text{ext}}(\vec{r}) = V_0 a^3 \delta(\vec{r})$. Then, we find that in the long wavelength limit $(\vec{Q} \to 0)$, $\langle V_{\text{tot}} \rangle_{11}(\vec{Q})$ will vanish while $\langle V_{\text{ext}} \rangle_{11}(\vec{Q})$ had a constant limit $V_0 a^3$.

As an application of this formalism let us compute at the Born approximation in the ground subband the level lifetime and the velocity relaxation time due to coulombic scatterers located on the plane $z = z_{\text{imp}}$ assuming the initial state is $|E_1, \vec{k}\rangle$. There is:

$$\frac{\hbar}{2\pi\tau_{1\vec{k}}^{\text{scatt}}} = \sum_{\vec{k}'} |\langle E_1, \vec{k}| - e\varphi_{\text{tot}} |E_1, \vec{k}'\rangle|^2 \delta\left(\frac{\hbar^2}{2m_1^*}(k^2 - k'^2)\right)$$

$$(\text{II.4.21})$$

$$\frac{\hbar}{2\pi\tau_{1\vec{k}}^{\text{veloc}}} = \sum_{\vec{k}'} |\langle E_1, \vec{k}| - e\varphi_{\text{tot}} |E_1, \vec{k}'\rangle|^2 \left(\frac{\vec{k}-\vec{k}'}{k}\right) \delta\left(\frac{\hbar^2}{2m_1^*}(k^2 - k'^2)\right)$$

$$(\text{II.4.22})$$

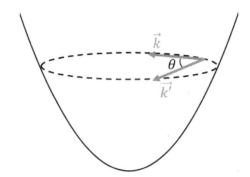

Figure II.4.1.   Sketch of the electronic wavevector during an intra-subband elastic scattering.

Due to the conservation of the modulus of $\vec{k}$ during the elastic scattering $\frac{\vec{k}-\vec{k'}}{k} = (1 - \cos\theta)$ where θ is the angle between $\vec{k}$ and $\vec{k'}$ (see Fig. II.4.1). Using the 2D Fourier decomposition, it is easily checked that:

$$\langle E_1, \vec{k}| - e\varphi_{tot}|E_1, \vec{k'}\rangle = -e\langle\varphi_{tot}\rangle_{11}(\vec{Q} = \vec{k} - \vec{k'})$$

$$= -e\frac{\langle\varphi_{ext}\rangle_{11}(\vec{Q})}{1 + \chi_{11}(\vec{Q})}\delta_{\vec{Q},\vec{k}-\vec{k'}} \qquad (II.4.23)$$

Inserting (II.4.23) in (II.4.21) and (II.4.22) leads, after getting rid of the summation over $\vec{k'}$, to the expression:

$$\frac{\hbar}{2\pi\tau_{1\vec{k}}^{scatt}} = \frac{N_{imp}2m_1^*}{S\hbar^2}\left(\frac{e^2}{4\pi\varepsilon_0\varepsilon_r}\right)^2\int_0^\pi d\theta\frac{[g_{imp}^{11}(Q, z_{imp})]^2}{[Q + Q_0(Q)]^2} \qquad (II.4.24)$$

$$\frac{\hbar}{2\pi\tau_{1\vec{k}}^{veloc}} = \frac{N_{imp}2m_1^*}{S\hbar^2}\left(\frac{e^2}{4\pi\varepsilon_0\varepsilon_r}\right)^2\int_0^\pi d\theta 2\sin^2\left(\frac{\theta}{2}\right)\frac{[g_{imp}^{11}(Q, z_{imp})]^2}{[Q + Q_0(Q)]^2}$$
$$(II.4.25)$$

where $Q = 2k\sin(\frac{\theta}{2})$ and g_{imp} is the impurity form factor:

$$g_{imp}^{11}(Q, z_{imp}) = \int_{-\infty}^{+\infty} dz\chi_1^2(z)e^{-Q|z-z_{imp}|} \qquad (II.4.26)$$

while at high temperature for non-degenerate carriers:

$$Q_0(Q) = g_s^{11}(Q)Q_{Db} \qquad (II.4.27)$$

where g_s^{11} is the screening form factor and Q_{Db} the 2D Debye wavevector defined in (II.4.17). Note that the pre-factor in (II.4.24) and (II.4.25) can be rewritten $4R^* N_{imp}/S$ where R^* is the effective Rydberg. Applications of Eqs. (II.4.24) and (II.4.25) to actual situations will be presented in the results parts (see Chapter II.5).

II.4.2. Case of many subbands occupation

Often, carriers occupy several subbands in heterostructures, in particular the quantum cascade structures comprise many subbands that are close in energy compared to $k_B T$ at room temperature. Thus, the previous analysis should be extended. We label the subbands by $p = 1, 2, \ldots$ and assume thermal equilibrium specific to each subband (chemical potential μ_p, temperature T_p). Equations (II.4.3) and (II.4.4) are generalised into:

$$\left(-\frac{\hbar^2 \nabla_2^2}{2m^*} - e\langle \varphi_{tot}\rangle_{pp}(\vec{\rho})\right) g_{\nu,p}(\vec{\rho}) = (\varepsilon_{\nu,p} - E_p) g_{\nu,p}(\vec{\rho}) \qquad \text{(II.4.28)}$$

$$\langle \varphi_{tot}\rangle_{pp}(\vec{\rho}) = \int_{-\infty}^{+\infty} dz \chi_p^2(z) \varphi_{tot}(\vec{r}) \qquad \text{(II.4.29)}$$

Equation (II.4.5) has now to be replaced by:

$$\varepsilon_{\nu,p} = E_p - \langle \varphi_{tot}\rangle_{pp}(\vec{\rho}) + \frac{\hbar^2 k^2}{2m_p^*} \qquad \text{(II.4.30)}$$

The 2D electron density in the pth subband is equal to:

$$n_{2,p}(\vec{\rho}) = -\frac{2e}{S} \sum_{\vec{k}} \frac{1}{1 + \exp\left[\beta_p \left(E_p - e\langle \varphi_{tot}\rangle_{pp}(\vec{\rho}) + \frac{\hbar^2 k^2}{2m_p^*} - \mu_p\right)\right]}$$

$$= -\frac{e m_p^* k_B T_p}{\pi \hbar^2} \ln(1 + e^{\beta_p(\mu_p + e\langle \varphi_{tot}\rangle_{pp}(\vec{\rho}) - E_p)}) \qquad \text{(II.4.31)}$$

Hence, the 3D charge density is $n_3(\vec{r}) = \sum_p n_{2,p}(\vec{\rho}) \chi_p^2(z)$. The 3D induced charge density is the difference between the charge density with and without φ_{tot}:

$$\delta n_{\text{ind}}(\vec{r}) = \sum_p \delta n_{\text{ind},p}(\vec{r}) = \sum_p \chi_p^2(z) \delta n_{2,\text{ind},p}(\vec{\rho}) \tag{II.4.32}$$

$$\delta n_{2,\text{ind},p}(\vec{\rho}) = -\frac{e m_p^* k_B T_p}{\pi \hbar^2} \ln\left(\frac{1 + e^{\beta_p(\mu_p + e\langle\varphi_{\text{tot}}\rangle_{pp}(\vec{\rho}) - E_p)}}{1 + e^{\beta_p(\mu_p - E_p)}}\right) \tag{II.4.33}$$

The induced electrostatic potential is equal to

$$\varphi_{\text{ind}}(\vec{r}) = \int d^3 r' \frac{\delta n_{\text{ind}}(\vec{r'})}{4\pi\varepsilon_0\varepsilon_r |\vec{r} - \vec{r'}|}$$

$$= \frac{1}{2\varepsilon_0\varepsilon_r S} \sum_{p,\vec{Q}} \frac{e^{i\vec{Q}\cdot\vec{\rho}}}{Q} \int dz' e^{-Q|z-z'|} \chi_p^2(z') \int d^2\rho' e^{-i\vec{Q}\cdot\vec{\rho'}} \delta n_{2,\text{ind},p}(\vec{\rho'})$$

$$\tag{II.4.34}$$

$$g_{\text{screen}}^{j,p}(\vec{Q}) = \iint dz\,dz' \chi_j^2(z) \chi_p^2(z') e^{-Q|z-z'|} \tag{II.4.35}$$

After linearisation of the induced charge density with respect to the total potential energy and defining as before the Fourier transforms of $\langle\varphi_{\text{ind}}\rangle_{jj}$ and $\langle\varphi_{\text{tot}}\rangle_{pp}$, we get:

$$\langle\varphi_{\text{ind}}\rangle_{jj}(\vec{Q}) = -\frac{e^2}{2\pi\hbar^2\varepsilon_0\varepsilon_r} \sum_p m_p^* \frac{e^{\beta_p(\mu_p - E_p)}}{1 + e^{\beta_p(\mu_p - E_p)}} \frac{g_{\text{screen}}^{j,p}(\vec{Q})}{Q} \langle\varphi_{\text{tot}}\rangle_{pp}(\vec{Q}) \tag{II.4.36}$$

Using $\varphi_{\text{ind}} = \varphi_{\text{tot}} - \varphi_{\text{ext}}$, we finally obtain:

$$\langle\varphi_{\text{ext}}\rangle_{jj}(\vec{Q}) = \sum_p [\delta_{j,p} + \chi_{j,p}(\vec{Q})]\langle\varphi_{\text{tot}}\rangle_{pp}(\vec{Q}) \tag{II.4.37}$$

$$\chi_{j,p}(\vec{Q}) = \frac{2}{a_p^* Q} g_s^{j,p}(\vec{Q}) \frac{e^{\beta_p(\mu_p - E_p)}}{1 + e^{\beta_p(\mu_p - E_p)}} \tag{II.4.38}$$

where a_p^* is the effective Bohr radius calculated with the in-plane mass of the pth subband m_p^*. Thus, the multi-subband occupation by carriers transforms the screening problem from a scalar to a matrix-like one. This leads to tedious calculations. Only the two occupied subbands case is easily tractable. We get:

$$\langle \varphi_{\text{tot}} \rangle_{11}(\vec{Q}) = \frac{(1 + \chi_{22})\langle \varphi_{\text{ext}} \rangle_{11}(\vec{Q}) - \chi_{12}\langle \varphi_{\text{ext}} \rangle_{22}(\vec{Q})}{(1 + \chi_{22})(1 + \chi_{11}) \quad \chi_{12}\chi_{21}} \qquad \text{(II.4.39)}$$

$$\langle \varphi_{\text{tot}} \rangle_{22}(\vec{Q}) = \frac{(1 + \chi_{11})\langle \varphi_{\text{ext}} \rangle_{22}(\vec{Q}) - \chi_{21}\langle \varphi_{\text{ext}} \rangle_{11}(\vec{Q})}{(1 + \chi_{22})(1 + \chi_{11}) - \chi_{12}\chi_{21}} \qquad \text{(II.4.40)}$$

When many subbands are occupied the induced charge density displays a z shape that is more and more uniform along the z-axis with increasing the number of occupied subbands. In this limit, it has been shown by Nelander *et al.* [49] that, instead of the complicated expressions of (II.4.37) and (II.4.39)–(II.4.40), the matrix elements of screened coulombic potential $\varphi_{\text{tot}}(\vec{r})$ can reasonably be replaced by those of a Yukawa potential, like in the 3D case:

$$\langle n\vec{k}| - e\varphi_{\text{tot}}(\vec{r})|n'\vec{k'}\rangle \approx \langle n\vec{k}| - \frac{Ze^2}{4\pi\varepsilon_0\varepsilon_r r}e^{-r/r_D}|n'\vec{k'}\rangle \qquad \text{(II.4.41)}$$

$$r_D = \sqrt{\frac{\varepsilon_0\varepsilon_r k_B T}{e^2 n_{3\text{D}}}} \qquad \text{(II.4.42)}$$

This compact form offers a considerable simplification over the intricate (II.4.37)–(II.4.40), in particular in the case of inter-subband scattering as we shall see below.

II.4.3.   Screening of inter-subband matrix elements

Take a multi-well structure and assume that one is interested in evaluating an inter-subband scattering rate due to an external potential $-e\varphi_{\text{ext}}(\vec{r})$. So far, we have handled intra-subband effects and found a convenient relationship between $\langle \varphi_{\text{tot}} \rangle_{11}$ and $\langle \varphi_{\text{ext}} \rangle_{11}$. The situation we envision is the computation of $\langle n\vec{k}| - e\varphi_{\text{tot}}|n'\vec{k'}\rangle$ knowing that electrons occupy the subbands $1, 2, \ldots, p$. The induced charge density due to the total potential will therefore involve the $\chi_1^2(z), \ldots, \chi_p^2(z)$ charge distributions and there is no longer a nice fitting between the matrix element of the external potential and that of the induced electrostatic potential. To tackle this difficulty, we split φ_{tot} into

$\varphi_{\text{ext}} + \varphi_{\text{ind}}$. φ_{ind} will be obtained from δn_{ind} by:

$$\varphi_{\text{ind}}(\vec{r}) = \int d^3r' \frac{\delta n_{\text{ind}}(\vec{r'})}{4\pi\varepsilon_0\varepsilon_r|\vec{r} - \vec{r'}|} \tag{II.4.43}$$

Suppose we take as external potential the one created by a point charge e_i located at $(\vec{\rho}_i, z_i)$. Then, we find the inter-subband matrix element of the external potential:

$$\langle n\vec{k}| - e\varphi_{\text{ext}}|n'\vec{k'}\rangle = -\frac{ee_i}{2\varepsilon_0\varepsilon_r S} \sum_{\vec{Q}} \frac{e^{-i\vec{Q}\cdot\vec{\rho}_i}}{Q} g_{\text{imp}}^{nn'}(Q, z_i)\delta_{\vec{Q},\vec{k}-\vec{k'}} \tag{II.4.44}$$

$$g_{\text{imp}}^{nn'}(Q, z_i) = \int dz\chi_n(z)\chi_{n'}(z)e^{-Q|z-z_i|} \tag{II.4.45}$$

To compute the matrix element of $\varphi_{\text{ind}}(\vec{r})$ we shall assume a simple situation; namely that all the mobile electrons occupy the ground subband. Hence:

$$\delta n_{\text{ind}}(\vec{r'}) = \chi_1^2(z')\delta n_{2,\text{ind},1}(\vec{\rho'}) \tag{II.4.46}$$

This leads to:

$$\varphi_{\text{ind}}(\vec{r}) = \int d^2\rho' \delta n_{2,\text{ind},1}(\vec{\rho'}) \int dz' \frac{\chi_1^2(z')}{4\pi\varepsilon_0\varepsilon_r|\vec{r} - \vec{r'}|} \tag{II.4.47}$$

Using (II.4.11), we get:

$$\varphi_{\text{ind}}(\vec{r}) = -\frac{e^2 m_1^*}{2\varepsilon_0\varepsilon_r\pi\hbar^2}\frac{e^{\beta_1(\mu_1-E_1)}}{1 + e^{\beta_1(\mu_1-E_1)}} \sum_{\vec{Q'}} \frac{e^{i\vec{Q'}\cdot\vec{\rho}}}{Q'}\langle\varphi_{\text{tot}}\rangle_{11}(\vec{Q'})$$

$$\times \int dz'\chi_1^2(z')e^{-Q'|z-z'|} \tag{II.4.48}$$

where $\langle\varphi_{\text{tot}}\rangle_{11}(\vec{Q'})$ is the total electrostatic potential that arises from intra-subband 1 contributions only. The inter-subband matrix element of the induced electrostatic potential is found to be equal to:

$$\langle n\vec{k}| - e\varphi_{\text{ind}}|n'\vec{k'}\rangle = \frac{e^3 m_1^*}{2\varepsilon_0\varepsilon_r\pi\hbar^2}\frac{e^{\beta_1(\mu_1-E_1)}}{1 + e^{\beta_1(\mu_1-E_1)}}\delta_{\vec{Q'},\vec{k}-\vec{k'}}$$

$$\times \frac{g_{nn'}^{11}(\vec{Q'})}{Q'} \frac{\langle \varphi_{\text{ext}} \rangle_{11}(\vec{Q'})}{1 + \chi_{11}(\vec{Q'})} \tag{II.4.49}$$

$$g_{nn'}^{11}(\vec{Q'}) = \iint dz dz' \chi_1^2(z) \chi_n(z') \chi_{n'}(z') e^{-Q'|z-z'|} \tag{II.4.50}$$

Thus, we explicitly obtain the inter-subband matrix element of the induced electrostatic potential as:

$$\langle n\vec{k}| - e\varphi_{\text{ind}}|n'\vec{k'}\rangle = \frac{e^2 m_1^*}{2\varepsilon_0 \varepsilon_r \pi \hbar^2 |\vec{k} - \vec{k'}|} \frac{e^{\beta_1(\mu_1 - E_1)}}{1 + e^{\beta_1(\mu_1 - E_1)}} \delta_{\vec{Q'}, \vec{k} - \vec{k'}} g_{nn'}^{11}(\vec{Q'})$$

$$\times \frac{ee_i}{2\varepsilon_0 \varepsilon_r S} \frac{e^{-i\vec{Q'} \cdot \vec{\rho}_i}}{Q'} \frac{g_{\text{imp}}^{11}(Q', z_i)}{1 + \chi_{11}(Q')} \tag{II.4.51}$$

This can also be rewritten as:

$$\langle n\vec{k}| - e\varphi_{\text{ind}}|n'\vec{k'}\rangle = -\langle n\vec{k}| - e\varphi_{\text{ext}}|n'\vec{k'}\rangle \frac{2}{a_B^* |\vec{k} - \vec{k'}|} \frac{e^{\beta_1(\mu_1 - E_1)}}{1 + e^{\beta_1(\mu_1 - E_1)}}$$

$$\times \delta_{\vec{Q'}, \vec{k} - \vec{k'}} \frac{g_{nn'}^{11}(Q')}{1 + \chi_{11}(Q')} \frac{g_{\text{imp}}^{11}(Q', z_i)}{g_{\text{imp}}^{nn'}(Q', z_i)} \tag{II.4.52}$$

As expected, we find that the induced electrostatic potential displays inter-subband matrix elements with a sign that is opposite to the sign of the external potential ones. We also find an expression where the impurity and screening form factors are a mixture of intra-subband 1 effects (like $\chi_{11}(Q)$, $g_{11}^{\text{imp}}(Q, z_i)$) and inter-subband contributions such as $g_{\text{imp}}^{nn'}(Q', z_i)$, $g_{nn'}^{11}(Q')$. Finally, note that the sum of (II.4.44) and (II.4.52) reduce to (II.4.19) when we set $n = n' = 1$.

When several subbands are occupied by electrons, the screening of inter-subband transitions becomes very tedious to evaluate. Like in the case of a single occupied subband, one has to express the induced charge density in the various subbands to obtain an explicit form of $\varphi_{\text{ind}}(\vec{r})$.

Chapter II.5

Results for Static Scatterers

II.5.1. Scattering by static disorder

In this paragraph, we give a few results of level lifetimes limited by static scatterers. We shall illustrate four salient features:

(1) The importance of screening effects for coulombic scatterers.
(2) The importance of the doping engineering (i.e., judiciously placing the dopants to minimise (or enhance) a specific feature (e.g., the level lifetime)).
(3) The comparison between the strengths of the interface defects and the ionised impurities scatterings.
(4) The comparison between the strengths of the intra- and the inter-subband scatterings.

For the points (1)–(4), we take the simplest possible structure, i.e., a single GaAs/Ga$_{0.7}$Al$_{0.3}$As quantum well with the following material parameters: $m^* = 0.07m_0$, $V_b = 0.22$ eV, $L = 15$ nm and $\varepsilon_r = 12.4$. We shall assume a fixed (against the temperature T) electronic concentration $n/S = 5 \times 10^{10}$ cm^{-2}. This is a low concentration, typical of THz emitting quantum cascade lasers. For point (1) the impurities are assumed to sit on a plane located at the centre of the well ($z_i = 0$). Their areal concentration is $N_{\mathrm{imp}}/S = 10^{10}$ cm^{-2}. The temperature T will be varied between 10 K and 300 K. For point (2) T and n/S are fixed (100 K, 5×10^{10} cm^{-2}) and z_i is varied from the well centre to the barrier.

We recall that, when the initial electron state is $|E_1, \vec{k}\rangle$, the intra-subband scattering time due to screened coulombic impurities is equal to:

$$\frac{\hbar}{2\tau_{1\vec{k}}} = \frac{e^2 e_i^2}{(4\pi\varepsilon_0\varepsilon_r)^2} \frac{N_{\text{imp}}}{S} \frac{2m^*\pi}{\hbar^2} \int_0^\pi \frac{g_{\text{imp}}^2(Q = |\vec{k} - \vec{k}'|, z_i)}{(Q + Q_s(Q))^2} d\theta \quad \text{(II.5.1)}$$

$$Q^2 = 2k^2 - 2k^2 \cos\theta = 4k^2 \sin^2\left(\frac{\theta}{2}\right) \quad \text{(II.5.2)}$$

$$Q_s(Q) = Q\chi_{11}(Q) = \frac{2g_s^{11}(Q)}{a_{\text{B}}^*} \times \frac{1}{1 + \exp[\beta(E_1 - \mu)]}$$

$$= \frac{2g_s^{11}(Q)}{a_{\text{B}}^*}\left[1 - \exp\left(-\frac{n\pi\hbar^2}{Sm^*k_BT}\right)\right] \quad \text{(II.5.3)}$$

where e_i is the charge of a single impurity, a_{B}^* is the effective Bohr radius, g_{imp} and g_s are the impurity and screening form factors, respectively (see Eqs. (II.4.26) and (II.4.10) respectively). We note that the level lifetime can also be expressed in terms of the effective Rydberg R^* ($R^* = \frac{m^*e^4}{2\hbar^2(4\pi\varepsilon_0\varepsilon_r)^2} = 13600\frac{m^*}{m_0\varepsilon_r^2}$ meV) for single charged donors and:

$$\frac{\hbar}{2\tau_{1\vec{k}}} = 4\pi R^* \frac{N_{\text{imp}}}{S} \int_0^\pi d\theta \frac{g_{\text{imp}}^2(Q = |\vec{k} - \vec{k}'|, z_i)}{(Q + Q_s(Q))^2} \quad \text{(II.5.4)}$$

We show in Fig. II.5.1 the k-dependence ($0 \leq k \leq 3/a_{\text{B}}^*$) of the level lifetime for a fixed carrier concentration, on-centre coulombic impurities and various temperatures. We recover the classical result that fast electrons (large k) are less scattered by charged impurities. We also find that unscreened coulombic impurities lead to a diverging level broadening (if $Q_s = 0$ the expression in the angular integral in (II.5.1)) diverges like $1/\theta^2$ near $\theta = 0$). As seen from (II.5.3), $Q_s(Q)$, and thus the screening efficiency decreases with increasing temperature leading to a decreasing $\tau_{1\vec{k}}(T)$.

Figure II.5.2 illustrates the idea of doping engineering. We show at $T = 100$ K, the k-dependences of the level lifetime for several z_i. As expected, we find for any fixed k a pronounced increase of $\tau_{1\vec{k}}$ when the impurity plane is increasingly separated from the centre of gravity of the electronic wavefunction (here $z = 0$).

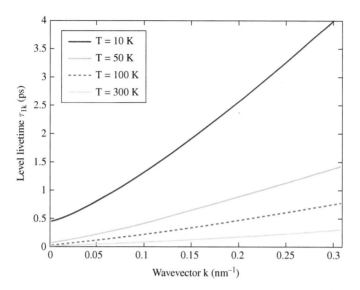

Figure II.5.1. k-Dependence $(0 \leq k \leq 3/a_B^*)$ of the level E_1 lifetime for a fixed carrier concentration, on-centre screened coulombic impurities and various temperatures.

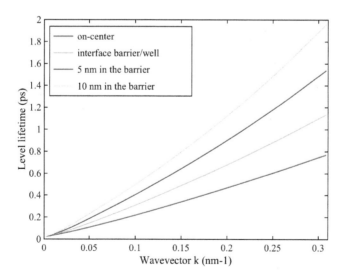

Figure II.5.2. k-Dependence of the level E_1 lifetime for several impurity locations: at the centre of the quantum well, at the barrier/well interface, 5 nm and 10 nm in the barrier. $T = 100$K. Note that at $k = 0$ the curves extrapolate at the value $\tau_{k=0} = \frac{\hbar S}{2\pi^2 R^* a_B^2 N_{imp}} [1 - \exp(\frac{n\pi\hbar^2}{Sm^* k_B T})]^2$.

To tackle point (3) we need to model the interface defects that are scatterers specific to the heterostructures. They unavoidably arise because the frontier between two epitaxially grown layers is never perfectly plane. Very often, the deviations from the perfect interface relate interface roughness potential to correlated in-plane fluctuations on the position of the interface. Let $\Delta(\vec{\rho})$ be the deviation of the interface from a plane. Then, the model rests on the assumption that two fluctuations at point $\vec{\rho}$ and $\vec{\rho}'$ admit a correlation function whose average over the possible configurations decays like a Gaussian (or an exponential, etc.):

$$\langle \Delta(\vec{\rho})\Delta(\vec{\rho}')\rangle_{\mathrm{av}} = \Delta^2 \exp\left(-\frac{(\vec{\rho}-\vec{\rho}')^2}{\Lambda^2}\right) \qquad (\mathrm{II.5.5})$$

where Λ is a correlation length often found equal to several nm's by fitting this model to the mobility data [12]. A nearly equivalent model consists in assuming that the interface defects consist of laterally localised protrusions that are either attractive when the well material protrudes in the barrier material or repulsive when the barrier material protrudes in the well. These protrusions are characterised by a depth h_{def} (one monolayer in the good cases such as GaAs/(Ga,Al)As), their lateral extension σ and their concentration $n_{\mathrm{def}} = (N_{\mathrm{att}} + N_{\mathrm{rep}})/S$ (where N_{att} and N_{rep} denote the number of attractive and repulsive defects respectively) or the fractional coverage of the surface S: $f = \pi\sigma^2 n_{\mathrm{def}}$. Take the ideal interface at $z = z_0$. Then the potential energy associated with interface defects is written:

$$\delta V(\vec{\rho}, z) = V_b\, g(z) \sum_{\vec{\rho}_i} \exp\left(-\frac{(\vec{\rho}-\vec{\rho}_i)^2}{2\sigma^2}\right) \qquad (\mathrm{II.5.6})$$

$$g_{\mathrm{rep}}(z) = +Y(z - z_0)Y(z_0 + h_{\mathrm{def}} - z) \qquad (\mathrm{II.5.7})$$

$$g_{\mathrm{att}}(z) = -Y(z - h_{\mathrm{def}} - z_0)Y(z_0 - z) \qquad (\mathrm{II.5.8})$$

where the function $g(z)$ is different (g_{rep}, g_{att}) depending on the nature (repulsive or attractive) of the defect. Assuming uncorrelated attractive and repulsive defects, we finally obtain the level lifetime limited by intra-subband transitions generated by these defects:

$$\frac{\hbar}{2\tau_{1\vec{k}}} = \frac{2m^*\pi\sigma^4}{\hbar^2}V_b^2\left(\frac{N_{\mathrm{rep}}}{S}\left|\int_{z_0-h_{\mathrm{def}}}^{z_0}dz\chi_1^2(z)\right|^2\right.$$

$$\left.+\frac{N_{\mathrm{att}}}{S}\left|\int_{z_0}^{z_0+h_{\mathrm{def}}}dz\chi_1^2(z)\right|^2\right)\int_0^\pi d\theta\frac{Q^2}{(Q+Q_s(Q))^2}e^{-\sigma^2Q^2}$$

$$(\mathrm{II.5.9})$$

Often, the envelope functions vary slowly at the scale of h_{def} and (II.5.9) simplifies in:

$$\frac{\hbar}{2\tau_{1\mathrm{k}}} = \frac{2m^*\sigma^2}{\hbar^2}V_b^2h_{\mathrm{def}}^2f\chi_1^4(z_0)\int_0^\pi d\theta\frac{Q^2}{(Q+Q_s(Q))^2}e^{-\sigma^2Q^2}$$

$$(\mathrm{II.5.10})$$

A comparison between the strengths of the scattering by coulombic and interface defects is shown in Fig. II.5.3 at $T = 100$ K with $n/S = 5 \times 10^{10}$ cm^{-2}, $z_i = L/2$ and $n_{\mathrm{imp}}/S = 10^{10}$ cm^{-2}. The interface defects are characterised by $f = 0.3$, $h_{\mathrm{def}} = 0.283$ nm,

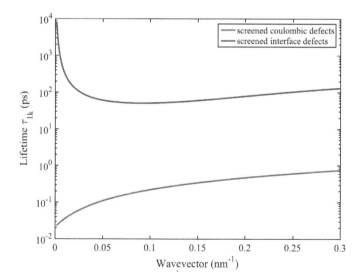

Figure II.5.3. Comparison between the level E_1 lifetimes by screened coulombic impurities ($z_i = \frac{L}{2}$) (lower curve) and screened interface defects (upper curve). We consider the same quantum well structure as in Figs. II.5.1 and II.5.2.

$\sigma = 3.6$ nm. We show the k-dependence $(0 \leq k \leq 3/a_{\mathrm{B}}^*)$ of the scattering time. We see that although very numerous, the interface defects are not as efficient as diluted screened ionised impurities (see Fig. II.5.1 for comparison). This is because interface defects are short range scatterers.

Finally, we would like to compare the intra-subband and the inter-subband efficiencies for a given scattering mechanism. In the form factor analysis, we have already shown that the inter-subband form factors vanish near zero wavevector while the intra-subband ones go to one in this limit. The inter-subband scattering contributions are thus anticipated to be less efficient than the intra-subband ones. In particular, the broadening due to the inter-subband scattering triggered by coulombic scatterers is finite even if there is no screening while that due to intra-subband transitions diverges in the same limit. We illustrate this feature in Fig. II.5.6, where we compare the intra-subband contributions to the level broadening to the inter-subband ones. We work this time without carriers (and thus without screening) using the same single quantum well parameters as defined above, and consider unscreened interface defects as scatterers. We compare the broadening due to the $E_2 \rightarrow E_1$ and $E_2 \rightarrow E_2$ elastic transitions (see Figs. II.5.4 and II.5.5). The relation between k_2 and

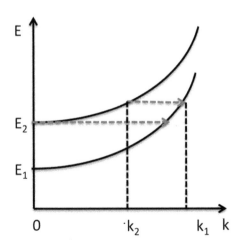

Figure II.5.4.   Sketch of the E_1 and E_2 dispersions. The dashed arrows indicate inter-subband $E_2 \rightarrow E_1$ elastic transitions.

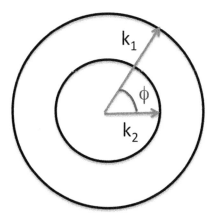

Figure II.5.5. Iso-energy surface in the E_2 (inner circle) and E_1 (outer circle) subbands. The angle ϕ is the angle between the two vectors $\vec{k}_2$ and $\vec{k}_1$.

k_1 is:

$$k_1 = \sqrt{k_2^2 + \frac{2m^*}{\hbar^2}(E_2 - E_1)} \qquad \text{(II.5.11)}$$

The broadening due to intra-E_2 transitions and due to inter-$E_2 \rightarrow E_1$ are given by the expressions:

$$\frac{\hbar}{2\tau_{2\vec{k}}^{\text{intra}}} = \frac{2m^*\pi\sigma^4}{\hbar^2}V_b^2 \left(\frac{N_{\text{rep}}}{S} \left| \int_{z_0-h_{\text{def}}}^{z_0} dz \chi_2^2(z) \right|^2 \right.$$
$$\left. + \frac{N_{\text{att}}}{S} \left| \int_{z_0}^{z_0+h_{\text{def}}} dz \chi_2^2(z) \right|^2 \right) \int_0^\pi d\theta e^{-\sigma^2 Q^2}$$

$$\text{(II.5.12)}$$

$$\frac{\hbar}{2\tau_{2\vec{k}}^{\text{inter}}} = \frac{2m^*\pi\sigma^4}{\hbar^2}V_b^2 \left(\frac{N_{\text{rep}}}{S} \left| \int_{z_0-h_{\text{def}}}^{z_0} dz \chi_1(z)\chi_2(z) \right|^2 \right.$$
$$\left. + \frac{N_{\text{att}}}{S} \left| \int_{z_0}^{z_0+h_{\text{def}}} \chi_1(z)\chi(z) \right|^2 \right) \int_0^\pi d\phi e^{-\sigma^2 K^2}$$

$$\text{(II.5.13)}$$

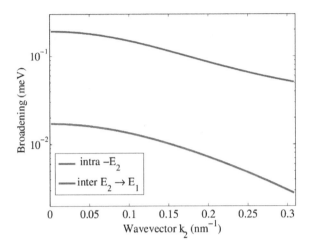

Figure II.5.6. k_2-Dependence of the intra-subband ($E_2 \to E_2$, upper curve) and inter-subband ($E_2 \to E_1$, lower curve) broadenings ($\frac{\hbar}{2\tau_{\vec{k}}}$) for unscreened interface defects.

where we have taken the same in-plane effective mass for the two subbands and where:

$$Q = 2k_2 \sin\left(\frac{\theta}{2}\right) \tag{II.5.14}$$

$$K = \sqrt{2k_2^2 + \frac{2m^*}{\hbar^2}(E_2 - E_1) - 2k_2 \cos\phi \sqrt{k_2^2 + \frac{2m^*}{\hbar^2}(E_2 - E_1)}} \tag{II.5.15}$$

Figure II.5.6 shows the k_2-dependences of the intra-subband and inter-subband scattering times. As expected the intra-subband contributions are more effective than the inter-subband ones.

II.5.2. Scattering of composite particles/excitons at the Born approximation

In semiconductor heterostructures or bulk materials, it may happen that different elementary excitations hybridise to produce a composite excitation/particle that is sufficiently long lived to affect the physical characteristics of the device. Among other composite particles there are the exciton complexes that comprise n electrons and

p holes bound into a single entity. The case of $n = p = 1$ (excitons) is the most frequently encountered when semiconductor heterostructures are shined with interband light [50]. Excitons govern the optical response at low temperature and remain important in the analysis as long as their binding energy are larger or comparable to the thermal agitation energy $k_B T$. In wide bandgap materials, such as the nitride compounds GaN, AlN, they remain dominant till room temperature. That is why it is interesting to investigate, at least partly, their scattering by imperfections and to analyse to which extent the scattering of an electron by static scatterers is different or not when the electron is free or when it is bound to a hole in an excitonic complex. Bi-excitons are formed when the interband light is sufficiently intense. Exciton complexes (trions: 2 electrons + 1 hole or 1 electron + 2 holes, charged bi-excitons) are weakly bound (a few meV's) and are only observed at low temperature (with again the notable exception of the nitrides, ZnO etc.). Polarons are a mixture of electrons and vibrations states. They are overwhelming in alkali halides but are not so important in the less polar III–V materials except when quantum dots are involved because of the reduction of the phase space for the electronic motion [51]. Polaritons are hybrids between excitons and photons and appear when the electromagnetic field modes are made discrete by enclosing the fields in cavities.

In this section, we limit ourselves to excitons and use very simple models to describe the bound electron–hole pairs (in particular holes will be assumed to display quadratic dispersions relations). We would like to ascertain how the binding of the two particles into an exciton affects the scattering of one of them by static scatterers compared to the situation where the scattered particle would be alone.

We need first to define the two carrier states. We work in the strong z quantisation limit and assume that the two particles wavefunctions can be written:

$$\psi(\vec{r}_e, \vec{r}_h) = \chi_n(z_e)\xi_m(z_h)\varphi(\vec{\rho}_e, \vec{\rho}_h) \qquad (II.5.16)$$

where $\chi_n(z_e)$ and $\xi_m(z_h)$ are the bound state wavefunctions for the electron and the hole respectively. The in-plane wavefunctions are the solutions of the effective Schrdinger equation:

$$\left(\frac{p_{xe}^2 + p_{ye}^2}{2m_e} + \frac{p_{xh}^2 + p_{yh}^2}{2m_h} - \frac{e^2}{4\pi\varepsilon_0\varepsilon_r} \left\langle \frac{1}{|\vec{r}_e - \vec{r}_h|} \right\rangle_{n,m} \right) \varphi(\vec{\rho}_e, \vec{\rho}_h)$$

$$= (\varepsilon - E_n - H_m)\varphi(\vec{\rho}_e, \vec{\rho}_h) \qquad (\text{II.5.17})$$

where E_n and H_m are the confinement energies of the nth (respectively, mth) electron (respectively, hole) subband and:

$$\left\langle \frac{1}{|\vec{r}_e - \vec{r}_h|} \right\rangle_{n,m} = \iint dz_e dz_h \chi_n^2(z_e)\xi_m^2(z_h) \frac{1}{\sqrt{(\vec{\rho}_e - \vec{\rho}_h)^2 + (z_e - z_h)^2}}$$

$$(\text{II.5.18})$$

We introduce the centre of mass $\vec{R}$ and the reduced $\vec{\rho}$ in-plane motions of the pair:

$$m_e\vec{\rho}_e + m_h\vec{\rho}_h = (m_e + m_h)\vec{R}; \quad \vec{\rho}_e - \vec{\rho}_h = \vec{\rho} \qquad (\text{II.5.19})$$

Equation (II.5.17) becomes:

$$\left(\frac{P^2}{2M} + \frac{p^2}{2\mu} - \frac{e^2}{4\pi\varepsilon_0\varepsilon_r} \iint dz_e dz_h \chi_n^2(z_e)\xi_m^2(z_h) \right.$$

$$\left. \frac{1}{\sqrt{\rho^2 + (z_e - z_h)^2}} \right) \varphi(\vec{\rho}, \vec{R}) = (\varepsilon - E_n - H_m)\varphi(\vec{\rho}, \vec{R})$$

$$(\text{II.5.20})$$

where M and μ are the total and reduced masses for the in-plane motion of the electron and the hole:

$$M = m_e + m_h \qquad (\text{II.5.21})$$

$$\mu = \left(\frac{1}{m_e} + \frac{1}{m_h} \right)^{-1} \qquad (\text{II.5.22})$$

Thus, we get readily that $\vec{\rho}$ and $\vec{R}$ separate and the centre of mass is free:

$$\varphi(\vec{\rho}, \vec{R}) = \frac{1}{\sqrt{S}} e^{i\vec{K}\cdot\vec{R}} f(\vec{\rho}) \qquad (\text{II.5.23})$$

The reduced motion admits bound and extended states. We concentrate on the bound states since the Coulomb correlations between the electron and the hole are expected to have a larger effect on the scattering efficiency in this case. We shall first look at the intra-subband scatterings that leave unchanged the z_e, z_h and in-plane reduced motions and then look at processes where the z subband for the electron changes.

We must first express the defects potential energy as a function of $\vec{\rho}$ and $\vec{R}$. Suppose we have a coulombic defect located at $(\vec{\rho}_i, z_i)$. Then, it is say attractive for the electron and repulsive for the hole:

$$V_{\text{imp}}(\vec{r}_e, \vec{r}_h) = -\frac{Zee_i}{2\varepsilon_0\varepsilon_r S}\sum_{\vec{Q}}\frac{1}{Q}$$

$$\times [e^{i\vec{Q}\cdot(\vec{\rho}_e-\vec{\rho}_i)}e^{-Q|z_e-z_i|} - e^{i\vec{Q}\cdot(\vec{\rho}_h-\vec{\rho}_i)}e^{-Q|z_h-z_i|}]$$

$$(\text{II.5.24})$$

where Ze_i is the positive charge of the donor. We first average V_{imp} over the (n,m) charge distributions and finally get the effective potential corresponding to the scattering of the centre of mass:

$$V_{\text{imp}}(\vec{\rho}, \vec{R}) = -\frac{Zee_i}{2\varepsilon_0\varepsilon_r S}\sum_{\vec{Q}}\frac{1}{Q}e^{i\vec{Q}\cdot(\vec{R}-\vec{\rho}_i)}(-e^{-i\vec{Q}\cdot\vec{\rho}\frac{m_e}{M}}\langle e^{-Q|z_h-z_i|}\rangle_{mm}$$

$$+ e^{i\vec{Q}\cdot\vec{\rho}\frac{m_h}{M}}\langle e^{-Q|z_e-z_i|}\rangle_{nn})$$

$$(\text{II.5.25})$$

with:

$$\langle e^{-Q|z_e-z_i|}\rangle_{nn} = \int dz_e\chi_n^2(z_e)e^{-Q|z_e-z_i|}$$

$$(\text{II.5.26})$$

$$\langle e^{-Q|z_h-z_i|}\rangle_{mm} = \int dz_h\xi_m^2(z_h)e^{-Q|z_h-z_i|}$$

$$(\text{II.5.27})$$

Finally, after averaging over the bound in-plane reduced motion (say the $1S$ state), we get:

$$V_{\text{eff}}(\vec{R}) = \left\langle V_{\text{imp}}(\vec{\rho}, \vec{R})\right\rangle_{1S}$$

$$= -\frac{Zee_i}{2\varepsilon_0 \varepsilon_r S} \sum_{\vec{Q}} \frac{1}{Q} e^{i\vec{Q}\cdot(\vec{R}-\vec{\rho}_i)}$$

$$\times \left(-\langle e^{-Q|z_h - z_i|}\rangle_{mm} \int d^2\rho |f_{1S}(\vec{\rho})|^2 e^{-i\vec{Q}\cdot\vec{\rho}\frac{m_e}{M}} \right.$$

$$\left. + \langle e^{-Q|z_e - z_i|}\rangle_{nn} \int d^2\rho |f_{1S}(\vec{\rho})|^2 e^{i\vec{Q}\cdot\vec{\rho}\frac{m_h}{M}} \right) \qquad \text{(II.5.28)}$$

We are now in position to compute the exciton scattering time in the $1S$ subband using the Fermi golden rule:

$$\frac{\hbar}{2\pi\tau_{1S}^{nm}(K)} = \sum_{\vec{K'}} |\langle \vec{K}|V_{\text{eff}}(\vec{R})|\vec{K'}\rangle|^2 \delta\left(\frac{\hbar^2}{2M}(K'^2 - K^2)\right) \qquad \text{(II.5.29)}$$

Introducing the angle θ between $\vec{K}$ and $\vec{K'}$, we find:

$$\frac{\hbar}{2\pi\tau_{1S}^{nm}(K)} = \frac{M}{\hbar^2} \left(\frac{Zee_i}{4\pi\varepsilon_0\varepsilon_r}\right)^2 \frac{N_{\text{imp}}}{2SK^2} \int_0^\pi \frac{d\theta}{\sin^2\left(\frac{\theta}{2}\right)}$$

$$\times \left(-\langle e^{-Q|z_h - z_i|}\rangle_{mm} \int d^2\rho |f_{1S}(\vec{\rho})|^2 e^{-i\vec{Q}\cdot\vec{\rho}\frac{m_e}{M}} \right.$$

$$\left. + \langle e^{-Q|z_e - z_i|}\rangle_{nn} \int d^2\rho |f_{1S}(\vec{\rho})|^2 e^{i\vec{Q}\cdot\vec{\rho}\frac{m_h}{M}} \right)^2$$

$$\text{(II.5.30)}$$

where $Q = 2K|\sin(\theta/2)|$ and N_{imp}/S is the areal concentration of spatially uncorrelated impurities in the plane $z = z_i$. Choosing a simple exponential for the $1S$ state: $f_{1S}(\rho) = \sqrt{\frac{2}{\pi\lambda^2}}\exp(-\frac{\rho}{\lambda})$, we find readily:

$$\int d^2\rho |f_{1S}(\rho)|^2 e^{i\alpha\vec{Q}\cdot\vec{\rho}} = \frac{1}{\left[1 + \left(\alpha\frac{Q\lambda}{2}\right)^2\right]^{3/2}} \qquad \text{(II.5.31)}$$

where α denotes either m_h/M or $-m_e/M$. The remarkable result of the intra-exciton subband scattering due to coulombic impurities is the fact that even unscreened coulombic scattering leads to a finite result for the scattering time. For a charged carrier (electron or hole), the unscreened coulombic scattering leads to a divergency

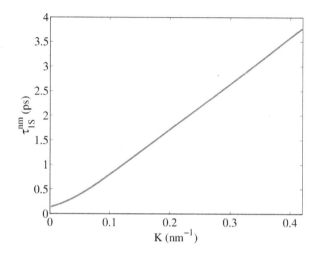

Figure II.5.7. Lifetime $\tau_{1S}^{nm}(K)$ versus wavevector K for a 11/2/6-nm GaAs/Al$_{0.15}$ Ga$_{0.85}$As double quantum well (DQW) structure. Intra-subband scattering in the lowest subbands: $n = m = 1$.

of the scattering frequency as we discussed earlier. Hence, blocking the relative motion of the electron and the hole drastically changes the nature of the scattering. But in a way, this is no surprise since sufficiently far away (compared to λ) from the coulombic centre (i.e., looking at the small Q limit of Eq. (II.5.30)), the exciton is a neutral particle and therefore can hardly be scattered by a coulombic centre. Figure II.5.7 shows a plot of $\tau_{1S}^{nm}(K)$ versus K for a double quantum well (DQW) structure. One sees that intra-subband scattering of excitons is extremely fast (subpicosecond).

We now examine the case of inter-subband exciton scatterings. Initially the electron is in the nth subband, the hole in the mth sub-band and we look for transitions where electrons will be transferred to the n'th subband while the hole will remain in the mth subband. This type of events can be put into a one-to-one correspondence with the electronic inter-subband $n \to n'$ scattering. Note that the inter-subband scatterings assisted by impurities, defects, phonons happen recurrently in DQW (see Fig. II.5.8) and multi-QW structures. We note that it allows a displacement of the mean electron position along the growth axis.

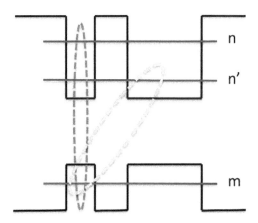

Figure II.5.8.   Conduction and valence band profiles of a double quantum well structure (electronic representation). The (n, m) exciton is scattered by coulombic defects and ends up as a spatially indirect exciton (n', m).

As seen in Fig. II.5.8, the final states correspond to a situation where the electron and the hole are spatially separated. Hence, the binding energy has to be expected smaller for the $1S$ (n', m) exciton than for the (n, m) one. The Fermi golden rule reads:

$$\frac{\hbar}{2\pi \tau_{1S}^{nm}(K)} = \sum_{\nu, \vec{K}'} |\langle n, m, 1S, \vec{K} | V_{\text{imp}} | n', m, \nu, \vec{K}' \rangle|^2$$

$$\times \delta \left(E_n - E_{n'} + \frac{\hbar^2}{2M}(K^2 - K'^2) - R_{1S}^{nm} + R_{\nu}^{n'm} \right)$$

$$(\text{II.5.32})$$

where ν labels the states of the in-plane reduced motion (in principle bound or extended) and R_{1S}^{nm}, $R_{\nu}^{n'm}$ the binding energy of the initial and final exciton states respectively. Note that unbound final exciton states correspond to negative binding energies (if they are approximated by plane waves $|k\rangle$, this negative binding is equal to $-\frac{\hbar^2 k^2}{2\mu}$).

The matrix element in (II.5.32) is:

$$\langle n, m, 1S, \vec{K} | V_{\text{imp}} | n', m, \nu, \vec{K}' \rangle$$

$$= -\frac{Zee_i}{2\varepsilon_0 \varepsilon_r S |\vec{K}' - \vec{K}|} \delta_{\vec{Q}, \vec{K} - \vec{K}'}$$

$$\times ((\langle 1S | e^{i \frac{m_h}{M} \vec{Q} \cdot \vec{\rho}} | \nu \rangle \langle e^{-Q|z_e - z_i|} \rangle_{nn'}$$

$$- \langle 1S | e^{-i \frac{m_e}{M} \vec{Q} \cdot \vec{\rho}} | \nu \rangle \langle e^{-Q|z_h - z_i|} \rangle_{mm})$$

$$(\text{II.5.33})$$

And at the end we get:

$$\frac{\hbar}{2\pi \tau_{1S}^{nm}(K)} = \frac{M}{\hbar^2} \left(\frac{Zee_i}{4\pi\varepsilon_0\varepsilon_r} \right)^2 \frac{N_{\text{imp}}}{S} \sum_\nu I_\nu(\vec{K} - \vec{K'}) \qquad (\text{II.5.34})$$

$$I_\nu(\vec{K} - \vec{K'}) = \int_0^{2\pi} \frac{d\theta}{|\vec{K'} - \vec{K}|^2} \delta_{\vec{Q}, \vec{K} - \vec{K'}}$$

$$\times \left(- \langle e^{-Q|z_h - z_i|} \rangle_{mm} \int d^2\rho f_{1s}(\vec{\rho}) f_\nu(\vec{\rho}) e^{-i\vec{Q} \cdot \vec{\rho} \frac{m_e}{M}} \right.$$

$$\left. + \langle e^{-Q|z_e - z_i|} \rangle_{nn'} \int d^2\rho f_{1S}(\vec{\rho}) f_\nu(\vec{\rho}) e^{i\vec{Q} \cdot \vec{\rho} \frac{m_h}{M}} \right)$$

$$(\text{II.5.35})$$

$$K' = \sqrt{K^2 + \frac{2M}{\hbar^2}(E_n - E_{n'} - R_{1S}^{nm} + R_\nu^{n'm})} \qquad (\text{II.5.36})$$

$$|\vec{K} - \vec{K'}|^2 = K^2 + K'^2 - 2KK' \cos\theta \qquad (\text{II.5.37})$$

This expression has to be compared with the lifetime of an electronic state $|n\vec{k}\rangle$ due to the $|n\vec{k}\rangle \to |n'\vec{k'}\rangle$ transitions assisted by coulombic impurities. Applying the same formalism as above to the single particle case, we get:

$$\frac{\hbar}{2\pi \tau_{nn'}(k)} = \frac{m_e}{\hbar^2} \left(\frac{Zee_i}{4\pi\varepsilon_0\varepsilon_r} \right)^2 \frac{N_{\text{imp}}}{S} \int_0^{2\pi} \frac{d\theta}{|\vec{k'} - \vec{k}|^2} \langle e^{-|\vec{k'} - \vec{k}||z_e - z_i|} \rangle_{nn'}^2$$

$$(\text{II.5.38})$$

$$k' = \sqrt{k^2 + \frac{2m_e}{\hbar^2}(E_n - E_{n'})}; \quad |\vec{k'} - \vec{k}|^2 = k^2 + k'^2 - 2kk' \cos\theta$$

$$(\text{II.5.39})$$

If we compare (II.5.34) and (II.5.38), we note the ratio M/m_e in favour of the excitonic process. It arises from the constant density of in-plane centre of mass states compared to the density of in-plane electronic states. However, the wavevector exchange $\vec{K'} - \vec{K}$, which is

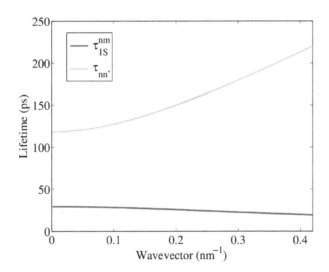

Figure II.5.9.   Comparison between the excitonic lifetime $\tau_{1S}^{nm}(K)$ versus wavevector K (red line) and the electronic inter-subband lifetime $\tau_{nn'(k)}$ versus wavevector k (green line) for a 11/2/6 nm GaAs/Al$_{0.15}$Ga$_{0.85}$As DQW structure; $n = 2$, $n' = 1$, $m = 1$.

in general non-vanishing, is detrimental to the excitonic process compared to the exchange of electron in-plane wavevector $\vec{k'} - \vec{k}$. At the onset $(K = 0$ or $k = 0)$, we note that $\frac{K'^2}{k'^2} \approx \frac{M}{m_e}$ thus cancelling the density of states factor. Therefore, no obvious trend shows up before a numerical computation. Figure II.5.9 shows a plot of $\frac{\hbar}{2\pi\tau_{1S}^{nm}(K)}$ versus K and $\frac{\hbar}{2\pi\tau_{nn'(k)}}$ versus k for a DQW structure. We have confined ourselves to the $1S \rightarrow 1S$ transfer and taken an exponential for the $1S'$ state with a characteristic length λ'. Hence, we get:

$$\int d^2\rho f_{1S}(\vec{\rho}) f_{1S'}(\vec{\rho}) e^{i\alpha\vec{Q}\cdot\vec{\rho}} = \frac{(4\lambda\lambda')}{(\lambda + \lambda')^2} \frac{1}{\left[1 + \left(\frac{\alpha Q\lambda\lambda'}{\lambda + \lambda'}\right)^2\right]^{3/2}}$$

$$(II.5.40)$$

The intra-subband transitions are found very efficient (see Fig. II.5.7). Their efficiency decreases with increasing K due to an increasingly smaller Fourier transform of $f_{1s}^2(\rho)$. The scattering time associated with a change of the electron subband index (red curve in Fig. II.5.9) is significantly longer than that where there is no change in the subband index. Finally, the electron inter-subband scattering is found less efficient by a factor comprised between 5 and 10 than when there is a hole bound to the electron. We note that all these times remain much smaller than a typical recombination time (a few 10^2 ps). Hence, the excitonic escape due to the electronic inter-subband transition is an important phenomenon one has to take into account in analysing cw or time-resolved photo-luminescence experiments.

II.5.3. Scattering on magnetic impurities

II.5.3.1. The "spin"-flip scattering of electrons

Magnetic impurities are found as dopants in semiconductors (e.g., Fe or Mn in GaAs). In addition, diluted magnetic semiconductor alloys such as $Cd_{1-x}Mn_xTe$ or $Ga_{1-x}Mn_xAs$ contain very large numbers of magnetic impurities. They have attracted attention because some of them can undergo a magnetic phase transition ($Ga_{1-x}Mn_xAs$ becomes ferromagnetic with a transition temperature that increases with x at low x). Magnetic impurities differ from the regular impurities by the existence of unfilled shells. These shells (e.g., the d shell in the case of transition metals) are characterised by very localised orbitals (in the Mn case the d orbitals). As a result of Hund rules, the localised d electrons give rise to localised spins at the site $\vec{R}_i$. The states of a localised spin will be labelled $|S_i, m_i\rangle$, $-S_i \leq m_i \leq +S_i$. In the case of Mn, $S_i = \frac{5}{2}$. To shorten the notations we shall admit that all the S_i's are identical. Thus, the states of the N localised spins are labelled by $|m_1, m_2, \ldots, m_N\rangle$.

A quasi-2D conduction electron is characterised by a state $|n, \vec{k}, \sigma_z\rangle$, where n is the subband index, $\vec{k}$ is the in-plane wavevector and $\sigma = \pm\frac{1}{2}$ is the dimensionless operator for the projection of the electron spin along the z direction. The electron interacts with the localised spins by a very short-range interaction, one part being spin independent and the other spin dependent. The effective Hamiltonian acting on the conduction envelope function is written

$$H_{s-d} = A(\vec{r} - \vec{R}_i) + J(\vec{r} - \vec{R}_i)\vec{S}_i \cdot \vec{\sigma} = A\delta(\vec{r} - \vec{R}_i) + J\delta(\vec{r} - \vec{R}_i)\vec{S}_i \cdot \vec{\sigma}$$
$$(II.5.41)$$

where A and J are constants that depend on the material under consideration. We are interested in the spin-flip scattering of a conduction electron, that is to say in the change of the initial electron spin projection along the z-axis because of the interaction with the magnetic impurities. In contrast to the previous elastic scattering mechanisms (alloys, impurities, etc.), the spin-flip scattering is inelastic (even though there might be no energy change for the spin system or the electron). This is because the quantum state of the scatterers changes.

We want to use the Fermi golden rule to compute the lifetime of $|n, \vec{k}, +\frac{1}{2}\rangle$ due to the spin-flip scattering to all states $|n', \vec{k}', -\frac{1}{2}\rangle$ ($n' = n$ or $n' \neq n$). However, the fact that the states of the scatterers will change during the spin flip implies that we have to keep track of the states of the localised spins both in the initial and in the final states. The initial state will be specified by giving the quantum numbers of the mobile electron: $|n, \vec{k}, \sigma_z\rangle$ as well as those of the localised spins: $|m_1, m_2, \ldots, m_N\rangle$. The final states are similarly labelled by $|n', \vec{k}', \sigma_z'\rangle$ and $|m_1', m_2', \ldots, m_N'\rangle$. In the Fermi Golden rule, we have to sum over all the possible final states, including the states of the localised spins. We get:

$$\frac{\hbar}{2\pi \tau_{\text{in}}} = \sum_{n', \vec{k}', -\frac{1}{2}} \sum_{m_1', m_2', \ldots, m_N'}$$

$$\times \left| \langle \psi_{\text{in}} | \sum_{\vec{R}_i} A\delta(\vec{r} - \vec{R}_i) + J\delta(\vec{r} - \vec{R}_i)\vec{S}_i \cdot \vec{\sigma} |\psi_{\text{fin}}\rangle \right|^2$$

$$\times \delta\left(E_n + \varepsilon - E_{n'} - \varepsilon' + \frac{\hbar^2 k^2}{2m^*} - \frac{\hbar^2 k'^2}{2m^*} \right) \qquad \text{(II.5.42)}$$

$$|\psi_{\text{in}}\rangle = \left| n, \vec{k}, +\frac{1}{2}, m_1, m_2, \ldots, m_N \right\rangle,$$

$$|\psi_{\text{fin}}\rangle = \left| n', \vec{k}', -\frac{1}{2}, m_1', m_2', \ldots, m_N' \right\rangle \qquad \text{(II.5.43)}$$

$$\varepsilon = \varepsilon(m_1, m_2, \ldots, m_N), \quad \varepsilon' = \varepsilon'(m_1', m_2', \ldots, m_N')$$

$$\text{(II.5.44)}$$

where m^* is the electron effective mass. We now expand the squared modulus and retain only the diagonal terms in the summation (assumption of ideally randomly located scatterers). We obtain:

$$\frac{\hbar}{2\pi\tau_{\text{in}}} = \sum_{n', \vec{k}', -\frac{1}{2}} \sum_{m_1', m_2', \ldots, m_N'} \sum_{\vec{R}_i}$$

$$\times |\langle \psi_{\text{in}} | A\delta(\vec{r} - \vec{R}_i) + J\delta(\vec{r} - \vec{R}_i)\vec{S}_i \cdot \vec{\sigma} | \psi_{\text{fin}} \rangle|^2$$

$$\times \delta\left(E_n + \varepsilon - E_{n'} - \varepsilon' + \frac{\hbar^2 k^2}{2m^*} - \frac{\hbar^2 k'^2}{2m^*}\right) \quad \text{(II.5.45)}$$

In order to compute the matrix elements easily, we introduce:

$$\vec{S}_i \cdot \vec{\sigma} = S_{iz}\sigma_z + \frac{1}{2}(S_{i+}\sigma_- + S_{i-}\sigma_+) \quad \text{(II.5.46)}$$

where S_{i+}, S_{i-} are the raising and lowering operators for m_i. These operators are such that:

$$S_{i+}|S_i, m_i\rangle = \sqrt{S_i(S_i + 1) - m_i(m_i + 1)}|S_i, m_i + 1\rangle \quad \text{(II.5.47)}$$

$$S_{i-}|S_i, m_i\rangle = \sqrt{S_i(S_i + 1) - m_i(m_i - 1)}|S_i, m_i - 1\rangle \quad \text{(II.5.48)}$$

$$\sigma_+|\uparrow\rangle = 0; \ \sigma_+|\downarrow\rangle = |\uparrow\rangle; \ \sigma_-|\uparrow\rangle = |\downarrow\rangle; \ \sigma_-|\downarrow\rangle = 0 \quad \text{(II.5.49)}$$

We can now compute versus the m_i's the scattering time of a conduction electron with spin $\uparrow$ to states where the mobile electron will have a spin $\downarrow$. The spin-independent part (A) contributes to nothing to the spin-flip scattering because of the orthogonality of the initial and final spin states of the mobile electron. As for the spin-dependent scattering term (J), we note that for a given spin scattering at $\vec{R}_i$ all the other spins are spectators and therefore their m's are conserved. We are left with:

$$\frac{\hbar}{2\pi\tau_{\text{in}}} = \sum_{n', \vec{k}'} \sum_{\vec{R}_i} |\langle n, \vec{k}, \uparrow, m_i | J\delta(\vec{r} - \vec{R}_i)\vec{S}_i \cdot \vec{\sigma} | n', \vec{k}', \downarrow, m_i' \rangle|^2$$

$$\times \delta\left(E_n + \varepsilon - E_{n'} - \varepsilon' + \frac{\hbar^2 k^2}{2m^*} - \frac{\hbar^2 k'^2}{2m^*}\right) \quad \text{(II.5.50)}$$

This expression can be rewritten as:

$$\frac{\hbar}{2\pi\tau_{in}} = \frac{J^2}{4S^2} \sum_{n',\vec{k}'} \sum_{\vec{R}_i} \chi_n^2(z_i)\chi_{n'}^2(z_i) \left[S_i(S_i+1) - m_i(m_i+1)\right] \delta_{m_i',m_i+1}$$

$$\times \delta\left(E_n + \varepsilon - E_{n'} - \varepsilon' + \frac{\hbar^2 k^2}{2m^*} - \frac{\hbar^2 k'^2}{2m^*}\right) \qquad \text{(II.5.51)}$$

where we have assumed the z-dependent wavefunction to be real. We can immediately perform the summation over $\vec{k}'$ and get:

$$\frac{\hbar}{2\pi\tau_{in}} = \frac{J^2 m^*}{8S\hbar^2} \sum_{n'} \sum_{\vec{R}_i} \chi_n^2(z_i)\chi_{n'}^2(z_i)[S_i(S_i+1) - m_i(m_i+1)]\delta_{m_i',m_i+1}$$

$$\times Y\left(E_n + \varepsilon(m_i) - E_{n'} - \varepsilon'(m_i+1) + \frac{\hbar^2 k^2}{2m^*}\right) \qquad \text{(II.5.52)}$$

We now assume that the localised spins are not polarised, hence:

$$\varepsilon(m_i) = \varepsilon'(m_i+1) \qquad \text{(II.5.53)}$$

Thus, in principle, the spin-flip scattering frequency of the conduction electron depends of the states of the all localised spins. However, these states are not known *a priori*. Moreover, the localised spins interact with their surrounding and most often it is reasonable to assume that they have reached thermal equilibrium. In other words, this thermalisation of the localised spins implies that we have to perform an average of $\frac{1}{\tau_{in}}$ over all the possible spin states of the initial states, each configuration $(m_1, m_2, \ldots, m_N)$ being weighted by the probability $P(m_1, m_2, \ldots, m_N)$. As so often for dilute impurities, it is fair (or convenient) to assume that the averaging over N spins is the product of the averaging over one single spin:

$$P(m_1, m_2, \ldots, m_N) = \prod_i P(m_i) \qquad \text{(II.5.54)}$$

Under such circumstances and for unpolarised spins, we get $P(m_i) = (2S_i+1)^{-1}$. Thus, we find that the spin-flip scattering averaged over the m_i is equal to:

$$\left\langle \frac{\hbar}{2\pi\tau_{\text{in}}} \right\rangle_{m_1,m_2,\ldots,m_N} = \frac{J^2 m^*}{8S\hbar^2} \sum_{z_i} N_{\text{loc}}(z_i) \sum_{n'} Y\left(E_n - E_{n'} + \frac{\hbar^2 k^2}{2m^*}\right)$$

$$\times \chi_n^2(z_i)\chi_{n'}^2(z_i) \frac{1}{2S_i + 1} \sum_{-S_i}^{+S_i}$$

$$\times [S_i(S_i + 1) - m_i(m_i + 1)] \qquad (\text{II.5.55})$$

We note that $\langle m_i \rangle = 0$ because of the assumption of unpolarised spins. Thus, for spin $S_i = 5/2$, we find:

$$\frac{1}{2S_i + 1} \sum_{-S_i}^{+S_i} [S_i(S_i + 1) - m_i(m_i + 1)] = \frac{35}{4} - \frac{29}{12} = \frac{19}{3} \qquad (\text{II.5.56})$$

Note that for a classical spin (limit obtained for $S_i \to \infty$) we would have gotten $2S^2/3 = 35/6$, a result very close from $19/3$.

The spin-flip scattering shares several common features with the alloy scattering. This is due to the very localised nature of the individual scatterers, as witnessed by the delta functions in (II.5.41). As a result, we find that the spin-flip rate is proportional to the density of states of the carriers, like the lifetime of conduction electron limited by alloy scattering. If the localised spins are not placed on a single plane z_0, we can, like in the alloy case, replace the discrete summation over the planes z_i by an integral:

$$\left\langle \frac{\hbar}{2\pi\tau_{\text{in}}} \right\rangle_{m_1,m_2,\ldots,m_N}$$

$$= \frac{J^2 m^*}{8Sa\hbar^2} \left(\frac{1}{2S_i + 1} \sum_{-S_i}^{+S_i} [S_i(S_i + 1) - m_i(m_i + 1)] \right)$$

$$\times \sum_{n'} Y\left(E_n - E_{n'} + \frac{\hbar^2 k^2}{2m^*}\right) \int dz_i N_{\text{loc}}(z_i)\chi_n^2(z_i)\chi_{n'}^2(z_i)$$

$$(\text{II.5.57})$$

where a is the distance between two consecutive planes. In the case of intra-subband scattering ($n = n'$) and a single quantum well structure, we recover the known result from the alloy scattering analysis that the spin-flip time for a given initial state is roughly proportional to the well thickness.

We can now introduce the population effects by summing over all the initial electron states weighted by the occupation function of these initial states and multiplying by the non-occupation function of the final states. We denote by $\langle\frac{1}{\tau_\uparrow(n_{s\uparrow})}\rangle$ the scattering frequency averaged over the mobile electrons, where $n_{s\uparrow}$ is the spin $\uparrow$ population and divide the result by $n_{s\uparrow}$, to obtain the average spin-flip rate per spin $\uparrow$ electron.

$$
\left\langle \frac{\hbar}{2\pi\tau_\uparrow(n_{s\uparrow})} \right\rangle = \frac{J^2 m^*}{8 S a \hbar^2 n_{s\uparrow}} \left(\frac{1}{2S_i + 1} \sum_{-S_i}^{+S_i} [S_i(S_i + 1) - m_i^2] \right)
$$

$$
\times \sum_{n,\vec{k}} f_\uparrow \left(E_n + \frac{\hbar^2 k^2}{2m^*} \right) \sum_{n'} \left[1 - f_\downarrow \left(E_n' + \frac{\hbar^2 k^2}{2m^*} \right) \right]
$$

$$
\times Y \left(E_n - E_{n'} + \frac{\hbar^2 k^2}{2m^*} \right) \int dz_i N_{\text{loc}}(z_i) \chi_n^2(z_i) \chi_{n'}^2(z_i)
$$

$$
\tag{II.5.58}
$$

where at thermal equilibrium:

$$
n_{s\uparrow} = \sum_{n\vec{k}} f_\uparrow \left(E_n + \frac{\hbar^2 k^2}{2m^*} \right) = \sum_{n,\vec{k}} \frac{1}{1 + \exp\left[\beta\left(E_n + \frac{\hbar^2 k^2}{2m^*} - \mu_\uparrow \right) \right]}
$$

$$
= \frac{m^* S k_B T}{2\pi\hbar^2} \ln(1 + e^{\beta(\mu_\uparrow - E_n)}) \tag{II.5.59}
$$

$$
n_{s\downarrow} = \sum_{n\vec{k}} f_\downarrow \left(E_n + \frac{\hbar^2 k^2}{2m^*} \right) = \sum_{n,\vec{k}} \frac{1}{1 + \exp\left[\beta\left(E_n + \frac{\hbar^2 k^2}{2m^*} - \mu_\downarrow \right) \right]}
$$

$$
= \frac{m^* S k_B T}{2\pi\hbar^2} \ln(1 + e^{\beta(\mu_\downarrow - E_n)}) \tag{II.5.60}
$$

In the previous expressions, $\mu_\uparrow$ and $\mu_\downarrow$ are, respectively, the chemical potentials of the $\uparrow$ and $\downarrow$ populations in the nth subband. Note that we have put the same T for both spin populations because the thermalisation involves electron–electron and electron–phonon interaction and should be much the same for both spins except perhaps in case of very strong spin imbalance.

Similarly, we can define an average spin ↓ scattering rate:

$$\left\langle \frac{\hbar}{2\pi\tau_\downarrow(n_{s\downarrow})} \right\rangle = \frac{J^2 m^*}{8 S a \hbar^2 n_{s\downarrow}} \left(\frac{1}{2S_i + 1} \sum_{-S_i}^{+S_i} [S_i(S_i + 1) - m_i^2] \right)$$

$$\times \sum_{n,\vec{k}} f_\downarrow \left(E_n + \frac{\hbar^2 k^2}{2m^*} \right) \sum_{n'} \left[1 - f_\uparrow \left(E_n + \frac{\hbar^2 k^2}{2m^*} \right) \right] Y$$

$$\times \left(E_n - E_{n'} + \frac{\hbar^2 k^2}{2m^*} \right) \int dz_i N_{\text{loc}}(z_i) \chi_n^2(z_i) \chi_{n'}^2(z_i)$$

$$(II.5.61)$$

We note that for unpolarised spins (and spin unpolarised mobile electrons: $\mu_\uparrow = \mu_\downarrow$), there is:

$$n_{s\uparrow} = n_{s\downarrow} = \frac{n_s}{2}; \quad \frac{1}{\tau_\downarrow} = \frac{1}{\tau_\uparrow} \qquad (II.5.62)$$

Suppose that by some means (spin orientation by optical pumping, spin injection from a ferromagnetic electrode, etc.) one has succeeded in creating a spin imbalance in the nth subband. Because there were initially more spins ↑, their population will undergo more spin-flip scatterings than the spin ↓ population, thereby leading to a decay of the spin imbalance. The spin imbalance $\langle \Sigma_z = (n_{s\uparrow} - n_{s\downarrow})/2 \rangle$ follows the time evolution:

$$\frac{d\langle \Sigma_z \rangle}{dt} = -\frac{J^2 m^* \pi}{8 S a \hbar^3} \left(\frac{1}{2S_i + 1} \sum_{-S_i}^{+S_i} [S_i(S_i + 1) - m_i^2] \right)$$

$$\times \sum_{n,n',\vec{k}} \left[f_\uparrow \left(E_n + \frac{\hbar^2 k^2}{2m^*} \right) - f_\downarrow \left(E_n + \frac{\hbar^2 k^2}{2m^*} \right) \right]$$

$$\times Y \left(E_n - E_{n'} + \frac{\hbar^2 k^2}{2m^*} \right) \int dz_i N_{\text{loc}}(z_i) \chi_n^2(z_i) \chi_{n'}^2(z_i)$$

$$(II.5.63)$$

Let us estimate this time constant for a population of electrons in the nth subband. Furthermore, if we restrict our considerations to intra-subband processes ($n = n'$) and assume thermalised populations of

↑ and ↓ spins with the same temperature, we obtain readily:

$$\frac{d\langle \Sigma_z \rangle}{dt} = -\frac{\langle \Sigma_z \rangle}{\tau_{\text{spin}}} \tag{II.5.64}$$

$$\frac{1}{\tau_{\text{spin}}} = \frac{J^2 m^* \pi}{4 S a \hbar^3} \left(\frac{1}{2S_i + 1} \sum_{-S_i}^{+S_i} \left[S_i(S_i + 1) - m_i^2 \right] \right) \int dz_i N_{\text{loc}}(z_i) \chi_n^4(z_i) \tag{II.5.65}$$

A typical magnitude of τ_{spin} is obtained with a single quantum well $L = 20\,\text{nm}$, an exchange constant $J = eV \times \frac{a_0^3}{4}$, a volume concentration of localised spins $\frac{N_{\text{loc}}}{S a_0} = x \frac{4}{a_0^3}$ with $x = 10\,\%$ and a carrier effective mass $m^* = 0.1 m_0$. With $a_0 = 0.566$ nm and for the ground state of a quantum well with infinite barriers, we find a spin-flip time ≈ 30 ps, which is short on account of the very large number of localised spins. Figure II.5.10 shows the L-dependence of the spin-flip relaxation time in $Cd_{0.935}Mn_{0.065}Te/Cd_{0.62}Mn_{0.38}Te$ quantum wells

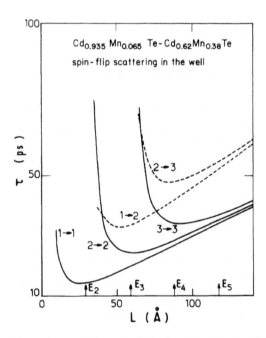

Figure II.5.10. L-dependence of the spin-flip relaxation time in $Cd_{0.935}Mn_{0.065}Te/$ $Cd_{0.62}Mn_{0.38}Te$ quantum wells both for intra-subband and inter-subband contributions.
Source: Bastard and Chang [52].

both for intra-subband and inter-subband contributions. The parameters are $a_0 = 0.6487$ nm, $m^* = 0.096m_0$ and $J = (0.22)\text{eV}a_0^3/4$ [52]. When both initial and final subbands are tightly bound to the well, the spin-flip times increase linearly with L.

II.5.3.2. The "spin"-flip scattering of holes

So far, we have mostly discussed the relaxation processes of conduction electrons in semiconductor heterostructures. The hole-scattering mechanisms are in contrast much less documented. This is due to the more intricate valence band structure than the conduction one due to the fourfold degenerate valence states at $k = 0$ in bulk zinc blende materials compared to the twofold spin degeneracy for the conduction band. However, many experiments, such as transport in p type materials or interband absorption/emission experiments, involve the holes in the valence band. Thus, we need to inquire whether the valence bands intricacies add something peculiar to the scattering frequencies compared to what we get with conduction band dispersions or whether they barely amount to algebraical complications without so much of novel physics. Here, we concentrate on the "spin"-flip scattering, that is to say the scattering between two Kramers conjugate states induced by static scatterers because, in fact, a novel physics emerges from the genuine complexity of the valence dispersion relations.

Due to a large spin–orbit coupling in most of the III–V or II–VI compounds, the hole spin is not a good quantum number. In bulk materials, this leads to a very short (picosecond or less) spin relaxation time. In quantum wells, we have seen (see Chapter II.2) that the size quantisation along the growth axis gives rise to eigenstates, which are also eigenstates of J_z the projection along the growth axis of the (pseudo) total angular momentum J ($J = 3/2$) if the in-plane wavevector $\vec{k} = (k_x, k_y)$ vanishes (subband edges). The heavy (light) hole HH_n (LH_m) states correspond to $J_z = \pm 3/2$ ($\pm 1/2$). In the absence of a magnetic field each of the states are twice degenerate (Kramers degeneracy). At $\vec{k} = 0$, this means that the $+3/2$ and $-3/2$ heavy hole states are degenerate as well as the $+1/2$ and

$-1/2$ light hole states. Away from the subband edges ($\vec{k} \neq 0$), the heavy and light hole nature of the energy eigenstates becomes mixed, the so-called valence band-mixing effect, but the Kramers degeneracy remains. In a quantum well structure, there exists an in-plane wavevector range Δk where the band-mixing is not very large and where the eigenstates remain approximate eigenstates of J_z. Then, what will matter for the "spin"-flip scattering are the magnitudes of the matrix elements of the perturbing potentials between the two eigenstates of opposite J_z at each subband edge. For the $J_z = \pm 3/2$ states, it turns out that these matrix elements are zero for several energy-conserving perturbations, such as those due to ionised impurities, alloy fluctuations, or even s-d exchange (when there exist localised magnetic moments in the heterostructure). This means that if one is able to create a $+3/2$ state at $\vec{k} = 0$, it will never flip to $J_z = -3/2$ and at small $\vec{k}$ the "spin" flip will occur after a long time. Hence, in stark contrast with bulk materials, heavy holes in quantum wells should be characterised by a suppression of "spin" flip when the hole energy approaches the subband edges, a situation reminiscent of the case of uniaxially stressed bulk materials.

Let us more quantitatively analyse the hole "spin"-flip scattering time in quantum wells and demonstrate that it can be very large near the HH_1 edge, despite the fact that there exist magnetic impurities in the well-acting material. Thus, we concentrate on $Cd_{1-x}Mn_xTe$ quantum wells (we saw above that these magnetic impurities are very efficient scatterers (picosecond) of the conduction electron spin).

The "spin"-flip mechanism is described by the following interaction:

$$V_{\text{exc}}(\vec{r}) = J_h \Omega_0 \sum_{\vec{R}_i} \delta(\vec{r} - \vec{R}_i) \vec{S}_i \cdot \vec{\sigma} \qquad (\text{II}.5.66)$$

J_h is the exchange constant for holes in diluted magnetic semiconductors and $\Omega_0 = \frac{a_0^3}{4}$ where a_0 is the lattice parameter of the magnetic sublattice. $\vec{S}_i$ is the localised spin at site $\vec{R}_i$. Note that the summation in (II.5.66) runs only on the "free" spins, i.e., those that are not anti-ferromagnetically locked to their neighbours in a singlet state. The $J_z = \pm 3/2$ states are $\frac{1}{\sqrt{2}}(X + iY) \uparrow$, $\frac{1}{\sqrt{2}}(X - iY) \downarrow$.

Hence, with the delta functions acting on the envelope functions (a bound state for the z motion and a plane wave for the in-plane motion), the matrix elements of the "spin"-flip scattering near the HH_1 band edge are zero either because $\langle \uparrow |v_z| \downarrow \rangle = 0$ or because $\langle X - iY|X + iY \rangle = 0$. Thus, the "spin"-flip lifetime should diverge when $\vec{k} \to 0$. To go beyond this qualitative remark and quantitatively estimate the "spin"-flip lifetime, we diagonalise the off-diagonal terms of the 4×4 Luttinger matrix and write in a three subbands model (HH_1, $LH1$ and HH_2) that:

$$\Psi_{\vec{k}\uparrow} = \frac{e^{i\vec{k}\cdot\vec{\rho}}}{\sqrt{S}}[a_{3/2}\chi_1(z), \ b_{-1/2}\varphi_1(z), \ 0, \ c_{-3/2}\chi_2(z)] \qquad \text{(II.5.67)}$$

$$\Psi_{\vec{k}\downarrow} = \frac{e^{i\vec{k}\cdot\vec{\rho}}}{\sqrt{S}}[c^*_{-3/2}\chi_2(z), \ 0, \ b^*_{-1/2}\varphi_1(z), \ a^*_{3/2}\chi_1(z)] \qquad \text{(II.5.68)}$$

In Eqs. (II.5.67) and (II.5.68), the basis $[u_{3/2}, u_{-1/2}, u_{1/2}, u_{-3/2}]$ has been used and the small terms linear in $\vec{k}$ associated with the inversion asymmetry have been neglected. The coefficients a, b and c can be expressed in terms of the off-diagonal terms of the valence Hamiltonian [53] and the energy denominators between the subband edges.

Figure II.5.11 shows the k-dependence of the "spin"-flip scattering time in (Cd, Mn)Te quantum wells for several well thicknesses. Owing to the pronounced hole localisation in the well, the "spin" flip by the magnetic ions in the barrier is negligible. With increasing the well thickness L, the energy separation between HH_1 and LH_1 decreases and for a given $\vec{k}$ the band-mixing becomes more important. This results in a faster "spin"-flip scattering for the localised spins in the well. For those located in the barrier, the inverse trend takes place due to the prevalent effect of decreasing wavefunction penetration into the barrier with increasing L. Figure II.5.11 gives a quantitative support to the qualitative finding that the hole "spin" flip should markedly increase when $\vec{k} \to 0$. Micro-second relaxation times can easily be obtained, which shows that the "spin" is almost a good quantum number in quantum well structures with enough energy separation between HH_1 and LH_1.

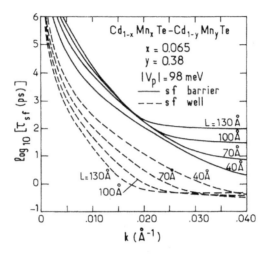

Figure II.5.11. Calculated in-plane dependence of the "spin"-flip scattering in $Cd_{1-x}Mn_xTe/Cd_{1-y}Mn_yTe$ quantum wells with $x = 6.5\%$ and $y = 38\%$ for different well thicknesses; $J_h = 0.88$ eV [54].

Source: Ferreira and Bastard [53].

As can be anticipated from (II.5.67) and (II.5.68), the "spin"-flip scattering exists even in the presence of non-magnetic scatterers (coulombic impurities, interface roughness, etc.). It arises from spin-mixing in a given "spin" state. We show in Fig. II.5.12 the calculated "spin"-flip times between the Kramers conjugates of the HH_1 and LH_1 subbands of a GaAs/AlAs quantum well versus the in-plane wavevector k for several well thicknesses. The scatterers are 10^{10} cm^{-2} ionised impurities located at one interface between GaAs and AlAs. One sees the same trend as found for magnetic scattering, namely a divergency of the "spin"-flip times when approaching the subband edges. Note the very short "spin"-flip times reached for the LH_1 subbands for some k values. These are due to the camel back shape of the LH_1 subband dispersion and leads to a divergent density of states at the maximum of the LH_1 edge (see Exercise 4) and therefore to very short "spin"-flip relaxation times.

Returning to the spin flip of conduction electrons, we anticipate from the previous discussion that the band non-parabolicity that mixes the spin states of the eigenstates will lead to a spin flip (the so-called Elliot–Yafet mechanisms). But other spin-flip terms

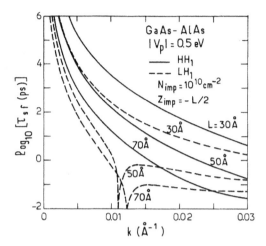

Figure II.5.12.   Calculated "spin"-flip time in the HH_1 and LH_1 subbands versus the in-plane wavevector k in GaAs/AlAs quantum wells of different thicknesses. The scatterers are ionised impurities located at one interface of the well.

Source: Ferreira and Bastard [53].

exist (Dresselhaus, Rashba terms). For a more complete account, the reader is referred to [55, 56].

II.5.4.   Three-body collisions

There exist situations where the regular Born approximation leads to a vanishing result or to values for the scattering times that are very long, too long compared to experiments. In order to interpret the experiments and obtain predictive outcomes, one has to consider going further than the two-body scattering (scattering of electrons by phonons or photons by electrons) and involve a third partner to enhance the scattering efficiency; e.g., replacing "electron + phonons" by "electrons + phonons + static disorder" or "photons + electrons" by "photons + electrons + static disorder/phonons". The two quoted examples are related to the free carrier absorption (FCA) in semiconductors (bulk and heterostructures) and more recently to the electronic cooling in lightly doped graphene (this three-body collision is in the graphene studies called the "super-collision theory").

Here, we merely give a sketchy discussion of these two phenomena (more details can be found in [57, 58]).

II.5.4.1.   FCA in imperfect bulks and heterostructures

Consider an electron with a wavevector $\vec{k}$ and a photon characterised by an angular frequency ω and wavevector $\vec{q}$. After interaction the photon has disappeared and the electron wavevector is $\vec{k'} = \vec{k} + \vec{q}$. It is well known [59] that this process is forbidden because it is impossible to simultaneously ensure the energy and wavevector conservations (except in the non-interesting situation where both ω and q vanish). The result also holds in a relativistic description of the electronic motion. Hence, to get an electronic transition by photon absorption, some third part should intervene to supply the wavevector difference $\Delta \vec{k} = \vec{k'} - \vec{k}$. For a 2D heterostructures (QW, QCL, etc.), only the in-plane components of the electron wavevector are involved. The $\Delta \vec{k}$ supplier actually breaks the translation invariance in the layer plane. These are the static defects and/or the phonons that, ultimately, lead to the photon absorption associated with an electronic transition oblique in the $\vec{k}$ space.

Before embarking in quantum mechanical calculations of the FCA, let us discuss a classical (or rather semi-classical) model of FCA based on the Drude model. The electron, with effective mass m^* and charge $-e$, is subjected to an electric force due to the electric field of the electromagnetic (em) wave and to a friction force due to the defects/phonons, etc. This force is written $-\frac{m^* \vec{v}}{\tau}$. One calculates the ω-dependent conductivity by looking at the permanent regime of:

$$m^* \frac{d\vec{v}}{dt} = -e\vec{F}e^{-i\omega t} - \frac{m^* \vec{v}}{\tau} \tag{II.5.69}$$

which leads to a conductivity $\sigma(\omega)$:

$$\sigma(\omega) = \frac{\sigma_{\text{dc}}}{1 - i\omega\tau} \tag{II.5.70}$$

where $\sigma_{\text{dc}} = \frac{n_{3D}e^2\tau}{m^*}$ is the static conductivity and n_{3D} is the 3D electron concentration. The absorption coefficient $\alpha(\omega)$ associated with this ω-dependent conductivity is equal to:

$$\alpha_{\mathrm{FCA}}(\omega) = \frac{n_{3\mathrm{D}}e^2}{n_r m^* c \varepsilon_0 \omega^2 \tau} \qquad (\mathrm{II.5.71})$$

where n_r is the refractive index at the angular frequency ω and $\omega\tau \gg 1$.

In the large $\omega\tau$ limit, the conductivity decreases like $\omega^{-2}\tau^{-2}$ showing that FCA can lead to a strong absorption mainly in the far infrared part of the spectrum. In fact, for GaAs-like parameters ($m^* = 0.07m_0$, $n_r = 3.5$, $n_{3\mathrm{D}} = 10^{16}$ cm^{-3}, $\tau = 1$ ps), one finds $\alpha \approx 0.12$ cm^{-1} for a wavelength $\lambda = 10$ μm. For mid-infrared semiconductor lasers operating through interband transitions, Haug *et al.* [60] showed that FCA is not an efficient loss mechanism. In the Drude analysis (II.5.69) and (II.5.70), τ is a phenomenological parameter of unknown strength that cannot be associated with any particular scattering mechanism. To go further, one needs to proceed with a quantum mechanical calculation of the transition rates [61] leading to a quantitative agreement between experiments and modelling in bulk semiconductors.

In quasi-2D heterostructures, a Drude-like approach is meaningful only if the electric field of the em wave has a non-vanishing component in the layer plane (see Fig. II.5.13). This is not the em

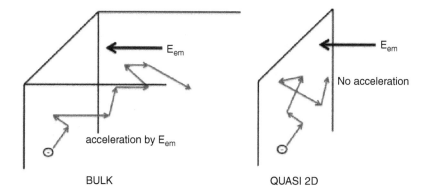

Figure II.5.13. Comparison between the bulk and quasi-2D classical situations. When the em electric field is parallel to the growth axis, there cannot be compensation between the electrical and friction forces. If the em electric field was applied in the layer plane, the Drude analysis would again be effective [62].

polarisation met in QCL's or QWIP's since they involve interband contributions activated by em waves that propagate in the layer plane with their electric fields lying along the growth direction. Translating this remark in the semi-classical analysis, we see that the requirement of the Drude model that the friction force is collinear with the electric force is impossible to achieve in QCL and QWIP structures since the z motion is discretised while the friction lies in the layer plane where the electron free motion takes place. A quantum calculation of FCA is thus needed.

Let us derive a general strategy of a quantum mechanical calculation of FCA in quasi-2D heterostructures. We work at the dipole approximation (long wavelength limit) and write the electric field of the em wave in the form:

$$\vec{E}_{\text{em}}(t) = (E_x\vec{\varepsilon}_x + E_y\vec{\varepsilon}_y + E_z\vec{\varepsilon}_z)\cos(\omega t) \qquad (\text{II.5.72})$$

where $\vec{\varepsilon}$ is a dimensionless polarisation vector. Hence, the time-dependent effective Hamiltonian is:

$$H = H_0 + e\vec{A}_{\text{em}}(t)\cdot\frac{\vec{p}}{m^*} + V_{\text{def}}(\vec{r}) + h.c; \quad \vec{E}_{\text{em}}(t) = \frac{\partial \vec{A}_{\text{em}}(t)}{\partial t} \quad (\text{II.5.73})$$

where V_{def} is a potential energy associated with the static defects/impurities (electron–phonon interaction could have also been considered [57]). To evaluate the absorption coefficient of the em wave at the dipole approximation, one needs to handle the time-dependent light-matter coupling by perturbation and by using the Fermi golden rule derive the transition probability per unit of time that an electron undergoes a $|n\vec{k}\rangle \rightarrow |n'\vec{k'}\rangle$ transition.

The matrix elements of the $\vec{p}$ operator in the unperturbed basis are:

$$\langle n\vec{k}|\varepsilon_x p_x + \varepsilon_y p_y + \varepsilon_z p_z|n'\vec{k'}\rangle = \delta_{nn'}\delta_{\vec{k},\vec{k'}}(\varepsilon_x\hbar k_x + \varepsilon_y\hbar k_y)$$

$$+ \varepsilon_z\delta_{\vec{k},\vec{k'}}\langle n|p_z|n'\rangle \qquad (\text{II.5.74})$$

Thus, the in-plane wavevector is conserved (translation invariance) and one deals either with intra-subband transitions (ε_x, ε_y polarisations) or to inter-subband transitions, the latter ones are only allowed in the ε_z polarisation.

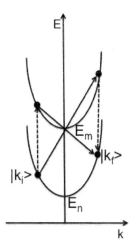

Figure II.5.14. Sketch of the virtual paths followed by an electron when going from $|k_i\rangle$ to $|k_f\rangle$ inside the subband E_n (intra-subband transition) in the z polarisation. The dashed vertical arrows correspond to virtual photon absorbing or emitting transitions while the oblique solid lines arise from the defects that are involved in virtual inter-subband transitions. Note that the virtual photon transitions are necessarily inter-subband since all optical transitions (virtual or real) inside the E_n subband are forbidden due to the vanishing of $\langle n|p_z|n\rangle$.

With $V_{\text{def}} = 0$, we know that the Fermi golden rule applied to the $\vec{A}\cdot\vec{p}$ coupling between the electron and the em wave gives a zero absorption in case of intra-subband transitions when the em electric field is parallel to the z-axis. Hence, we shall use V_{def} to perturb the electronic wavefunctions and then handle the $\vec{A}\cdot\vec{p}$ couplings between the V_{def}-perturbed eigenstates (see Fig. II.5.14). At the end of the calculations, we shall get a scattering time (an energy loss rate) that will be proportional to the square of the em electric field and to the defects concentration.

The peculiarity of the electron–photon coupling is that it is vertical in the $\vec{k}$ space while the impurity scattering leads to oblique inter-subband transitions. Realistic defects (coulombic impurities, interface defects and phonons) have been considered in the literature [57, 62] and must be put in the calculations to quantitatively describe the experiments. Once again in this textbook, we shall use uncorrelated delta scatterers in order to get simple analytical results. These scatterers have an areal concentration N_{def}/S and they are located on the plane $z = z_0$ at the sites $\vec{\rho}_i$. Thus:

$$V_{\text{def}}(\vec{r}) = V_0 a^3 \delta(z - z_0) \sum_{\vec{\rho}_i} \delta(\vec{\rho} - \vec{\rho}_i) - V_0 a^3 \frac{N_{\text{def}}}{S} \chi_n^2(z_0) \quad \text{(II.5.75)}$$

where V_0 is an energy, a a length and where the constant term ensures that all the diagonal elements of V_{def} vanish after averaging over the positions of the scatterers. To the lowest order, the perturbed wavefunctions are:

$$|\tilde{\Psi}_{n\vec{k}}\rangle = |n\vec{k}\rangle + \sum_{\vec{k}' \neq \vec{k}} |n\vec{k}'\rangle \frac{\langle n\vec{k}'|V_{\text{def}}|n\vec{k}\rangle}{\frac{\hbar^2(k^2 - k'^2)}{2m^*}}$$

$$+ \sum_{m \neq n, \vec{k}', \vec{k}} |m\vec{k}'\rangle \frac{\langle m\vec{k}'|V_{\text{def}}|n\vec{k}\rangle}{E_n - E_m + \frac{\hbar^2(k^2 - k'^2)}{2m^*}} \quad \text{(II.5.76)}$$

or:

$$|\tilde{\Psi}_{n\vec{k}}\rangle = |n\vec{k}\rangle + \frac{2m^*}{\hbar^2 S} V_0 a^3 \left[\sum_{\vec{k}_3 \neq \vec{k}} \left(|n\vec{k}_3\rangle \frac{\chi_n^2(z_0)}{(k^2 - k_3^2)} \right. \right.$$

$$\left. \left. + \sum_{m \neq n} |m\vec{k}_3\rangle \frac{\chi_n(z_0)\chi_m(z_0)}{\frac{2m^*}{\hbar^2}(E_n - E_m) + (k^2 - k_3^2)} \right) \sum_{\vec{\rho}_i} e^{i(\vec{k} - \vec{k}_3) \cdot \vec{\rho}_i} \right]$$

$$\text{(II.5.77)}$$

where S is the sample area.

z **polarisation.** To compute the transition rate for an intra-subband transition $|n\vec{k}\rangle \to |n\vec{k}'\rangle$, we first evaluate $\langle \tilde{\Psi}_{n\vec{k}'}|p_z|\tilde{\Psi}_{n\vec{k}}\rangle$ and obtain:

$$\langle \tilde{\Psi}_{n\vec{k}'}|p_z|\tilde{\Psi}_{n\vec{k}}\rangle$$

$$= \frac{2m^*}{\hbar^2 S} V_0 a^3 \sum_{\vec{\rho}_i} e^{i(\vec{k} - \vec{k}') \cdot \vec{\rho}_i} \chi_n(z_0)\chi_m(z_0)$$

$$\times \left[\frac{\langle n|p_z|m\rangle}{\frac{2m^*}{\hbar^2}(E_n - E_m) + (k^2 - k'^2)} + \frac{\langle m|p_z|n\rangle}{\frac{2m^*}{\hbar^2}(E_n - E_m) + (k'^2 - k^2)} \right]$$

$$\text{(II.5.78)}$$

As expected, we find that a non-zero intra-subband p_z element is induced by the disorder. Note that, after averaging over the defect/impurity positions, we shall find a vanishing average $\langle\langle\tilde{\Psi}_{n\vec{k}'}|p_z|\tilde{\Psi}_{n\vec{k}}\rangle\rangle_{\vec{\rho}_i}$ but a non-zero $\langle|\langle\tilde{\Psi}_{n\vec{k}'}|p_z|\tilde{\Psi}_{n\vec{k}}\rangle|^2\rangle_{\vec{\rho}_i}$ and this will lead to a net photon absorption. Due to the sinusoidal variation of the em field, we can compute the rate of emitted energy by the electrons using:

$$P^z_{\text{emiss}} = \frac{\pi e^2 E^2_{\text{em}}}{2m^{*2}\omega} 2\sum_{\vec{k},\vec{k}'} f_{n\vec{k}}(1 - f_{n\vec{k}'})\langle|\langle\tilde{\Psi}_{n\vec{k}'}|p_z|\tilde{\Psi}_{n\vec{k}}\rangle|^2\rangle_{\vec{\rho}_i}$$

$$\times \delta\left(\frac{\hbar^2(k^2 - k'^2)}{2m^*} - \hbar\omega\right) \tag{II.5.79}$$

where $f_{n\vec{k}}$ is the occupation factor of the state $|n\vec{k}\rangle$. Note that we have introduced a factor of 2 in front of the double sum to account for the electron spin:

$$P^z_{\text{abs}} = \frac{\pi e^2 E^2_{\text{em}}}{2m^{*2}\omega} 2\sum_{\vec{k},\vec{k}'} f_{n\vec{k}}(1 - f_{n\vec{k}'})\langle|\langle\tilde{\Psi}_{n\vec{k}'}|p_z|\tilde{\Psi}_{n\vec{k}}\rangle|^2\rangle_{\vec{\rho}_i}$$

$$\times \delta\left(\frac{\hbar^2(k^2 - k'^2)}{2m^*} + \hbar\omega\right) \tag{II.5.80}$$

By interchanging $\vec{k}$ and $\vec{k}'$ in (II.5.80) and subtracting (II.5.79) from (II.5.80), we get the energy loss rate of the em wave associated with intra-subband n transitions:

$$P^z_{\text{loss}} = P^z_{\text{abs}} - P^z_{\text{emiss}} = \frac{\pi e^2 E^2_{\text{em}}}{2m^{*2}\omega} 2\sum_{\vec{k},\vec{k}'} (f_{n\vec{k}'} - f_{n\vec{k}})\langle|\langle\tilde{\Psi}_{n\vec{k}'}|p_z|\tilde{\Psi}_{n\vec{k}}\rangle|^2\rangle_{\vec{\rho}_i}$$

$$\times \delta\left(\frac{\hbar^2(k^2 - k'^2)}{2m^*} - \hbar\omega\right) \tag{II.5.81}$$

Using (II.5.78) we obtain:

$$P^z_{\text{loss}} = \frac{\pi e^2 E^2_{\text{em}}}{2m^{*2}\omega} \frac{V_0^2 a^6}{S^2} N_{\text{def}}\chi^2_n(z_0)$$

$$\times \sum_m \chi_m^2(z_0) |\langle n|p_z|m\rangle|^2 \left(\frac{1}{E_n - E_m + \hbar\omega} - \frac{1}{E_n - E_m - \hbar\omega} \right)^2$$

$$\times 2 \sum_{\vec{k}, \vec{k}'} (f_{n\vec{k}'} - f_{n\vec{k}}) \delta \left(\frac{\hbar^2(k^2 - k'^2)}{2m^*} - \hbar\omega \right) \qquad (\text{II.5.82})$$

Let us first assume that the electron concentration is small enough and the temperature is high enough to ensure that $f_{n\vec{k}}$ is well approximated by a Boltzmann distribution (classical limit). Then, the double sum in (II.5.82) simplifies as:

$$2 \sum_{\vec{k}, \vec{k}'} (f_{n\vec{k}'} - f_{n\vec{k}}) \delta \left(\frac{\hbar^2(k^2 - k'^2)}{2m^*} - \hbar\omega \right) = \frac{n}{S} \frac{m^* S^2}{2\pi\hbar^2} \left(1 - e^{-\frac{\hbar\omega}{k_B T}} \right)$$

$$(\text{II.5.83})$$

$$n = 2 \sum_{\vec{k}} f_{n\vec{k}} \qquad (\text{II.5.84})$$

where n/S is the areal concentration of electrons. With the explicit results (II.5.82, II.5.83) we find that, as it should, P_{loss}^z is an extensive quantity: if we double the area S, the number of electrons and the number of impurities, the emitted power is multiplied by 2.

In the (extreme) opposite limit of a degenerate electron gas at $T = 0$ K, we find that:

$$2 \sum_{\vec{k}, \vec{k}'} (f_{n\vec{k}'} - f_{n\vec{k}}) \delta \left(\frac{\hbar^2(k^2 - k'^2)}{2m^*} - \hbar\omega \right)$$

$$= \frac{n}{S} \frac{m^* S^2}{2\pi\hbar^2} \left[Y(\hbar\omega - \varepsilon_F) + \frac{\hbar\omega}{\varepsilon_F} Y(\varepsilon_F - \hbar\omega) \right] \qquad (\text{II.5.85})$$

$$n = 2 \sum_{\vec{k}} f_{n\vec{k}} = \frac{m^* S}{\pi\hbar^2} \varepsilon_F \qquad (\text{II.5.86})$$

The $T = 0$ K limit is interesting in that the occupation factors are either 0 or 1. It can be readily seen that the emitted power P_{emiss} is zero due to the 0/1 occupation factors. In fact at $T = 0$ K the initial state must be occupied which implies that the electrons have an in-plane kinetic energy smaller than the Fermi energy ε_F. On the other hand, the final states have to be empty and at $T = 0$ K this implies that their in-plane kinetic energy should be larger than ε_F. The energy conservation requires that each final state is reached by electrons whose initial states have energies larger than $\varepsilon_F + \hbar\omega$. There is no such state as noted above. As for absorption, we immediately see that if $\hbar\omega > \varepsilon_F$, all the electrons participate in the absorption process. Hence, if $\hbar\omega > \varepsilon_F$, the absorption saturates. On the other hand, if $\hbar\omega < \varepsilon_F$, not all the electrons can contribute to absorption: the effective electron concentration that contributes to absorption is the one comprised between $\varepsilon_F - \hbar\omega$ and ε_F. This concentration is equal to $\left(\frac{m^* S}{\pi \hbar^2}\right)\hbar\omega = n\frac{\hbar\omega}{\varepsilon_F}$; hence the result.

It is quite remarkable that the energy loss rate of the em wave shows no divergence when $\omega \to 0$. Instead, we find a vanishing P^z_{loss} in this limit. This is in striking contrast with the Drude results which show a ω^{-p} $p \approx 2 - 3$ divergence in the same limit. Instead, P^z_{loss} displays a singularity when the photon energy approaches the energy separation between subbands. No such a feature could appear in the Drude analysis that ignores size quantisation.

We show in Fig. II.5.15 the calculated energy loss rate versus $\hbar\omega$ for a GaAs single quantum well with $L = 20$ nm and a conduction

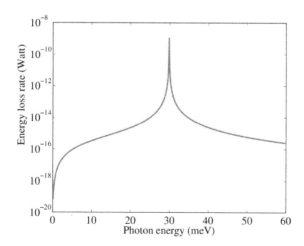

Figure II.5.15. Energy loss rate versus $\hbar\omega$ in the z polarisation for a GaAs single quantum well with $L = 20$ nm; $V_0 = 0.6$ eV, $a = 0.3$ nm, $z_0 = L/4$ $n/S = 2 \times 10^{10}$ cm^{-2} and $N_{\text{def}}/S = 10^{11}$ cm^{-2}; $E_{\text{em}} = 1$ kV/cm; $T = 100$ K.

band offset of 0.22 eV. $m^* = 0.07m_0$; $V_0 = 0.6$ eV, $a = 0.3$ nm, $n/S = 2 \times 10^{10}$ cm^{-2} and $N_{\mathrm{def}}/S = 10^{11}$ cm^{-2}; $E_{\mathrm{em}} = 1$ kV/cm; $T = 100$ K. We assume all the electrons are in the $n = 1$ subband. Hence, $n = 1$ and $m = 2$ in (II.5.82). We have chosen $z_0 = L/4$. We note again the "modulation" doping aspect of FCA. In particular, if the delta scatterers were placed in the middle of the well, the FCA would vanish. This very strong modulation doping effect reflects the physical reality but is magnified by the short range aspect of the scatterers.

In-plane polarisation. Instead of the x or y polarisation that privileges a direction of the plane while our problem is essentially isotropic, we consider a polarisation $\vec{\varepsilon}_+ = \frac{1}{\sqrt{2}}(\vec{\varepsilon}_x + i\vec{\varepsilon}_y)$ that holds x and y on equal footing (see Fig. II.5.16). This will ease the calculations. Proceeding as above, we get the squared modulus of the $\frac{p_x + ip_y}{\sqrt{2}}$ matrix element averaged over the impurity positions:

$$\left\langle \left| \langle \tilde{\Psi}_{n\vec{k}'} | \frac{p_x + ip_y}{\sqrt{2}} | \tilde{\Psi}_{n\vec{k}} \rangle \right|^2 \right\rangle_{\vec{\rho}_i} = N_{\mathrm{def}} \left(\frac{\sqrt{2}m^* V_0 a^3}{\hbar S} \right)^2 \chi_n^4(z_0) \frac{(\vec{k} - \vec{k}')^2}{(k^2 - k'^2)^2}$$

$$(\mathrm{II.5.87})$$

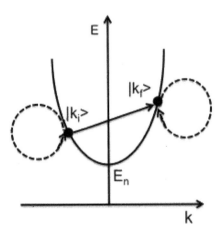

Figure II.5.16.   Sketch of the virtual paths followed by an electron when going from $|k_i\rangle$ to $|k_f\rangle$ inside the subband E_n (intra-subband transition) in the parallel polarisation. The dashed circles correspond to virtual photon absorbing or emitting transitions while the oblique solid lines arise from the defects that are involved in virtual inter-subband transitions.

For non-degenerate carriers, we obtain the energy loss rate for the in-plane polarisation:

$$P_{\text{loss}}^{x,y} = S \frac{e^2 E_{\text{em}}^2 (1 - e^{-\beta\hbar\omega})}{4m^*\hbar^2\omega^3} \frac{N_{\text{def}}}{S} \chi_n^4(z_0) V_0^2 a^6 \frac{n}{S}$$

$$\times \left(\frac{2m^* k_B T}{\hbar^2} + \frac{m^*\omega}{\hbar} \right) \tag{II.5.88}$$

The opposite limit of $P_{\text{loss}}^{x,y}$ arising from delta scatterers and a degenerate electron gas at $T = 0$ K is left as an exercise (see Exercise 52). We have recovered in (II.5.88) a Drude-like behaviour since our calculation predicts that the energy loss rate diverges when $\omega \to 0$ and furthermore shows no further singularity like the one we found in the z polarisation (see Fig. II.5.17 calculated with the same material parameter as used in Fig. II.5.15). We stress again that this feature results from the optical selection rules that prevents the existence of transition within a given subband in z polarisation.

Finally, it is worth comparing the magnitude of P_{loss} obtained in either z or in-plane polarisations assuming identical electron and

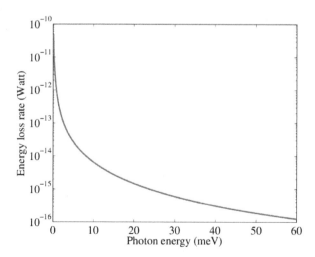

Figure II.5.17. Energy loss rate versus $\hbar\omega$ in the in-plane polarisation for a GaAs single quantum well with $L = 20$ nm. $V_0 = 0.6$ eV, $a = 0.3$ nm, $z_0 = L/4$ $n/S = 2 \times 10^{10}$ cm^{-2} and $N_{\text{def}}/S = 10^{11}$ cm^{-2}; $E_{\text{em}} = 1$ kV/cm; $T = 100$ K.

defect/impurities concentrations. In the non-degenerate limit we find:

$$\frac{P_{\text{loss}}^z}{P_{\text{loss}}^{x,y}} = \hbar^2 \omega^2 \frac{|\langle n|p_z|m\rangle|^2}{m^*(\hbar\omega + 2k_B T)} \frac{\chi_m^2(z_0)}{\chi_n^2(z_0)}$$

$$\times \left(\frac{1}{E_n - E_m + \hbar\omega} - \frac{1}{E_n - E_m - \hbar\omega} \right)^2 \quad \text{(II.5.89)}$$

Equation (II.5.89) demonstrates very clearly that the in-plane polarisation is more efficiently absorbed than the z polarisation when $\hbar\omega \ll E_n - E_m$. This absorption anisotropy is due to the fact that oblique in $\vec{k}$ intra-subband transitions are forbidden in the parallel polarisation because they would lead to a violation of the in-plane translation invariance. In the z polarisation instead we find these oblique intra-subband transitions doubly forbidden in ideal materials since (1) they violate the in-plane translation invariance but in addition (2) they are forbidden since $\langle n|p_z|n\rangle = 0$. Figure II.5.18 shows the ω-dependence of the ratio $\frac{P_{\text{loss}}^z}{P_{\text{loss}}^{x,y}}$ and establish the existence of a strong anisotropy of the optical absorption when $\omega \to 0$.

The previous results have been established using idealised scatterers. It turns out that handling realistic scatterers leads to similar features: the non-Drude aspects of FCA for the parallel (z)

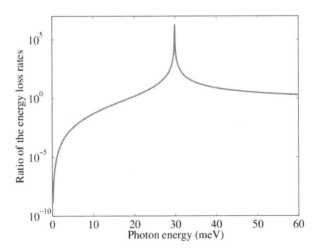

Figure II.5.18. Ratio of the energy loss, rates $P_{\text{loss}}^z/P_{\text{loss}}^{x,y}$ versus $\hbar\omega$ for a GaAs single quantum well with $L = 20$ nm; $V_0 = 0.6$ eV, $a = 0.3$ nm, $z_0 = L/4$ $n/S = 2 \times 10^{10}$ cm^{-2} and $N_{\text{def}}/S = 10^{11}$ cm^{-2}; $E_{\text{em}} = 1$ kV/cm; $T = 100$ K.

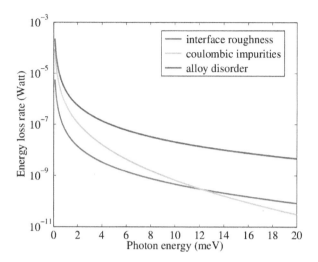

Figure II.5.19. Energy loss rate for intra $n = 2$ oblique transitions in the parallel polarisation assisted by interface roughness, coulombic impurities and alloy disorder; $T = 100$ K.

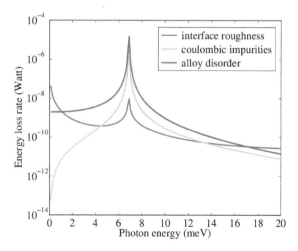

Figure II.5.20. Energy loss rate for intra $n = 2$ oblique transitions in the z polarisation assisted by interface roughness, coulombic impurities and alloy disorder. $T = 100$ K.

polarisation as well as a pronounced optical anisotropy in the long wavelength limit. Figures II.5.19–II.5.21 show the ω-dependence of the energy loss rate in both polarisations as well as their ratio for an asymmetric 26/3.1/12.6 nm double quantum well structure

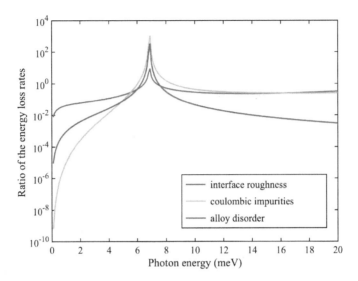

Figure II.5.21.   Ratio between the energy loss rates in the z polarisation to that in the parallel polarisation versus photon energy.

[63]. The conduction band offset is 0.36 eV corresponding to the $In_{0.53}Ga_{0.47}As/GaAs_{0.51}Sb_{0.49}$ ternary system. The carrier effective mass is $0.045m_0$ in the barrier material and $0.043m_0$ in the well material respectively; $n/S = 2.17 \times 10^{10}$ cm^{-2}. Interface defects are modelled as Gaussian protrusions with lateral extension of 5.6 nm and a fractional coverage of the surface equal to $f = 0.3$. Donors are placed in the wide well and $N_{def}/S = n/S$. The area $S = 200$ nm $\times 200$ nm.

II.5.4.2.   Phonon scattering in the presence of static scatterers

In contrast to the forbidden photon absorption/emission associated with intra-subband transitions, the absorption/emission of acoustical (or optical) phonons is allowed (energy permitting) inside a given subband (see Fig. II.5.22). Usually, the part played by static defects amounts to blurring the delta function that ensures the conservation of the energy of the {electron + phonon} system. Unless one deals with heavy doping, this is a small effect and the calculations

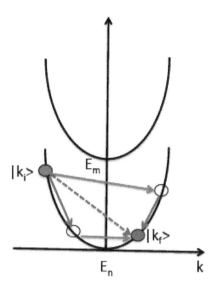

Figure II.5.22. Sketch of the virtual paths followed by an electron when going from $|k_i\rangle$ to $|k_f\rangle$ inside the subband E_n (intra-subband transition) due to the combined actions of impurities/defects (red arrows) and phonon emission (blue arrows). The dashed blue arrow is the real $|k_i\rangle \to |k_f\rangle$ transition assisted by phonon emission. Note that in contrast to FCA, the virtual phonon transitions can be intra-subband. In addition to the virtual process shown here, it may also exist virtual processes where the intermediate states (open circles) are in a different subband from the E_n one.

made by taking the matrix elements of the electron–phonon interaction between unperturbed electron states are sufficiently accurate for most purposes. In the case of acoustical phonons, we know that the phonon energy exchange with the electron is typically 1–2 meV. Enhancing the amount of energy exchange would improve the energy loss rate of electrons and fasten the electronic thermalisation.

The strategy to follow to compute the enhancement is the same as the one followed for the FCA: one perturbs the ideal electron states by the static scatterers and then computes the lifetime due to the emission/absorption of acoustical phonons between these perturbed states. One starts from:

$$H = H_{\text{el}} + H_{\text{ph}} + H_{\text{el-ph}} \tag{II.5.90}$$

$$H_{\text{el}} = \frac{p^2}{2m^*} + V_{\text{conf}}(z) + V_{\text{def}}(\vec{r}) \tag{II.5.91}$$

$$H_{\text{ph}} = \sum_{\vec{Q}} \left(a_{\vec{Q}}^{\dagger} a_{\vec{Q}} + \frac{1}{2} \right) \hbar \omega_{\vec{Q}}; \quad \hbar \omega_{\vec{Q}} = \hbar c_s Q \tag{II.5.92}$$

$$H_{\text{el-ph}} = \sum_{\vec{Q}} (v_{\vec{Q}}^* e^{-i\vec{Q}\cdot\vec{r}} a_{\vec{Q}}^{\dagger} + v_{\vec{Q}} e^{i\vec{Q}\cdot\vec{r}} a_{\vec{Q}}) \tag{II.5.93}$$

where a 3D model for the longitudinal acoustical phonons with an isotropic dispersion (c_s is the sound velocity) has been assumed. $v_{\vec{Q}}$ is the deformation potential coupling and $V_{\text{def}}(\vec{r})$ the defect potential that will mix $|n\vec{k}'\rangle \neq |n\vec{k}\rangle$ states in the unperturbed $|n\vec{k}\rangle$ states.

Using for V_{def} the uncorrelated delta scatterers, one perturbs the electron wavefunction at the first order in V_{def} as in Eq. (II.5.76). Specialising to low k vectors (such that the in-plane kinetic energy remains smaller than the subband spacing $E_n - E_m$) one can neglect the third term with respect to the second one in (II.5.76). Then, with the delta scatterers of Eq. (II.5.75), one gets:

$$\langle \vec{r} | \tilde{\Psi}_{n\vec{k}} \rangle = \chi_n(z) \left[\frac{e^{i\vec{k}\cdot\vec{\rho}}}{\sqrt{S}} + \chi_n^2(z_0) \frac{2m^* V_0 a^3}{\hbar^2 S} \sum_{\vec{k}_3 \neq \vec{k}} \sum_{\vec{\rho}_i} \frac{e^{i(\vec{k}-\vec{k}_3)\cdot\vec{\rho}_i}}{k^2 - k_3^2} \frac{e^{i\vec{k}_3\cdot\vec{\rho}}}{\sqrt{S}} \right]$$

$$= \langle \vec{r} | n\vec{k} \rangle + \sum_{\vec{k}_3} \alpha_{n,\vec{k},\vec{k}_3} \langle \vec{r} | n\vec{k}_3 \rangle \tag{II.5.94}$$

$$\alpha_{n,\vec{k},\vec{k}_3} = \chi_n^2(z_0) \frac{2m^* V_0 a^3}{\hbar^2 S} \sum_{\vec{\rho}_i} \frac{e^{i(\vec{k}-\vec{k}_3)\cdot\vec{\rho}_i}}{k^2 - k_3^2} \tag{II.5.95}$$

The lifetime of an electron with energy $E_n + \frac{\hbar^2 k^2}{2m^*} + \langle n\vec{k} | V_{\text{def}} | n\vec{k} \rangle$ and wavefunction $\langle \vec{r} | \tilde{\Psi}_{n\vec{k}} \rangle$ due to the emission of acoustical phonons is equal to:

$$\frac{\hbar}{2\pi \tau_{n\vec{k}}^{\text{emiss}}} = \sum_{\vec{Q}} (1 + n_{\vec{Q}}) |v_{\vec{Q}}|^2 |\langle \tilde{\Psi}_{n\vec{k}'} | e^{-i\vec{Q}\cdot\vec{r}} | \tilde{\Psi}_{n\vec{k}} \rangle|^2$$

$$\times \delta \left(\frac{\hbar^2 (k^2 - k'^2)}{2m^*} - \hbar c_s Q \right) \tag{II.5.96}$$

Expanding the electron–phonon coupling matrix element up to the first order in $V_0 a$, we find:

$$\langle \tilde{\Psi}_{n\vec{k}'} | e^{-i\vec{Q}\cdot\vec{r}} | \tilde{\Psi}_{n\vec{k}} \rangle = \langle n | e^{-iQ_z z} | n \rangle (\delta_{\vec{k}',\vec{k}-\vec{q}} + \alpha_{n,\vec{k},\vec{k}'+\vec{q}} + \alpha^*_{n,\vec{k}',\vec{k}-\vec{q}})$$

(II.5.97)

$$\vec{Q} = (\vec{q}, Q_z)$$

(II.5.98)

Then:

$$\langle \tilde{\Psi}_{n\vec{k}'} | e^{-i\vec{Q}\cdot\vec{r}} | \tilde{\Psi}_{n\vec{k}} \rangle$$

$$= \langle n | e^{-iQ_z z} | n \rangle \left[\delta_{\vec{k}',\vec{k}-\vec{q}} + \left(\chi_n^2(z_0) \frac{2m^* V_0 a^3}{\hbar^2 S} \right) \right.$$

$$\left. \times \sum_{\vec{\rho}_i} e^{i(\vec{k}-\vec{k}'-\vec{q})\cdot\vec{\rho}_i} \left(\frac{1}{k^2 - (\vec{k}'+\vec{q})^2} + \frac{1}{k'^2 - (\vec{k}-\vec{q})^2} \right) \right]$$

(II.5.99)

We see clearly that the matrix element involved in the phonon emission comprises a contribution that is defect/impurity-independent and one that is linear in $V_0 a^3$ and is proportional to the impurity structure factor at a wavevector which is equal to the total (electron + phonon) wavevector change. With (II.5.99) one can apply the Fermi golden rule by taking the squared matrix element of $e^{-i\vec{Q}\cdot\vec{r}}$. A zeroth-order term is first obtained; it coincides with the "usual" relaxation frequency of the ideal electron system. The next term displays a singularity when $\vec{k}' = \vec{k} - \vec{q}$ but actually this equality cannot show up since it would mean the intermediate vector $\vec{k}_3$ coincides either with $\vec{k}$ or $\vec{k}'$ in the perturbation expansion of the initial and final states. We note that the second term is proportional to the structure factor at $\vec{k}' - \vec{k} + \vec{q}$, a non-zero vector by assumption. Hence, it will vanish after averaging over the impurities positions. Finally, one gets a third contribution that will be proportional to N_{def} after performing the same averaging over the positions of the impurities.

One therefore obtains for phonon emission:

$$\frac{\hbar}{2\pi \tau_{n\vec{k}}^{(0)}} = \sum_{Q_z, \vec{q}, \vec{k}'} \left(1 + n_{\vec{Q}} \right) \left| \langle n | e^{-iQ_z z} | n \rangle \right|^2 |v_{\vec{Q}}|^2 \delta_{\vec{k}',\vec{k}-\vec{q}}$$

$$\times \, \delta \left(\frac{\hbar^2 (k^2 - k'^2)}{2m^*} - \hbar c_s Q \right) \tag{II.5.100}$$

$$\frac{\hbar}{2\pi \tau_{n\vec{k}}^{(1)}} = \frac{N_{\text{imp}}}{S} \sum_{Q_z, \vec{q}, \vec{k}'} \left(1 + n_{\vec{Q}} \right) \left| \langle n | e^{-iQ_z z} | n \rangle \right|^2 |v_{\vec{Q}}|^2$$

$$\times \, \delta \left(\frac{\hbar^2 (k^2 - k'^2)}{2m^*} - \hbar c_s Q \right) A(\vec{k}, \vec{k}', \vec{q}) \tag{II.5.101}$$

where:

$$A(\vec{k}, \vec{k}', \vec{q}) = \frac{1}{S} \left(\chi_n^2(z_0) \frac{2m^* V_0 a^3}{\hbar^2} \right)^2$$

$$\times \left(\frac{1}{k^2 - (\vec{k}' + \vec{q})^2} + \frac{1}{k'^2 - (\vec{k} - \vec{q})^2} \right)^2 \tag{II.5.102}$$

The calculations become numerically involved and will not be attempted here. In the case of doped graphene, the three-body collisions (electrons, acoustical phonons, impurities) have enabled the understanding of the energy loss rate of hot electrons while the regular two-body processes (interacting electrons and phonons) failed to do so [58]. It may be that the importance of three-body collisions in doped graphene arise from the (linearly) decreasing density of states versus the electron energy which renders the quasi-elastic processes increasingly inefficient at low energies.

Chapter II.6

Results for Electron–Phonon Interaction

We give in this chapter a few results regarding the level broadening and energy loss rate due to electron–phonon interaction. In contrast with static scatterers, we shall not include screening effects. This is because the static screening model developed in Chapter II.4 is reasonably accurate for the electron–acoustical phonon interaction but is not reliable for the electron–optical phonon interaction. The LO phonons are so quickly oscillating (period $T \approx 1.2 \times 10^{-13}$ s in GaAs) that the electrostatic perturbations they create require a dynamical approach of the screening action that is beyond the scope of our introductory textbook (see e.g., [64]). We therefore deal with the electron–phonon Hamiltonian (II.3.36) and (II.3.51):

$$H_{e-ph} = \sum_{\vec{Q}} u_\alpha(\vec{Q}) e^{-i\vec{Q}\cdot\vec{r}} a^\dagger_{\alpha,\vec{Q}} + u^*_\alpha(\vec{Q}) e^{i\vec{Q}\cdot\vec{r}} a_{\alpha,\vec{Q}} \qquad \text{(II.6.1)}$$

where $\vec{Q} = (Q_z, \vec{q})$ is the 3D phonon wavevector, α denotes the phonon species (acoustical, optical, longitudinal, transverse, etc.) and the u's the way the electron interacts with a particular phonon mode. Here, we shall deal with longitudinal optical (LO) and longitudinal acoustical (LA) phonons. The u's in (II.6.1) are respectively equal to the Fröhlich and deformation potential terms:

$$u_{\text{Frohlich}}(\vec{Q}) = -i\frac{C_F}{Q};$$

$$C_{\mathrm{F}} = e \sqrt{\frac{\hbar\omega_{\mathrm{LO}}}{2\Omega\varepsilon_0}\left(\frac{1}{\varepsilon_r(\infty)} - \frac{1}{\varepsilon_r(0)}\right)} \qquad \text{(II.6.2)}$$

$$u_{\mathrm{DP}}(\vec{Q}) = D_c \sqrt{\frac{\hbar Q}{2\Omega\rho c_s}} \qquad \text{(II.6.3)}$$

We shall be discussing both the inter-subband and intra-subband scatterings.

II.6.1.   Optical phonon scattering

Let us first examine the inter-subband case which is technologically very important for the quantum cascade lasers as it is the most effective way to empty the lower level of the lasing transition at low carrier concentration (see Fig. II.6.1).

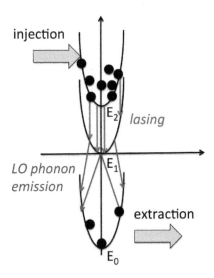

Figure II.6.1.   Schematics of one stage of a three subbands quantum cascade laser. Electrons are injected from the previous stage in the E_2 subband. Under population inversion between E_2 and E_1, photons are emitted at the energy $E_2 - E_1$. The E_1 subband is quickly depopulated by LO phonon emission to the E_0 subband. The carriers in the latter subband are extracted from this stage to the next one where they are injected in the E_2 subband of the next stage. For this scheme to be viable, the depopulation of the E_1 subband should be very efficient.

The lifetime of an electron in the state $|n\vec{k}\rangle$ due to LO phonon emission to any state $|n'\vec{k'}\rangle$ is given by:

$$\frac{1}{\tau_{n\vec{k}}} = \frac{m^* e^2}{8\pi\varepsilon_0\hbar^2} \left(\frac{1}{\varepsilon_r(\infty)} - \frac{1}{\varepsilon_r(0)} \right) (1 + n_{\mathrm{LO}})\omega_{\mathrm{LO}} Y$$

$$\times \left(E_n + \frac{\hbar^2 k^2}{2m^*} - E_{n'} - \hbar\omega_{\mathrm{LO}} \right)$$

$$\times \int_0^{2\pi} d\theta' \frac{I_{nn'}(|\vec{k} - \vec{k'}|)}{|\vec{k} - \vec{k'}|} \tag{II.6.4}$$

$$I_{nn'}(|\vec{k} - \vec{k'}|) = \iint dz dz' \chi_n(z)\chi_{n'}^*(z)\chi_n^*(z')\chi_{n'}(z')$$

$$\times \exp(-|\vec{k} - \vec{k'}||z - z'|) \tag{II.6.5}$$

where n_{LO} is the phonon occupation function and θ' is the angle between $\vec{k}$ and $\vec{k'}$. The Heaviside function Y ensures that $k'^2 > 0$ while:

$$k' = \sqrt{k^2 + \frac{2m^*}{\hbar^2}(E_n - E_{n'} - \hbar\omega_{\mathrm{LO}})} \tag{II.6.6}$$

$$q = |\vec{k} - \vec{k'}| = \sqrt{k^2 + k'^2 - 2kk'\cos\theta'} \tag{II.6.7}$$

It will also be useful to consider the average escape time from subband n by a thermalised population:

$$\frac{1}{\langle\tau_n\rangle} = \frac{\int_0^\infty k dk \frac{1}{\tau_{n\vec{k}}} \exp\left(-\frac{\hbar^2 k^2}{2m^* k_B T}\right)}{\int_0^\infty k dk \exp\left(-\frac{\hbar^2 k^2}{2m^* k_B T}\right)} \tag{II.6.8}$$

The time $\langle\tau_n\rangle$ is the characteristic decay time of the population in the nth subband due to the $n \to n'$ transitions assisted by the LO phonon emission (note that the refilling of the nth subband by LO phonon absorption has not been taken into account in (II.6.8)).

Expressions similar to (II.6.4)–(II.6.7) can be derived for LO phonon absorption by changing $(1 + n_{\mathrm{LO}})$ into n_{LO} in (II.6.4) and $-\hbar\omega_{\mathrm{LO}}$ into $+\hbar\omega_{\mathrm{LO}}$ in (II.6.7). In general, the emission times is significantly smaller than the phonon absorption time because the LO phonon energy is large (36 meV in GaAs) compared to $k_B T$, even

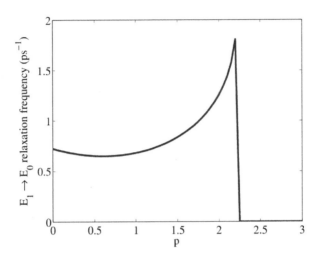

Figure II.6.2.   The LO phonon-assisted inter-subband relaxation frequency between E_1 and E_0 in a GaAs/Ga$_{0.75}$Al$_{0.25}$As $9/2/(3+p)$ nm double quantum well is plotted versus p; $k = 0$; $T = 0$ K ($n_{\mathrm{LO}} = 0$).

at room temperature and thus $n_{\mathrm{LO}} < 1$. We show in Fig. II.6.2 the LO phonon-assisted relaxation frequency between E_1 and E_0 in a GaAs/Ga$_{0.75}$Al$_{0.25}$As $9/2/(3+p)$ nm double quantum well where $p = 0, 1, \ldots$. The initial state is the E_1 edge ($k = 0$). Increasing p leads to a situation where it becomes impossible to get a LO phonon emission at low temperature once $E_1 < E_0 + \hbar\omega_{\mathrm{LO}}$. The inter-subband relaxation can become very effective at resonance, in contrast with the inter-subband relaxation due to elastic mechanisms. This is because when $E_2 - E_1 = \hbar\omega_{\mathrm{LO}}$ both $\vec{k}$ and $\vec{k}'$ can vanish, implying a vanishing $\vec{q}$ while in the case of an elastic inter-subband transition $\vec{q}$ never vanishes.

When $E_1 - E_0 < \hbar\omega_{\mathrm{LO}}$, the relaxation can only proceed from $k \neq 0$ initial states in the E_1 subband. We show in Fig. II.6.3, the k-dependence of the inter-subband relaxation frequency in such a situation. One finds a threshold of the relaxation efficiency at

$$k_{\mathrm{th}} = \sqrt{\frac{2m^*(\hbar\omega_{\mathrm{LO}} + E_1 - E_2)}{\hbar^2}} \qquad (\mathrm{II.6.9})$$

Thus, at low temperature, one does not expect any inter-subband relaxation since the $k > k_{\mathrm{th}}$ states are not populated. The relaxation

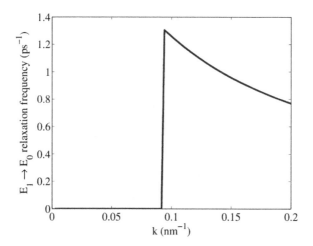

Figure II.6.3. The $E_1 \to E_0$ inter-subband relaxation frequency due to LO phonon emission is plotted versus the initial wavevector k in the E_1 subband for a 9/2/5.6 nm double quantum well; $T = 0$ K $(n_{\mathrm{LO}} = 0)$.

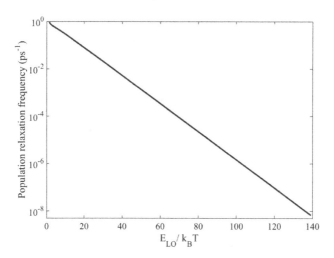

Figure II.6.4. The population relaxation frequency due to $E_1 \to E_0$ inter-subband transitions in a 9/2/5.6-nm double quantum well is plotted versus $\frac{E_{\mathrm{LO}}}{k_B T} = \frac{\hbar\omega_{\mathrm{LO}}}{k_B T}$ displaying a clear thermo-activation.

is thermo-activated as shown in Fig. II.6.4 where the T-dependence of the $1 \to 0$ relaxation is shown. In case of the $0 \to 1$ transition due to LO phonon absorption, the thermo-activation takes place when $E_1 - E_0 > \hbar\omega_{\mathrm{LO}}$.

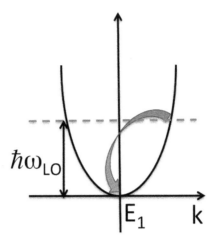

Figure II.6.5. E_1 dispersion relation showing the onset of the intra-subband transitions assisted by the emission of one LO phonon at low temperature ($k_B T \ll \hbar\omega_{LO}$). The initial wavevector should be larger than k_{ph}.

The intra-subband scattering time is usually very short (subpicosecond). Its shortest value is reached when the final wavevector $\vec{k}'$ nearly vanishes (see Fig. II.6.5). In this case we get:

$$\frac{1}{\tau_{n\vec{k}_{\min}}} \approx \frac{m^* e^2}{4\varepsilon_0 \hbar^2} \left(\frac{1}{\varepsilon_r(\infty)} - \frac{1}{\varepsilon_r(0)} \right) (1 + n_{LO})\omega_{LO} \frac{I_{nn}(k_{ph})}{k_{ph}} \quad (II.6.10)$$

$$k_{ph} = \sqrt{\frac{2m^*}{\hbar}\omega_{LO}} \quad (II.6.11)$$

$$I_{nn}(k_{ph}) = \iint dz dz' \chi_n^2(z)\chi_n^2(z') \exp(-k_{ph}|z - z'|) \quad (II.6.12)$$

Taking the approximation $\exp(-k_{ph}|z - z'|) \approx \frac{2}{k_{ph}}\delta(z - z')$ (which is the more valid for the larger k_{ph}'s), we end up with:

$$\frac{1}{\tau_{n\vec{k}_{ph}}} \approx \frac{e^2}{4\varepsilon_0 \hbar} \left(\frac{1}{\varepsilon_r(\infty)} - \frac{1}{\varepsilon_r(0)} \right) (1 + n_{LO}) \int dz \chi_n^4(z) \quad (II.6.13)$$

This expression shows that the intra-subband relaxation time at the onset is nearly m^* and ω_{LO}-independent (apart from the Bose factor). The polarity of the material enters in (II.6.13) through the difference between $1/\varepsilon_r$ and $1/\varepsilon_\infty$ which is the larger when the material is the more polar.

II.6.2. Acoustical phonon scattering

The scattering by LA phonons leads to the relaxation time:

$$\frac{1}{\tau_{n\vec{k}}} = \frac{D_c^2}{8\pi^2 \rho c_s^2 \hbar} \int_{-\infty}^{+\infty} dQ_z |f(Q_z)|^2$$

$$\times \int_0^{2\pi} d\theta' \int_0^\infty k'dk' \hbar\omega_{LA}[1 + n_{LA}(\hbar\omega_{LA})]$$

$$\times \delta\left(E_n - E_{n'} - \hbar\omega_{LA} + \frac{\hbar^2(k^2 - k'^2)}{2m^*}\right) \qquad \text{(II.6.14)}$$

$$\hbar\omega_{LA}(Q_z, \vec{q}) = \hbar c_s \sqrt{Q_z^2 + q^2}; \quad \vec{q} = \vec{k'} - \vec{k} \qquad \text{(II.6.15)}$$

$$q^2 = k^2 + k'^2 - 2kk' \cos\theta' \qquad \text{(II.6.16)}$$

where c_s is the sound velocity, isotropic acoustical dispersions have been assumed and:

$$f(Q_z) = \int_{-\infty}^{+\infty} dz \chi_n(z)\chi_{n'}^*(z)e^{-iQ_z z} \qquad \text{(II.6.17)}$$

The typical phonon energy that is absorbed or emitted is $\approx 1-2$ meV. Hence, when the electronic energies exceed, say, 10 meV, it is a good approximation to neglect the acoustical phonon energy in the delta function that ensures the energy conservation in (II.6.14). Also, at high temperature, there are many acoustical phonons and

$$n_{LA} \approx \frac{k_B T}{\hbar\omega_{LA}} \gg 1 \qquad \text{(II.6.18)}$$

These two approximations allow for a significant simplification of (II.6.14):

$$\frac{1}{\tau_{n\vec{k}}} = \frac{D_c^2 m^* k_B T}{4\pi \hbar^3 \rho c_s^2} \int_{-\infty}^{+\infty} dQ_z |f(Q_z)|^2$$

$$= \frac{D_c^2 m^* k_B T}{2\hbar^3 \rho c_s^2} \int_{-\infty}^{+\infty} dz \chi_n^2(z)\chi_{n'}^2(z) \qquad \text{(II.6.19)}$$

The LA phonon absorption rate is given by the same expression as (II.6.19) to the extent that $n_{LA} \gg 1$ and that the acoustical phonon energy has been neglected in the energy conservation. This feature (almost equal absorption and emission rates) is in sharp contrast with the LO phonon case. We recover in (II.6.19) a familiar trend, which is the linear increase of the electron–LA phonon scattering rate upon T. The scattering frequency is proportional to the carrier effective mass, a feature reminiscent of the proportionality of the density of final states to m^*. For a single quantum well with infinite height both the intra-subband and inter-subband contributions in (II.6.19) are proportional to $1/L$ (by dimensionality argument or a direct calculation). Hence, both the intra-subband and inter-subband scattering rates grow linearly with the quantum well thickness. For actual QW structures, this trend remains correct, except when one of the states becomes marginally bound. This is illustrated in Fig. II.6.6 where we show the intra-subband and inter-subband scattering times versus the QW thickness L. The calculations were performed using the full Eqs. (II.6.14)–(II.6.17) at $T = 0$ K and GaAs-like material parameters. For $L = 10$ nm and GaAs material parameters one

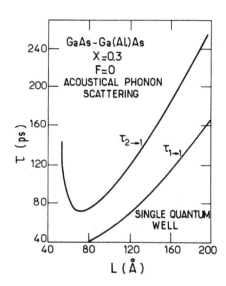

Figure II.6.6.   Quantum well thickness (L) dependence of the inter-subband $2 \to 1$ and intra-subband $1 \to 1$ relaxation times due to LA phonon scattering emission; $T = 0$ K. GaAs-like parameters were used: $D_c = 8.6$ eV, $\rho = 5.3$ g.cm^{-3}, $c_s = 3700$ m.s^{-1}, $m^* = 0.07m_0$, $V_b = 213.8$ meV.

Source: Ferreira and Bastard [65].

calculates at room temperature using (II.6.19) an intra-E_1 subband scattering time of 2.3 ps and an inter-subband $E_2 \rightarrow E_1$ subband scattering time that is 3/2 longer. The latter trend roughly agrees with the numerical data shown in Fig. II.6.6.

II.6.3. Energy loss rate

When a phonon of energy E_{ph} is emitted (absorbed), the electron gas loses (gains) this energy at a rate equal to the inverse of the corresponding scattering times. Manipulating the emission/absorption scattering times and averaging over the distribution functions of the initial states and non-occupation functions of the final states leads to the net power $\langle P \rangle$ given by the electrons to the LO phonons equal to:

$$\langle P \rangle = \frac{2\pi}{\hbar} \hbar \omega_{\text{LO}} C_{\text{F}}^2 \sum_{n,n'} \sum_{\vec{k},\vec{k'}} \delta(\varepsilon_{n\vec{k}} - \varepsilon_{n'\vec{k'}} - \hbar\omega_{\text{LO}}) A(k,k')$$

$$\times [(1 + n_{\text{LO}}) f(\varepsilon_{n\vec{k}})(1 - f(\varepsilon_{n'\vec{k'}}))$$
$$- n_{\text{LO}} f(\varepsilon_{n'\vec{k'}})(1 - f(\varepsilon_{n\vec{k}}))] \quad \text{(II.6.20)}$$

$$A(k,k') = \sum_{Q_z} \frac{|\langle \chi_n | e^{iQ_z z} | \chi'_n \rangle|^2}{Q_z^2 + (k^2 + k'^2 - 2\vec{k} \cdot \vec{k'})} = \frac{L_z}{2q_0} I_{nn'}(q_0) \quad \text{(II.6.21)}$$

where $q_0 = |\vec{k} - \vec{k'}|$ and L_z is the macroscopic length of the sample along the growth axis. For a thermalised electronic distribution, the bracket in (II.6.20) can be rewritten:

$$[\,] = n_{\text{LO}} e^{-\beta\mu} f(\varepsilon_{n\vec{k}}) f(\varepsilon_{n'\vec{k'}}) [e^{\beta_{\text{ph}}\hbar\omega_{\text{LO}}} e^{\beta\varepsilon_{n'\vec{k'}}} - e^{\beta\varepsilon_{n\vec{k}}}] \quad \text{(II.6.22)}$$

$$f(\varepsilon_{\vec{k}}) = \frac{1}{1 + \exp[\beta(\varepsilon_{n\vec{k}} - \mu)]} \quad \text{(II.6.23)}$$

where μ is the chemical potential of the electrons and T their temperature, $\beta = \frac{1}{k_B T}$, $\beta_{\text{ph}} = \frac{1}{k_B T_{\text{ph}}}$ where T_{ph} is the phonon bath temperature. Thus, if the thermalised electron distribution is at the same temperature as the phonon bath there is no net average power given by (or received from) the electrons to the LO phonons. This important result defines a dynamical thermal equilibrium between the electron and phonon subsystems. Also, as expected, if the electron temperature is larger (respectively, smaller) than the lattice temperature, the net power given to the phonon bath will be positive (respectively, negative). This implies that if a thermalised distribution of electrons has to be maintained at a temperature larger than the one of the lattice, an external source of energy should heat up the electron gas.

A significantly lighter algebra results when the carrier statistics is non-degenerate (high temperature, low density) and that a single subband, the ground one $n = 1$, contributes to the energy loss rate. Then, after some calculations, one finds that the energy loss rate per carrier can be written:

$$\frac{\langle P \rangle}{n_s} = \frac{\hbar \omega_{\mathrm{LO}}}{\tau_{\mathrm{eff}}} \tag{II.6.24}$$

$$\frac{1}{\tau_{\mathrm{eff}}} = \frac{e^2 k_{\mathrm{ph}}^2}{32\pi\hbar\varepsilon_0} \left(\frac{1}{\varepsilon_\infty} - \frac{1}{\varepsilon_r} \right) \tilde{\alpha}_{11} e^{-\beta\hbar\omega_{\mathrm{LO}}} (1 - e^{(\beta - \beta_{\mathrm{ph}})\hbar\omega_{\mathrm{LO}}})(1 + n_{\mathrm{LO}}) \tag{II.6.25}$$

$$\tilde{\alpha}_{11} e^{-\beta\hbar\omega_{\mathrm{LO}}} = \frac{\int_{k_{\mathrm{ph}}}^{\infty} k \, dk \, \alpha_{11}(k)^{-\beta\frac{\hbar^2 k^2}{2m^*}}}{\int_0^{\infty} k \, dk \, e^{-\beta\frac{\hbar^2 k^2}{2m^*}}} \tag{II.6.26}$$

$$\alpha_{11}(k) = \int_0^{2\pi} d\theta' \frac{I_{11}(q_0)}{q_0} \tag{II.6.27}$$

where k_{ph} has been defined in (II.6.11). In (II.6.27) $q_0 = |\vec{k} - \vec{k}'|$ has to be evaluated for $k' = \sqrt{k^2 - \frac{2m^*\omega_{\mathrm{LO}}}{\hbar}}$. Finally, because the optical phonons are quasi-monochromatic, the net energy loss rate can be simply cast into the ratio of a characteristic energy exchange (here the LO phonon energy) between the electrons and the phonons divided by a typical time τ_{eff}. The typical scattering frequency τ_{eff}^{-1} is proportional to the Boltzmann factor $\exp(-\beta\hbar\omega_{\mathrm{LO}})$ because only energetic enough electrons can emit an LO phonon. Depending on whether these electrons are numerous or not makes the cooling efficient or inefficient. Therefore, at low carrier temperature, the effective scattering frequency that enters the energy loss rate has to be less or much less than the reciprocal of the level lifetime that were calculated above and displayed in Fig. II.6.2. In addition, the scattering frequency vanishes when the thermal equilibrium is reached between the electrons and the phonons.

To get an order of magnitude of the effect, we approximate $\alpha_{11}(k)$ by $\frac{6\pi}{Lk_{\text{ph}}^2}$ (assuming perfect confinement for the electrons in the well and $k_{\text{ph}}L \gg 1$ where L is the quantum well thickness) to obtain:

$$\frac{1}{\tau_{\text{eff}}} \approx \frac{3e^2}{16\hbar\varepsilon_0 L}\left(\frac{1}{\varepsilon_r(\infty)} - \frac{1}{\varepsilon_r(0)}\right)e^{-\beta\hbar\omega_{\text{LO}}}\left(1 - e^{(\beta-\beta_{\text{ph}})\hbar\omega_{\text{LO}}}\right)(1+n_{\text{LO}})$$

$$(\text{II.6.28})$$

With numbers appropriate to carriers in a 20-nm GaAs quantum well and an electronic temperature of 42 K, we find an effective scattering frequency $1/\tau_{\text{eff}}$ of 1.27×10^8 s^{-1} and an energy loss rate of 0.73×10^{-12} W per carrier. Such figures are in qualitative agreement with experiments [44] (see Fig II.6.7). The discrepancy between

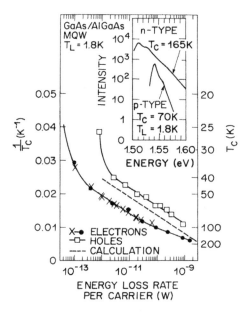

Figure II.6.7. The carrier temperature T_c (right scale) and its inverse $1/T_c$ (left scale) are plotted versus the energy loss rate per carrier either for electrons or for holes in modulation-doped GaAs/(Ga,Al)As quantum wells at a lattice temperature $T_L = 1.8$ K. The inset shows the photoluminescence intensity of n-doped or p-doped quantum wells versus the photon energy E. The high energy tails of these curves are proportional to $\exp(-\frac{\hbar\omega}{k_B T_c})$, thereby giving a direct access to T_c. Note the two parallel straight lines for the two kinds of carriers in the semi-log plots of $1/T_c$ versus the energy loss rate. The slope is $(\hbar\omega_{\text{LO}})^{-1}$.

Source: Shah *et al.* [44].

theory and experiments for electrons may originate from the incorrect assumption of a Boltzmann distribution for the electron gas. On the other hand, notice that the measured exponential decrease of $\langle P \rangle$ with decreasing T is nicely reproduced by the model. The energy loss rate has been measured versus the effective carrier temperature by Shah *et al.* [44]. To this end, the photoluminescence signal of n-doped or p-doped quantum wells was measured versus the photon energy while in-plane contacts ensured a Joule heating of the electron or hole gases. The high energy tail of the photoluminescence signal directly provided the heated carrier temperature T_c. The Joule energy loss rate was measured knowing the resistivity of the doped quantum well and the applied in-plane voltage. The Joule heat transferred to the carriers ultimately goes to the phonons. Hence, under thermal equilibrium among the carriers, the curves T_c versus the energy loss rate could be measured (see Fig. II.6.6). Shah *et al.* have attributed the marked difference between electron and hole energy loss rate to hot phonon effects that affect differently the electrons and holes energy loss rates curves.

Chapter II.7

Beyond the Born Approximation

In the previous chapters we have investigated the level lifetimes obtained by handling the electron defects/phonons interaction at the Born approximation (Fermi golden rule). Here, we wish to extend our analysis beyond the Born approximation because there exist situations where a more elaborate modelling is required (e.g., scattering involving bound states, scattering between Landau levels, etc.).

The multi-subband situation of quasi-2D (or 1D) materials enhances the need to pay more attention to the bound (or quasi-bound) states that are completely absent from the Born description of scattering. In a bulk material, coulombic impurities create bound states below (above) the edge of the conduction (valence) band. These bound states do not participate in the transport since the average velocity in a bound state is zero. They participate in the population evolution by trapping/de-trapping carriers but they can never be the final states of an elastic scattering (in a single band approximation), when there exists secondary minima not far in energy from the main one (as e.g., in GaSb) a situation somewhat similar to the one discussed below can show up. In contrast, it is quite frequent in a heterostructure that an electron in an extended state of one subband undergoes an elastic scattering on a static defect and ends up in a final state that is an impurity/a defect quasi-bound state attached to another subband.

We need to design a tool to handle such a situation because a bound state results from an infinite number of electron/impurity interactions and not only two like the scattering at the Born approximation. Besides, we noticed that usually the intra-subband scatterings are more efficient than the inter-subband ones. In other words, before undergoing an inter-subband transition, the electron experiences several intra-subband scatterings. Therefore, it is not fully coherent to handle both scatterings at the same level of approximation and to assume in the case of inter-subband scattering that the initial state is a plane wave, i.e., a state that has not been perturbed by the interactions with the defects.

Consider the projectors P_n and $P_{n'}$ on the nth and n'th subband:

$$P_n = \sum_\nu |n\nu\rangle\langle n\nu|; \quad P_{n'} = \sum_{\nu'} |n'\nu'\rangle\langle n'\nu'| \qquad \text{(II.7.1)}$$

where $|\nu\rangle$, $|\nu'\rangle$ are the eigenstates of an in-plane Hamiltonian; for instance the free particle Hamiltonian where $|n\nu\rangle$ is equal to $|n\vec{k}\rangle$ or another one that will be convenient for our purpose. We approximate the identity operator by $P_n + P_{n'}$, all the other subbands being uninvolved. Thus, in the time-dependent Schrödinger equation we get:

$$(P_n + P_{n'})(H_0 + V)(P_n + P_{n'})\psi = i\hbar\frac{\partial\psi}{\partial t}$$

$$[P_n(H_0 + V)P_n + P_{n'}(H_0 + V)P_{n'} + P_n V P_{n'} + P_{n'} V P_n]\psi = i\hbar\frac{\partial\psi}{\partial t}$$
$$\text{(II.7.2)}$$

It follows from Eq. (II.7.2) that the ψ projections $P_n\psi$ and $P_{n'}\psi$ on the nth and n'th subbands fulfil the coupled sets of equations:

$$P_n\left(H_0 + V - i\hbar\frac{\partial}{\partial t}\right)P_n(P_n\psi) + P_n V P_{n'}(P_{n'}\psi) = 0$$

$$P_{n'}\left(H_0 + V - i\hbar\frac{\partial}{\partial t}\right)P_{n'}(P_{n'}\psi) + P_{n'} V P_n(P_n\psi) = 0 \qquad \text{(II.7.3)}$$

Thus, the two components $P_n\psi$ and $P_{n'}\psi$ are coupled through the interband terms $P_n V P_{n'}$ and $P_{n'} V P_n$.

We choose the states $|\nu\rangle$ as the solutions of the intra-subband n (or n') in-plane Hamiltonian:

$$\begin{cases} (H_0 + \langle n|V|n\rangle)|\nu\rangle = (E_n + \varepsilon_\nu)|\nu\rangle \\ (H_0 + \langle n'|V|n'\rangle)|\nu'\rangle = (E_{n'} + \varepsilon_{\nu'})|\nu'\rangle \end{cases} \qquad \text{(II.7.4)}$$

We can now solve the t-dependent Schrödinger equation by using the Born approximation for the inter-subband term $P_n V P_{n'}$. We find the level lifetime of the initial state $|n\nu\rangle$ as:

$$\frac{\hbar}{2\pi\tau_{n\nu}} = \sum_{\nu'} |\langle n\nu|V_{\text{def}}|n'\nu'\rangle|^2 \delta(E_n - E_{n'} + \varepsilon_\nu - \varepsilon_{\nu'}) \qquad \text{(II.7.5)}$$

We see in Eq. (II.7.5) that the coupling matrix element accounted for the changes due to intra-subband scattering of the initial and final states compared to their unperturbed (plane waves) values, but also that the intra-subband scattering has led to new spectra compared to the parabolic dispersions of the 2D subbands. These spectra comprise bound (or quasi-bound) states below the edges E_n and $E_{n'}$ (see Fig. II.7.1).

The "new" Fermi golden rule produces results that are qualitatively different from those obtained by the "regular" Born approximation. This is in particular true in the vicinity of the subband edges where the intra-subband effects produce bound states. For THz emitters or detectors based on these quasi-2D heterostructures, the effect of these quasi-bound states on the transport (and thus I–V characteristics) will have to be studied (resonance scattering). All

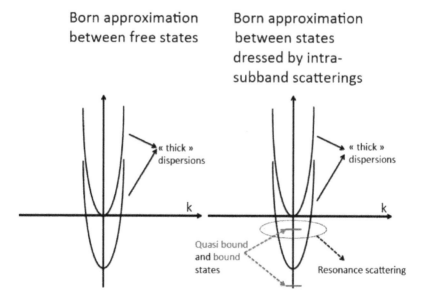

Figure II.7.1.   Comparison between Born approximation between plane wave states versus that between states dressed by the intra-subband scattering. "Thick" dispersion refers to broadened states.

these effects are enhanced when one goes towards subband spacings $E_n - E_{n'}$ that become comparable to the impurity binding energy ($\approx$5–8 meV in GaAs-based materials). In these nanostructures potentially useful for THz emission, the part played by the resonance scattering should become prevalent.

II.7.1. Scattering between Landau levels

We saw previously that a magnetic field applied parallel to the growth axis of a quasi-2D heterostructure Landau-quantises the electronic motion. When the Landau gauge $\vec{A} = (0, Bx, 0)$ is used, the eigenstates of the ideal system labelled $|n, p, k_y\rangle$ are

$$\psi_{n,p,k_y}(\vec{r}) = \frac{e^{ik_y y}}{\sqrt{L_y}}\chi_n(z)\varphi_p(x + \lambda^2 k_y); \quad \lambda = \sqrt{\frac{\hbar}{eB}}; \; p = 0, 1, 2, \ldots$$

$$\text{(II.7.6)}$$

The eigenenergies corresponding to Eq. (II.7.6) are:

$$\varepsilon_{n,p}(k_y) = E_n + \left(p + \frac{1}{2}\right)\hbar\omega_c; \quad \omega_c = \frac{eB}{m^*} \qquad \text{(II.7.7)}$$

where the effective mass mismatch has been neglected for simplicity. These energies are macroscopically degenerate since the degeneracy of a given Landau level is $g_{np} = \frac{L_x L_y}{2\pi\lambda^2}$ (spin excluded).

In addition to g_{np}, we see that two Landau levels p_1, p_2 belonging to two different subbands n_1, n_2 can cross if:

$$E_{n_1} + p_1\hbar\omega_c = E_{n_2} + p_2\hbar\omega_c \qquad \text{(II.7.8)}$$

These "accidental" degeneracies are unimportant for ideal systems because the system cannot evolve if at $t = 0$ it was placed in one of the eigenstates given in Eq. (II.7.6). In the presence of disorder these degeneracies lead to very significant population transfers because of the mixing between different Landau levels and different subbands. These population transfers may have catastrophic consequences on the behaviour of the device: for instance they can (reversibly) switch off the emission of a Quantum Cascade Laser [66]. We shall analyse the disorder induced population transfers later in this chapter.

Even when the magnetic field is far from the values that fulfil Eq. (II.7.8), the scattering between Landau levels cannot be handled by the usual Born-like approximation. To analyse this remarkable feature, we expand the unknown wavefunction on the basis of Eq. (II.7.6) and to simplify the analysis as much as possible, we restrict the expansion to intra-Landau level interactions by keeping n and p fixed:

$$\psi_{n,p}(\vec{r}, t) = \sum_{k_y} c_{n,p}(k_y, t) \exp\left(-i\frac{\varepsilon_{n,p,k_y} t}{\hbar}\right) \psi_{n,p,k_y}$$

$$i\hbar\frac{dc_{n,p}(k_y, t)}{dt} = \sum_{k_y'} c_{n,p}(k_y', t)\langle n, p, k_y|V_{\text{def}}|n, p, k_y'\rangle \qquad \text{(II.7.9)}$$

We see that the Landau level degeneracy leads to the absence in the right-hand side of Eq. (II.7.9) of any oscillating term unlike the situation where ε_{n,p,k_y} would depend on k_y. Suppose that we attempt to implement the reasoning that has led to the Fermi golden rule. To this end, we take the boundary condition at $t = 0$ as: $c_{n,p}(k_y, t = 0) = \delta_{k_y,k_0}$. Then, assuming the V_{def} matrix elements to be small, we truncate the differential system (Eq. (II.7.9)) and obtain (see Section I.3.3):

$$c_{n,p}(k_y, t) = \langle n, p, k_y|V_{\text{def}}|n, p, k_0\rangle\frac{t}{i\hbar}; \quad k_y \neq k_0 \qquad \text{(II.7.10)}$$

Thus, irrespective of the strength of the matrix elements, there will exist a time where the $c_{n,p}(k_y, t)$ are no longer small and all what we analysed at zero magnetic field to derive the Fermi golden rule no longer applies.

It is not easy to find a tractable model of Landau levels perturbed by defects. To start with we take a single delta scatterer since it often leads to an exactly solvable model. We take:

$$V_{\text{def}}(\vec{r}) = V_0 a^3 \delta(x - x_0)\delta(y)\delta(z - z_0) \qquad \text{(II.7.11)}$$

where a is a length. We obtain:

$$i\hbar\frac{dc_{n,p}(k_y, t)}{dt} = \frac{V_0 a^3 \chi_n^2(z_0)}{L_y}\varphi_p(x_0 + \lambda^2 k_y)\sum_{k_y'} c_{n,p}(k_y', t)\varphi_p(x_0 + \lambda^2 k_y')$$

$$\text{(II.7.12)}$$

A non-trivial solution of Eq. (II.7.12) can be found, we introduce the function:

$$Z_{n,p}(t) = \sum_{k_y} c_{n,p}(k_y, t)\phi_p(x_0 + \lambda^2 k_y) \tag{II.7.13}$$

and get:

$$i\hbar\frac{dZ_{n,p}(t)}{dt} = \frac{V_0 a^3 \chi_n^2(z_0)}{2\pi\lambda^2}Z_{n,p}(t) \tag{II.7.14}$$

So either $Z_{n,p}(t) = 0$ at any t or we obtain:

$$Z_{n,p}(t) = Z_{n,p}(0)e^{-i\Omega t}$$

$$\Omega = \frac{V_0 a^3 \chi_n^2(z_0)}{2\pi\lambda^2\hbar}; \quad Z_{n,p}(0) = \phi_p(x_0 + \lambda^2 k_0) \tag{II.7.15}$$

Thus, a single non-trivial frequency appears in the time-dependent problem. To get a further insight into te physical meaning of such frequency, let us examine the stationary problem. We expand the solution like in Eq. (II.7.9):

$$\psi_{n,p}(\vec{r}) = \sum_{k_y} c_{n,p}(k_y)\psi_{n,p,k_y}(\vec{r}) \tag{II.7.16}$$

Then, proceeding as above we define $\tilde{Z}_{n,p} = \sum_{k_y} c_{n,p}(k_y)\varphi_p(x_0 + \lambda^2 k_y)$ to obtain:

$$\left[E_n + \left(p + \frac{1}{2}\right)\hbar\omega_c + \hbar\Omega - \varepsilon\right]\tilde{Z}_{n,p} = 0 \tag{II.7.17}$$

Thus, either $\tilde{Z}_{n,p} = 0$ or

$$\varepsilon = E_n + \left(p + \frac{1}{2}\right)\hbar\omega_c + \hbar\Omega \tag{II.7.18}$$

The condition $\tilde{Z}_{n,p} = 0$ implies that the N possible values of $c_{n,p}(k_y)$ are linked by a single linear constraint. Hence, one may take $N - 1$ arbitrary values of these c's and the constraint allows expressing the Nth c as a function of the $N-1$ others. All these solutions correspond to the unperturbed energy $E_n + (p + \frac{1}{2})\hbar\omega_c$.

When $\tilde{Z}_{n,p} \neq 0$ and Eq. (II.7.18) is fulfilled, $\hbar\Omega$ appears as the "binding energy" of an electron around the delta scatterer in the presence of a strong magnetic field. There is a single bound state per Landau level, like in all 1D problems with delta scatterer (here the problem is effectively 1D because we have neglected the coupling between Landau levels). We note that Ω increases linearly with B. What is remarkable in Eqs. (II.7.16)–(II.7.17) is the fact that a repulsive potential (if $V_0 > 0$) creates a bound state above the unperturbed continuum (in other word its binding energy is negative). At $B = 0$ where there are 2D subbands, a repulsive potential does not create bound states: it scatters the plane waves but an attractive delta scatterer does bind a state below the subband edge ($\Omega < 0$ if $V_0 < 0$). In strong field, similarly, an attractive delta scatterer creates one bound state below the unperturbed Landau energy. The existence of bound states created by repulsive potentials is of course due to the suppression of the subband continuum thanks to the Landau quantisation. Such a feature is also found in quantum dots (quasi-0D systems) where unbound complexes (i.e., with a negative binding energy) are routinely observed (and calculated). The previous remarks are not only valid for the rather unrealistic case of delta scatterers (except for alloy scattering) but remain true if, for instance, one investigates dilute 2D gases in the presence of a strong magnetic field and realistic disorder. There, it is found that ionised donors (respectively, acceptors) create bound states below (respectively, above) the unperturbed Landau level energies [67].

We have not yet handled the case of Landau levels perturbed by randomly distributed impurities. The necessity to use non-perturbative approaches for a single impurity foresees the need of powerful techniques of quantum transport theory to handle the case of many impurities. The foundations of these techniques (mostly diagrammatic) are beyond the scope of this introductory textbook (see e.g., [68]).

Let us give the result of the self-consistent Born approximation very often used to analyse quasi-2D materials at zero or non-zero magnetic field (see e.g., [69]). We define the unperturbed Green function G_0 of the system as the operator inverse of $(\varepsilon - H_0)$. Similarly, G is the Green function of the system with randomly distributed scatterers:

$$G_0(\varepsilon) = (\varepsilon - H_0)^{-1}; \quad G(\varepsilon) = (\varepsilon - H_0 - V_{\text{def}})^{-1} \tag{II.7.19}$$

G_0 is obviously diagonal on the unperturbed basis. An important property of the G's is their relationships with the density of states. Indeed:

$$\lim_{\eta \to 0} \frac{1}{\varepsilon + i\eta - H_0} = P\left(\frac{1}{\varepsilon - H_0}\right) - i\pi\delta(\varepsilon - H_0) \qquad \text{(II.7.20)}$$

Now we see that

$$-\frac{1}{\pi}\text{Im}(\text{Tr}G_0) = \sum_{\nu} \delta(\varepsilon - \varepsilon_{0\nu}) = \rho_0(\varepsilon) \qquad \text{(II.7.21)}$$

where $\varepsilon_{0\nu}$ are the eigenvalues of the unperturbed Hamiltonian and ρ_0 is the unperturbed density of states. A similar expression would be obtained for G. G and G_0 are linked by the exact relationship:

$$\begin{aligned}
G(\varepsilon_+) &= G_0(\varepsilon_+) + G_0(\varepsilon_+)V_{\text{def}}G(\varepsilon_+) \\
G(\varepsilon_+) &= G_0(\varepsilon_+) + G_0(\varepsilon_+)V_{\text{def}}G_0(\varepsilon_+) \\
&\quad + G_0(\varepsilon_+)V_{\text{def}}G_0(\varepsilon_+)V_{\text{def}}G_0(\varepsilon_+)V_{\text{def}}G_0(\varepsilon_+) + \cdots
\end{aligned}$$
$$\text{(II.7.22)}$$

where $\varepsilon_+ = \varepsilon + i\eta$, $\eta \to 0$. G is an implicit function of the disorder (since it is a function of the Hamiltonian H that contains disorder). For a given realisation of the disorder, there is a particular H and thus a particular G. What is however physically more significant is $\langle G \rangle_{\text{aver}}$ the Green function averaged over the disorder (e.g., the positions of the impurities/defects). Again, the idea is that if the sample is large enough to be subdivided in many micro-samples where different realisations of the disorder show up, $\langle G \rangle_{\text{aver}}$ allows to compute the averaged density of states etc.

The degeneracy of the unperturbed Landau levels makes the series of Eq. (II.7.22) formally simple to resum. In fact, we note that inside the subspace with dimension g_{np} of such an unperturbed Landau level, all the diagonal matrix elements of the G_0 reduce to the c number $(\varepsilon + i\eta - \varepsilon_{np})^{-1}$ while all the off-diagonal matrix elements vanish. Thus, Eq. (II.7.22) can as well be rewritten:

$$G(\varepsilon + i\eta) = G_0(\varepsilon + i\eta) + G_0(\varepsilon + i\eta)$$

$$\times \left(V_{\text{def}} + \frac{V_{\text{def}}^2}{(\varepsilon + i\eta - \varepsilon_{np})} + \frac{V_{\text{def}}^3}{(\varepsilon + i\eta - \varepsilon_{np})^2} + \cdots \right)$$

$$\times \; G_0(\varepsilon + i\eta)$$

$$G(\varepsilon + i\eta) = G_0(\varepsilon + i\eta) + G_0(\varepsilon + i\eta)V_{\text{def}}$$

$$\times \left(1 - \frac{V_{\text{def}}}{(\varepsilon + i\eta - \varepsilon_{np})}\right)^{-1} G_0(\varepsilon + i\eta) \qquad \text{(II.7.23)}$$

However, averaging Eq. (II.7.23) over the positions of the impurities is not so easy since we have difficulties in computing $V_{\text{def}}[1 - V_{\text{def}}(\varepsilon + i\eta)^{-1}]^{-1}$. We should thus search for an approximate resummation of Eq. (II.7.23). It is furnished by the self-consistent Born approximation [12]: the quantity $\langle G \rangle_{\text{aver}}$ is linked to the self-energy $\Sigma(\varepsilon)$ operator by the Dyson equation:

$$\left\langle \langle \nu | G | \nu' \rangle \right\rangle_{\text{aver}}$$

$$= \delta_{\nu\nu'} \langle \nu | G_0(\varepsilon) | \nu \rangle + \langle \nu | G_0(\varepsilon) | \nu \rangle \sum_{\nu''} \langle \nu | \Sigma | \nu'' \rangle \left\langle \langle \nu'' | G | \nu' \rangle \right\rangle_{\text{aver}}$$

$$\text{(II.7.24)}$$

At the self-consistent Born approximation there is [69]:

$$\langle \nu | \Sigma | \nu' \rangle = \sum_{\beta, \beta'} \left\langle \langle \nu | V_{\text{def}} | \beta \rangle \langle \beta' | V_{\text{def}} | \nu' \rangle \right\rangle_{\text{aver}} \left\langle \langle \beta | G | \beta' \rangle \right\rangle_{\text{aver}} \qquad \text{(II.7.25)}$$

Equations (II.7.24) and (II.7.25) have to be solved self-consistently.

Let us try to make a connexion with the scattering times we calculated at the Born approximation in the previous chapters. To this end, suppose we replace G by G_0 in Eq. (II.7.25) and use the ideal Landau level basis to compute the matrix elements. In doing so, we get for the imaginary part of the self-energy a familiar result, namely:

$$G \to G_0 \Rightarrow \text{Im}(\langle \nu | \Sigma | \nu' \rangle) = -\pi \sum_{\beta} \left\langle \langle \nu | V_{\text{def}} | \beta \rangle \langle \beta | V_{\text{def}} | \nu' \rangle \right\rangle_{\text{aver}} \delta(\varepsilon - \varepsilon_{0\beta})$$

$$\text{(II.7.26)}$$

Hence, if we are interested in the diagonal part ($\nu = \nu'$) of Σ, we recover a formula that is reminiscent of the broadening of a level ν due to all transitions to levels β. The difficulty with Landau levels is of course that $\varepsilon_{0\beta}$ is β-independent. This makes Eq. (II.7.26) inapplicable because $\text{Im}(\langle \nu | \Sigma | \nu \rangle)$ is either zero or infinite. Let us now apply the formal results (Eqs. (II.7.24) and (II.7.25)) to an actual situation. We consider a single quantum well [70] in a strong magnetic field. The scatterers are the alloy fluctuations since the well is $Ga_{1-x}In_xAs$. Hence:

$$V_{def} \equiv V_{alloy} = \Delta V \omega_0 \left(\sum_{\vec{R}_{Ga}} x \delta(\vec{r} - \vec{R}_{Ga}) - \sum_{\vec{R}_{In}} (1 - x) \delta(\vec{r} - \vec{R}_{In}) \right)$$
(II.7.27)

where ω_0 is the volume of the unit cell and ΔV an energy related to the difference between the atomic potential of Ga and In averaged over the unit cell ω_0. We find:

$$\langle\langle n, p, k_y | G | n, p, k_y' \rangle\rangle_{aver} = \frac{1}{\varepsilon + i0 - \varepsilon_{np} - \Sigma_{np}(\varepsilon)} \delta_{k_y, k_y'} \qquad (II.7.28)$$

$$\Sigma_{np}(\varepsilon) = \overline{V}^2_{np,np} \langle\langle n, p, k_y | G | n, p, k_y \rangle\rangle_{aver} \qquad (II.7.29)$$

$$\overline{V}^2_{np,np} = \left\langle \sum_{k_y'} |\langle n, p, k_y | V_{alloy} | n, p, k_y' \rangle|^2 \right\rangle_{aver} \qquad (II.7.30)$$

$$\langle n, p, k_y | V_{alloy} | n, p, k_y' \rangle = \int d^3r \psi^*_{n,p,k_y}(\vec{r}) V_{alloy} \psi_{n,p,k_y'}(\vec{r}) \qquad (II.7.31)$$

The quantity $\Sigma_{np}(\varepsilon)$ acquires a clear physical meaning: if we look at the poles of the averaged Green function we see that they occur at:

$$\varepsilon = \varepsilon_{np} + \Sigma_{np}(\varepsilon) \qquad (II.7.32)$$

while of course for an ideal material the poles of G_0 occurs at the unperturbed energies: $\varepsilon = \varepsilon_{np}$. So, $\Sigma_{np}(\varepsilon)$ appears as the effect of the disorder on the propagating electron: it provides a shift (real part) and a damping (imaginary part) to the unperturbed energies. At the lowest order the poles of the averaged Green function occur at $\varepsilon = \varepsilon_{np} + \Sigma_{np}(\varepsilon)$ and as we mentioned above the connexion between $Im(\Sigma_{np})$ and lifetime τ_{np} becomes more transparent.

Finally, we obtain the energy dependence of the averaged self-energy:

$$\Sigma_{n,p}(\varepsilon) = \frac{\varepsilon - \varepsilon_{n,p}}{2} - i \sqrt{\overline{V}^2_{np,np} - \left(\frac{\varepsilon - \varepsilon_{n,p}}{2} \right)^2} \qquad (II.7.33)$$

Hence, the density of states averaged over the disorder is half an ellipse:

$$\rho_{n,p}(\varepsilon) = -\frac{1}{\pi}\text{Im}(\text{Tr}\langle G\rangle_{\text{aver}}) = -\frac{eBL_xL_y}{2\pi^2\hbar\overline{V}^2_{np,np}}\text{Im}(\Sigma_{n,p}(\varepsilon)) \quad \text{(II.7.34)}$$

As expected, the disorder that breaks the in-plane translation invariance has lifted the macroscopic degeneracy of the unperturbed Landau levels. Instead of a delta function we have now pockets of finite energy width. The total Landau level width is $4\sqrt{\overline{V}^2_{np,np}}$. It is easily checked that each pocket contains as many states as an unperturbed Landau level. In the specific case of alloy scattering the matrix elements can be entirely calculated:

$$\overline{V}^2_{np,np} = \frac{x(1-x)\omega_0(\Delta V)^2}{2\pi\lambda^2}\int dz f_{\text{alloy}}(z)\chi_n^4(z) \quad \text{(II.7.35)}$$

where the function f_{alloy} is one where the alloy scattering takes place and zero otherwise. We note that the alloy scattering is independent of the Landau level index p. It is also independent of the subband index n if the quantum well has an infinite height. We also find that the Landau level width grows like $\sqrt{B}$ and not like B (as does the degeneracy of the unperturbed spectrum).

Let us express $\text{Im}(\Sigma)$ in terms of a lifetime: $\text{Im}(\Sigma_{np}) = \frac{\hbar}{2\tau_{np}}$. Then, we find that $1/\tau_{np}$ is not proportional to the number of scatterers N_{def} (here $x(1-x)$ in the case of alloy scattering) but to its square root. Similarly, the width of the broadened Landau level is not proportional to N_{def} but to $\sqrt{N_{\text{def}}}$. These striking results arise from the self-consistency requirement since in the Σ_{np} expression, the quantity to be found also appears at the denominator of $\langle\beta|G|\beta'\rangle_{\text{aver}}$. This, in turn, implies that if we consider the scattering within (or between) a (two) Landau level(s) arising from the sum of two kinds of uncorrelated scatterers, the self-energy and broadening will not be the sum of the widths due to each kinds of scatterers. Hence, the very singular density of unperturbed states leads to spectacular effects on broadening. One can as well handle the case of the accidental degeneracies between Landau levels that belong to different subbands (see Eq. (II.7.8)). This time, there are intra-Landau level couplings as well as inter-Landau levels couplings.

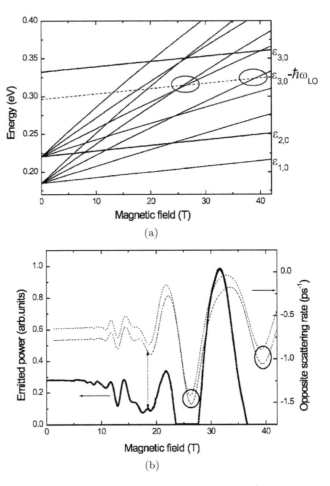

Figure II.7.2.   Magnetic field dependence of the output power of a GaAs-based QCL.
Note the oscillations when the field strength varies. Around $B = 25$ T note the B range
where the QCL no longer emits any light. Above 35 T there exists another B range
where the device will be turned off.

Courtesy A. Vasanelli, from [66].

As mentioned above, the particular magnetic fields where two
Landau levels attached to two different subbands have the same ener-
gies play basically no part in ideal samples. In real samples instead,
these degeneracies lead to spectacular effects. We illustrate this in
Fig. II.7.2 where the output power of a Quantum Cascade Laser
(QCL) is plotted versus the magnetic field strength B. A QCL is

an unipolar device where the radiative recombination takes place between two subbands of the conduction (or more rarely valence) band. The magnetic field is applied parallel to the growth axis and thus Landau-quantises the electron in-plane motion.

The layer sequence of a QCL is very involved (injection-active-extraction regions, etc.) because one should ensure efficient filling (emptying) of the upper (lower) state of the lasing transition but in the active region one may for a quantitative analysis restrict the consideration to only two subbands, the ones one wants to be population-inverted in order to produce lasing. Suppose this has been achieved at zero magnetic field. We want to understand why applying a strong magnetic field may change the situation. Firstly, one should remember that the lasing action is strongly dependent upon the optical selection rules. QCL's lase only when the electric vector of the electromagnetic field is parallel to the growth axis. Hence, the matrix element of the dipole operator $-ez$ ($e > 0$) should be non-zero between the initial and final subbands. At $B = 0$, the conservation of the in-plane electron wavevector must also be ensured for the dipole operator to have non-vanishing matrix elements. Under Landau quantisation (and using Landau gauge) the conservation of the in-plane wavevector is replaced by the conservation of the centre of the Landau orbit and of the harmonic oscillator index. We denote by 1 (respectively, 2) the lower (respectively, upper) subbands. In a simplified approach, we assume that the subband (1) is depopulated at a very fast rate (indeed one of the key ingredient to get a QCL lasing is to design an efficient extraction). Let us investigate the B-dependence of the upper state population and compare to the $B = 0$ situation. The steady state regime for the population n_2 in the upper subband when it is populated at a rate γ and depopulated at a rate $\frac{1}{\tau_{\text{rad}}} + \frac{1}{\tau_{\text{def}}}$ due to the radiative recombination and to defect/impurities/phonons is:

$$n_2 = \gamma \frac{\tau_{\text{rad}}}{1 + \frac{\tau_{\text{rad}}}{\tau_{\text{def}}}} \tag{II.7.36}$$

The laser gain g of a QCL is proportional to $n_2 - n_1$: $g = a(n_2 - n_1)$. Because there exist unavoidable losses, the output power P emitted by the QCL is proportional to the difference between gain and losses.

Neglecting the population of the lower subband, we find in this simplified analysis $P \approx an_2 - b$ as long as $P \geq 0$ where b is associated to the losses. Thus, we see that if it happens that n_2 becomes too small, P may vanish. In Eq. (II.7.36), the radiative lifetime τ_{rad} has no particular reason to vary with B since for allowed transitions the initial and final in-plane wavefunctions should be identical. Hence, we are led to the conclusion that the B-dependence of the QCL output power gives information on the variation with B of the non-radiative channels. In fact, a complete spectroscopy of the non-radiative transitions in QCL's has been made possible by this technique (see [66]). For fields which are not equal to those that line up different Landau levels of different subbands (see Eq. (II.7.8)), the situation is *a priori* better for the lasing action since there is no other state where an electron with a given kinetic energy in the upper subband (i.e., a given Landau level index p) could go by elastic scattering with defects/impurities (see Fig. II.7.3). On the other hand, near the fields where an accidental degeneracy $(n, p/n', p')$ takes place, new channels (n', p') become available to the electrons in the initial Landau level (n, p). The important point is that if f is the fraction of the n_2 population that has been transferred to the p' Landau level of the subband n' that is different from the upper one, then this fraction becomes optically dark since even if the z-dependent dipole matrix element between the n' subband and the ground subband of the lasing transition is non-zero, the in-plane wavefunction will be orthogonal to that of the ground subband lasing transition $(p' \neq p)$.

Looking again at Fig. II.7.2 with these remarks in mind, we clearly see that two effects are observed: (1) a spectacular decrease of the QCL output power is achieved near those fields where an accidental degeneracy takes place leading even to the QCL not lasing any more ($B_{n0/n'1}$ in Fig. II.7.3) while (2) the emitted power becomes larger or much larger than at $B = 0$ when the initial Landau is energetically far away from any other Landau levels (B_{off} in Fig. II.7.3).

The theoretical analysis of the magnetic field-dependent effects on the non-radiative losses in QCL is complicated not only because of the intricacies of the scattering between Landau levels but also because there actually exist two "kinds" of broadenings: the homogeneous and

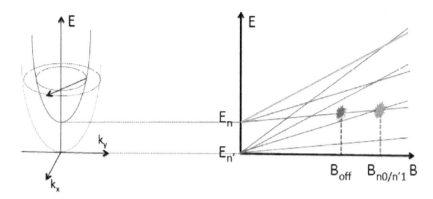

Figure II.7.3. Comparison between the elastic inter-subband scattering at $B = 0$ (lhs sketch) and $B \neq 0$ (rhs sketch). While at $B = 0$, there is always possibilities to elastically scatter an electron from the subband n to subband n' irrespective of its in-plane kinetic energy, it is in general impossible to do so at non-zero B (like B_{off}) except for the particular magnetic fields that line up different Landau levels that belong to different subbands (here $p = 0$ from the nth subband with $p' = 1$ of the n'th subband). In this resonant situation, the scattering is more efficient than at $B = 0$ because of the large density of the final states.

inhomogeneous broadenings. The homogeneous broadening considers the microscopic scattering of carriers in an otherwise homogeneous/uniform sample. The inhomogeneous broadening instead considers that the actual sample consists in a myriad of micro-samples whose material parameters randomly fluctuate from one place to the other in the sample. Consequently, a macroscopic response such as the light emission by the device displays a broadening that results from these random fluctuations. Leuillet *et al.* [66] were able to interpret their data within the framework of the inhomogeneous broadening model. Here, we examine the homogeneous broadening.

Like for intra-Landau level couplings due to defects, the $(n, p/n', p')$ transitions cannot be described by the Born approximation. Besides, since there are at least two Landau levels that come into play, the self-energy is no longer diagonal in the subband/Landau level indexes. We restrict our considerations to the two Landau levels analysis. Equations (II.7.31) are generalised into:

$$\Sigma_{np}(\varepsilon) = \left\langle \sum_{k'_y} V^{k_y, k'_y}_{np, np} \frac{1}{\varepsilon + i\eta - \varepsilon_{np} - \Sigma_{np}(\varepsilon)} V^{k'_y, k_y}_{np, np} \right\rangle_{\mathrm{aver}}$$

$$+\left\langle \sum_{k_y'} V_{np,n'p'}^{k_y,k_y'} \frac{1}{\varepsilon + i\eta - \varepsilon_{n'p'} - \Sigma_{n'p'}(\varepsilon)} V_{n'p',np}^{k_y',k_y} \right\rangle_{\text{aver}}$$

(II.7.37)

$$\Sigma_{n'p'}(\varepsilon) = \left\langle \sum_{k_y'} V_{n'p',n'p'}^{k_y,k_y'} \frac{1}{\varepsilon + i\eta - \varepsilon_{n'p'} - \Sigma_{n'p'}(\varepsilon)} V_{np,np}^{k_y',k_y} \right\rangle_{\text{aver}}$$

$$+\left\langle \sum_{k_y'} V_{n'p',np}^{k_y,k_y'} \frac{1}{\varepsilon + i\eta - \varepsilon_{np} - \Sigma_{np}(\varepsilon)} V_{np,n'p'}^{k_y',k_y} \right\rangle_{\text{aver}}$$

(II.7.38)

$$\langle n,p,k_y|\langle G(\varepsilon)\rangle_{\text{aver}}|n,p,k_y'\rangle = \frac{\delta_{k_y,k_y'}}{\varepsilon + i\eta - \varepsilon_{np} - \Sigma_{np}(\varepsilon)}$$

(II.7.39)

$$\langle n',p',k_y|\langle G(\varepsilon)\rangle_{\text{aver}}|n',p',k_y'\rangle = \frac{\delta_{k_y,k_y'}}{\varepsilon + i\eta - \varepsilon_{n'p'} - \Sigma_{n'p'}(\varepsilon)}$$

(II.7.40)

These coupled self-consistent equations for Σ can be reduced to a quartic algebraic equation [70]. The latter can be solved numerically. Analytical results can be obtained in few special cases. Let us discuss the resonance field case: $\varepsilon_{np} = \varepsilon_{n',p'}$, $B = B_{np/n'p'}$. If, in addition, we look at the centre of the broadened Landau levels ($\tilde{\varepsilon} = \varepsilon_{np} = \varepsilon_{n'p'}$), we get:

$$\Sigma_{np}(\tilde{\varepsilon}) = -\frac{\bar{V}_{np,np}^2}{\Sigma_{np}(\tilde{\varepsilon})} - \frac{\bar{V}_{np,n'p'}^2}{\Sigma_{n'p'}(\tilde{\varepsilon})} \;\; ; \;\; \Sigma_{n'p'}(\tilde{\varepsilon}) = -\frac{\bar{V}_{n'p',n'p'}^2}{\Sigma_{n'p'}(\tilde{\varepsilon})} - \frac{\bar{V}_{n''p',np}^2}{\Sigma_{np}(\tilde{\varepsilon})}$$

(II.7.41)

$$\bar{V}_{np,n'p'}^2 = \bar{V}_{n'p',np}^2 = \frac{x(1-x)\omega_0(\Delta V)^2}{2\pi\lambda^2 L_z}$$

(II.7.42)

$$\bar{V}_{np,np}^2 = \bar{V}_{n'p',n'p'}^2 = \frac{3}{2}\bar{V}_{np,n'p'}^2$$

(II.7.43)

and therefore:

$$\Sigma_{np}(\tilde{\varepsilon}) = -i\sqrt{\bar{V}_{np,np}^2 + \bar{V}_{np,n'p'}^2}$$

(II.7.44)

The density of states at the particular energy is:

$$\rho(\tilde{\varepsilon}) = \rho_{np}(\tilde{\varepsilon}) + \rho_{n'p'}(\tilde{\varepsilon}) = \frac{L_x L_y}{2\pi\lambda^2} \frac{2}{\pi\sqrt{\overline{V}_{np,np}^2 + \overline{V}_{np,n'p'}^2}} \qquad (\text{II.7.45})$$

This has to be compared to twice the value at the maximum of the density of states for a single broadened Landau level:

$$\rho(\tilde{\varepsilon}) = \rho_{n'p'}(\tilde{\varepsilon}) = \frac{L_x L_y}{2\pi\lambda^2} \frac{1}{\pi\sqrt{\overline{V}_{np,np}^2}} \qquad (\text{II.7.46})$$

Hence, we find that doubling the number of available channels for elastic scattering has a nonlinear effect on the maximum of the perturbed density of state since:

$$\frac{\rho(\tilde{\varepsilon})}{\rho_{np}(\tilde{\varepsilon})} = 2\sqrt{\frac{3}{5}} \qquad (\text{II.7.47})$$

This contrasts with e.g., a Lorentzian lineshape where doubling the width decreases the maximum by a factor of 2 since the product of the height by the full width at half maximum is a constant.

The previous analytical results can be ascertained by a numerical computation of the eigenstates and eigenenergies [70]. The Hamiltonian including the alloy fluctuations is diagonalised in a large volume (100 nm $\times$100 nm $\times L_z$). The large box is partitioned into tiny cubes (0.5 nm side). In each cube the defect potential energy is a random variable equal to $x\Delta V$ with probability $(1 - x)$ and to $-(1 - x)\Delta V$ with probability x. For each realisation of the computer-generated disorder, the eigenvalues and eigenvectors are calculated. Then, the density of states is numerically evaluated. Another realisation of the disorder is generated and the density of states is again calculated, etc. After N trials an average density of states is obtained. In the results shown in Fig. II.7.4, $N = 100$. The material parameters are $L_z = 12.5$ nm, $m^* = 0.05m_0$, $x = 0.53$, $E_2 - E_1 = 143$ meV and thus $B_{20/12} = 30.9$ T. Three magnetic fields are considered which correspond to two decoupled situations (18T and 35T) where the two Landau levels $n = 1, p = 2$ and $n = 2, p = 1$ are farther apart than their widths due to intra-Landau level broadening and the resonance field $B_{20/12}$. In addition, the $n = 1, p = 0$ density of states has been

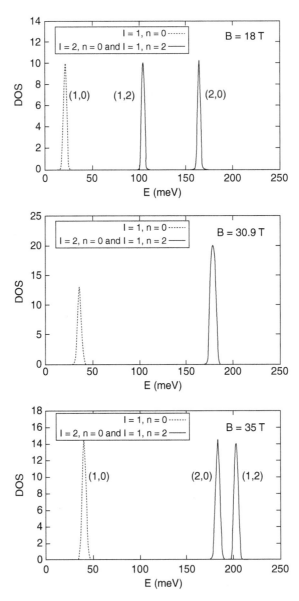

Figure II.7.4.   Calculated density of states for three Landau levels broadened by alloy scattering in a (Ga,In)As single quantum well with $L_z = 12.5$ nm. $B = 30.9$ T corresponds to an accidental degeneracy between the $n = 2, p = 0$ and $n = 1, p = 2$ Landau levels. The $n = 1, p = 0$ Landau level is also shown for comparison. In the insets the subband index is 1 and the Landau level index is p. From [70].

displayed since the $n = 1, p = 0$ Landau level is well isolated at these large fields ($\hbar\omega_c \gg$ broadening). In the non-resonant situations, the density of states exhibits three almost identical peaks, the shape of the density of states depend neither on the subband index nor on the Landau level index. This identity results from the short-range nature of the scatterers (see Eq. (II.7.43)) and would not be true for scatterers with finite range. At the resonance field instead, the two $n = 1, p = 2$ and $n = 2, p = 1$ peaks have coalesced. We note the good agreement between the numerically calculated ratio of the two peaks heights and the self-consistent Born approximation result.

PART III

Exercises

1. Average position and velocity

Compute the average position of a particle in a state $|\varphi\rangle$ such that

$$\varphi(\vec{r}) = \left(\frac{\sqrt{2}}{\sigma\sqrt{\pi}}\right)^{3/2} \exp\left[-\left(\frac{\vec{r}-\vec{r}_0}{\sigma}\right)^2\right] \tag{III.1.1}$$

What is the average particle velocity in the state $|\varphi\rangle$?

Solution

The average position is $\vec{r}_0$ obviously. The average velocity is zero because $|\varphi\rangle$ is a bound state. To see that, write:

$$
\begin{aligned}
\langle \vec{v} \rangle &= -\frac{i\hbar}{m} \int d^3r\, \varphi(\vec{r}) \nabla_{\vec{r}}\varphi(\vec{r}) \\
&= -\frac{i\hbar}{m} \int d^3r\, \nabla_{\vec{r}}(\varphi^2(\vec{r})) - \varphi(\vec{r})\nabla_{\vec{r}}\varphi(\vec{r}) \\
&= \frac{i\hbar}{m} \int d^3r\, \varphi(\vec{r}) \nabla_{\vec{r}}\varphi(\vec{r})
\end{aligned}
\tag{III.1.2}
$$

Hence, $\langle \vec{v} \rangle = 0$. This property is the equivalent of the classical result that states that the average velocity over a period is zero if the motion is periodic in time. Note that the vanishing of $\langle \vec{v} \rangle$ does not require $\varphi(\vec{r})$ to have a definite parity.

2. Average velocity in a bound state

We consider a Hamiltonian $H = \frac{p^2}{2m^*} + V(\vec{r})$. Show that:

$$\vec{p} = \frac{1}{2i\hbar}[\vec{r}, H] \quad \text{where } [A, B] = AB - BA \tag{III.2.1}$$

We assume that the eigenenergies E_n of H are discrete and their associated wavefunctions $\varphi_n(\vec{r})$ are sufficiently decaying functions of r at large $r = |\vec{r}|$. Prove that $\langle \varphi_n | \vec{p} | \varphi_n \rangle = 0$.

Solution

We only need to know the canonical result $[\vec{r}_\alpha, \vec{p}_\beta] = i\hbar\delta_{\alpha\beta}$. Then:

$$\langle\varphi_n|\vec{p}|\varphi_n\rangle = \frac{1}{i\hbar}\langle\varphi_n|\vec{r}H - H\vec{r}|\varphi_n\rangle = \frac{E_n}{i\hbar}\left[\langle\varphi_n|\vec{r}|\varphi_n\rangle - \langle\varphi_n|\vec{r}|\varphi_n\rangle\right] = 0 \tag{III.2.2}$$

If the diagonal matrix elements of $\vec{r}$ are finite, we find the expected result. But if the integrals diverge we cannot conclude. For extended states the average values of x, y or z are diverging and the previous reasoning does not work. In fact for a plane wave $|\vec{k}\rangle$, $\langle\vec{k}|\vec{p}|\vec{k}\rangle = \hbar\vec{k}$.

3. Density of states

(1) Let H be a Hamiltonian that can be split into two independent Hamiltonians H_1 and H_2 (i.e., acting on two independent subspaces). The H spectrum and eigenfunctions can therefore be written:

$$\varepsilon_l = \varepsilon_\nu + \varepsilon_\mu; \quad H|l\rangle = \varepsilon_l|l\rangle; \quad |l\rangle = |\nu\rangle \otimes |\mu\rangle \tag{III.3.1}$$

$$H_1|\nu\rangle = \varepsilon_\nu|\nu\rangle; \quad H_2|\mu\rangle = \varepsilon_\mu|\mu\rangle \tag{III.3.2}$$

Show that:

$$\rho(\varepsilon) = \sum_l \delta(\varepsilon - \varepsilon_l) = \int_{\text{Min}\,\varepsilon_\nu}^{\varepsilon - \text{Min}\,\varepsilon_\mu} d\varepsilon' \rho_1(\varepsilon')\rho_2(\varepsilon - \varepsilon') \tag{III.3.3}$$

where $\text{Min}\,\varepsilon_\nu$ (respectively, $\text{Min}\,\varepsilon_\mu$) is the lowest eigenvalue of H_1 (respectively, H_2) and ρ_1, ρ_2 are the densities of states, respectively, associated with H_1 and H_2.

Example: Compute the density of states for a free particle moving in one dimension (spin excluded). Deduce that for a free particle moving in two dimensions.

(2) We consider a one-dimensional (1D) chain. In the tight binding approximation limited to nearest neighbours, the electron dispersion relation can be written:

$$\varepsilon(k) = -\frac{\Delta}{2}\cos(kd) \tag{III.3.4}$$

Find the density of states (spin included) of these electrons.

(3) Electrons in graphene display "ultra-relativistic" dispersion relations: for one valley, there is:

$$\varepsilon(\vec{k}) = \hbar c_s k; \quad k = \sqrt{k_x^2 + k_y^2} \tag{III.3.5}$$

Let g_v be the number equivalent valleys, compute the density of states of the electrons in graphene (spin included).

Solution

By definition:

$$\rho(\varepsilon) = \sum_l \delta(\varepsilon - \varepsilon_l) = \sum_\nu \sum_\mu \delta((\varepsilon - \varepsilon_\nu) - \varepsilon_\mu) \tag{III.3.6}$$

We recognise in the $\sum_\mu$ the density of states $\rho_2(\varepsilon - \varepsilon_\nu)$: Thus:

$$\rho(\varepsilon) = \sum_\nu \rho_2(\varepsilon - \varepsilon_\nu) \tag{III.3.7}$$

But:

$$\rho_2(\varepsilon - \varepsilon_\nu) = \int^{\varepsilon - \text{Min}\,\varepsilon_\mu} d\varepsilon' \delta(\varepsilon' - \varepsilon_\nu) \rho_2(\varepsilon - \varepsilon') \tag{III.3.8}$$

where the upper bound accounts for the fact that $\varepsilon - \varepsilon'$ should be larger than $\text{Min}\,\varepsilon_\mu$ to get a non-zero ρ_2: Therefore:

$$\rho(\varepsilon) = \int^{\varepsilon - \text{Min}\,\varepsilon_\mu} d\varepsilon' \rho_2(\varepsilon - \varepsilon') \sum_\nu \delta(\varepsilon' - \varepsilon_\nu)$$

$$= \int_{\text{Min}\,\varepsilon_\nu}^{\varepsilon - \text{Min}\,\varepsilon_\mu} d\varepsilon' \rho_1(\varepsilon') \rho_2(\varepsilon - \varepsilon') \tag{III.3.9}$$

where we have made use of the fact that $\rho_1(\varepsilon) = 0$ if $\varepsilon < \text{Min}\,\varepsilon_\nu$.

(1) We write the definition of the density of states. For a spinless particle in 1D

$$\rho_{1D}(\varepsilon) = \frac{L_x}{2\pi} \int_{-\infty}^{+\infty} dk_x \delta\left(\varepsilon - \frac{\hbar^2 k_x^2}{2m^*}\right) = \frac{m^* L_x}{\pi \hbar^2 \sqrt{\frac{2m^* \varepsilon}{\hbar^2}}} \tag{III.3.10}$$

Thus, by applying the convolution formulae given in the text:

$$\rho_{2D}(\varepsilon) = \frac{L_x L_y m^*}{2\pi^2 \hbar^2} \int_0^\varepsilon \frac{d\varepsilon'}{\sqrt{\varepsilon'}\sqrt{\varepsilon - \varepsilon'}} = \frac{m^* L_x L_y}{2\pi^2 \hbar^2} \int_0^1 \frac{dt'}{\sqrt{t'}\sqrt{1 - t'}} \tag{III.3.11}$$

With the change of variables $t' = u^2$ we get the result:

$$\rho_{2D}(\varepsilon) = \frac{m^* L_x L_y}{2\pi\hbar^2}; \quad \text{if } \varepsilon > 0 \qquad \text{(III.3.12)}$$

(2) For the linear chain:

$$\rho(\varepsilon) = \frac{L_z}{\pi} \int_{-\pi/d}^{+\pi/d} dk\delta\left(\varepsilon + \frac{\Delta}{2}\cos(kd)\right) = \frac{2L_z}{\pi d} \int_0^\pi dx\delta\left(\varepsilon + \frac{\Delta}{2}\cos x\right)$$

$$= \frac{4L_z}{\pi d\Delta} \frac{1}{\sqrt{1 - \left(\frac{2\varepsilon}{\Delta}\right)^2}}; \quad \text{if } -\frac{\Delta}{2} \leq \varepsilon \leq \frac{\Delta}{2} \qquad \text{(III.3.13)}$$

Note the existence of two singularities that display the same shape as that found above for 1D free particle. This had to be expected in so far as the dispersion relation can be approximated by parabolas both near $q = 0$ and $q = \pi/d$.

(3) Graphene:

$$\varepsilon(\vec{k}) = \hbar c_s k \qquad \text{(III.3.14)}$$

$$\rho(\varepsilon) = 2g_v \frac{S}{4\pi^2} \int_0^\infty 2\pi k dk\delta(\varepsilon - \hbar c_s k) = \frac{g_v S}{\pi\hbar c_s}\left(\frac{\varepsilon}{\hbar c_s}\right) \qquad \text{(III.3.15)}$$

4. Density of states of a camel back shaped dispersion relation

The valence band of heterostructures often displays non-monotonic dispersion relations. We analyse in this exercise the consequence of such a feature using a simplified model.

Consider the ground light hole band LH_1 of a quantum well that is not too narrow. It displays a camel back shape (see Fig. 4.1). In the following, we analyse the camel back shaped LH_1 using the simplified dispersion relation:

$$\varepsilon(k) - LH_1 = \frac{\hbar^2 k^2}{2m_1}\left(1 - \frac{\hbar^2 k^2}{2m_1\Delta}\right) \qquad \text{(III.4.1)}$$

Compute the density of states associated with such a dispersion.

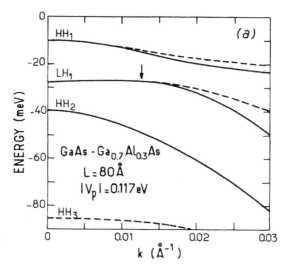

Figure 4.1. Calculated in-plane dispersion relations of the topmost valence subbands in a 8-nm thick GaAs/Ga$_{0.7}$Al$_{0.3}$As quantum well versus k the modulus of the electron wavevector (isotropic dispersions). Note the camel back shape of LH_1.

Source: Ferreira and Bastard [53].

Solution

We define the two dimensionless energies:

$$x = \frac{\hbar^2 k^2}{2m_1 \Delta}; \quad \eta(k) = \frac{\varepsilon(k) - LH_1}{\Delta} \qquad \text{(III.4.2)}$$

In terms of these dimensionless variables, the dispersion relation is:

$$\eta(k) = x(1 - x) \qquad \text{(III.4.3)}$$

The quantity x is positive but the dimensionless energy η covers the range $-\infty < \eta \leq \frac{1}{4}$. The dispersion is monotonically decreasing for $\eta < 0$, i.e., if $\varepsilon < LH_1$ there is a single $k \geq 0$ such that:

$$\varepsilon - LH_1 = \frac{\hbar^2 k^2}{2m_1} \left(1 - \frac{\hbar^2 k^2}{2m_1 \Delta}\right) \qquad \text{(III.4.4)}$$

Note that at a large k these dispersions are rather inaccurate ($\varepsilon(\vec{k}) \approx -\alpha k^4$). However, in the energy segment of our interest where the camel back exists ($\frac{1}{4} \geq \eta \geq 0$) this dispersion relation is plausible and two possible values of x exist for a given η, namely:

$$x_\pm = \frac{1 \pm \sqrt{1 - 4\eta}}{2} \tag{III.4.5}$$

To compute the density of states, we write:

$$\rho(\varepsilon) = 2 \sum_{\vec{k}} \delta(\varepsilon - \varepsilon(\vec{k})) = \frac{2S}{4\pi^2} \iint d^2k \, \delta(\varepsilon - \varepsilon(\vec{k})) \tag{III.4.6}$$

where the factor 2 accounts for the Kramers degeneracy. Since the dispersion is isotropic in k, $d^2k = 2\pi k dk$ and:

$$\rho(\varepsilon) = \frac{S}{\pi} \int_0^\infty kdk \, \delta\left(\varepsilon - LH_1 - \Delta\eta(k)\right)$$

$$= \frac{S}{\pi} \sum_{k_i} \frac{k_i}{\left|\frac{d\varepsilon}{dk}\right|_{k=k_i}} = \frac{S}{\pi\Delta} \sum_{k_i} \frac{k_i}{\left|\frac{d\eta}{dk}\right|_{k=k_i}} \tag{III.4.7}$$

$$\rho(\varepsilon) = \frac{Sm_1}{\pi\hbar^2} \sum_{k_i} \frac{1}{\left|\frac{d\eta}{dx}\right|_{k=k_i}} = \frac{2Sm_1}{\pi\hbar^2} \frac{1}{\sqrt{1 - 4\eta}}$$

$$= \frac{2Sm_1}{\pi\hbar^2} \frac{1}{\sqrt{1 - \frac{4(\varepsilon - LH_1)}{\Delta}}} \tag{III.4.8}$$

The k_i are the zeros of the argument of the delta function. In the final expression, the factor 2 now comes from the two possible k's that make the argument of the delta function vanishing. The previous result is valid for $0 \leq \eta \leq \frac{1}{4}$. Hence, the density of states diverges in the vicinity of the local maximum of the density of states. This result is more general than the chosen dispersion relation. Actually, the only thing that is needed to get a divergent behaviour is that the isotropic dispersion displays a local maximum around a certain k_0. Indeed, let us expand the isotropic dispersion around k_0:

$$\varepsilon(k) \approx \varepsilon(k_0) - \frac{\hbar^2(k - k_0)^2}{2m^*} \tag{III.4.9}$$

We get immediately:

$$\rho(\varepsilon) = \frac{S}{\pi} \int_0^\infty kdk \, \delta\left(\varepsilon - \varepsilon(k_0) + \frac{\hbar^2(k - k_0)^2}{2m^*}\right)$$

$$= \frac{Sm^*}{\pi \hbar^2} \sum_{\pm} \frac{k_\pm}{|k_\pm - k_0|} \tag{III.4.10}$$

$$k_\pm - k_0 = \pm \sqrt{\frac{2m^*}{\hbar^2}[-\varepsilon + \varepsilon(k_0)]} \tag{III.4.11}$$

and therefore the result:

$$\rho(\varepsilon) = \frac{Sm^*}{\pi \hbar^2} \sum_{\pm} \frac{k_\pm}{|k_\pm - k_0|} \approx \frac{2m^* S k_0}{\pi \hbar^2 \sqrt{\frac{2m^*}{\hbar^2}[-\varepsilon + \varepsilon(k_0)]}} \tag{III.4.12}$$

where we have approximated $k_\pm$ by k_0 in the numerator since $k_\pm - k_0$ is small when ε approaches $\varepsilon(k_0)$. The presence of these singular densities of states implies that the intra-LH_1 scattering or the scattering between different valence subbands with LH_1 final states become extremely efficient for energies corresponding to the local maxima of the LH_1 subbands. This explains that the "spin"-flip relaxation time in the valence subband can be very short when the final states approach the local maximum of the LH_1 dispersion.

5. Heisenberg inequality in a quantum well with infinitely high barriers

We consider a particle with mass m^* moving in a 1D quantum well (QW) with width L. The QW barriers are taken infinitely high. The boundary conditions fulfilled by the eigenfunctions $\chi_n(z)$ are $\chi_n(0) = \chi_n(L) = 0$.

(1) Compute the energy eigenvalues E_n and the normalised eigenstates.
(2) Suppose the electron is in the nth eigenstates of the Hamiltonian, $n = 1, 2, \ldots$ Compute $\Delta z \Delta p_z$ versus n. How does this compare to $\frac{\hbar}{2}$?
(3) Same question for the 1D harmonic oscillator of angular frequency ω.

Solution

(1) We take the z origin at the centre of the QW and write that inside the QW the particle is free. Hence, the eigenfunctions of the

Hamiltonian are necessarily of the form:

$$\chi_k(z) = C\sin(kz) + D\cos(kz); \quad |z| \le \frac{L}{2} \qquad \text{(III.5.1)}$$

$$E = \frac{\hbar^2 k^2}{2m^*} \qquad \text{(III.5.2)}$$

Now, the parity operator commutes with the Hamiltonian. Thus, we can choose the χ's as being even or odd in z. So either $C = 0$ or $D = 0$.

If $C = 0$ (even χ's), then making the wavefunction to vanish at $z = L/2$ (or $-L/2$) leads to the quantisation of the allowed k's:

$$\frac{kL}{2} = (2p + 1)\frac{\pi}{2}; \quad p = 0, 1, \dots \qquad \text{(III.5.3)}$$

If $D = 0$, we obtain eigenstates that are odd functions of z and making them to vanish at $z = L/2$ (or $-L/2$) leads to the quantised k values:

$$\frac{kL}{2} = j\pi \qquad \text{(III.5.4)}$$

The quantisation of k implies that of the energies since the electron has only kinetic energy:

$$E_n = \frac{\hbar^2 n^2 \pi^2}{2m^* L^2}; \quad n = 1, 2, \dots \qquad \text{(III.5.5)}$$

Even (respectively, odd) wavefunctions in z correspond to $n = 2p+1$ (respectively, $n = 2j$). The normalised eigenfunctions are:

$$\chi_{2p+1}(z) = \sqrt{\frac{2}{L}} \cos\left((2p+1)\frac{\pi z}{L}\right) \qquad \text{(III.5.6)}$$

$$\chi_{2j}(z) = \sqrt{\frac{2}{L}} \sin\left(2j\frac{\pi z}{L}\right) \qquad \text{(III.5.7)}$$

(2) We compute:

$$\Delta z_n \Delta p_{zn} = \sqrt{\langle z^2 \rangle_n - \langle z \rangle_n^2} \times \sqrt{\langle p_z^2 \rangle_n - \langle p_z \rangle_n^2} \qquad \text{(III.5.8)}$$

The eigenstates have a given parity. Hence, $\langle z \rangle_n = 0$. All the states are bound. Hence, $\langle p_z \rangle_n = 0$. In addition, since the carrier has only kinetic energy there is:

$$\Delta p_z = \frac{n\pi\hbar}{L}, \quad n = 1, 2, \dots \tag{III.5.9}$$

Finally, we get after some calculations:

$$n = 2p + 1 \rightarrow \langle z^2 \rangle_{2p+1} = \frac{L^2}{12} - \frac{L^2}{2\pi^2(2p+1)^2} \tag{III.5.10}$$

$$n = 2j \rightarrow \langle z^2 \rangle_{2j} = \frac{L^2}{12} - \frac{L^2}{2\pi^2(2j)^2} \tag{III.5.11}$$

Hence for the ground state ($p = 0$), there is:

$$\Delta z \Delta p_z = \frac{\hbar}{\sqrt{2}}\sqrt{\frac{\pi^2}{6} - 1} \approx 0.57\hbar \tag{III.5.12}$$

We also find that when $n \rightarrow \infty$, $\Delta z \Delta p_z \approx \frac{n\pi\hbar}{2\sqrt{3}} \rightarrow \infty$.

(3) For the 1D harmonic oscillator there is no calculation to make thanks to the virial theorem that states that for a quadratic potential energy the averaged kinetic and potential energies are equal to 1/2 of the total energy (see Exercise 10):

$$\left\langle \frac{p_z^2}{2m^*} \right\rangle_n = \left\langle \frac{1}{2}m^*\omega^2 z^2 \right\rangle_n = \frac{1}{2}E_n = \frac{1}{2}\left(n + \frac{1}{2}\right)\hbar\omega \tag{III.5.13}$$

Since the potential energy is even in z, the eigenstates have a definite parity. Thus $\langle z \rangle_n = 0$ and:

$$\Delta z_n = \sqrt{\left(n + \frac{1}{2}\right)\frac{\hbar}{m^*\omega}} \tag{III.5.14}$$

All the states are bound. Thus $\langle p_z \rangle_n = 0$ and:

$$\Delta p_{zn} = \sqrt{m^*\hbar\omega\left(n + \frac{1}{2}\right)} \tag{III.5.15}$$

Thus, in the nth state, there is:

$$\Delta z_n \Delta p_{zn} = \left(n + \frac{1}{2}\right)\hbar \tag{III.5.16}$$

In particular for $n = 0$, $\Delta z_n \Delta p_{zn} = \frac{\hbar}{2}$, the lowest possible value. Like in the square well case $\Delta z_n \Delta p_{zn}$ diverges when $n \rightarrow \infty$. In both cases this is associated with the ever increasing total energy with increasing quantum number n.

6. Manipulating Slater determinants

We consider a self-organised quantum dot with nanometric sizes (an InAs dot looks like a truncated cone with height ≈ 3 nm and basis radius ≈ 10 nm). In a first approximation for the envelope function the system is rotationally invariant around the z-axis.

The shell structure of the electron states in these dots is well established: the ground state is S-like and the first excited state is (in a first approximation) orbitally degenerate corresponding to $|P_x\rangle$, $|P_y\rangle$ symmetries.

(1) Show that it is impossible to store three electrons in such a dot with two in the S state for the orbital motion and one in the P_x state for the orbital motion and all being spin up ($\sigma_z = +1/2$).

(2) Same question if two electrons are spin up ($\sigma_z = +1/2$) one in an S state and the other in a P_x state for the orbital motion and one spin down ($\sigma_z = -1/2$) in an S state for the orbital motion.

Solution

(1) The Slater determinant has two identical lines. Thus, it vanishes. It was clear that the proposal amounted to violate the Pauli principle by putting two electrons in exactly the same quantum state $\left(\varphi_S(\vec{z})|\sigma_z = +\frac{1}{2}\rangle\right)$.

(2) We write the Slater determinant:

$$\psi_{AS} = \frac{1}{\sqrt{6}} \begin{vmatrix} S(1)\uparrow_1 & S(2)\uparrow_2 & S(3)\uparrow_3 \\ S(1)\downarrow_1 & S(2)\downarrow_2 & S(3)\downarrow_3 \\ P_x(1)\uparrow_1 & P_x(2)\uparrow_2 & P_x(3)\uparrow_3 \end{vmatrix} \qquad (\text{III.6.1})$$

Expanding the determinant, we find readily:

$$\psi_{AS} = \frac{1}{\sqrt{3}} \left[S(1)S(2)P_x(3)\frac{1}{\sqrt{2}}(\uparrow_1\downarrow_2 - \downarrow_1\uparrow_2)\uparrow_3 \right.$$

$$-S(1)P_x(2)S(3)\frac{1}{\sqrt{2}}(\uparrow_1\downarrow_3 - \downarrow_1\uparrow_3)\uparrow_2$$

$$\left. + P_x(1)S(2)S(3)\frac{1}{\sqrt{2}}(\uparrow_2\downarrow_3 - \downarrow_2\uparrow_3)\uparrow_1\right] \qquad \text{(III.6.2)}$$

A way to interpret this result is to remark that if we had only two electrons the S shell would be filled. The orbital part being symmetrical in the exchange of the two electrons, the spin part would have to be antisymmetrical with $\uparrow$ and $\downarrow$ spins. The only way to realise this is to write the two spins state as $\frac{1}{\sqrt{2}}(\uparrow_1\downarrow_2 - \downarrow_1\uparrow_2)$. With a third electron with spin $\uparrow$ in the P_x orbital state, we see that the three electrons state is actually built by keeping the frozen core of two electrons in a spin state identical to what was found for two electrons and placing the third electron in the P_x state with spin $\uparrow$. There are three different ways to put one of the three electrons in the P_x state and the two others in S state.

7. Pauli principle for two weakly interacting electrons in 1D

(1) Two electrons with mass m^* are free to move along the z-axis. Apply the Pauli principle to find the possible two electrons states if it is known that their wavevectors are k_1 and k_2 respectively. Use the center of mass and relative motion coordinates to express the Hamiltonian of the problem and show that the possible states are organised into a triplet and a singlet. Write the normalised ψ_{AS}.

(2) These two electrons interact weakly via a screened Coulomb potential. For simplicity, we write this interaction potential:

$$V(z) = \begin{cases} V_0, & |z| < \lambda \\ 0, & |z| \geq \lambda \end{cases} \qquad \text{(III.7.1)}$$

where $z = z_1 - z_2$ and $k\lambda \ll 1$, k being the wavevector that characterises the reduced free motion. Show at the lowest order of perturbation theory that the triplet is lower in energy than the singlet. Compute the energy difference.

Solution

(1)

$$H = \frac{P^2}{2M} + \frac{p^2}{2\mu}; \quad M = 2m^*, \ \mu = \frac{m^*}{2} \qquad \text{(III.7.2)}$$

We have:

$$Z = \frac{z_1 + z_2}{2}; \quad z = z_1 - z_2 \qquad \text{(III.7.3)}$$

The Hamiltonian is separable into two Hamiltonians acting on different variables. Hence, we can search for eigenfunctions of the orbital motion in the form $f(Z)g(z)$. Both f and g can be chosen as plane waves or linear combinations of plane waves:

$$f(Z) = \frac{1}{\sqrt{L}} \exp(iKZ); \quad g(z) = \frac{N}{\sqrt{L}}[A \exp(ikz) + B \exp(-ikz)]$$

$$\text{(III.7.4)}$$

$$K = k_1 + k_2; \quad k = \frac{k_1 - k_2}{2} \qquad \text{(III.7.5)}$$

Since the Hamiltonian is spin independent, we can search for anti-symmetrical two electrons wavefunctions that are products of spin function times the function $f(Z)g(z)$. We can antisymmetrise the spin and orbital functions separately ensuring at the end that the total wavefunction ψ_{AS} is antisymmetrical when the two electrons are interchanged. Since the center of mass wavefunction is symmetrical with respect to the interchange of the two electrons whatever its shape, the final symmetry of the orbital wavefunction is furnished by $g(z)$.

To get a definite symmetry for $g(z)$ with respect to the interchange of the two electrons we should have $A = \pm B = \frac{1}{2}$. Then $g(z)$ is either $\cos(kz)$ or $i\sin(kz)$ and in both cases $N = (2/L)^{1/2}$. Finally

- if $g(z)$ is $\cos(kz)$:

$$\psi_{AS}^{\text{singlet}} = \frac{1}{\sqrt{2}}(\uparrow_1\downarrow_2 - \downarrow_1\uparrow_2)\frac{1}{\sqrt{L}} \exp(iKZ)\sqrt{\frac{2}{L}} \cos(kz) \quad \text{(III.7.6)}$$

- if $g(z)$ is $i\sin(kz)$ there are three possible symmetrical combinations of the spins of the two electrons: $|\uparrow_1\uparrow_2\rangle$, $|\downarrow_1\downarrow_2\rangle$, $\frac{1}{\sqrt{2}}(|\uparrow_1\downarrow_2\rangle + |\downarrow_1\uparrow_2\rangle)$. Dropping the i (which is a pure phase), we finally get the triplet states:

$$
\psi_{AS}^{\text{triplet}} = \begin{cases} (\uparrow_1\uparrow_2)\dfrac{1}{\sqrt{L}}\exp(iKZ)\sqrt{\dfrac{2}{L}}\sin(kz) \\[2ex] (\downarrow_1\downarrow_2)\dfrac{1}{\sqrt{L}}\exp(iKZ)\sqrt{\dfrac{2}{L}}\sin(kz) \\[2ex] \dfrac{1}{\sqrt{2}}(\uparrow_1\downarrow_2 + \downarrow_1\uparrow_2)\dfrac{1}{\sqrt{L}}\exp(iKZ)\sqrt{\dfrac{2}{L}}\sin(kz) \end{cases} \qquad \text{(III.7.7)}
$$

(2) The singlet and triplet states are degenerate in the absence of electron–electron interaction. We shall see that putting any repulsive interaction between the two electrons will lower the triplet states compared to the singlet. This effect originates from the Pauli principle that forces the wavefunction for the relative motion to vanish at the origin for the triplet state.

If the interaction is weak it can be handled by perturbation calculus. Although there are four degenerate states we see readily that there is no coupling between any of these states due to $V(z)$ on account of the orthogonality of the spin functions.

Using first-order non-degenerate perturbation theory, we find the shift of the singlet and triplet states:

$$
\begin{aligned}
\delta\varepsilon_{\text{triplet}} &= \langle \psi_{AS}^{\text{triplet}}|V(z)|\psi_{AS}^{\text{triplet}}\rangle \\
&= \frac{2V_0}{L}\int_{-\lambda}^{+\lambda} dz\,\sin^2(kz) = \frac{2V_0\lambda}{L}\left[1 - \frac{\sin(2k\lambda)}{2k\lambda}\right] \quad \text{(III.7.8)}
\end{aligned}
$$

$$
\begin{aligned}
\delta\varepsilon_{\text{singlet}} &= \langle \psi_{AS}^{\text{singlet}}|V(z)|\psi_{AS}^{\text{singlet}}\rangle \\
&= \frac{2V_0}{L}\int_{-\lambda}^{+\lambda} dz\,\cos^2(kz) = \frac{2V_0\lambda}{L}\left[1 + \frac{\sin(2k\lambda)}{2k\lambda}\right] \quad \text{(III.7.9)}
\end{aligned}
$$

Hence, the singlet-triplet splitting Δ is equal to:

$$
\Delta = \frac{4V_0\lambda}{L}\left[\frac{\sin(2k\lambda)}{2k\lambda}\right] \approx \frac{4V_0\lambda}{L} \qquad \text{(III.7.10)}
$$

Note that Δ is very small since L is a macroscopic quantity.

8.   Calculation with Pauli matrices

We consider a localised electron interacting with a magnetic field $\vec{B} \| \hat{x}$. Its Hamiltonian is therefore:

$$H = -\vec{\mu} \cdot \vec{B} = -\frac{g_e \mu_B B}{\hbar} \sigma_x \tag{III.8.1}$$

$\vec{\mu}$ is the magnetic moment of this localised electron and all the other degrees of freedom of the electron have been re-absorbed in the energy zero. We give σ_x in the basis where σ_z is diagonal:

$$\sigma_x = \frac{\hbar}{2} \begin{pmatrix} 0 & 1 \\ 1 & 0 \end{pmatrix} \tag{III.8.2}$$

Compute the eigenvalues and the trace of the operator $\exp(-\beta H)$ where $\beta = 1/(k_B T)$. The trace is the partition function of this localised spin if considered at thermal equilibrium at temperature T.

Solution

We take advantage that:

$$\sigma_x = \frac{\hbar}{2} \begin{pmatrix} 0 & 1 \\ 1 & 0 \end{pmatrix} \Rightarrow \sigma_x^2 = \left(\frac{\hbar}{2}\right)^2 \begin{pmatrix} 1 & 0 \\ 0 & 1 \end{pmatrix} = \left(\frac{\hbar}{2}\right)^2 Id \tag{III.8.3}$$

$$\Rightarrow \quad \sigma_x^{2n} = \left(\frac{\hbar}{2}\right)^{2n} Id; \quad \sigma_x^{2n+1} = \frac{2}{\hbar}\left(\frac{\hbar}{2}\right)^{2n+1} \sigma_x \tag{III.8.4}$$

Thus:

$$\exp(-\beta H) = \exp(\alpha \sigma_x); \quad \alpha = \frac{\beta g_e \mu_B B}{\hbar} \tag{III.8.5}$$

We expand the exponential in Taylor series:

$$\exp(\alpha \sigma_x) = 1 + \alpha \sigma_x + \frac{(\alpha \sigma_x)^2}{2!} + \cdots \tag{III.8.6}$$

and get finally:

$$\exp(-\beta H) = \cosh\left(\frac{\beta g_e \mu_B B}{2}\right) Id + \frac{2}{\hbar} \sigma_x \sinh\left(\frac{\beta g_e \mu_B B}{2}\right) \tag{III.8.7}$$

Thus:

$$\exp(-\beta H) = \begin{pmatrix} \cosh t & \sinh t \\ \sinh t & \cosh t \end{pmatrix}; \quad t = \frac{\beta g_e \mu_B B}{2} \tag{III.8.8}$$

The eigenvalues λ fulfil:

$$\lambda^2 - 2\lambda \cosh t + 1 = 0 \;\Rightarrow\; \lambda_\pm = \exp(\pm t) \qquad \text{(III.8.9)}$$

The trace is the partition function and is equal to:

$$Z = 2\cosh t \qquad \text{(III.8.10)}$$

Note that this result could have been obtained with much less calculation by noting that the scalar product $-\vec{\mu} \cdot \vec{B}$ is a number and therefore rotation invariant. By rotating x to z (in other words by using the basis where σ_x is diagonal) we would have gotten $\exp(-\beta H)$ diagonal with eigenvalues $\lambda_\pm$.

9. Moss–Burstein shift of interband absorption

We consider a quantum well where the electrons and the holes are confined in the same material. We denote by E_1 and H_1 the lowest (topmost) bound state for the conduction (valence) state and by m_c and m_v the effective masses of the E_1 and H_1 subbands for the in-plane motion.

We admit that the $p_{x,y,z}$ matrix elements between the valence and conduction states are such that:

$$\langle u_c \chi_{c1} \vec{k}_c | p_{x,y,z} | u_v \chi_{v1} \vec{k}_v \rangle = \langle u_c | p_{x,y,z} | u_v \rangle \langle \chi_{c1} | \chi_{v1} \rangle \langle \vec{k}_c | \vec{k}_v \rangle \qquad \text{(III.9.1)}$$

with

$$\langle \vec{\rho} | \vec{k}_{c,v} \rangle = \frac{1}{\sqrt{S}} \exp(i\vec{k}_{c,v} \cdot \vec{\rho}) \qquad \text{(III.9.2)}$$

Neglecting any electron–electron interaction, the absorption probability of light by a single quantum well is proportional to:

$$\alpha(\omega) \propto 2 \sum_{\vec{k}_c, \vec{k}_v} f(\vec{k}_v)[1 - f(\vec{k}_c)] |\langle u_v \chi_{c1} \vec{k}_c | p_{x,y,z} | u_v \chi_{v1} \vec{k}_v \rangle|^2$$

$$\times \delta \left(\varepsilon_g + E_1 + \frac{\hbar^2 k_c^2}{2m_c} + H_1 + \frac{\hbar^2 k_v^2}{2m_v} - \hbar\omega \right) \qquad \text{(III.9.3)}$$

where the 2 accounts for the electron spin, ε_g is the bandgap of the bulk well-acting material and f is the Fermi–Dirac function.

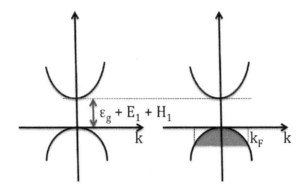

Figure 9.1. Dispersion relations for a quantum well structure either undoped (left panel) or doped with acceptors (right panel). The acceptors are assumed ionised and their holes are in the H_1 subband.

(1) Compute the absorption probability for the $H_1 \to E_1$ transitions.

  We work at very low temperature: $T \to 0$. The quantum well has been doped with acceptors in such way that instead of being completely filled, the H_1 subbands is filled only for $k \geq k_F$ (see Fig. 9.1).

(2) Compute the absorption probability for the $H_1 \to E_1$ transitions in this situation and show that its onset is blue shifted with respect to the result found in (1) (Moss–Burstein shift). Show that the shift is proportional to the areal concentration of holes.

Solution

(1) The absorption coefficient is a staircase that starts at the onset:

$$\hbar\omega_{\text{onset}} = \varepsilon_g + E_1 + H_1 \qquad\qquad \text{(III.9.4)}$$

because the optical transitions are vertical in the k space. In fact, for all the valence levels $f = 1$ while all the conduction levels are empty. Thus:

$$\alpha(\omega) \propto 2 \sum_{\vec{k}_c, \vec{k}_v} f(\vec{k}_v)[1 - f(\vec{k}_c)] |\langle u_v \chi_{c1} \vec{k}_c | p_{x,y,z} | u_v \chi_{v1} \vec{k}_v \rangle|^2$$

$$\times \, \delta \left(\varepsilon_g + E_1 + \frac{\hbar^2 k_c^2}{2m_c} + H_1 + \frac{\hbar^2 k_v^2}{2m_v} - \hbar\omega \right)$$

$$= 2|\langle u_c|p_{x,y,z}|u_v\rangle|^2|\langle \chi_{c1}|\chi_{v1}\rangle|^2$$

$$\times \sum_{\vec{k}_v} \delta\left(\varepsilon_g + E_1 + \frac{\hbar^2 k_c^2}{2m_c} + H_1 + \frac{\hbar^2 k_v^2}{2m_v} - \hbar\omega\right)$$

$$= 2|\langle u_c|p_{x,y,z}|u_v\rangle|^2|\langle \chi_{c1}|\chi_{v1}\rangle|^2 \frac{\mu S}{2\pi\hbar^2} Y(\hbar\omega - \varepsilon_g + E_1 + H_1)$$

$$\text{(III.9.5)}$$

where $\frac{1}{\mu} = \frac{1}{m_c} + \frac{1}{m_v}$ and $Y(x)$ is the step function.

(2) The reasoning is the same as in (1) except that $f(k_v) = 1$ for $k_v \geq k_F$ and $f(k_v) = 0$ for $k_v \leq k_F$. The conduction subband is empty: $f(k_c) = 0$. The absorption onset is blue shifted with respect to the onset of undoped materials by an amount $\frac{\hbar^2 k_F^2}{2\mu}$.

(3) It is easy to see that this shift is proportional to the areal concentration of holes p since:

$$p = \frac{2}{4\pi^2}\pi k_F^2 = \frac{k_F^2}{2\pi} \qquad \text{(III.9.6)}$$

Although this simple one electron description provides results that are close from the experiments (existence of a blue shift), they prove short to quantitatively interpret the whole experimental features. The many-body effects are responsible for these shortcomings as they produce two main departures from the above description. Firstly, on a quantitative basis the absorption onset does not reduce to what we have calculated in (2). The reason is that electron–electron interaction shifts the onset (the so-called exchange-correlation effects/bandgap renormalisation). Secondly, the lineshape of the absorption spectrum is not a step function since, very often, it displays a peak (the so-called Fermi edge singularity), more or less blurred. More details can be found in [71] and in [72].

10. Virial theorem

The virial theorem connects the averages of the kinetic energy $\langle T \rangle$ to the one of the potential energy $\langle V \rangle$ when the particle is in a stationary bound state of the Hamiltonian (i.e., characterised by a

wavefunction $\varphi(\vec{r})$ that decays sufficiently rapidly when $|\vec{r}| \to \infty$).
It is very useful in that it does not require an explicit knowledge
of $\varphi(\vec{r})$.

We denote by $[A, B] = AB - BA$ the commutator of the two opera-
tors A and B. To establish the virial theorem, compute $\langle \varphi | [H, xp] | \varphi \rangle$
where $|\varphi\rangle$ is an eigenstate of H. Show that this quantity is equal to
zero provided $\varphi(\vec{r})$ decays sufficiently rapidly to zero at large r.

(1) Show that $[H, xp] = [H, x]p + x[H, p]$.
(2) Show that $[H, x] = -i\hbar \frac{p}{m}$ and $[H, p] = i\hbar \frac{\partial V}{\partial x}$.
(3) Conclude that:

$$2\langle T \rangle = \left\langle x \frac{\partial V}{\partial x} \right\rangle \qquad (III.10.1)$$

(4) We consider the case where $V(x) = V_0(\frac{|x|}{L})^p$. Show that $2\langle T \rangle = p\langle V \rangle$.
(5) As a result, show that the average mechanical energy of the par-
ticle is equal to:

$$\langle H \rangle = \langle T + V \rangle = \left(1 + \frac{p}{2}\right)\langle V \rangle \qquad (III.10.2)$$

Solution

(1)

$$\langle \varphi | [H, xp] | \varphi \rangle = \langle \varphi | Hxp - xpH | \varphi \rangle = E\left(\langle xp \rangle - \langle xp \rangle\right) = 0 \quad (III.10.3)$$

Note that this result requires the integrals to be convergent. If
instead, $\varphi(x)$ is unbound, as for example happens if we deal with
plane waves, the integral of xp diverges and no firm conclusion can
be drawn.

(2)

$$[H, xp] = Hxp - xpH = Hxp - xHp + xHp - xpH \qquad (III.10.4)$$
$$[H, xp] = [H, x]p + x[H, p] \qquad (III.10.5)$$

(3)

$$[H, x] = \left[\frac{p^2}{2m}, x\right] = \frac{1}{2m}(p^2 x - pxp + pxp - xp^2) \qquad (III.10.6)$$

Using $[x, p] = i\hbar$, we obtain readily:

$$[H, x] = -i\hbar\frac{p}{m} \tag{III.10.7}$$

Along the same line:

$$[H, p] = [V(x), p] = V(x)\frac{\hbar}{i}\frac{\partial}{\partial x} - \frac{\hbar}{i}\frac{\partial}{\partial x}V(x). \tag{III.10.8}$$

Applying this identity to any bound state leads to the result:

$$[H, p] = i\hbar\frac{\partial V}{\partial x} \tag{III.10.9}$$

(4) We obtain readily from (1)–(3) that:

$$2\langle T \rangle = \left\langle x\frac{\partial V}{\partial x} \right\rangle \tag{III.10.10}$$

(5) In the case of a power law variation $V(x) = V_0(\frac{|x|}{L})^p$ there is $x\frac{\partial V(x)}{\partial x} = pV(x)$ and we obtain:

$$2\langle T \rangle = p\langle V \rangle. \tag{III.10.11}$$

Since $H = T + V$ the previous result can also be written:

$$\langle H \rangle = \langle T + V \rangle = \left(1 + \frac{p}{2}\right)\langle V \rangle \tag{III.10.12}$$

Examples:

- For a harmonic oscillator where $p = 2$, all the states are bound and the virial theorem states that the average kinetic and potential energies are equal to half the average total mechanical energy.
- For a particle bound in a symmetrical triangular well $V(x) = eF|x|$ there is $p = 1$ and we find that:

$$\langle T \rangle = \frac{\langle H \rangle}{3} = \frac{\langle V \rangle}{2} \tag{III.10.13}$$

The same is true in the triangular well:

$$V(x) = \infty \quad \text{if } x < 0 \tag{III.10.14}$$
$$V(x) = eFx \quad \text{if } x \geq 0 \tag{III.10.15}$$

Namely, we find that: $\langle T \rangle = \frac{\langle H \rangle}{3} = \frac{\langle V \rangle}{2}$.

- For a three-dimensional (3D) coulombic potential calling $r = \sqrt{x^2 + y^2 + z^2} > 0$ there is $p = -1$ and:

$$\langle V \rangle = -2\langle T \rangle = 2\langle H \rangle \qquad \text{(III.10.16)}$$

As a counter-example, note that $p = 0$ (constant potential energy) seemingly leads to the absurd result $\langle T \rangle = 0$. But of course in a constant potential there is no bound state and the whole machinery of the virial theorem collapses.

11.   Absence of degeneracy for the 1D bound states

We consider the 1D Ben Daniel and Duke Hamiltonian:

$$H = \frac{1}{2}p_z \left(\frac{1}{m(z)} \right) p_z + V(z) \qquad \text{(III.11.1)}$$

Prove that the bound states of H are non-degenerate.

Hint: Assume that φ_1 and φ_2 are two independent solutions of H with the same energy E and show that the function

$$W(\varphi_1, \varphi_2) = \varphi_1 \left(\frac{1}{m(z)} \right) \frac{d\varphi_2}{dz} - \varphi_2 \left(\frac{1}{m(z)} \right) \frac{d\varphi_1}{dz} \qquad \text{(III.11.2)}$$

has a zero derivative.

Conclude that this implies that φ_1 and φ_2 are proportional if φ_1 and φ_2 are bound states in contradiction with the assumption of their independence.

Solution

We write the time independent Schrödinger equation for φ_1 and φ_2:

$$\frac{1}{2}p_z \left(\frac{1}{m(z)} \right) p_z\varphi_1(z) = [E - V(z)]\varphi_1(z) \qquad \text{(III.11.3)}$$

$$\frac{1}{2}p_z \left(\frac{1}{m(z)} \right) p_z\varphi_2(z) = [E - V(z)]\varphi_2(z) \qquad \text{(III.11.4)}$$

We multiply on the left (III.11.3) by $\varphi_2(z)$ and (III.11.4) by $\varphi_1(z)$ and subtract. We obtain:

$$\varphi_2(z)\frac{d}{dz}\left(\frac{1}{m(z)}\right)\frac{d}{dz}\varphi_1(z) - \varphi_1(z)\frac{d}{dz}\left(\frac{1}{m(z)}\right)\frac{d}{dz}\varphi_2(z) = 0$$

$$\text{(III.11.5)}$$

Let us compute $dW(\varphi_1,\varphi_2)/dz$. We obtain:

$$\frac{dW(\varphi_1,\varphi_2)}{dz} = \varphi_1\frac{d}{dz}\left[\frac{1}{m(z)}\frac{d\varphi_2}{dz}\right] - \varphi_2\frac{d}{dz}\left[\frac{1}{m(z)}\frac{d\varphi_1}{dz}\right]$$

$$+\frac{d\varphi_1}{dz}\left(\frac{1}{m(z)}\right)\frac{d\varphi_2}{dz} - \frac{d\varphi_2}{dz}\left(\frac{1}{m(z)}\right)\frac{d\varphi_1}{dz}$$

$$\text{(III.11.6)}$$

The first bracket cancels because of (III.11.5). The last two terms cancel one another. Hence:

$$\frac{dW(\varphi_1,\varphi_2)}{dz} = 0 \Rightarrow W(\varphi_1,\varphi_2) = C \qquad \text{(III.11.7)}$$

Since φ_1 and φ_2 are bound states, their wavefunctions decay to zero at infinity. Thus, the constant C is actually equal to zero. But if $W = 0$ this means that for all z:

$$\frac{d\varphi_1(z)}{\varphi_1(z)} = \frac{d\varphi_2(z)}{\varphi_2(z)} \Rightarrow \varphi_1(z) = A\varphi_2(z) \qquad \text{(III.11.8)}$$

Thus, the two eigenfunctions of H with the same energy E are in fact proportional. Therefore, the bound states of 1D Hamiltonians are non-degenerate.

Note the crucial part played by the assumption of having bound states: it has allowed us to set $C = 0$ and finally deduce the proportionality between φ_1 and φ_2. As a counter-example take the 1D free motion where $H = \frac{p_z^2}{2m^*}$. For a given energy $E > 0$ we know that there are two degenerate eigenstates:

$$\varphi_1(z) = \frac{1}{\sqrt{L}}e^{ikz}; \quad \varphi_2(z) = \frac{1}{\sqrt{L}}e^{-ikz} \qquad \text{(III.11.9)}$$

where $E = \frac{\hbar^2 k^2}{2m^*}$. We readily compute that the function $W(\varphi_1,\varphi_2)$ is the non-vanishing constant $W(\varphi_1,\varphi_2) = -2ik/L$.

When the effective mass is position-independent W is called the Wronskian of φ_1 and φ_2. It is extensively used in theory of second-order differential equations, in particular to obtain a second solution if one is known.

The rule of non-degeneracy for bound states has many consequences, in particular on the variation of the eigenstates versus a parameter. Take for instance a biased double quantum well. Then, increasing (or decreasing) the bias will make a level to cross another one. The non-degeneracy rule makes that crossing impossible and actually the two levels anti-cross [73].

12. Variational method: hydrogen atom

Consider the hydrogen atom problem. Find the variational estimate of the ground $1s$ state if the trial wavefunction is a Gaussian:

$$\psi_{1s}(\vec{r}) = N \exp\left(-\frac{r^2}{2\lambda^2}\right) \qquad \text{(III.12.1)}$$

where N is a normalisation constant that you will have to evaluate.

Hint: the expression of the Laplacian operator in spherical coordinates is:

$$\Delta = \frac{1}{r^2}\frac{\partial}{\partial r}\left(r^2\frac{\partial}{\partial r}\right) + \frac{1}{r^2 \sin\theta}\frac{\partial}{\partial \theta}\left(\sin\theta\frac{\partial}{\partial \theta}\right) + \frac{1}{r^2 \sin^2\theta}\frac{\partial^2}{\partial\varphi^2} \tag{III.12.2}$$

Solution

$$N^2 = \frac{1}{(\lambda\sqrt{\pi})^3}; \quad \langle T \rangle = \frac{3\hbar^2}{4m\lambda^2}; \quad \langle V \rangle = -\frac{2}{\sqrt{\pi}}\frac{e^2}{4\pi\varepsilon_0\lambda} \tag{III.12.3}$$

The best trial wavefunction is obtained by minimising $\langle H \rangle$ with respect to λ. We find:

$$\lambda_{\min} = \frac{3\sqrt{\pi}}{4}a_0, \quad a_0 = \frac{4\pi\varepsilon_0\hbar^2}{me^2} \tag{III.12.4}$$

$$E_{\min} = -\frac{8R^*}{3\pi} \approx -0.848R^*, \quad R^* = \frac{\hbar^2}{2ma_0^2} = \frac{e^2}{8\pi\varepsilon_0 a_0} \tag{III.12.5}$$

a_0 is the Bohr radius (about 0.053 nm) and R^* the Rydberg constant (about 13.6 eV). Note that coulombic potentials fulfil the "virial theorem" (see Exercise 10) namely that $\langle T \rangle = -E_{min} = -\langle V \rangle/2$.

13. Variational method: electron in a triangular potential

Consider the bound motion of an electron moving in a linearly varying potential eFz for $z \geq 0$. For $z < 0$ there is an infinitely high repulsive barrier.

(1) Show that the eigenenergies vary like $F^{2/3}$.

(2) We attempt a variational solution

$$\chi_1(z) = Nz \exp\left(-\frac{bz}{2}\right) \tag{III.13.1}$$

Compute N, then

$$E_1(b) = \langle \chi_1 | H | \chi_1 \rangle \tag{III.13.2}$$

as functions of b. Minimise $E_1(b)$ to find the lowest confinement energy. Compute its value for $m^* = 0.07m_0$ and $F = 50$ kV/cm.

Solution

(1) Take the Schrödinger equation for $z \geq 0$. Try to change z into ax where a is a length and x is dimensionless. Express the energy in terms of $\frac{\hbar^2}{2m^*a^2}$. The only way to get a dimensionless equation is $2eFa^3/\hbar^2$ to be a c-number, say 1. Then the energies will scale like $F^{2/3}$.

(2)

$$N^2 = \frac{b^3}{2}; \quad T = \frac{\hbar^2 b^2}{8m^*}; \quad \langle eFz \rangle = \frac{3eF}{b} \tag{III.13.3}$$

$$b_{min} = \left(\frac{12m^*eF}{\hbar^2}\right)^{1/3}; \quad E_{min} = \frac{3}{8}(12eFL)^{2/3}\left(\frac{\hbar^2}{m^*L^2}\right)^{1/3} \tag{III.13.4}$$

where L is an arbitrary length. In the 3/8, 1/8 goes to kinetic and 2/8 to potential energy (to comply with the virial theorem, see Exercise 10).

14.   Variational method: anharmonic oscillator

Consider a one-dimensional anharmonic oscillator with Hamiltonian:

$$H = \frac{p^2}{2m} + \frac{1}{2}m\omega^2 x^2 \left(1 + \frac{x^2}{L^2}\right) \tag{III.14.1}$$

We search for a variational estimate of its ground state by using the trial wavefunction:

$$\psi_\lambda(x) = N \exp\left(-\frac{x^2}{2\lambda^2}\right) \tag{III.14.2}$$

where λ is the variational parameter. We denote by a the length associated with the harmonic oscillator: $a = \sqrt{\frac{\hbar}{m\omega}}$.

Compute $E(\lambda) = \langle\psi_\lambda|H|\psi_\lambda\rangle$. By minimising with respect to λ, find the equation fulfilled by the optimal λ. Solve it to the lowest order in a/L.

Solution

$$N^2 = \frac{1}{\lambda\sqrt{\pi}}; \quad \langle T \rangle = \frac{\hbar^2}{4m^*\lambda^2}; \quad \langle V \rangle = \frac{1}{2}m^*\omega^2\left(\frac{\lambda^2}{2} + \frac{3\lambda^4}{4L^2}\right) \tag{III.14.3}$$

$$\frac{dE(\lambda)}{d\lambda} = -\frac{\hbar^2}{2m^*\lambda^3} + \frac{1}{2}m^*\omega^2\left(\lambda + \frac{3\lambda^3}{L^2}\right) \tag{III.14.4}$$

In the absence of anharmonic term in H, the optimal λ is $\lambda = a$. Hence, we let $\lambda = at$ and get:

$$\frac{dE(\lambda)}{d\lambda} = \frac{1}{2}m\omega^2 a\left(-\frac{1}{t^3} + t + 3\frac{a^2}{L^2}t^3\right) = 0 \tag{III.14.5}$$

This is a cubic equation in t^2. Hence, the roots can be gotten analytically (if not quickly). Assuming $a \ll L$ allows an easy computation of the lowest (second) order change the optimal t:

$$t_{\text{opt}} = 1 - \frac{3a^2}{4L^2} \tag{III.14.6}$$

and a blue shift of the lowest eigenvalue $\frac{1}{2}\hbar\omega$ by a quantity $\frac{3a^2}{4L^2}\hbar\omega$. Both the blue shift and the shortening of the characteristic length of the wavefunction had to be expected: the quartic term is positive; so its only effect is to increase the energy. Since the overall potential is steeper than the harmonic one, it confines the electron more. Thus, the characteristic length of the bound states should decrease.

15. Screened coulombic bound states

In semiconductor at thermal equilibrium, there exist free carriers if $T \neq 0$. If the semiconductor is doped with impurities, the free carriers will modify the binding energy of these impurities because they screen the coulombic potential that generates the bound states. The physics of the screening appears simple: the mobile electrons have a tendency to pile up where the donors are located. This accumulation of electrons in turn modifies the potential experienced by an extra electron, making it weaker since the extra electron is attracted by the bare coulombic potential of the donor but repelled by the cloud of electrons that has piled up nearby the impurity site. The weakened attraction leads to shallower binding, and more so if the concentration of mobile electrons is larger. But at thermal equilibrium a decrease of the electron binding energy implies necessarily (see below) an increase of free electron concentration, which itself leads to a decrease of the binding energy. Hence, we feel that two situations may exist depending of the extension of the screening cloud. If the electronic concentration is weak enough, there will exist an equilibrium concentration of mobile electrons such that the coulombic potential plus the repulsion of the piled electrons still produce a deep enough bound state. On the other hand, if the electron concentration nearby the donor is too large, the screening will be so effective that no bound state will survive.

We examine in this exercise the binding energy of a screened Coulomb donor potential for several values of the screening length. Then, at a given temperature, for each value of screened donor binding energy, we compute the equilibrium concentration of mobile electrons, a self-consistent requirement will determine the actual equilibrium concentration of mobile electrons and in turn the equilibrium screened donor binding energy. We consider a bulk semiconductor because in heterostructures the screening problem becomes much complicated by the formation of bound states in one (or several) dimensions.

Part I

Admit that the screened electrostatic potential created by a positively charged impurity located at $\vec{R}_i$ is of the Debye–Huckel shape:

$$\varphi(\vec{r}) = \frac{e}{4\pi\varepsilon_0\varepsilon_r|\vec{r} - \vec{R}_i|} \exp\left(-\frac{|\vec{r} - \vec{R}_i|}{\lambda}\right) \qquad \text{(III.15.1)}$$

where ε_0 and ε_r are the vacuum and relative dielectric constant and λ is the screening length:

$$\lambda = \left(\frac{\varepsilon_0\varepsilon_r k_B T}{e^2 n_{3D}}\right)^{1/2} \qquad \text{(III.15.2)}$$

while n_{3D} is the volume concentration of mobile electrons.

Find a variational estimate of the binding energy of an electron bound to such a donor by using the trial wavefunction:

$$\psi_a(\vec{r}) = N \exp\left(-\frac{|\vec{r} - \vec{R}_i|}{a}\right) \qquad \text{(III.15.3)}$$

where a is the trial parameter and N a normalisation constant to be evaluated. Compute:

$$E(a) = \langle\psi_a|\frac{p^2}{2m^*} - e\varphi(\vec{r})|\psi_a\rangle \qquad \text{(III.15.4)}$$

and minimise it with respect to a.

Part II

In a second stage write the thermal equilibrium between the electrons bound to the donors and the mobile electrons. For such a purpose assume that the donor has a single bound state calculated in the first part. We recall that the occupation function of a bound state is (see e.g., [42]):

$$f(\varepsilon_d) = \frac{1}{1 + \frac{1}{2}\exp[-\beta(\varepsilon_d + \mu)]}; \quad \beta = \frac{1}{k_B T} \qquad \text{(III.15.5)}$$

where ε_d is the binding energy, i.e., the lowest energy that should be given to the electron bound to the donor to be promoted in the conduction band. The factor $1/2$ in the denominator comes from the impossibility for the donor to bind two electrons (the existence of the negatively charged donor is neglected because of its very shallow binding).

Write down the charge neutrality equation and show that the unknown $z = e^{-\beta\mu}$ is solution of the equation:

$$\frac{1}{2\pi^2}\left(\frac{2m^*k_BT}{\hbar^2}\right)^{3/2}\int_0^\infty dt\frac{\sqrt{t}}{1+ze^t} = N_d\frac{z}{z+2e^{\beta\varepsilon_d}} \qquad \text{(III.15.6)}$$

where N_d is the donor volume concentration and ε_d the donor binding energy.

For simplicity, we take the classical limit in the integral (i.e., we assume z is large). Show that the volume concentration of electrons n is equal to:

$$n = \frac{1}{4z}\left(\frac{2m^*k_BT}{\pi\hbar^2}\right)^{3/2} \qquad \text{(III.15.7)}$$

We give:

$$\int_0^\infty dxe^{-x^2} = \frac{\sqrt{\pi}}{2} \qquad \text{(III.15.8)}$$

Deduce that at thermal equilibrium:

$$n = \frac{2N_d}{1+\sqrt{1+32N_d\left(\frac{\pi\hbar^2}{2m^*k_BT}\right)^{3/2}e^{\beta\varepsilon_d}}} \qquad \text{(III.15.9)}$$

This is a self-consistent equation since the binding energy ε_d decreases with n as established in the first part of the problem.

Solution

Part I

The energy zero corresponds to an electron at rest and located at infinite distance from the coulombic centre. The eigenvalues spectrum comprises a continuum (positive energies) and, possibly, bound states at negative energies. The binding energy ε_d is the energy necessary to promote the electron from the lowest state to the lowest extended state (vanishing kinetic energy). Hence, $\varepsilon_d = -\text{Min}_a \, E(a)$.

One finds readily that:

$$N^2 \pi a^3 = 1; \quad \left\langle -\frac{\hbar^2}{2m}\Delta \right\rangle = \frac{\hbar^2}{2ma^2} \tag{III.15.10}$$

$$\left\langle \frac{-e^2 e^{-|\vec{r}-\vec{R}_i|/\lambda}}{4\pi\varepsilon_0\varepsilon_r |\vec{r} - \vec{R}_i|} \right\rangle = -\frac{e^2}{4\pi\varepsilon_0\varepsilon_r a \left(1 + \frac{a}{2\lambda}\right)^2} \tag{III.15.11}$$

Expressing a in terms of the effective Bohr radius a_B: $a = xa_B$ ($a_B = \frac{4\pi\varepsilon_0\varepsilon_r\hbar^2}{m^*e^2} \approx (0.053 \text{ nm})\frac{\varepsilon_r m_0}{m^*}$) and the energy in terms of the effective Rydberg R_B:

$$R_B = \frac{m^*e^4}{2\hbar^2(4\pi\varepsilon_0\varepsilon_r)^2} \approx \frac{m^*}{m_0\varepsilon_r^2}(13600) \text{ meV} \tag{III.15.12}$$

one finds:

$$\frac{E(x)}{R_B} = \left(\frac{1}{x^2} - \frac{2}{x\left(1 + \frac{a_B}{2\lambda}x\right)^2} \right) \tag{III.15.13}$$

If a_B/λ is vanishingly small, one recovers the (exact) result $x_{min} = 1$; $E_{min} = -R_B$. For increasing a_B/λ the attractive part diminishes (since the large x behaviour falls like x^{-3} instead of x^{-1}). For small a_B/λ one finds easily that:

$$x_{min} \approx 1; \quad E_{min} = -R_B\left(1 - 2\frac{a_B}{\lambda}\right) \tag{III.15.14}$$

As expected the negative screening cloud that surrounds the donor weakens the binding energy of the extra electron.

When the screening length decreases enough the binding energy vanishes. For this particular value $a_B/2\lambda$ there is $E(a_{min}) = 0$ and $\frac{dE}{da}\big|_{a=a_{min}} = 0$. It can be readily checked that this happens when:

$$x_{min} = 2 \quad \text{and} \quad \lambda = a_B \tag{III.15.15}$$

A complete study of the problem requires a numerical finding of the minimum (it is given by solving a cubic equation which is doable but

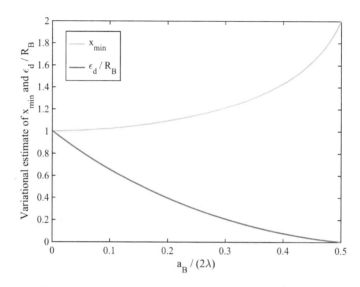

Figure 15.1. Variations of $x_{\min}$ and ε_d versus the dimensionless parameter $a_B/2\lambda$. When the screening length decreases enough, i.e., the parameter $a_B/2\lambda$ is large enough, the binding energy, as obtained from the variational principle, vanishes. An exact numerical calculation would probably lead to a non-zero (but small) binding energy.

painful). We show in Fig. 15.1 a plot of $x_{\min}$ and of the dimensionless binding energy ε_d/R_B versus the dimensionless parameter $a_B/2\lambda$.

Part II

The volume concentration of free electrons n is given by:

$$n = \frac{1}{2\pi^2}\left(\frac{2m^*k_BT}{\hbar^2}\right)^{3/2}\int_0^\infty \frac{dx\,x^{1/2}}{1+ze^x} \qquad \text{(III.15.16)}$$

Working in the classical limit, we find readily:

$$n = \left(\frac{2m^*k_BT}{\pi\hbar^2}\right)^{3/2}\frac{1}{4z} \qquad \text{(III.15.17)}$$

The volume concentration of ionised donors N_{d+} is $N_d[1-f(\varepsilon_d)]$:

$$N_{d+} = N_d\frac{z}{z+2\exp(\beta\varepsilon_d)} \qquad \text{(III.15.18)}$$

By equating n to N_{d+} we get:

$$z = \frac{1 + \sqrt{1 + 32e^{\beta\varepsilon_d}n_d}}{8n_d} \; ; \; n_d = N_d \left(\frac{\pi\hbar^2}{2m^*k_BT} \right)^{3/2} \qquad \text{(III.15.19)}$$

n_d is the number of donors in a volume whose radius is roughly the thermal wavelength $\sqrt{\frac{\hbar^2}{2m^*k_BT}}$. This length is of the order of 8.12 nm at $T = 100$ K if $m^* = 0.07m_0$. Finally, one ends up with the self-consistent equation on n:

$$n = \frac{2N_d}{1 + \sqrt{1 + 32n_de^{\beta\varepsilon_d}}} \qquad \text{(III.15.20)}$$

On the right-hand side, the n-dependence is due to the decrease of ε_d with increasing n (see Fig. 15.1). Note that (III.15.20) does not always admit a solution with non-zero ε_d: if at a given T, N_d is too large, n will exceed the critical concentration where the binding energy vanishes and the solution of (III.15.20) will be $n = N_d$.

It must be pointed out that this exercise does not exhaust (by far) the problem of bound states in the presence of mobile electrons. Two effects have been left over. Firstly, the fact that in the presence of mobile electrons the Pauli principle acts by preventing the occupied states to contribute to the build-up of the impurity wavefunction. In other words if at $n = 0$ we wrote the impurity trial wavefunction (Eq. (III.15.3)) on the basis of the plane wave:

$$\psi(\vec{r}) = \sum_{\vec{k}} c(\vec{k}) \frac{\exp(i\vec{k} \cdot \vec{r})}{\sqrt{\Omega}} \qquad \text{(III.15.21)}$$

the participation of a given $\vec{k}$ to the summation should be weighed by the probability that it is empty. Secondly, the assumption of ideal dilution may become wrong because of multi-impurity effects (heavy doping). So, the present exercise should rather be viewed as a very rough description of a phenomenon that occurs in all semiconductors and their heterostructures: the decrease of the impurity binding energy with increasing concentration of mobile charges.

16. A two-dimensional coulombic problem

(1) We consider the bi-dimensional motion of an electron on the plane $z = 0$. This electron is attracted by a coulombic center located at the origin. Find its binding energy by minimising $\langle \psi_\lambda | H | \psi_\lambda \rangle$ with respect to λ where:

$$\langle \vec{\rho} | \psi_\lambda \rangle = N_\lambda e^{-\frac{\rho}{\lambda}}; \quad H = -\frac{\hbar^2}{2m^* \rho} \frac{d}{d\rho} \left(\rho \frac{d}{d\rho} \right) - \frac{e^2}{4\pi\varepsilon_0\varepsilon_r \rho} \quad \text{(III.16.1)}$$

where ε_r is the relative dielectric permittivity of the material. The results obtained in this question are exact.

(2) The donor is now located at a distance D from the plane $z = 0$ where the electron moves. Show that in the limit of large D, the electron energy can exactly be written:

$$E(D) = -\frac{e^2}{4\pi\varepsilon_0\varepsilon_r D} + \hbar\sqrt{\frac{e^2}{4\pi\varepsilon_0\varepsilon_r D^3 m^*}} \quad \text{if} \quad \sqrt{\frac{a_B}{D}} \ll 1 \quad \text{(III.16.2)}$$

where a_B is the effective Bohr radius and m^* the electron mass.

Solution

(1) The binding energy is minus the expectation value of the Hamiltonian over the exact wavefunction because the lowest lying dissociated state consists in having the electron at rest infinitely far away from the attractive center. Our variational ansatz consists in guessing a plausible shape for the wavefunction and in finding the best among them by minimising E. One calculates readily:

$$N_\lambda^2 = \frac{2}{\pi\lambda^2}; \quad \langle \psi_\lambda | H | \psi_\lambda \rangle = \frac{\hbar^2}{2m^*\lambda^2} - \frac{e^2}{2\pi\varepsilon_0\varepsilon_r\lambda}$$

$$\text{(III.16.3)}$$

$$\lambda_{\min} = \frac{2\pi\varepsilon_0\varepsilon_r\hbar^2}{m^*e^2} = \frac{a_B}{2}; \quad E_{\min} = -2\frac{m^*e^4}{(4\pi\varepsilon_0\varepsilon_r)^2\hbar^2} = -4R_B$$

$$\text{(III.16.4)}$$

where a_B and R_B are the 3D effective Bohr radius and Rydberg, respectively.

(2) When the impurity is far enough away the characteristic in-plane distance will be small compared to D. Thus we can expand the coulombic potential and the lowest order in ρ/D we find:

$$-\frac{e^2}{4\pi\varepsilon_0\varepsilon_r\sqrt{\rho^2+D^2}} \approx -\frac{e^2}{4\pi\varepsilon_0\varepsilon_r D} + \frac{e^2\rho^2}{8\pi\varepsilon_0\varepsilon_r D^3} \qquad \text{(III.16.5)}$$

Thus, apart from a constant, the electron moves in a two-dimensional (2D) harmonic potential with an angular frequency:

$$\Omega = \sqrt{\frac{e^2}{4\pi\varepsilon_0\varepsilon_r D^3 m^*}} \qquad \text{(III.16.6)}$$

Thus, in the limit of large D one finds exactly:

$$E(D) \approx -\frac{e^2}{4\pi\varepsilon_0\varepsilon_r D} + \hbar\Omega \qquad \text{(III.16.7)}$$

For this to be valid, we need that the in-plane extension of the wave-function remains much smaller than D. But because of the equipartition (virial) theorem we know that:

$$\frac{1}{2}m^*\Omega^2\langle\rho^2\rangle = \frac{1}{2}\hbar\Omega \qquad \text{(III.16.8)}$$

It follows that the condition of validity of the previous expansion is:

$$\sqrt{\frac{a_B}{D}} \ll 1 \qquad \text{(III.16.9)}$$

Thus, the impurity has to be remote (40 nm with GaAs parameters if $1/2$ is considered $\ll 1$). The binding will be very shallow (2 meV or less) and in practice (i.e., above 77 K) these remote donors will be ionised on average. However, they can temporarily trap carriers and therefore induce random fluctuations in the carrier concentrations and currents of the device (flicker noise).

In the opposite limit $(D \ll a_B)$, we find with the same trial wavefunction:

$$\langle V \rangle_\lambda = -\frac{e^2}{4\pi\varepsilon_0\varepsilon_r}\left(\frac{4D}{\lambda^2}\int_0^\infty \frac{x\,dx}{\sqrt{1+x^2}}c^{-\mu x}\right); \quad \mu - \frac{2D}{\lambda} \quad \text{(III.16.10)}$$

This integral is expressible in terms of the Struve (H_1) and Neumann (Y_1) functions of order 1:

$$\int_0^\infty \frac{x}{\sqrt{1+x^2}}e^{-\mu x}dx = \frac{\pi}{2}[H_1(\mu) - Y_1(\mu)] - 1 \quad \text{(III.16.11)}$$

Thus, expressing the energy in terms of R_B and λ in terms of the radius a_B, we find:

$$\frac{E(x,D)}{R_B} = \frac{1}{x^2} - \frac{8D}{a_Bx^2}\left\{\frac{\pi}{2}\left[H_1\left(\frac{2D}{a_Bx}\right) - Y_1\left(\frac{2D}{a_Bx}\right)\right] - 1\right\}$$
$$\text{(III.16.12)}$$

Figure 16.1 shows the minimum energy $E_{\min}$ versus the dimensionless ratio D/a_B. One sees, as expected, a continuous decrease of the binding $(-E_{\min})$ with increasing D/a_B.

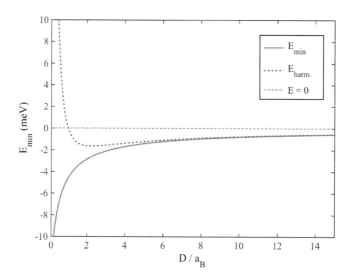

Figure 16.1. The energy $E_{\min}$ versus the dimensionless ratio D/a_B. The binding decreases continuously with increasing D/a_B. Moreover, we note a good agreement between the variational estimate (solid line) and the harmonic approximation (dashed line) when D/a_B is large enough.

17. Inter-subband transitions in cubic GaN/AlN quantum wells: information on the conduction band offset

The very existence of inter-subband optical transitions between the conduction subbands in quantum well (QW) structure gives information on a key material parameter: the conduction band offset. In this exercise we examine why this is so.

Consider a rectangular QW of thickness L and barrier height V_b. The carrier effective mass is m^* $(m^* = 0.11m_0)$.

(1) We choose the origin of the x coordinate at the center of the QW. Show that $[P, H] = 0$ where H is the 1D QW Hamiltonian and P the parity operator such that:

$$P\psi(x) = \psi(-x) \qquad \text{(III.17.1)}$$

(2) Find the eigenvalues and eigenvectors of P.

(3) Compute the equation that determines the bound states of the QW that are even in x. Same question for the bound states that are odd in x.

(4) What is the critical thickness where the last odd bound state disappears? Same question for the disappearance of the last even bound state.

(5) We denote by $E_1, E_2, \ldots$ the bound states of the QW. We consider a QW with thickness L_c that corresponds to the disappearance of the last odd bound state E_2. Show that $E_1(L_c)$ fulfils:

$$\xi = \cos\left(\frac{\xi\pi}{2}\right) \qquad \text{(III.17.2)}$$

where ξ is the dimensionless parameter defined by:

$$\xi = \sqrt{\frac{2m^* E_1 L_c^2}{\hbar^2 \pi^2}} \qquad \text{(III.17.3)}$$

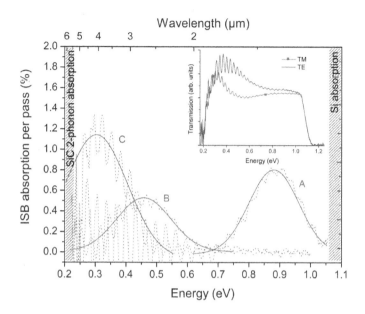

Figure 17.1. Inter-subband absorption measurements in cubic GaN/AlN QW's. *Source*: Machhadani *et al.* [74].

(6) Show that the solution of this equation is in between $1/2$ and $2/3$. Show that approximately there is:

$$\xi = \frac{4}{\pi^2}\left(-1 + \sqrt{1 + \frac{\pi^2}{2}}\right) \qquad \text{(III.17.4)}$$

Hint: expand $\cos(x)$ up to the second order in x and check *a posteriori* that the expansion was justified.

(7) If one admits that an inter-subband transition $E_i \rightarrow E_j$ is allowed only if both the initial and final subbands are bound to the QW, what information can one get if the transition $E_1 \rightarrow E_2$ is experimentally observed in a QW with thickness $L_{\exp}$?

(8) Figure 17.1 shows a recent result of inter-subband absorption measurements in cubic GaN/AlN QW's (Machhadani *et al.* [74]) versus photon energy. The three samples labelled A, B, C, respectively, correspond to QW thicknesses equal to 2 nm, 3 nm and 5 nm. Comment this figure in light of question (7).

Solution

(1) It is clear that the potential energy $V(x)$ is an even function of x if one chooses the x origin at the middle of the well. Then, if $P(x)$ is the parity operator with respect to the center of the QW, there is $PH = HP$. It follows that one can find eigenfunctions of H among the eigenfunctions of P.

(2) The parity operator is such that $P^2 = 1$. This operator identity implies that the eigenvalues of P are ± 1. The $+1$ eigenvalue corresponds to eigenfunctions that are even in x while the eigenvalue -1 corresponds to eigenfunctions that are odd in x.

(3) For the even eigenfunctions, we choose:

$$\psi(x) = A\cos(kx), \quad |x| \leq \frac{L}{2}; \quad k = \sqrt{\frac{2m^*\varepsilon}{\hbar^2}} \quad \text{(III.17.5)}$$

$$\psi(x) = B\exp\left[-\kappa\left(z - \frac{L}{2}\right)\right], \quad x \geq \frac{L}{2}; \quad \kappa = \sqrt{\frac{2m^*(V_b - \varepsilon)}{\hbar^2}}$$
$$\text{(III.17.6)}$$

We write the continuity of $\psi(x)$ and $\psi'(x)$ at $z = L/2$:

$$A\cos\left(\frac{kL}{2}\right) = B; \quad Ak\sin\left(\frac{kL}{2}\right) = \kappa B \quad \text{(III.17.7)}$$

$$\Rightarrow k\sin\left(\frac{kL}{2}\right) = \kappa\cos\left(\frac{kL}{2}\right) \quad \text{(III.17.8)}$$

Note that accounting for the parity of the eigenstates has allowed us to use only one interface instead of the two interfaces that separate well and barriers.

For the odd states, we choose:

$$\psi(x) = C\sin(kx), \quad |x| \leq \frac{L}{2}; \quad k = \sqrt{\frac{2m^*\varepsilon}{\hbar^2}} \quad \text{(III.17.9)}$$

$$\psi(x) = D\exp\left[-\kappa\left(z - \frac{L}{2}\right)\right], \quad x \geq \frac{L}{2}; \quad \kappa = \sqrt{\frac{2m^*(V_b - \varepsilon)}{\hbar^2}}$$
$$\text{(III.17.10)}$$

Proceeding as above, we get for the odd states:

$$k\cos\left(\frac{kL}{2}\right) = -\kappa\sin\left(\frac{kL}{2}\right) \quad \text{(III.17.11)}$$

(4) The last odd bound state disappears when its energy becomes equal to the barrier height (the energy origin has been taken in the well-acting material). Thus κ_b vanishes.

From (3) we see that: $Lk(V_b) = (2j + 1)\pi$ is fulfilled. Thus, the last odd state that disappears in the continuum is E_2 when $Lk(E_2 = V_b) = \pi$.

A similar analysis can be performed for the even bound states, leading to $Lk(V_b) = 2j\pi$. Hence, the last one disappears at vanishing QW thickness.

(5) The equation that determines E_1 for this particular thickness L_c is:

$$\cos[k(E_1)]\frac{L_c}{2} = \sqrt{\frac{E_1}{V_b - E_1}} \sin[k(E_1)]\frac{L_c}{2} \Rightarrow E_1 = V_b \cos^2\left[k(E_1)\frac{L_c}{2}\right]$$
(III.17.12)

By using the suggested dimensionless variable and taking into account the fact that at L_c there is $E_2 = V_b$ and $k(V_b = E_2)L_c = \pi$, one finally gets easily the proposed equation:

$$\xi = \cos\left(\frac{\xi\pi}{2}\right)$$
(III.17.13)

(6) To solve numerically Eq. (III.17.13), we compute the right-hand side (rhs) and the left-hand side (lhs) for a few values of ξ.

ξ	0	1/2	2/3	3/4	1
lhs	0	1/2	2/3	3/4	1
rhs	1	$\sqrt{2}/2$	1/2	$\cos\left(\frac{3\pi}{8}\right)$	0

Hence, the root is in between 1/2 and 2/3. Numerically, we find: $\xi \approx 0.59$ by linear interpolation of the function $x - \cos(\pi x/2)$. The approximate value obtained by expanding $\cos x$ up to the second order is close from this value.

It is worth pointing out that the finite barrier height effect is particularly sizeable. Indeed, if the barriers were infinitely high the $E_2 - E_1$ transition energy would (always) be equal to $\frac{3\hbar^2\pi^2}{2m^*L^2}$. Here instead when E_2 disappears in the continuum we have:

$$E_2 - E_1 = \frac{\hbar^2 \pi^2}{2m^* L^2} - (0.59)^2 \frac{\hbar^2 \pi^2}{2m^* L^2} \approx 0.64 \frac{\hbar^2 \pi^2}{2m^* L^2} \qquad \text{(III.17.14)}$$

(7) and (8) If the $E_2 - E_1$ transition is observed for a QW thickness L_{exp}, this means that at worse the E_2 level is just at the top of the well. Thus $E_2 = V_b$ and $\frac{2m^* V_b L_{\text{exp}}^2}{\hbar^2} = \pi^2$. Thus at least we know that:

$$V_b \geq \frac{\hbar^2 \pi^2}{2m^* L_{\text{exp}}^2} \qquad \text{(III.17.15)}$$

Even more, let us denote by $\hbar \omega_{\text{exp}}$ the value of the transition energy. It is equal to:

$$\hbar \omega_{\text{exp}} = E_2 - E_1 = V_b - E_1 = \frac{\hbar^2 \pi^2}{2m^* L_{\text{exp}}^2} (1 - \xi^2) \qquad \text{(III.17.16)}$$

$$\Rightarrow V_b = E_2 = \frac{\hbar^2 \pi^2}{2m^* L_{\text{exp}}^2} = \frac{\hbar \omega_{\text{exp}}}{1 - \xi^2} = \frac{\hbar \omega_{\text{exp}}}{0.64} \qquad \text{(III.17.17)}$$

We know that if E_2 is at (or very near) the top of the well, the band offset is directly related to a measurable quantity.

For $L = 2$ nm there is an absorption peak at 0.88 eV. If we assume that E_2 coincides with the top of the well we get from the previous question $V_b = 1.38$ eV. Thus, the cubic GaN is a material suitable for inter-subband transitions operating in the infrared part of the electromagnetic spectrum. Of course, many issues have to be solved (line broadening, etc.) before a real device shows up.

18.   Asymmetrical square quantum well

Consider a 1D rectangular quantum well with a left (respectively, right) barrier height equal to V_l (respectively, $V_r > V_l$). The effective masses are, respectively, m_l, m_w and m_r. Use the Ben Daniel–Duke form for the kinetic energy. We will have to write the boundary conditions at $z = 0$ and $z = L$. Assume there exists one bound state. Find the transcendental equation fulfilled by the bound state. Does the asymmetrical quantum well always bind a state? Same question if $V_l = V_r$.

Solution

We assume there exists one bound state and look for its envelope function in the form:

$$\chi(z) = a e^{\kappa_1 z}, \quad z \leq 0 \tag{III.18.1}$$
$$\chi(z) = b \sin(k_w z) + c \cos(k_w z), \quad 0 \leq z \leq L \tag{III.18.2}$$
$$\chi(z) = d \exp[-\kappa_r(z - L)], \quad z \geq L \tag{III.18.3}$$

where $z = 0$ and $z = L$ denote the boundaries between the well and the barriers. The three wavevectors appearing in $\chi(z)$ are respectively equal to:

$$k_w = \sqrt{\frac{2m_w \varepsilon}{\hbar^2}}; \quad \kappa_{l,r} = \sqrt{\frac{2m_{l,r}(V_{l,r} - \varepsilon)}{\hbar^2}} \tag{III.18.4}$$

Let us denote by C and S the quantities:

$$C = \cos(k_w L); \quad S = \sin(k_w L) \tag{III.18.5}$$

We write the boundary conditions at $z = 0$ and $z = L$ (continuity of the envelope and of the current) and get:

$$a = c \tag{III.18.6}$$

$$a = b \frac{k_w m_l}{m_w \kappa_l} \tag{III.18.7}$$

$$bS + cC = d \tag{III.18.8}$$

$$bC - cS = -d \frac{\kappa_r m_w}{m_r k_w} \tag{III.18.9}$$

Finally, a non-trivial solution exists if:

$$C \left(1 + \frac{\kappa_l m_r}{m_l \kappa_r} \right) + S \left(\frac{\kappa_l m_w}{m_l k_w} - \frac{k_w m_r}{m_w \kappa_r} \right) = 0 \tag{III.18.10}$$

When L decreases, we know that the confinement energies will increase (cf. Heisenberg inequality). At some critical L_c the last bound state will have its confinement energy equal to V_l. Its evanescent wavevector in the left barrier will vanish and the state will become unbound. Letting $\kappa_l = 0$ in the previous equation leads to L_c since:

$$\tan\left[L_c k_w(\varepsilon = V_l)\right] = \sqrt{\frac{m_w}{m_r}} \sqrt{\frac{V_r}{V_l} - 1} \qquad \text{(III.18.11)}$$

For barrier heights that are not too different, we find:

$$L_c \approx \sqrt{\frac{\hbar^2}{2 m_w V_l}} \sqrt{\frac{m_w}{m_r}} \sqrt{\frac{V_r}{V_l} - 1} \qquad \text{(III.18.12)}$$

In particular, we recover that the last bound state of a symmetrical quantum well disappears only if $L = 0$. As an example, let us take $V_r = 240$ meV, $V_l = 200$ meV, $m_w = 0.07 m_0$, $m_r = 0.08 m_0$. We get $L_c = 0.69$ nm.

19.   Spherical quantum dots

We are used to the fact that attractive potentials admit bound states. This is always the case in classical mechanics. In quantum mechanics, the one-dimensional (1D) rectangular quantum wells have at least one bound state. However, we saw that an asymmetrical 1D quantum well, if narrow enough, has no bound state (see Exercise 18). The 3D situation is more difficult to assess. We know that attractive coulombic potentials have an infinite number of bound states due to their long range and $1/r$ decay. What about 3D isotropic quantum wells where:

$$V(r) = -V_b, \quad 0 \leq r \leq R \qquad \text{(III.19.1)}$$
$$V(r) = 0, \quad r \geq R \qquad \text{(III.19.2)}$$

This question is not only academic but also directly applies to an important class of existing semiconductor quantum dots: the nanocrystals[1] (see [75] for reviews).

We consider the 3D quantum states of a particle with mass m^* (we neglect for simplicity the effective mass mismatch). We are interested in the ground bound state that will have no node. In addition, since

---

[1] https://en.wikipedia.org/wiki/Core-shellsemiconductornanocrystal.

the attractive potential is spherically symmetric, it is sensible to look for a solution such that $\psi(\vec{r}) \equiv \psi(r)$; in other words we look for an S state corresponding to a zero angular momentum (only S state can be nodeless).

(1) Find the equation fulfilled by $\psi(r)$.

We let:

$$\psi(r) = \frac{u(r)}{r} \tag{III.19.3}$$

(2) Show that $u(r)$ fulfils:

$$-\frac{\hbar^2}{2m^*} \frac{d^2 u(r)}{dr^2} + V(r)u(r) = \varepsilon u(r) \tag{III.19.4}$$

It can be shown that $u(r)$ must vanish at $r = 0$ (see [9]). In addition $u(r)$ should decay to zero when $r \to \infty$ since it corresponds to a bound state where $\psi(r \to \infty) \to 0$. At $r = R$ the probability density and current must be continuous. Hence, $u(r)$, $u(r')$ should be continuous.

(3) Find the equation governing the bound states.

(4) Deduce that there exists a lowest radius $R_{\min}$ below which the last bound state disappears in the continuum (defined as the states such that $\varepsilon \geq 0$).

(5) Compute $R_{\min}$ if $m^* = 0.07m_0$, $V_0 = 0.4$ eV (corresponding roughly to InAs embedded in a GaAs matrix).

Solution

(1) By remarking that $\frac{dr}{d(x,y,z)} = \frac{x,y,z}{r}$; $r = \sqrt{x^2 + y^2 + z^2}$, we find easily that:

$$-\frac{\hbar^2}{2m^*} \left(r \frac{d^2\psi}{dr^2} + 2\frac{d\psi}{dr} \right) + [V(r) - \varepsilon]\, r\psi(r) = 0 \tag{III.19.5}$$

(2) Then, the function $u(r) = r\psi(r)$ fulfils:

$$-\frac{\hbar^2}{2m^*} \frac{d^2 u(r)}{dr^2} + V(r)u(r) = \varepsilon u(r) \tag{III.19.6}$$

This equation is therefore identical to the Schrödinger equation of a 1D rectangular quantum well with the exception that in our case r can only be ≥ 0. The boundary condition $u(0) = 0$ reflects that r can never become negative; everything behaves as if there were an infinite potential barrier that prevents the particle to enter the forbidden region $r < 0$.

(3) For a bound state we write:

$$u(r) = A\sin(k_w r), \quad 0 \leq r \leq R \tag{III.19.7}$$

$$u(r) = B\exp(-\kappa_b(r - R)), \quad r \geq R \tag{III.19.8}$$

$$k_w = \sqrt{\frac{2m^*(\varepsilon + V_b)}{\hbar^2}}; \quad \kappa_b = \sqrt{\frac{-2m^*\varepsilon}{\hbar^2}} \tag{III.19.9}$$

(4) We know that the last odd bound state of the 1D rectangular quantum well disappears in the continuum when $k_w L = \pi$ where k_w is evaluated at the top of the well. The same condition allows determining $R_{\min}$ for the spherical quantum dot:

$$R_{\min} = \sqrt{\frac{\hbar^2 \pi^2}{2m^* V_0}} \tag{III.19.10}$$

(5) For the parameters given in the text we find $R_{\min} = 3.68$ nm. In reality InAs dots do not grow with a spherical shape: they rather look like discs with radius $R \approx 10$ nm and height $h \approx 2$ nm. They accommodate several bound states.

20.   Delta quantum well

The delta potential is very popular among theoreticians because it allows easy calculations. Whether it represents an acceptable approximation of the real physical phenomenon one wants to investigate depends on the situation. In this exercise we study the 1D motion of a carrier with mass m that moves under the action of a potential energy:

$$V(x) = -V_0 a\delta(x - x_0) \tag{III.20.1}$$

where a is a length and V_0 an energy. The singularity in the potential energy suggests that we revisit the boundary conditions, i.e., the stationary solutions of the Schrödinger equation must fulfil. To do so, integrate the Schrödinger equation across the singularity at $x = x_0$.

(1) Besides the continuity of the wavefunction $\chi(x)$ that results from the necessary physical requirement that the probability density must be continuous, find that the derivative of the wavefunction $\chi'(x)$ should have a discontinuity at x_0, namely that:

$$\frac{d\chi}{dx}(x_0^+) - \frac{d\chi}{dx}(x_0^-) = -\frac{2m}{\hbar^2}aV_0\chi(x_0) \tag{III.20.2}$$

(2) Show that $\chi(x)$ can be chosen with a definite parity with respect to x_0, i.e., that:

$$\chi(x - x_0) = \pm\chi(x_0 - x) \tag{III.20.3}$$

(3) We take the energy zero at the onset of the conduction band. If there exists a bound state, its wavefunction should be evanescent in the barrier. Hence, we look for a solution:

$$\chi(x) = A\exp[-\kappa(x - x_0)], \quad x \geq x_0 \tag{III.20.4}$$
$$\chi(x) = A\exp[\kappa(x - x_0)], \quad x \leq x_0 \tag{III.20.5}$$

$$\kappa = \sqrt{-\frac{2m\varepsilon}{\hbar^2}} \tag{III.20.6}$$

Argue qualitatively why we have to choose an even wavefunction in $x - x_0$ rather than an odd one if we search for a bound state.

Find that there exists a single bound state to the problem of a 1D attractive delta potential and that this state has an energy:

$$\varepsilon = -\frac{V_0^2 ma^2}{2\hbar^2} \tag{III.20.7}$$

(4) Consider a square well of depth V_0 and thickness L. We take the energy zero at the top of the well. Find the equation that determines the even bound states of the well. Study the $L \to 0$ limit. What should be the relationship between L and a if one wants the result of (4) to coincide with (3).

Solution

(1) A delta potential is an idealisation of a very narrow and deep potential. As we shall see in question (4) it is a good approximation of a very thin square quantum well. The fact that it is so singular versus x (technically speaking $\delta(x)$ is actually a distribution: "the Dirac mass". In more plain term it is the limit of a sequence of function $f_\sigma(x)$ that are more and more spatially concentrated and at the same time display a maximum that is steeper and steeper in such a way that $\int_{-\infty}^{+\infty} f_\sigma(x)dx = 1$). There is:

$$\int_{x_0-c}^{x_0+b} \delta(x-x_0)g(x) = g(x_0), \quad c,b > 0 \tag{III.20.8}$$

Then by integrating the Schrödinger equation in the vicinity of x_0 we get:

$$-\frac{\hbar^2}{2m}\int_{x_0-c}^{x_0+b} dx \frac{d^2\chi}{dx^2} - V_0 a \int_{x_0-c}^{x_0+b} \delta(x-x_0)\chi(x)dx = \varepsilon \int_{x_0-c}^{x_0+b} \chi(x)dx \tag{III.20.9}$$

In the limit of $c,b \to 0$ we find the required identity:

$$\frac{d\chi}{dx}(x_0^+) - \frac{d\chi}{dx}(x_0^-) = -\frac{2m}{\hbar^2} a V_0 \chi(x_0) \tag{III.20.10}$$

(2) The delta function is even with respect to the inversion of its argument. Hence the parity operator with respect to x_0 commutes with the Hamiltonian. We can therefore search for eigenfunctions that are also eigenfunctions of this parity operator. But the latter are well known. These are the functions that are either even or odd in $(x-x_0)$.

(3) So we look for bound states. These states will be evanescent everywhere (since the bound states are at lower energy than any of the continuum states associated with the free motion). We can either choose the bound states functions even or odd. But note that an odd wavefunction cannot lead to a bound state for a delta potential, since it will never experience any attractive potential (including at x_0 for

the probability density vanishes at that point). Thus, we should look if an even wavefunction in $(x - x_0)$ can lead to a bound state:

$$\chi(x) = A \exp[-\kappa(x - x_0)], \quad x \geq x_0 \tag{III.20.11}$$

$$\chi(x) = A \exp[\kappa(x - x_0)], \quad x \leq x_0 \tag{III.20.12}$$

$$\kappa = \sqrt{-\frac{2m\varepsilon}{\hbar^2}} \tag{III.20.13}$$

Making the boundary conditions explicit, we get readily that a non-trivial solution $(A \neq 0)$ exists provided:

$$\kappa = \frac{mV_0 a}{\hbar^2}; \quad \varepsilon = -V_0^2 \frac{ma^2}{2\hbar^2} \tag{III.20.14}$$

(4) We take the energy zero at the top of the well and we look for an even bound states. The quantum well extends from $x_0 - L/2$ to $x_0 + L/2$.

$$\chi(x - x_0) = A \cos[k(x - x_0)], \quad 0 \leq x - x_0 \leq \frac{L}{2} \tag{III.20.15}$$

$$\chi(x - x_0) = B \exp[-\kappa(x - x_0)], \quad x - x_0 \geq \frac{L}{2} \tag{III.20.16}$$

$$\kappa = \sqrt{-\frac{2m\varepsilon}{\hbar^2}}; \quad k = \sqrt{\frac{2m(\varepsilon + V_0)}{\hbar^2}} \tag{III.20.17}$$

Writing that χ and χ' are continuous at $x = L/2$ we find readily:

$$k \sin\left(\frac{kL}{2}\right) = \kappa \cos\left(\frac{kL}{2}\right) \tag{III.20.18}$$

For a very narrow well, we know that both ε and $L \to 0$. Thus, one should get:

$$k^2 \frac{L}{2} \approx \kappa \Rightarrow \varepsilon \approx -\frac{mV_0^2 L^2}{2\hbar^2} \tag{III.20.19}$$

Hence, we recover the delta function potential if we set $a = L$. It is very difficult to grow extremely thin quantum well structures (say one or two monolayers thick) of high quality. Suppose such a growth has been successful and let $L = 0.566$ nm for $V = 0.24$ eV and $m = 0.07m_0$, we find $\varepsilon = -8.45$ meV, hence a very weak binding of this shallow bound state. Note also that the binding is a quadratic function of the quantum well thickness when L is small.

21. Wavefunction amplitude at the interfaces

We consider a single quantum well of width L. V_b is the barrier height. The electron effective mass is m_w (respectively, m_b) in the well (respectively, barrier) material. It has been found that, often, impurities/defects appear near the interfaces between the well and the barriers. Under such circumstances we write for short range scatterers located near the $z = L/2$ interface that the analytical shape of the defect potential is:

$$V(\vec{\rho}, z) = g(z)u(\vec{\rho}); \quad \vec{\rho} = (x, y) \tag{III.21.1}$$

$$g(z) = 1 \quad \text{if} \ \left| z - \frac{L}{2} \right| \leq \frac{\delta}{2} \tag{III.21.2}$$

$$g(z) = 0 \quad \text{if} \ \left| z - \frac{L}{2} \right| \geq \frac{\delta}{2} \tag{III.21.3}$$

Any matrix element between $|n\vec{k}\rangle$ and $|n'\vec{k'}\rangle$ where $\vec{k}$, $\vec{k'}$ are the 2D vectors that label the free motion in the layer plane will be such that:

$$\langle n\vec{k}|V(\vec{\rho}, z)|n'\vec{k'}\rangle = \langle \vec{k}|u(\vec{\rho})|\vec{k'}\rangle \langle n|g(z)|n'\rangle$$

$$\approx \delta\langle \vec{k}|u(\vec{\rho})|\vec{k'}\rangle \chi_n^* \left(\frac{L}{2}\right) \chi_{n'} \left(\frac{L}{2}\right) \tag{III.21.4}$$

in the limit of small δ. Thus, the scattering efficiency will depend markedly on the amplitude of the wavefunctions at the interfaces.

From now on, we look at the case $n = n' = 1$ (the ground subband). We write:

$$\chi_1(z) = A\cos(k_w z); \quad |z| \leq \frac{L}{2} \tag{III.21.5}$$

$$\chi_1(z) = B\exp\left[-\kappa_b\left(z - \frac{L}{2}\right)\right]; \quad |z| \geq \frac{L}{2} \tag{III.21.6}$$

$$\chi_1(z) = \chi_1(-z) \tag{III.21.7}$$

Find the asymptotic behaviour of $\chi_1(L/2)$ when $L \to 0$, $L \to \infty$ and deduce that there exists (at least) one maximum of $\chi_1(L/2)$ versus L. Explain physically this result.

Solution

By writing the continuity of the wavefunction and of the probability current at $z = L/2$, one gets readily that the ground energy E_1 (which corresponds to even wavefunctions) fulfils:

$$\frac{k_w}{m_w} \sin\left(\frac{k_w L}{2}\right) = \frac{\kappa_b}{m_b} \cos\left(\frac{k_w L}{2}\right) \tag{III.21.8}$$

$$k_w = \left(\frac{2 m_w E_1}{\hbar^2}\right)^{1/2}; \quad \kappa_b = \left[\frac{2 m_b (V_b - E_1)}{\hbar^2}\right]^{1/2} \tag{III.21.9}$$

where m_b and m_w are the masses in the barrier and in the well, respectively.

The wavefunction amplitude at the interface is $B = A \cos(k_w L/2)$. By writing the normalisation of the wavefunction χ_1, one gets:

$$A = \sqrt{\frac{2}{L}} \left[1 + \frac{\sin(k_w L)}{k_w L} + \frac{2}{L \kappa_b} \cos^2\left(\frac{k_w L}{2}\right)\right]^{-1/2} \tag{III.21.10}$$

When L becomes very large we know that the decreasing $E_1(L)$ approaches zero like L^{-2}. More precisely, we can set $k_w L = \pi - x$, $x \ll 1$. With this ansatz as input, we get:

$$x = \frac{2 k_w}{\kappa_b} \frac{m_b}{m_w} \approx \frac{2 \pi m_b}{m_w L \kappa_b}; \quad \kappa_b \approx \left(\frac{2 m_b V_b}{\hbar^2}\right)^{1/2} \tag{III.21.11}$$

Then we find:

$$L \to \infty, \quad \chi_1\left(\frac{L}{2}\right) = A \cos\left(\frac{k_w L}{2}\right) \approx \sqrt{\frac{2}{L}} \frac{\pi m_b}{m_w L \kappa_b} \propto L^{-3/2} \tag{III.21.12}$$

In the opposite limit when L is very small, we know that E_1 approaches V_b from below:

$$L \to 0 \quad k_w \approx \sqrt{\frac{2 m_w V_b}{\hbar^2}}; \quad \kappa_b \approx \frac{L V_b m_b}{\hbar^2}; \quad E_1 \approx V_b - \frac{m_b V_b^2 L^2}{2 \hbar^2} \tag{III.21.13}$$

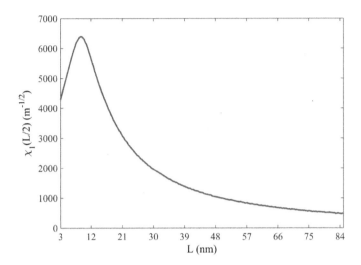

Figure 21.1.   Wavefunction amplitude of the ground state $(\chi_1(L/2))$ at the interface versus the quantum well thickness (L). The material parameters are: $m_w = 0.07m_0$, $m_b = 0.08m_0$ and $V_b = 0.23$ eV.

Inserting in the definition of A, we get:

$$L \to 0, \quad \chi_1\left(\frac{L}{2}\right) \approx A \approx \sqrt{\frac{2}{L}}\left(2 + \frac{2\hbar^2}{L^2 V_b m_b}\right)^{-1/2} \approx \left(\frac{L V_b m_b}{\hbar^2}\right)^{1/2}$$
$$\text{(III.21.14)}$$

Thus, the function $\chi_1\left(L/2\right)$ has a constant sign, goes to zero at both ends of the segment $[0, \infty]$, it has therefore one maximum (at least). Physically, this means that the interface is "not so important" when the well is either very broad or very narrow.

In Fig. 21.1, we illustrate the previous consideration by showing the wavefunction amplitude at the interface versus L when $m_w = 0.07m_0$, $m_b = 0.08m_0$ and $V_b = 0.23$ eV.

22.   Interface state in HgTe/CdTe heterojunctions

We have mentioned that there is usually no allowed energy states in an A/B heterojunction when the electron is evanescent in both kinds of layers. There exist counter-examples to this generally correct statement.

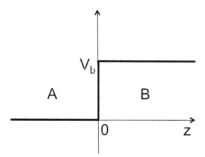

Figure 22.1. Conduction band profile of the heterojunction.

We work using the Ben Daniel–Duke model. The carrier effective mass is m_A (m_B) in the A (B) material. The energy zero is taken at the edge of the conduction band of the A material. V_b is the offset between the two materials (see Fig. 22.1).

(1) Take the case where both effective masses are positive. Find that there exists no allowed energy state with a negative energy.

(2) We consider the case where $m_A = -|m_A|$ is now negative. Hence, we now deal with a valence band in A. To get an evanescent propagation in both kinds of layers we need to consider the energy segment $[0, V_b]$. Show that there always exists one allowed solution in this energy range.

Solution

We should match the envelope and the probability current at the interface $z = 0$. To get normalisable wavefunctions with evanescent states, the only possibility is to choose:

$$\chi(z) = A \exp(\kappa_A z); \quad \kappa_A = \sqrt{\frac{-2m_A \varepsilon}{\hbar^2}}; \quad z \leq 0 \qquad \text{(III.22.1)}$$

$$\chi(z) = B \exp(-\kappa_B z); \quad \kappa_B = \sqrt{\frac{2m_B(V_b - \varepsilon)}{\hbar^2}}; \quad z \geq 0 \qquad \text{(III.22.2)}$$

By matching $\chi(z)$, $\frac{1}{m(z)}\chi'(z)$ at $z = 0$, we get:

$$A = B; \quad \frac{\kappa_A}{m_A} A = -\frac{\kappa_B}{m_B} B \qquad \text{(III.22.3)}$$

These two equations have no solution but the trivial one $A = B = 0$. The reason is that it is not possible to have simultaneously curvatures (second-order derivative of the envelope function) of the same sign in both materials and decaying envelope functions on both sides of the interface.

(2) The effective mass is now negative in the A material. Hence, we deal with a valence band at $z \leq 0$. To get evanescent propagation in both layers is possible only in the energy segment $[0, V_b]$. Proceeding as in (1), we get readily:

$$A = B; \quad \frac{1}{m_B}\sqrt{\frac{2m_B(V_b - \varepsilon)}{\hbar^2}} = \frac{1}{|m_A|}\sqrt{\frac{2|m_A|\varepsilon}{\hbar^2}} \qquad \text{(III.22.4)}$$

$$\Rightarrow \varepsilon = \frac{V_b}{1 + \frac{m_B}{|m_A|}} \qquad \text{(III.22.5)}$$

We note that such an interface state exists for any value of the ratio $m_B/|m_A|$ and V_b. This curiosity exists in the system HgTe/CdTe for the light particles (electron for HgTe and light hole for CdTe) but also in several IV–VI heterostructures such as (Pb, Sn)Se/(Pb,Ev)Se quantum wells. Interface states signal that the materials belong to the class of "topological insulators".

23.   Step quantum well

We consider a step quantum well (see Fig. 23.1). The potential energy is zero in region II, equal to v in region III and equal to V in regions I and IV. The carrier effective mass is m_0 in regions I and IV. It is

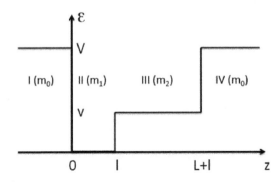

Figure 23.1.   Conduction band profile of a step quantum well.

equal to m_1 in region II and to m_2 in region III. We note:

$$C_1 = \cos(k_1 l), \quad S_1 = \sin(k_1 l) \tag{III.23.1}$$
$$C_2 = \cos(k_2 L), \quad S_2 = \sin(k_2 L) \tag{III.23.2}$$

where k_1 and k_2 are the wavevectors of propagating electron waves in regions II and III, respectively. Find the bound state(s) for this potential profile.

(2) The step quantum well (QW) is one the simpler heterostructure that lacks for inversion symmetry. As a result, the probability densities of the different eigenstates are unevenly distributed in the two halves of the large QW (thickness $L + l$). In our step QW the probability to find the electron in the left-hand side of the large QW is larger than to find it in the right-hand side. In addition, it can be checked that the average position $\langle z \rangle_n = \langle \chi_n | z | \chi_n \rangle$ increases with increasing eigenenergies ε_n. The lack of inversion centre implies the existence of specific physical features that have been experimentally demonstrated, notably a linear Stark effect at low electric field and a non-vanishing second-order nonlinear susceptibility. The reader is referred to [76–79] for more details.

Let us analyse the origin of the linear Stark effect. We shall use the Hellmann–Feynman theorem for that purpose [80]. The Hamiltonian of the biased step QW is:

$$H_F = H^{\text{Step QW}} + eFz \tag{III.23.3}$$

Its eigenfunctions (respectively, eigenenergies) are $\chi_n(F, z)$ (respectively, $\varepsilon_n(F)$). By definition there is:

$$\varepsilon_n(F) = \langle \chi_n(F) | H_F | \chi_n(F) \rangle \tag{III.23.4}$$

Prove the Hellmann–Feynman theorem:

$$\frac{d\varepsilon_n}{dF} = \left\langle \chi_n(F) \left| \frac{\partial H_F}{\partial F} \right| \chi_n(F) \right\rangle = e\langle \chi_n(F) | z | \chi_n(F) \rangle \tag{III.23.5}$$

Hint:

(a) There is no difficulty in interchanging d/dF and $\int dz$.
(b) H_F being hermitian, there is $H_F | \chi_n(F) \rangle = \varepsilon_n(F) | \chi_n(F) \rangle$; $\langle \chi_n(F) | H_F = \varepsilon_n(F) \langle \chi_n(F) |$.

(3) At low electric field $\chi_n(F, z) \approx \chi_n(F = 0, z)$. Deduce that:

$$\varepsilon_n(F) = \varepsilon_n(0) + eF\langle z \rangle_n^{F=0} \qquad \text{(III.23.6)}$$

(4) Instead of the step QW suppose that the potential energy at $F = 0$ admits an inversion centre z_0: $V(z - z_0) = V(z_0 - z)$. Then, show by an appropriate choice of the origin of the electrostatic potential that there exists no linear Stark shift and therefore that at the lowest order in F there is:

$$\varepsilon_n(F) = \varepsilon_n(0) + \beta_n F^2 \qquad \text{(III.23.7)}$$

(5) Apply the Hellmann–Feynman theorem to the triangular potential well:

$$V(z) = \infty, \quad z < 0 \qquad \text{(III.23.8)}$$
$$V(z) = eFz, \quad z \geq 0 \qquad \text{(III.23.9)}$$

and deduce that $\langle z \rangle_n \approx F^{-1/3}$.

Solution

Since we look for bound states the energy ε is $\leq V$. Besides if $0 \leq \varepsilon \leq v$ ($\varepsilon \geq v$), the wave is evanescent (propagative) in region III. Let us discuss the case where the wave is propagative between $z = 0$ and $z = L$. Then we write:

$$\chi(z) = A \exp(\kappa_0 z), \quad z \leq 0 \qquad \text{(III.23.10)}$$
$$\chi(z) = B \cos(k_1 z) + C \sin(k_1 z), \quad 0 \leq z \leq l \qquad \text{(III.23.11)}$$
$$\chi(z) = D \cos[k_2(z - l)] + E \sin[k_2(z - l)], \quad l \leq z \leq l + L \qquad \text{(III.23.12)}$$
$$\chi(z) = F \exp[-\kappa_0(z - l - L)], \quad z \geq L + l \qquad \text{(III.23.13)}$$

Writing the continuity of the envelope functions and of the current at the different interfaces we get:

$$A = B; \quad A\frac{\kappa_0}{m_0} = C\frac{k_1}{m_1} \qquad \text{(III.23.14)}$$

$$BC_1 + CS_1 = D; \quad \frac{k_1}{m_1}(-BS_1 + CC_1) = E\frac{k_2}{m_2} \qquad \text{(III.23.15)}$$

$$DC_2 + ES_2 = F; \quad \frac{k_2}{m_2}(-DS_2 + EC_2) = -F\frac{\kappa_0}{m_0} \qquad \text{(III.23.16)}$$

Manipulating these expressions, we arrive at:

$$D \left(\frac{k_2}{m_2} C_2 + \frac{\kappa_0}{m_0} S_2 \right) = E \left(\frac{k_2}{m_2} S_2 - \frac{\kappa_0}{m_0} C_2 \right) \qquad \text{(III.23.17)}$$

$$D \left(S_1 + \frac{k_1 m_0}{m_1 \kappa_0} C_1 \right) = E \left(C_1 - S_1 \frac{k_1 m_0}{m_1 \kappa_0} \right) \frac{k_1 m_2}{m_1 k_2} \qquad \text{(III.23.18)}$$

Finally, the bound states are the solutions of:

$$\frac{k_1 m_2}{m_1 k_2} \left(C_1 - S_1 \frac{k_1 m_0}{m_1 \kappa_0} \right) \left(C_2 + S_2 \frac{\kappa_0 m_2}{m_0 k_2} \right)$$

$$- \left(S_1 + C_1 \frac{k_1 m_0}{m_1 \kappa_0} \right) \left(S_2 - C_2 \frac{\kappa_0 m_2}{m_0 k_2} \right) = 0 \text{ (III.23.19)}$$

It can be checked that if $l = 0$, Eq. (III.23.19) reduces as it should to the equation governing the bound state of a single rectangular quantum well with thickness L, namely:

$$C_2 + \frac{1}{2} \left(\xi - \frac{1}{\xi} \right) S_2 = 0; \quad \xi = \frac{\kappa_0 m_2}{m_0 k_2} \qquad \text{(III.23.20)}$$

Similarly, one checks that Eq. (III.23.19) reduces to the bound state equation for a rectangular quantum well with thickness $l + L$ if $v = 0$.

When the electron wave is evanescent in layer III ($\varepsilon < v$) we change k_2 into $i\kappa_2$ where:

$$\kappa_2 = \sqrt{\frac{2m_2(v - \varepsilon)}{\hbar^2}} \qquad \text{(III.23.21)}$$

Then, the trigonometric functions change into:

$$S_2 \to i\tilde{S}_2 = i \sinh(\kappa_2 L); \quad C_2 \to \tilde{C}_2 = \cosh(\kappa_2 L) \qquad \text{(III.23.22)}$$

and Eq. (III.23.19) becomes:

$$\frac{k_1 m_2}{m_1 \kappa_2} \left(C_1 - S_1 \frac{k_1 m_0}{m_1 \kappa_0} \right) \left(\tilde{C}_2 + \tilde{S}_2 \frac{\kappa_0 m_2}{m_0 \kappa_2} \right)$$

$$+ \left(S_1 + C_1 \frac{k_1 m_0}{m_1 \kappa_0} \right) \left(\tilde{S}_2 + \tilde{C}_2 \frac{\kappa_0 m_2}{m_0 \kappa_2} \right) = 0 \text{ (III.23.23)}$$

We show in Fig. 23.2 the variation of the bound state energies in a step quantum well with $l = 7$ nm, $L = 8$ nm versus $x = v/V$ where

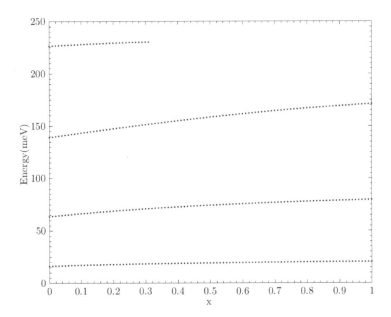

Figure 23.2.   Bound states energies of a step QW versus $x = v/V$. The energy zero is at the bottom of the conduction band of the material II. The other parameters are described in the text.

$V = 230$ meV, $m_0 = 0.08m_e$, $m_1 = 0.07m_e$ and

$$m_2 = m_1 + (m_0 - m_1)x \qquad\qquad (III.23.24)$$

At $x = 0$ (respectively, $x = 1$), the levels are those of a square QW with barrier V and thickness $L + l = 15$ nm (respectively, $l = 7$ nm). At small x the variations of bound states energies are quasi-linear with x while there is a clear tendency to saturation once the energies become smaller than v. The quasi-linearity suggests a linear Stark shift, although the magnitude of the effective electric field is difficult to assess. Looking for instance at the second bound state, we obtain:

$$E_2(v) \approx E_2(0) + \alpha_2 v \qquad\qquad (III.23.25)$$

with $\alpha_2 \approx 0.68$. As expected on physical grounds α_2 decreases with increasing $y = \frac{l}{l+L}$. Keeping $l + L = 15$ nm, we find $\alpha \approx 0.31$ (0.11) for $v = 0.73$ (0.87).

(2) We interchange the order of the integration over z and of the derivative with respect to F:

$$\frac{d\varepsilon_n}{dF} = \frac{d}{dF}\langle\chi_n(F)|H_F|\chi_n(F)\rangle$$

$$= \frac{d}{dF}\int dz\chi_n^*(F,z)H_F\chi_n(F,z)$$

$$= \int dz\frac{d}{dF}[\chi_n^*(F,z)H_F\chi_n(F,z)] \qquad \text{(III.23.26)}$$

$$\frac{d\varepsilon_n}{dF} = \int dz\chi_n^*(F,z)\frac{\partial H_F}{dF}\chi_n(F,z) + \int dz\frac{\partial\chi_n^*(F,z)}{\partial z}H_F\chi_n(F,z)$$

$$+ \int dz\chi_n^*(F,z)H_F\frac{\partial\chi_n(F,z)}{dF} \qquad \text{(III.23.27)}$$

But

$$\int dz\frac{\partial\chi_n^*(F,z)}{\partial z}H_F\chi_n(F,z) = \varepsilon_n(F)\int dz\frac{\partial\chi_n^*(F,z)}{\partial z}\chi_n(F,z)$$

$$\text{(III.23.28)}$$

$$\int dz\chi_n^*(F,z)H_F\frac{\partial\chi_n(F,z)}{dF} = \varepsilon_n(F)\int dz\chi_n^*(F,z)\frac{\partial\chi_n(F,z)}{\partial z}$$

$$\text{(III.23.29)}$$

Therefore:

$$\frac{d\varepsilon_n}{dF} = \int dz\chi_n^*(F,z)\frac{\partial H_F}{\partial F}\chi_n(F,z)$$

$$+\varepsilon_n(F)\int dz$$

$$\times \left[\frac{\partial\chi_n^*(F,z)}{\partial F}\chi_n(F,z) + \chi_n^*(F,z)\frac{\partial\chi_n(F,z)}{dF}\right] \qquad \text{(III.23.30)}$$

$$\frac{d\varepsilon_n}{dF} = \int dz\chi_n^*(F,z)\frac{\partial H_F}{dF}\chi_n(F,z)$$

$$+\varepsilon_n(F)\left[\int dz\frac{\partial}{\partial F}(\chi_n^*(F,z)\chi_n(F,z))\right]$$

$$= \int dz \chi_n^*(F,z) \frac{\partial H_F}{\partial F} \chi_n(F,z)$$

$$+ \varepsilon_n(F) \frac{\partial}{\partial F} \int dz \chi_n^*(F,z) \chi_n(F,z) \qquad \text{(III.23.31)}$$

The last term vanishes because the integral is equal to 1 for any square integrable $\chi_n(F,z)$. Therefore:

$$\frac{d\varepsilon_n}{dF} = \int dz \chi_n^*(F,z) \frac{\partial H_F}{\partial F} \chi_n(F,z) \qquad \text{(III.23.32)}$$

If we apply this theorem to the biased step QW, we find:

$$\frac{d\varepsilon_n}{dF} = e \int dz \chi_n^*(F,z) z \chi_n(F,z) = e\langle z \rangle_n^F \qquad \text{(III.23.33)}$$

(3) When F is small enough we expect $\chi_n(F,z) \approx \chi_n(F=0,z)$. This implies the linear Stark effect:

$$\varepsilon_n(F) = \varepsilon_n(0) + eF\langle z \rangle_n^{F=0} \qquad \text{(III.23.34)}$$

Note that this result makes sense only for bound states since $\langle z \rangle_n^{F=0}$ needs to exist. The continuum states of the step QW are excluded from this analysis. Also since the linearly varying electrostatic potential precludes the existence of true bound states we need to enclose the step QW into impenetrable barriers far away from the active zone.

Note also that the result (III.23.34) could have been obtained by applying the first-order perturbation calculus to the zero field eigenstates, the perturbation being eFz.

(4) If the structure admits an inversion centre at z_0 (symmetrical heterostructure), then the eigenstates at $F = 0$ admit a definite parity in $(z - z_0)$. By choosing the origin of the electrostatic potential at z_0, one finds readily that $\langle z - z_0 \rangle_n = 0$. Therefore, for symmetrical structures:

$$\varepsilon_n(F) = \varepsilon_n(0) + \beta_n F^2 \qquad \text{(III.23.35)}$$

The coefficient β_n can be obtained by applying the second-order perturbation calculus to the zero field eigenstates.

(5) In the triangular potential we know that the eigenenergies vary like $F^{2/3}$:

$$\varepsilon_n(F) = A_n F^{2/3} \qquad \text{(III.23.36)}$$

Then the Hellmann–Feynman theorem tells us that:

$$\frac{d\varepsilon_n}{dF} = \frac{2}{3} A_n F^{-1/3} = e\langle z \rangle_n \qquad \text{(III.23.37)}$$

and therefore $\langle z \rangle_n$ varies likes $F^{-1/3}$. Note that this result could have also been obtained from the virial theorem $(eF\langle z \rangle_n = \frac{2\varepsilon_n(F)}{3})$.

24. Application of the Bohr–Sommerfeld quantisation rule to 1D confining potential: digital alloying

The Schrödinger equation did not show up all of a sudden on top of the failing classical description of the atomic systems. There have been attempts to improve the classical formalism (mostly in its most elaborate form of the Hamiltonian–Jacobi equations) to force the classical systems (where the allowed energies form a continuum) to have discrete energy levels (to explain the line spectra of atoms) for a conservative forces (time-independent potential energies). Without entering into technical intricacies (see e.g., [73]), it is accepted that at large quantum numbers the quantum mechanics should reduce to classical results (the semi-classical limit). Quantisation still remains in this limit, based on the so-called Bohr–Sommerfeld formula. For the 1D bound motions, it reads:

$$\frac{2}{h} \int_a^b p(x)dx = \left(n + \frac{1}{2} \right); \quad n = 0, 1, \ldots \qquad \text{(III.24.1)}$$

where h is the Planck constant ($h \approx 6.64 \times 10^{-34}$ Js) and $p(x)$ is the linear momentum for the particle with mass m and energy E at point x:

$$p(x) = \sqrt{2m[E - V(x)]} \qquad \text{(III.24.2)}$$

The factor 2 that appears in (III.24.1) means that the integration is over a complete period of the motion. a and b are the classical turning points of the motion where $p(a) = p(b) = 0$. The way (III.24.1) is established is the so-called semi-classical description of the wavefunctions of the Schrödinger equation that requests the potential energy to vary very little over the de Broglie wavelength of the particle $\lambda(x) = \frac{h}{p(x)}$. This approximation always fails near the classical turning points where p vanishes and one has to replace $V(x)$ near these points by linear functions and match the wavefunctions on each side of a or b. Thus, (III.24.1) requires a smoothly varying potential (continuous with continuous derivative) in order to be able to replace the actual shape of $V(x)$ by such linear variations near a and b.

When there is instead a potential step at a and/or b, or discontinuous derivative $V'(x)$ at these points, the semi-classical motion assumption runs into trouble (the potential energy no longer varies smoothly enough), and often the factor $\frac{1}{2}$ in (III.24.1) changes into a factor ν_p ($0 \leq \nu_p \leq 1$) that depends on the nature of the $V(x)$ discontinuity at the turning points. Note also that (III.24.1) is often used for any n, despite the fact that only the large values of n make sense.

Nevertheless, the Bohr–Sommerfeld formula is convenient to analyse in a qualitative manner certain characteristics of the bound states of potential wells. Here, we apply this approximate quantisation rule to the specific problem of the sensitivity of the eigenvalues to the shape of a 1D potential well. This question is relevant to the determination of the conduction (valence) discontinuity V_b between a pair of semiconductor materials assembled into a heterostructure. When it is unknown (and granted that one can artificially construct, at least approximately, $V(x)$, say by using, e.g., the digital alloying technique, see below and [20]), one would like, by measuring the energy difference between the eigenvalues of $V(x)$, to have an idea of V_b because a great deal of the optical properties and technological future of such a pair of heterostructure relies on the magnitude of V_b.

We consider a potential well $V(x)$ depth V_b which is an even function of x:

$$V(x) = V_b \left(\frac{|x|}{L} \right)^p \tag{III.24.3}$$

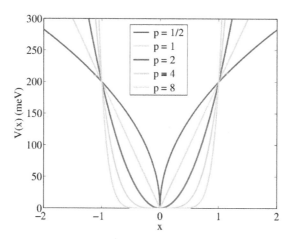

Figure 24.1. Potential energy profile $V(x)$ versus x/L for $p = \frac{1}{2}, 1, 2, 4, 8$. Note that $V(x)$ increasingly resembles a square potential when p increases.

where L is a characteristic length and $p > 0$. Figure 24.1 shows the shape of these potentials for several values of p. In principle, one should restrict (III.24.3) to $|x| \leq L$ and complete $V(x)$ by stating that $V(x) = V_b$ for $|x| \geq L$. However, this would complicate the algebra significantly and we keep (III.24.3) for all x.

The easiest heterostructure to grow is a square quantum well. It corresponds to the limit $p \to \infty$ since if $|x| < L$, $V(x) \to 0$ while if $|x| > L$, $V(x) \to \infty$. We shall examine thanks to the Bohr–Sommerfeld quantisation rule whether it is a convenient profile for our goal of determining V_b from the knowledge of the functional dependency of the eigenvalues upon V_b.

(1) Is it better to have a small or a large p if we want the eigenenergies to be the more sensitive to V_b?

(2) Examine the cases $p = 1$, $p = 2$, $p = 4$ and $p \to \infty$.

Solution

(1) In order to account for possible difficulties near $x = 0$ (divergent derivative at $x = 0$), we replace the $\frac{1}{2}$ in (III.24.1) by ν_p when $p \leq 1$.

We take advantage of the evenness in x of $V(x)$ and get:

$$\int_0^{x_0} dx\sqrt{2m\left[E - V_b\left(\frac{x}{L}\right)^p\right]^{1/2}} = (n + \nu_p)\frac{h}{4}; \quad \frac{x_0}{L} = \left(\frac{E}{V_b}\right)^{1/p}$$

$$\text{(III.24.4)}$$

In the integral, we make the change of variable $x = tx_0$ and after some manipulations we readily obtain:

$$E_n = V_b^{\frac{2}{p+2}}(n + \nu_p)^{\frac{2p}{p+2}}\left(\frac{h}{4LI_p\sqrt{2m}}\right)^{\frac{2p}{p+2}}; \quad I_p = \int_0^1 dt\sqrt{1 - t^p}$$

$$\text{(III.24.5)}$$

Hence, the eigenenergies depend on V_b in a rather neat fashion: $V_b^{\frac{2}{p+2}}$. This immediately suggests that the eigenenergies and their differences (the quantities one can hopefully measure by spectroscopic or electrical, e.g., capacitance, techniques) will be the more sensitive to V_b when p is small. We note that we need to request the existence of several bound states $(E_n < V_b)$ to effectively achieve the possibility of transitions between them. This can always be realised by increasing the width $2L$ of the well to force it to accommodate as many bound states as we want.

(2) We now discuss a few cases. Let us first estimate the dimensionless integral I_p. There is:

p	$1/2$	1	2	4	$\cdots$	$\rightarrow \infty$
I_p	$8/15$	$2/3$	$\pi/4$	≈ 0.081	$\cdots$	1

Thus, I_p varies by less than a factor 2 when p increases from $\frac{1}{2}$ to ∞.

(a) The case $p = 1$ also describes the motion of an electron in a piecewise constant electric field $F = V_b/(eL)$ between 0 and L and to a reversal of that field between $-L$ and 0. The Bohr–Sommerfeld quantisation is:

$$E_n = \left(\frac{h^2}{2mL^2}\right)^{1/3}\left[\frac{3}{8}(n + \nu_1)eFL\right]^{2/3} \quad \text{(III.24.6)}$$

and we retrieve the well-known $F^{2/3}$ dependency of the eigenenergies versus the electric field strength.

(b) The case $p = 2$ is the harmonic oscillator case with an angular frequency ω:

$$\omega = \sqrt{\frac{2V_b}{mL^2}} \qquad \text{(III.24.7)}$$

In that case the Bohr–Sommerfeld quantisation is exact since we find:

$$E_n = \left(n + \frac{1}{2}\right)\hbar\omega \qquad \text{(III.24.8)}$$

(c) The case $p = 4$ (quartic potential) leads to:

$$E_n = V_b^{1/3}\left(n + \frac{1}{2}\right)^{4/3}\left(\frac{1}{4I_4}\sqrt{\frac{h^2}{2mL^2}}\right)^{4/3} \qquad \text{(III.24.9)}$$

(d) The case $p \to \infty$ (square well) leads to:

$$E_n = V^0\frac{\hbar^2\pi^2}{2mL^2}(n+\alpha)^2; \quad 0 \le \alpha \le 1 \qquad \text{(III.24.10)}$$

where the term α comes this time from the sharp potential step at $x = \pm L$. Despite being the easiest structure to grow among the class of wells analysed here, the rectangular quantum well is the most ill-suited to band offset determination. Note that, in reality, the excited states of the well should be more sensitive to V_b than the ground one (see Exercise 17). This is because the electron wave penetrates more the barrier when its energy increases whereas the classical particle, at work in the Bohr–Sommerfeld formulae, undergoes the same sign inversion of its velocity at the classical turning point, irrespective of its kinetic energy. Comparing the different cases, we see that the harmonic oscillator, $n = 2$, is the border that splits the energy spacing into two categories; those which are sublinear in n ($p < 2$) and those which are superlinear in n ($p > 2$).

The feasibility of non-square quantum wells has been addressed by a number of authors. A shape that is both simple and effective for band offset determination is the two-step well or narrow Separate Confinement Heterostructure [81]. In a way, it looks like a primitive version of the $p = 1$ well (see Fig. 24.2). Note that the effective electrical fields for conduction and valence electrons have opposite signs and different magnitudes.

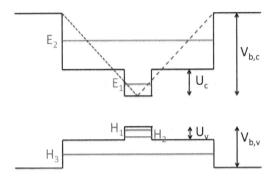

Figure 24.2.   Conduction and valence band profiles of a narrow separate confinement heterostructure (SCH). It consists of a narrow and shallow well embedded into a larger and deeper one. The dashed line is the conduction band profile of an equivalent $p = 1$ well. Note however that the equivalent electric field is somewhat arbitrary: one could have drawn different straight dashed lines (e.g., joining the middles of the well and of the intermediate barriers). Optical transitions $H_1 - E_1$ are strong since they involve initial and final states that are localised in the same region of space. Their energies show however little dependence upon U_c and U_v. Transitions $H_2 - E_2$ are weaker because the initial and final states little overlap due to their different spatial localisations. Their energies are quite sensitive to U_c and U_v.

In addition, by squeezing the narrow well, one makes levels popping out from it. By studying the optical transitions that involve both a level mostly localised in the narrow well and another that spills over the whole structure, one gets a transition energy that is very sensitive to the intermediate offsets U_c and U_v.

In the canonical system $GaAs/Ga_{1-x}Al_xAs$, one could envision during the MBE growth to let the alloy content x varying continuously with the position in a prescribed fashion by controlling the shutters of the heated Ga and Al cells with time. This is because the conduction band discontinuity between GaAs and $Ga_{1-x}Al_xAs$ is a linear function of x to an excellent approximation reaching about 0.22 eV for $x = 0.3$. Thus, increasing the Al content proportionally to say $\sqrt{t}$ at a constant MBE growth rate is equivalent to raise the potential barrier proportionally to the square root of the layer thickness. But this is technically very demanding because the shutters that open and close the MBE effusion cells (and therefore control the effective Al content of the alloy that impinges the heated GaAs substrate) do not respond instantaneously.

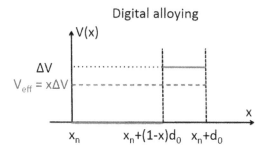

Figure 24.3. Principle of digital alloying. If d_0 is smaller than the length scale where the wavefunction varies significantly, the motion between x_n and $x_n + d_0$ takes place in the constant potential profile V_{eff}.

It has been proven more effective to replace the true $Ga_{1-x}Al_xAs$ alloy by a digital version. Starting from the position x_n, the digital alloy corresponds to growing a very short GaAs/AlAs (d_1/d_2) layer where d_1 and d_2 are a few monolayers thick. If $d_1 + d_2 = d_0$ remains small compared to the length scale where the wavefunction varies significantly, then by choosing $d_1 = [1 - x(x_n)]d_0$ and $d_2 = x(x_n)d_0$, the effective barrier height seen by the carriers between x_n and x_n+d_0 will be $x(x_n)\Delta V$ where ΔV is the conduction band offset between GaAs and AlAs (we have taken the energy zero in the GaAs layer).

In the next step, at $x_{n+1} = x_n + d_0$, x is changed to $x(x_{n+1})$ and, at the end of the growth, one gets a staircase potential variation whose envelope is the prescribed potential profile upon position (see Fig. 24.3). This solution offers the advantage of not requiring constant changes of the shutters with time.

Very nice pseudo-parabolic wells have been grown by the digital alloy technique [20]. Figure 24.4 shows how a pseudo-parabolic well has been realised by the digital alloy technique by the TU Wien group.

We are very much indebted to Pr. G. Strasser for insightful remarks on the digital alloy technique.

25. Transmission/reflection in a delta quantum well

We consider the 1D attractive delta well of Exercise 20 and compare the structure of the continuum states of this well to that of a square

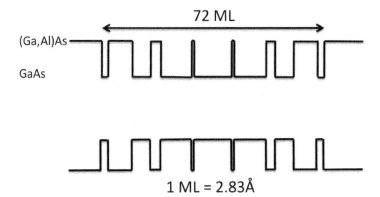

Figure 24.4.   Conduction and valence band profiles of an actual pseudo-parabolic well grown by the digital alloy technique. Courtesy of G. Strasser, J. Darmo and K. Unterrainer.

quantum well with thickness L.

(1) The delta potential well is:

$$V(x) = -V_0 a \delta(x - x_0) \qquad \text{(III.25.1)}$$

We are interested in the continuum states (with an energy $\varepsilon > 0$). We write down the wavefunction for $x \leq 0$ and $x \geq 0$ separately:

$$\chi(z) = A e^{ik(x-x_0)} + B e^{-ik(x-x_0)}, \quad x \leq x_0 \qquad \text{(III.25.2)}$$

$$\chi(z) = C e^{ik(x-x_0)} + D e^{-ik(x-x_0)}, \quad x \geq x_0 \qquad \text{(III.25.3)}$$

So, *a priori* we have four unknown coefficients. But we have only two relations (the two boundary conditions at $x = x_0$). Hence, the problem is under-determined. However, we have not really used all our boundary conditions since we have not chosen how we want to proceed at $x = \pm\infty$: how are the particles shot to the potential well: either from $-\infty$ or from $+\infty$ as we would do in a real experiment. Suppose now we have chosen to shoot particles on the potential well from $-\infty$ (respectively, $+\infty$). Then in the expression of the wavefunction, D (respectively, A) should be set equal to zero. Once this is taken into account we seem to have three unknowns still. However, it is clear that the linearity between the various coefficients found in the boundary conditions makes that only the ratios B/A $(= r)$ and C/A $(= t)$ are meaningful. Thus, we write the continuum wavefunctions in the form:

$$\chi_+(x) = e^{ik(x-x_0)} + r(k)e^{-ik(x-x_0)}, \quad x \le x_0 \tag{III.25.4}$$

$$\chi_+(x) = t(k)e^{ik(x-x_0)}, \quad x \ge x_0 \tag{III.25.5}$$

for the situation where the particles impinge from $-\infty$. For particles impinging from $+\infty$ we write:

$$\chi_-(x) = te^{-ik(x-x_0)}, \quad x \le x_0 \tag{III.25.6}$$

$$\chi_-(x) = re^{ik(x-x_0)} + e^{-ik(x-x_0)} \tag{III.25.7}$$

Deduce r and t from the boundary conditions at $x = x_0$ (Exercise 20). Check that $R + T = 1$ where $R = |r|^2$, $T = |t|^2$.

(2) We consider now a rectangular quantum well with thickness L and barrier height V. We take the energy origin at the bottom of the barrier continuum. The potential energy is therefore:

$$V(x) = -VY(x)Y(L - x) \tag{III.25.8}$$

The effective masses are m_w and m_b in the well and in the barrier, respectively. The boundary conditions arising from the Ben Daniel and Duke kinetic energy term $(p_x[1/2m(x)]p_x)$ are that the wavefunction $\chi(x)$ and $m^{-1}(x)d\chi/dx$ are continuous across the interfaces.
We search $\chi(x)$ in the form:

$$\chi(x) = e^{ik_b x} + re^{-ik_b x}, \quad x \le 0 \tag{III.25.9}$$

$$\chi(x) = A\cos(k_w x) + B\sin(k_w x), \quad 0 \le x \le L \tag{III.25.10}$$

$$\chi(x) = te^{ik_b x}, \quad x \ge L \tag{III.25.11}$$

$$\varepsilon = \frac{\hbar^2 k_b^2}{2m_b}; \quad \varepsilon + V = \frac{\hbar^2 k_w^2}{2m_w} \tag{III.25.12}$$

Apply the boundary conditions at $x = 0$ and $x = L$ to find t and r. Compute $T = |t|^2$.

Solution

(1)

$$t = \frac{1}{1 - i\frac{\kappa}{k}}; \quad r = t - 1 = i\frac{\kappa}{k\left(1 - i\frac{\kappa}{k}\right)} \tag{III.25.13}$$

$$\kappa = \frac{maV}{\hbar^2} \tag{III.25.14}$$

The fact that $R + T = 1$ means that no particle is lost (in other words there is no dissipation) and every particle that impinges the well is either transmitted or reflected. We note that there is neither transmission nor reflection resonances, i.e., particular energies where either T or $R = 1$. This is due to the fact that there are no possible interference/diffraction effects in a delta potential because it has no characteristic geometrical length. In a square quantum well instead, the continuum states display transmission (Fabry–Perot) resonances any time $kL = j\pi$, $j = 1, 2, 3, \ldots$, where L is the quantum well thickness (see below).

(2) To establish the Fabry–Perot resonance condition in the continuum of a rectangular quantum well, we match the wavefunction and the current at the $x = 0$ and $x = L$ interfaces:

We let $C = \cos(k_w L)$, $S = \sin(k_w L)$ and $\eta = (k_b/m_b)(m_w/k_w)$. We find readily:

$$1 + r = A; \quad 1 - r = \frac{B}{i\eta} \tag{III.25.15}$$

$$A = t(C - i\eta S); \quad B = t(S + i\eta C) \tag{III.25.16}$$

and after some manipulations:

$$t = \frac{1}{C - \frac{iS}{2}\left(\eta + \frac{1}{\eta}\right)}; \quad r = -1 + \frac{C - i\eta S}{C - \frac{iS}{2}\left(\eta + \frac{1}{\eta}\right)} \tag{III.25.17}$$

$$T = |t|^2 = \frac{1}{1 + \frac{S^2}{4}\left(\eta - \frac{1}{\eta}\right)^2} \tag{III.25.18}$$

Hence, we indeed find that any time $k_w L = j\pi$, $j = 1, 2, \ldots, T$ reaches unity (and $R = 0$). For these particular energies, everything is such as if there were no well on account of interferences between the various transmitted and reflected rays at the two interfaces. A remarkable analysis of the transmission resonances in 1D potential wells can be found in [82].

26. Static perturbation of a harmonic oscillator

Consider a charged 1D harmonic oscillator with angular frequency ω. Its charge is $-e$. It interacts with a static and homogeneous electric field F applied parallel to its unperturbed motion.

(1) Compute by perturbation calculus the shift of the nth unperturbed eigenvalues up to the second-order in F.

(2) The problem of a harmonic oscillator perturbed by a linearly varying potential can be solved exactly. Find the new eigenvalues. By comparing to the results obtained in (1) what do you conclude?

Solution

(1) The spectrum of the harmonic oscillator is evenly spaced:

$$\varepsilon_n = \left(n + \frac{1}{2}\right)\hbar\omega \tag{III.26.1}$$

The potential energy associated with a constant electric field applied parallel to the x-axis is eFx if one chooses the electrostatic potential energy zero at the rest position of the oscillator. Let us express the operator x in terms of the creation and annihilation operators:

$$x = \sqrt{\frac{\hbar}{2m\omega}}(a + a^\dagger) \tag{III.26.2}$$

Then we find immediately that the average value x is zero since:

$$a|n\rangle = \sqrt{n}|n-1\rangle; \quad a^\dagger|n\rangle = \sqrt{n+1}|n+1\rangle \tag{III.26.3}$$

Along the same line the second-order shift of ε_n is:

$$\delta_2 = \frac{e^2 F^2}{\hbar\omega} \sum_{m \neq n} \frac{|\langle n|x|m\rangle|^2}{(n-m)} = -\frac{e^2 F^2}{2m\omega^2} \tag{III.26.4}$$

We note that the shift δ_2 is n-independent and does not depend on $\hbar$, evidencing its classical origin.

(2) When a harmonic oscillator is perturbed by a linearly varying potential, we know that a shift of its equilibrium position will ensue. But we also know from classical mechanics that the frequency of a harmonic oscillator does not depend on its equilibrium position. Hence, we expect evenly spaced levels by the same quantity as at $F = 0$. Proving this is very easy since:

$$V(x) = \frac{1}{2}m\omega^2 x^2 + eFx = \frac{1}{2}m\omega^2 \left(x + \frac{eF}{m\omega^2}\right)^2 - \frac{e^2 F^2}{2m\omega^2} \quad \text{(III.26.5)}$$

Hence the exact new spectrum will be:

$$\lambda_n = \left(n + \frac{1}{2}\right)\hbar\omega - \frac{e^2 F^2}{2m\omega^2} \quad \text{(III.26.6)}$$

So by comparing the exact result to the second-order perturbation estimate, we are led to the conclusion that all perturbation orders higher that 2 give a vanishing contribution to the energy. This situation is very rare since the perturbation theory usually gives terms that decrease in magnitude when the perturbation order increase but usually do not vanish.

27. Static perturbation (degenerate case)

Consider a 2D harmonic oscillator described by the Hamiltonian

$$H_0 = H_{0x} + H_{0y} = \frac{p_x^2}{2m^*} + \frac{1}{2}m^*\omega^2 x^2 + \frac{p_y^2}{2m^*} + \frac{1}{2}m^*\omega^2 y^2 \quad \text{(III.27.1)}$$

It is perturbed by a term:

$$\lambda V(x, y) = \lambda A m^* \omega^2 xy \quad \text{(III.27.2)}$$

We consider the degenerate triplet of states with energy $3\hbar\omega$. Diagonalise $H_0 + \lambda V$ in this subspace.

Solution

The unperturbed spectrum is $(n + m + 1)\hbar\omega$; $n = m = 0, 1, \ldots$. The ground state $(n = m = 0)$ is non-degenerate. Then, there is a doublet with energy $2\hbar\omega$; then a triplet with energy $3\hbar\omega$. The unperturbed states of the triplet are $|2, 0\rangle$, $|0, 2\rangle$, $|1, 1\rangle$. In this basis we have:

$$H_0 + \lambda V = \begin{pmatrix} 3\hbar\omega & 0 & \beta \\ 0 & 3\hbar\omega & \beta \\ \beta & \beta & 3\hbar\omega \end{pmatrix}; \quad \beta = \langle 2, 0|\lambda V|1, 1\rangle = \langle 0, 2|\lambda V|1, 1\rangle$$

(III.27.3)

The eigenenergies and eigenstates are:

$$\varepsilon_1 = 3\hbar\omega; \quad \psi_1 = \begin{pmatrix} \frac{1}{\sqrt{2}} \\ -\frac{1}{\sqrt{2}} \\ 0 \end{pmatrix}; \quad \varepsilon_\pm = 3\hbar\omega \pm \beta\sqrt{2}; \quad \psi_\pm = \frac{1}{2}\begin{pmatrix} 1 \\ 1 \\ \pm\sqrt{2} \end{pmatrix}$$

(III.27.4)

28. Degenerate perturbation calculus applied to quantum dots with cylindrical symmetry

Consider a quantum dot with cylindrical symmetry and assume it binds only one S state $|S\rangle$ and two P states $|P_+\rangle$ and $|P_-\rangle$.

This quantum dot is subjected to an electric field $\vec{F}$ applied in the xOy plane. Show that this induces a lifting of the P state degeneracy. Compute it to the lowest order in F by retaining only the bound states in your analysis. It will be more convenient to use a $|P_x\rangle$, $|P_y\rangle$ basis instead of the $|P_+\rangle$, $|P_-\rangle$ one. This is because the electric perturbation has created a preferential direction x.

(1) We define:

$$|P_x\rangle = \frac{1}{\sqrt{2}}(|P_+\rangle + |P_-\rangle); \quad |P_y\rangle = -\frac{i}{\sqrt{2}}(|P_+\rangle - |P_-\rangle) \quad \text{(III.28.1)}$$

Check that $|P_x\rangle$, $|P_y\rangle$ are ortho-normalised. What is the mean value of L_z in a $|P_x\rangle$ state? In a $|P_y\rangle$ state?

(2) Diagonalise the perturbation in the $|S\rangle$, $|P_x\rangle$, $|P_y\rangle$ basis.

Solution

Because of the assumed cylindrical symmetry, one can take $\vec{F} \| \hat{x}$. On account of the cylindrical symmetry at $F = 0$, the eigenstates can be classified according to the value of L_z. The fact $L_z = +1$ and $L_z = -1$ states are degenerate comes from the time reversal symmetry. If one breaks the time reversal symmetry by applying a magnetic field $\vec{B}$ parallel to z the P_+, P_- degeneracy is lifted (paramagnetic orbital Zeeman effect).

It is more convenient to analyse this problem in terms of P_x and P_y states. The latter are linear combinations of P_+ and P_- such that P_x is $xf(r)$ and P_y is $yf(r)$ where $r = \sqrt{x^2 + y^2}$.

(1) One finds without difficulty that $|P_x\rangle$ and $|P_y\rangle$ are orthogonal and that each of them is normalised. In this basis the angular momentum is quenched since both $\langle P_x|L_z|P_x\rangle$ and $\langle P_y|L_z|P_y\rangle$ vanish.

Then in a 3×3 basis spanned by $|S\rangle$, $|P_x\rangle$, $|P_y\rangle$ we find that $|P_y\rangle$ remains unchanged while we have to diagonalise a 2×2 matrix for the coupled $|S\rangle$, $|P_x\rangle$ states:

$$\begin{pmatrix} (\varepsilon_P - \varepsilon) & eF\langle P_x|x|S\rangle \\ eF\langle S|x|P_x\rangle & \varepsilon_S - \varepsilon \end{pmatrix} = 0 \qquad \text{(III.28.2)}$$

$$\varepsilon_\pm = \frac{(\varepsilon_S + \varepsilon_P)}{2} \pm \sqrt{\left(\frac{\varepsilon_P - \varepsilon_S}{2}\right)^2 + e^2 F^2 |\langle P_x|x|S\rangle|^2} \qquad \text{(III.28.3)}$$

Thus, to the lowest order in F the P_x state will be blue shifted by a quantity proportional to F^2:

$$\varepsilon_+ \approx \varepsilon_P + \frac{e^2 F^2 |\langle S|x|P_x\rangle|^2}{\varepsilon_P - \varepsilon_S} \qquad \text{(III.28.4)}$$

We note that (III.28.4) is what would have predicted the non-degenerate perturbation theory applied to the two levels $|S\rangle$ and $|P_x\rangle$. By using the symmetry of the perturbation to carefully eliminate one of the two degenerate levels ($|P_y\rangle$) of the unperturbed basis, we have recovered a much simpler scheme to analyse. In order to get a quick order of magnitude of the effect we shall assume that the confinement is parabolic. Since the cylindrical symmetry is broken by the electric field it is easier to use Cartesian coordinates than polar coordinates. Then:

$$\psi_S(\rho,\theta) \to \psi_{00}(x,y) = \varphi_0(x)\varphi_0(y) \qquad \text{(III.28.5)}$$

$$\psi_{P_x}(\rho,\theta) \to \psi_{10}(x,y) = \varphi_1(x)\varphi_0(y) \qquad \text{(III.28.6)}$$

where φ_n is the nth Hermite function, solution of the 1D harmonic oscillator problem with energy $(n+1/2)\hbar\omega$ where ω is the angular frequency of the oscillator.

The matrix element we are looking for is:

$$\langle P_x|x|S \rangle = \langle \varphi_1|x|\varphi_0 \rangle = \sqrt{\frac{\hbar}{2m\omega}} \qquad \text{(III.28.7)}$$

Hence, the blue shift of the P state affected by the field is:

$$\varepsilon_+ - \varepsilon_P = \frac{e^2 F^2}{\hbar\omega}\frac{\hbar}{2m\omega} \qquad \text{(III.28.8)}$$

For a typical InAs dot, the $S - P$ energy is 50 meV, the electron effective mass is $0.07m_0$. If the electric field strength is 10 kV/cm we obtain a blue shift of ≈ 0.22 meV. This very small shift evidences the rigidity of the InAs dots to external perturbations as a result of their strong spatial confinement [25, 26, 51].

29. Quantum well and a delta potential: perturbative estimate

We consider a quantum well with thickness L and infinite barrier height. H_0 is the electronic Hamiltonian. We take the origin at the centre of the well. m^* is the electron effective mass assumed to be position-independent.

(1) Find the eigenstates and eigenenergies of H_0.

(2) The electronic motion is perturbed by a localised perturbation located at the centre of the well. It is constant (V_0) and extends over $[-a/2, +a/2]$ with $a \ll L$. Explain why and how it can be approximated by $V(z) = V_0 a\delta(z)$.

(3) Study $[P, H]$ where P is the parity operator and $H = H_0 + V$. What can you deduce from your finding regarding the effect of the perturbation $V(z)$ on the unperturbed eigenstates?

(4) Compute the shift of the unperturbed energies up to the second order in V_0. Give a numerical estimate of this shift for the ground state if $V_0 = 0.1$ eV, $a = 0.283$ nm, $L = 10$ nm.

(5) There is another way to compute exactly the eigenenergies of this problem. Expand the wavefunctions of $H_0 + V$ on the basis of the eigenstates of H_0. Project on one of the unperturbed eigenstates. What can you say of a matrix element $\langle \varphi_m | V(z) | \varphi_n \rangle$? Exploit this property to show that the perturbed energies ε of the problem are the solutions of:

$$1 = \frac{2V_0 a}{L E_1} \sum_j \frac{1}{\frac{\varepsilon}{E_1} - (2j+1)^2} \qquad \text{(III.29.1)}$$

where E_1 is the lowest eigenvalue of the unperturbed problem.

(6) We look for an iterative solution of Eq. (III.29.1) around E_1. Show that the correction to E_1 up to the second order in V_0 coincides with the perturbative estimate of (4).

Solution

(1) With the z origin at the middle of the well we know that the eigenfunctions will be either $\cos(kz)$ or $\sin(kz)$. By writing the boundary condition at $z = L/2$, we find readily:

$$\varphi_{2j}(z) = \sqrt{\frac{2}{L}} \sin\left(\frac{2j\pi z}{L}\right); \quad E_{2j} = 4j^2 E_1; \quad j = 1, 2, \ldots \qquad \text{(III.29.2)}$$

$$\varphi_{2j+1}(z) = \sqrt{\frac{2}{L}} \cos\left(\frac{(2j+1)\pi z}{L}\right); \quad E_{2j+1} = (2j+1)^2 E_1; \quad j = 0, 1, \ldots$$
$$\text{(III.29.3)}$$

where $E_1 = \frac{\hbar^2 \pi^2}{2m^* L^2}$.

(2) Let us investigate the matrix element of the perturbation on the cosines basis:

$$\langle \varphi_{2j+1} | V(z) | \varphi_{2j'+1} \rangle$$

$$= \frac{4}{L} V_0 \int_0^{a/2} dz \cos\left(\frac{(2j+1)\pi z}{L}\right) \cos\left(\frac{(2j'+1)\pi z}{L}\right)$$

$$= \frac{2}{L} V_0 \left[\frac{L}{\pi(2j+2j'+2)} \sin\left(\frac{(2j+2j'+2)\pi a}{2L}\right) \right.$$

$$\left. + \frac{L}{\pi(2j-2j')} \sin\left(\frac{(2j-2j')\pi a}{2L}\right) \right] \tag{III.29.4}$$

Up to which $j - j'$, $j + j'$ can we go to replace the sines by their arguments? Typically, the term $\sin(\pi\alpha)$ can be approximated by its argument $\pi\alpha$ if $\alpha < 1/10$. Thus, the larger $j+j'$ will be of the order of 11 if $L = 10$ nm and $a = 0.283$ nm. As we shall see this is sufficient to get a fair estimate of the perturbation replacement. We find readily that the matrix element is equal to:

$$\langle \varphi_{2j+1} | V(z) | \varphi_{2j'+1} \rangle \approx \frac{2a}{L} V_0 \tag{III.29.5}$$

But this result coincides with that obtained by replacing the perturbing potential by $V_0 a \delta(z)$.

(3) The parity operator commutes with H_0. It also commutes with the perturbation because the δ function is even in z (it is the limit of a sequence of functions that are even in z, e.g., Gaussians). Therefore, if we start from the eigenstates of H_0 the even (odd) eigenstates will be admixed with even (odd) eigenstates but there will be no mixing between the even and the odd eigenstates. In addition, the odd eigenstates vanish at $z = 0$. Hence, they are insensitive to the perturbation. We have not to consider the odd states any longer since to any order in V_0, they will remain the same as at $V_0 = 0$.

(4) The second-order perturbation to the energy $E_{2j+1} = E_1(2j+1)^2$ is equal to:

$$\tilde{E}_{2j+1} = E_{2j+1} + 2\frac{V_0 a}{L} + \left(\frac{2V_0 a}{L}\right)^2 \frac{1}{E_1} \sum_{j' \neq j} \frac{1}{(2j+1)^2 - (2j'+1)^2} \tag{III.29.6}$$

For the ground state, we find readily:

$$\tilde{E}_1 = E_1 + 2\frac{V_0 a}{L} - \left(\frac{2V_0 a}{L}\right)^2 \frac{1}{4E_1} \sum_{j'=1} \frac{1}{j'(j'+1)} \qquad \text{(III.29.7)}$$

The numerical series amounts to be equal to 1. The first-order energy shift is equal to 5.66 meV. The second-order energy shift is much smaller (a few % of the first order). We note, once again, that the second-order energy shift of the ground state is negative. This property is general.

(5) There is actually an exact solution to the problem (and that is again thanks to the delta-shaped potential energy). We expand the wavefunction of the perturbed quantum well on the basis of the eigensolutions of H_0 with an even parity:

$$|\psi\rangle = \sum_j c_{2j+1}|\varphi_{2j+1}\rangle \qquad \text{(III.29.8)}$$

and after projecting on $\langle\varphi_{2j+1}|$ we get:

$$c_{2j+1}(E_{2j+1} - \varepsilon) + 2\frac{V_0 a}{L}\sum_{j'} c_{2j'+1} = 0 \qquad \text{(III.29.9)}$$

Define $S = \sum_j c_{2j+1}$. Then:

$$S = S\frac{2V_0 a}{L}\sum_j \frac{1}{\varepsilon - E_1(2j+1)^2} \qquad \text{(III.29.10)}$$

So either $S = 0$ (which is uninteresting because V_0-independent), or ε must be the solution of the equation:

$$1 = \frac{2V_0 a}{L E_1}\sum_j \frac{1}{\frac{\varepsilon}{E_1} - (2j+1)^2} \qquad \text{(III.29.11)}$$

We have made no approximation on the strength of V_0. Let us suppose that we are in the perturbative regime where V_0 is somehow small and let us concentrate on the vicinity of the lowest unperturbed eigenvalue E_1. We write:

$$1 = \frac{2V_0 a}{LE_1} \left(\frac{1}{\frac{\varepsilon}{E_1} - 1} + \sum_{j \geq 1} \frac{1}{\frac{\varepsilon}{E_1} - (2j+1)^2} \right) \qquad \text{(III.29.12)}$$

$$\frac{\varepsilon}{E_1} - 1 = \frac{2V_0 a}{LE_1} \left[1 + \left(\frac{\varepsilon}{E_1} - 1 \right) \sum_{j \geq 1} \frac{1}{\frac{\varepsilon}{E_1} - (2j+1)^2} \right] \qquad \text{(III.29.13)}$$

From this expression we check readily that the expansion versus ascending power V_0 nicely reduces to the results given in Eq. (III.29.7).

Actually, the insertion of very localised perturbations in a quantum well is not only an academic exercise. During the MBE epitaxy of the GaAs well, one can insert a monolayer of AlAs or of InAs. Al and In are isovalent to Ga. Hence, the perturbation they create will be short-ranged (spatially limited to the unit cells of the dopant plane) since each of the Al or In atom will not display a long range coulombic tail as exhibited by the donors (e.g., Zn a group VI element substituting As) or acceptors (e.g., C a group IV element substituting As).

The shift of the energy levels produced by these monolayer insertions leads to shifts of the optical transition energies, either interband or intraband. For instance, the ground quantum well transition $E_1 \rightarrow E_2$ is dipole allowed in the z polarisation. In the presence of an on-centre perturbation and owing to the prevalence of the first-order energy shift over the second order (and to the fact that E_2 is unaffected by the perturbation), we see that using $V_0 > 0$ (Al monolayer) we blue shift the E_1 level and therefore red shift the $E_1 - E_2$ transition energy. On the contrary, if we insert an In monolayer it creates an attractive potential for the electron. Thus E_1 will be red shifted and the transition $E_1 - E_2$ will be blue shifted.

Moreover (and this was the key ingredient used by Marzin *et al.* [83]), we can as well dope any part of the quantum well (or of its barrier) by this planar doping. Using the first-order results for the shift (anticipating that it will play the leading part), we get a shift

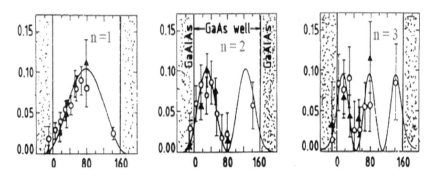

« Measurements » of the the shape
of the n = 1,2,3 lower lying states of a square QW

Figure 29.1.   Reconstruction of the three lowest bound states of a GaAs/(Ga,Al)As quantum well as obtained by measuring the interband transition energies of wells selectively doped by In or Al (planar doping).

of both the even and odd states (because now for an off-centre doping the parity is no longer conserved). These shifts are proportional to the squared envelope function at the dopant plane. Repeating this operation many times both with attractive (In) and repulsive (Al) potentials, measuring the transition energy shifts one should be able to reconstruct the envelope function for the ground and the few excited states. This was done by Marzin and Gerard and their measurements confirm that the envelope function approximation works very well at least for the quantum well they were investigating (see Fig. 29.1).

30.   Quantum dot anisotropy

Isotropic quantum dot. A popular model for representing the electronic structure of self-organised Quantum Dots (QD) (e.g., InAs QD's embedded into a GaAs substrate) is to identify the electronic confinement in the xOy plane to an isotropic harmonic potential. Thus, it is tacitly assumed that the (x, y) and z motions decouple; which is a sensible approximation since the QD height ($h \approx 2 - 3$ nm) is usually much smaller than the in-plane dimensions of the QD (diameter $D \approx 20-30$ nm).

From now on, we admit that the one electron Hamiltonian can be approximated by:

$$H_0 = \frac{p_z^2}{2m^*} + V_{\text{conf}}(z) + \frac{p_x^2 + p_y^2}{2m^*} + \frac{1}{2}m^*\omega^2(x^2 + y^2) \qquad \text{(III.30.1)}$$

(1) Show that the eigenstates of H_0 factorise:

$$\psi_{nlm}(\vec{r}) = \langle \vec{r}|E_l, n_x, n_y\rangle = \chi_l(z)\varphi_{n_x}(x)\varphi_{m_y}(y) \qquad \text{(III.30.2)}$$

where the φ's are the Hermite functions, the eigenfunctions of the 1D harmonic oscillator (their explicit form is given in Chapter I.4 in Part II dealing with the Landau quantisation).

(2) Find the degeneracy of an $|E_l, n_x, n_y\rangle$ state.

(3) Suppose we know the diameter D of the QD and that the electron is in the lowest bound state of the QD. Relate ω to D. If $D = 20$ nm and $m^* = 0.07m_0$ evaluate ω. Which part of the electromagnetic spectrum corresponds to the angular frequency ω?

Since the z motion plays no part, we assume it is frozen into its ground state and concentrate on the (x, y) motion.

(4) The QD is shined by a linearly polarised electromagnetic wave tuned in frequency to the energy difference between the two lowest eigenvalues of the in-plane Hamiltonian. Admit that the absorption of the electromagnetic wave is proportional to $|\langle \psi_{\text{in}}|\vec{\varepsilon}\cdot\vec{r}|\psi_{\text{fin}}\rangle|^2$, where $\vec{\varepsilon}$ is the polarisation vector of the light with components $(\cos\alpha, \sin\alpha)$ in the layer plane. Show that this matrix element is in fact independent of α.

Anisotropic quantum dot. Figure 30.1 shows the result of an absorption measurement performed at low temperature on an ensemble of InAs self-organised QD's in a GaAs matrix. It is seen that the predicted isotropy is not observed. Instead, two peaks show up corresponding to the two orthogonal directions [110] and [1−10]. This suggests that the QD's are slightly anisotropic since the two peaks

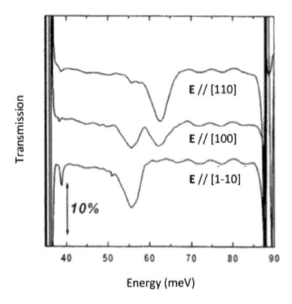

Figure 30.1. Transmission spectra of an ensemble of InAs quantum dots. The electromagnetic wave is linearly polarised. $T = 5$ K.

Source: Hameau *et al.* [84].

are shifted by $\approx \pm 3.5$ meV on each side of an average transition energy of ≈ 60 meV. To explain these features, we write that there exist two different characteristic frequencies for the harmonic confinements $\omega_0(1 - \frac{\varepsilon}{2})$ and $\omega_0(1 + \frac{\varepsilon}{2})$ where $\varepsilon \ll 1$. Evidently, we know immediately the exact spectrum for the in-plane motion:

$$E(n_x, n_y) = \left(n_x + \frac{1}{2}\right)\hbar\omega_0\left(1 + \frac{\varepsilon}{2}\right) + \left(n_y + \frac{1}{2}\right)\hbar\omega_0\left(1 - \frac{\varepsilon}{2}\right)$$
$$(\text{III.30.3})$$

Therefore, the lowest lying transition (from $|0_x 0_y\rangle$ to either $|1_x 0_y\rangle$ or $|0_x 1_y\rangle$) will be split and the splitting will be equal to $\varepsilon\hbar\omega_0$.

Our purpose is to exercise the reader with the perturbative approach. So, we shall start from the Hamiltonian, extract a perturbation Hamiltonian and handle this perturbation.

(5) Rewrite the in-plane Hamiltonian as $H_0 + V_{\text{anis}}$ where H_0 is ε-independent and V_{anis} depends on ε.

(6) Diagonalise V_{anis} in the 3×3 subspace generated by $|0_x 0_y\rangle$, $|1_x 0_y\rangle$, $|0_x 1_y\rangle$.

(7) From your findings and by comparison with the experimental data, deduce the anisotropy dimensionless parameter ε for the InAs QD's.

Solution

(1) Since the Hamiltonian is the sum of the x, y, z parts, its eigenfunctions factorise.

(2) The degeneracy is $(n + m + 1)$. It is equal to the number of possibilities of getting the sum of two terms n and m equal to a certain value M: if we fix M and the first number there is no room left to the second number. Hence, the degeneracy reduces to the number of possible numbers between 0 and M, thus $M + 1$.

(3) In a 1D harmonic oscillator, it is known that the average potential energy is half the total energy (virial theorem). Hence:

$$\left\langle n \left| \frac{1}{2} m^* \omega^2 x^2 \right| n \right\rangle = \frac{1}{2} \left(n + \frac{1}{2} \right) \hbar \omega \tag{III.30.4}$$

and

$$\left\langle 0 \left| \frac{1}{2} m^* \omega^2 x^2 \right| 0 \right\rangle = \frac{\hbar \omega}{4} \tag{III.30.5}$$

Now the uncertainty over the x position can roughly be identified with the size of the object. Therefore:

$$D \approx \sqrt{\frac{\hbar}{2 m^* \omega}} \tag{III.30.6}$$

With the material parameters given in the text, we find $\hbar \omega \approx$ 1.35 meV. This energy corresponds to the submillimetre part of the electromagnetic spectrum ($\lambda \approx 0.9$ mm).

(4) For a 2D isotropic harmonic oscillator, we find that the absorption coefficient is proportional to:

$$|\langle 0_x 0_y | x \cos \alpha + y \sin \alpha | 0_x 1_y \rangle|^2 + |\langle 0_x 0_y | x \cos \alpha + y \sin \alpha | 1_x 0_y \rangle|^2$$

$$= \sin^2 \alpha |\langle 0_y | y | 1_y \rangle|^2 + \cos^2 \alpha |\langle 0_x | x | 1_x \rangle|^2 \qquad \text{(III.30.7)}$$

But the two matrix elements are identical. Hence, we find that any linearly polarised light should induce the same absorption.

(5) We concentrate on the in-plane Hamiltonian and write:

$$\frac{1}{2} m^* \omega_0^2 \left[x^2 \left(1 + \frac{\varepsilon}{2} \right)^2 + y^2 \left(1 - \frac{\varepsilon}{2} \right)^2 \right]$$

$$= \frac{1}{2} m^* \omega_0^2 (x^2 + y^2) + \frac{1}{2} m^* \omega_0^2 \varepsilon (x^2 - y^2) + \frac{1}{2} m^* \omega_0^2 \frac{\varepsilon^2}{4} (x^2 + y^2)$$

$$\text{(III.30.8)}$$

$$\Rightarrow H_0 = \frac{p_x^2}{2m^*} + \frac{p_y^2}{2m^*} + \frac{1}{2} m^* \omega_0^2 (x^2 + y^2) \qquad \text{(III.30.9)}$$

$$V_{\text{anis}} = \frac{1}{2} m^* \omega_0^2 \left[\varepsilon \left(x^2 - y^2 \right) + \frac{\varepsilon^2}{4} (x^2 + y^2) \right] \qquad \text{(III.30.10)}$$

To conveniently handle V_{anis}, we shall make a heavy reliance on the symmetry properties of the eigenstates of H_0 and of the perturbation.

The H_0 eigenstates are eigenstates of the parity operator both for the x and y directions. The two components of the perturbations are even both in x and y. Moreover, the interchange of x and y changes the sign of the term linear in ε but not the sign of the quadratic term in ε.

The unperturbed eigenstates we deal with are $|0_x 0_y\rangle$, $|0_x 1_y\rangle$, $|1_x 0_y\rangle$. Let us first examine the effect of the linear term in ε. Its diagonal elements are zero in the ground state (which is invariant in the x, y interchange). It has opposite effects on $|0_x 1_y\rangle$ and $|1_x 0_y\rangle$. It has no non-vanishing element between the ground state and the two degenerate excited states because it is even in x and y while the connected states are of opposite parities. Finally, the term linear in ε has no non-vanishing element between the two excited states (by parity).

Let us now examine the effect of the quadratic term in ε. The diagonal terms are very easy to handle since they are proportional to the potential energy of the unperturbed problem. Hence, by application of the virial theorem $\langle n|\frac{1}{2}m^*\omega_0^2 x^2|n\rangle = \frac{1}{2}\left(n+\frac{1}{2}\right)\hbar\omega_0$, we get readily:

$$\langle 0_x 0_y|\frac{1}{2}m^*\omega_0^2(x^2+y^2)|0_x 0_y\rangle = \frac{\hbar\omega_0}{2} \tag{III.30.11}$$

$$\langle 1_x 0_y|\frac{1}{2}m^*\omega_0^2(x^2+y^2)|1_x 0_y\rangle = \langle 0_x 1_y|\frac{1}{2}m^*\omega_0^2(x^2+y^2)|0_x 1_y\rangle = \hbar\omega_0 \tag{III.30.12}$$

The quadratic term in ε has no off-diagonal matrix element (from parity consideration in x and y) between the three states under consideration.

(6) Thus, we arrive at the remarkable results that in the subspace spanned by the three lowest eigenstates, V_{anis} is diagonal. The $H_0 + V_{\text{anis}}$ matrix reads:

$$\begin{pmatrix} \hbar\omega_0 + \eta & 0 & 0 \\ 0 & 2\hbar\omega_0 + \xi + \beta & 0 \\ 0 & 0 & 2\hbar\omega_0 + \xi - \beta \end{pmatrix} \begin{pmatrix} |0_x 0_y\rangle \\ |0_x 1_y\rangle \\ |1_x 0_y\rangle \end{pmatrix} \tag{III.30.13}$$

where η, ξ (β) are quadratic (linear) in ε. The transition energy will thus display a splitting that is equal to 2β and which is linear in ε:

$$\beta = \langle 1_x 0_y|\frac{1}{2}m^*\omega_0^2\varepsilon(x^2-y^2)|1_x 0_y\rangle$$

$$= \frac{1}{2}m^*\omega_0^2\varepsilon\langle 1_x|x^2|1_x\rangle - \frac{1}{2}m^*\omega_0^2\varepsilon\langle 0_y|y^2|0_y\rangle$$

$$= \varepsilon\left(\frac{3}{4}\hbar\omega_0 - \frac{1}{4}\hbar\omega_0\right) = \varepsilon\frac{\hbar\omega_0}{2} \tag{III.30.14}$$

It has to be stressed that, despite the line broadening due to fluctuations in the QD sizes, the QD responses to a polarised light very much points out to a fairly reproducible anisotropy from one QD to another one. By comparing the theoretical splitting to the experimental one, we get $\varepsilon \approx 5\%$.

Now, the careful reader will remark (and wonder why) that our perturbative estimate predicts a shift (η) of the ground state energy that is quadratic in ε. But the exact results (see text) show no such shift of the ground state. So, where is the mistake, if any? It lays in our unfinished job with the perturbation calculus. What we did was to diagonalise exactly the perturbation inside a 3×3 subspace. In doing so, we actually got diagonal corrections. We would have gotten the same result for the ground state $|0_x 0_y\rangle$ by treating V_{anis} to the first order on the ground state. The missing term comes from not treating the term of V_{anis} that is linear in ε to the second order of perturbation theory. This neglect has made that we have gotten consistent results for the term that is linear in ε but not for the quadratic terms in ε.

Let us repair this shortcoming and handle the linear terms in ε to the second order. Specifically, we express x and y in terms of the creation and annihilation operators and get:

$$\frac{1}{2} m^* \omega_0^2 \varepsilon (x^2 - y^2)$$

$$= \frac{\varepsilon \hbar \omega_0}{4} (a_x a_x^\dagger + a_x^\dagger a_x + a_x^2 + a_x^{\dagger 2} - a_y a_y^\dagger - a_y^\dagger a_y - a_y^2 - a_y^{\dagger 2})$$

$$\text{(III.30.15)}$$

We handle this contribution up to the second order on the ground state:

$$\Delta \varepsilon_{00} = -\frac{\varepsilon^2}{16} \hbar \omega_0 \sum_{n_x, n_y \neq 0_x, 0_y}$$

$$|\langle 0_x 0_y | a_x a_x^\dagger + a_x^\dagger a_x + a_x^2 + a_x^{\dagger 2} - a_y a_y^\dagger$$

$$\times \frac{- a_y^\dagger a_y - a_y^2 - a_y^{\dagger 2} | n_x n_y \rangle |^2}{n_x + n_y} \quad \text{(III.30.16)}$$

Firstly, we notice that the contribution is negative, as it should (perturbation of the ground state). Secondly, we see readily that the only non-vanishing terms arise from the squared a and $a^\dagger$. Hence, they could not have shown up in the 3×3 matrix where the n's only differ by one unit. Finally, when we express the value of the matrix element, we find:

$$\Delta\varepsilon_{00} = -\frac{\varepsilon^2}{8}\hbar\omega_0 \qquad\qquad (\text{III}.30.17)$$

This contribution exactly offsets the first-order term coming from the ε^2 part of the perturbation. Thus, there is actually no η in the 3×3 matrix. The reader will also check that there is no ξ term as well.

So, to summarise, when the perturbation involves several terms that display different powers of a small parameter, one should always make sure that the results display consistent handling of that small parameter.

31. Defect in a superlattice: tight binding approach

Part I: Ideal superlattice

We consider the electron states in a binary AB superlattice (SL) that we handle in a tight binding approach. In an ideal SL we write the Hamiltonian as:

$$H_0 = \sum_n \varepsilon_0|n\rangle\langle n| - \lambda|n-1\rangle\langle n| - \lambda|n+1\rangle\langle n| \qquad (\text{III}.31.1)$$

where $|n\rangle$ is an orbital centred on the nth period of the superlattice. Orbitals centred on different periods are assumed orthogonal: $\langle n|m\rangle = \delta_{nm}$. $\langle x|n\rangle = \varphi(x - nd)$ looks much like the ground bound state of the well-acting layer in the nth period.

(I1) Comment this choice for H_0. It may prove useful to compute $\langle j|H_0|j'\rangle$.

(I2) We look for stationary states of H_0 in the form:

$$|\psi\rangle = \frac{1}{\sqrt{2N+1}}\sum_n \beta_n|n\rangle \qquad\qquad (\text{III}.31.2)$$

where $2N + 1$ is the macroscopic number of unit cells in the superlattices (labelled $-N, -N+1, \ldots, -1, 0, 1, \ldots, N-1, N$). Show that the β_n's are the solutions of:

$$\beta_n(\varepsilon_0 - \varepsilon) - \lambda(\beta_{n+1} + \beta_{n-1}) = 0 \qquad \text{(III.31.3)}$$

where ε is the eigenenergy associated with $|\psi\rangle$.

(I3) Since the superlattice is a periodic stacking of A layers and B layers, all A and all B layers being of the same thicknesses (L_A and L_B respectively with $L_A + L_B = d$), the Bloch theorem should apply. Deduce that $\beta_n = \exp(iqnd)$ where q is the electron wavevector along the x-axis that one can restrict to the first Brillouin zone: $-\pi/d \leq q \leq \pi/d$.

From now on we shall denote by $|\psi_q\rangle$ the stationary state of H_0 which is also an eigenfunction of the translation operator T_d with eigenvalue $\exp(iqd)$.

(I4) What is the electron dispersion relation $\varepsilon(q)$ where $\varepsilon(q)$ is the eigenvalue of H_0 associated with $|\psi_q\rangle$?

(I5) By expanding $\varepsilon(q)$ in the vicinity of $q = 0$ and $q = \pi/d$ respectively, find the carrier effective mass in the vicinity of these two points. The effective mass m^* is such that one can write in the vicinity of $q = 0$:

$$\varepsilon(q) \approx \varepsilon(0) + \frac{\hbar^2 q^2}{2m^*} \qquad \text{(III.31.4)}$$

Discuss the functional relationship $m^*(\lambda)$, in particular the limit $\lambda \to 0$.

Part II: Superlattice with a defect

We consider now the case of a modified SL where the quantum well of the $n = 0$ unit cell is different. This means that the Hamiltonian we are considering is:

$$H = H_0 + \Delta|0\rangle\langle 0| \qquad \text{(III.31.5)}$$

(II1) How should the anomalous quantum well thickness vary to get $\Delta > 0$, $\Delta < 0$?

(II2) We look for a solution of H in the form:

$$|\chi\rangle = \sum_q \alpha_q |\psi_q\rangle \qquad \text{(III.31.6)}$$

By projecting H on the $|\psi_q\rangle$ basis find that the eigenenergies of H fulfil:

$$1 = \frac{\Delta}{2N+1} \sum_q \frac{1}{\varepsilon - \varepsilon(q)} \qquad \text{(III.31.7)}$$

(II3) We consider the case $\varepsilon < \varepsilon_0 - 2\lambda$. Under which condition does the equation in II3 admit a solution. Same question if $\varepsilon > \varepsilon_0 + 2\lambda$.

(II4) Do you see an analogy between the imperfect SL situation and that of doped semiconductors?

(II5) Compute explicitly ε in the case where either $\varepsilon < \varepsilon_0 - 2\lambda$ or $\varepsilon > \varepsilon_0 + 2\lambda$. We give:

$$\int_0^\pi \frac{dx}{1 + a\cos x} = \begin{cases} \dfrac{\pi}{\sqrt{1-a^2}} & \text{if } |a| < 1 \\ 0 & \text{if } |a| > 1 \end{cases} \qquad \text{(III.31.8)}$$

Solution

(I1) We compute $\langle j|H_0|j'\rangle = \varepsilon_0\delta_{jj'} - \lambda(\delta_{j,j'+1} + \delta_{j,j'-1})$. Thus, ε_0 is the on-site energy of the electron in any period of the superlattice; typically the confinement energy of the isolated quantum well out of which the superlattice is built. λ represents the transfer from one period to the next due to the tunnelling across the barrier separating two consecutive wells. Note that the sign of λ corresponds to hybridisation of the lowest bound states of the well giving rise to the lowest superlattice subband. For the first excited subband λ is negative most of the times.

(I2) We start from $|\psi\rangle = \frac{1}{\sqrt{2N+1}} \sum_n \beta_n |n\rangle$ and let H_0 act on it.

We find:

$$0 = \sum_p (\varepsilon_0 - \varepsilon)|p\rangle\langle p| - \lambda|p-1\rangle\langle p| - \lambda|p+1\rangle\langle p|\frac{1}{\sqrt{2N+1}}\left(\sum_n \beta_n|n\rangle\right)$$

$$= \frac{1}{\sqrt{2N+1}}\sum_p \beta_p(\varepsilon_0 - \varepsilon)|p\rangle - \lambda\beta_p|p-1\rangle - \lambda\beta_p|p+1\rangle$$

$$= \sum_p [\beta_p(\varepsilon_0 - \varepsilon) - \lambda(\beta_{p+1} + \beta_{p-1})]\,|p\rangle \qquad \text{(III.31.9)}$$

Thus, we get:

$$\beta_p(\varepsilon_0 - \varepsilon) - \lambda(\beta_{p+1} + \beta_{p-1}) = 0 \qquad \text{(III.31.10)}$$

(I3) For $|\psi\rangle$ to be a Bloch state such that $T_d|\psi\rangle = e^{iqd}|\psi\rangle$, one should write $\beta_n = e^{iqnd}$ where q is the superlattice wavevector that can be restricted to the first Brillouin zone:

$$-\frac{\pi}{d} \le q \le \frac{\pi}{d} \qquad \text{(III.31.11)}$$

(I4) By inserting the Bloch ansatz into (I2) one gets readily:

$$\varepsilon(q) = \varepsilon_0 - 2\lambda\cos(qd) \qquad \text{(III.31.12)}$$

In the vicinity of $q = 0$ one gets the band minimum:

$$\varepsilon(q) \approx \varepsilon_0 - 2\lambda + \lambda q^2 d^2 \equiv \varepsilon_0 - 2\lambda + \frac{\hbar^2 q^2}{2m^*} \qquad \text{(III.31.13)}$$

$$\frac{1}{m^*} = \frac{2\lambda d^2}{\hbar^2} \qquad \text{(III.31.14)}$$

In the vicinity of the zone boundary $q = \pi/d$ one finds the band maximum:

$$\varepsilon(q) \approx \varepsilon_0 + 2\lambda - \lambda q^2 d^2 \equiv \varepsilon_0 + 2\lambda + \frac{\hbar^2 q^2}{2m^*} \qquad \text{(III.31.15)}$$

$$\frac{1}{m^*} = -\frac{2\lambda d^2}{\hbar^2} \qquad \text{(III.31.16)}$$

Hence the effective mass is negative in the vicinity of the band maximum.

Both masses go to infinity when $\lambda \to 0$. Without tunnel coupling the particle undergoes periodic oscillations inside a given well say the nth well. As for its displacement over the whole superlattice, it is less and less efficient resulting in an effective mass for the z motion that is heavier and heavier.

In this simple tight binding description of the electron motion, we have a first encounter on the physical meaning of an effective mass. We shall find other situations where the effective mass concept receives other physical interpretations.

(II1) If the anomalous well in the zeroth cell is narrower than the wells of the SL one gets $\Delta > 0$. In the case where the anomalous well is thicker than the others one gets $\Delta < 0$.

(II2) We let H to act on $|\chi\rangle$:

$$(H_0 + \Delta|0\rangle\langle0| - \varepsilon)\sum_{q'}\alpha_{q'}|\psi_{q'}\rangle = 0 \qquad \text{(III.31.17)}$$

$$\sum_{q'}\alpha_{q'}\{[\varepsilon(q') - \varepsilon]\,|\psi_{q'}\rangle + \Delta|0\rangle\langle0|\psi_{q'}\rangle\} = 0 \qquad \text{(III.31.18)}$$

But $\langle0|\psi_q\rangle = (2N+1)^{-1/2}$. If we now multiply by the bra $\langle\psi_q|$ and taking into account that $\langle\psi_q|\psi_{q'}\rangle = \delta_{qq'}$ we get:

$$\alpha_q\,[\varepsilon(q) - \varepsilon] + \frac{\Delta}{2N+1}\sum_{q'}\alpha(q') = 0 \qquad \text{(III.31.19)}$$

$$I = I\frac{\Delta}{2N+1}\sum_q\frac{1}{\varepsilon - \varepsilon(q)}; \quad I = \sum_q\alpha(q) \qquad \text{(III.31.20)}$$

Then, assuming $I \neq 0$, we find that the perturbed energies are the solutions of the equation:

$$1 = \frac{\Delta}{2N+1}\sum_q\frac{1}{\varepsilon - \varepsilon(q)} \qquad \text{(III.31.21)}$$

Note that the expression $\sum_q\frac{1}{\varepsilon-\varepsilon(q)}$ must in the continuous limit $(N \to \infty)$ be understood as a distribution: $PP\sum_q\frac{1}{\varepsilon-\varepsilon(q)} - i\pi\delta[\varepsilon - \varepsilon(q)]$ [1]. On the other hand if the q's are discretised the sum is well defined.

(II3) and (II4) For $\varepsilon < \varepsilon_0 - 2\lambda$, the sum is negative (because all its terms are negative). Hence Δ must be negative to get a possible solution. That corresponds to an anomalous well thicker than all others. Symmetrically for $\varepsilon > \varepsilon_0 + 2\lambda$ the sum is positive and Δ has to be positive if there is a solution. Hence states above (respectively, below) the band are created by anomalous well that are thinner (respectively, thicker) than the others. In the vicinity of the band maximum (respectively, minimum) the effective mass is negative (respectively, positive). So we get an analogy with the doped semiconductors by stating that narrower (respectively, thicker) wells create acceptor-like (respectively, donor-like) states.

The computation of the summation is straightforward. First we introduce the binding energy x and let

$$\varepsilon = \varepsilon_0 - 2\lambda - x, \quad x > 0 \qquad \text{(III.31.22)}$$

We then convert the sum into an integral by the usual rule:

$$\sum_q f(q) \to \frac{(2N+1)d}{2\pi} \int_{-\pi/d}^{\pi/d} f(q)dq \qquad \text{(III.31.23)}$$

We get:

$$1 = \frac{-\Delta}{\sqrt{x^2 + 4\lambda x}} \Rightarrow x = -2\lambda + \sqrt{\Delta^2 + 4\lambda^2} \qquad \text{(III.31.24)}$$

Note (as a check) that Δ must be negative to get a solution.

If we look at the solution above the band, we again introduce the (hole) binding energy x and let:

$$\varepsilon = \varepsilon_0 + 2\lambda + x, \quad x > 0 \qquad \text{(III.31.25)}$$

and get:

$$1 = \frac{\Delta}{\sqrt{x^2 + 4\lambda x}} \Rightarrow x = -2\lambda + \sqrt{\Delta^2 + 4\lambda^2} \qquad \text{(III.31.26)}$$

As a check we find that Δ must be positive to get a solution above the band. Note the symmetry between what happens below and what happens above the band. This is the result of the assumption of nearest neighbour tunnel coupling that makes the dispersion symmetrical with respect to its center (here ε_0).

For actual superlattices such as GaAs/Ga(Al)As, usually λ is larger or much larger than Δ and to a reasonable approximation there is in both cases: $x \approx \frac{\Delta^2}{4\lambda}$. Thus the binding energy of an electron bound to an anomalous well in a superlattice is significantly smaller than the change in the confinement energy of the anomalous well if it were isolated. We find here a smoothening of the attractive (or repulsive) effect of the anomalous well because of the delocalisation of the electrons states in the superlattice due to tunnelling between the anomalous well and its neighbours.

32. Bound states created by two delta scatterers in a Landau level

We consider the problem of the Landau level states perturbed by two scatterers. These scatterers are short-ranged:

$$V(\vec{r}) = V_0 a^3 \delta(\vec{r} - \vec{r}_0) + V_1 a^3 \delta(\vec{r} - \vec{r}_1) \qquad \text{(III.32.1)}$$

We have already solved the one impurity problem in Chapter II.7 of Part II and wish to extend the results to take into account the interaction between impurities. As before we neglect the defects-induced coupling between different subbands and between different Landau levels. Thus, we expand the wavefunction on the basis spanned by one Landau level (using the Landau gauge):

$$\psi_{n,p}(\vec{r}) = \sum_{k_y} c_{n,p}(k_y) \frac{e^{ik_y y}}{\sqrt{L_y}} \varphi_p(x + \lambda^2 k_y) \chi_n(z) \qquad \text{(III.32.2)}$$

(1) Find the equation fulfilled by the coefficients $c_{n,p}(k_y)$.

(2) Like before (see Chapter II.7), we define the functions:

$$A_0^{n,p} = \sum_{k_y} c_{n,p}(k_y) e^{ik_y y_0} \varphi(x_0 + \lambda^2 k_y) \qquad \text{(III.32.3)}$$

$$A_1^{n,p} = \sum_{k_y} c_{n,p}(k_y) e^{ik_y y_1} \varphi(x_1 + \lambda^2 k_y) \qquad \text{(III.32.4)}$$

Show that these functions are the solutions of the 2×2 linear system:

$$\begin{pmatrix} B_{00} & B_{01} \\ B_{10} & B_{11} \end{pmatrix} \begin{pmatrix} A_0^{n,p} \\ A_1^{n,p} \end{pmatrix} = 0 \qquad \text{(III.32.5)}$$

where:

$$B_{00} = 1 - \frac{V_0 a^3 \chi_n^2(z_0)}{2\pi\lambda^2(\varepsilon - \varepsilon_{n,p})}; \quad B_{11} = 1 - \frac{V_1 a^3 \chi_n^2(z_1)}{2\pi\lambda^2(\varepsilon - \varepsilon_{n,p})}$$

(III.32.6)

$$B_{01} = -\frac{V_1 a^3 \chi_n^2(z_1)}{2\pi\lambda^2(\varepsilon - \varepsilon_{n,p})} e^{iX(y_1 - y_0)} I_p$$

(III.32.7)

$$B_{10} = -\frac{V_0 a^3 \chi_n^2(z_0)}{2\pi\lambda^2(\varepsilon - \varepsilon_{n,p})} e^{iX(y_1 - y_0)} I_p^*$$

(III.32.8)

$$X = \frac{x_1 + x_0}{2}; \quad x = \frac{x_1 - x_0}{2}$$

(III.32.9)

$$I_p(x) = \int_{-\infty}^{+\infty} dt \varphi_p(t + x)\varphi_p(t - x) e^{it\left(\frac{y_0 - y_1}{\lambda^2}\right)}$$

(III.32.10)

$$\varepsilon_{np} = E_n + \left(p + \frac{1}{2}\right)\hbar\omega_c$$

(III.32.11)

(3) Deduce the energies of the bound states. How many bound states show up for fixed n and p? If there are N allowed k_y values, how many states have the unperturbed energy $\varepsilon_{n,p}$?

(4) The integrals I_p can be expressed in terms of Laguerre polynomials. Let us investigate the defect states created in the $p = 0$ Landau level. We give:

$$I_0(x) = \exp\left(-\frac{1}{4\lambda^2}\left[(x_0 - x_1)^2 + (y_0 - y_1)^2\right]\right)$$

(III.32.12)

Discuss qualitatively the behaviour of the states versus the in-plane distance between the impurities when the two delta scatterers have the same sign and strength (e.g., an "acceptor" pair) and when they have the same strength but opposite sign ("donor–acceptor" pair).

Solution

(1)

$$c_{n,p}(k_y)(-\varepsilon_{n,p} + \varepsilon)$$

$$= \sum_{k'_y} c_{n,p}(k'_y)$$

$$\times \left[\frac{V_0 a^3}{L_y} \chi_n^2(z_0) e^{i(k'_y - k_y)y_0} \varphi_p(x_0 + \lambda^2 k_y) \varphi_p(x_0 + \lambda^2 k'_y) \right]$$

$$+ \sum_{k'_y} c_{n,p}(k'_y)$$

$$\times \left[\frac{V_1 a^3}{L_y} \chi_n^2(z_1) e^{i(k'_y - k_y)y_1} \varphi_p(x_1 + \lambda^2 k_y) \varphi_p(x_1 + \lambda^2 k'_y) \right]$$

$$\text{(III.32.13)}$$

Because of the Landau level degeneracy, the diagonal term in k_y do not depend on k_y. This is the key factor that allows the problem to be solved in closed form. Consider for instance the first off diagonal term:

$$\sum_{k'_y} c_{n,p}(k'_y) \frac{V_0 a^3}{L_y} \chi_n^2(z_0) e^{i(k'_y - k_y)y_0} \varphi_p(x_0 + \lambda^2 k_y) \varphi_p(x_0 + \lambda^2 k'_y)$$

$$\text{(III.32.14)}$$

We find it equal to:

$$\frac{V_0 a^3}{L_y} \chi_n^2(z_0) \varphi_p(x_0 + \lambda^2 k_y) e^{-ik_y y_0} A_0^{n,p} \qquad \text{(III.32.15)}$$

Similarly, the second off diagonal term is equal to:

$$\frac{V_1 a^3}{L_y} \chi_n^2(z_1) \varphi_p(x_1 + \lambda^2 k_y) e^{-ik_y y_1} A_1^{n,p} \qquad \text{(III.32.16)}$$

Hence:

$$c_{n,p}(k_y) = \frac{1}{\varepsilon - \varepsilon_{n,p}} \left[\frac{V_0 a^3}{L_y} \chi_n^2(z_0) \varphi_p(x_0 + \lambda^2 k_y) e^{-ik_y y_0} A_0^{n,p} \right.$$

$$\left. + \frac{V_1 a^3}{L_y} \chi_n^2(z_1) \varphi_p(x_1 + \lambda^2 k_y) e^{-ik_y y_1} A_1^{n,p} \right] \quad \text{(III.32.17)}$$

We can now make $A_0^{n,p}$ and $A_1^{n,p}$ appearing:

$$A_0^{n,p} = \frac{1}{\varepsilon - \varepsilon_{n,p}} \left[\frac{V_0 a^3}{L_y} \chi_n^2(z_0) A_0^{n,p} \sum_{k_y} \varphi_p^2(x_0 + \lambda^2 k_y) \right.$$

$$+ \frac{1}{\varepsilon - \varepsilon_{n,p}} \left[\frac{V_1 a^3}{L_y} \chi_n^2(z_1) A_1^{n,p} \sum_{k_y} \varphi_p(x_0 + \lambda^2 k_y) \right.$$

$$\left. \left. \times \varphi_p(x_1 + \lambda^2 k_y) e^{ik_y(y_0 - y_1)} \right] \right] \tag{III.32.18}$$

Then, we transform the summation over k_y into an integral. We define:

$$X = \frac{x_0 + x_1}{2}; \quad x = \frac{x_1 - x_0}{2} \tag{III.32.19}$$

$$x_1 = x + X; \quad x_0 = X - x \tag{III.32.20}$$

$$A_0^{n,p} = \frac{1}{\varepsilon - \varepsilon_{n,p}} \frac{V_0 a^3}{2\pi\lambda^2} \chi_n^2(z_0) A_0^{n,p}$$

$$+ \frac{1}{\varepsilon - \varepsilon_{n,p}} \left(\frac{V_1 a^3}{2\pi\lambda^2} \chi_n^2(z_1) A_1^{n,p} e^{-iX \frac{(y_0 - y_1)}{\lambda^2}} \right.$$

$$\left. \times \int_{-\infty}^{+\infty} dt \varphi_p(-x + t) \varphi_p(x + t) e^{it \frac{(y_0 - y_1)}{\lambda^2}} \right) \tag{III.32.21}$$

Or:

$$A_0^{n,p} \left(1 - \frac{V_0 a^3}{2\pi\lambda^2(\varepsilon - \varepsilon_{n,p})} \chi_n^2(z_0) \right)$$

$$- \frac{V_1 a^3}{2\pi\lambda^2(\varepsilon - \varepsilon_{n,p})} \chi_n^2(z_1) e^{-iX \frac{(y_0 - y_1)}{\lambda^2}} I_p A_1^{n,p} = 0 \tag{III.32.22}$$

We could proceed in the same way to express A_1^{np}. So, thanks to the degeneracy of the unperturbed Landau levels with respect to k_y, we are able to find that the two impurity bound states fulfil

$$\begin{pmatrix} B_{00} & B_{01} \\ B_{10} & B_{11} \end{pmatrix} = \begin{pmatrix} A_0^{np} \\ A_1^{np} \end{pmatrix} = 0 \qquad (\text{III.32.23})$$

(2) Thus, we have to solve:

$$B_{00}B_{11} - B_{01}B_{10} = 0 \qquad (\text{III.32.24})$$

The other solutions where the determinant is non-zero correspond to $A_0^{n,p} = A_1^{n,p} = 0$. There are $g_{n,p} - 2$ such solutions with the unperturbed energy if $g_{n,p}$ is the number of allowed k_y values at fixed n and p $\left(g_{n,p} = \frac{L_x L_y}{2\pi\lambda^2}\right)$.

(3) By expressing the B coefficients and after some manipulations, we get:

$$\varepsilon - \varepsilon_{n,p} = \frac{1}{4\pi\lambda^2}(S \pm \sqrt{D^2 + 4V_0 V_1 a^6 \chi_n^2(z_0)\chi_n^2(z_1)|I_p|^2})$$

$$(\text{III.32.25})$$

$$S = V_0 a^3 \chi_n^2(z_0) + V_1 a^3 \chi_n^2(z_1); \quad D = V_0 a^3 \chi_n^2(z_0) - V_1 a^3 \chi_n^2(z_1)$$

$$(\text{III.32.26})$$

Like in the single impurity problem (see Chapter II.5 of Part II) we find a departure from the unperturbed energy that is proportional to B. However, there is an extra B-dependence that comes from I_p term.

(4) It is clear that I_p gives a measure of the spatial correlation between the two single impurity solutions. These are:

$$\varepsilon_0 - \varepsilon_{n,p} = \frac{V_0 a^3 \chi_n^2(z_0)}{2\pi\lambda^2}; \quad \varepsilon_1 - \varepsilon_{n,p} = \frac{V_1 a^3 \chi_n^2(z_1)}{2\pi\lambda^2} \qquad (\text{III.32.27})$$

With $p = 0$ there is: $I_0 = \exp\left(-\frac{1}{4\lambda^2}[(x_0 - x_1)^2 + (y_0 - y_1)^2]\right)$. Hence, the two single impurity solutions will have overlap if the in-plane distance ρ_{01} is $\approx$ or $< \lambda$.

Suppose the two impurities have the same strength and sign. Thus, $D = 0$ and if we consider two "acceptor"-like scatterers

$(V_0 > 0)$, there is:

$$\varepsilon - \varepsilon_{n,p=0} = \frac{V_0 a^3 \chi_n^2(z_0)}{2\pi\lambda^2}(1 \pm |I_0|) \qquad \text{(III.32.28)}$$

We recognise a familiar bonding-antibonding splitting between the two identical impurity levels. A remarkable feature is the Gaussian (and not exponential) decrease of the splitting with the impurity distance.

In the case of a "donor–acceptor" pair, there is $S = 0$ and $D = 2V_0 a^3 \chi_n^2(z_0)$. Taking $D > 0$, we get:

$$\varepsilon_0 - \varepsilon_{n,p} = \pm\frac{V_0 a^3 \chi_n^2(z_0)}{2\pi\lambda^2}\sqrt{1 - I_0^2} \qquad \text{(III.32.29)}$$

We show in Fig. 32.1 the variation of the defect-related eigenstates versus the defect distance in the two cases of two identical "acceptors" and a "donor–acceptor" pairs.

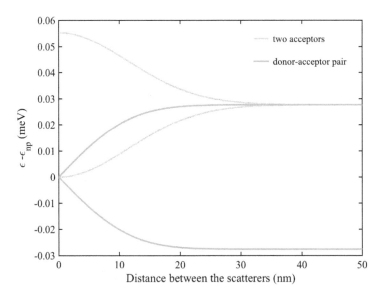

Figure 32.1.   Variation of the defect related eigenstates versus the defect distance in the case of two acceptors and a donor–acceptor pair. The calculation is done for a single GaAs/Ga$_{0.7}$Al$_{0.3}$As quantum well of thickness 3 nm. $V_0 = 0.2$ eV, $a = 0.6$ nm and the magnetic field is set at 10 T. The location of the scatterers z_0 coincides with the centre of the quantum well.

When there is a pair of remote point-like acceptors, the pair spectrum consists of two nearly degenerate levels. Decreasing the distance between the acceptors leads to the well-known bonding/antibonding splitting. At vanishing distance between the acceptors, the bonding state has become a double acceptor while the antibonding state has a vanishing effective V_0.

The donor–acceptor pair displays a very similar behaviour. At large distance between the donor and the acceptor, the acceptor (respectively, donor) bound state lays above (respectively, below) the centre of the Landau level by the same energy distance. When the donor–acceptor pair distance decreases, the binding energy of each component decreases (in a symmetrical fashion) due to the repulsive interaction with the other component of the pair. When the donor and the acceptor coalesce, the effective V_0 vanishes and the resulting pair energy coincides with the centre of the unperturbed Landau level.

33. Time-dependent evolution in an infinitely deep quantum well

Consider a quantum well with infinite barriers and thickness L. At $t = 0$ an electron is placed in a state that is an equal mixture of the ground and first excited state of the quantum well. Find the time evolution of its position.

Solution

A quantum well with thickness L and infinite barriers has a spectrum:

$$\varepsilon_n = n^2 \hbar \omega_0; \quad \omega_0 = \frac{\hbar \pi^2}{2mL^2} \tag{III.33.1}$$

with the associated eigenfunctions:

$$\chi_n(x) = \sqrt{\frac{2}{L}} \sin\left(\frac{n\pi x}{L}\right) \tag{III.33.2}$$

According to the text, the normalised electron wavefunction at time $t = 0$ is:

$$\chi(x, 0) = \frac{1}{\sqrt{L}} \left[\sin\left(\frac{\pi x}{L}\right) + \sin\left(\frac{2\pi x}{L}\right) \right] \tag{III.33.3}$$

Then, according to the general rule, its wavefunction at time t will be:

$$\chi(x,t) = \frac{1}{\sqrt{L}}\left[\sin\left(\frac{\pi x}{L}\right)e^{-i\omega_0 t} + \sin\left(\frac{2\pi x}{L}\right)e^{-4i\omega_0 t}\right] \qquad \text{(III.33.4)}$$

Hence:

$$\langle x\rangle(t) = \langle\chi(t)|x|\chi(t)\rangle = \frac{1}{L}\int_0^L dx\, x\left[\sin^2\left(\frac{\pi x}{L}\right) + \sin^2\left(\frac{2\pi x}{L}\right)\right.$$

$$\left. +2\cos(3\omega_0 t)\sin\left(\frac{\pi x}{L}\right)\sin\left(\frac{2\pi x}{L}\right)\right]$$

$$= \frac{L}{2}\left[1 - \frac{32}{9\pi^2}\cos(3\omega_0 t)\right] \qquad \text{(III.33.5)}$$

We note that this oscillating dipole will couple to the electric field of an electromagnetic (em) wave. Resonant absorption/emission will show up when ω, the angular frequency of the em wave, is equal to $3\omega_0$: Or, equivalently, when the photons of the em wave have an energy equal to the energy difference between ε_1 and ε_2:

$$\hbar\omega = \varepsilon_2 - \varepsilon_1 = 3\hbar\omega_0 \qquad \text{(III.33.6)}$$

34. Time-dependent problem: evolution

We consider the time-dependent evolution of a particle with mass m. The particle can move only along the x-axis. It is subjected to a time-dependent potential energy $V(x,t)$ such that:

$$V(x,t) = 0, \quad t \leq 0 \qquad \text{(III.34.1)}$$
$$V(x,t) = -Va\delta(x), \quad 0 \leq t \leq \tau \qquad \text{(III.34.2)}$$
$$V(x,t) = 0, \quad t \geq \tau \qquad \text{(III.34.3)}$$

When t is large and negative ($t = -T$) the particle is in the state $|k_0\rangle$ corresponding to a positive velocity (i.e., $k_0 > 0$). What is the probability that it will be found in the same state $|k_0\rangle$ when $t \gg \tau$?

Hint: It might be helpful to expand $|\psi(t)\rangle$ over the $|k\rangle$ basis or over the $|\nu\rangle$ basis generated by the eigenstates of $p^2/2m - Va\delta(x)$.

Solution

For $-T \leq t \leq 0$ the particle is free. Since its initial state is an eigenstate of the free particle Hamiltonian, it will remain in this state. At time t, there is:

$$|\psi(-T \leq t \leq 0)\rangle = |k_0\rangle \exp\left[-i(t+T)\frac{\hbar k_0^2}{2m}\right] \qquad \text{(III.34.4)}$$

Thus at $t = 0$ we have:

$$|\psi(t=0)\rangle = |k_0\rangle \exp\left(-iT\frac{\hbar k_0^2}{2m}\right) \qquad \text{(III.34.5)}$$

For $0 \leq t \leq \tau$ the Hamiltonian of the system is now:

$$H = \frac{p^2}{2m} - Va\delta(x) \qquad \text{(III.34.6)}$$

As we have seen before this Hamiltonian admits one bound state and extended states.

We denote $|\nu\rangle$ the eigenstates of H. Suppose $|\psi(t=0)\rangle$ is known. Then, we project $|\psi(t=0)\rangle$ onto the $|\nu\rangle$ basis:

$$|\psi(t=0)\rangle = \sum_\nu |\nu\rangle\langle\nu|\psi(t=0)\rangle \qquad \text{(III.34.7)}$$

The state at time t $|\psi(0 \leq t \leq \tau)\rangle$ is then known:

$$|\psi(0 \leq t \leq \tau)\rangle = \sum_\nu |\nu\rangle\langle\nu|\psi(t=0)\rangle \exp\left(-i\frac{\varepsilon_\nu t}{\hbar}\right) \qquad \text{(III.34.8)}$$

and we have:

$$|\psi(\tau)\rangle = \sum_\nu |\nu\rangle\langle\nu|\psi(t=0)\rangle \exp\left(-i\frac{\varepsilon_\nu \tau}{\hbar}\right) \qquad \text{(III.34.9)}$$

For $t \geq \tau$ the particle is again free and its state at $t = \tau$ is a super-position of plane wave states:

$$|\psi(\tau)\rangle = \sum_k c(k)|k\rangle \text{ with } c(k) = \sum_\nu \langle k|\nu\rangle\langle\nu|\psi(t=0)\rangle \exp\left(-i\frac{\varepsilon_\nu \tau}{\hbar}\right) \qquad \text{(III.34.10)}$$

So finally:

$$|\psi(t)\rangle = \sum_k c(k)|k\rangle \exp\left[-i(t-\tau)\frac{\hbar k^2}{2m}\right] \qquad \text{(III.34.11)}$$

The probability to find the particle at time t in the same state as at $t = -T$ is $P_S(t) = |\langle k_0 | \psi(t) \rangle|^2$:

$$P_S(t) = |c(k_0)|^2 = \left| \sum_\nu \langle k_0 | \nu \rangle \langle \nu | \psi(t=0) \rangle \exp\left(-i\frac{\varepsilon_\nu \tau}{\hbar}\right) \right|^2$$

$$= \left| \sum_\nu |\langle k_0 | \nu \rangle|^2 \exp\left(-i\frac{\varepsilon_\nu \tau}{\hbar}\right) \right|^2 \tag{III.34.12}$$

We note that, as expected, $P_S(t)$ is 1 if $\tau = 0$ since in this limit the particle has remained in the $|k_0\rangle$ eigenstate.

The states $|\nu\rangle$ comprise a single bound state and continuum states. The latter are analysed in terms of scattering states. Each of the continuum energy is twice degenerate. This degeneracy corresponds to having either at large distance in the left an impinging plane wave $f_+(x) = e^{ikx}$, $k > 0$, which is partially reflected and partially transmitted at $x = 0$ and finally moves on towards $+\infty$ or a particle that comes from $+\infty$ as $f_-(x)e^{-ikx}$ and is partially transmitted and partially reflected at $x = 0$ to move on at constant speed $-\hbar k/m$ towards $-\infty$:

$$f_+(x) = e^{ikx} + re^{-ikx}, \quad x \leq 0; \; f_+(x) = te^{ikx}, \quad x \geq 0 \tag{III.34.13}$$

$$f_-(x) = te^{-ikx}, \quad x \leq 0; \; f_-(x) = e^{-ikx} + re^{ikx}, \quad x \geq 0 \tag{III.34.14}$$

$$\varepsilon_\pm = \frac{\hbar^2 k^2}{2m} \tag{III.34.15}$$

The reflection coefficient R and transmission coefficient T are, respectively, equal to $R = |r|^2$ and $T = |t|^2$. They fulfil the conservation law: $R + T = 1$. f_+ and f_- need to be normalised over a macroscopic length L (like a regular plane wave). It is easily checked that the normalisation constant is $L^{-1/2}$ like a plane wave. We immediately compute:

$$\langle k_0 | f_+ \rangle = \frac{1}{2}[1 + t(k_0)]\delta_{k,k_0} + \frac{r(-k_0)}{2}\delta_{k,-k_0} \tag{III.34.16}$$

$$\langle k_0 | f_- \rangle = \frac{1}{2}[1 + t(-k_0)]\delta_{k,-k_0} + \frac{r(k_0)}{2}\delta_{k,k_0} \tag{III.34.17}$$

In the P_S expression, the summation over ν implies a summation over the two continuum states $f_\pm$ in addition to the inclusion of the bound state. Because of the Kronecker delta symbols, the summation over ν actually reduces to a summation over $\pm$. This results in:

$$|\langle k_0|f_+\rangle|^2 + |\langle k_0|f_-\rangle|^2 = \frac{1}{4}\{2 + 2\mathrm{Re}[t(k_0)]\} \tag{III.34.18}$$

$$P_S = |A_S|^2; \quad A_s = A_S^{\mathrm{cont}} + A_S^{\mathrm{bound}} \tag{III.34.19}$$

$$A_S^{\mathrm{cont}} = \frac{1}{4}\{2 + 2\,\mathrm{Re}[t(k_0)]\}\exp\left(-i\frac{\tau\hbar k_0^2}{2m}\right) \tag{III.34.20}$$

where:

$$t(k_0) = \left(1 - i\frac{maV}{\hbar^2 k_0^2}\right)^{-1} \tag{III.34.21}$$

As for the bound state contribution to P_S, we expand the bound state wavefunction on the plane wave basis:

$$|\varphi_{\mathrm{bound}}\rangle = \sum_k \varphi_k|k\rangle \tag{III.34.22}$$

This leads to:

$$\varphi_{k_0} = \frac{2\kappa}{\kappa^2 + k_0^2}\sqrt{\frac{\kappa}{L}}; \quad \kappa = V\frac{ma}{\hbar^2} \tag{III.34.23}$$

$$A_S^{\mathrm{bound}} = |\varphi_{k_0}|^2\exp\left(\frac{i\tau\eta}{\hbar}\right); \quad \eta = V^2\frac{ma^2}{2\hbar^2} \tag{III.34.24}$$

$$P_S(\tau) = \left|\,|\varphi_{k_0}|^2\exp\left(\frac{i\tau\eta}{\hbar}\right) + \frac{1}{4}\{2 + 2\,\mathrm{Re}[t(k_0)]\}\exp\left(-i\frac{\tau\hbar k_0^2}{2m}\right)\right|^2 \tag{III.34.25}$$

where $-\eta$ is the energy of the bound state and κ the characteristic length of its exponential decay.

We note that $P_S \to 1$ when $k_0 \to \infty$: the bound state wavefunction has increasingly smaller Fourier components at increasingly larger k_0 on the one hand while the transmission goes to one at large kinetic energy. We also notice that the bound state contribution is negligible in the macroscopic limit ($L \to \infty$). It would have a significant weight only if the initial state had a localisation length comparable to κ^{-1}.

35.   A touch of interaction representation

The time-dependent Schrödinger equation

$$i\hbar\frac{\partial|\psi(t)\rangle}{\partial t} = [H_0 + V(t)]|\psi(t)\rangle; \quad |\psi(t_0)\rangle = |\eta\rangle \qquad \text{(III.35.1)}$$

can be conveniently solved by eliminating the time-dependent contributions due to H_0.

Define the new state vector:

$$|\varphi(t)\rangle = e^{\frac{i}{\hbar}H_0(t-t_0)}|\psi(t)\rangle \qquad \text{(III.35.2)}$$

(1) What is the equation fulfilled by $|\varphi(t)\rangle$? What is the boundary condition at $t = t_0$?

(2) Project this equation on the basis $|n\rangle$ of the H_0 eigenstates.

Solution

By injecting the chosen $|\varphi(t)\rangle$ we get readily:

$$i\hbar\frac{\partial|\varphi(t)\rangle}{\partial t} = e^{\frac{i}{\hbar}H_0(t-t_0)}V(t)e^{-\frac{i}{\hbar}H_0(t-t_0)}|\varphi(t)\rangle; \quad |\varphi(t_0)\rangle = |\eta\rangle$$
$$\text{(III.35.3)}$$

H_0 has disappeared from the time evolution of $|\varphi(t)\rangle$. Let us project this new Schrödinger equation on the basis of H_0:

$$|\varphi(t)\rangle = \sum_n c_n(t)|n\rangle; \quad c_n(t_0) = \langle n|\varphi\rangle \qquad \text{(III.35.4)}$$

We find:

$$i\hbar\frac{dc_n}{dt} = \sum_m \langle n|V(t)|m\rangle e^{i\frac{t}{\hbar}(\varepsilon_n - \varepsilon_m)(t-t_0)}c_m(t) \qquad \text{(III.35.5)}$$

This set of equations is very useful when $V(t)$ is a small perturbation to H_0. Since we have managed to eliminate the fast evolutions associated with H_0, (III.35.5) is a convenient way to search for solutions $(c_n(t))$ in ascending powers of $V(t)$ (see Section I.3.3 for time-dependent perturbation calculus).

36. Time evolution if A and H commute

We consider a time-independent Hamiltonian H and we let A be a self-adjoint operator (a similar exercise can be found in [85]). We consider the two operators:

$$U(t) = \exp\left(-\frac{i}{\hbar}Ht\right); \quad G(\alpha) = \exp\left(-\frac{i}{\hbar}A\alpha\right) \quad \text{(III.36.1)}$$

Let $[C, D] = CD - DC$ be the commutator of the two operators C and D.

(1) Suppose

$$[H, A] = 0 \quad \text{(III.36.2)}$$

Show that

$$[U(t), A] = 0; \quad [G(t), A] = 0; \quad [G(t), U(t)] = 0 \quad \text{(III.36.3)}$$

Hint: Taylor-expand $G(t)$ and $U(t)$.

(2) Derive from $[H, A] = 0$ that $\langle\psi(t)|A|\psi(t)\rangle$ is time independent: the average value of an operator which commutes with a time-independent Hamiltonian is independent of time if this average is taken over the state $|\psi(t)\rangle$ that results from the evolution governed by H.

Solution

(1) Let us expand $U(t)$ and $G(t)$ in Taylor series (we are entitled to do that at any time t because the exponential function is nicely behaved: its Taylor expansion has an infinite convergence radius). Thus:

$$U(t) = \sum_{n=0}^{\infty}\left(-\frac{it}{\hbar}\right)^n \frac{H^n}{n!}; \quad G(t) = \sum_{m=0}^{\infty}\left(-\frac{it}{\hbar}\right)^m \frac{A^m}{m!} \quad \text{(III.36.4)}$$

We now use the fact that if $[A, B] = 0$ then $[A, B^p] = 0$ and $[A^m, B] = 0$ (this is easily proven by induction on p or m). Then we get right away $[U(t), A] = 0$. $G(t)$ being a function of A it commutes with A and at any t there is $[G(t), A] = 0$.

As for $[G(t), U(t)]$, we Taylor-expand say G to get:

$$[G(t), U(t)] = \sum_{m=0}^{\infty} \left(-\frac{it}{\hbar}\right)^m \frac{1}{m!} [A^m, U(t)] \qquad \text{(III.36.5)}$$

Since $[A, U(t)] = 0$, then $[A^2, U(t)] = 0$ and as well $[A^m, U(t)] = 0$. Hence, we get the required $[G(t), U(t)] = 0$.

(2) This small piece of linear algebra has consequences. Notably if $[A, H] = 0$ then we shall prove that the average of the operator A over the quantum state that evolves due to H is actually time independent. In effect, the formal solution of $i\hbar \partial \psi / \partial t = H|\psi\rangle$ is:

$$|\psi(t)\rangle = U(t - t_0)|\psi(t_0)\rangle \qquad \text{(III.36.6)}$$

Thus:

$$\langle \psi(t)|A|\psi(t)\rangle = \langle \psi(t_0)|U^\dagger(t - t_0)AU(t - t_0)|\psi(t_0)\rangle \qquad \text{(III.36.7)}$$

$$\langle \psi(t_0)|U^\dagger(t - t_0)U(t - t_0)A|\psi(t_0)\rangle = \langle \psi(t_0)|A|\psi(t_0)\rangle \qquad \text{(III.36.8)}$$

Note the crucial part played by the assumption of a time-independent Hamiltonian. Suppose in fact that H depends on t. Then, if at a certain time t_0 there was $[H(t_0), A] = 0$, there is no warrantee that this will still be true at another time because the Hamiltonian will be different. A simple example is provided by:

$$H(t) = H_0 + eFz \cos(\omega t); \quad [A, H_0] = 0 \qquad \text{(III.36.9)}$$

Then for $t_n = (2n+1)\pi/(2\omega)$ there is $[H[(2n+1)\pi/(2\omega)], A] = 0$ but in general $[H(t), A] \neq 0$ (try e.g., $A = p_z$, $H_0 = p_z^2/(2m)$).

37. Oscillator: time evolution of averages

Find the time evolution of the operator x and p if:

$$H(t) = \frac{p^2}{2m^*} + \frac{1}{2}m^*\Omega^2 x^2 + eFx + efx \cos(\omega t) + Ax^3 \qquad \text{(III.37.1)}$$

(1) First let $A = 0$. The Hamiltonian corresponds to a charged harmonic oscillator interacting with both static and a time-dependent electric field. Compare this quantum analysis to the classical one.

(2) Let $A \neq 0$. The Hamiltonian corresponds to a charged anharmonic oscillator interacting with both a static and a time-dependent electric field. Compare the quantum analysis to the classical one.

Solution

(1)

$$\frac{d\langle x \rangle}{dt} = \frac{\langle p \rangle}{m^*}; \quad \frac{d\langle p \rangle}{dt} = -m^* \Omega^2 \langle x \rangle - eF - ef \cos(\omega t) \quad \text{(III.37.2)}$$

$$\Rightarrow m^* \frac{d^2 \langle x \rangle}{dt^2} = -m^* \Omega^2 \langle x \rangle - eF - ef \cos(\omega t) \quad \text{(III.37.3)}$$

Hence the equations governing the time evolution of the average position (linear momentum) are exactly the same as found in classical mechanics for the particle trajectory. Note that this is not a general result as one may find easily by replacing the quadratic potential by a higher power in x. The harmonic oscillator (or the linearly varying potential energy) has a quantum behaviour that leads to averages that are very close from the classical description.

(2) If $A \neq 0$, we find easily that:

$$m^* \frac{d^2 \langle x \rangle}{dt^2} = -m^* \Omega^2 \langle x \rangle - eF - ef \cos(\omega t) - 3A \langle x^2 \rangle \quad \text{(III.37.4)}$$

This time the exact correspondence between the classical and quantum results is lost because $\langle x^2 \rangle \neq \langle x \rangle^2$ (otherwise that would mean that there is no mean square deviation on the position of the particle).

38. Time evolution of a system where one level is coupled to N degenerate levels

We consider a level $|l\rangle$ and N degenerate levels $|i\rangle$, $1 \leq i \leq N$. The energy associated with $|l\rangle$ is ε_l. The N levels are degenerate. Their energy is ε_0 and $\langle i|j \rangle = \delta_{ij}$. The level $|l\rangle$ is coupled to the levels $|i\rangle$ by a matrix element:

$$\langle l|H|i \rangle = \lambda_i \quad \text{(III.38.1)}$$

At $t = 0$ the system is in the state $|l\rangle$. Find the survival probability in this state $P(t)$, i.e., the probability that the system will be found in the state $|l\rangle$ at time t.

Solution

We write the $(N + 1) \times (N + 1)$ matrix representing H in the basis spanned by $|l\rangle$ and $|i\rangle$, $1 \le i \le N$

$$
H = \begin{pmatrix}
\varepsilon_l & \lambda_1 & \lambda_2 & \cdots & \lambda_{N-1} & \lambda_N \\
\lambda_1^* & \varepsilon_0 & 0 & 0 & 0 & 0 \\
\lambda_2^* & 0 & \varepsilon_0 & 0 & 0 & 0 \\
\vdots & 0 & 0 & \ddots & 0 & 0 \\
\lambda_{N-1}^* & 0 & 0 & 0 & \varepsilon_0 & 0 \\
\lambda_N^* & 0 & 0 & 0 & 0 & \varepsilon_0
\end{pmatrix}
\tag{III.38.2}
$$

The general form of the eigenstates is:

$$
|\psi\rangle = c_l |l\rangle + \sum_{i=1} d_i |i\rangle
\tag{III.38.3}
$$

There are $N - 1$ eigenvalues that correspond to $c_l = 0$. They are degenerate and coincide with the unperturbed solutions $\varepsilon = \varepsilon_0$. The only constraint that the N unknown coefficients d_i must fulfil is:

$$
\sum_{i=1}^{N} \lambda_i d_i = 0
\tag{III.38.4}
$$

We can for instance choose:

$$
\vec{v}_1 = \frac{1}{\sqrt{1 + \left(\frac{\lambda_1}{\lambda_2}\right)^2}} \left(0, 1, -\frac{\lambda_1}{\lambda_2}, 0, 0, \dots, 0, 0\right)
\tag{III.38.5}
$$

$$
\vec{v}_2 = \frac{1}{\sqrt{2 + \left(\frac{\lambda_1 + \lambda_2}{\lambda_3}\right)^2}} \left(0, 1, 1, -\frac{\lambda_1 + \lambda_2}{\lambda_3}, 0, \dots, 0, 0\right)
\tag{III.38.6}
$$

$$\vec{v}_3 = \frac{1}{\sqrt{3 + \left(\frac{\lambda_1 + \lambda_2 + \lambda_3}{\lambda_4}\right)^2}} \left(0, 1, 1, 1, -\frac{\lambda_1 + \lambda_2 + \lambda_3}{\lambda_4}, 0, \ldots, 0, 0\right)$$

$$(\text{III.38.7})$$

$$\vdots$$

Note that these vectors are not orthogonal to each other and a subsequent work would be to render them orthogonal by a suitable procedure (e.g., Gram–Schmidt). With our example, this gives:

$$\vec{u}_1 = \vec{v}_1 \qquad (\text{III.38.8})$$

$$\vec{u}_2 = \frac{\vec{v}_2 - (\vec{v}_2 \cdot \vec{u}_1)\vec{u}_1}{\|\vec{v}_2 - (\vec{v}_2 \cdot \vec{u}_1)\vec{u}_1\|} \qquad (\text{III.38.9})$$

$$\vec{u}_3 = \frac{\vec{v}_3 - (\vec{v}_3 \cdot \vec{u}_1)\vec{u}_1 - (\vec{v}_3 \cdot \vec{u}_2)\vec{u}_2}{\|\vec{v}_3 - (\vec{v}_3 \cdot \vec{u}_1)\vec{u}_1 - (\vec{v}_3 \cdot \vec{u}_2)\vec{u}_2\|} \qquad (\text{III.38.10})$$

$$\vdots$$

Besides these $N - 1$ solutions there are two solutions where $c_1 \neq 0$. One eliminates all the d_i's to the benefit of c_l and get:

$$d_i = \frac{\lambda_i^*}{\varepsilon - \varepsilon_0} c_l \qquad (\text{III.38.11})$$

So, we obtain either $c_l = 0$ (not interesting since d_i is also 0) or:

$$(\varepsilon_l - \varepsilon) + \sum_i \frac{|\lambda_i|^2}{-\varepsilon_0 + \varepsilon} = 0 \qquad (\text{III.38.12})$$

hence, the two solutions:

$$\varepsilon_\pm = \frac{\varepsilon_0 + \varepsilon_l}{2} \pm \sqrt{\left(\frac{\varepsilon_0 - \varepsilon_l}{2}\right)^2 + \sum_i |\lambda_i|^2} \qquad (\text{III.38.13})$$

What is interesting in Eq. (III.38.13) is the fact that the coupling with the continuum selects a single particular linear combination of degenerate states to hybridise it with the localised state. The coupling (which has an arbitrary shape/length in our discussion through the λ_i) in all cases effectively transforms our problem into a 2-level system problem. Moreover, the strength of the repulsion at resonance is proportional to $\sqrt{N}$ if the coupling constants λ_i are of the same order of magnitude. Hence, it is no wonder that the time evolution of the discrete level $|l\rangle$ reveals Rabi-like oscillations as we shall see below.

For the two solutions $\varepsilon_\pm$, the normalised states are such that:

$$c_{l\pm} = \left(1 + \frac{\sum_i |\lambda_i|^2}{(\varepsilon_\pm - \varepsilon_0)^2} \right)^{-1/2} \tag{III.38.14}$$

The time evolution of the survival probability $P_s(t)$ is obtained by applying the evolution operator to the initial state:

$$P_s(t) = |\langle l|\psi(t)\rangle|^2 = |\langle l|e^{-i\frac{H}{\hbar}t}|l\rangle|^2 \tag{III.38.15}$$

Only the two interacting states display a non-zero component on $|l\rangle$. Hence, Eq. (III.38.15) becomes:

$$P_s(t) = ||\langle l|+\rangle|^2 e^{-i\frac{\varepsilon_+}{\hbar}t} + |\langle l|-\rangle|^2 e^{-i\frac{\varepsilon_-}{\hbar}t}|^2$$

$$= |\langle l|+\rangle|^4 + |\langle l|-\rangle|^4 + 2|\langle l|+\rangle|^2|\langle l|-\rangle|^2 \cos\left(\frac{\varepsilon_+ - \varepsilon_-}{\hbar}\right)t \tag{III.38.16}$$

Equation (III.38.16) shows very clearly that in this *a priori* complicated time evolution there is nothing but the Rabi oscillations between the two only possible states that have a non-zero projection on $|l\rangle$. In the case of a degeneracy between ε_0 and ε_l we find:

$$\varepsilon_\pm = \varepsilon_l \pm \sqrt{\sum_i |\lambda_i|^2}; \quad c_{l\pm} = \frac{1}{\sqrt{2}} \tag{III.38.17}$$

$$P_s(t) = \frac{1}{2} + \frac{1}{2}\cos\left(\frac{2t}{\hbar}\sqrt{\sum_i |\lambda_i|^2}\right) \tag{III.38.18}$$

This model applies to a very large number of physical situations. For instance, the polaron effect in quantum dots can be analysed using Eqs. (III.38.13)–(III.38.16). In this problem there is a resonant coupling of a continuum that arises from an electron state (S) and one longitudinal optical (LO) phonon (energy $\hbar\omega_0$ in many possible modes labelled by the phonon wavevector Q_i, $i = 1, 2, \ldots, N$) and a discrete level that comprises an excited electron state (P_-) with zero phonons [86]. Since $|P_-\rangle$ can be pulled down in energy to approach the one LO phonon replica of the ground state $|S\rangle$, it is possible to study in detail how the electron–phonon coupling will affect the interacting levels.

The discrete level ($|l\rangle$ in our notations) is:

$$|l\rangle = |P_-\rangle \otimes \prod_i \otimes |0_{\vec{Q}_i}\rangle \qquad (\text{III.38.19})$$

while the N degenerate states are:

$$|i\rangle = |S\rangle \otimes |1_{\vec{Q}_i}\rangle \otimes \prod_{j \neq i} |0_{\vec{Q}_j}\rangle \qquad (\text{III.38.20})$$

These $|l\rangle$ and $|i\rangle$ are eigenstates of the non-interacting electron and phonon Hamiltonian:

$$H = H_{\text{e}} + \hbar\omega_0 \sum_{\vec{Q}} \left(a_{\vec{Q}}^\dagger a_{\vec{Q}} + \frac{1}{2} \right) \qquad (\text{III.38.21})$$

The states $|l\rangle$ and $|i\rangle$ are coupled because of the electron–phonon interaction

$$H_{\text{e-ph}} = \sum_{\vec{Q}} u_\alpha(\vec{Q}) e^{-i\vec{Q}\cdot\vec{r}} a_{\alpha\vec{Q}}^\dagger + u_\alpha^*(\vec{Q}) e^{i\vec{Q}\cdot\vec{r}} a_{\alpha\vec{Q}} \qquad (\text{III.38.22})$$

where α denotes the LO phonon mode and the $u_\alpha(\vec{Q})$'s are the Fröhlich terms (see Eq. (II.3.36) in Part II).

The λ_i are therefore equal to:

$$\lambda_i = u_\alpha(\vec{Q}_i)\langle P_-|e^{i\vec{Q}_i\cdot\vec{r}}|S\rangle \langle 0_{\vec{Q}_i}|a_{\alpha\vec{Q}_i}|1_{\vec{Q}_i}\rangle = u_\alpha(\vec{Q}_i)\langle P_-|e^{i\vec{Q}_i\cdot\vec{r}}|S\rangle \qquad (\text{III.38.23})$$

39. Time-dependent Hamiltonian: an exactly solvable model

Suppose the time-dependent Hamiltonian governing the evolution of a system can be factorised in the form:

$$H(t) = H_0 f(t) \qquad (\text{III.39.1})$$

where $f(t)$ is arbitrary.

We call E_n and $|\varphi_n\rangle$, respectively, the eigenenergies and eigenfunctions of H_0. Solve the TDSE knowing that at $t = 0$, the system was in state $|\alpha\rangle$.

Compute the average energy of the system at time t.

Solution

We note that at any t the functions $|\varphi_n\rangle$ remain eigenfunctions of $H(t)$ with eigenvalues $E_n f(t)$. Hence, we look for a solution:

$$|\psi(t)\rangle = \sum_n c_n(t) \exp\left(-\frac{iE_n}{\hbar} \int_0^t f(t')dt'\right) |\varphi_n\rangle \qquad \text{(III.39.2)}$$

Inserting into the TDSE and projecting on $\langle\varphi_n|$ we get readily that

$$\dot{c}_n(t) = 0 \Rightarrow c_n(t) = \text{cste} \qquad \text{(III.39.3)}$$

The c_n values are determined by the initial condition:

$$|\alpha\rangle = \sum_n c_n|\varphi_n\rangle \Rightarrow c_n = \langle\varphi_n|\alpha\rangle \qquad \text{(III.39.4)}$$

Thus:

$$|\psi(t)\rangle = \sum_n \exp\left(-\frac{iE_n}{\hbar} \int_0^t f(t')dt'\right) |\varphi_n\rangle\langle\varphi_n|\alpha\rangle \qquad \text{(III.39.5)}$$

The average energy at time t is:

$$E(t) = \langle\psi(t)|H_0 f(t)|\psi(t)\rangle = \sum_n |\langle\varphi_n|\alpha\rangle|^2 E_n f(t) \qquad \text{(III.39.6)}$$

There are unfortunately not so many Hamiltonians that can be factorised in terms of a function of time times a t-independent hermitian operator. An example is:

$$H(t) = H_0 \cos(\omega t) = g\mu_B B\sigma_z \cos(\omega t) \qquad \text{(III.39.7)}$$

where σ_z is the dimensionless spin (with eigenvalues $\pm 1/2$), g the Landé factor and μ_B the Bohr magneton. The eigenfunctions of H_0 are:

$$|\psi_+\rangle = \begin{pmatrix} 1 \\ 0 \end{pmatrix}; \quad |\psi_-\rangle = \begin{pmatrix} 0 \\ 1 \end{pmatrix} \qquad \text{(III.39.8)}$$

They are associated with the eigenvalues $E_+ = +\frac{1}{2}g\mu_B B$, $E_- = -\frac{1}{2}g\mu_B B$ respectively. If the initial state is $|\alpha\rangle = \cos\theta|\psi_+\rangle + \sin\theta|\psi_-\rangle$, then the average energy at time t is:

$$E(t) = \frac{1}{2}g\mu_B B(\cos^2\theta - \sin^2\theta)\cos(\omega t) \qquad \text{(III.39.9)}$$

40. Time evolution of superlattice states

We consider a superlattice state ψ_q and we assume that it is well described by the nearest neighbour tight binding approximation:

$$\psi_q(z) = \frac{1}{\sqrt{2N+1}}\sum_{-N}^{+N} e^{iqnd}\varphi_{\text{loc}}(z-nd); \quad \varepsilon(q) = -\frac{\Delta}{2}\cos(qd) \qquad \text{(III.40.1)}$$

where N is very large, $-\pi/d \le q \le \pi/d$ and the φ_{loc} are taken as ortho-normalised:

$$\int_{-\infty}^{\infty} \varphi_{\text{loc}}^*(z-nd)\varphi_{\text{loc}}(z-md) = \delta_{nm} \qquad \text{(III.40.2)}$$

We are dealing exclusively with intraband effects and the band index has been dropped. Then, the completeness of the $|\Psi_q\rangle$ states reads:

$$\sum_q |\Psi_q\rangle\langle\Psi_q| = 1 \qquad \text{(III.40.3)}$$

(1) At $t=0$ the electron is in the state $\langle z|\psi(0)\rangle = \varphi_{\text{loc}}(z)$. Compute $|\psi(t)\rangle$ and its projection $A_n(t)$ on $\varphi_{\text{loc}}(z-nd)$:

$$A_n(t) = \int_{-\infty}^{\infty} dz\psi(z,t)\varphi_{\text{loc}}^*(z-nd) \qquad \text{(III.40.4)}$$

Hint: the formal solution of the time-dependent Schrödinger equation is

$$|\Psi(t)\rangle = \exp\left(-i\frac{Ht}{\hbar}\right)|\Psi(0)\rangle \qquad \text{(III.40.5)}$$

It will prove useful to express the completeness of the $|\Psi_q\rangle$ states.

(2) Same question if:

$$\langle z|\psi(0)\rangle = \frac{1}{\sqrt{2}}\left[\varphi_{\text{loc}}(z) + e^{i\alpha}\varphi_{\text{loc}}(z-d)\right] \qquad \text{(III.40.6)}$$

where α is a real number. Examine the case $n > 2$.

We give:

$$e^{iz\cos x} = J_0(z) + 2\sum_{k=1} i^k J_k(z)\cos(kx) \qquad \text{(III.40.7)}$$

where J_p is the Bessel function of order p which admits the Taylor expansion:

$$J_p(z) = \left(\frac{z}{2}\right)^p \sum_{k=0}(-1)^k \left(\frac{z}{2}\right)^{2k} \frac{1}{k!(p+k)!} \qquad \text{(III.40.8)}$$

As seen on the Taylor expansion J_{2n} and J_{2n+1} are, respectively, even and odd functions of their arguments. Besides:

$$J_{\pm p}(z) \approx \sqrt{\frac{2}{\pi z}}\cos\left(z \pm p\frac{\pi}{2} - \frac{\pi}{4}\right), \quad |z| \to \infty \qquad \text{(III.40.9)}$$

$$J_0^2(z) + 2\sum_{k=1} J_k^2(z) = 1 \qquad \text{(III.40.10)}$$

Solution

(1) Firstly because of the orthogonality of the φ_{loc}'s, one find easily that:

$$\int_{-\infty}^{+\infty} dz\psi_q(z)\varphi_{\text{loc}}^*(z-nd) = \frac{1}{\sqrt{2N+1}}e^{iqnd} \qquad \text{(III.40.11)}$$

Then, the formal solution of the time-dependent Schrödinger equation is in our case:

$$|\psi(t)\rangle = e^{-i\frac{Ht}{\hbar}}|\psi(0)\rangle = e^{-i\frac{Ht}{\hbar}}\sum_q |\psi_q\rangle\langle\psi_q|\psi(0)\rangle$$

$$= \sum_q |\psi_q\rangle\frac{1}{\sqrt{2N+1}}e^{-i\frac{\varepsilon(q)t}{\hbar}} \qquad \text{(III.40.12)}$$

where $\varepsilon(q)$ is the electron dispersion relation. Using the tight binding form

$$\varepsilon(q) - -\frac{\Delta}{2}\cos(qd) \qquad \text{(III.40.13)}$$

we get:

$$A_n(t) = \frac{d}{2\pi}\int_{-\pi/2}^{+\pi/2} dq\, e^{iqnd}\exp\left[i\left(\frac{\Delta t}{2\hbar}\right)\cos(qd)\right] \qquad \text{(III.40.14)}$$

By using the formulae given in the text, we obtain readily:

$$A_n(t) = \delta_{n0}J_0(x) + i^{-n}J_{-n}(x)Y(n<0) + i^n J_n(x)Y(n>0); \quad x = \frac{\Delta t}{\hbar}$$
$$\text{(III.40.15)}$$

where $Y(n<0) = 1$ if $n<0$ and $Y(n<0) = 0$ if $n>0$ and similarly for $Y(n>0)$.

Thus, we see that $|A_{-n}(t)|^2 = |A_n(t)|^2$: as time flows the state spreads symmetrically on each side of the cell $n = 0$. This is a breathing mode where there would not be any net current to the right or to the left.

A feature is noteworthy: it is the oscillatory structure displayed by the $|A_n(t)|^2$ versus time since the Bessel functions vanish an infinite number of times. This is in striking contrast with the free particle case where the departure from a given point is monotonic upon time. The main difference comes from the existence in the superlattice case of a natural energy scale: the bandwidth Δ and therefore of a natural time scale $T = h/\Delta$. We illustrate the non-monotonic departure from the $n = 0$ unit cell in Fig. 40.1 where we plot $J_0^2(x)$ versus $x = \frac{\Delta t}{2\hbar}$.

We show in Fig. 40.2 the time evolution of $|A_{10}|^2 = J_{10}^2(x)$ which is the probability to find the particle in the state localised around the tenth period at time t if it was localised around the period $n = 0$ at $t = 0$.

We see that at early time the probability is very small: classically the particle did not have time to reach the tenth period. Note that the initial state $\varphi_{\text{loc}}(z)$ corresponds to an energy which is at the center of the band. If it were a Bloch state it would have a maximum velocity of $v = \Delta d/(2\hbar)$. But being a localised state it has no average

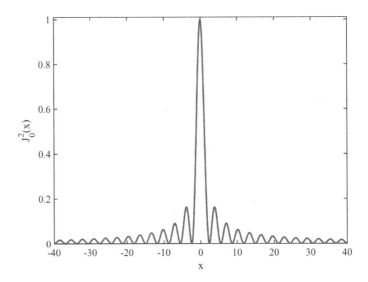

Figure 40.1.   Plot of the J_0^2 function versus $x = \frac{\Delta t}{2\hbar}$.

velocity at initial time:

$$
\begin{aligned}
\langle\psi(0)|v|\psi(0)\rangle &= \sum_{q,q'}\langle\psi(0)|\Psi_q\rangle\langle\Psi_q|v|\Psi_{q'}\rangle\langle\Psi_{q'}|\psi(0)\rangle \\
&= \sum_{q,q'}\langle\psi(0)|\Psi_q\rangle\frac{1}{\hbar}\frac{\partial\varepsilon(q)}{\partial q}\delta_{q,q'}\langle\Psi'_q|\psi(0)\rangle \\
&= \sum_{q}|\langle\psi(0)|\Psi_q\rangle|^2\frac{1}{\hbar}\frac{\partial\varepsilon(q)}{\partial q} \\
&= \frac{1}{2N+1}\sum_{q}\frac{1}{\hbar}\frac{\partial\varepsilon(q)}{\partial q} = 0 \qquad\qquad \text{(III.40.16)}
\end{aligned}
$$

where the last identity comes from the evenness in q of the dispersion relation, a feature due to the time reversal symmetry.

A classical free particle with velocity $v = \frac{\Delta d}{2\hbar}$ will need a time $10d/v$ to cover a distance of $10d$. Thus, the value of x corresponding to the arrival of the classical particle is $x_{\text{class}} = \frac{\Delta}{2\hbar}\frac{10d}{\Delta d}\times 2\hbar = 10$.

More generally the classical particle will arrive at the pth period at $x_{\text{class}} = p$. The quantum calculation provides a first maximum that is slightly larger (but surprisingly close) from the classical expectation as can be seen on Fig. 40.2. Of course, at longer times the classical

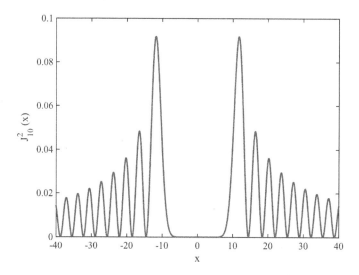

Figure 40.2. Time evolution of the probability $|A_{10}|^2 = J_{10}^2(x)$.

and quantum calculations differ radically since the classical probability would drop to zero after the particle has crossed the entire pth period while we see a non-monotonic quantum probability. The oscillations shown by $|A_p(t)|^2$ reflect the constructive and destructive interferences between the waves that are partially transmitted and partially reflected at the various boundaries. Note the decreasing envelopes which reflect the $1/t$ fall of J_{10}^2 at long time.

(2) We consider the case $n \geq 2$. Using the same method as in (1) we find:

$$A_n(t) = \frac{i^{p-1}}{\sqrt{2}}[iJ_n(x) + e^{i\alpha}J_{n-1}(x)]; \quad x = \frac{\Delta t}{2\hbar} \qquad \text{(III.40.17)}$$

and therefore:

$$|A_n(t)|^2 = \frac{1}{2}\left[J_n^2(x) + J_{n-1}^2(x) + 2\sin(\alpha)J_n(x)J_{n-1}(x)\right] \quad \text{(III.40.18)}$$

In contrast to the breathing mode, the initial state may have a non-zero velocity depending on α. In fact, proceeding as above one finds:

$$\langle\psi(0)|v|\psi(0)\rangle = \frac{d\Delta\sin\alpha}{4\hbar} \qquad \text{(III.40.19)}$$

If $\alpha = 0$ we find an even function of time for the squared projection on the localised state $\varphi_{loc}(z - 10d)$ since:

$$|A_{10}|^2 = \frac{1}{2}\left[J_{10}^2(z) + J_9^2(z)\right] \tag{III.40.20}$$

The difference with the case 1 is that the destructive interferences do not completely cancel $|A_{10}|^2$. For $\alpha = \pi/6$, $\pi/2$, the initial velocity is non-vanishing and the curve $|A_{10}|^2$ is no longer an even function of time. Actually if $\alpha = \pi/2$, there is:

$$|A_{10}(z)|^2 = \frac{1}{2}\left[J_{10}(z) + J_9(z)\right]^2 \tag{III.40.21}$$

and the difference between $t > 0$ and $t < 0$ becomes obvious since J_{10} and J_9 have opposite parities.

41.   Wavepackets

Consider the 1D wavepacket:

$$\langle z|\psi\rangle = \psi(z) = \sum_k \alpha(k)\frac{e^{ikz}}{\sqrt{L}} \to \frac{L}{2\pi}\int_{-\infty}^{\infty} dk\alpha(k)\frac{e^{ikz}}{\sqrt{L}} \tag{III.41.1}$$

where $\alpha(k)$ is a function that peaks at k_0 with a width $2\Delta k$ around k_0.

(1) Show by using the property of the Fourier transform that $\psi(z)$ is the product of a plane wave $\frac{e^{ik_0 z}}{\sqrt{L}}$ times an envelope $f(z)$ that extends over $\Delta z \approx \frac{1}{2\Delta k}$.

(2) Check this property by calculating explicitly $\psi(z)$ if $\alpha(k) = N\exp\left(-\frac{|k-k_0|}{\Delta k}\right)$ where N is a normalisation constant that ensures $\langle\psi|\psi\rangle = \int_{-\infty}^{\infty} dz|\psi(z)|^2 = 1$.

(3) What is the average velocity over the state $|\psi\rangle$ defined in 2?

(4) What is the average kinetic energy in the state $|\psi\rangle$ defined in 2?

Solution

(1)

$$\Delta z \Delta k \approx 1 \tag{III.41.2}$$

$$\psi(z) = e^{ik_0 z} \int_{-\infty}^{\infty} dq \alpha(k_0 + q) e^{iqz} \tag{III.41.3}$$

The function $\alpha(q)$ is maximum at $q = 0$ and it extends over $2\Delta k$ in the reciprocal space. Thus, its Fourier transform will extend over a length $\Delta z \approx 1/(2\Delta k)$.

(2) In the chosen example:

$$\psi(z) = \sqrt{\frac{2}{\pi}} (\Delta k)^{-3/2} e^{ik_0 z} \frac{1}{z^2 + \left(\frac{1}{\Delta k}\right)^2} \tag{III.41.4}$$

This function is indeed in agreement with the expected properties.

(3)

$$
\begin{aligned}
\langle \psi | v | \psi \rangle &= \sum_{k,k'} \alpha^*(k) \alpha(k') \frac{1}{L} \int dz e^{-ikz} \frac{p}{m^*} e^{ik'z} \\
&= \sum_{k,k'} \alpha^*(k) \alpha(k') \frac{1}{L} \frac{\hbar k'}{m^*} L \delta_{kk'} \\
&= \sum_{k} |\alpha(k)|^2 \frac{\hbar k}{m^*} = \frac{\hbar k_0}{m^*}
\end{aligned} \tag{III.41.5}
$$

since the wavepacket is an even function of $k - k_0$.

(4) Naïvely speaking we expect $\frac{\hbar^2 k_0^2}{2m^*}$. We shall see that this naïve expectation needs to be slightly revised.

$$\langle \psi | T | \psi \rangle = \sum_{k} |\alpha(k)|^2 \frac{\hbar^2 k^2}{2m^*} \tag{III.41.6}$$

$$k^2 = (k - k_0 + k_0)^2 = k_0^2 + (k - k_0)^2 + 2k_0(k - k_0) \tag{III.41.7}$$

The term linear in $k - k_0$ does not contribute. We are left with the first term that gives rise to the intuitive result. As for the last term, it can be written:

$$\sum_k |\alpha(k)|^2 \frac{\hbar^2(k-k_0)^2}{2m^*} \rightarrow \frac{L}{2\pi} N^2 \int dk \frac{\hbar^2(k-k_0)^2}{2m^*} e^{-2\frac{|k-k_0|}{\Delta k}}$$

$$= \frac{L}{\pi} N^2 \frac{\hbar^2}{m^*} \left(\frac{\Delta k}{2}\right)^3 \qquad \text{(III.41.8)}$$

$$1 = \frac{L}{2\pi} N^2 \Delta k \Rightarrow \sum_k |\alpha(k)|^2 \frac{\hbar^2(k-k_0)^2}{2m^*} \rightarrow \frac{\hbar^2}{2m^*} \frac{(\Delta k)^2}{2} \qquad \text{(III.41.9)}$$

$$\Rightarrow \langle \psi | T | \psi \rangle = \frac{\hbar^2 k_0^2}{2m^*} + \frac{\hbar^2}{2m^*} \frac{(\Delta k)^2}{2} \qquad \text{(III.41.10)}$$

42. Average velocity of a wavepacket

We consider 1D motions along the x-axis. $|k\rangle$ is a 1D plane wave:

$$\langle x | k \rangle = \frac{1}{\sqrt{L}} e^{ikx} \qquad \text{(III.42.1)}$$

$$\langle k | k' \rangle = \delta_{kk'} \qquad \text{(III.42.2)}$$

where L is the macroscopic length. The plane waves are idealisations of the actual situations because they correspond to electron states that are uniformly spread. They are not normalised in the usual sense. In reality, one should consider wavepackets, e.g., Gaussian, for $\langle x | k \rangle$:

$$\langle x | k \rangle_G = A \int_{-\infty}^{\infty} dq \exp(iqx) \exp\left[-\frac{(q-k)^2}{2\sigma^2}\right] \qquad \text{(III.42.3)}$$

where A is a normalisation constant to be determined. For these states there is:

$$_G\langle k | p_x | k' \rangle_G = \hbar k \delta_{k,k'} \qquad \text{(III.42.4)}$$

where δ is the Kronecker symbol:

$$\delta_{k,k'} = 1 \text{ if } k = k'; \quad \delta_{k,k'} = 0 \text{ if } k \neq k' \qquad \text{(III.42.5)}$$

To this end, compute the required matrix element between two Gaussian wavepackets $|k\rangle_G$ and $|k'\rangle_G$ and then let the spreading parameter σ going to zero.

Solution

By normalising the wavepacket to 1 over the x-axis we find readily that:

$$\langle x|k\rangle_G = \frac{\sqrt{\sigma}}{\pi^{1/4}} \exp\left(-\frac{\sigma^2 x^2}{2}\right) \exp(ikx) \qquad \text{(III.42.6)}$$

Then:

$$_G\langle k|p_x|k\rangle_G = -\frac{i\hbar\sigma}{\sqrt{\pi}} \int_{-\infty}^{+\infty} dx e^{ix(k'-k)} e^{-\sigma^2 x^2} (ik' - \sigma^2 x) \qquad \text{(III.42.7)}$$

$$\begin{aligned}
_G\langle k|p_x|k'\rangle_G &= \frac{\sigma}{\sqrt{\pi}} \exp\left(-\frac{(k-k')^2}{4\sigma^2}\right) \int_{-\infty}^{\infty} dx \\
&\quad \times \exp\left(-\left[\sigma x - i\frac{(k'-k)}{2\sigma}\right]^2\right) \\
&\quad \times (\hbar k' + i\hbar\sigma^2 x) \\
&= \hbar\frac{(k+k')}{2} \exp\left(-\frac{(k-k')^2}{4\sigma^2}\right) \qquad \text{(III.42.8)}
\end{aligned}$$

Now when σ goes to zero either $k \neq k'$ or $k = k'$. If $k \neq k'$ we find a vanishing matrix element in the limit of vanishing σ. If $k = k'$ the matrix element is equal to $\hbar k$ in particular when σ goes to zero. Hence, we are justified in stating that the matrix element in the limit of vanishing σ is equal to $\hbar k \delta_{kk'}$. The limit of vanishing σ is that of an envelope that spreads over an increasingly large distance and is modulated by the plane wave $\exp(ikx)$.

43. Time-dependent perturbation in a 2-level system

We consider a 2-level system $|a\rangle$, $|b\rangle$ with energies ε_a, ε_b. This system is weakly perturbed by an electromagnetic pulse whose electric field at the dipole approximation is written[2]:

$$\vec{F}(t) = \vec{e}_z F_0 e^{-\frac{|t|}{\tau}} \cos(\omega_L t) \qquad (\text{III.43.1})$$

Since the system has discrete states, we chose the gauge where $\vec{A} = 0$ and where the interaction between the 2-level system and the electromagnetic wave is written as:

$$V(t) = eF_0 z e^{-\frac{|t|}{\tau}} \cos(\omega_L t) \qquad (\text{III.43.2})$$

We assume $\langle a|z|a \rangle = \langle b|z|b \rangle = 0$ and $\langle a|z|b \rangle = \langle b|z|a \rangle \neq 0$.

We look for a solution of the time-dependent Schrödinger equation in the form:

$$|\psi(t)\rangle = c_a(t) e^{-i\frac{t}{\hbar}\varepsilon_a}|a\rangle + c_b(t) e^{-i\frac{t}{\hbar}\varepsilon_b}|b\rangle \qquad (\text{III.43.3})$$

Find the equations fulfilled by $c_a(t)$ and $c_b(t)$.

The boundary conditions are that $c_a(-\infty) = 1$, $c_b(-\infty) = 0$. Simplify the equations assuming that the perturbation is weak (i.e., that $c_b \ll c_a \approx 1$).

Compute the probability $P_b(t = +\infty)$ that the 2-level system is found in the $|b\rangle$ state at $t = +\infty$.

Study $P_b(t = +\infty)$ versus ω_L.

Solution

$$i\hbar \dot{c}_a = eF \langle a|z|b \rangle \cos(\omega_L t) e^{-\frac{|t|}{\tau}} c_b e^{-i\omega_{ba} t} \qquad (\text{III.43.4})$$

$$i\hbar \dot{c}_b = eF \langle b|z|a \rangle \cos(\omega_L t) e^{-\frac{|t|}{\tau}} c_a e^{i\omega_{ba} t} \qquad (\text{III.43.5})$$

If the perturbation is weak c_a remains ≈ 1 and we get:

$$c_b(t) \approx \frac{eF}{i\hbar} \langle b|z|a \rangle \int_{-\infty}^{t} dt' \cos(\omega_L t') e^{-\frac{|t'|}{\tau}} e^{i\omega_{ba} t'} \qquad (\text{III.43.6})$$

---

[2]Note that this $e^{-\frac{|t|}{\tau}}$ functional dependence has been chosen for computational conveniences. Actual pulses are rather Gaussian-shaped, i.e., vary like e^{-t^2/δ^2}

The probability to find the system in the $|b\rangle$ state at long time is $P_b(t \to \infty) = |c_b(t \to \infty)|^2$ where:

$$c_b(t \to \infty) \approx \frac{eF}{i\hbar} \langle b|z|a \rangle \int_{-\infty}^{+\infty} dt' \cos(\omega_L t') e^{-\frac{|t'|}{\tau}} \cos(\omega_{ba} t')$$

$$= \frac{eF}{i\hbar} \langle b|z|a \rangle \left(\int_0^{\infty} dt' e^{-\frac{t'}{\tau}} \cos[(\omega_L + \omega_{ba})t'] \right.$$

$$+ \left. \int_0^{\infty} dt' e^{-\frac{t'}{\tau}} \cos[(\omega_L - \omega_{ba})t'] \right)$$

$$= \frac{eF}{i\hbar} \langle b|z|a \rangle \mathrm{Re} \left(\int_0^{\infty} dt' e^{-\frac{t'}{\tau}} e^{i(\omega_L + \omega_{ba})t'} \right.$$

$$+ \left. \int_0^{\infty} dt' e^{-\frac{t'}{\tau}} e^{i(\omega_L - \omega_{ba})t'} \right)$$

$$= \frac{eF\tau}{i\hbar} \langle b|z|a \rangle \left(\frac{1}{1 + \tau^2(\omega_L + \omega_{ba})^2} + \frac{1}{1 + \tau^2(\omega_L - \omega_{ba})^2} \right)$$

$$(\text{III.43.7})$$

The coefficient c_b is the sum of the two Lorentzian functions associated with the two components of the electromagnetic wave. One will display a resonance when the centre of the pulse will coincide with the Bohr frequency of the material while the anti-resonant component will be featureless. To be consistent with our assumption $|c_b| \ll 1$ one should get $\frac{eF\tau}{\hbar} \langle b|z|a \rangle \ll 1$.

44. Universal absorption probability for interband transitions in graphene

Graphene is a 2D crystal with a honeycomb lattice. The unit cell comprises two carbon atoms. In the following, we shall assume that the $2p_z$ orbitals of the two carbon atoms in the unit cell have a zero overlap.

The effective Hamiltonian when written on the basis of the two (orthogonal) p_z functions is:

$$H_0 = \begin{pmatrix} 0 & v_F(p_x - ip_y) \\ v_F(p_x + ip_y) & 0 \end{pmatrix} \qquad (\text{III.44.1})$$

(1) Find the eigenstates of H_0 and show that they correspond to linear dispersions:

$$\vec{\psi}_{v\vec{k}} \rightarrow \varepsilon_v(\vec{k}) = -v_F\hbar k \qquad (III.44.2)$$

$$\vec{\psi}_{c\vec{k}} \rightarrow \varepsilon_c(\vec{k}) = +v_F\hbar k \qquad (III.44.3)$$

$$\vec{k} = k(\cos\theta, \sin\theta) \qquad (III.44.4)$$

Here the arrows on the state $\vec{\psi}$ recall that they are 2×1 column vectors on the basis of the two (orthogonal) p_z functions. Compute explicitly these (normalised) column vectors.

(2) In order to handle the coupling with light, we shall use the $\vec{A} \cdot \vec{p}$ gauge. Then, we have to replace $\vec{p}$ by $\vec{p} + e\vec{A}$, $e > 0$. We write:

$$\vec{E}(t) = -\frac{\partial\vec{A}}{\partial t} = \vec{\varepsilon}F_0\cos(\omega t) \;\Rightarrow\; \vec{A}(t) = -\vec{\varepsilon}\frac{F_0}{\omega}\sin(\omega t) \qquad (III.44.5)$$

where $\vec{\varepsilon}$ is a dimensionless polarisation vector.

Show that the Hamiltonian can now be written $H = H_0 + V(t)$ where:

$$V(t) = \begin{pmatrix} 0 & \frac{eF_0v_F}{\omega}(-\varepsilon_x + i\varepsilon_y)\sin(\omega t) \\ \frac{eF_0v_F}{\omega}(-\varepsilon_x - i\varepsilon_y)\sin(\omega t) & 0 \end{pmatrix}$$

$$(III.44.6)$$

(3) We assume that at $t = 0$, the electron is in the state $\vec{\psi}_{v\vec{k}_0}$ with an energy $\varepsilon_{v\vec{k}_0} = -v_F\hbar k_0$. Our goal is to compute the energy loss rate of the electromagnetic wave because of the interband transitions that will bring it to the conduction band. We search for:

$$\vec{\psi}(t) = \sum_{\vec{k}} \alpha_{c\vec{k}}(t)\vec{\psi}_{c\vec{k}}e^{-i\frac{t}{\hbar}\varepsilon_{c\vec{k}}} + \alpha_{v\vec{k}}(t)\vec{\psi}_{v\vec{k}}e^{-i\frac{t}{\hbar}\varepsilon_{v\vec{k}}} \qquad (III.44.7)$$

and we insert this ansatz into the Schrödinger equation.

Show that the unknown function $\alpha_{c,v}(t)$ are the solutions of the coupled system:

$$i\hbar\frac{d\alpha_{c\vec{k}}}{dt}e^{-i\frac{t}{\hbar}\varepsilon_{c\vec{k}}} = \sum_{\vec{k}'}\alpha_{c\vec{k}'}\langle\vec{\psi}_{c\vec{k}}|V(t)|\vec{\psi}_{c\vec{k}'}\rangle e^{-i\frac{t}{\hbar}\varepsilon_{c\vec{k}'}}$$

$$+ \sum_{\vec{k}'}\alpha_{v\vec{k}'}\langle\vec{\psi}_{c\vec{k}}|V(t)|\vec{\psi}_{v\vec{k}'}\rangle e^{-i\frac{t}{\hbar}\varepsilon_{v\vec{k}'}} \qquad \text{(III.44.8)}$$

and similarly for $\alpha_{v\vec{k}}(t)$.

(4) Make the usual approximation of the weak coupling: the only large coefficient is $\alpha_{v\vec{k}_0}$ that has kept the same value at $t = 0$, namely 1. All the other coefficients are small (they are at least linear in V). Show that at the first order in V the previous system simplifies into:

$$i\hbar\frac{d\alpha_{c\vec{k}}}{dt}e^{-i\frac{t}{\hbar}\varepsilon_{c\vec{k}}} = \langle\vec{\psi}_{c\vec{k}}|V(t)|\vec{\psi}_{v\vec{k}_0}\rangle e^{-i\frac{t}{\hbar}\varepsilon_{v\vec{k}_0}} \qquad \text{(III.44.9)}$$

(5) Show that:

$$\langle\vec{\psi}_{c\vec{k}}|V(t)|\vec{\psi}_{v\vec{k}_0}\rangle = \delta_{\vec{k},\vec{k}_0}\left(-\frac{ieF_0v_F\sin(\omega t)}{\omega}\right)(\varepsilon_x\sin\theta_0 - \varepsilon_y\cos\theta_0) \qquad \text{(III.44.10)}$$

(6) Deduce that:

$$\frac{d\alpha_{c\vec{k}_0}}{dt} = -\frac{eF_0v_F}{2i\hbar\omega}(\varepsilon_x\sin\theta_0 - \varepsilon_y\cos\theta_0)[e^{it(\omega+2v_Fk_0)} - e^{it(-\omega+2v_Fk_0)}] \qquad \text{(III.44.11)}$$

(7) In terms of unknown coefficients $\alpha_{c\vec{k}}$ what is the probability $P_{v\vec{k}_0}^{c\vec{k}}$ to find the system in the state $\vec{\psi}_{c\vec{k}}$ at time t if it were in the state $\vec{\psi}_{v\vec{k}_0}$ at $t = 0$?

(8) In (6) there is a resonant and a non-resonant contribution. Drop the latter and compute $P_{v\vec{k}_0}^{c\vec{k}}$.

(9) Compute the transitions rate as the time derivative of $P_{v\vec{k}_0}^{c\vec{k}}$.

(10) Evaluate $W_{v \to c} = \sum_{\vec{k}_0} \dfrac{dP^{c\vec{k}}_{v\vec{k}_0}}{dt}$ and convert

$$\sum_{\vec{k}_0} u(\vec{k}_0) \to \frac{S}{4\pi^2} \int_0^{2\pi} d\theta_0 \int_0^\infty k_0 dk_0 u(k_0, \theta_0) \qquad \text{(III.44.12)}$$

where S is the macroscopic sample area.

(11) Now there is the mathematical result that:

$$\lim_{t \to \infty} \frac{A \sin[t(-\omega + 2v_F k_0)]}{(-\omega + 2v_F k_0)} = \pi A \delta(-\omega + 2v_F k_0) \qquad \text{(III.44.13)}$$

Take this into account, as well as the existence of two spin directions and two non-equivalent valleys to show that:

$$W_{v \to c} = \frac{e^2 F_0^2 S(\varepsilon_x^2 + \varepsilon_y^2)}{8\hbar^2 \omega} \quad \text{with } k_0 = \frac{\omega}{2v_F} \qquad \text{(III.44.14)}$$

(12) If we are interested in absorption probability we should multiply this rate W by the occupation functions:

$$f_D(\varepsilon_{v\vec{k}_0})[1 - f_D(\varepsilon_{c\vec{k}_0})] - f_D(\varepsilon_{c\vec{k}_0})[1 - f_D(\varepsilon_{v\vec{k}_0})] \qquad \text{(III.44.15)}$$

where the second term accounts for the stimulated emission. Moreover, we get the energy loss rate $\langle W \rangle_{\text{net abs}}$ by multiplying this weighted rate W by the photon energy $\hbar\omega$. Finally show that:

$$\langle W \rangle_{\text{net abs}} = \frac{e^2 F_0^2 S(\varepsilon_x^2 + \varepsilon_y^2)}{8\hbar}$$

$$\times \left[\frac{1}{1 + \exp\left[\beta\left(-\frac{\hbar\omega}{2} - \mu\right)\right]} - \frac{1}{1 + \exp\left[\beta\left(\frac{\hbar\omega}{2} - \mu\right)\right]} \right] \qquad \text{(III.44.16)}$$

(13) Now, for one experiment where there is a single graphene sheet in vacuum and under normal incidence, the electromagnetic power deposited on the surface by the electromagnetic wave is given by the

flux of the Poynting vector. This averaged Poynting vector is:

$$\langle R \rangle = \frac{Sc\varepsilon_0 F_0^2}{2} \qquad \text{(III.44.17)}$$

The absorption probability P_{abs} is the ratio between $\langle W \rangle_{\text{net abs}}$ and $\langle R \rangle$. Introducing the fine structure constant $\alpha = \frac{e^2}{4\pi\varepsilon_0\hbar c}$, show that:

$$P_{\text{abs}} = \pi\alpha(\varepsilon_x^2 + \varepsilon_y^2)$$

$$\times \left[\frac{1}{1 + \exp\left[\beta\left(-\frac{\hbar\omega}{2} - \mu\right)\right]} - \frac{1}{1 + \exp\left[\beta\left(\frac{\hbar\omega}{2} - \mu\right)\right]} \right]$$

$$\text{(III.44.18)}$$

(14) In light of (13) can you comment the often written statement that the absorption probability of one graphene sheet is the universal constant $\pi\alpha$?

Solution

(1) Written on the same basis as H_0, the eigenstates of H_0 are the 2×1 spinors:

$$\vec{\psi}_{v\vec{k}} = \frac{1}{\sqrt{2}} \begin{pmatrix} -e^{-i\theta} \\ 1 \end{pmatrix} \frac{1}{\sqrt{S}} e^{i\vec{k}\cdot\vec{\rho}}, \quad \varepsilon_v(\vec{k}) = -v_F k \qquad \text{(III.44.19)}$$

$$\vec{\psi}_{c\vec{k}} = \frac{1}{\sqrt{2}} \begin{pmatrix} e^{-i\theta} \\ 1 \end{pmatrix} \frac{1}{\sqrt{S}} e^{i\vec{k}\cdot\vec{\rho}}, \quad \varepsilon_c(\vec{k}) = +v_F k \qquad \text{(III.44.20)}$$

(2) By using the vector potential given in the text, one finds readily that:

$$V(t) = \begin{pmatrix} 0 & \frac{eF_0 v_F}{\omega}(-\varepsilon_x + i\varepsilon_y)\sin(\omega t) \\ \frac{eF_0 v_F}{\omega}(-\varepsilon_x - i\varepsilon_y)\sin(\omega t) & 0 \end{pmatrix}$$

$$\text{(III.44.21)}$$

(3) By inserting the ansatz wavefunction in the Schrödinger equation and by multiplying by the bras $\langle \vec{\psi}_{c\vec{k}} |$, $\langle \vec{\psi}_{v\vec{k}} |$, one finds:

$$i\hbar \frac{d\alpha_{c\vec{k}}}{dt} e^{-i\frac{t}{\hbar}\varepsilon_{c\vec{k}}} = \sum_{\vec{k}'} \alpha_{c\vec{k}'} \langle \vec{\psi}_{c\vec{k}} | V(t) | \vec{\psi}_{c\vec{k}'} \rangle e^{-i\frac{t}{\hbar}\varepsilon_{c\vec{k}'}}$$

$$+ \sum_{\vec{k}'} \alpha_{v\vec{k}'} \langle \vec{\psi}_{c\vec{k}} | V(t) | \vec{\psi}_{v\vec{k}'} \rangle e^{-i\frac{t}{\hbar}\varepsilon_{v\vec{k}'}} \qquad \text{(III.44.22)}$$

(4) The weak coupling means that the larger element is at t like at $t = 0$ the projection on the initial valence state $\alpha_{v\vec{k}_0}$ which is taken equal to 1 while all the other projections are small (of the order of V). As we are interested in interband transitions we just have to retain on the left-hand side the projection on the conduction states. Thus

$$i\hbar \frac{d\alpha_{c\vec{k}}}{dt} e^{-i\frac{t}{\hbar}\varepsilon_{c\vec{k}}} = \langle \vec{\psi}_{c\vec{k}}|V(t)|\vec{\psi}_{v\vec{k}_0}\rangle e^{-i\frac{t}{\hbar}\varepsilon_{v\vec{k}_0}} \qquad \text{(III.44.23)}$$

The big advantage with this approximation is the disentanglement between the various projections of the wavefunctions as time flows. The time evolution of the conduction band projection is given by a first-order differential equation with a right-hand side that is a given function of time. Hence, it is easily integrated.

(5) We compute the $V(t)$ matrix element as:

$$\langle \vec{\psi}_{c\vec{k}}|V(t)|\vec{\psi}_{v\vec{k}_0}\rangle$$

$$= \delta_{\vec{k},\vec{k}_0} \left\langle \frac{e^{i\theta}}{\sqrt{2}}, \frac{1}{\sqrt{2}} \middle| V(t) \middle| \begin{array}{c} -\frac{e^{-i\theta}}{\sqrt{2}} \\ \frac{1}{\sqrt{2}} \end{array} \right\rangle$$

$$= \delta_{\vec{k},\vec{k}_0} \left\langle \frac{e^{i\theta}}{\sqrt{2}}, \frac{1}{\sqrt{2}} \middle| \begin{array}{c} -\frac{eF_0 v_F}{\omega\sqrt{2}}(-\varepsilon_x + i\varepsilon_y) \\ \frac{eF_0 v_F e^{-i\theta_0}}{\omega\sqrt{2}}(+\varepsilon_x + i\varepsilon_y) \end{array} \right\rangle$$

$$= \delta_{\vec{k},\vec{k}_0} \left(-\frac{ieF_0 v_F \sin(\omega t)}{\omega}(\varepsilon_x \sin\theta_0 - \varepsilon_y \cos\theta_0) \right) \qquad \text{(III.44.24)}$$

(6) Evidently, we find that the only conduction state coupled to the valence state $\vec{\psi}_{v\vec{k}_0}$ is $\vec{\psi}_{c\vec{k}_0}$ because of the in-plane translation invariance.

Thus

$$\frac{d\alpha_{c\vec{k}_0}}{dt} = -\frac{eF_0 v_F}{2i\hbar\omega}(\varepsilon_x \sin\theta_0 - \varepsilon_y \cos\theta_0)[e^{it(\omega+2v_F k_0)} - e^{it(-\omega+2v_F k_0)}]$$

$$\text{(III.44.25)}$$

(7) The probability $P^{c\vec{k}}_{v\vec{k}_0}$ to find the system in the state $\vec{\psi}_{c\vec{k}}$ if it were in the state $\vec{\psi}_{v\vec{k}_0}$ at $t = 0$ is:

$$P^{c\vec{k}}_{v\vec{k}_0}(t) = \delta_{\vec{k},\vec{k}_0} |\alpha_{c\vec{k}_0}(t)|^2 \qquad (\text{III.44.26})$$

(8) By inspection of the time evolution of $\alpha_{c\vec{k}_0}(t)$, we recognise a resonant and a non-resonant contribution. The latter will be negligibly small because it will oscillate at a high frequency while the former may have a very small evolution frequency. So we drop the non-resonant term at once and get:

$$\alpha_{c\vec{k}_0}(t) = -\frac{eF_0 v_F}{2\hbar\omega(-\omega + 2v_F k_0)}(\varepsilon_x \sin\theta_0 - \varepsilon_y \cos\theta_0)[e^{it(-\omega+2v_F k_0)} - 1]$$
$$(\text{III.44.27})$$

Thus, the probability to find the system in the state $\vec{\psi}_{c\vec{k}_0}$ at time t while it is was in the state $\vec{\psi}_{v\vec{k}_0}$ at $t = 0$ is $|\alpha_{c\vec{k}_0}|^2$:

$$|\alpha_{c\vec{k}_0}(t)|^2 = \frac{e^2 F_0^2 v_F^2}{\hbar^2 \omega^2(-\omega + 2v_F k_0)^2}$$

$$\times (\varepsilon_x^2 \sin^2\theta_0 + \varepsilon_y^2 \cos^2\theta_0 - 2\varepsilon_x\varepsilon_y \sin\theta_0 \cos\theta_0)$$

$$\times \sin^2\left(\frac{t}{2}[-\omega + 2v_F k_0]\right) \qquad (\text{III.44.28})$$

(9) The transition rate is the derivative of this expression with respect to time:

$$\frac{d|\alpha_{c\vec{k}_0}|^2}{dt} = \frac{e^2 F_0^2 v_F^2}{2\hbar^2 \omega^2(-\omega + 2v_F k_0)}$$

$$\times (\varepsilon_x^2 \sin^2\theta_0 + \varepsilon_y^2 \cos^2\theta_0 - 2\varepsilon_x\varepsilon_y \sin\theta_0 \cos\theta_0)$$

$$\times \sin(t[-\omega + 2v_F k_0]) \qquad (\text{III.44.29})$$

(10) and (11) Now there is the mathematical result that:

$$\lim_{t\to\infty} \frac{A\sin[t(-\omega + 2v_F k_0)]}{(-\omega + 2v_F k_0)} = \pi A\delta(-\omega + 2v_F k_0) \qquad (\text{III.44.30})$$

We convert the summation into an integration and average over the θ_0 angle:

$$\sum_{\vec{k}_0} \cdots \rightarrow \frac{S}{4\pi^2} \int_0^{2\pi} d\theta_0 \int_0^{\infty} k_0 dk_0 \cdots \qquad \text{(III.44.31)}$$

$$\int_0^{2\pi} d\theta_0 \sin^2 \theta_0 = \int_0^{2\pi} d\theta_0 \cos^2 \theta_0 = \pi; \quad \int_0^{2\pi} d\theta_0 \sin \theta_0 \cos \theta_0 = 0$$

$$\text{(III.44.32)}$$

All the calculations so far were done for one spin direction (either up or down). In addition, there are two degeneracy points (K and K') in graphene (see [87]). Summing over these possibilities amounts to a multiplication by four and finally we get:

$$W_{v \to c} = \frac{e^2 F_0^2 S(\varepsilon_x^2 + \varepsilon_y^2)}{8\hbar^2 \omega} \quad \text{with } k_0 = \frac{\omega}{2v_F} \qquad \text{(III.44.33)}$$

(12) If we are interested in absorption probability we should multiply this rate W by the occupation functions:

$$f_D(\varepsilon_{v\vec{k}_0})[1 - f_D(\varepsilon_{c\vec{k}_0})] - f_D(\varepsilon_{c\vec{k}_0})[1 - f_D(\varepsilon_{v\vec{k}_0})] \qquad \text{(III.44.34)}$$

where the second term accounts for the stimulated emission. Moreover, we get the energy loss rate by multiplying this weighted rate W by the photon energy. Finally we get the energy loss rate $\langle W \rangle_{\text{net abs}}$:

$$\langle W \rangle_{\text{net abs}} = \frac{e^2 F_0^2 S(\varepsilon_x^2 + \varepsilon_y^2)}{8\hbar}$$

$$\times \left[\frac{1}{1 + \exp\left[\beta\left(-\frac{\hbar\omega}{2} - \mu\right)\right]} - \frac{1}{1 + \exp\left[\beta\left(\frac{\hbar\omega}{2} - \mu\right)\right]} \right] \qquad \text{(III.44.35)}$$

(13) Now, for one experiment where there is a single graphene sheet in vacuum and under normal incidence, the electromagnetic power deposited on the surface by the electromagnetic wave is given by the

flux of the Poynting vector. This averaged Poynting vector is:

$$\langle R \rangle = \frac{Sc\varepsilon_0 F_0^2}{2} \tag{III.44.36}$$

The absorption probability P_{abs} is the ratio between $\langle W \rangle_{\text{net abs}}$ and $\langle R \rangle$. Introducing the fine structure constant $\alpha = \frac{e^2}{4\pi\varepsilon_0\hbar c}$, we get:

$$P_{\text{abs}} = \pi\alpha(\varepsilon_x^2 + \varepsilon_y^2)$$

$$\times \left[\frac{1}{1 + \exp\left[\beta\left(-\frac{\hbar\omega}{2} - \mu\right)\right]} - \frac{1}{1 + \exp\left[\beta\left(\frac{\hbar\omega}{2} - \mu\right)\right]} \right] \tag{III.44.37}$$

So, we made two approximations. The first one is assuming a zero overlap between the two $2p_z$ carbon atomic functions. The second one is the blind application of the weak coupling between the material system and the electromagnetic wave. Actually there is no continuum for the final state since its wavevector should be identical (translation invariance) to the initial one. This is the same problem as in bulk crystalline semiconductors where there is also a single final state for any given initial state. We still apply weak coupling because we argue that the resulting polariton splitting would be small compared to broadening.

Note of course that the "universal result" becomes violated at low enough energy because of the occupation functions.

Clearly for an ideal graphene there is $\mu = 0$. But in actual material one should take into account the doping to determine μ. For degenerate statistics $\frac{|\mu|}{k_B T} \geq 3$, the ideal value will be reached for photon energy larger than $2\mu + dk_B T$ with $d = 2 - 3$.

Figure 44.1 taken from Orlita and Potemski shows the excellent agreement between the modelling and the experiment [87].

45. Scattering by N random impurity dimmers

In this exercise we examine how fixing the position of some impurities instead of letting them uncorrelated modifies the magnitude of the level lifetime.

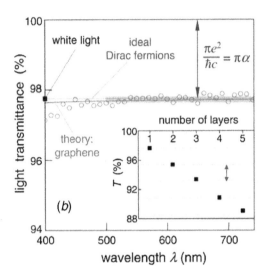

Figure 44.1.   Comparison between the transmittance spectrum of single-layer graphene and the theoretical transmission for ideal massless Dirac fermions (i.e., with linear dispersions).

Source: Orlita *et al.* [87]. In the figure e^2 should be understood as $\frac{e^2}{4\pi\varepsilon_0}$.

(1) Consider $2N$ impurities randomly located on the plane $z = z_0$ of a quasi-2D heterostructure (see Fig. 45.1). Compute the level lifetime $\tau_{n\vec{k}}$ of the eigenstates $|n\vec{k}\rangle$ of the ideal heterostructure limited by intra-subband scattering on these $2N$ impurities in the nth subband. Assume parabolic dispersion relations for the in-plane motion. Use the Born approximation and take the scattering potential associated with one impurity located at $\vec{R}_i = (\vec{\rho}_i, z_0)$, $\vec{\rho}_i = (x_i, y_i)$ as:

$$V(\vec{\rho} - \vec{\rho}_i, z - z_0) = Va^3\delta(\vec{\rho} - \vec{\rho}_i)\delta(z - z_0) \qquad \text{(III.45.1)}$$

(2) We consider now that the $2N$ impurities are not completely uncorrelated (see Fig. 45.1). In fact, they are grouped in N independent and randomly located impurity dimmers: the two impurities of each dimmer are separated by the 2D vector $\vec{\tau} = \tau(\cos\varphi, \sin\varphi)$. Compute the level lifetime $\tau_{n\vec{k}}$ of the state $|n\vec{k}\rangle$ limited by intra-subband scattering on these N impurity dimmers in the nth subband. The scattering potential is the same as in (1).

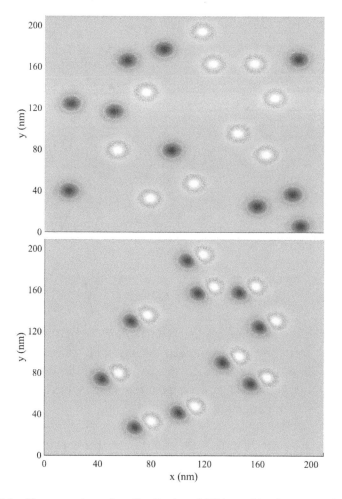

Figure 45.1. Upper panel: random distribution of $2N$ impurities. Lower panel: random distribution of N impurity dimmers containing two correlated impurities. $N = 10$ and the surface of the sample is 210×210 nm^2.

We give:

$$e^{iz\cos\alpha} = \sum_{n=-\infty}^{+\infty} i^n J_n(z)e^{in\alpha}; \quad e^{iz\sin\alpha} = \sum_{n=-\infty}^{+\infty} J_n(z)e^{in\alpha}$$

$$(\text{III}.45.2)$$

where $J_n(z)$ is the nth Bessel function.

Solution

(1) We apply the rule on the scattering by $2N$ independent and randomly located impurities to write the level lifetime $\tau_{n\vec{k}}$ as:

$$\left\langle \frac{\hbar}{2\pi\tau_{n\vec{k}}} \right\rangle_{av} = 2N \sum_{\vec{k}'} |\langle n\vec{k}|Va^3\delta(\vec{\rho}-\vec{\rho}_i)\delta(z-z_0)|n\vec{k}'\rangle|^2 \delta$$

$$\times \left(\frac{\hbar^2}{2m^*}(k'^2 - k^2) \right)$$

$$= 2N \frac{V^2 a^6}{S^2} \chi_n^4(z_0) \frac{S}{4\pi^2} \int_0^\infty 2\pi k' dk' \delta \left(\frac{\hbar^2}{2m^*}(k'^2 - k^2) \right)$$

$$= \frac{2N}{S} V^2 a^6 \chi_n^4(z_0) \frac{m^*}{2\pi\hbar^2} \qquad \text{(III.45.3)}$$

where $\langle\ \rangle_{av}$ means that the averaging over the positions of the $2N$ uncorrelated impurities has been taken.

We recover the familiar result that the inverse of the level lifetime due to scattering is proportional to the impurity concentration $2N/S$. Here it does not depend on the energy because the density of states is a constant and the averaged squared matrix element of a delta scatterer is also a constant.

(2) When there are N independent dimmers, there is for each dimmer the same form factor $f_{\vec{k}'-\vec{k}}$ that arises from the summation over the two scatterers of the dimmer: one at $(0,0)$ and the other located at $\vec{\tau} = \tau(\cos\varphi, \sin\varphi)$ from the first one:

$$f_{\vec{k}'-\vec{k}} = 1 + e^{i(\vec{k}'-\vec{k})\cdot\vec{\tau}} \qquad \text{(III.45.4)}$$

The level lifetime $\tau_{n\vec{k}}$ is now given by:

$$\left\langle \frac{\hbar}{2\pi\tau_{n\vec{k}}} \right\rangle_{av} = N \sum_{\vec{k}'} \left| \langle n\vec{k}|Va^3\delta(\vec{\rho}-\vec{\rho}_i)\delta(z-z_0)|n\vec{k}'\rangle \right|^2 \left| f_{\vec{k}'-\vec{k}} \right|^2$$

$$\times \delta \left(\frac{\hbar^2}{2m^*}(k'^2 - k^2) \right)$$

$$= 2N \frac{V^2 a^6}{S^2} \chi_n^4(z_0) \frac{S}{4\pi^2} \int_0^{2\pi}$$

$$\times d\theta' \left\{ 1 + \cos(k\tau[(\cos\theta' - 1)\cos\varphi + \sin\theta'\sin\varphi]) \right\}$$

$$\times \int_0^\infty k' dk' \delta \left(\frac{\hbar^2}{2m^*}(k'^2 - k^2) \right) \tag{III.45.5}$$

where the initial wavevector is $\vec{k} = (k, 0)$ and where we have taken into account that $k' = k$ to simplifies the form factor. The k' integral is the same as in (1) and we get:

$$\left\langle \frac{\hbar}{2\pi\tau_{n\vec{k}}} \right\rangle_{\text{av}} = \frac{2N}{S} V^2 a^6 \chi_n^4(z_0) \frac{m^*}{2\pi\hbar^2} G(k, \vec{\tau}) \tag{III.45.6}$$

$$G(k, \vec{\tau}) = \frac{1}{2\pi} \int_0^{2\pi} d\theta' \left\{ 1 + \cos(k\tau[(\cos\theta' - 1)\cos\varphi + \sin\theta'\sin\varphi]) \right\}$$

$$= 1 + \frac{1}{2\pi} \int_0^{2\pi} d\theta' \cos\left\{ k\tau[(\cos\theta' - 1)\cos\varphi + \sin\theta'\sin\varphi] \right\}$$

$$= 1 + \frac{1}{2\pi} \int_0^{2\pi} d\theta' \cos\left\{ k\tau[\cos(\theta' - \varphi) - \cos\varphi] \right\}$$

$$= 1 + \frac{1}{2\pi} \int_0^{2\pi} d\theta' \left\{ \cos[k\tau\cos(\theta' - \varphi)]\cos(k\tau\cos\varphi) \right.$$

$$\left. + \sin[k\tau\cos(\theta' - \varphi)]\sin(k\tau\cos\varphi) \right\} \tag{III.45.7}$$

The latter integral can be evaluated thanks to the Bessel expansion. We obtain:

$$\cos[k\tau\cos(\theta' - \varphi)] = \text{Re}(e^{i[k\tau\cos(\theta' - \varphi)]})$$

$$= \text{Re} \left(\sum_{n=-\infty}^{+\infty} i^n J_n(k\tau) e^{in(\theta' - \varphi)} \right) \tag{III.45.8}$$

$$\sin(k\tau\cos[\theta' - \varphi]) = \text{Im}(e^{i[k\tau\cos(\theta' - \varphi)]})$$

$$= \text{Im} \left(\sum_{n=-\infty}^{+\infty} i^n J_n(k\tau) e^{in(\theta' - \varphi)} \right) \tag{III.45.9}$$

The integral over θ' leaves only the $n = 0$ term in the summation over n. Thus, at the end one gets:

$$G(k, \vec{\tau}) = 1 + J_0(k\tau) \cos(k\tau \cos \varphi) \qquad \text{(III.45.10)}$$

Therefore:

$$\left\langle \frac{\hbar}{2\pi \tau_{n\vec{k}}} \right\rangle_{\text{av}}^{\text{dim}} = \frac{2N}{S} V^2 a^6 \chi_n^4(z_0) \frac{m^*}{2\pi \hbar^2} [1 + J_0(k\tau) \cos(k\tau \cos \varphi)]$$

$$\text{(III.45.11)}$$

This result, although not really applicable to actual materials (impurity dimmers are hard to make!), shows very clearly that the usual rule that the scattering by $2N$ impurities is $2N$ times that by a single one rests on the very strong assumption that the impurities are uncorrelated. The case of dimmers in this exercise is an extreme one where there is no uncertainty on the position of the second impurity with respect to the first one. This fixed position of the two companions of the dimmer completely invalidates the usual approach.

We note that there exist specific energies where the difference between dimmers and completely uncorrelated impurities vanishes. This happens when $k\tau$ is a zero of J_0 or when $k\tau \cos \varphi = (2p + 1)\pi/2$. We also note that in contrast with 1), the level broadening varies with the energy of the initial state. It is only at high energy $k\tau \gg 1$ that the uncorrelated impurity limit is reached ($|J_0(x)| \leq \frac{1}{\sqrt{x}}$ when $x \to \infty$): the electron wavelength $2\pi/k$ becomes $\ll \tau$, the distance between the two companions of the dimmer which results in an effective decoupling between the consecutive scatterings on these two impurities (Fig. 45.2 shows a plot of G versus $x = k\tau$ for $\varphi = \frac{\pi}{3}$).

46. A tractable example of selective doping by delta scatterers

We consider a quasi-2D heterostructure. The growth axis is z and the bound states for the z motion are $E_1, E_2, \ldots$. The heterostructure contains N_{imp} randomly distributed scatterers in the plane $z = z_i$. They are delta-like scatterers: for a scatterer located at the position

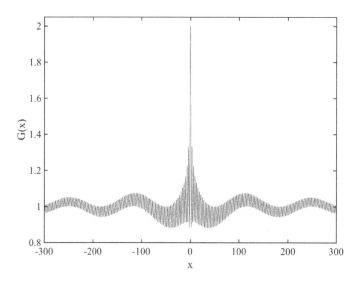

Figure 45.2.   Plot of the function G versus $x = k\tau$ for $\varphi = \frac{\pi}{3}$, see (III.45.10).

$(\vec{\rho}_i, z_i)$, there is:

$$V(\vec{\rho} - \vec{\rho}_i, z - z_i) = V_0 a^3 \delta(\vec{\rho} - \vec{\rho}_i)\delta(z - z_i) \qquad \text{(III.46.1)}$$

(1) Find the expression of the level lifetime of an electron placed in the ground subband E_1. Assume that its in-plane kinetic energy is smaller than $E_2 - E_1$.

(2) Same question if its in-plane kinetic energy is larger than $E_2 - E_1$.

Solution

Cases (1) and (2) differ in that only intra-subband transitions are possible in (1) while in (2) both intra- and inter-subband transitions are possible.

(1) We use the assumption of random locations on the $z = z_i$ plane to get:

$$\frac{\hbar}{2\pi\tau_{1\vec{k}}}\bigg|_{\text{intra 11}} = N_{\text{imp}} \sum_{\vec{k}'} |\langle 1\vec{k}|V(\vec{\rho} - \vec{\rho}_i, z - z_i)|1\vec{k}'\rangle|^2 \delta\left(\varepsilon_{1\vec{k}} - \varepsilon_{1\vec{k}'}\right)$$

$$= \frac{N_{\text{imp}} V_0^2 a^6}{S^2} \chi_1^4(z_i) \sum_{\vec{k'}} \delta \left(\varepsilon_{1\vec{k}} - \varepsilon_{1\vec{k'}} \right)$$

$$= \frac{N_{\text{imp}} V_0^2 a^6}{2\pi S} \chi_1^4(z_i) \int_0^\infty k' dk' \delta \left(\varepsilon_{1\vec{k}} - \varepsilon_{1\vec{k'}} \right)$$

$$= \frac{N_{\text{imp}} V_0^2 a^6 m^*}{2\pi S \hbar^2} \chi_1^4(z_i) \qquad \text{(III.46.2)}$$

The selective doping concept appears here very clearly since we can make these scatterers very effective by placing them on a plane located at the maximum of the probability density of the ground subband. Conversely, they can have a negligible influence if they are placed in the barriers where $\chi_1^4(z_i)$ is very small.

(2) When the in-plane kinetic energy of the initial state is larger than $E_2 - E_1$, inter-subband scattering shows up, in addition to the intra-subband one. Hence, we have to add the contribution:

$$\left. \frac{\hbar}{2\pi \tau_{1\vec{k}}} \right|_{\text{inter } 12} = N_{\text{imp}} \sum_{\vec{k'}} \left| \langle 1\vec{k} | V(\vec{\rho} - \vec{\rho}_i, z - z_i) | 2\vec{k'} \rangle \right|^2 \delta \left(\varepsilon_{1\vec{k}} - \varepsilon_{2\vec{k'}} \right)$$

$$= \frac{N_{\text{imp}} V_0^2 a^6}{S^2} \chi_1^2(z_i) \chi_2^2(z_i) \sum_{\vec{k'}} \delta \left(\varepsilon_{1\vec{k}} - \varepsilon_{2\vec{k'}} \right)$$

$$= \frac{N_{\text{imp}} V_0^2 a^6}{2\pi S} \chi_1^2(z_i) \chi_2^2(z_i) \int_0^\infty k' dk' \delta \left(\varepsilon_{1\vec{k}} - \varepsilon_{2\vec{k'}} \right)$$

$$= \frac{N_{\text{imp}} V_0^2 a^6 m^*}{2\pi S \hbar^2} \chi_1^2(z_i) \chi_2^2(z_i) Y \left(\frac{\hbar^2 k^2}{2m^*} - E_2 + E_1 \right)$$

$$\text{(III.46.3)}$$

where $Y(x)$ is the step function. We see that the level lifetime $\tau_{1\vec{k}}$ has a jump when the in-plane kinetic energy passes through the inter-subband energy distance. This is due to the constant density of states of 2D subbands joined to the fact that the scattering efficiency of delta scatterers is constant and therefore does not vanish at the subband edge.

There are experimental observations of this jump [88]. It was the velocity relaxation time (through the electron mobility) and not the level lifetime and the scatterers were likely ionised impurities and not delta scatterers. But the essential of the physics is the same as in this exercise, namely the constant density of states associated with quasi-2D motions.

47. Comparison between Born and self-consistent Born approximations

We have pointed out that it is sometimes mandatory to go beyond the Born approximation. In this exercise, we wish to compare both approximations in a regime that is algebraically tractable and where it is often expected that the regular Born approximation is sufficient.

To this end, we consider a quantum wire (z is the wire axis). The transverse (x, y) motion is bound and we consider a single channel. Hence, the eigenstates and eigenenergies are:

$$\psi_{\nu, k_z}(\vec{r}) = \varphi_\nu(\vec{\rho}) \frac{e^{ik_z z}}{\sqrt{L}}; \quad \varepsilon_\nu(k_z) = E_\nu + \frac{\hbar^2 k_z^2}{2m^*} \qquad (\text{III.47.1})$$

where L is the macroscopic length of the wire. This wire contains N_{def} delta scatterers randomly positioned at $(\vec{\rho}_0, z_i)$:

$$V_{\text{def}}(\vec{r}) = \sum_i V_0 a^3 \delta(\vec{\rho} - \vec{\rho}_0) \delta(z - z_i) \qquad (\text{III.47.2})$$

where a is a length and V_0 an energy. If we compute the first-order energy shift of a $|\nu, k_z\rangle$ state due to V_{def}, we find a constant $V_0 a^3 |\psi_\nu(\vec{\rho}_0)|^2 \frac{N_{\text{def}}}{L}$. This constant (with respect to k_z) is absorbed in the definition of E_ν. Hence, our new defect potential is:

$$\tilde{V}_{\text{def}}(\vec{r}) = V_{\text{def}}(\vec{r}) - V_0 a^3 |\psi_\nu(\vec{\rho}_0)|^2 \frac{N_{\text{def}}}{L} \qquad (\text{III.47.3})$$

(1) Compute the lifetime τ_ν of a state $|\nu, k_z\rangle$ at the Born approximation on $\tilde{V}_{\text{def}}(\vec{r})$ considering that all the z_i are uncorrelated random variables.

(2) The self-consistent Born approximation for the self-energy averaged over the defect configuration $\Sigma(\varepsilon)$ leads to the equation:

$$\Sigma(\varepsilon) = \left\langle \sum_{k_z'} \frac{\langle \nu, k_z | \sum_i V_0 a^3 \delta(\vec{\rho} - \vec{\rho}_0) \delta(z - z_i) | \nu, k_z' \rangle \times \langle \nu, k_z' | \sum_j V_0 a^3 \delta(\vec{\rho} - \vec{\rho}_0) \delta(z - z_j) | \nu, k_z \rangle}{\varepsilon + i\eta - \Sigma(\varepsilon) - E_\nu - \frac{\hbar^2 k_z'^2}{2m^*}} \right\rangle_{\text{average}}$$

(III.47.4)

where $\eta \to 0$. We set the energy zero at E_ν: $\varepsilon' = \varepsilon - E_\nu$. Show that $\Sigma(\varepsilon')$ is the solution of:

$$\Sigma(\varepsilon') = \frac{N_{\text{def}}}{2\pi L} |\psi_\nu(\vec{\rho}_0)|^4 V_0^2 a^6 \int_{-\infty}^{+\infty} dk' \frac{1}{\varepsilon' + i\eta - \Sigma(\varepsilon') - \frac{\hbar^2 k_z'^2}{2m^*}}$$

(III.47.5)

(3) We let $\Sigma = \Sigma_1 - i\Sigma_2$, $\Sigma_2 \geq 0$. Write the two equations fulfilled by Σ_1 and Σ_2.

(4) Show that in the limit of large ε', there is:
  (a) $|\Sigma_1| \ll \Sigma_2$,
  (b) $\Sigma_2(\varepsilon') \to \frac{\hbar}{\tau_\nu(\varepsilon')}$.

We give:

$$I(a) = \int_{-\infty}^{+\infty} \frac{dt}{1 + (t^2 - a)^2} = \frac{\pi}{\sqrt{1 + a^2}} \frac{1}{\sqrt{2}} \sqrt{a + \sqrt{1 + a^2}}$$

(III.47.6)

At large $a > 0$, $I(a)$ behaves like $\pi a^{-1/2}$.

Solution

(1) We write the Born approximation for an initial state $|\nu, k_z\rangle$ that is scattered by V_{def} to all the $|\nu, k_z'\rangle$:

$$\frac{\hbar}{2\pi \tau_{\nu, k_z}^{\text{Born}}} = \sum_{k_z'} \langle |\langle \nu, k_z | V_{\text{def}} | \nu, k_z' \rangle|^2 \rangle_{\text{aver}} \delta\left(\frac{\hbar^2(k_z^2 - k_z'^2)}{2m^*} \right)$$

(III.47.7)

The average is on the positions of the scatterers along the wire axis. If there is no correlation on their positions, the previous expression reduces to:

$$\frac{\hbar}{2\pi\tau_{\nu,k_z}^{\text{Born}}} = \frac{V_0^2 a^6 N_{\text{def}}}{2\pi L}|\psi_\nu(\vec{\rho}_0)|^4 \int_{-\infty}^{+\infty} dk'_z \delta\left(\frac{\hbar^2(k_z^2 - k_z'^2)}{2m^*}\right)$$

$$= \frac{V_0^2 a^6 N_{\text{def}}}{2\pi L}|\psi_\nu(\vec{\rho}_0)|^4 \frac{m^*}{\hbar^2|k_z|} \tag{III.47.8}$$

Note that we have only retained the solution $k'_z = -k_z$ since $k'_z = k_z$ corresponds to no scattering at all. The broadening diverges in the vicinity of the subband edge as a consequence of the divergent density of states of the 1D free motion. This divergence should be a matter of concern because we expect in the weak disorder limit that the approximate eigenenergies in the presence of the disorder will display imaginary parts of the eigenenergies that remain much smaller than their real parts if one wants to describe the system in terms of weakly damped plane waves. Clearly, this is violated close from the subband edge but should be true at elevated energies. As it is well known, fast particles are less affected by disorder than slow ones, the latter one being much more sensitive to the potential landscape.

(2) The handling of the averaging is the same in (1). Hence, we get readily the required expression.

(3) We let $\Sigma(\varepsilon') = \Sigma_1(\varepsilon') - i\Sigma_2(\varepsilon')$, $\Sigma_2 > 0$ and get:

$$\Sigma_1(\varepsilon') = \frac{N_{\text{def}}}{2\pi L}|\psi_\nu(\vec{\rho}_0)|^4 V_0^2 a^6 \int_{-\infty}^{+\infty} dk'_z \frac{\varepsilon' - \Sigma_1(\varepsilon') - \frac{\hbar^2 k_z'^2}{2m^*}}{\left(\varepsilon' - \Sigma_1(\varepsilon') - \frac{\hbar^2 k_z'^2}{2m^*}\right)^2 + \Sigma_2^2(\varepsilon')} \tag{III.47.9}$$

$$1 = \frac{N_{\text{def}}}{2\pi L}|\psi_\nu(\vec{\rho}_0)|^4 V_0^2 a^6 \int_{-\infty}^{+\infty} dk'_z \frac{1}{\left(\varepsilon' - \Sigma_1(\varepsilon') - \frac{\hbar^2 k_z'^2}{2m^*}\right)^2 + \Sigma_2^2(\varepsilon')} \tag{III.47.10}$$

We introduce the dimensionless variables:

$$t^2 = \frac{\hbar^2 k_z'^2}{2m^* \Sigma_2(\varepsilon')}; \quad a = \frac{\varepsilon' - \Sigma_1(\varepsilon')}{\Sigma_2(\varepsilon')} \tag{III.47.11}$$

and obtain:

$$\Sigma_1(\varepsilon') = \frac{N_{\text{def}}}{2\pi L}|\psi_\nu(\vec{\rho}_0)|^4 V_0^2 a^6 \sqrt{\frac{2m^*}{\hbar^2 \Sigma_2(\varepsilon')}} \int_{-\infty}^{+\infty} dt \frac{(a - t^2)}{(a - t^2)^2 + 1}$$

$$\text{(III.47.12)}$$

$$1 = \frac{N_{\text{def}}}{2\pi L}|\psi_\nu(\vec{\rho}_0)|^4 V_0^2 a^6 \sqrt{\frac{2m^*}{\hbar^2 \Sigma_2^3(\varepsilon')}} \int_{-\infty}^{+\infty} dt \frac{1}{(a - t^2)^2 + 1}$$

$$\text{(III.47.13)}$$

If we compute the ratio between the real and imaginary parts of the self-energies, we see that it is equal to the ratio of the two integrals. The integral in Σ_2 is that of a double bell-shaped function centred at $\pm\sqrt{a}$ (when $a > 0$) while the integral appearing in Σ_1 is that of a double S-shaped curve centred at $\pm\sqrt{a}$ and that changes sign at $\pm\sqrt{a}$. It has to be smaller than Σ_2 and in a first approximation it is zero: as so often Σ_1 that represents a level shift (since the poles of the Green function occur no longer at the unperturbed energies but are shifted by Σ_1 from them) is much smaller than the level broadening Σ_2.

Based on that remark, we get an iterative scheme:
(a) At the zeroth-order $\Sigma_1 = 0$ and Σ_2 is given by the second equation.
(b) Next, we plug the zeroth-order Σ_2 to get Σ_1 from the first equation etc. There is one noticeable feature in the coupled equations that link Σ_1 and Σ_2; namely, the possible existence of solutions at negative ε'.

We can make a qualitative estimate of the integral I_2 appearing in Σ_2. We consider the limit of large $a > 0$. The integral can be rewritten:

$$I_2 = \frac{2}{a^{3/2}} \int_0^\infty \frac{dx}{(x^2 - 1)^2 + \frac{1}{a^2}} \qquad \text{(III.47.14)}$$

It has a maximum equal to a^2 at $x = 1$. The full width at half maximum is $\approx 1/a$. Hence the integral is of the order of $I_2 \approx 2a^{-3/2}\alpha a =$

$2\alpha a^{-1/2}$ where α is a c number. Thus:

$$\Sigma_2(\varepsilon') \approx \frac{N_{\text{def}}}{2\pi L}|\psi_\nu(\vec{\rho}_0)|^4 V_0^2 a^6 \sqrt{\frac{2m^*}{\hbar^2}} \frac{2\alpha}{\sqrt{\varepsilon' - \Sigma_1(\varepsilon')}}; \quad \varepsilon' \to \infty$$

(III.47.15)

If we neglect Σ_1 with respect to ε', we indeed (because in fact $\alpha = \frac{\pi}{2}$) retrieve that at large energy $(\varepsilon \gg \Sigma_2(\varepsilon'))$:

$$\Sigma_2(\varepsilon') = \frac{\hbar}{\tau_\nu(\varepsilon')}$$

(III.47.16)

Thus, the self-consistent Born approximation reduces to the regular Born approximation when the scattering is weak.

Note that for quasi-2D and 3D materials the limit of very weak disorder would be $\Sigma_2 \approx \frac{\hbar}{2\tau_{k_z}}$ and not $\frac{\hbar}{\tau_{k_z}}$. This is because in quasi-1D materials an elastic scattering can be realised in a single way: $k'_z = -k_z$, the other possibility $k'_z = k_z$ being excluded (not a scattering). In higher dimensions instead, an elastic scattering can be realised in a myriad of fashions in such a way that the $\vec{k}' = \vec{k}$ case has no weight (mathematically speaking has a zero measure). Thus, in 2 or 3 dimensions, the Born approximation leads to a scattering frequency that is proportional to the density of states, while in a quasi-1D situation the scattering frequency is proportional to half of the density of states. The lack of available final states may, in fact, signal the marginal applicability of the Born approximation in 1D situations.

Let us investigate the case $a \leq 0$. We note that $I(a = 0) = \frac{\pi}{\sqrt{2}}$. Hence, $\Sigma_2(a = 0)$ is well defined. For $a < 0$, I_2 is now equal to:

$$I_2 = \frac{2}{|a|^{3/2}} \int_0^\infty \frac{dx}{(x^2 + 1)^2 + \frac{1}{a^2}}$$

(III.47.17)

At large $|a|$, $I_2(a) \approx \frac{\pi}{|a|^{3/2}}$. This means that the disorder has created states below the unperturbed states and that the self-consistent Born approximation partially account for them. Note however that the bound states, possibly created by the disorder potential, cannot be described by the self-consistent Born approximation since the bound states result from an infinite number of interactions between the electron and the disorder potential. We also note that the asymptotic form of $I_2(a)$ when $a \to -\infty$ prevents to determine $\Sigma_2(\varepsilon)$ since (III.47.3) becomes Σ_2 independent in this limit. Actually, for energies far below the subband edge, we cannot expect to find any state (and thus a non-vanishing Σ_2) because we deal with a finite number of short range scatterers.

We thank Dr. Leyronas for insightful remarks.

48. Influence of a fast emptying of the final subband on the equilibrium between two subbands

We consider a system with three subbands 1, 2 and 3. We mentioned that the refilling of 1 by 2 due to elastic collisions can be perturbed by a quick depletion of subband 2. We examine here a very simple example of such a situation. Call N_1, N_2 and N_3 the population of subbands 1, 2 and 3. Because of elastic transitions the rates of change of N_1 and N_2 are proportional to N_1 and N_2 with the same coefficient $1/\tau_{12} = 1/\tau_{21}$. In addition, the electrons in subband 2 undergo inelastic collisions that amount to decreasing N_2 at a rate N_2/τ_{23}. Finally, the population of the subband 3 decreases at a rate $(\alpha + \beta)$ due to refilling of subbands 1 and 2 respectively.

Find the stationary populations of the three subbands and the value of the ratio $\rho = \dfrac{N_1^\infty}{N_2^\infty}$.

Solution

We write the system of equations:

$$
\begin{pmatrix} \dfrac{dN_1}{dt} \\[2ex] \dfrac{dN_2}{dt} \\[2ex] \dfrac{dN_3}{dt} \end{pmatrix} = \begin{pmatrix} -\dfrac{1}{\tau_{12}} & \dfrac{1}{\tau_{12}} & \alpha \\[2ex] \dfrac{1}{\tau_{12}} & -\dfrac{1}{\tau_{12}} - \dfrac{1}{\tau_{23}} & \beta \\[2ex] 0 & \dfrac{1}{\tau_{23}} & -(\alpha + \beta) \end{pmatrix} \begin{pmatrix} N_1 \\[2ex] N_2 \\[2ex] N_3 \end{pmatrix} \qquad \text{(III.48.1)}
$$

We let

$$t = x\tau_{12}; \quad a = \alpha\tau_{12}; \quad b = \beta\tau_{12}; \quad \xi = \frac{\tau_{12}}{\tau_{23}} \tag{III.48.2}$$

$$\begin{pmatrix} \dfrac{dN_1}{dx} \\[2mm] \dfrac{dN_2}{dx} \\[2mm] \dfrac{dN_3}{dx} \end{pmatrix} = \begin{pmatrix} -1 & 1 & a \\[1mm] 1 & -1-\xi & b \\[1mm] 0 & \xi & -(a+b) \end{pmatrix} \begin{pmatrix} N_1 \\[2mm] N_2 \\[2mm] N_3 \end{pmatrix} \tag{III.48.3}$$

We note that the total population $N_1 + N_2 + N_3$ is a constant. In the permanent regime, we can express N_1, N_2 in terms of N_3 and there is:

$$N_2^\infty = (\alpha + \beta)\tau_{23}N_3^\infty \; ; \; N_1^\infty = \tau_{12}\alpha\left[1 + \frac{\tau_{23}}{\tau_{21}}\left(1 + \frac{\beta}{\alpha}\right)\right]N_3^\infty \tag{III.48.4}$$

$$\rho = \frac{N_1^\infty}{N_2^\infty} = \left(\frac{\alpha}{\alpha + \beta}\right)\left(1 + \frac{\tau_{12}}{\tau_{23}} + \frac{\beta}{\alpha}\right) \tag{III.48.5}$$

Thus, a fast emptying of the subband 2 leads to a large imbalance of the steady state populations N_1 and N_2.

On the other hand if we cut the escape from subband 2 to subband 3 by letting τ_{23} to go to infinity, we find the ratio of the equilibrium populations that no longer depends on τ_{12}: the exchanges between subbands 1 and 2 are so fast that the final population ratio depends only on the refilling from subband 3 to subband 1 compared to that from subband 3 to subband 2. In fact, when $\tau_{23} \to \infty$, $\rho \to 1$. Figure 48.1 shows the time dependence of the normalised populations N_1, N_2, N_3 knowing that at $t = 0$, $N_1 = 1$, $N_2 = N_3 = 0$. Two values of the parameters $\xi = \frac{\tau_{12}}{\tau_{23}}$ have been considered. For $\xi = 0.1$ N_1 and N_2 become equal ($\frac{1}{2}$) at long time while if $\xi = 10$ there is a substantial imbalance between the asymptotic values of N_1 and N_2.

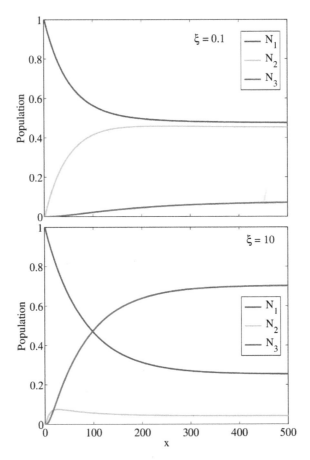

Figure 48.1.   Time dependence of the normalised populations N_1, N_2, N_3. Two values of the parameters $\xi = \frac{\tau_{12}}{\tau_{23}}$ have been considered: $\xi = 0.1$ (upper panel) and $\xi = 10$ (lower panel).

49.   Phonon-mediated equilibration of the electronic temperature to the lattice temperature

We consider a 2D electron gas with N_s electrons on an area S. It occupies a single electronic subband and we neglect any intersubband transition. We call E_1 the edge energy of this subband. The electrons have reached an internal equilibrium with temperature T_e while the lattice is at the temperature T_L. We consider a situation where the electron gas is classical, that is to say where the distribution function can safely be approximated by a Boltzmann law: $f_{n\vec{k}} = \exp\left[-\beta_e(\varepsilon_{n\vec{k}} - \mu)\right] \ll 1$, where μ is the chemical potential.

(1) Express N_s in terms of S, β_e, μ and E_1.

(2) What is the relationship between the average energy $\langle E \rangle$ of the N_s electrons and β_e?

(3) The energy loss rate of the electron gas is given by:

$$\frac{d\langle E \rangle}{dt} = -2 \sum_{\vec{k},\vec{k}'} \left[W_{\vec{k}\to\vec{k}'} f_{\vec{k}}(1 - f_{\vec{k}'}) - W_{\vec{k}'\to\vec{k}} f_{\vec{k}'}(1 - f_{\vec{k}}) \right] \left(\varepsilon_{\vec{k}} - \varepsilon_{\vec{k}'} \right)$$

$$(\text{III.49.1})$$

We assume that the phonons that are coupled to the electrons are bulk-like longitudinal optical (LO) phonons and we neglect their dispersion:

$$\omega_{LO}(\vec{Q}) = \omega_{LO} \Rightarrow \frac{1 + n_{LO}}{n_{LO}} = e^{\beta_L \hbar \omega_{LO}} \qquad (\text{III.49.2})$$

where n_{LO} is the Bose–Einstein distribution function. To further simplify the algebra we write:

$$W_{\vec{k}\to\vec{k}'}^{\text{emi}} = \left(\frac{2\pi}{\hbar} \right) W_0^2 (1 + n_{LO}) \delta(\varepsilon_{1\vec{k}} - \varepsilon_{1\vec{k}'} - \hbar\omega_{LO}) \qquad (\text{III.49.3})$$

$$W_{\vec{k}\to\vec{k}'}^{\text{abs}} = \left(\frac{2\pi}{\hbar} \right) W_0^2 n_{LO} \delta(\varepsilon_{1\vec{k}} - \varepsilon_{1\vec{k}'} + \hbar\omega_{LO}) \qquad (\text{III.49.4})$$

$$(\text{III.49.5})$$

where W_0 is a constant with the dimension of an energy.

Establish the differential equation fulfilled by the time-dependent electronic temperature $T_e(t)$. All the integrals are exactly computable.

(4) We let:

$$T_e = T_L(1 + x) \qquad (\text{III.49.6})$$

Linearise the differential equation assuming $x \ll 1$ and show that x exponentially relaxes towards zero.

Solution

(1) We write:

$$N_s = \frac{2S}{4\pi^2} \int_0^\infty 2\pi k dk \exp\left[-\beta_e\left(E_1 + \frac{\hbar^2 k^2}{2m_1} - \mu\right)\right] \qquad \text{(III.49.7)}$$

$$\Rightarrow N_s = \frac{Sm_1}{\pi\hbar^2\beta_e} \exp\left[-\beta_e(E_1 - \mu)\right] \qquad \text{(III.49.8)}$$

where E_1 is the edge of the first subband, m_1 the in-plane effective mass in the E_1 subband and $\beta_e = 1/(k_B T_e)$. The condition for the Boltzmann approximation to be justified is that the electron gas is non-degenerate; i.e., the chemical potential μ is well below E_1 compared to $1/\beta_e$.

(2) If the electron has a Boltzmann distribution function, the equipartition theorem of the old kinetic theory applies (every quadratic degree of freedom in the Hamiltonian contributes to $1/(2\beta_e)$). Since the free motion is 2D we have:

$$\langle E \rangle = N_s\left(E_1 + \frac{1}{\beta_e}\right) \qquad \text{(III.49.9)}$$

(3) We start from the definition of the energy loss rate. We neglect the occupation $f_{\vec{k}}$, $f_{\vec{k}'}$ compared to 1 and get:

$$\frac{d\langle E\rangle}{dt} = -2\sum_{\vec{k},\vec{k}'}\left(W_{\vec{k}\to\vec{k}'}f_{\vec{k}} - W_{\vec{k}'\to\vec{k}}f_{\vec{k}'}\right)\left(\varepsilon_{\vec{k}} - \varepsilon_{\vec{k}'}\right) \qquad \text{(III.49.10)}$$

since the only way to vary the energy of the electron gas is through absorption/emission of LO phonons. We have to account for absorption and emission processes:

$$\frac{d\langle E\rangle}{dt} = -2\sum_{\vec{k},\vec{k}'}[(W^{\text{emi}}_{\vec{k}\to\vec{k}'} + W^{\text{abs}}_{\vec{k}\to\vec{k}'})f_{\vec{k}} - (W^{\text{emi}}_{\vec{k}'\to\vec{k}} + W^{\text{abs}}_{\vec{k}'\to\vec{k}})f_{\vec{k}'}](\varepsilon_{\vec{k}} - \varepsilon_{\vec{k}'})$$

$$\text{(III.49.11)}$$

$$\frac{d\langle E\rangle}{dt} = \frac{d\langle E\rangle_{\text{emi}}}{dt} + \frac{d\langle E\rangle_{\text{abs}}}{dt} \qquad \text{(III.49.12)}$$

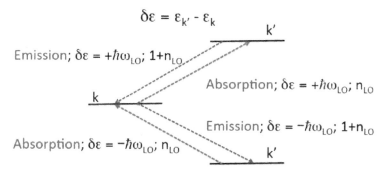

Figure 49.1. Sketch of the different electronic transitions by the emission/absorption of a LO phonon.

Starting from $\vec{k}$ going to $\vec{k'}$ an electron can (see Fig. 49.1 below)

(1) either absorb a phonon. The electron gas increases its energy by $\hbar\omega_{LO}$. The rate is proportional to n_{LO} and the energy conservation is $\varepsilon_{\vec{k'}} = \varepsilon_{\vec{k}} + \hbar\omega_{LO}$.

(2) or emit a phonon. The electron gas decreases its energy by $\hbar\omega_{LO}$. The rate is proportional to $1 + n_{LO}$ and the energy conservation is $\varepsilon_{\vec{k'}} = \varepsilon_{\vec{k}} - \hbar\omega_{LO}$.

Summing these contributions, putting appropriate signs (+ for energy gains, − for energy losses by the electron gas), we get after some manipulations:

$$N_s \frac{dk_B T_e}{dt} = -4(1 + n_{LO})2\pi\omega_{LO}W_0^2 \sum_{\vec{k},\vec{k'}} f_{\vec{k}} \left[\delta(\varepsilon_{\vec{k'}} - \varepsilon_{\vec{k}} + \hbar\omega_{LO}) \right.$$

$$\left. - e^{-\beta_L \hbar\omega_{LO}} \delta(\varepsilon_{\vec{k'}} - \varepsilon_{\vec{k}} - \hbar\omega_{LO}) \right] \tag{III.49.13}$$

$$n_{LO} = (1 + n_{LO})e^{-\beta_L \hbar\omega_{LO}} \tag{III.49.14}$$

We note that

$$N_s = 2\sum_{\vec{k}} f_{\vec{k}}; \quad 2\sum_{\vec{k}} f_{\vec{k}} Y(\varepsilon_{\vec{k}} - \hbar\omega_{LO}) = N_s \exp(-\beta_e \hbar\omega_{LO})$$

$$\tag{III.49.15}$$

since f_k is a Boltzmann distribution. So finally:

$$k_B \frac{dT_e}{dt} = -2(1 + n_{\mathrm{LO}})\omega_{\mathrm{LO}}W_0^2 \frac{Sm_1}{\hbar^2}$$
$$\times \exp(-\beta_e \hbar\omega_{\mathrm{LO}})\{-1 + \exp[(\beta_L - \beta_e)\hbar\omega_{\mathrm{LO}}]\} \quad \text{(III.49.16)}$$

We note that the energy loss rate is the difference between two Boltzmann-like terms. They both reflect thermally activated processes: as seen from the electron, absorbing a phonon increases its energy but requires the phonon presence; hence n_{L0} and at the end an exponentially small phonon number $\exp(-\beta_L \hbar\omega_{\mathrm{LO}})$ compared to an emission process.

For the emission process, that leads to a decrease of the energy of the electron gas, there is a factor $1 + n_{\mathrm{LO}}$ but to emit an LO phonon an electron should be energetic enough; hence a factor $\exp(-\beta_e \hbar\omega_{\mathrm{LO}})$ compared to an absorption process (which is always possible for a non-degenerate electron gas).

(4) We note that the differential equation is (formally) integrable since the variables t and T_L are separated. But an exact integration can only be done numerically. On the other hand, close from equilibrium we can use the proposed linearisation scheme. We get to the lowest order in x:

$$\frac{dx}{dt} = -\frac{x}{\tau}; \quad \frac{1}{\tau} = 2(1 + n_{\mathrm{LO}})\left(\frac{\hbar\omega_{\mathrm{LO}}}{k_B T_L}\right)^2 \frac{W_0^2}{\hbar}\frac{m^* S}{\hbar^2} \quad \text{(III.49.17)}$$

So x decays to zero exponentially with time with a time constant τ. Note that the sample area S is in actual calculation of W_0 cancelled by a term coming from the strength of the electron–phonon Hamiltonian.

50. Inter-subband scattering by unscreened coulombic impurities

We consider a quantum well (QW) with thickness L and height V_b. It has been delta-doped by coulombic impurities (areal concentration $N_{\mathrm{imp}}/S = 10^{11}$ cm^{-2}) on the plane $z = z_{\mathrm{imp}}$. This QW binds several bound states $E_1, E_2, \ldots$.

(1) The z origin is taken at the middle of the QW. Evaluate the lifetime of an electron (effective mass m^*) placed at the edge of the E_2 subband due to its scattering to E_1 states. Assume V_b is infinite. Take (1a) $z_{imp} = 0.1L$, (1b) $z_{imp} = 2L/\pi$. We give:

$$\int dx \sin(\alpha x) e^{\beta x} = \frac{e^{\beta x}}{\alpha^2 + \beta^2} [\beta \sin(\alpha x) - \alpha \cos(\alpha x)] \qquad \text{(III.50.1)}$$

(2) Compute the magnitude of this lifetime if $m^* = 0.07 m_0$, $L = 50$ nm, $\varepsilon_r = 12.4$, $1/4\pi\varepsilon_0 \approx 9 \times 10^9$ SI, $e = 1.6 \times 10^{-19}$ C.

(3) Will (1a) and (1b) remain true if the barrier height is finite?

(4) Will (1b) change if a constant and homogeneous electric field F is applied parallel to the z-axis? Can you elaborate a model to handle the $F \neq 0$ case?

Solution

Applying the Fermi golden rule, we have

$$\frac{\hbar}{2\pi\tau_{2,k=0}} = \sum_{\vec{k}'} |\langle 2\vec{k} = 0|V_{imp}|1\vec{k}'\rangle|^2 \delta\left(E_2 - E_1 - \frac{\hbar^2 k'^2}{2m^*}\right)$$

$$\text{(III.50.2)}$$

$$V_{imp}(\vec{r}) = -\sum_{\vec{\rho}_i} \frac{e^2}{4\pi\varepsilon_0\varepsilon_r \sqrt{(\vec{\rho} - \vec{\rho}_i)^2 + (z - z_{imp})^2}}$$

$$= -\frac{2\pi e^2}{\kappa S} \sum_{\vec{\rho}_i} \sum_{\vec{q}} \frac{e^{-q|z - z_{imp}|}}{q} e^{i\vec{q}\cdot(\vec{\rho} - \vec{\rho}_i)} \qquad \text{(III.50.3)}$$

where $\kappa = 4\pi\varepsilon_0\varepsilon_r$ and $\vec{q}$ is a 2D wavevector. Assuming the impurities are randomly distributed and diluted, the average over their positions amounts to multiplying the rate of scattering by one impurity by

N_{imp}. Then:

$$\frac{\hbar}{2\pi \tau_{2,k=0}} = N_{\text{imp}} \left(\frac{2\pi e^2}{\kappa S}\right)^2 \sum_{\vec{q}} \frac{|\langle 2|e^{-q|z-z_{\text{imp}}|}|1\rangle|^2}{q^2}$$

$$\times \delta\left(E_2 - E_1 - \frac{\hbar^2 q^2}{2m^*}\right)$$

$$= \frac{N_{\text{imp}}}{S} \left(\frac{e^2}{\kappa}\right)^2 \int_0^\infty 2\pi q\, dq \frac{|\langle 2|e^{-q|z-z_{\text{imp}}|}|1\rangle|^2}{q^2}$$

$$\times \delta\left(E_2 - E_1 - \frac{\hbar^2 q^2}{2m^*}\right)$$

$$= \frac{N_{\text{imp}}}{S} \left(\frac{e^2}{\kappa}\right)^2 \frac{2\pi m^*}{\hbar^2 q_{21}^2} |\langle 2|e^{-q_{21}|z-z_{\text{imp}}|}|1\rangle|^2;$$

$$q_{21} = \sqrt{\frac{2m^*(E_2 - E_1)}{\hbar^2}} \tag{III.50.4}$$

And finally:

$$\frac{\hbar}{2\pi \tau_{2,k=0}} = \pi \frac{N_{\text{imp}}}{S} \left(\frac{e^2}{\kappa}\right)^2 \frac{1}{E_2 - E_1} |\langle 2|e^{-q_{21}|z-z_{\text{imp}}|}|1\rangle|^2 \tag{III.50.5}$$

(a) The form factor can be readily evaluated. If z_{imp} coincides with the middle of the well the impurity potential is an even function of z. Consequently, it cannot connect subbands with different parities and there is no inter-subband scattering associated with on-center coulombic impurities.

(b) If the delta doping occurs in the barrier (e.g., $z_{\text{imp}} > L/2$), we can calculate the form factor by noting that:

$$\frac{2}{L} \int_{-L/2}^{L/2} dz \sin\left(\frac{2\pi z}{L}\right) \cos\left(\frac{\pi z}{L}\right) \exp[-q_{21}(z_{\text{imp}} - z)]$$

$$= \frac{1}{\pi} \exp[-q_{21}(z_{\text{imp}})] \int_{-\pi/2}^{\pi/2} dx [\sin(3x) + \sin(x)] \exp\left(\frac{q_{21} L}{\pi} x\right) \tag{III.50.6}$$

Therefore, we get:

$$\langle 2|e^{-q_{21}|z-z_{\text{imp}}|}|1\rangle = \frac{2\beta \cosh(\beta\pi/2)}{\pi}\left(\frac{1}{\beta^2+1} - \frac{1}{\beta^2+9}\right)$$

$$\times \exp(-q_{21}z_{\text{imp}}) \quad\quad \text{(III.50.7)}$$

$$\beta = \frac{q_{21}L}{\pi} \quad\quad \text{(III.50.8)}$$

where cosh is the hyperbolic cosine:

$$\cosh x = \frac{e^x + e^{-x}}{2} \quad\quad \text{(III.50.9)}$$

We note that the form factor vanishes if $q_{21} = 0$ (which is actually not possible) and it decays exponentially at large $z_{\text{imp}} - L/2$. This is another example of modulation doping: if we place the impurities further and further in the barrier, any scattering becomes increasingly inhibited, was it either intra-subband (as displayed in the velocity relaxation time and evidenced in the mobility enhancement) or inter-subband (the present calculation). We find an exponential decay that is faster when q_{21} is larger ($\frac{\hbar}{\tau} \propto e^{-2q_{21}(z_{\text{imp}}-\frac{L}{2})}$); this is another example of the weakness of the coulombic scattering at large wavevector transfer.

(2) Let us evaluate an order of magnitude of the inter-subband scattering time. For the parameters given in the text, we find: 0.34 ps for $z_{\text{imp}} = 2L/\pi$ and 0.10 ps for $z_{\text{imp}} = 0.1L$.

(3) If the QW has a finite height, (1a) remains true because the conclusions arise from symmetry arguments that keep holding in the finite barrier case; (1b) instead is no longer quantitatively true since the wavefunctions, form factors, etc. are different in the finite barrier case. However, the trend on the weakening of the matrix element when the impurity plane is farther and farther away from the QW remains valid.

(4) We consider on-center impurities ($z_{\text{imp}} = 0$). If a longitudinal electric field is applied to the QW, irrespective of its intensity, it will break the mirror symmetry of the potential energy that exists

at $F = 0$. Hence, the impurity form factor that used to vanish due to this symmetry should in principle be non-vanishing at $F \neq 0$.

It is possible to evaluate it in the limit of weak electric field $(eFL \ll E_2 - E_1)$. In this case we use first-order perturbation calculus:

$$|\psi_1\rangle = |1\rangle + \sum_{n \neq 1} |n\rangle \frac{\langle n|eFz|1\rangle}{E_1 - E_n};$$

$$|\psi_2\rangle = |2\rangle + \sum_{n \neq 2} |n\rangle \frac{\langle n|eFz|2\rangle}{E_2 - E_n} \qquad \text{(III.50.10)}$$

$$\langle \psi_1| \exp(-q_{21}|z|)|\psi_2\rangle \approx \sum_{n \neq 2} \langle 1| \exp(-q_{21}|z|)|n\rangle \frac{\langle n|eFz|2\rangle}{E_2 - E_n}$$

$$+ \sum_{m \neq 1} \langle m| \exp(-q_{21}|z|)|2\rangle \frac{\langle 1|eFz|m\rangle}{E_1 - E_m}$$

$$\text{(III.50.11)}$$

$(z_{\text{imp}} = 0)$. In the two terms contributing to the form factor, the first one requires n to be even while in the second one m has to be odd. At the lowest order in F we find that the inter-subband scattering time will vary like F^2. We can numerically evaluate this form factor. But a reasonable estimate of the magnitude of the induced scattering time is obtained by retaining the first terms in the two summations: $n = 1$ and $m = 2$. If one does so, one obtains:

$$\langle \psi_1| \exp(-q_{21}|z|)|\psi_2\rangle \approx eF \frac{\langle 1|z|2\rangle}{3E_1} \left[\langle 1| \exp(-q_{21}|z|)|1\rangle \right.$$

$$\left. - \langle 2| \exp(-q_{21}|z|)|2\rangle \right] \qquad \text{(III.50.12)}$$

At this approximation the inter-subband impurity form factor at $F \neq 0$ appears proportional to the difference between the two intra-subband ones at $F = 0$. There is $\langle 1|z|2\rangle = \frac{16L}{9\pi^2}$ and:

$$\langle 1| \exp(-q_{21}|z|)|1\rangle$$

$$= \frac{1}{\pi}\left[\frac{2\pi}{q_{21}L}(1-e^{-\frac{q_{21}L}{2}}) + \frac{\frac{q_{21}L}{2\pi}}{1+\left(\frac{q_{21}L}{2\pi}\right)^2}(1+e^{-\frac{q_{21}L}{2}})\right]$$

(III.50.13)

$$\langle 2| \exp(-q_{21}|z|)|2\rangle$$

$$= \frac{1}{2\pi}\left[\frac{4\pi}{q_{21}L}(1-e^{-\frac{q_{21}L}{2}}) - \frac{\frac{q_{21}L}{4\pi}}{1+\left(\frac{q_{21}L}{4\pi}\right)^2}(1-e^{-\frac{q_{21}L}{2}})\right]$$

(III.50.14)

We note the correct limiting values of these intra-subband form factors, namely that they extrapolate to one when $q_{21} \to 0$ and that they go to zero when $q_{21} \to \infty$ (faster for the excited states because its envelope function vanishes at $z = 0$).

We show in Fig. 50.1 two intra-subband factors for on-center impurities versus $q_{21}L/2\pi$ and the inter-subband one at $F = 20$ kV/cm. Despite the fact that the inter-subband transition induced by impurities has become allowed, the efficiency of this inter-subband transfer clearly lags behind the intra-subband one.

51. Evaluation of a double sum appearing in the free carrier absorption

When discussing the free carrier absorption in the z polarisation (Chapter II.5.4), we had to compute an expression:

$$I(\omega) = 2\sum_{\vec{k},\vec{k'}}(f_{n\vec{k'}} - f_{n\vec{k}})\delta\left(\frac{\hbar^2(k^2 - k'^2)}{2m^*} - \hbar\omega\right)$$

(III.51.1)

where:

$$f_{n\vec{k}} = \frac{1}{1 + \exp\left[\beta\left(\frac{\hbar^2k^2}{2m^*} - \mu\right)\right]}$$

(III.51.2)

μ is the chemical potential counted from the subband edge E_n. Expressions for $I(\omega)$ were given in the limits of very dilute or

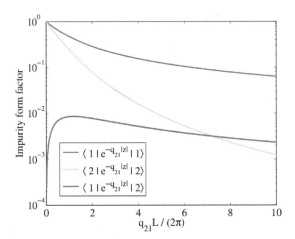

Figure 50.1.   Variation of the two intra-subband form factors $\langle 1|\exp(-q_{21}|z|)|1\rangle$ (blue line) and $\langle 2|\exp(-q_{21}|z|)|2\rangle$ (green line) for on-center impurities and the inter-subband one $\langle 1|\exp(-q_{21}|z|)|2\rangle$ (red line) at $F = 20$ kV/cm versus $q_{21}L/2\pi$. $L = 10$ nm.

degenerate carriers densities. Because the in-plane motion is bi-dimensional, it is actually possible to compute $I(\omega)$ exactly.

Evaluate $I(\omega)$ versus the chemical potential μ. Express μ in terms of the carrier density n/S and the temperature T.

Check that the $T \to 0$, $T \to \infty$ limits at fixed n/S coincide with the results given in Chapter II.5.4.

Solution

In evaluating $I(\omega)$ it is better to get rid of k because the argument of the delta function will vanish for a $k(k', \omega)$ that has no restriction on k' and ω. Thus:

$$I(\omega) = 2\sum_{\vec{k'}} \frac{S}{2\pi} \int_0^\infty k\,dk$$

$$\times \left[\frac{1}{1 + \exp\left[\beta\left(\frac{\hbar^2 k'^2}{2m^*} - \mu\right)\right]} - \frac{1}{1 + \exp\left[\beta\left(\frac{\hbar^2 k^2}{2m^*} - \mu\right)\right]} \right]$$

$$\times \delta\left(\frac{\hbar^2 k^2}{2m^*} - \frac{\hbar^2 k'^2}{2m^*} - \hbar\omega\right) \tag{III.51.3}$$

$$= 2\frac{m^*S}{2\pi\hbar^2}\sum_{\vec{k}'}$$

$$\times\left[\frac{1}{1+\exp\left[\beta\left(\frac{\hbar^2k'^2}{2m^*}-\mu\right)\right]}-\frac{1}{1+e^{\beta\hbar\omega}\exp\left[\beta\left(\frac{\hbar^2k'^2}{2m^*}-\mu\right)\right]}\right]$$

$$\text{(III.51.4)}$$

We convert the summation over k' into an integration and let

$$\beta\frac{\hbar^2k'^2}{2m^*}=x \qquad\qquad\text{(III.51.5)}$$

We obtain:

$$I(\omega)=2\frac{m^{*2}S^2k_BT}{4\pi^2\hbar^4}\int_0^\infty dx\left(\frac{e^{-x}}{e^{-x}+e^{-\beta\mu}}-\frac{e^{-x}}{e^{-x}+e^{\beta\hbar\omega}e^{-\beta\mu}}\right)$$

$$\text{(III.51.6)}$$

$$=2\frac{m^{*2}S^2k_BT}{4\pi^2\hbar^4}[\ln(1+e^{\beta\mu})-\ln(1+e^{\beta(\mu-\hbar\omega)})] \qquad\text{(III.51.7)}$$

The electron concentration is related to the chemical potential by:

$$\frac{n}{S}=\frac{m^*k_BT}{\pi\hbar^2}\ln(1+e^{\beta\mu}) \qquad\qquad\text{(III.51.8)}$$

Thus:

$$I(\omega)=\frac{m^*S^2}{2\pi\hbar^2}\frac{n}{S}\left[1-\frac{\ln(1+e^{\beta(\mu-\hbar\omega)})}{\ln(1+e^{\beta\mu})}\right] \qquad\text{(III.51.9)}$$

The classical (Boltzmann limit) is achieved when $\beta\mu\ll 0$ (the chemical potential is well below the subband edge). Then the exponentials in the arguments of the logarithms are very small and we may expand the ln's to obtain:

$$I_{\text{classical}}(\omega)\approx\frac{m^*S^2}{2\pi\hbar^2}\frac{n}{S}(1-e^{-\beta\hbar\omega}) \qquad\text{(III.51.10)}$$

On the contrary at low temperature, for a fixed n/S, the chemical potential is well above the subband edge compared to k_BT. $e^{\beta\mu}$ is very large. So is $e^{\beta(\mu-\hbar\omega)}$ if $\mu-\hbar\omega>0$. On the other hand, if

$\mu - \hbar\omega < 0$, the corresponding exponential will be very small. Thus, in the $T \to 0$ limit for a fixed n/S, we find:

$$I_{T\to0}(\omega) = \frac{m^* S^2}{2\pi\hbar^2} \frac{n}{S} \left[\frac{\hbar\omega}{\mu} Y(\mu - \hbar\omega) + Y(\hbar\omega - \mu) \right] \qquad \text{(III.51.11)}$$

and at $T = 0$ K μ coincides with the Fermi energy ε_F. Thus, both high and low temperature limits found in Chapter II.5.4 are recovered.

52. Energy loss rate for the in-plane polarisation $T = 0$ K

The energy loss rate due to absorption for the in-plane polarisation is given by the expression:

$$P_{\text{loss}}^{x,y} = \frac{\pi e^2 E_{\text{em}}^2}{2m^{*2}\omega} 2 \sum_{\vec{k},\vec{k}'} f_{n\vec{k}} (1 - f_{n\vec{k}'}) \langle |\langle \tilde{\Psi}_{n\vec{k}'} | p_{x,y} | \tilde{\Psi}_{n\vec{k}} \rangle|^2 \rangle_{\bar{\rho}_i} \delta$$

$$\times \left(\frac{\hbar^2(k^2 - k'^2)}{2m^*} - \hbar\omega \right) \qquad \text{(III.52.1)}$$

where for uncorrelated delta scatterers there is:

$$\left\langle \left| \langle \tilde{\Psi}_{n\vec{k}'} | \frac{p_x + ip_y}{\sqrt{2}} | \tilde{\Psi}_{n\vec{k}} \rangle \right|^2 \right\rangle_{\bar{\rho}_i}$$

$$= N_{\text{def}} \left(\frac{\sqrt{2}m^* V_0 a^3}{\hbar S} \right)^2 \chi_n^4(z_0) \frac{(\vec{k} - \vec{k}')^2}{(k^2 - k'^2)^2} \qquad \text{(III.52.2)}$$

Taking into account the photon absorption, one is led to evaluating the double sum:

$$I = \sum_{\vec{k},\vec{k}'} (f_{n\vec{k}'} - f_{n\vec{k}}) \frac{(\vec{k} - \vec{k}')^2}{(k^2 - k'^2)^2} \delta \left(\frac{\hbar^2(k^2 - k'^2)}{2m^*} - \hbar\omega \right) \qquad \text{(III.52.3)}$$

We consider a 2D gas with a given electron concentration n/S. Compute I at $T = 0$ K using the previous expressions. *Hint*: in the double sum it is easier to start by the sum over $\vec{k}$.

Solution

We compute:

$$I = \sum_{\vec{k},\vec{k}'}(f_{n\vec{k}'} - f_{n\vec{k}})\frac{(\vec{k} - \vec{k}')^2}{(k^2 - k'^2)^2}\delta\left(\frac{\hbar^2(k^2 - k'^2)}{2m^*} - \hbar\omega\right) \quad \text{(III.52.4)}$$

We first integrate over $\vec{k}$. We note that

$$(\vec{k} - \vec{k}')^2 = k^2 + k'^2 - 2kk'\cos\theta \quad \text{(III.52.5)}$$

where θ is the angle between $\vec{k}$ and $\vec{k}'$. There is no other angular dependence in I. Hence, after integrating over θ, we are left with an integration over the modulus $k = |\vec{k}|$. This modulus is given by the zero of the argument of the delta function. Finally, we obtain:

$$I = \frac{S^2}{4\pi^2}\left(\frac{\hbar}{2m^*\omega}\right)^2\frac{2m^*}{\hbar^2}\int_0^\infty k'dk'\left(k'^2 + \frac{m^*\omega}{\hbar}\right)$$

$$\times\left[\frac{1}{1 + \exp\left(\frac{\hbar^2 k'^2}{2m^* k_B T}\right)e^{-\beta\mu}} - \frac{1}{1 + \exp\left(\frac{\hbar^2 k'^2}{2m^* k_B T}\right)e^{-\beta(\mu - \hbar\omega)}}\right]$$

$$\text{(III.52.6)}$$

We make the change of variable:

$$\frac{\hbar^2 k'^2}{2m^*} = \varepsilon \quad \text{(III.52.7)}$$

and obtain:

$$I = \left(\frac{S\hbar}{4\pi m^*\omega}\right)^2\left(\frac{2m^*}{\hbar^2}\right)^2\frac{m^*}{\hbar^2}\int_0^\infty d\varepsilon\left(\varepsilon + \frac{\hbar\omega}{2}\right)$$

$$\times\left(\frac{1}{1 + e^{\beta(\varepsilon - \mu)}} - \frac{1}{1 + e^{\beta(\varepsilon - \mu + \hbar\omega)}}\right) \quad \text{(III.52.8)}$$

In the integral, the second bracket > 0 is the difference between two Fermi–Dirac functions characterised by chemical potentials μ and $\mu - \hbar\omega$. They look like Heaviside functions blurred by $k_B T$ around the chemical potentials. Hence, in the limit $T \to 0$, we can limit the

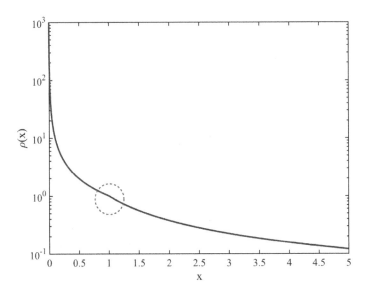

Figure 52.1.   Evolution of the dimensionless ratio ρ versus $x = \hbar\omega/\varepsilon_F$; $n/S = 2 \times 10^{10}$ cm^{-2}, $m* = 0.07m_0$, $N_{\text{def}}/S = 10^{11}$ cm^{-2}, $V_0 = 0.6$ eV and $a = 0.3$ nm; $S = 200$ nm$\times$200 nm; $E_{\text{em}} = 1$ kV/cm.

integration to the segment $[0, \mu]$ and $[0, \mu - \hbar\omega]$ (if $\mu - \hbar\omega > 0$) to obtain:

$$I(\omega) = \frac{S^2}{8\pi^2\hbar^2\omega^2} \frac{m^*\mu}{\hbar^2} \left[\mu + \hbar\omega - (\mu - \hbar\omega)\left(1 - \frac{\hbar\omega}{2\mu}\right)Y(\mu - \hbar\omega) \right]$$

$$(\text{III.52.9})$$

where $Y(x) = 1$ if $x > 0$ and $Y(x) = 0$ if $x < 0$.

At small ω, $I(\omega)$ diverges like ω^{-2}. We show in Fig. 52.1 the dimensionless ratio:

$$\rho = \frac{I(T = 0, \hbar\omega)}{I(T = 0, \mu)} \qquad (\text{III.52.10})$$

versus $x = \hbar\omega/\varepsilon_F$:

$$\rho(x) = \frac{1}{2x^2}[1 + x - (1 - x)Y(1 - x)] \qquad (\text{III.52.11})$$

The Drude-like behaviour is clearly evidenced and there is a faint kink when $\hbar\omega = \varepsilon_F$.

53. Inter-subband absorption versus carrier concentration in an ideal heterostructure

The inter subband absorption coefficient associated with vertical transitions between parabolic subbands 1 and 2 with the same in-plane effective mass in an ideal heterostructure is given by:

$$\alpha_{\text{inter}}^{1\to 2}(\omega) = \frac{\pi e^2}{m^{*2}\omega\varepsilon_0 c n_r L}|\langle 1|p_z|2\rangle|^2 (n_1 - n_2)\delta(E_2 - E_1 - \hbar\omega)$$

$$(\text{III.53.1})$$

where n_r is the refraction index, n_1 and n_2 are the populations of subbands 1 and 2, respectively, and L is the length of the heterostructure. We assume thermal equilibrium at temperature $T \approx 0$ K.

(1) Suppose one can control the total electronic population n. Compute the absorption coefficient versus n and show that it saturates at large n.

(2) Compute the matrix element $\langle 1|p_z|2\rangle$ in the case of a quantum well with infinite barriers.

Solution

(1) Suppose that the total 2D electron concentration n is given. Its repartition between the different subbands depends on the temperature T and the subband spacing. We write:

$$n = \sum_j n_j; \quad n_j = \frac{2}{4\pi^2}2\pi \int_0^\infty \frac{k dk}{1 + \exp[\beta(E_j - \mu)]\exp\left(\beta\frac{\hbar^2 k^2}{2m^*}\right)}$$

$$(\text{III.53.2})$$

The change of variable $\beta\frac{\hbar^2 k^2}{2m^*} = x$ leads to:

$$n_j = \frac{m^* k_B T}{\pi \hbar^2}\int_0^\infty dx \frac{e^{-x}}{e^{-x} + \lambda_j} = \frac{m^* k_B T}{\pi \hbar^2}\ln\left(1 + \frac{1}{\lambda_j}\right) \quad (\text{III.53.3})$$

$$\lambda_j = \exp[\beta(E_j - \mu)] \quad (\text{III.53.4})$$

Equations (III.53.2)–(III.53.4) are implicit equations in $\mu(n, T)$. At low temperature, the λ_j are either very small if $\mu > E_j$ or very large if $\mu < E_j$. Then:

$$n_j \approx \frac{m^*}{\pi\hbar^2}(\mu - E_j) \quad \text{if } \mu > E_j \tag{III.53.5}$$

$$n_j \approx \frac{m^* k_B T}{\pi\hbar^2 \lambda_j} \quad \text{if } \mu < E_j \tag{III.53.6}$$

In the limit $T \to 0$, we find:

$$n = \sum_j \frac{m^*}{\pi\hbar^2}(\varepsilon_F - E_j)Y(\varepsilon_F - E_j) \tag{III.53.7}$$

where $Y(x)$ is the step function. In the same $T \to 0$ limit, the intersubband absorption coefficient becomes:

$$\alpha_{\text{inter}}^{1\to 2}(\omega) = \begin{cases} \dfrac{e^2(\varepsilon_F - E_1)}{m^*\hbar^2\omega\varepsilon_0 c n_r L}|\langle 1|p_z|2\rangle|^2 & E_1 \leq \varepsilon_F \leq E_2 \\ \quad \delta(E_2 - E_1 - \hbar\omega); \\ \dfrac{e^2(E_2 - E_1)}{m^*\hbar^2\omega\varepsilon_0 c n_r L}|\langle 1|p_z|2\rangle|^2 & \varepsilon_F \geq E_2 \\ \quad \delta(E_2 - E_1 - \hbar\omega); \end{cases} \tag{III.53.8}$$

Thus, $\alpha(\omega)$ as a function of the electron concentration n is first proportional to n and saturates as soon as the final subband becomes populated. This behaviour is a direct consequence of the 2D free motion that leads to an energy-dependent density of states

$$\varepsilon_F = E_1 + \frac{\hbar^2 k_{F1}^2}{2m^*} = E_2 + \frac{\hbar^2 k_{F2}^2}{2m^*} \tag{III.53.9}$$

When $\varepsilon_F \leq E_2$, the whole population of electrons contributes to absorption and because the in-plane dispersions are parallel, all electrons contribute with the same delta peak. However, when $\varepsilon_F \geq E_2$, the absorption corresponding to $k \leq k_{F2}$ becomes blocked and the absorption now results from the electron states that are located between k_{F2} and k_{F1}. The concentration of these electrons is proportional to the orange area shown in Fig. 53.1 (left panel).

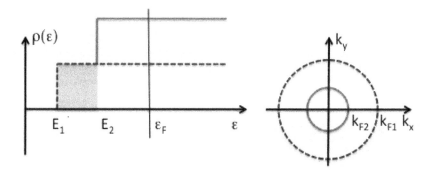

Figure 53.1. Left panel: density of states ρ versus the energy of the state ε. Right panel: Schematic representation of the wavevector k_{F1} and k_{F_2} in the 2D k-space.

(2) We take advantage of the parity of the potential energy with respect to z (origin at the centre of the well) to write that the wavefunctions are:

$$\chi_{2j+1}(z) = \sqrt{\frac{2}{L}} \cos\left([2j+1]\frac{\pi z}{L}\right), \quad j = 0, 1, 2 \qquad \text{(III.53.10)}$$

$$\chi_{2j}(z) = \sqrt{\frac{2}{L}} \sin\left(2j\frac{\pi z}{L}\right), \quad j = 1, 2 \qquad \text{(III.53.11)}$$

Thus, to compute $\langle 1|p_z|2\rangle$, we write:

$$\langle 1|p_z|2\rangle = -i\hbar\frac{2}{L}\int_{-L/2}^{L/2} dz \cos\left(\frac{\pi z}{L}\right)\frac{d}{dz}\left[\sin\left(\frac{2\pi z}{L}\right)\right] \qquad \text{(III.53.12)}$$

$$= -i\hbar\frac{4\pi}{L^2}\int_{-L/2}^{L/2} dz \cos\left(\frac{\pi z}{L}\right)\cos\left(\frac{2\pi z}{L}\right) \qquad \text{(III.53.13)}$$

$$= -i\hbar\frac{4\pi}{L^2}\int_{0}^{L/2} dz \left[\cos\left(\frac{\pi z}{L}\right) + \cos\left(\frac{3\pi z}{L}\right)\right] = -\frac{8i\hbar}{3L} \qquad \text{(III.53.14)}$$

We note that since there is a single characteristic length L in this problem, the matrix element of p_z is necessarily proportional to $\frac{\hbar}{L}$. We also note that despite p_z being a hermitian operator, its off-diagonal matrix elements are purely imaginary. The diagonal elements are all real and in fact all are equal to zero because there is no average velocity for a bound state. A secondary reason is that the eigenstates have a definite parity. But we stress that the diagonal elements of p_z always vanish for bound states independently of the commutation of the parity operator with the Hamiltonian.

54. Electron–LO phonon interaction: dimensionality dependence

Using the Fermi golden rule, the lifetime due to emission of LO phonons from a state $|\vec{k}_i\rangle$ with the energy ε_i can be written at $T = 0$ K:

$$\frac{\hbar}{2\pi\tau_i} = A^2 \sum_{\vec{Q}, \vec{k}'} \frac{|\langle\Psi_i|e^{i\vec{Q}\cdot\vec{r}}|\Psi_{\vec{k}'}\rangle|^2}{Q^2} \delta(\varepsilon_i - \varepsilon(\vec{k}') - \hbar\omega_{\text{LO}}) \quad \text{(III.54.1)}$$

$$A^2 = e^2 \frac{\hbar\omega_{\text{LO}}}{2\Omega\varepsilon_0}\left(\frac{1}{\varepsilon_r(\infty)} - \frac{1}{\varepsilon_r(0)}\right) \quad \text{(III.54.2)}$$

where $\vec{Q}$ is the 3D wavevector of the optical phonons with energy $\hbar\omega_{\text{LO}}$ (LO phonons are assumed dispersionless). A is a constant that is expressible in terms of the dielectric constants: high frequency $\varepsilon_r(\infty)$ and static $\varepsilon_r(0)$; ε_0 is the vacuum dielectric constant. $\vec{k}'$, $\vec{k}_i$ are electronic wavevectors whose dimensions vary depending on whether we deal with a bulk material ($D = 3$), a quantum well ($D = 2$) or a wire ($D = 1$). At $T \neq 0$ K, one has to multiply the previous expression by $1 + n_{\text{LO}}$, where n_{LO} is the Bose–Einstein occupation function at the LO phonon energy.

In the following, we look at transitions close from the threshold of LO phonon emission (see Fig. 54.1): $\varepsilon_i = \hbar\omega_{\text{LO}} + \eta$, $\eta \to 0$, where depending on D, the energy zero is the bottom of the conduction band ($D = 3$), of a quantum well subband ($D = 2$) or of a 1D subband ($D = 1$). Then, $\varepsilon(\vec{k}') \to 0$, $\vec{k}' \to 0$. Let $\vec{k}_i$ be the initial wavevector.

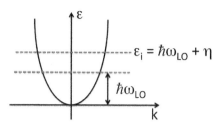

Figure 54.1. Sketch of the LO phonon emission near the threshold: an electron initially at energy ε_i emits an LO phonon. Its final state is near $k = 0$: $\eta \to 0$.

(1) Bulk material ($D = 3$)

Starting from the Fermi golden rule, show that:

$$\frac{\hbar}{2\pi\tau_i} = A^2(1 + n_{\text{LO}}) \sum_{\vec{Q},\vec{k'}} \frac{1}{Q^2} \delta_{\vec{Q},\vec{k_i}-\vec{k'}} \delta\left(\varepsilon_i - \varepsilon(\vec{k'}) - \hbar\omega_{\text{LO}}\right)$$

$$= A^2(1 + n_{\text{LO}}) \sum_{\vec{k'}} \frac{1}{|\vec{k'} - \vec{k_i}|^2} \delta\left(\eta - \frac{\hbar^2 k'^2}{2m^*}\right) \qquad (\text{III.54.3})$$

where n_{LO} is the number of LO phonons at temperature T. By evaluating the required 3D integral over $\vec{k'}$ find the η dependence of $1/\tau_i$. We give:

$$\int_0^\pi d\theta \frac{\sin\theta}{a + b\cos\theta} = \frac{1}{b} \ln\left(\left|\frac{a+b}{a-b}\right|\right) \qquad (\text{III.54.4})$$

(2) Quasi-2D structures ($D = 2$)

The phonons are considered as being 3D, $\vec{Q} = (Q_z, \vec{q})$, but the electron free motion occurs only in the layer plane ($D = 2$). Starting from the Fermi golden rule show that for transitions in the nth subband there is

$$\frac{\hbar}{2\pi\tau_i} = \frac{A^2\Omega(1 + n_{\text{LO}})}{8\pi^3} \int_{-\infty}^{+\infty} dQ_z |\langle\chi_n|e^{iQ_z z}|\chi_n\rangle|^2$$

$$\times \int_0^{2\pi} d\varphi \int_0^\infty \frac{k'}{Q_z^2 + k_i^2 + k'^2 - 2k_i k' \cos\varphi} \delta\left(\eta - \frac{\hbar^2 k'^2}{2m^*}\right) dk'$$

$$(\text{III.54.5})$$

where φ is the angle between $\vec{k}$ and $\vec{k'}$ and χ_n the envelope function for the motion along z. We recall that:

$$\int_0^\infty k'b(k')\delta\left(\eta - \frac{\hbar^2 k'^2}{2m^*}\right)dk' = \frac{m^*}{\hbar^2}Y(\eta)b\left(\sqrt{\frac{2m^*\eta}{\hbar^2}}\right) \qquad (\text{III}.54.6)$$

where $b(x)$ is an arbitrary (smooth) function of x and $Y(x)$ is the step function. Deduce that:

$$\frac{\hbar}{2\pi\tau_i} = \frac{A^2\Omega m^*}{8\pi^3\hbar^2}(1 + n_{LO})Y(\eta)\int_{-\infty}^{+\infty}dQ_z|\langle\chi_n|e^{iQ_{zz}}|\chi_n\rangle|^2$$

$$\times \int_0^{2\pi}d\varphi\frac{1}{Q_z^2 + k_i^2 + k'^2 - 2k_ik'\cos\varphi}; \quad k' = \sqrt{\frac{2m^*\eta}{\hbar}}$$

$$(\text{III}.54.7)$$

The integral over φ can be calculated analytically. But, being interested in the $\eta \to 0$ limit, we may as well let $k' = 0$ in the previous formula. Show that we obtain:

$$\frac{\hbar}{2\pi\tau_i} = \frac{A^2\Omega m^*}{4\pi^2\hbar^2}(1 + n_{LO})Y(\eta)\int_{-\infty}^{+\infty}dQ_z\frac{|\langle\chi_n|e^{iQ_{zz}}|\chi_n\rangle|^2}{Q_z^2 + k_i^2} \qquad (\text{III}.54.8)$$

Comment on the difference with the $D = 3$ case.

(3) Quantum wire $(D = 1)$

We assume the quantum wire, parallel to the z-axis has an arbitrary cross section defined by $f(x,y) = 0$ with an closed boundary $y(x)$. Find the $\eta \to 0$ behaviour of τ_i when the electron is in the ground 1D subband of the wire.

Solution

(1) $D = 3$. To evaluate the scattering time we need to sum over the 3D phonon wavevectors $\vec{Q}$ and final 3D electron wavevectors $\vec{k'}$.

The Kronecker delta that expresses the translation invariance along the three directions of space allows to get rid of one of the two summations and to obtain:

$$\frac{\hbar}{2\pi\tau_i} = A^2(1+n_{\text{LO}})\frac{\Omega}{8\pi^3}\iiint d^3k' \frac{\delta\left(\eta - \frac{\hbar^2 k'^2}{2m^*}\right)}{|\vec{k}_i - \vec{k'}|^2} \qquad \text{(III.54.9)}$$

To perform the integration we use spherical coordinates with the k'_z direction parallel to the initial vector $\vec{k}_i$. We write:

$$|\vec{k'} - \vec{k}_i|^2 = k'^2 + k_i^2 - 2k_i k' \cos\theta; \quad 0 \le \theta \le \pi \qquad \text{(III.54.10)}$$

Then:

$$\frac{\hbar}{2\pi\tau_i} = A^2\frac{\Omega}{4\pi^2}(1+n_{\text{LO}})\int_0^\pi d\theta \frac{\sin\theta}{k'^2 + k_i^2 - 2k_i k' \cos\theta}$$

$$\times \int_0^\infty k'^2 dk' \delta\left(\eta - \frac{\hbar^2 k'^2}{2m^*}\right)$$

$$= A^2\frac{\Omega m^* k'(\eta)}{4\pi^2\hbar^2}(1+n_{\text{LO}})\int_0^\pi d\theta \frac{\sin\theta}{k'^2 + k_i^2 - 2k_i k' \cos\theta}$$

$$\text{(III.54.11)}$$

where $k'(\eta) = \sqrt{\frac{2m^*\eta}{\hbar^2}}$. Finally:

$$\frac{\hbar}{2\pi\tau_i} = A^2(1+n_{\text{LO}})\frac{\Omega m^*}{4\pi^2\hbar^2 k_i} \ln\left(\frac{1 + \frac{k'(\eta)}{k_i}}{1 - \frac{k'(\eta)}{k_i}}\right) \qquad \text{(III.54.12)}$$

In the vicinity of the onset $\eta \to 0$, $k_i \approx \sqrt{\frac{2m^*\omega_{\text{LO}}}{\hbar}}$, $\ln(\ldots) = 2\sqrt{\frac{\eta}{\hbar\omega_{\text{LO}}}}$ and:

$$\frac{\hbar}{2\pi\tau_i} = A^2(1+n_{\text{LO}})\frac{\Omega m^*}{2\pi^2\hbar^2 k_i}\sqrt{\frac{\eta}{\hbar\omega_{\text{LO}}}} \qquad \text{(III.54.13)}$$

Expressing A^2 leaves us with a particularly simple expression:

$$\frac{\hbar}{\tau_i} = \frac{e^2}{4\pi\varepsilon_0}(1+n_{\text{LO}})\sqrt{\frac{2m^*\eta}{\hbar^2}}\left(\frac{1}{\varepsilon_r(\infty)} - \frac{1}{\varepsilon_r(0)}\right) \qquad \text{(III.54.14)}$$

(2) $D = 2$. Starting from the Fermi golden rule, we have just to explicit the matrix elements of the electron–LO phonon interaction

to arrive at the proposed formula:

$$\frac{\hbar}{2\pi\tau_i} = \frac{A^2\Omega m^*}{8\pi^3\hbar^2}(1 + n_{\text{LO}})\int_{-\infty}^{+\infty} dQ_z |\langle\chi_n|e^{iQ_z z}|\chi_n\rangle|^2$$

$$\times \int_0^{2\pi} d\varphi \frac{Y(\eta)}{Q_z^2 + k_i^2 + k'^2 - 2k_i k' \cos\varphi}; \quad \eta = \frac{\hbar^2 k'^2}{2m^*}$$

$$(\text{III.54.15})$$

The angular integral can be found in tables. But we are asked about the $\eta \to 0$ behaviour where $k' = 0$. It is therefore easy to derive the required expression:

$$\frac{\hbar}{2\pi\tau_i} = \frac{A^2\Omega m^*}{4\pi^2\hbar^2}(1 + n_{\text{LO}})Y(\eta)\int_{-\infty}^{+\infty} dQ_z \frac{|\langle\chi_n|e^{iQ_z z}|\chi_n\rangle|^2}{Q_z^2 + k_i^2}$$

$$(\text{III.54.16})$$

We can manipulate the Q_z integral by writing the squared modulus explicitly and by using:

$$\int_{-\infty}^{\infty} dQ_z \frac{e^{iQ_z(z-z')}}{Q_z^2 + k_i^2} = \frac{\pi}{k_i}\exp(-k_i|z - z'|) \qquad (\text{III.54.17})$$

to get finally:

$$\frac{\hbar}{2\pi\tau_i} = \frac{A^2\Omega m^*}{4\pi\hbar^2 k_i}(1 + n_{\text{LO}})Y(\eta)\iint dz dz' \chi_n^2(z)\chi_n^2(z')\exp(-k_i|z - z'|)$$

$$(\text{III.54.18})$$

or

$$\frac{\hbar}{2\pi\tau_i} = \frac{e^2}{16\pi\varepsilon_0}(1 + n_{\text{LO}})\left(\frac{1}{\varepsilon_r(\infty)} - \frac{1}{\varepsilon_r(0)}\right)\sqrt{\frac{2m^*\omega_{\text{LO}}}{\hbar}}Y(\eta)$$

$$\times \iint dz dz' \chi_n^2(z)\chi_n^2(z')\exp(-k_i|z - z'|) \qquad (\text{III.54.19})$$

We note that the level broadening at the onset is non-vanishing in stark contrast with the 3D situation. We also note that for a given material, the broadening at the onset depends also on the quantum well thickness. The reader will check that for a quantum well with infinitely high barriers and assuming $k_i L \gg 1$, one finds $\tau_i \propto L$.

(3) $D = 1$. Proceeding exactly as before we arrive at:

$$\frac{\hbar}{2\pi\tau_i} = A^2 \frac{\Omega}{8\pi^3}(1 + n_{LO})Y(\eta)\sqrt{\frac{m^*}{2\hbar^2\eta}}\sum_{\pm}\iint dQ_x dQ_y$$

$$\times \frac{|\langle nm|e^{i\vec{q}\cdot\vec{\rho}}|nm\rangle|^2}{q^2 + (k_i \pm k_z)^2} \qquad\qquad (III.54.20)$$

$$\vec{q} = (Q_x, Q_y); \quad k_z = \sqrt{\frac{2m^*\eta}{\hbar^2}} \qquad\qquad (III.54.21)$$

where n and m denote the quantum numbers required to specify the bound electron states in the plane perpendicular to the wire. Note the $\sum_{\pm}$ over the two possible values of k_z. Here, k_z cannot be equal to k_i, hence $\pm k_z$ have to be retained. This contrasts with elastic scattering where the solution $k_z = k_i$ has to be excluded because the initial and final states would coincide. We could go one step further in the calculations and transform the double integral over $\vec{q}$ (a K_0 Bessel function with an imaginary argument would show up). But the central point is the $\eta^{-1/2}$ behaviour. This combined with the results obtained in (1) and (2) shows that the broadening at the onset of the LO phonon scattering emission is proportional to the density of states of the free electron motion. In a way, this could have been expected although the Fröhlich Hamiltonian is singular at $Q = 0$. But, in the intra-subband scattering Q can never vanish: near the onset it is equal to k_i, which is never zero because of the energy conservation. Thus, we could have as well simplify the qualitative aspect of the intra-subband scattering by writing that the Fröhlich matrix elements are constant, resulting in a broadening that is proportional to the density of final states. Note that the inter-subband scattering cannot *a priori* be handled by the same simplification since in the latter case k, k', q can all vanish near the threshold (when the subband spacing is equal to the LO phonon energy).

Finally, the 1D case raises a fundamental problem that is the divergence of the broadening near the onset. This invalidates the regular Born approximation and requires to go beyond this simple approach (e.g., using the self-consistent Born approximation, see Exercise 47).

A similar difficulty exists with Landau levels, either in bulk materials where the electron motion recalls the quantum wire case, or in quantum well systems where the electron density of states is a delta function when the magnetic field is parallel to the growth axis (see Chapter I.4).

Bibliography

[1] A. Messiah. *Quantum Mechanics*. Dover Publications, 1961.

[2] C. Davisson and L. H. Germer. The scattering of electrons by a single crystal of nickel. *Nature* 119:558, 1927.

[3] O. Nairz, B. Brezger, M. Arndt and A. Zeilinger. Diffraction of complex molecules by structures made of light. *Phys. Rev. Lett.* 87:160401, 2001.

[4] G. C. Goertzel and N. Tralli. *Some Mathematical Methods of Physics*. McGraw-Hill, 1960.

[5] K. Jacob. *Quantum Measurement Theory and its Applications*. Cambridge University Press, 2014.

[6] M. Born. *Atomic Physics*. Dover Publications, 1969.

[7] J. C. Slater. *Quantum Theory of Matter*. McGraw-Hill, 1951.

[8] D. Bouwmeester, A. Ekert and A. Zeilinger. *The Physics of Quantum Information, Quantum Cryptography, Quantum Teleportation, Quantum Computation*. Springer, 2000.

[9] C. Cohen-Tannoudji, B. Diu and F. Laloe. *Quantum Mechanics*. Hermann, 1997.

[10] J. Joachain. *Quantum Collision Theory*. North-Holland, 1975.

[11] J.-L. Basdevant and J. Dalibard. *Quantum Mechanics*. Springer, 2002.

[12] T. Ando, A. B. Fowler and F. Stern. Electronic properties of two-dimensional systems. *Rev. Mod. Phys.* 54:437–672, 1982.

[13] S. L. Chuang. *Physics of photonic devices*. Wiley, 2009.

[14] C. R. Pidgeon, D. L. Mitchell and R. N. Brown. Interband magnetoabsorption in InAs and InSb. *Phys. Rev.* 154:737–742, 1967.

[15] L. I. Schiff. *Quantum Mechanics*. McGraw-Hill 1968.

[16] G. H. Döhler. Electron states in crystals with nipi-superstructure. *Phys. Stat. Sol. (b)* 52:79, 1972.

[17] Z. Schlesinger, S. J. Allen, J. C. M. Hwang, P. M. Platzman and N. Tzoar. Cyclotron resonance in two dimensions. *Phys. Rev. B* 30:435–437, 1984.

[18] T. Nishinaga. *Handbook of Crystal Growth: Fundamentals*, 2nd edn. Elsevier, 2015.

[19] J. Y. Tsao. *Material Fundamentals of Molecular Beam Epitaxy*. Academic Press, 1993.

[20] A. C. Gossard, M. Sundaram and P. F. Hopkins. Epitaxial microstructures. In *Semiconductor and Semimetals*, Vol. 40, p. 153. Academic Press, 1994.

[21] M. Razeghi. *The MOCVD Challenge: A Survey of GaInAsP–InP and GaInAsP–GaAs for Photonic and Electronic Device Applications*. CRC Press, 2011.

[22] A. Pimpinelli and J. Villain. *Physics of Crystal Growth*. Cambridge University Press, 1998.

[23] C. B. Murray and C. R. Kagan. Synthesis and characterization of monodisperse nanocrystals and close-packed nanocrystal assemblies. *Ann. Rev. Mater. Sci.* 30:545–610, 2000.

[24] Q. Pang, L. J. Zhao, Y. Cai, D. P. Nguyen, N. Regnault, N. Wang, S. H. Yang, W. K. Ge, R. Ferreira, G. Bastard and J. N. Wang. CdSe nanotetrapods: controllable synthesis, structure analysis and electronic and optical properties. *Chem. Mater.* 17(21):5263–5267, 2005.

[25] F. Rossi and P. Zanardi. *Semiconductor Macroatoms*. Imperial College Press, 1995.

[26] D. Bimberg, M. Grundmann and N. N. Ledentsov. *Quantum Dot Heterostructures*. Wiley, 1998.

[27] F. Capasso. Band-gap engineering: from physics and materials to new semiconductor devices. *Science* 235(4785):172–176, 1987.

[28] C. Weisbuch and B. Vinter. *Quantum Semiconductor Structures: Fundamentals and Applications*. Academic Press, 1991.

[29] J. Faist. *Quantum Cascade Lasers*. Oxford University Press, 2013.

[30] A. Baldereschi, S. Baroni and R. Resta. Band offsets in lattice-matched heterojunctions: a model and first-principles calculations for GaAs/AlAs. *Phys. Rev. Lett.* 61:734–737, 1988.

[31] C. Delerue and M. Lannoo. *Nanostructures. Theory and Modelling*. Springer, 2003.

[32] Olivier Krebs and Paul Voisin. Giant optical anisotropy of semiconductor heterostructures with no common atom and the quantum-confined pockels effect. *Phys. Rev. Lett.* 77:1829–1832, 1996.

[33] R. Benchamekn, N. Nestoklon, J. P. Jancu and P. Voisin. Theory of modeling for the nanoscale: The spds* tight binding approach. In *Semiconductor Modeling Techniques*, eds. X. Marie and N. Balkan, Springer Series in Materials Science, Vol. 159, Springer, 2012.

[34] G. Bastard. *Wave Mechanics Applied to Semiconductor Heterostructures*. EDP Science, 1996.

[35] J. Luttinger and W. Kohn. Motion of electrons and holes in perturbed periodic fields. *Phys. Rev.* 97:869–883, 1955.

[36] E. O. Kane. Band structure of indium antimonide. *J. Phys. Chem. Solids* 1(4):249–261, 1957.

[37] P. Y. Yu and M. Cardona. *Fundamentals of Semiconductors*. Springer, 1999.

[38] G. L. Bir and G. Pikus. *Symmetry and Strain induced Effects in Semiconductors*. Wiley, 1974.

[39] M. G. Burt. Fundamentals of envelope function theory for electronic states and photonic modes in nanostructures. *J. Phys.: Conden. Matter* 11(9):53, 1999.

[40] B. A. Foreman. Valence-band mixing in first-principles envelope-function theory. *Phys. Rev. B* 76:045327, 2007.

[41] D. BenDaniel and C. Duke. Space-charge effects on electron tunneling. *Phys. Rev.* 152:683–692, 1966.

[42] N. W. Ashcroft and N. D. Mermin. *Solid State Physics*. Harcourt, 1976.

[43] A. Wacker, M. Lindskog and D. O. Winge. Nonequilibrium Green's function model for simulation of quantum cascade laser devices under operating conditions. *IEEE J. Select. Topics Quantum Electron.* 19(5):1200611, 2013.

[44] J. Shah, A. Pinczuk, A. C. Gossard and W. Wiegmann. Energy-loss rates for hot electrons and holes in GaAs quantum wells. *Phys. Rev. Lett.* 54:2045–2048, 1985.

[45] R. Dingle, H. L. Störmer, A. C. Gossard and Wiegmann W. Electron mobilities in modulation-doped semiconductor heterojunction superlattices. *Appl. Phys. Lett.* 33(7):665–667, 1978.

[46] P. Giannozzi, S. de Gironcoli, P. Pavone and S. Baroni. *Ab initio* calculation of phonon dispersions in semiconductors. *Phys. Rev. B* 43:7231–7242, 1991.

[47] M. A. Stroscio and M. Dutta. *Phonons in Nanostructures*. Cambridge University Press, 2001.

[48] B. K. Ridley. *Quantum Processes in Semiconductors*. Clarendon Press, 1988.

[49] R. Nelander and A. Wacker. Temperature dependence and screening models in quantum cascade structures. *J. Appl. Phys.* 106(6):063115, 2009.

[50] Y. Toyozawa. *Optical Processes in Solids*. Cambridge University Press, 2003.

[51] R. Ferreira and G. Bastard. *Capture and Relaxation in Self-Assembled Semiconductor Quantum Dots*. London edn. Morgan and Claypool Publishers, IOP Concise Physics, 2015.

[52] G. Bastard and L. L. Chang. Spin-flip relaxation time of conduction electrons in Cd1-xMnxTe quantum wells. *Phys. Rev. B* 41:7899–7902, 1990.

[53] R. Ferreira and G. Bastard. "Spin"-flip scattering of holes in semiconductor quantum wells. *Phys. Rev. B* 43:9687–9691, 1991.

[54] J. A. Gaj, R. Planel and G. Fishman. Relation of magneto-optical properties of free excitons to spin alignment of Mn^{2+} ions in $Cd_{1-x}Mn_xTe$. *Solid State Commun.* 29(5):435–438, 1979.

[55] G. C. La Rocca and E. A de Andrada e Silva. Spin splittings in nanostructures without inversion symmetry. *Pure Appl. Chem.* 69(6):1187–1194, 1997.

[56] E. L. Ivchenko and G. Pikus. *Superlattices and Other Heterostructures: Symmetry and Optical Phenomena*. Springer, 1995.

[57] C. Ndebeka-Bandou, F. Carosella, R. Ferreira, A. Wacker and G. Bastard. Free carrier absorption and inter-subband transitions in imperfect heterostructures. *Semiconductor Sci. Technol.* 29(2):023001, 2014.

[58] A. C. Betz, S. H. Jhang, E. Pallecchi, R. Ferreira, G. Feve, J.-M. Berroir and B. Placais. Supercollision cooling in undoped graphene. *Nature Phys.* 9(2):109–112, 2013.

[59] H. Haug and S. Koch. *Quantum Theory of the Optical and Electronic Properties of Semiconductors*. World Scientific, 2004.

[60] H. Haug. Free-carrier absorption in semiconductor lasers. *Semiconductor Sci. Technol.* 7(3):373, 1992.

[61] W. Walukiewicz, L. Lagowski, L. Jastrzebski, M. Lichtensteiger and H. C. Gatos. Electron mobility and free-carrier absorption in GaAs: Determination of the compensation ratio. *J. Appl. Phys.* 50(2):899–908, 1979.

[62] F. Carosella, C. Ndebeka-Bandou, R. Ferreira, E. Dupont, K. Unterrainer, G. Strasser, A. Wacker and G. Bastard. Free-carrier absorption in quantum cascade structures. *Phys. Rev. B* 85:085310, 2012.

[63] C. Ndebeka-Bandou, F. Carosella, R. Ferreira and G. Bastard. Free-carrier absorption in asymmetric double quantum well structures due to static scatterers in the in-plane polarization. *Phys. Rev. B* 89:075313, 2014.

[64] Paul Harrisson. *Quantum Wells, Wires and Dots. Theoretical and Computational Physics of Semiconductor Nanostructures.* Wiley-Interscience, 2005.

[65] R. Ferreira and G. Bastard. Evaluation of some scattering times for electrons in unbiased and biased single- and multiple-quantum-well structures. *Phys. Rev. B* 40:1074–1086, 1989.

[66] A. Leuliet, A. Vasanelli, A. Wade, G. Fedorov, D. Smirnov, G. Bastard and C. Sirtori. Electron scattering spectroscopy by a high magnetic field in quantum cascade lasers. *Phys. Rev. B* 73:085311, 2006.

[67] W. Zawadzki, A. Raymond and M. Kubisa. Conduction electrons in acceptor-doped GaAs/(Ga,Al)As heterostructures: a review. *Semiconductor Sci. Technol.* 31(5):053001, 2016.

[68] E. Ackermanns and M. Montambaux. *Mesoscopic Physics of Electrons and Photons.* Cambridge University Press, 2011.

[69] N. H. Shon and T. Ando. Quantum transport in two-dimensional graphite system. *J. Phys. Soc. Japan* 67(7):2421–2429, 1998.

[70] N. Regnault, R. Ferreira and G. Bastard. Broadening effects due to alloy scattering in a quantum cascade laser. *Phys. Rev. B* 76:165121, 2007.

[71] M. Bugajski, K. Reginski, M. Godlewski, M. Wesolowski, P. O. Holtz, A. V. Buyanov and B. Monemar. Fermi-edge singularity in excitonic spectra of modulation doped AlGaAs/GaAs quantum wells. *Acta Phys. Polon. A* 90:751, 1996.

[72] W. Maslana. Carrier induced ferromagnetism in (Cd, Mn)Te quantum wells: a spectroscopic study. PhD thesis, https://tel.archives-ouvertes.fr/tel-00159510/document.

[73] L. D. Landau and E. M. Lifshitz. *Quantum Mechanics: Non-relativistic Theory*, Vol. 3. Pergamon Press, 1958.

[74] H. Machhadani, M. Tchernycheva, S. Sakr, L. Rigutti, R. Colombelli, E. Warde, C. Mietze, D. J. As and F. H. Julien. Intersubband absorption of cubic GaN/Al(Ga)N quantum wells in the near-infrared to terahertz spectral range. *Phys. Rev. B* 83:075313, 2011.

[75] P. Reiss, M. Protière and L. Li. Core/Shell semiconductor nanocrystals. *Small* 5(2):154–168, 2009.

[76] E. Rosencher and Ph. Bois. Model system for optical nonlinearities: asymmetric quantum wells. *Phys. Rev. B* 44:11315–11327, 1991.

[77] C. Sirtori, F. Capasso, D. L. Sivco, A. L. Hutchinson and A. Y. Cho. Resonant Stark tuning of second-order susceptibility in coupled quantum wells. *Appl. Phys. Lett.* 60(2):151–153, 1992.

[78] A. Bonvalet, J. Nagle, V. Berger, A. Migus, J.-L. Martin and M. Joffre. Femtosecond infrared emission resulting from coherent charge oscillations in quantum wells. *Phys. Rev. Lett.* 76:4392–4395, 1996.

[79] E. Rosencher, A. Fiore, B. Vinter, V. Berger, Ph. Bois and J. Nagle. Quantum engineering of optical nonlinearities. *Science* 271(5246):168–173, 1996.

[80] https://en.wikipedia.org/wiki/Hellmann-Feynman_theorem.

[81] M. H. Meynadier, C. Delalande, G. Bastard, M. Voos, F. Alexandre and J. L. Liévin. Size quantization and band-offset determination in GaAs–GaAlAs separate confinement heterostructures. *Phys. Rev. B* 31:5539–5542, 1985.

[82] D. Bohm. *Quantum Theory.* Prentice-Hall, 1951.

[83] J.-Y. Marzin and J.-M. Gérard. Experimental probing of quantum-well eigenstates. *Phys. Rev. Lett.* 62:2172–2175, 1989.

[84] S. Hameau, Y. Guldner, O. Verzelen, R. Ferreira, G. Bastard, J. Zeman, A. Lemaitre and J. M. Gérard. Strong electron–phonon coupling regime in quantum dots: evidence for everlasting resonant polarons. *Phys. Rev. Lett.* 83:4152–4155, 1999.

[85] http://laurent.sexy/epfl/quantique_I/exercice/Serie08.pdf.

[86] S. Hameau, J. N. Isaia, Y. Guldner, E. Deleporte, O. Verzelen, R. Ferreira, G. Bastard, J. Zeman and J. M. Gérard. Far-infrared magnetospectroscopy of polaron states in self-assembled InAs/GaAs quantum dots. *Phys. Rev. B* 65:085316, 2002.

[87] M. Orlita and M. Potemski. Dirac electronic states in graphene systems: optical spectroscopy studies. *Semiconductor Sci. Technol.* 25(6):063001, 2010.

[88] H. L. Störmer, A. C. Gossard and W. Wiegmann. Observation of intersubband scattering in a 2-dimensional electron system. *Solid State Commun.* 41(10):707–709, 1982.

Index